VALIDITY IN SURVEY RESEARCH

Dedicated to Harry Henry, BSc(Econ), FIS, FSS, Professor of Marketing and Media Policy, The Management Centre from Buckingham,

my tough-minded, provocative colleague,

whose forthright questioning of the National Readership Survey procedure provided me with the opportunity to develop the intensive interviewing and the progressive modification techniques — the key elements in the studies reported in this book

Validity in Survey Research

With Special Reference to the Techniques
of Intensive Interviewing and Progressive
Modification for Testing and Constructing
Difficult or Sensitive Measures for Use
in Survey Research

A report by
WILLIAM A. BELSON, BA, PhD

*Based upon research under the direction
and control of William Belson with participation by:*

J. G. Cleland, BA
P. J. Didcott, BA, Dip.Crim.
C. McNaughton, BA (later C. Collis)
G. L. Millerson, BA, PhD
D. W. Osborne, BSc
S. B. Quinn, BA
B. M. Speak, BSc, PhD, Dip.Psych.
V. R. Thompson (computer design and management)
V. R. Yule, BA

Gower

Published by

Gower Publishing Company Limited
Gower House, Croft Road
Aldershot, Hants GU11 3HR
England

Gower Publishing Company,
Old Post Road
Brookfield, Vermont 05036
USA

British Library Cataloguing in Publication Data

Belson, William A.
    Validity in survey research.
    1. Social surveys   2. Surveys
    I. Title
    001.4'33   HN29

    ISBN 0-566-00510-7

Library of Congress Cataloging in Publication Data

Belson, William A.
    Validity in survey research.

    Bibliography: p.
    Includes index.
1. Public opinion polls — evaluation. 2. Public opinion — Great Britain.
3. Social sciences — methodology.   I. Title.
HM261.B347   1985   303.3'8072   84-13681

ISBN 0-566-00510-7

Printed in Great Britain at the University Press, Cambridge

Contents

PART I

INVESTIGATING THE ACCURACY OF THE MEASURING PROCEDURES USED IN SURVEY RESEARCH

v

vi

Microfiche supplement

ERRATA
p. 5, line 16, for 'trade' read 'grade'
p. 61, line 27, for 'for the first' read 'tested in the second'
p. 131, Table 4.22, column 4 should include another
       brace:

$$\left.\begin{array}{l} 3 \\ 12 \\ 9 \\ 3 \\ 0 \\ 14 \\ 3 \end{array}\right\} 44$$

p. 134, line 21, for '(column 3)' read '(column 6)'
p. 238, Figure 5.7 caption, for '. . .' read 'used'
p. 341, line 26, the heading 'What any method must
       overcome' should occur before line 31,
       beginning 'Having made this point . . .'
p. 511, line 29, insert 'pp. 512-18'

List of tables

xi

List of figures

Foreword and acknowledgements

The studies reported in this book were designed by the author and conducted under his direction. They were carried out through the Survey Research Centre of the London School of Economics and Political Science. The personnel working on the different projects were numerous and those principally involved in each are named in the introductions to the different studies reported herein.

The concept of the intensive interview developed out of the author's planning of a check on the accuracy of the National Readership Survey of 1959, and it went on developing through later studies, some of which are described or listed in this book. It is hoped that the development of intensive interviewing will continue through the work of others engaged in accuracy checking. Progressive modification has probably been around, in an informal way, for a long time. However, its use as a consciously cyclical process geared to the emergence of an accurate procedure probably had its origin in the (author's) modification of the National Readership Survey procedures.

Funds for the different investigations came from many sources and together were very substantial. The donors included the Home Office of the United Kingdom; the Institute of Practitioners in Advertising through the contributions of its members; the Columbia Broadcasting System (CBS) of the USA; a large consortium of business houses, research establishments, advertising agencies, government agencies based mainly in the UK but also in other countries. Members of this consortium are listed below.

Anglia Television Ltd
Ashridge Management College
Aspro-Nicholas Ltd (Nicholas Products Ltd)
Attwood Statistics Ltd
Audience Studies Ltd (later Market Decisions Ltd)
Audits of Great Britain Holdings Ltd
Audits & Surveys, Inc. USA
Australian Broadcasting Commission
Australian Broadcasting Control Board
Bass Charrington Ltd
Beecham Products (UK)
Benton & Bowles Ltd
Birkbeck College, Department of Occupational Psychology
Boots Pure Drug Company Ltd
Bovril Ltd
British-American Tobacco Co. Ltd
British Broadcasting Corporation
British Market Research Bureau Ltd and J. Walter Thompson Ltd
British Petroleum Ltd
Brown & Polson Ltd
Bureau of Commercial Research and Wasey Quadrant Ltd
Bureau of the Census (US Dept of Commerce)
Bureau of Social Science Research, Inc. USA
Cadbury Schweppes Ltd
California State College
Chesebrough-Pond's Ltd
Colgate Palmolive Ltd
Columbia Broadcasting System Inc.
Communications Research Ltd
Doyle, Dane, Bernbach Ltd
Doyle, Dane, Bernbach Inc. Advertising, USA
The Economist and the Economist Intelligence Unit Ltd
The Electricity Council
Enskilder Utrednings Institutet AB (Consultants on Survey Research Methods)
Esso Petroleum Company Ltd
Fisons Pharmaceuticals Ltd
Ford Motor Co. Ltd
The Gas Council
Gillette Safety Razor Company
The Health Education Council Ltd
H.J. Heinz Company Ltd
Hobson Bates & Partners Ltd
Universidad Iberoamericana, Mexico
Imperial Chemical Industries Ltd (Paints Division)
Imperial Tobacco Co. Ltd
Independent Television Authority
Independent Television Companies Association Ltd
Institute of Statistics, University of Stockholm
IPC (Group Management) Ltd
Intercontinental Medical Statistics Ltd
Jours de France

KBMS Limited
The University of Kent at Canterbury
Kimberley-Clark Ltd
Kodak Ltd
University of Lancaster
University of Technology, Loughborough
J. Lyons Ltd (Tea Division)
Market Analysis (Australasia) Pty Ltd
Makrotest Ltd
Market Facts of Canada Ltd
Market Information Services Ltd
MIL Research Ltd
Marketing Advisory Services Ltd
Marketing and Economic Research Ltd
Marplan Ltd
Mars Ltd
Masius, Wynne-Williams Ltd
Mass-Observation Ltd
Merck Sharp & Dohme Ltd
National Central Bureau of Statistics, Sweden
National Criminal Justice Statistics Center, USA
National Opinion Polls Ltd
National Opinion Research Center, USA
Newcastle upon Tyne Polytechnic
The University of New South Wales
Norman Craig & Kummel Ltd
North East London Polytechnic
ODEC, Spain (Consultants on Survey Research Methods)
Office of Economic Opportunity, USA
Ogilvy, Benson & Mather Ltd
The Open University
Petfoods Ltd
Philips Electrical Ltd
Portsmouth Polytechnic, Applied Linguistics Research Unit
The Post Office
Proctor & Gamble Ltd
The Rank Organisation
Reader's Digest Association Ltd
Reckitt & Sons Ltd
Research Services Ltd
Response Analysis Corporation, USA
Roche Products Ltd
Rowntree Mackintosh Ltd
Sales Research Services Ltd
Sandoz Products Ltd
University of Saskatchewan Regina Campus, Communications Programme
Schweppes (Home) Ltd
The Scott & Turner Company and Phillips Laboratories Ltd
G.D. Searle & Co. Ltd
Shell International Petroleum Co. Ltd
Shell-Mex & BP Ltd
Smith Kline & French Laboratories Ltd
Social Science Research Council, Survey Unit
Southern Television Ltd
Spillers Ltd
Swedish Broadcasting Corporation

Tate & Lyle Refineries Ltd
The Tavistock Institute of Human Relations
Tilastointi, Finland (Consultants on Survey
    Research Methods)
Henry Telfer Ltd
The Thompson Organisation Ltd

The Toni Company
Transmark (British Rail)
Unilever Ltd
United States Information Agency
Wasey, Prichard Wood & Quadrant Ltd
The University of York

The author wishes to express his appreciation for the financial support given to the series and his thanks to the many members of staff whose painstaking work lies behind the series of investigations presented in this volume.

1 The coverage of the book

This book is principally concerned with two key procedures for use in the continuing development of a scientifically based survey research methodology. The first is the method of the intensive interview, which may be used to investigate the accuracy of an existing questioning or measuring procedure. The second is the method of progressive modification, which may be used, in conjunction with the intensive interviewing method, for constructing procedures for carrying out complex or sensitive or demanding measurements.

These two procedures must of course be seen in the context of the many other research tactics and methods that are available for the pursuit of accuracy in survey research: the use of the existing principles of question design; questionnaire piloting; methods for determining how questions are understood; a large range of checks on and controls over interviewer performance; sampling strategies and bias reduction through matching; checks against some (occasionally) available criterion of truth; internal consistency and item analysis; indicator technology. In fact I have attempted to summarise this context in Chapter 2. However for various reasons I have chosen to focus this book upon those two techniques: intensive interviewing and progressive modification. My first reason is that whereas they have been described in various small-circulation reports, they have never been presented and published as methods in their own right. The second reason is that they are very demanding techniques, dependent upon a research rigour that is all too easily lost in the absence of a readily available and fully illustrated documentation. Thirdly, I think that as methods they fill a gap which in the past has left the survey researcher with no means of testing (and then of increasing) the accuracy level of many of his measures or questioning procedures.

This book is in three parts. Part I is called 'Investigating the accuracy of measuring procedures used in survey research'. It starts with Chapter 2 which (a) presents the case for evaluating our questioning methods with regard to accuracy and (b) sets out the principal evaluative and testing techniques that are available. After this come reports of three studies, each concerned with assessing the accuracy level of a measuring procedure. Two of them deal with behavioural information[1,2] and the third with opinion information.[3] Each study was based on the intensive interviewing method.

Part II deals with the modification of faulty measuring procedures towards greater accuracy. There is an introductory chapter followed by two illustrations of the technique in use. One of these illustrations involves the progressive modification towards accuracy of the National Readership Survey as it was at the start of 1959.*[2] The second illustration concerns the progressive modification of a radio diary being used in Canada by the Bureau of Broadcasting Measurement.[4]

Part III deals with the development of a valid measuring technique where none previously existed. Chapter 10 describes the main tactics used for such developmental work, and Chapter 11 presents an example of this procedure in operation.[5]

The whole book, then, is about accuracy of the tools or measuring techniques or questions used in survey research and particularly of the more sophisticated tools. It concerns accuracy level in existing techniques; the modification of inadequate procedures towards greater accuracy; and the development of totally new measuring techniques with an acceptable level of accuracy. The technology described is applicable to the general run of survey questions, but the main thrust and concern of the book is with the more difficult measuring tasks.

THE CONCEPT OF MEASUREMENT IN SURVEY RESEARCH

For some, the very idea of *measurement* in survey research may seem strange. Surely it is just a matter of questions being asked and answered! In fact I will argue that 'measurement' in survey research (and in the social sciences generally) is not different in principle from measurement in the physical sciences. Measurement in social research is

*This report was originally presented as the second part of *Studies in Readership*, published in 1962.[2]

a process whereby we validly classify people according to their position in relation to some specified characteristic or variable. If we ask the respondent for her (say) age and get a correct reply we may designate that respondent as belonging to one of some (say) four or more age groups. If a respondent makes accurate use of a rating scale to say what she thinks of a particular product or of a specified public service, then we may place that respondent in one of the five or so categories defined by that rating scale. Similarly with respect to questions about income, number of some particular branded item bought in a specified period of time, frequency of church attendance, educational level achieved, miles driven in the last week, attitudes towards a particular racial minority, and so on. Provided we get accurate answers to our questions, we can sort or grade the respondent into one or another category with respect to the subject matter of the question asked. The process is in principle the same as measuring the length of some item, weighing something, and so on.

THE LIMITATIONS OF THE MEASUREMENTS AVAILABLE TO THE SURVEY RESEARCHER

However, of course there are differences too. The principal difference is that techniques used in survey research tend both to be crude and underdeveloped — more so, that is, than measures used in the physical sciences. In addition, many of our measures are subject to influence by the conditions under which we apply them so that they lack the stability of many of the measures used in the physical sciences.

Indeed the survey researcher is limited to direct observation of behaviour and to the responses of people to survey questions. Let me detail this limitation more fully by listing all the kinds of information commonly sought by the survey researcher — all of them involving 'measurement' as I am using that term, but most of them subject to limitations.

Visibly obvious characteristics　Examples are: colour of eyes and hair, clothing worn, household facilities (if allowed to explore the household), characteristics of housing, sex. The survey interviewer may be in a position to make a number of such observations and hence to grade or classify a respondent in terms of them. However, very few of the items of information sought by the survey interviewer are likely to be of this 'visibly obvious' kind.

Visibly obvious behaviour　Examples are: shopping behaviour, street crossing behaviour, illegal driving, work patterns on the factory floor, and so on. This is a valuable source of measurement or classification. Of course, observable behaviour of such things may not always give us a full understanding of what is happening and in any case there is much that the survey researcher will want to know that is not open to observation. On top of that we have to take care that the observation process itself does not affect the observed behaviour.

Information about the respondent's own characteristics and situations — of the sort that the respondent might reasonably be expected to be able to provide to the survey interviewer Examples are: age, country of origin, family composition, whether working and in what occupation, ownership of various goods, marital state, and so on. Such information is frequently called for and the respondent should be able to give it. However, we cannot always be sure for all respondents: sometimes the question may be misunderstood and sometimes the respondent may not choose or bother to give a fully accurate reply.

Opinions on some seemingly innocent and non-threatening matter Examples are: views about road traffic; reactions to some product just tasted; ideas about housing, prices of goods, some visible aspects of youth culture, schools; and so on. But even at this seemingly innocent level, one cannot be wholly sure that a respondent will always answer fully and openly.

Information about behaviour that calls for memory effort or that may be subject to confusion Examples are: miles driven in some specified recent period; when did the respondent last look at some given publication; number of periods lasting a week or more that the respondent was absent from work in the last 12 months; prices of goods bought during the week; what was viewed on television yesterday. Such information is notoriously open to forgetfulness and confusion. Simply asking for it in a survey interview may well be to ask for erroneous information.

Information that the respondent won't want to admit because it is dangerous or shameful to admit it, or because he considers that it is private This information may relate to behaviour or to opinions — for example: drinking behaviour; extra-marital sexual activity; involvement in illegal behaviour of even a minor kind; failure in some task or resolution; harsh treatment of others; behaviour that departs from one's own norms or professional ideals; certain attitudes about some minority group; ideas about one's employer; views about strict honesty. The researcher who is not aware of such difficulties is naive indeed.

Attitudes and tendencies and personality traits about which the respondent is not fully aware — perhaps not aware at all Examples are: fear of failure; an inferiority complex; a tendency to say 'no' to any question or proposition; a bullying approach; superstitiousness; latent cowardice; thoughtlessness; sadism; irrationality; altruism.

So whereas measurement in survey research can often be quite easy, it can also face some very difficult tasks, and with these the possibility of error can be much greater than with many measurements in the physical sciences. This in turn makes it desirable to take very seriously indeed the formulation of any questioning procedures that the survey researcher must rely upon.

But having said all that, the fact remains that measurement is as much a feature of survey research as it is of any other branch of the sciences. Moreover, a short simple question that allows us to grade or categorise people is a measuring instrument in just the same way as is a complex question or complex of questions that allows us to trade or categorise people.

NOT PSYCHOLOGICAL MEASURES

One thing that I must make clear is that in this book I am not concentrating upon psychological measures of the kind constructed and used by psychologists in test work for vocational guidance, clinical diagnosis or other purposes. Such measures are more in the mode of those made by the physical scientists in that they involve precise or small interval measurements or gradings. In addition, they are concerned with the measurement of individuals in order to assist decisions made for or about those particular individuals, whereas survey measures are made for the development of population distributions or segmentations.

However, the reasons for not dealing with psychological measures in this book are that (1) they are not normally used in survey work and (2) they are already the subject of very considerable attention by psychologists concerned with the issue of valid measurement.

Point (2) is not meant to imply that the validity of psychological measures is beyond challenge. Indeed Chapter 2 argues otherwise. However, from a validity standpoint, the psychological measures tend to be in a much stronger position than the often intuitively derived measures currently used in survey research.

FOR BOTH COMMERCIAL AND NON-COMMERCIAL READERS

The methods and principles put forward in this book are equally relevant and applicable to the work of the market researcher and to the work of the social researcher. Sometimes a social researcher may feel that some depicted inadequacy in a purely commercial study could not have any relevance to his own purely social research problems; and vice versa. In fact he is very likely to be wrong in this opinion. Large scale misunderstanding of ordinary commercial-type questions almost certainly means that there will be misunderstanding of ordinary social-type questions. A technique that is effective in detecting misunderstanding in commercial-type questions is very likely to be of use in detecting misunderstanding in social-type questions. The repertory grid method that is applicable in some social-type work has major value for commercial-type research; and so on right across the research scene.

The thing to do when faced with some methodological operation or finding is to ask oneself how that finding or method might be of relevance to one's own specialised field of enquiry. I ask that the reader do this throughout this book. If he does this I think he will find that most of it has relevance for his own research actions and interests.

PART I
INVESTIGATING THE ACCURACY OF THE MEASURING PROCEDURES USED IN SURVEY RESEARCH

2 The case and the methods for measuring the accuracy of questioning or measuring procedures that have been prepared for use in survey research

For a measuring technique to be of any use in survey research, it must produce results that are sufficiently accurate and relevant for the operation in hand. In other words, the measure must be sufficiently *valid** for that purpose. The whole thrust of this book has to do with the validity of the measures we use; and its focus is on those measures of behaviour and opinion that are used in survey research.

The term *validity* should not be confused with *reliability* — which refers to the power of a measuring procedure to produce the same results each time it is applied to the same thing or situation. Reliability is a concept with which I take issue,† but for the present it is sufficient that I point out that a given faulty measuring technique may produce the same (inaccurate) result each time it is used on equivalent samples of people. A valid measure is one that produces accurate results about

---

*A valid measure is one that accurately measures what it is supposed to measure.
†In the first place, the idea of a survey measure yielding the same result each time it is applied to the same person is challengeable — the first application of the test may well affect its second application. The common view of reliability assumes no such test—re-test effect, and it assumes no difference in the two testing situations. However, if that were the case, then *any* test would have total reliability. It would be a denial of scientific determinism to suggest otherwise. So what are we left with? I think the best meaning we can give to the concept is that of 'stability' — does the measure produce the same result each time it is used in spite of the inevitable variability of testing situations? In other words, is it stable in the face of variations in testing conditions? This concept is appealing, but it still leaves out of account the whole issue of the effect of one testing process upon the next. Reliability as it applies to the individual would thus seem to be an impracticable concept. It is only when applied to equivalent samples that it takes a feasible form — and in that case it is best converted to 'stability'. If we do this, then we can test stability in the context of normal day-to-day differences in testing conditions.

the matter being investigated. A valid measure will be reliable (in the sense in which I have just used this term), but a reliable measure will not necessarily be a valid measure.

VALIDITY CANNOT BE TAKEN FOR GRANTED

Contrary to what seems in practice to be assumed by many survey researchers, the validity of a measuring procedure cannot be taken for granted. This applies whether the measuring procedure is a simple looking single question or a set of questions dealing with some complex issue.

There are many reasons why validity cannot be taken for granted, particularly when the measuring procedure involves questioning people in the survey situation about their own behaviour and opinions. These reasons have in general been established through research and have been adequately documented. I have summarised them briefly below.

THE INTERVIEWER CHANGES THE WORDING OF THE QUESTION(S)

The writer's first major experience with this process occurred in the context of the study of the accuracy of the National Readership Survey of the UK back in 1960.[2] One of the elements of this study was the tape-recording of interviewers delivering the readership question. There was evidence of major deviation from the required wording of the questions and of interviewer procedure generally. Details of these deviations are given in Chapter 4 of this book.

Interviewer changes of question wording were also clearly present in a study by the Survey Research Centre of the dependability of interviewer behaviour in a common form of commercial survey.* It was based on 332 tape-recorded interviews with a quota sample of London female adults. There were 15 different interviewers, one from each of 15 different market research teams. A large degree of word changing occurred for all the experimental questions. Word changes occurred for all the interviewers, though to varying degrees. In a great many cases, the changes could hardly have altered the meaning of the question for

---

*The first part of this study (dealing with the faithfulness of interviewers in reporting what was said to them) was published as a report to the Market Research Society Conference in March 1983 ('The accuracy of interviewer reporting of respondent replies to open and to fully structured questions', W.A. Belson).[6] The second part, dealing with the accuracy of interviewers' deliveries of questions, has yet to be published, but the examples given here are drawn from that part of the enquiry.

the respondent, but in other cases they could hardly have failed to do so. For all questions, there were word omissions, word additions, changes in wording, changes in the order of the words of the question. Here are two examples.

The question asked   'Where do you usually buy your shampoo?'

This question was delivered quite unchanged in only 37% of the deliveries. Most of the changes were of no obvious consequence; for example, 'Now where do you . . . ' 'Now you can tell me where . . . '. However, (a) in 12% of the deliveries the interviewer added something of the sort 'what sort of shop?'; (b) in 9% of the deliveries, the term 'usually' was lost.

The question asked   'On average, how often do you yourself buy a shampoo?'

This question was delivered quite unchanged in 23% of the deliveries. Here again, the great bulk of the changes were of no obvious consequence; for example, the interviewer added 'Um' . . . 'Er' . . . 'And now'. However, (i) the term 'on average' was lost in 11% of the deliveries; (ii) the term 'yourself' was either lost or substantially changed in 12% of the deliveries. The mis-delivery of the term 'yourself' (7% of the deliveries) is especially noteworthy; for example, 'On average how often do you buy a shampoo for yourself?'/. . . 'for your own hair?'.

Throughout the whole questionnaire the same process of change went on, very often of no obvious consequence, but occasionally likely to affect the reply. This applied to the non-commercial questions equally with the commercial ones. For example, the question 'What is the job of the head of this household?' did on occasions take such forms as: 'And, er, what is your husband's job?'/ 'Can I ask you your husband's job?'/'Now do you have a pension — the state pension? . . . And do you have any other income at all?'/ 'Now your husband's retired, is he? Would it be alright to put what he's retired from?'.

Consider another question   'Are you, yourself, in a paid job?' IF YES . . . 'Is it a full-time or a part-time job?'. This question did on occasions become: 'Now are you in a paid job? . . . Full-time or part-time?'/'You don't do a paid job yourself?' . . . 'You do??' . . . 'Full time or part time?'/'And are . . . you yourself in business?'/'Are you in any paid occupation?'.

11

Another study of deviation from question wording,[7] involved the tape-recorded delivery of the instructions for completing the so-called Semantic Differential scaling system to a systematically derived sub-sample (238 cases) of a representative sample of 1069 London adults. The instructions for this system were long — as they normally are. Only 2% of the recorded deliveries* were more or less verbatim, and the overall length of what was delivered was 70% of what should have been delivered. Omissions and distortions took these forms: deliberately designed repetitions of key instructions to the respondent were frequently omitted; quite often key instructions were lost altogether; the delivery involved a jumbling of the different parts of the instructions so that they became unclear to the respondent; terms were changed and added (for example the word 'scale' was substituted for the term 'this line'). Occasionally the changes were massive — and there was one case in which the interviewer said only 'You'll get the idea as you go along'.

SUMMING UP ON WORD CHANGING

Indeed, wherever the Survey Research Centre recorded interviewers at work, deviation from question wording tended to emerge as a fairly common feature of interviewer behaviour. It appeared to be a natural tendency of many interviewers and to be heightened as a process by badly designed questions and by poor training and control of interviewers. The Survey Research Centre investigators were left in no doubt that the reduction of interviewer deviation to a minor or negligible level would call for careful selection of interviewers in the first place, followed by training and by regular supervisory control. In the absence of those precautions, interviewer deviation from question wording is likely to be a significant factor in the survey research mix.

Much the same can be said of interviewer deviation from the printed instructions with respect to the use of visual aids, the application of a general instruction to probe in certain recurrent situations, the delivery of reminders to the respondent of certain rules.

To sum up: the constant likelihood of interviewer deviation from instructions is a threat to the validity of any questioning procedure. It must not be left uncurbed.

*280 of the 1069 interviews were recorded and of these 238 were fully audible.

THE RESPONDENT FAILS TO INTERPRET THE
QUESTION IN THE WAY INTENDED BY ITS DESIGNER

Let us suppose that a question was in fact delivered as intended. Another kind or level of risk must now be considered. It is the risk that a respondent will fail to interpret the question as intended by its designer. In studies of the nature and extent of such a danger, the writer has used a testing procedure which involves questioning respondents who have just answered a survey question in order to find out how they interpreted its different elements and concepts. This procedure is described briefly on pages 29–32 of this chapter, and in addition in an earlier publication.[8] In that study, which was based on double interviews* with a random sample of 265 London adults, and on 29 experimental questions, a high degree of misinterpretation of the survey questions was found, with less than a third (on average) of sample members interpreting an experimental question as intended. The results for several of the experimental questions follow.

> An experimental question was: 'Do you think that children suffer any ill effects from watching programmes with violence in them, other than ordinary Westerns?' On a liberal marking, 8% interpreted this question more or less as intended. Over half *included* Westerns in their understanding of the question. Here are a few of the individual interpretations: 'children' was interpreted all the way from 'babies' to 'teenagers' — even up to the age of 20 years; there were also some rather exclusive interpretations, such as: 'children who have been brought up properly'; 'your own grandchildren'; 'nervous children'; 'children such as your own'; and so on.

> Another experimental question was: 'Do you think any programmes have a bad effect on young people by teaching them slang?' Twenty per cent interpreted this question more or less as intended. There was major variability in the interpretation of 'young people', with the ages considered ranging from five years to over 20 years. The term 'slang' was interpreted by some as 'bad grammar' or 'poor pronunciation'; by some as 'swearing or bad talk'; by others as 'crime, violence, bad sex life, bad manners'. The term 'any programme' was interpreted by some as programmes showing crime or violence.

The findings for all 29 experimental questions are given in considerable detail in the report of the enquiry.[8] That report leaves no room for doubt that respondents can and do misinterpret survey questions, often quite seriously.

---

*An ordinary and an intensive interview.

Whereas this particular study was based on experimental questions into each of which some commonly occurring difficulty had been built, tests of questions as they normally occur in questionnaires bring out the same sort of problems — substantial misunderstanding of the question put to the respondent.[9-15]

The tendency of respondents to misunderstand is very much heightened by quite common practices in question design; for example: the use of a lot of information-carrying words in the one question; complex constructions; the use of long alternatives; the use of a qualifying clause at the end of the question; the use of words that are not the common property of the respondents; asking a memory-dependent question; asking about behaviour in some specified recent period (the respondent being prone to answer in terms of her *usual* behaviour); and so on. Here are some survey questions that the writer expects to be subject to misunderstanding. The reader may wish to evaluate them in terms of the principles of question design set out later in this chapter.

Some commonly occurring classification questions

- How many persons are there in your household?
- How many rooms do you or your family have for your own use — not counting bathrooms, hall, landings?
- What is your job?/What is the occupation of the head of this household?
- Have you had any further education since leaving full-time school?
- Are you a cigarette smoker?

A key question in the National Readership Survey of the UK

- 'I want you to go through this booklet with me, and tell me for each paper roughly how many issues you have read or looked at recently — it doesn't matter where. As I show you each card, will you tell me which of the statements applies?'

  NOW EXPLAIN 'read or look at'/'it doesn't matter where'/'any copy'

  The respondent is shown a card with the name of a paper on it and, underneath that name, a choice of the following kind:

  'IN AN AVERAGE MONTH I SEE THIS NUMBER OF ISSUES:

  4 / 3 / 2 / 1 / Less than one / None'

(The reader of this book should look not only for the possibility of the respondent misunderstanding this question, but also for several nonsenses in it.)

Some questions from published opinion polls

- 'If a centre party was formed by the moderates and right-wing members of the Labour Party splitting away from the left wing *and* they put up a candidate in your constituency, which of the following candidates would you be inclined to vote for?'

    PASS CARD SHOWING THE FOLLOWING CHOICES: Conservative candidate/Labour candidate/Liberal candidate/Centre Party candidate/Nationalist or other party candidate/would not vote.

- 'Some people believe that there is a lot of misuse of social security benefits, with people drawing benefits while they are earning money. Others believe that by and large people treat the social security system responsibly. Do you think . . . ?'

(READ OUT)

The system is misused

OR That people treat it responsibly

Don't know

Some questions from the Family Expenditure Survey in Great Britain

- 'Do (any of) you pay for anything by means of a standing order or direct debit through a bank or through a National (Post Office) Giro account or by bank budget account?' (C2, Q39)
- 'Do (any of) you hold a current weekly or season ticket for any form of transport for which you yourself paid, including any you have bought for a child?' (C2, Q36)
- 'What was your wage/salary, including overtime, bonus, commission or tips, after all deductions, the last time you were paid?'
- 'Has Inland Revenue allowed you, or will you be claiming, tax relief or expenses incurred as a result of your employment, such as overalls, clothing, tools, subscriptions to professional societies?' (D2, Q18)
- 'What proportion of your expenditure which you have already told me about have you claimed/will you be claiming as a business expense for tax purposes?' (D2, Q28)
(Separate proportions are asked for with respect to rent, mortgage payments on structure, rates, water charges. . . .)

A question from the General Household Survey

- 'Thinking now about the four weeks ending last Sunday, that is, between . . . and . . . (SHOW CALENDAR), have you had any other spells away from work because of your own illness or injury, apart from the one(s) which meant you were away last week?' (Question 11)

yes, other spells of illness
no other spells of illness

**A question from the Survey of Drinking
in England and Wales, 1980 (DHSS)**

● 'Before you were aged 18, did you ever have a drink on a special occasion like a birthday party, a wedding, or on Christmas Day, or did you not have anything alcoholic to drink before you were aged 18?'

It is suggested that the reader makes a practice of looking critically at the form of the questions that lie behind the findings formulated in reports of surveys. More important, this critical activity should start with the questions that he himself formulates.

Where questions are designed in accordance with established principles of design,[8, 15] misinterpretation of them is very much less likely to occur. With really good question design, misunderstanding can be reduced to a very minor level. That, however, is a rather big 'if', and the danger of misinterpretation remains a real threat to validity.

Of course, misunderstanding of some part of the question may not lead to an erroneous answer being given in a particular case. Thus for a young married couple living alone in a dwelling, it would not matter if they thought a question about 'size of household' involved excluding lodgers. The answer would still be 'two'. However, one cannot count on being saved by that sort of fortuitous circumstance.

THE QUESTION ASKED MAY BE
LEADING OR LOADED OR SUGGESTIVE

Researchers are generally aware of the dangers of leading or loaded or suggestive questions. Here is one that was asked in a government survey of attitudes towards the Metropolitan (London) police force in a study reported in 1962.[16]

'The police have sometimes been accused of such things as taking bribes, using unfair methods to get convictions, using too much force on people. Considering bribery first, do you think there is any truth in the suggestion that the police sometimes take bribes or do you think it most unlikely that they would?'

Can you identify the bias in that question? Its first sentence involves what is probably preliminary conditioning. It might well produce a negative set in the respondent. On top of this, the class of answer offered seems likely to lead respondents to answer to the effect that police take bribes. In the document concerned, there were a lot of other questions with an obvious bias in them. The reader is invited to examine it.[16]

Here is another example from more recent times:

'Some people say that attitudes towards marriage have been changing and that recently women have tended to get married at a slightly later age than they used to. What do you think is the best age for women to get married nowadays?' (Question 11 Family information section of 'General Household Survey 1981').

The perceptive reader of questionnaires will find many cases where question bias is present to one degree or another.

Though, in general, biased questions are easy enough to recognise, they can also take quite subtle forms. Consider these:

- 'Do you agree or disagree with the view that " . . . "?'
- 'How often do you . . . ?'
- 'When was the last time you . . . ?'
- 'Some people say that too much money is being spent on new motorways. Do you agree or disagree?'
- 'Do you agree with the common view that . . . ?'

Now try adding others you have seen around.

There is a special problem about loaded and leading questions. Researchers generally recognise them as dangerous practice. However, methodological research on the effects of such characteristics of questions is vague and often of dubious value. The principal exception is the work of Rugg and Cantril way back in 1944. Rugg and Cantril investigated the effects on response of using 'big names' in questions.[17] They found that in some instances this made a meaningful difference to the answers given but that in other instances it did not. In fact the best that one can say of the research to date is that there is no single general thing one can say about the effect on response distributions of leading or loaded questions. It appears that 'it all depends' on the circumstances. However, it is also clear that on occasions it *can matter*, and this should be enough to warn the researcher away from such questions — as a matter of principle. On this approach, the possibility that a question is leading or loaded or suggestive constitutes a threat to its validity as a measuring instrument.

ORDER EFFECTS

There is one form of question bias that is very likely indeed to affect the answers of survey respondents. This concerns the order in which choice of answer elements are offered, especially the order of presentation of the items in a rating scale. In a study of the effect on responses of presenting rating scales in traditional versus reversed order, Belson[18] found a major tendency for the scale items presented first to get greater endorsement than the same items presented last. That study had been conducted under test room conditions. Quinn and Belson (1969) found the same marked tendency when the enquiry was repeated under doorstep interview conditions.[19]

The National Readership Survey was likewise subject to order effects, there being a major difference in the readership figures for monthly publications when these were presented in the two orders: monthlies, weeklies, Sundays, dailies — versus dailies, Sundays, weeklies, monthlies.[2]

I must make it clear that in speaking of order effects, I have not been referring to the order in which separate questions are presented in a questionnaire. For that issue, order effects are simply variable.[20,21]

OTHER REASONS FOR ERROR

There are numerous other reasons for wariness about taking accuracy of reply for granted, all of them bound up in the respondent's mental and emotional processes. Several of these follow.

A careless reply   In the first place, there is no good reason, in the general case, for expecting a respondent to formulate a careful reply to questions put to her by a stranger who calls at the door, perhaps at an unsuitable hour, and asks questions of no particular interest to the respondent. Getting a careful reply calls for something special in a situation — an interesting subject, an interviewer capable of sparking off helpfulness in the respondent, a suitable time for the respondent, a set of simple questions. The details in Chapters 3—5 provide evidence on this matter.

Memory decay   Another threat to accuracy is the general decay of respondent memory, leading to confusion and to failure to produce accurate recall of one's own behaviour. There is nothing new or surprising about this and evidence of it is given in plenty in several of the studies reported in this book and in the literature of memory research.[22-30]

Consider the following requests to the respondent:

- When did he last look at publication X?
- Number of some specified item he bought in the last seven days
- Price paid for some minor commodity
- Size of last bill for gas or for car repair or for telephone use
- Brands of a commodity used in the last month/frequency of purchase of some branded article
- The amount of the last rate rebate.

Try adding more from your reading of questionnaires.

There is much one can do about memory failure through an intelligent use of different aids; for example: visuals of product packages; cards listing all the different reasons for some form of behaviour so that the respondent can draw from it; careful verbal or visual descriptions of situations or events; refraining from asking for the impossible or for a memory-dependent effort on the doorstep. But if the researcher blunders in with an unaided question calling for memory-dependent information, error is almost certain to occur. Human beings are not recording machines to be turned on by an interviewer's doorstep questioning.

Unwillingness to admit   Another threat to accuracy is an unwillingness on the part of the respondent to make certain kinds of admissions. The respondent has only to be sensitive on the matter asked about for withholding to occur. In some cases it can be dangerous from a psychological or a legal viewpoint to make a particular admission, and the sensible respondent knows better than to do so. Problems like this can be largely overcome by careful preparation which includes making it *safe* for the respondent to talk out. However this can take time, calls for interviewer skills, and it may also involve costly technique development. The reaction of many would-be investigators is to avoid research problems that involve the collection of delicate information. Some, however, barge in. Consider these examples:

- drinking and smoking behaviour
- frequency of teeth cleaning

- frequency of taking a bath or a shower/of changing clothes/of shoe cleaning
- sexual aberrations
- reasons for absence from work
- frequency of reading one's preferred newspaper
- rent paid by lodgers
- negative views about some racial minority
- earnings from all sources.

OTHER INTERVIEWER-BASED PROBLEMS

In this short overview of possible causes of error in survey research, at least some reference should be made to other faults of interviewers. Deviation from instructions has already been mentioned. However, in addition there are misdemeanours such as unfaithful reporting of replies given;[6, 31] interview bias and expectation;[32-34] sampling failures in the form of lost interviews. With poor selection of the interviewers, and with poor training of them, many faults do commonly occur. On the other hand, careful selection, training and quality control can reduce the occurrence of such faults, particularly when a fieldwork department sets out to develop craftsmanship in its interviewers. Whereas some researchers take great care over interviewer training and control, others do not.

SUMMING UP ON ERROR-MAKING FACTORS

The upshot of these warnings is as obvious as the weaknesses to which the warnings refer: *accuracy from survey questions or measuring instruments cannot be taken for granted.* Accuracy is an achievement. Sometimes it is an achievement against the odds. Its achievement calls for the use of question design technology and often for a high degree of it. I am not saying that accuracy cannot occur in careless hands. With luck and the balancing of errors, accuracy may *happen* as it were. However it cannot be guaranteed. Nor is high intelligence in the question designer enough to guarantee accuracy. Its achievement calls for the application of a technology readily available to researchers in the literature of research and referred to frequently in this book.

YET SOMEHOW ACCURACY IS TAKEN FOR GRANTED

In spite of the problems I have outlined, accuracy in survey research is frequently taken for granted. Whereas survey research practitioners are in general well aware of problems in securing accurate data about a respondent's views and behaviour, that awareness does not appear generally to have been translated into regular or even occasional checking of the accuracy of the data they gather.

Just as in Chapter 1, I am talking about validity in *survey research* and not about the validity of the tests that psychologists construct for use on individuals for vocational, clinical or other purposes. Whereas I consider that such tests are not taken far enough in the pursuit of validity, I am sure that they are taken much further in that direction than are the measures used in survey research. This is done through an adherence to a validity principle in their construction, and the application of that principle is strengthened by a validity concern on the part of many of those who apply such tests.

By contrast, many survey researchers appear to rely almost entirely upon their armchair skills in writing questions and in putting together some choice of answer. Many act as if they believe that some particular threat of error will be overcome by their own bright ideas for formulation — by that alone. Somehow these armchair formulations are thought to be good enough to ensure that the measure is accurate. Once made and in use, a measure tends to be recognised as established and accurate, and it may well stay in use for years without serious challenge.

How has this dangerous situation come about? At the speculative level I suspect such factors as these:

- The designer regards it as obvious that the questions asked are indeed about the sort of behaviour under investigation — that is, they mean the sorts of things that they are intended to measure.
- The designer fails to recognise the high degree of fallibility in a respondent in interpreting a question and in formulating a reply when the issue asked about is memory-dependent or sensitive or seemingly too trivial for effort or embarrassing.
- The designer fails to realise that an issue of validity is in fact involved.
- The designer has an untested faith in his own ability to communicate.
- There is a commercial pressure to get a measure into operation as soon as possible — with every show of confidence in the accuracy of the questions asked.
- There is often a resistance to any attempt to check on the accuracy of a behavioural or opinion measure once it is in use — because to start checking it at that stage may well be destructive of the confidence of those who buy or use the results of the survey.

- Behavioural and opinion measures in survey research usually relate to population groups or samples (even though collected through individuals) whereas tests of ability are often conducted in order to reach decisions about *individuals* — who may be capable of challenging any results they don't like.
- Sometimes a questioning procedure or measure is designed by an industry committee — a committee with its mixture of vested interests, lack of training and skill for this sort of work, lack of concern for the securement of accuracy, a desire to reach a concensus.
- And of course there is, on the rare occasion, that 'Who's going to check?' mentality in some dubious researcher.

At the purely speculative level, I have heard it asked if perhaps the chief origin of the naively confident attitudes I have complained of is a failure of the academic discipline from which many researchers are drawn — a failure to immerse them, as students, in the psychology of information securement and of human error-making. Consider this view in relation to the teaching of economics, statistics, mathematics and sociology.

Whatever the reason for the absence of the validity principle in constructing a measure of behaviour or opinion, and for failure to test any procedures once put together, the fact is that many of our measures are put together without anything approaching a major use of the validity principle, and the great bulk of them are not tested for validity in any meaningful way.

Studies of voting intentions have sometimes been suspect because election results have challenged their accuracy. One wonders what might happen with many other questions or measures if the day of apparent reckoning was equally present for them.

THE NEED TO CHECK

Bearing in mind the known problems or hazards of securing accurate information about respondent behaviour and opinion, it is essential that we be prepared to challenge and to check the accuracy of the behavioural and opinion data that we collect or have collected for us.

Techniques for getting information about *behaviour* are prime targets for checking, especially where costly decisions are based on the collected information. However opinion-type questions should also be checked. Oddly enough, there is abroad a claim that, whereas one can talk about checking the accuracy of *behavioural* data, one cannot do so with respect to *opinion* data. The view appears to be that such a check is in some way inconceivable. The writer is totally unsympathetic to such a view and has carried out intensive checks on the accuracy of opinion data. One such check is described in Part I of this book in order to illustrate the methods available for doing such work.

THE METHODS AVAILABLE FOR CHECKING EXISTING METHODS FOR ACCURACY

The need to assess the validity of a data collection procedure used in survey research is clear enough. What is less than clear is just what techniques are available for doing this. Such techniques *are* available and I am going to introduce them in this chapter.

METHOD 1: EVALUATING A PROCEDURE IN TERMS OF THE KNOWN PRINCIPLES OF QUESTION FORMU-LATION AND QUESTIONNAIRE DESIGN

Over the decades, a great many principles of question formulation have been established by survey methodologists. Though they have not yet been brought together in a single text, the serious researcher will be aware of them and will use them not only to challenge his own design work but also to evaluate the question design work of others.

Much can be done this way. You have only to study a questioning procedure against a list of the established principles to be able to identify at least some of the weaknesses and strengths of that questioning procedure. I have set out below such a list and I suggest that the reader should start by using it to evaluate his own most recent question design work.

List 1: Some principles of question design for survey research

Before formulating the wording of a question

1   Before designing any question, see that you have identified the specific issues that the client wants investigated. *Write these down in the form of statements about what information you want to extract through your questions.* It can be very wasteful to start writing a question before you have specified the class of information which it is required to elicit. Always start by specifying what is wanted.

2   Be clear about whether you want an open-ended type of question

(for exploratory purposes) or a fully structured type (for the development of population distributions).

3   Where several different concepts are to be involved in a question and where the question will have to be complex, consideration should be given as to whether a short series of questions, linked by filters, should be asked instead.

Concerning the wording of questions

AVOID
- words likely to be unfamiliar to the respondent
- negative words and formulations
- the use of a lot of information-carrying words in the one question
- words that would sound like something else
- broad concepts (e.g. advertising, children, the government, cost of living)
- qualifying clause at the *end* of a question
- a question that the respondent can start to answer before the question has been fully read out
- two questions in one
- questions that offer long alternatives as a 'choice of answer'
- questions that invite replies in terms of the *usual*
- suggestion or leadingness in the question
- big names in the question
- questions that call for a lot of effort by the respondent as in memory dependent questions, questions involving working something out.

IN GENERAL   Keep the question short, simple, concrete.

ALWAYS   If in doubt, pre-test the question, and don't confuse pre-testing with piloting (see later).

Concerning the offering of a set of answers for the respondent to choose from

1   If at all possible, give the respondent a 'choice of answer' card rather than asking the interviewer *to read out* some list of possible answers.

2   Use large print on all 'choice of answer' cards.

3   Check the comprehensibility of all visual aids and all 'choice of answer' systems and make these as attention-getting as possible.

24

4   Use empirical methods to construct the rating scales you use.

5   Issue instructions sufficient to control *when* the interviewer presents the visual aids of the 'choice of answer' cards.

6   Wherever possible, rotate the order of presentation of the items appearing in a 'choice of answer' or visual aid system.

7   Take steps to prevent a respondent reading an answer card at the same time as the interviewer is asking her questions.

Concerning deviation by interviewers

1   Don't give interviewers questions that encourage them to change the wording of those questions or to ignore instructions.

2   Control the presentation of visual aids (by interviewers) through the design of the questioning system.

Also

1   Where you are going to ask about behaviour in a given period, plan preliminary questions to disarm any tendency by the respondent to extend the period for inclusion of such activity; for example:
    - ask about the average week before asking your question about the last seven days;
    - fix the furthermost limit of the recall period before asking about behaviour in that period.

2   Similarly, plan to disarm any unwarranted tendency to answer in terms of the 'usual'; for example, by asking about usual behaviour before asking about behaviour in a specific recent period.

3   Never combine the response distributions from open and closed question systems.

4   Make your questions as direct as possible. Where indirect questions or indices are used, see that they have been validated before putting any faith in the implied meaning of the responses they produce.

5   Preferably treat data comparatively rather than in an absolute sense. This applies particularly to rating scales.

As an exercise, I suggest the reader try evaluating the questions on pp. 14–16 against the above list of principles.

The reader may wish to extend his critical appraisal of his own questions or those of others by referring to the following well-grounded hypotheses about the way in which questions are distorted or misunderstood.[8]

1   When a respondent finds it difficult to answer a question, he is likely to modify it in such a way as to be able to answer it more easily.

2   If a broad term or concept is used, there will be a strong tendency for respondents to interpret it less broadly.

3   Under certain conditions a term or concept may be widened (for example: when the respondent feels he is too restricted by some very narrow concept or where he feels he is saying too little by dwelling upon only one specific point of detail; where a reference splits off a single aspect of some broad matter about which the respondent feels strongly; where a wide setting to a question leads the respondent to expect a wider concept than the one offered; where the *setting* of a narrow term is wide, leading the respondent to widen the narrower term 'to match').

4   Part of the question may be overlooked under certain conditions (for example: when, on first impression, an element of the question seems to be superfluous; when other parts of the question seem to make some particular part of it superfluous; where the respondent feels able to start answering the question before all of it is read out to him; where two long alternatives are offered as answers at the end of a question; where a qualifying clause postulates a condition that is unusual or imposes some odd qualification upon a familiar concept; where the wording of a question is such that ordinary mishearing is facilitated).

5   A respondent may distort a question to fit into his own situation or position or experience; or because he wants to create an opportunity to express an opinion, perhaps held strongly; or to avoid admitting anything that could show him in a poor light.

6   The general context or setting of a term in a question may wrongly influence the way that term is interpreted (for example: in a question about the impartiality or otherwise of news programmes in their treatment of political matters, a respondent may be led, because the question refers to political matters, to interpret news programmes as political programmes — such as a party political broadcast, political interviews).

7   Specific words or clauses, which are meant to define or qualify a wider term, may lead to the misinterpretation of that wider term (for example, the term 'programme' can become 'children's programmes' when the respondent is asked if TV programmes seen by children are appropriate for them).

8   A question may be wrongly interpreted if it has in it difficult words or words which mean different things to different people.

26

And so on. These hypotheses are drawn from the 15 put forward, with a rather full explanation in each case, in *The Design and Understanding of Survey Questions*.[8]

METHOD 2: PILOTING THE QUESTIONNAIRE

There is one checking procedure that good survey researchers carry out as a matter of course, namely the *piloting* of the questionnaire. What this procedure tends to involve is that interviewers deliver the questionnaire in the way planned to a small sample of people of the sort that the questionnaire was designed for. The interviewer notes carefully things like: how long the questionnaire took to deliver; evidence of the *respondent* finding anything in the questionnaire difficult or misleading; any difficulties experienced by the interviewer in delivering the questionnaire or any of its questions.

Here are some of the things that the piloting interviewers may note and report.

Concerning the respondent

- The respondent asks how much longer the interview is going to take
- The respondent seems irritated by some questions
- The respondent is seen to misuse a visual aid or a scale that she was instructed to use in some particular way
- The respondent says he doesn't understand, looks puzzled, says he cannot remember

The reports on respondents will be linked both to the questionnaire as a whole and to specific questions. However, the piloting procedure is less than dependable for identifying the difficulties that *respondents* may be having — and to this limitation I will be returning later on in the chapter.

Concerning the interviewers

On the other hand, what the piloting procedure is especially suited for is picking up evidence of *interviewer*-linked problems. After all, the interviewer who is delivering the procedure is in a very good position to note and report upon the difficulties that *she herself* experiences in delivering the question. With a good piloting team, problems of the sorts listed below may be detected.

List 2: The kinds of interviewer-linked problems that may be revealed through piloting

- Certain of her instructions are too vague
- The filtering system originating in a given question is confusing her
- Too little space is allowed for the answer to be written fully
- There is too big a gap (going across the page) between the list of answers offered and their corresponding code numbers
- It is impossible to keep up with the coding of certain open-ended replies as the respondent goes on speaking, possibly quite rapidly
- Too much information has to be fitted into a particular answer grid
- The printing on the questionnaire is too small
- Too many questions are packed into a single page of the questionnaire
- You need three hands to administer one of the visual aids (i.e. to hold the board, administer the card, write down the answer)
- The introduction is so long that the interviewer feels she will lose the interview before she gets to the first question
- The early questions seem to the interviewer to be too personal
- The question is very hard to say without carefully reading it (so that the interviewer is looking down and obviously reading instead of looking at the respondent)
- The interviewer feels that certain of the questions are silly or offensive or too difficult (for the respondent)
- The interviewer finds herself changing the wording of certain of the questions

A piloting team should have in it both 'run of the mill' interviewers and several really bright and discerning interviewers. The 'run of the mill' interviewers will be in a position to pick up the sorts of difficulties that the interviewers generally will have in administering the questionnaire. The brighter interviewers should pick up the threats to interviewer performance that the others will not discern.

For effective reporting of problems encountered, the piloting interviewers should have, at the very least, a report form at the end of each questionnaire. It should allow the interviewer to report on how long it took to deliver the questionnaire; all the difficulties the interviewer met with in delivering it; all the respondent-linked problems discerned. In addition, the interviewer should be required to link such difficulties to the question concerned wherever this is relevant. Better still, there should be space after each question for reporting any difficulties occurring in relation to it.

De-briefing and piloting interviewers is a skilled process, and it is essential to have at this session not only the researcher responsible for the survey, but the relevant members of the fieldwork and the analysis staffs. This increases the likelihood that action will be taken in relation to weaknesses in the survey questionnaire.

As already mentioned, standard piloting is the right method for picking up interviewer difficulties, but it is unreliable as a technique for detecting respondent problems or troubles. Thus whereas some respondents will ask what a question means or give evidence of meeting trouble in some way, it is very common for a respondent to misunderstand a question — to misinterpret it — without either the respondent or the interviewer being aware that this has happened. I say this on the basis of evidence of major misunderstanding of survey questions that have come very successfully through the piloting procedure.[8, 14] Sometimes the respondent will simply get the meaning of the question wrong; sometimes he will convert the question to something that will allow him to answer with what he *wants* to say; sometimes he won't mention a failure to grasp some word (perhaps because he is sensitive about admitting it) but will simply put the rest of the questions together to make some meaning — to which he gives his reply.

So piloting, though a necessary procedure, is a limited device best used for picking up interviewer difficulties. It is not a dependable detector of respondent misunderstanding of questions, but it is a very useful part of the researcher's battery of tactics for picking up defects in a research procedure.

METHOD 3: DETERMINING HOW THE QUESTION WAS INTERPRETED

To determine how a survey question is interpreted by respondents, a procedure usually called 'question testing' may be employed. It is applied when the question designer has reason to suspect that a question may be misunderstood by survey respondents. From time to time the wise question designer also applies the method to questions that he is confident about. In question testing, the interviewer (who will be a specialist by training) first delivers the questionnaire just as if she was piloting it. She writes down the answers to all questions. After this she asks the respondent for an extension of the interview for which a fee will be paid. She explains that her purpose is to 'find out if certain of our questions are likely to be misunderstood or misinterpreted'. She explains that this will mean finding out how the respondent did in fact interpret such questions. *She explains that this is not a test of the respondent but a test of 'our questions'.*

Once agreement is reached (and about 70% of London interviewees have tended so to agree) the question tester asks to continue the interview inside the house. She carefully explains her purposes, saying again that she is now trying to find out if certain of her questions were in fact understood as intended. She stresses once more that this is not a check on the respondent but a check on 'our questions' — 'because it is so easy for people to write questions that nobody can understand'. Against this background (and it is important to establish it) the question tester proceeds as follows.

First of all she reads the respondent the question once more and asks for a repeat of her original reply (reminding the respondent of her actual reply if she now gives a different reply — a very rare event). Next, the interviewer asks the respondent to explain how she got from that question to her answer and extended probing is used as necessary to get a full reply. This is done to get the respondent thinking about her own response processes at the time she first answered the question. The key part of the testing procedure now follows. The respondent is asked a series of questions designed to determine how each of the key concepts or words in the question was interpreted. For example, in a question about the effect of television on children, the question tester wants to know how the respondent interpreted the term 'children'. So she asks 'When you answered that question, *what* people did you have in mind? What people were you telling me about?' It might turn out that the respondent was thinking of her own children or perhaps of very young children or perhaps of well brought up children. This process is repeated for each of the concepts in the question that is to be investigated.

The whole of this testing process is tape-recorded, and the researcher is then in a position to reconstruct the respondent's interpretation of the original question.

The question tester then moves on to the next of the questions that she has been assigned to test for this respondent and repeats the operation.

In all, she tests about three questions on the one respondent. Thus one question tester will probably be limited to the testing of those three or so questions, whilst another question tester deals with three other questions in the questionnaire.

Here is an example of the checking system used in testing the survey question: 'Do you think that children suffer any ill effects from watching programmes with violence in them, other than ordinary Westerns?'.

Step 1

REPEAT THE QUESTION AND GET THE RESPONDENT TO REPEAT HER REPLY.

THEN SAY:

'Tell me exactly how you arrived at that answer . . . how did you work it out . . . how exactly did you get to it?'

PROBE FOR A FULL REPLY

Step 2

(a) To find out what were the ages of the people that the respondent was thinking of in answering the question.

'What ages were the people you had in mind when you gave your answer?

(b) To find out if the respondent was thinking of ill effects and, if so, which ones.

'What sorts of effects were you thinking of when you answered the question?'

(c) To find out what sorts of programmes the respondent had in mind.

'When you told me that children were/were not affected by these programmes, what sorts of programmes did you have in mind?'

PROBE FOR ALL TYPES. THEN ASK FOR EXAMPLES THAT MIGHT GET OFFERED.

(d) To find out if the respondent was including Westerns.

'Were you including Westerns when you answered the question?'

YES/NO/CAN'T SAY

IF YES OR NO, ASK:

'Why was that?'
'Did you think we wanted you to include Westerns?'

YES/NO/NOT SURE

And so on, for each of the concepts in the question.*

The reader may wish to formulate a question testing programme for finding out how the following question was interpreted.

'How many people are there in your household?'*

---

*For the *results* of testing this question see *The Design and Understanding of Survey Questions.*[8]

The limitations of question testing must be noted at this point. Where a respondent misunderstands a question, the likelihood of a correct reply being given is reduced — and sometimes ruled out altogether. However, even with a proper understanding of the question, a correct reply cannot be assumed. The occasional testing of the accuracy of a reply is necessary — see later.

METHOD 4: TESTING TO SEE THE INTERVIEWER DELIVERS THE QUESTION FAITHFULLY

It is wise, in the early stages of any new survey procedure, to tape-record a number of interviewers at work with the questionnaire. Either the interviewer or someone accompanying the interviewer makes the recording. This is a relatively easy thing to do with modern recording equipment, though it should never be done without the respondent knowing and agreeing. Such a recording will provide evidence of interviewer deviation where it is occurring. Obviously interviewers will avoid conscious deviation when the tape-recorder is running. But the author's experience has been that considerable deviation by the interviewers nonetheless shows up through such recording. A tape-recorder has the further advantage of picking up deviant behaviour in the interviewer's *reporting* of respondent replies.

METHOD 5: EVALUATING A MEASURING TECHNIQUE BY COMPARING THE RESULTS OF IT WITH SOME DIRECTLY AVAILABLE 'CRITERION OF TRUTH'

If an interviewer changes the question, or if the respondent misunderstands what the question actually is, there is a likelihood that she will give a reply other than that warranted by the question as designed. However it is still quite possible for the respondent to give an erroneous reply to a question that has been faithfully delivered and that is properly understood by the respondent. The reasons for this have already been given. So methods for testing the level of *accuracy* achieved are of considerable importance.

Occasionally a direct criterion of truth is available. Here are some examples.

● Out-patients of a particular hospital are available for interview and are questioned about, say, the time of their last call at the out-patients department, the frequency of such calls, the nature of their illness, and so on. If the hospital's records about these out-patients are available to the organisation responsible for the interviewing, a direct check may be made upon the accuracy of the replies of the respondents to the survey question. If the responses are thus shown to be accurate, the questions concerned will be regarded as safe for continuous usage in the survey situation.

- In a USA survey, respondents were asked if they had a torch (flash light) in use and, if so, what brand of batteries they had in it. At the end of the interview, the respondent was asked to get the torch and the batteries in it were examined.[35]

- If women shoppers are to be asked about the contents of their shopping baskets, a check on the accuracy that might be expected from the questions asked may be made by paying the respondent, after she has answered the survey question, to let the interviewer make a direct check on the contents of her basket.

- In special cases, it may be possible to observe the behaviour of a respondent (for example: behaviour in a supermarket; in a waiting room; in public transport) before asking her about that behaviour. However such a check does call for very considerable care on the part of the 'validator' if the latter is to get a faithful record of what actually happened and is to avoid the respondent becoming aware of the scrutiny being made of her behaviour. There is of course the obvious issue of the ethics of such surveillance.

- It is sometimes advocated that the accuracy of a survey result dealing with the quantities of some commodity bought be established by setting it against 'factory output' figures. However this is a dubious kind of check for fairly obvious reasons. Where possible it is much better to make the comparison with the results from systematic store audits, though here too there are problems: we have to be sure that the store audit data are correct and that they relate to the same buying period and area units as does the survey that is being checked against them.

- It is common practice for politicians and public to judge the accuracy of a pre-election survey of 'voting intention' . . . to judge its accuracy in terms of how votes were eventually cast. However, one must be very careful about this, because all the pollster is doing is measuring voting intentions at a specific point in time and he will say, quite rightly, that a great deal can happen between a survey and the actual vote. So perhaps voting outcome is not a very satisfactory 'criterion of truth' for judging the accuracy of 'voting intention' results. On the other hand, if (say) five surveys of voting intention all conducted at the same time give different results, then *that* is evidence that something is wrong with at least some of the results.

To sum up Opportunity should be taken, wherever possible, to check the results of a survey result against any available direct criterion of 'truth' — with proper humility with respect to the limitations of such a criterion. *The problem, however, is that a direct criterion of truth is rarely available for the measure we use or want to use.* If we are dealing with behaviour, then very likely there will exist no record of what *actually* occurred — as in readership research, petrol buying by individuals in the course of a week, food consumption, patterns of travel, honesty of transactions, illegal behaviour, and so on. So much happens without the possibility of record keeping or non-interfering observation going on. So many of the things we want to measure happen privately and tend not to happen if an observer is present. Nonetheless a direct criterion of truth should be used whenever it is available. Checking through such a criterion will tell us about the validity of the measuring instrument we are testing. It will also tell us quite a lot about the *principles* of question design — about what works and what does not work. Subsequent challenging of respondents found to be in error can contribute usefully to the development of that understanding.

METHOD 6: EVALUATION OF A TECHNIQUE BY COMPARING ITS RESULTS WITH A SIMULATION OF SOME KIND

Another method sometimes used to validate a measure used in survey research is to compare the results from that measure with those derived from a simulation of some kind — a substitute for a direct criterion where the simulation is thought to approximate to what really took place.

The glue spot simulation[36]   One such simulation is the glue spot technique used in readership research. With this method, a publication may be delivered to the home of a person who is scheduled (though he won't know this yet) for a readership interview. In the delivered copy, various of the pages will have been fixed together with a spot of glue. This glue spot can be broken without tearing the pages and without it being very obvious that gluings have taken place.

Subsequently an interviewer calls and puts the respondent through a noting and reading type of procedure. For each page spread, the respondent is asked to say if he/she had looked at it. If a page spread for which the glue spot is unbroken is claimed to have been looked at by the respondent, the interviewer concludes that the respondent is giving inaccurate evidence. If, on the other hand, the respondent claims to have seen a page spread for which the glue spot *is* broken, then the interviewer will regard that claim as not inconsistent with the evidence (that is, of broken glue spot).

However, there are certain obvious snags about such a criterion of truth. In the first place, the glue spot could have been broken by some other member of the household (perhaps even by rough handling of the paper at some point). Secondly, the respondent may have broken the glue spot in the process of page turning without having paused to look at anything in the page spread concerned. Over and above these arguments however the arrival of an un-ordered paper at the respondent's home is likely to be a rather atypical event and one that may well make for atypical use or reading of that paper. What this means is that the glue spot test is really no more than a negative test (useful in that sense of course) and that even *this* negative test may be upset to an extent by the atypicality of the testing situation.

The camera check [36]   In another check on the accuracy of a readership measuring procedure, respondents waited (in a waiting room), by appointment, to be put through a 'noting and reading' test (though they could not know of this test at the time of waiting). A respondent could pick up a publication to read while waiting. The seating in the waiting room was so positioned that a hidden camera could be used to photograph the pages through which the respondent turned. The respondent was eventually taken into her readership interview. Subsequently, the camera record of what pages the respondent opened and spent time with could be compared with her statements in her noting and reading test for that very same publication. If we assume that the camera evidence was quite unambiguous (and that is really an assumption), there is still the problem of how typical or representative was the simulated reading event. Certainly it was a long way from the normal 'reading at home' situation. It is even a bit of a strain to think of it as normal waiting room behaviour — where there is usually a choice of papers to look at. There is, of course, the obvious problem of the ethics of such a testing procedure — even where, as was done in the case I have cited, a respondent is eventually told what went on and given the opportunity to destroy the film.

The reader will no doubt be able to think of other simulated criteria that might be or have been used for checking on the accuracy of some measure. However the thing to do is to challenge any such criterion in terms of *how* similar to reality it is *and* in terms of whether or not the setting up of the simulation interferes with what is being studied.

METHOD 7:   EVALUATION THROUGH THE INTENSIVE INTERVIEW METHOD

A checking method that I have used in the studies reported in this text is a special form of intensive interview. The intensive interview is really a very high grade extended interview which is designed to overcome the many difficulties and sources of failures that do from time to time threaten information gathering through the survey method. I have set out below a generalised statement about its rationale and its methods.

1   The intensive interviewing procedure must be geared to a knowledge, on the part of the research designer, of the many factors that can lead survey respondents to give inaccurate replies. Such knowledge is readily available to the serious researcher and is summarised below. With such knowledge and sufficient time, the designer is in a position to make a sustained effort to avoid or to overcome those error-making factors. He should not expect to succeed completely in this objective, but he should quite easily do much better than through the ordinary survey interview.

2   In my experience of methodological research, the principal causes of error in the gathering of data through survey methods are as follows:

   - Respondent failure to understand the survey question in the way intended by the question designer
   - Lack of effort or interest on the part of the respondent (that is, he just tosses off a reply)
   - Unwillingness of the respondent to admit to his attitudinal (or his behavioural) situation
   - Failure of the respondent's memory and thinking processes in the stressed conditions of the doorstep interview
   - Interviewer failure of various kinds; for example: changes in the wording of set questions and of instructions; visual aid delivery failures; faulty reporting of what the respondent said

3   Against that background, *the whole thrust of the intensive interview is to reduce as much as possible the various sources of respondent error*. The tactics used in the intensive interview do vary from study to study. Here is a list of the principal tactics.

   (a)   The respondent is always told the purpose of the intensive investigation — namely to find out how good or bad 'our' questions are — *never* to test the respondent. This is necessary for getting the respondent to co-operate in the detective-like operation that is to follow.

   (b)   Quite often the intensive interview will then be moved on to extract from the respondent background information about the issue being investigated. This information is to be used as necessary for challenging; for example, in a check on the accuracy of the entries in a radio diary, the location and operating efficiency of all radios in the relevant environment of the respondent would be key information for challenging purposes.

(c) The respondent's grasp of the question(s) making up the measure is tested and corrected as necessary. Special delivery techniques, such as card sorting and major use of visual aids, are used to ensure communication of the intensive interviewer's questions.

(d) Familiarisation tactics may be used. An example is where a respondent is asked to turn through several issues of a given publication to ensure that he understands which publication it is he is being asked about. Or, for a question about different television programmes, the intensive interviewer may show the respondent several excerpts from the programme concerned before going on with her questions.

(e) Temporal reconstruction is also used, as when the respondent's 'yesterday' is reconstructed before she is asked about her, say, buying behaviour 'yesterday'.

(f) The technique of probing is almost always used as a method of getting the respondent to reveal more about some key issue — to go on pouring out her thoughts on some matter.

(g) Challenging is used to get the respondent out of the habit of careless or sloppy answering.

(h) Anonymity or at least strict confidentiality is stressed as a safety measure and in some cases quite elaborate steps will be taken to ensure that the respondent cannot be linked by name to what she is saying.

(i) Clarification is a standard tactic. It is used when a respondent gives a vague or even a contradictory reply.

(j) On occasions, a form of conditioning is used to overcome such resistances as the respondent may have to making an honest statement.

(k) Fatigue techniques can also be used. They involve repeating questions to respondents when they are tired or possibly off guard.

(l) There may at times be a check on the respondent's opportunity and motivation for doing whatever is being asked about.

The last step in the intensive interview is a confrontation process. In it, a comparison is made of the replies to the first and the intensive interviews. Where there is a difference, the respondent is asked to help the interviewer to understand how that difference came about — what lay behind it. The respondent is encouraged to talk out, and his replies are extensively probed and challenged. The reasons elicited in this way are seen as providing good indications of what lay behind the difference. If there are certain hypotheses (about the causes of differences) that the investigator wants to be considered, this can be done at the end of the confrontation process; that is, in addition to the normal pursuit of reasons for the difference through the confrontation process.

The method of the intensive interview is by no means finished and complete. Doubtless more tactics will be employed in the search for a criterion of truth in testing some measuring technique. However, certain principles should dominate any such further development.

- Intensive interviewing is meant to block off or obviate the errors and pitfalls that often feature in survey interviewing.
- Intensive interviewing is a detective-like process in which the methods of the detective and the psychologist are used and have much to offer.
- Intensive interviewing can go a long way to providing an accurate answer or criterion of truth. However the rigours of intensive interviewing are in practice frequently whittled away by careless operators who persist nonetheless in calling their version of the method an 'intensive interview'.
- Whatever the validity of the evidence provided by the intensive interview, scientific thinking requires that we see it as moving us *towards* accuracy, rather than allowing us to lay claim to a totally accurate result.

To conclude, then, there are a considerable number of different checks we can make in testing the accuracy of a survey research procedure. Sometimes we will be lucky enough for a *direct* check of 'truth' to be available to us — though we must take great care to ask if it is *really* such a criterion of truth. Sometimes there may be available to us some simulation of truth, though here too vigilance is needed. However, very often there is available nothing like a direct or even indirect criterion of truth and we will be forced to use the intensive interviewing method. Indeed I regard that method as a basic tool for checking the accuracy of survey measuring techniques. As such I think it must be developed further, and it must at all times be maintained as a sharp and detective-like tool.

Part I of this book is principally about the intensive interviewing method as an accuracy checking strategy.

3 Testing the accuracy of survey-based claims about purchases: purchases of different brands of chocolate confectionery in the last seven days

A STATEMENT BASED CLOSELY UPON A REPORT BY
WILLIAM BELSON OF THE SURVEY RESEARCH CENTRE

ORIGINAL RESEARCH BY

W.A. Belson, BA, PhD (Design and Direction)
B.M. Speak, BSc, PhD, Dip Psych.
D.W. Osborne, BSc (Econ.)
V.R. Yule, BA
V.R. Thompson (Analysis)

CONTENTS OF CHAPTER

AIMS OF THE ENQUIRY

During 1966, the Survey Research Centre initiated a series of studies of the accuracy of claims made by survey respondents. This series was undertaken in the wake of and in the manner of the Centre's study of the accuracy of Britain's National Readership Survey, completed in 1961.

The study reported here was an investigation of the accuracy of survey respondents' claims in a chocolate confectionery survey. More specifically, it had the following purposes.

1   To investigate the accuracy of respondents' answers to survey questions about their purchases of certain kinds of chocolate confectionery during the specified recent period — in fact the seven days prior to the day of the interview.

2   To investigate variations in accuracy level according to type of chocolate confectionery and characteristics of respondents.

3   To investigate the nature and the circumstances of such errors as respondents made.

Aim 1 was the principal purpose of the enquiry, but Aims 2 and 3 were meant to provide the sort of evidence that would help in the development of a more accurate procedure.

HOW THIS STUDY ORIGINATED

In discussions with Centre members, market research agencies and manufacturing companies had frequently expressed concern about the accuracy of quantitative estimates of market size derived from survey research. That concern lay behind the Centre's earlier and projected validity studies.

The choice of chocolate confectionery for such a study was the result of a number of considerations: the fact that chocolate confectionery was amongst the commodities often named by our discussants as subject to substantial survey error (in fact, in the form of over-estimates); the fact that ex-factory figures and retail audits, about which there was greater confidence, could not provide consumer profiles — so that manufacturers could not avoid suspect survey methods; the fact that Centre subscribers included a number of confectionery manufacturers who offered discussional and material facilities for the project.

The type of survey information of greatest interest to the different manufacturers was the amount of different products purchased over a specified short period of time. There were in operation surveys devoted to gathering just such information. If only this sort of information could be collected accurately, it would offer a simple and direct method of establishing market share for the different brands as well as purchaser profiles. Accordingly, the Centre's accuracy check was directed at assessing the accuracy of the information provided by such surveys. However, because the manufacturers wanted to reduce what they believed were inaccuracies in such data, a special feature of the accuracy check was to be the identification of the causes of such errors as were found. This particular study was focused upon one of these problem areas, namely, the purchase of chocolate confectionery.

THE METHODS OF RESEARCH – IN BRIEF

A total of 295 adults living in Greater London was double-interviewed during a six-week period in May and June 1965. These respondents were first interviewed by 'average' market research interviewers using an orthodox questionnaire concerning chocolate confectionery. Having thus made a series of statements or claims about their purchases of 36 products, these same respondents were re-interviewed later the same day/evening by specially trained intensive interviewers. This intensive interview consisted of lengthy and systematic probing to test the accuracy of the statements made in the first interview. In the intensive interview, each respondent was re-interviewed in respect of five chocolate confectionery products. By a system of rotation, a total of 12 products was 'tested' in this way, each product being 'tested' on 121–124 respondents.

THE METHODS OF RESEARCH – IN DETAIL

THE IMPORTANCE OF THE DESCRIPTION OF METHODS OF RESEARCH

The methods used in conducting a research project are always vital, for upon them depends the meaningfulness of the findings. They should be presented in the report with sufficient fullness to allow the discerning reader to judge the scientific adequacy of the study and to decide whether the findings are relatively unambiguous and workably accurate. In the present case, it is also vital that the testing procedure adopted be fully described because that is the principal purpose of this and the other illustrative reports included in this book.

THE NATURE OF THE PROPOSED ACCURACY CHECK

The basic design or rationale of the accuracy check

The rationale of the accuracy check was: (i) to administer the survey questionnaire in a normal way to ordinary survey respondents through ordinary survey interviewers; (ii) to put the same people, the same day/evening, through a specialised intensive procedure focused upon those parts of the original questionnaire that it is desired to check for accuracy; and (iii) to regard differences between the two sets of findings as approximating to evidence of error in the first interview. The intensive procedure was to be detective-like in character, to include challenging, probing and other tactics and to be administered by people trained for that job.

The search for a criterion of 'truth'

If a test of the accuracy of the survey procedure was to be made, it would, quite obviously, entail: (i) the administration of the chocolate confectionery survey under normal conditions; and (ii) the comparison of the findings from that survey with some measure of 'the truth'. However, securing a measure of the truth did in the present case raise major difficulty. Several possibilities were considered.

1 The first of these involved observing people's purchases of chocolate confectionery in a shop. However, what about their other purchases that day or that week? Could we hope to track them all day or all week? Over and above this formidable proposition, we would have to find out who these observed people were if an ordinary survey interview was to be carried out with them in the ordinary way. We might, of course, have the original observer or her partners conduct such an interview once the purchaser left the shop. But how normal is that? In real life, the ordinary interview is usually at home and it may occur as much as a week after the last purchase.

2   A second approach was to have people keep a diary in which they made a record of all purchases of chocolate confectionery, with the researcher regarding these diary records as presenting the truth. However, diarists often forget to make entries. Also, the very process of recording a purchase — of writing down its details — is likely to make it more memorable than it otherwise would be.

3   A third approach was to use the records of consumer panels as a benchmark with which to compare the survey-based results. In the first place, the records of the consumer panel members were ordinarily made through diary methods. However, over and above that, this approach would yield sample differences and not differences for individuals. Then, again, the two samples would have to be closely matched.

4   A fourth approach was to use a retail audit as a benchmark with which to compare the survey-based results. This method would not yield a comparison of results at the individual level. It would call for large scale retail and survey work. There were further problems over comparability.

For some investigations, there might of course be that well documented evidence that constitutes the desired criterion of the truth — such as hospital records, passport evidence of travel outside the country, or work absences. However, so often there is no such documented evidence and this is certainly so for the past purchases of chocolate confectionery by the individual members of a survey sample.

In the circumstances, we were left with intensive interviewing, used as a sort of detective operation, for trying to discover the truth of the matter. The ordinary survey interview was to be carried out with sample members. But straight after this, there would have to be a detective process, applied at length to a limited number of the survey claims of each respondent. Provided that detective operation was rigorous, differences between the respondent's estimates from the first and the intensive elicitation processes would, at best, be regarded as revealing error in the first interview. At worst, those differences would indicate unreliability in the survey system. In my view, the outcome is likely to be much nearer to the first of those two possibilities.

THE NATURE OF THE SURVEY PROCEDURE
THAT WAS TO BE CHECKED FOR ACCURACY

The form of the survey procedure

Unlike the National Readership Survey methodology tested by the Centre during 1961, there did not exist a single, well-established survey procedure for measuring purchasing of chocolate confectionery. There were several different procedures used by different organisations. Moreover, any one of them had tended to be varied (in form) over time. What was done in the circumstances was to adopt the more commonly used procedure, modifying it where necessary in line with good research practice. It was this procedure, whatever its weaknesses or strengths, that was to be tested. Accordingly, it is vital that the reader should study this particular procedure with care as a preliminary to reading the rest of the report. On the other hand, this feature of the study should in no way reduce the relevance of the reported enquiry as an illustration of the accuracy-testing method in operation.

The questioning procedure to be tested is set out on pages 46, 47.

Comments on features of the survey procedure

There are several features of this questionnaire that should be specially noted.

The time period   The time period within which respondents were required to answer was 'the last seven days, not counting today'. This was the period more commonly used in the survey procedures being employed by various research practitioners. It may be felt that using a seven-day period was 'asking for error' — better by far to ask about purchasing behaviour 'yesterday'. However, to have asked only about purchases 'yesterday' would have: (i) added to the cost of the survey because a larger sample would have been required to obtain sufficient numbers of purchasers for the estimation of market size and brand share; and (ii) excluded evidence of repeat buying by individuals. There was, therefore, an incentive for attempting to use as long a time period as the requirements for accuracy seemed to pe ᵐⁱᵗ Practitioners working in the chocolate confectionery industry ᵃ garded seven days as such a limit.

The exclusion of 'today' is standard procedure — replies could depend upon the time of day at w took place.

CHOCOLATE SURVEY

| Name (Mrs/Mr/Miss): | Address: . . . . |
| Sex: M / F   Age: . . . . | Social Class Grading: A / B / C / D / E |

FIRST INTERVIEW   Date: . . . . Time: . . . . Interviewer: . . . .
APPOINTMENT MADE FOR: Date: . . . . Time: . . . .
SECOND INTERVIEW   Date: . . . . Time: . . . . Interviewer: . . . .

'I'm doing a survey on *confectionery* and I'd like to ask you a few questions.'
'Here are the wrappers (SHOW FIRST PAGE OF VISUAL AIDS) of some different packs of chocolate.'
'I'm going to ask you, for each one, whether you have ever bought any, whether you have bought any in the last seven days, and how many you have bought.'

SHOW EACH WRAPPER IN TURN (HOLDING THE BUNDLE OF VISUAL AIDS YOURSELF) AND FOR EACH ONE ASK:

(a) 'Have you ever bought any . . . .' (SAY THE FULL NAME AS BELOW, STATING THE PRICE)

IF 'NO', CODE AND GO ON TO THE NEXT WRAPPER. IF 'YES', ASK:

(b) 'Have you definitely bought any of it in the last seven days — not counting today?'

IF 'NO', CODE AND GO ON TO NEXT WRAPPER. IF 'YES', ASK:

(c) 'And not counting today, how many bars of this have you bought in the last seven days?' (KEEP THE VISUAL AID SHOWING)

ONLY WHEN RESPONDENT BECOMES FAMILIAR WITH THE SYSTEM MAY THE (a), (b) and (c) QUESTIONS BE LIMITED (e.g. 'EVER BOUGHT', 'BOUGHT IN THE LAST SEVEN DAYS', 'HOW MANY')

BARS	Col	Ever bought		Bought in last 7 days		Number
		No	Yes	No	Yes	
CADBURY'S DAIRY MILK BAR at 6d	10	12	11	0	9	
CADBURY'S FRUIT AND NUT at 1/6	11	12	11	0	9	
CADBURY'S BOURNEVILLE CHOCOLATE at 1/3	12	12	11	0	9	
GALAXY FRUIT AND ALMOND at 1/-	13	12	11	0	9	
NESTLE'S ROYALS MILK CHOCOLATE at 1/-	14	12	11	0	9	
NESTLE'S MILKY BAR at 7d	15	12	11	0	9	
NESTLE'S FRUIT AND NUT at 6d	16	12	11	0	9	
FRY'S FIVE BOYS CHOCOLATE at 6d	17	12	11	0	9	
CARAMAC at 6d	18	12	11	0	9	
NESTLE'S MILK CHOCOLATE at 6d	19	12	11	0	9	
MARS BAR at 7d	20	12	11	0	9	
KIT KAT at 6d	21	12	11	0	9	
ROLO at 6d	22	12	11	0	9	
FRY'S CRUNCHIE at 6d	23	12	11	0	9	
FRY'S FIVE CENTRE at 6d	24	12	11	0	9	
FRY'S TURKISH DELIGHT at 6d	25	12	11	0	9	
FRY'S TIFFIN at 6d	26	12	11	0	9	
ROWNTREE'S PEPPERMINT CRACKNELL at 6d	27	12	11	0	9	
MACKINTOSH'S TOFFEE CRISP at 6d	28	12	11	0	9	
NESTLE'S CRACKERMILK at 6d	29	12	11	0	9	
FRY'S CHOCOLATE CREAM BAR at 6d	30	12	11	0	9	
MILKY WAY at 3½d	31	12	11	0	9	

REMINDER INSTRUCTIONS

(a) 'Have you ever bought any . . . . ' (SAY FULL NAME AS BELOW, STATING PRICE)

    IF 'NO', CODE AND GO ON TO THE NEXT WRAPPER. IF 'YES', ASK:

(b) 'Have you definitely bought any of it in the last seven days — not counting today?'

    IF 'NO', CODE AND GO ON TO NEXT WRAPPER. IF 'YES', ASK:

(c) 'And not counting today, how many packets/how much/how many boxes of this have you bought in the last seven days?' (KEEP THE VISUAL AID SHOWING)

PACKETS	Col	Ever bought		Bought in last 7 days		Number of
		No	Yes	No	Yes	packets
QUALITY STREET PACKETS at 1/4	32	12	11	0	9	
SMARTIES at 1/3	33	12	11	0	9	
MALTESERS at 6d	34	12	11	0	9	
PEANUT TREETS at 6d	35	12	11	0	9	
CHOCOLATE TREETS at 6d	36	12	11	0	9	

AFTER DEALING WITH THE PACKETS, SAY:

'Now we come to loose assortments of chocolates. I mean chocolate assortments which are sold by weight.'

ASSORTMENT	Col	Ever bought		Bought in last 7 days		Quantity
		No	Yes	No	Yes	
QUALITY STREET at 1/4 per ¼ lb.	37	12	11	0	9	
CADBURY'S ROSES CHOCOLATES at 1/5 per ¼ lb	38	12	11	0	9	
DUNCAN'S CHOCOLATES at 1/4 per ¼ lb	39	12	11	0	9	

AFTER DEALING WITH ASSORTMENTS, SAY:

'Finally, we come to boxes of chocolates.'

BOXES OF CHOCOLATES	Col	Ever bought		Bought in last 7 days		Number
		No	Yes	No	Yes	
ROWNTREES' DAIRY BOX at 3/9	40	12	11	0	9	
CADBURY'S MILK TRAY at 3/10	41	12	11	0	9	
NESTLE'S HOME MADE at 4/6	42	12	11	0	9	
GOOD NEWS at 4/-	43	12	11	0	9	
ROWNTREES' BLACK MAGIC at 4/3	44	12	11	0	9	
AFTER EIGHT ASSORTMENT at 6/6	45	12	11	0	9	

ABOUT THE RESPONDENT

1 (a) Do you have a TV set in your home?   YES/NO/?

  (b) (IF 'YES'): Can you get ITV on it?   YES/NO/?

2 (a) Including yourself, how many people are there in your home? . . . .
  (b) How many of these are children aged 15 or less? . . . .

3   What is your age? . . . .

4   ASK HOUSEWIVES: What is your husband's job?
. . . .
    ASK ALL OTHER ADULTS: What is/was your job?
. . . .

5   NOW CHECK THE NAME AND ADDRESS AND FIX THE APPOINTMENT FOR THE SECOND INTERVIEW. ENTER NAME, ADDRESS, SEX, SOCIAL CLASS AND APPOINTMENT ON TOP OF FIRST PAGE OF QUESTIONNAIRE.

The three questions about purchasers   These were in line with the practices of the time. The first question ('Have you ever bought . . . ?') was a broad screening item meant to eliminate non-purchasers. As a practice, this device has the backing of earlier research.* The second question ('Have you definitely bought any of it in the last seven days — not counting today?') was meant as a second level screen, designed to protect the all important third question from overclaims. If the respondent answered yes to that second question, the third question followed: 'And not counting today, how many bars of this have you bought in the last seven days?' (KEEP THE VISUAL AID SHOWING).

The visual aids   The visual aids used were coloured photographs of the confectionery itself. This arrangement was meant to reduce such confusion of one brand with another as seemed likely to occur with only verbal differentiation between them. The visual card presented not only a picture of the product concerned, but also its name and the price level of the item about which the question was being asked (for example, Cadbury's Dairy Milk Chocolate at 6d).

The confectionery items dealt with in the survey questionnaire   Some 36 chocolate confectionery products were included in the survey procedure. This was not out of line with common practice, and it allowed the use of an array that was well spread between the six main manufacturers and between the main groups of chocolate confectionery products (that is, block chocolates, filled bars, sweets in packets, chocolate assortments, boxed chocolates). Whereas the planned accuracy checking procedure was not intended to cover all 36, such a wide spread provided opportunity to assess accuracy for many different classes of chocolate confectionery. See pages 51, 52, for a description of those selected for accuracy checking.

The selection, briefing and control of the interviewers who would administer the survey

Selection of first interviewers   It was important for this enquiry to ensure that the quality of work done by the first interviewers was reasonably representative of normal interviewing standards in the type of market research survey they were replicating. To this end the market

---

*See *Studies in Readership*.[2] Only 1% of the readership claims by people who held that they 'never' read specific newspapers were found to be inaccurate.

research departments of four chocolate confectionery manufacturers each provided three experienced interviewers whom they considered to be of 'average' standard. In addition, six interviewers were provided by market research agencies or were selected from replies to an advertisement. As with the first 12, these six interviewers were chosen as being 'experienced' but 'average' market research interviewers.

Each week a team of three of these interviewers conducted interviews in one of the survey areas. Any one team of interviewers worked for only one week, being replaced the following week by another team. In the course of the six weeks over which fieldwork was spread, a total of 18 different market research interviewers took part. A member of the Survey Research Centre staff did a few interviews as a relief interviewer when interviewers were unavoidably absent.

This procedure meant that a relatively large number of interviewing talents and tendencies were introduced into the project. The chances of one or two interviewers' personal oddities in interviewing technique unduly influencing the results were thus reduced. The use of interviewers from several research organisations served a similar purpose.

Another reason for using any one interviewer for a relatively short time was to prevent the interviewers from becoming aware of the purpose of the interviews they were delivering and so perhaps becoming in some way atypical. The first interviewers received only the normal instructions on sampling and interviewing. They were *not* told the true purpose of their work (that is, to conduct 'normal' market research interviews which would then be 'tested' by intensive interviews).

Briefing of first interviewers and making appointments for intensive interviewer to call   Each Monday morning during the period of the fieldwork a new team of interviewers reported for briefing. At this briefing, which usually lasted about two hours, the first interview questionnaire was presented to the market research interviewers as a straightforward questionnaire about purchases of various chocolate confectionery lines. The interviewers were taken through the questionnaire and shown how to use the visual aids (one visual aid for each product). There was nothing on the questionnaire to reveal the true purpose of the operation.

A vital step in this project was the *making of an appointment* for a second interviewer (in fact, an intensive interviewer) to call on the respondent later on the same day. This had to be done by the first interviewer at the end of her interview. It was this unusual arrangement which made it necessary to take special steps to prevent the first interviewers from finding out about the true purpose of the project and so perhaps becoming conditioned and atypical. They were told that the purpose of the appointment was simply to allow a second interviewer to gather additional and detailed information about purchases and preferences of various lines of chocolate confectionery.

There were certain rules and requirements concerning the making of appointments. One of these was that the interviewer must not refer in any way to the appointment, nor to the second interview, until she had finished her own interview. Only then could she seek an appointment for the second interviewer. Another requirement was that appointments were to be sought with *all* respondents interviewed. The respondent was told that the second interviewer would be paying a small fee for the time given her and that she would be someone from the university who would be coming out specially to keep the appointment. The first interviewer was to leave with the respondent a card stating the time of the appointment and a letter introducing the second interviewer. This letter explained that the interview was part of an important inquiry being conducted from a university.

Appointments for the second interview were to be sought at times both to suit the respondent and to fit into the working schedules of the intensive interviewers. The number of appointments required of the first interviewer was three or four on any one day. They had to make specified numbers of appointments with men and with women. After each appointment was made, the first interviewer returned to the local centre (see later) with the questionnaire and the details of the appointment.

Each team of first interviewers was to work from Monday to Saturday inclusive. One member of the team was to work from 9.30 am to 3.30 pm and the other two from 1.30 pm to 7.30 pm. The shifts of the three were to be rotated in order.

The first interviewers were provided with identification cards marked 'Survey Research Centre' and instructed to tell respondents if asked that this was the research body for which they were working. They were told not to mention 'the university' until they had made an appointment for the intensive interviewer to call.

A list of 40 names was given to each of the first interviewers and they were told to make at least three calls on each address before giving up and *not* to accept any substitutes for the names on the list.

THE PURPOSES AND NATURE OF
THE INTENSIVE INTERVIEW

The purposes of the intensive interview

The purpose of the intensive interview was two-fold:

- To find out the exact quantities of the specified chocolate confectionery lines which had been bought by the respondent (either for himself or for others) in the seven days prior to (and exclusive of) the day of interview.
- If there were any differences between these amounts and the amounts stated by the respondent in the first interview, to find out how and why these differences occurred.

An introduction to the nature of the intensive interview

There was a clearly specified procedure for carrying out the intensive interview. It was administered by intensive interviewers specially selected and trained for the job.

The intensive interview was a detective process into which were incorporated: memory aids; systematic probing to find out about the respondents' purchases during the specified period; considerable challenging and cross-checking of respondents' replies. The intensive interview was fully tape-recorded.

The number of claims to be checked
through the intensive interview

In planning the intensive interview, two limits had to be imposed upon the testing of claims made in the first interview. These limits each stemmed from the fact that intensive interviewing is ordinarily a very demanding process in terms of *time* as well as in other ways. Past experience with the method, and preparatory work, had made it clear that no more than five first-interview claims could properly be checked in the interviewing time available for any one respondent. Under the right conditions, this time was about an hour. That was the first limitation: the checking of only five claims per intensive interview.

In the second place, the number of different chocolate confectionery products to be dealt with *between* the intensive interviewers was set at 12. It had been calculated that, with the available resources, this would allow the testing of approximately 120 claims about each of those 12 products. A smaller number of products (less than 12) would yield a larger numerical base for each, but less variety between the products tested.

The 12 products selected for tests through the intensive interview were:

Cadbury's Dairy Milk Chocolate	@	6d*	
Nestle's Fruit and Nut	@	6d	
Mars Bar	@	7d	
Mackintosh's Rolo	@	6d	
Fry's Tiffin	@	6d	
Rowntree's Peppermint Cracknell	@	6d	
Fry's Chocolate Creams	@	6d	
Peanut Treets	@	6d	
Mackintosh's Quality Street Assortment	@	1/4	per ¼ lb
Cadbury's Roses	@	1/5	per ¼ lb
Nestle's Home Made Chocolates	@	4/6	per box
Rowntree's Black Magic Chocolates	@	4/3	per box

The number of positive and zero claims to be checked for each chocolate confectionery product

Another question for settlement in relation to each of the 12 chocolate confectionery products selected for study was the proportion of the first interview claims that should be positive and a proportion that should be negative. Obviously it would be best to test *all* claims 'as they came' (positive or zero). However, it was equally obvious that there would be far too many of them for this to be practicable. Moreover, the great majority of those first-interview claims would be zero claims (that is, no purchase at all).

In these circumstances, a decision was taken:

- to test *all* positive claims for each of the 12 test products; and
- to make up the remainder of each interviewer's load (of product claims to be tested) with zero claims.

Taking an average over the whole 12 test products, this did in fact mean an average of about one positive claim and four zero claims per intensive interviewer. Allocation of zero claims was done by the local centre administrator working to a particular rule. Thus in allocating

*Prices at the time of fieldwork.

52

zero claims for testing, the objective was always to keep the total number of allocations (positive or zero) as near as possibly equal over the 12 test products. For each of them the allocations would fill up equally fast. In fact, the ultimate 'fill' for each was about 122. The balance between positive and zero claims for each of them is shown in Table 3.1.

It was clear at the time that re-weighting of the positive and zero balances back to normality would have to occur before the results were analysed. Details of this step are given on pages 61, 62.

The different stages of the intensive interview

There follows a detailed commentary on the stages of the intensive interview, and this should be linked to a study of the procedure itself, shown in the appendix to this chapter.

- After a brief informal conversation designed to put the respondent at ease, the interviewer introduced the interview as being about 'the way memory works', especially memory for the small things which are done and bought each day. The respondent was then asked to think back to the interview which had taken place earlier in the day.
- The second stage was aimed at finding out the precise period which the respondent had been thinking of when she was deciding whether or not she had bought any of the products she was asked about. She should, of course, have been thinking of the seven days which ended the night before the interview took place.
- When the period considered by the respondent had been determined as precisely as possible, it was necessary to establish in her mind the *correct* period she should have considered. This was done by using 'landmarks' which would help mark out the period for her. These consisted of events in the respondent's own life, television pro-grammes, public events, and so on. If the respondent kept a diary or had old shopping lists this was often found helpful.

  Having established as far as possible the correct period in the respondent's mind, it was essential to *fix* it, in case she should 'wander' out of it again. This was done by asking her to recollect, for each day of the period, something that had happened in her own life. These events were noted by the interviewer so that they could be used, if necessary, later in the interview (for example, '. . . you remember, Thursday was the day your mother came to lunch').
- The next stage was aimed at finding out whether the respondent had, in fact, bought any of the five test products in that seven day period and, if so, how much of each had been bought. The visual aids

(wrappers) of each of the five products were spread out in front of the respondent and for each one there was a process of checking and challenging the respondent's replies.

- When the interviewer and the respondent had agreed upon a figure of purchases for each of the five products 'tested' with that particular respondent, the problem was tackled in another way. The respondent was asked to go through the last seven days, starting with 'yesterday' and working backwards, telling the interviewer exactly what she did from the moment of rising to going to bed at night. Naturally, more time was spent on those occasions when the respondent was out of the house and could have made some purchases, although the possibility of house-to-house sales was not overlooked. The intensive interviewer had to be alert for every possibility of shopping, especially visits to sweet shops, newsagents, grocers, Woolworths, public houses, open markets and other places which might conceivably sell chocolate confectionery. Whenever a visit had been made to a possible buying point, the respondent was closely questioned as to whether any of the five test products could have been bought and, if so, what size, price, etc. it had been and whether it was bought by the respondent herself (that is, by actually asking for it herself).

- At the end of this day-by-day account of the respondent's activities, the amounts purchased of each product were totalled for the seven days. These totals were put before the respondent and she was asked whether or not she felt this was the correct amount for each product, whether it was not perhaps a little too much or not quite enough and whether these amounts consisted only of purchases made by herself. Any corrections which had to be made were made at this point.

- Finally, the amounts derived from the two intensive procedures were compared. To start with, the quantities claimed as purchased earlier in the interview were compared with the quantities just arrived at. The respondent was asked to explain any discrepancies. When a final figure had been agreed upon by the respondent and the interviewer, this figure was taken as the 'second interview total' for that product.

- When all second interview totals for the five products had been determined in this way, then (and only then) did the intensive interviewer open a sealed envelope containing the respondent's first interview questionnaire. For each product for which there was a difference between the first and second interview claims, the respondent was asked to explain how the difference came about.

In doing this, every effort was made to prevent her from feeling that she was being criticised or caught out. This was frequently unnecessary, however, because respondents themselves had usually become very interested in any discrepancies between the two sets of figures. For each product for which the claimed purchase(s) from the first interview differed from the second interview figure, the respondent was asked which was the correct figure. The respondent was also asked to explain how this discrepancy could have occurred. This process was repeated for each of the five products separately.

It must be noted that the intensive interviewer had not seen the respondent's first questionnaire before this point in the interview and hence had no idea what amounts had been claimed at the first interview.

- The intensive interviewer completed her interview by collecting biographical data and asking for ratings on certain scales dealing with product usage. (See appendices.)

The selection and training of the intensive interviewers

A total of six interviewers were employed on the intensive interviews in this study. It was necessary that interviewers doing this work should be of above-average intelligence, well educated, acceptable to respondents of all classes, and that they should have the mentality necessary for what was, in fact, a form of detective work. There were on the staff of the Survey Research Centre four people who had considerable experience in intensive interviewing. One of these became Assistant Office Manager and relief interviewer and another became Quality Controller and relief interviewer. The remaining two became full-time interviewers. Two further interviewers were selected from amongst the 20 applicants who replied to press advertisements. These two new interviewers joined the other four in a week's training course in the intensive interview method for this research.

Although only a week was allocated for *initial* training, in fact training went on throughout the survey. In the initial training week, the trainees were introduced to the purpose of the inquiry and to the first intensive interview on which most of the training period was spent. The method of training was, after verbal instruction in the technique of intensive interviewing and after classroom practice in its administration, to have trainees administer the intensive interview to ordinary members of the public in their homes. The trainees tape-recorded each interview, passing the recording to the person in charge of training. Each day, after interviewers had carried out their interviews, *one* of the tape-recordings was played back to the whole group of trainees and to the person in charge of training them. The trainees were required to ask for the play-back to be stopped each time they thought the interviewer concerned had gone wrong and each time they thought she had missed a promising lead. This apparent failure was then discussed by the trainees under the guidance of their instructor. If the trainees did not notice a particular failure in the recorded interview, the instructor stopped the play-back and focused attention of the trainees on the failure, saying what *should* have been done. After this, another recording (by a different trainee) was played back and criticised in the same way. In the course of a week, all the different trainees had about the same number of their interviews criticised in this way. One of the things the instructor tried to develop in the trainees was a willingness to accept criticism, and trainees were encouraged to join in with criticism of their own work. Ordinarily, people unwilling to accept criticism are dropped from the team.

The process of critical discussion was continued throughout the six-week survey period. It took place in the local centre at any time of the day when interviewers were not actually visiting respondents in their homes. The Quality Controller listened to the tape-recording of a proportion of the intensive interviews each day (approximately half the recordings were listened to in this way). He then took up failures with the interviewers concerned, telling them what was wrong and suggesting ways of correcting their failure. This tuition was limited to the interviewer concerned, but frequently other of the interviewers were able to join in criticism of the recorded interviews. Where difficulties of a recurrent kind showed up and where methods for dealing with them were developed, details of these modifications were passed on to all interviewers.

CONTROLLING BOTH THE FIRST AND THE INTENSIVE INTERVIEWING OPERATIONS THROUGH A MOBILE CENTRE

The use of a mobile control centre as a headquarters office

For the kind of operation that was planned, a local headquarters was essential. The first survey interviewers would have to pass in their appointments progressively during the day and the intensive interviewers would have to be based there and to receive very short-term notice of those appointments. The intensive interviewers would also need such a centre for transcribing their tape-recordings and for receiving corrective instructions from a Quality Controller. However, getting suitable local offices in all the localities drawn through random sampling processes is usually an extremely difficult thing to do and even fairly intensive searches often fail. In the face of such difficulties, a large office caravan was hired to serve as a mobile local centre. Though this was not ideal, it was possible to partition this caravan into two portions, one of which was used by the intensive interviewers and the other half used by market research interviewers for handing in the results of their interviews and the details of appointments made.

This caravan had to be situated in the midst of the polling district in which the team was currently working, otherwise too much time would be spent by interviewers in travelling to and from respondents' homes. Each week, the team worked in a fresh polling district. The caravan was moved to a new site early each Monday morning.

The first interviewers' use of the centre

When a market research interviewer had secured an appointment, she brought the completed first interview questionnaire to the local centre in time for the appointment to be kept by the intensive interviewer. At the same time, the market research interviewers reported any failures to contact respondents or to secure appointments. These first interviewers were also free to come to the local centre to have a cup of coffee or tea or to pick up fresh questionnaires or letters. However, they were not permitted to stay long at the centre and their contact there was always with the local centre manager or her assistant. As part of the effort to prevent market research interviewers finding out the real purpose of the enquiry, a separate door of the caravan was used for these interviewers and they were not allowed to go into the part of the caravan used by the intensive interviewers. Intensive interviewers were told *never* to engage with market research interviewers in discussion of the purpose of the survey.

The intensive interviewers' use of the centre

The intensive interviewers were based at the local centre (that is, the caravan). They returned to the caravan after each intensive interview. There, each of them collected her next appointment and finalised the report on the interview just made (working from the tape-recording of it and from notes made during it). Each day, before starting out to keep appointments, intensive interviewers had to spend some time with the Quality Controller, listening to his comments on the quality of their work, and listening to passages of the tape-recording he had selected for tuition. They were also given details of any modifications in their instructions and also any reminders which appeared to be necessary. Before going to their interviews each day all the intensive interviewers were given a list showing the important events of each of the past eight days (e.g. highlights in the television programmes, headlines from the newspapers, extremes of weather, etc.). These were to be used in helping respondents to focus memory on a particular day (for example, 'last Tuesday' was the day on which there was a sudden thunderstorm in London).

Before leaving for an interview the intensive interviewer had to ensure she had with her: a tape-recorder complete with microphone, batteries and extra tape; her instruction sheet (see Appendix 3.1); the second interview report form (see Appendix 3.2); the requisite visual aids; the first questionnaire (which was given her in a sealed envelope and not opened until the confrontation at the end of the interview); a small sum of money to pay the respondent for the time given.

The Quality Controller also worked at the local centre in the room used by the intensive interviewers. All tape-recorders were fitted with earphones, so that the Quality Controller was able to listen to the tapes as they came in without disturbing the other people working there.

The office manager's role at the centre

The office manager and her assistant were responsible for the general running of the local centre, which was open throughout the day until 10.30 pm Mondays to Saturdays inclusive. Each Monday morning, the office manager briefed the market research interviewers and after this they were taken to the local centre to begin their week's assignment. One of the office manager's jobs was to keep a record of the interviewing progress to date and to keep a tally of the number of people who had been tested in respect of each of the 12 products which were being tested.

When a market research interviewer reported back to the local office with an appointment, the office manager examined the questionnaire to find out which of the 12 products had been bought by the respondent. Only in a few cases had more than five of the test products been bought by the respondent. In these cases, the less commonly purchased products were chosen for testing in preference to the more commonly purchased products. If a respondent happened to have bought exactly five of the products, all five were assigned for testing. In the more usual case, where the respondent claimed to have bought less than five of the products, all of those which had been bought were assigned for testing and the number made up to five by selecting certain of the products which the respondent did not claim to have bought in the 'last seven days'. The allocation of the latter was designed to keep as even as possible the number of tests (whether of claims or of non-claims) carried out on each of the 12 test products.

Having selected an appropriate five products for testing, the office manager wrote the names of these products on the report form to be used in that intensive interview. She did not, of course, indicate which, if any, of these five products the respondent claimed to have bought in the first interview. The first interview questionnaire was then placed in an envelope and sealed. The respondent's name, address, age, time of appointment and a serial number were written on the intensive interview report form and on the sealed envelope, and these were passed to the appropriate intensive interviewer. The office manager saw all the market research interviewers as they reported in, noting failures and difficulties.

SAMPLING DETAILS

Selection of interviewing areas

The dependence of the enquiry upon establishing and operating local centres put a practical limit upon the number of different areas on which sampling could be based. In fact, six wards in the Greater London area were drawn. The six wards were drawn through systematic probability sampling, with probability proportional to size of electorate. Within each selected ward, one polling district was drawn, namely that one nearest to the ward in terms of economic level (as indicated at that time by the percentage of people in an area who were eligible for jury service).

The reason for using polling districts instead of the larger wards was that a ward was so large that the ordinary survey interviewers would have spent an impractical amount of time walking from the location of an interview to the local centre. Geographical and social grade controls were employed in order to increase the likelihood that the small sample of six polling districts* would yield a sample of people not unduly atypical of the population of Greater London in terms of personal characteristics. On the other hand, it would be great folly to expect the confectionery buying yield from these six polling districts to be typical of the confectionery buying for London as a whole. The difference could be very large.

---

*The six selected polling districts were as follows, with proportions of 'middle class' males in each ('middle class' = Registrar General's Occupation Groups I, II, III, IV and XIII):

Constituency	Ward	Polling District	Proportion of 'Middle Class'
Poplar	East	PP	5.69%
Camberwell, Peckham	Burgess	MA	5.88%
Hammersmith North	Addison	HA	11.76%
Wandsworth Putney	Thamesfield	E	17.16%
Hampstead	West End	I	32.56%
Woolwich West	Horn Park	23A	37.50%

Response rate for first interviews

From each selected polling district, 120 names were drawn from the Electoral Register by systematic random sampling. These names were split equally among the three market research interviewers working that week, so that each had 40 names. Since there were 18 market research interviewers operating in the course of the enquiry, the total number of names issued in this way was 720. Interviewers were told to make three calls before giving up trying to contact an individual named in the list.

When an interviewer reported that she had exhausted her list of potential contacts, she was given a supplementary list of 12 names which had been drawn in the same way. If this list, too, was exhausted, 12 more names were issued. A total of 537 extra names was issued in this way, making an overall total of 1257 names between the 18 market research interviewers. Of these 1257 a total of 35% were interviewed.*

The response rate of 35% is not comparable with the response rate on a normal random sample survey. This is because the need to obtain appointments for the second interviewers placed restrictions on how the first interviewers could make their calls. The first interviewers had not only to contact respondents and interview them in the normal way, but also to secure appointments for second interviews later that *same* day. Moreover, these appointments were to be with a specified number of men and of women. This meant that the first interviewers had to be selective in their calls and could not work after 7.30 in the evening. Also, after each appointment was fixed they had to return to the local centre to book it in.

*Non-contacts				
	moved	89		
	on holiday	47		
	sick, incapable, etc.	61		
	not known, house empty or demolished	48		
	All		245	19.5%
Refusals to undergo first interview			92	7.3%
Not available for first interview during interviewing hours (9.30 am–7.30 pm)			87	6.9%
Abandoned as 'not at home'				
	after one call	142†		
	after two calls	95†		
	after three calls	156†		
	All		393	31.2%
Contacted and interviewed			440	35.0%
TOTAL ATTEMPTED CONTACTS			1257	100.0%

†Premature abandonment necessitated because of need to fix intensive appointments on the same day.

The first interviewer, therefore, could not get through nearly as many call-backs as they would have done in an ordinary random sample survey. Lastly, the apparent response rate was reduced by the fact that the first interviewers, because of their need to obtain their quotas of appointments, tended to ask the local office manager for supplementary names, instead of pursuing with further calls potential respondents who appeared to be out. This meant that there was a much higher proportion than normal of names abandoned as 'not at home', frequently after only one or two calls.

Response rate for second interviewers

The 440 respondents contacted and interviewed by the first interviewers were asked to see a second interviewer that same day at a time agreed between the respondent and the interviewer. Of these, 80 (18%) respondents were either unwilling or unable to make this appointment.

Of the remaining 360 who made an appointment, a further 55 (12.5%) failed to keep it or refused to see the second interviewer when she called. Another six (1.4%) people started the interview but were unable to complete it and one other person was found to be the wrong respondent.

In all, 298 (68%) people went through the intensive interview and 295 (67%) of these were successfully tape-recorded.

An analysis of the characteristics of those going through the two interviews showed that they were closely similar to the adult population of Greater London.*

RE-WEIGHTING BEFORE ANALYSIS

The raw data produced by the enquiry could not be presented as they stood. This was because the positive and zero claims for the first

*Characteristic	This sample %	Greater London† %	Characteristic	This sample %	Greater London† %
Sex — male	49	49	Occupational level		
female	51	51	Professional,		
			Semi-professional,	13	6
Age — 21–30	18	21	Executive		
31–40	19	19	Highly skilled	13	13
41–50	22	19	Skilled	24	25
51–60	16	18	Moderately skilled	16	26
61–70	14	23	Semi-skilled	20	15
71+	11		Unskilled	14	15

†Age and sex distributions for Greater London are based on 1961 Census data. Occupational level distributions are based on data from the Audience Research Department of the BBC.

interview had been subject to weighting on the pattern shown in the first and intensive interview columns below.

Table 3.1
Showing initial underweighting of zero claims and
occasional underweighting of positive claims

Chocolate confectionery lines tested	First interview claims			Intensive interview claims		
	+	−	All	+	−	All
Cadbury's Dairy Milk (6d)	71	221	292	66	53	119
Nestle's Fruit and Nut (6d)	7	286	293	7	114	121
Mars Bars (7d)	78	214	292	76	48	124
Mackintosh's Rolo (6d)	51	242	293	48	75	123
Fry's Tiffin (6d)	7	288	295	7	117	124
Rowntree's Peppermint Cracknell (6d)	6	289	295	6	117	123
Fry's Chocolate Cream (6d)	46	246	292	45	76	121
Peanut Treets (6d)	14	279	293	14	108	122
Quality Street Assortment (1/4d)	16	278	294	16	105	121
Cadbury's Roses Assortment (1/5d)	13	281	294	13	108	122
Nestle's Home Made Chocolates (4/6d)	0	294	294	0	123	123
Rowntree's Black Magic (4/3d)	11	284	295	11	110	121
All	320	3202	3522	312	1154	1467

Before analysis could take place, however, re-weighting would have to occur. To this end, the second interview results for the under-represented zero claims would in effect have to be weighted to their first interview levels; similarly for the few cases where the number of tested positive claims was different from the first interview levels. The method of re-weighting is complex. Its description is illustrated in Table 3.1.1 and it is completed in three steps.

Step 1 For each score category (column a), calculate the ratio of the first interview number to the number actually put through the intensive interviews (e.g. 221:53; 29:29; . . .). This is entered in column (d) and is called the 'weighting ratio'.

Step 2 For each score category (column a), use its weighting ratio on each of the scores established through the intensive interview, for

Table 3.1.1
The weighting system illustrated through the results for Cadbury's Dairy Milk Chocolate*

Score in bars	First interview numbers	Number of cases tested in intensive interview	Weighting in ratio	(Raw scores in intensive interview (e) and weighted score (f))									Total intensive interview cases without weighting
				0	1	2	3	4	5	6	7	8	
(a)	(b)	(c)	(d)										(g)
0	221	53	4.17	(47) 196.0	(3) 12.5	(1) 4.2	(1) 4.2	(1) 4.2	0	0	0	0	221.1
1	29	29	1.00	(10) 10.0	(14) 14.0	(2) 2.0	(2) 2.0			(1) 1.0			29.0
2	16	14	1.14	(7) 8.0	(1) 1.1	(3) 3.4	(1) 1.1	(2) 2.3					15.9
3	10	7	1.43	(1) 1.4	(1) 1.4	(2) 2.9	(2) 2.9	(1) 1.4					10.0
4	7	7	1.00	(2) 2.0		(1) 1.0	(1) 1.0	(2) 2.0		(1) 1.0			7.0
5	2	2	1.00						(2) 2.0				2.0
6	2	2	1.00	(1) 1.0				(1) 1.0					2.0
7	3	3	1.00			(1) 1.0					(1) 1.0	(1) 1.0	3.0
11	1	1	1.00									(1) 1.0	1.0
12	1	1	1.00			(1) 1.0							1.0
All	292	119		218.4	29.0	15.5	11.2	10.9	2.0	2.0	1.0	2.0	292.0
													(h)

Weighted intensive scores = (218.4 x 0) + (29.0 x 1) + (15.5 x 2) + (. . . . = 182.2 bars*
Weighted first interview scores = (221.1 x 0) + (29.0 x 1) + (15.9 x 2) + (. . . = 184.8 bars*

63

example, 47, 3, 1, 1, 1 of the first row of figures entered under (e) and shown in brackets. Thus (47) is multiplied by 4.17, as are (3), (1), (1), (1); similarly, (7), (1), (3), (1), (2) are multiplied by 1.14 and so on. The new figures are used to calculate a cumulative purchase score of *182.2* bars, as shown above, which approximates to the true figure for the sample.

Step 3 The use of the weighting ratio on the frequencies yielded by the intensive interview produce case totals that are not quite the same as the totals shown in column (b). 'Trim' weighting is therefore done to complete the matching of the first interview and the intensive interview samples. The final score for the *first interview* thus becomes $(221.1 \times 0) + (29.0 \times 1) + (15.9 \times 2) + \ldots = $ *184.8* bars.

FINDINGS

ERRORS IN MEASURING THE TOTAL AMOUNT OF CHOCOLATE CONFECTIONERY PURCHASED

One of the purposes of conducting a chocolate confectionery survey is to establish the amounts of different chocolate confectionery being purchased in a given period. The different manufacturers want to know not only how they are going, but how they are going in relation to competition. They want to be able to calculate the market share of their own and of their competitors' products. The important question in the present context is one of how accurate the survey results actually are. Details are given in Table 3.2.

Taking all 12 tested products together, the number of bars, packs, etc. claimed in the first interview was about a fifth larger than the total number finally agreed in the intensive interview (which is interpreted as being nearer the truth). If the products are taken individually, however, it can be seen that the results are extremely variable from one product to another and that they range from large overestimates to large under-estimates.

Because of the relatively small sample sizes for individual products, it would be unwise to take at face value the *precise* extent of the inflation or deflation of purchases shown in Table 3.1 for the products separately. However, it is clear that there is considerable variability in

Table 3.2

The 'accuracy' of purchasing data yielded by the survey method:
a comparison of 12 chocolate confectionery products*

Chocolate confectionery products	Estimates of quantity purchased in 'last seven days, excluding today' (with weighting of the intensive interview data)*			Numerical base	
	Via standard survey method (a)	Via intensive interview (b)	(a) as % of (b)	Weighted number	Unweighted number
Fry's Chocolate Cream (6d)	91.1	39.9	228%	292	121
Mackintosh's Rolo (6d)	95.0	61.5	154%	293	123
Rowntree's Black Magic Chocolates (4/3d)	11.0	8.2	134%	295	121
Mars Bar (7d)	194.0	153.1	127%	292	124
Cadbury's Roses (1/5d qtr lb)	20.0	16.2	123%	294	122
Cadbury's Dairy Milk (6d)	184.8	182.2	101%	292	119
Mackintosh's Quality Street Assortment (1/4d qtr lb)	27.0	28.1	96%	294	121
Rowntree's Peppermint Cracknell (6d)	10.0	11.0	91%	295	123
Nestle's Fruit and Nut (6d)	7.0	8.0	88%	293	121
Peanut Treets (6d)	22.0	32.1	69%	293	122
Fry's Tiffin (6d)	9.0	15.8	57%	295	124
Nestle's Home Made Assortment (4/6d)	0	4.8	0%	294	123
All	670.9	560.9	120%		

*It would be most unwise to convert the above quantities to general population figures. They relate to only six polling districts in London. Individually they may be higher or lower for economic level than other polling districts in London and there is no way in which they may be re-weighted to yield an estimate for the whole of London. What they tell us about is what happened to the quantities claimed in the first interview when the intensive interview was used (relative results only).

the degree to which purchases of individual products are overstated or understated. If this is so, then there is a strong possibility that survey-based estimates of brand shares of the market might be distorted. To take the extreme case, the brand share of Fry's Chocolate Cream in the 'market' formed by the 12 products listed in Table 3.1 can be 14% or 7% depending on whether the first or the intensive interview figures are used.

ERRORS IN CLASSIFYING SURVEY RESPONDENTS AS PURCHASERS OR NON-PURCHASERS OF CHOCOLATE CONFECTIONERY PRODUCTS

Another important purpose of the chocolate confectionery survey is to allow classification of respondents as purchasers or non-purchasers of a given chocolate confectionery product. Descriptions of purchasers (as distinct from non-purchasers) may then be prepared as a basis for marketing policy. Clearly it is important that those classified as buyers should in fact *be* buyers.

Table 3.3 provides evidence about the adequacy of the recent buying survey as a basis for such classification.

Table 3.3

Showing the 'accuracy' of the survey method in classifying respondents as recent buyers of specific chocolate confectionery products

Chocolate confectionery products	Classified in int. interview as non-purchasers 'in last seven days'				Classified in int. interview as purchasers 'in last seven days'				Total in error	
	All	Check agrees	Check disagrees		All	Check agrees	Check disagrees			
	n	n	n	%	n	n	n	%	n	%
Cadbury's Dairy Milk	221	196	25	11	71	49	22	31	47	16
Nestle's Fruit and Nut	286	284	2	1	7	3	4	57	6	2
Mars Bar	214	196	18	8	79	50	29	37	47	16
Mackintosh's Rolo	242	236	6	2	51	33	18	35	24	8
Fry's Tiffin	288	281	7	2	7	3	4	57	11	4
Rowntree's Peppermint Cracknell	289	284	5	2	6	2	4	67	9	3
Fry's Chocolate Cream	246	240	6	2	46	17	29	63	35	12
Peanut Treets	279	266	13	5	14	7	7	50	20	7
Quality Street Assortment	279	274	5	2	16	9	7	44	12	4
Cadbury's Roses Assortment	281	276	5	2	13	6	7	54	12	4
Nestle's Home Made Assortment	294	289	5	2	0	0	0	(0%)	5	2
Rowntree's Black Magic	284	279	5	2	11	3	8	73	13	4
All	3203	3101	102	3%	321	182	139	43%	241	7

In the first place, those who denied purchasing a given chocolate confectionery product turned out to be predominantly just that, that is non-purchasers of it. For all 12 products considered together, the confirmation figure is 97%. Moreover, this is broadly the position product by product.

However, the situation is sharply different for those who claimed to be purchasers. For all 12 products considered together, 43% of those who claimed to be purchasers turned out to be non-purchasers. Moreover, mis-classification of this kind is at a high level for each of the 12 products considered separately.

The overall mis-classification figure of 7% (Table 3.3) hides the fact that 43% of those claiming to be purchasers were in fact non-purchasers.

COMPARING THE PROFILE OF THOSE CLAIMING IN THE FIRST INTERVIEW TO BE PURCHASERS WITH THE PROFILE OF THOSE IDENTIFIED AS PURCHASERS THROUGH THE INTENSIVE INTERVIEW

On the evidence so far presented, there is a case for wariness about the adequacy of consumer profiles based upon sample survey evidence. Table 3.4 compares the profile of those classified as purchasers through the first interview with the profile of those identified as purchasers through the intensive interview.

Table 3.4
Profiles of claimed purchasers compared with profile of
actual purchasers (12 products combined)*

Characteristics of respondents		Percentage of respondents claiming to have purchased in last seven days	Percentage of respondents actually purchasing in last seven days
		%	%
Sex	Male	46	43
	Female	54	57
Age	40 and under	43	45
	41 and over	57	55
Occupational level	More skilled	40	35
	Less skilled	60	65
Children under 15	None	44	39
	Some	56	61
Terminal education age	16 and over	15	19
	15 and under	85	81
Frequency of eating sweets	Most days	60	64
	Less often	40	36

*After application of the standard weighting up system.

Surprisingly, the two profiles are fairly similar.

If we are to try to explain this finding, there is at least one interesting possibility. This possibility is that the majority of those who wrongly claimed they were non-purchasers in the first interview (see column 3 in Table 3.3) and the majority of those who wrongly claimed they were purchasers in the first interview (see column 6 in Table 3.3) are really (both of them) long-term buyers and as such have similar characteristics. This possibility is by no means inconsistent with the 'reasons for error' put forward by respondents as set out in Table 3.9.

Whatever the case, the details in Table 3.4 relate to all 12 products considered together and provide no evidence about the individual products. So we must keep an open (and wary) mind on how the profiles might compare at the level of the individual product.

What matters above all else is that the recent purchasing survey did in this case lead to a substantial mis-classification of the survey respondents in terms of whether or not they bought specified chocolate confectionery in the 'last seven days excluding today'.

THE INNER MECHANICS OF ERROR-MAKING BY RESPONDENTS WHEN THE SURVEY METHOD IS USED FOR ESTIMATING QUANTITIES OF CHOCOLATE CONFECTIONERY PURCHASED

The enquiry has also provided evidence which, though of no obvious relevance to the marketing decision-maker, is of considerable relevance to the research practitioner. This evidence is about:

- The extent and nature of balancing errors — about how overclaims and underclaims partially balance each other out (Table 3.5)
- The reasons for error as seen by the respondent (Tables 3.7 and 3.8)

It is clear from Table 3.5 that over- and underclaiming is an intrinsic feature of the response processes in the survey concerned. Sometimes the two virtually balance each other out. However, more often they do not do so by any means and for some of the products the imbalance is of a major order. Moreover, there can be a net overclaim *or* a net underclaim.

It must be noted of course that over- and underclaiming is a feature of virtually any technique for measuring quantities through respondent recall. What is exceptional here is the sheer size of the overclaim/under-

Table 3.5
Showing the degree to which respondents' over- and underclaims balance out — or don't

Chocolate confectionery products	All bars claimed in first interview (a)	Bars OVER-claimed in first interview (b)	Bars UNDER-claimed in first interview (c)	Net OVER- or UNDER-claimed in first interview (b – c)	All bars actually purchased (intensive interview) (a) – (b – c)
Cadbury's Dairy Milk	185.0	74.0	71.2	2.8	182.2
Nestle's Fruit and Nut	7.0	4.0	5.0	–1.0	8.0
Mars Bar	194.0	94.9	54.0	40.9	153.1
Mackintosh's Rolo	95.0	46.1	12.6	33.5	61.5
Fry's Tiffin	9.0	5.5	12.3	–6.8	15.8
Rowntree's Peppermint Cracknell	10.0	6.5	7.5	–1.0	11.0
Fry's Chocolate Cream	91.1	61.7	10.5	51.2	39.9
Peanut Treets	22.0	14.0	24.1	–10.1	32.1
Mackintosh's Quality Street Assortment	27.0	11.0	12.1	–1.1	28.1
Cadbury's Roses Assortment	20.0	9.0	5.2	3.8	16.2
Nestle's Home Made Assortment	0.0	0.0	4.8	–4.8	4.8
Rowntree's Black Magic	11.0	8.0	5.2	2.8	8.2
All*	671.1	334.7	224.5	110.2	560.9

*All cell entries based on 'weighted' bars.

claim problem. That large size means two things. First, it indicates a basically unstable situation as regards measurement. Secondly, it suggests a direction for remedial effort to the methodologist who sets out to make the measuring technique more accurate. The latter point will be taken up again in later chapters.

THE POSSIBLE CAUSES OF ERROR

Whenever a test of the accuracy of a method is carried out, it is essential to learn as much as possible about the reasons for such errors as are discovered. Only when that is done is the technique designer in a position to modify the technique towards greater accuracy. To this end, certain checks were included in the intensive interview.

The enquiries made and the tabulation of findings

The interpretation of the qualifying time period   In stage I of the intensive interview, the respondent was told the purpose of the second interview and was in general prepared for what was to come. The intensive interviewer then asked the respondent to specify the actual period she had in mind in answering the question.

- 'When you told the first interviewer about any chocolates you had bought, what period were you thinking of?'
- 'Exactly when was the start of the period you were actually thinking of?'
- 'Which were the days you counted when you answered the first interviewer?'

This line of questioning produced evidence of considerable distortion of the time period (that is, the last seven days excluding 'today'), and this evidence is presented in Table 3.6 below.

Table 3.6
Concerning the time period actually considered in the first interview

1 Was the correct period considered?	3 Did respondent include 'today'?
Yes 6%	Yes 46%
No 89%	
Unclear 5%	4 When did the considered period start?
All 100%	Seven days ago excluding 'today'* 24%
	Earlier 40%
2 Length of period considered	Later 29%
1—3 days 6%	Unclear 6%
4—6 days 15%	
7 days 20%	5 When did the considered period end?
8—10 days. 37%	Today 46%
11—14 days 3%	Yesterday 25%
15 days—3 months 2%	Before yesterday 18%
Period not clear 17%	Unclear 11%
Overall average amongst those considering a particular period = 8.5 days	

*But not necessarily including all those seven days.

Explanations of how the respondent came to misinterpret the qualifying period Further information about respondent interpretation of the qualifying time period was available from the confrontation phase of the intensive interview. Thus once the intensive interviewer had established a difference between the quantity estimates from the first and the intensive interviews, the respondent was put through a mild form of interrogation to elicit the respondent's views about the causes of that difference. In the process of doing this, further evidence was collected about the ways in which the time period was interpreted and about how it came to be so interpreted. Details are given in Table 3.7.

Other factors named as responsible for discrepancies between the first and the intensive interviews

The confrontation stage of the intensive interview yielded 'ex-

Table 3.7
Explanation/elaborations of failure to think in terms of the specified time period ('last seven days excluding today')*

	Frequency with which this explanation was given
Where respondent included specific extra days	
Included 'today' because respondent thought this was required (55) / because today's shopping already done (3) / because interviewer told her to include it (1) / for other reasons (3)	62
The respondent wanted to include today's buying	34
Included special days (e.g. holidays) outside of the specified period	12
Thought an eight-day period was seven days	12
Where respondent extended the time period	
Thought back to last time bought (34) / thought in terms of *when* chocolates last bought (4)	38
Period extended to include special shopping days / usual shopping days	6
Thought back to the distant past (17) / last month (9)	26
Thought back to week before the present one (= 'last week')	19
Thought of week as seven 'shopping days'	1
Where there was a 'shift' of the time period	
Not much bought in last seven days, so respondent thought in terms of a period when buying *was* done	10
Respondent thought in terms of 'last week' but had a personal 'set' about the duration of 'last week' (e.g. Friday to Friday, Monday to Friday, shopping day to shopping day, pay day to pay day)	109
There was an exclusion of certain days	
Respondent excluded days when shops were closed (6) / where not at work (6) / when could not go out (8) / non-shopping days (8)	28
Considered only shopping days (10) / only days when chocolate *was* bought (52) / the weekends when chocolate was *usually* bought (14)	76
Considered only days when there was money for chocolate / when sweets were given to respondent	8
Thought interviewer wanted only a specific buying occasion within the last seven days	14
Thought a week meant only from Monday to 'yesterday' (3) / Monday to Friday (5)	8
Where only a vague period was considered or no period at all	
Respondent did not fix start (10) / or end (9) of the period	19
Respondent did not think of any particular period (45) / did not think the period mattered (4) / did not recall being asked about 'last seven days' (3) / respondent did not bother to apply the specified period (5)	57
Respondent was muddled over the days (2) / was not sure which days to include (4)	6
Respondent thought only of certain shopping days	7
Interviewer blamed for failure to specify correct time period	
Interviewer did not say 'last seven days' (9) / interviewer said 'bought recently' (7) / interviewer said 'seven days' but did not specify *which* seven days (2)	18
Interviewer asked only if 'ever bought'	3
Interviewer named some other period (e.g. weekends, during a couple of weeks)	12
Interviewer failed to say 'not counting today'	40
Interviewer did not correct the respondent when she got the period wrong	4
Other explanations for failure to think in terms of specified time period	
Respondent thought of *usual* buying pattern (11) / of buying generally (5)	16
Respondent had no time to think because he was in a hurry (5) / was rushed by the interviewer (1)	6
Respondent caught off guard (1) / confused (4)	5
Respondent annoyed at being interrupted for the interview	1

*A given respondent's failure to think in terms of the specified time period (a) could be on more than one 'front' (e.g. counted 'today's' buying *and* 'thought in terms of the last ten days'); (b) could take different forms for the different products that were subject to intensive interview check (e.g. thought in terms of last buying occasion for Quality Street, but in terms of today for Mars bars). For these reasons, the number of explanations given in this table is very large.

Table 3.8
Reasons offered for errors/discrepancies
(over and above mistaken time period)*

	Frequency with which this explanation was given
Explanations relating to time, place, occasion of first interview	
The doorstep interview did not permit concentrated thought	4
Time unsuitable (11) / occasion unsuitable (7)	18
Respondent was in a hurry (11) / did not take the interview seriously (8)	19
Explanations relating to performance of the first interviewer	
The first interviewer made mistakes in recording answer (22) / did not hear correctly (1)	23
First interviewer carried out the interview in muddled/hurried way (4) / made respondent muddled or flustered or confused (6)	10
First interviewer did not say 'in the last seven days' (13) / 'how many bars' (1)	14
First interviewer encouraged respondent to include 'today's' buying (1) / other people's buying (8)	9
First interviewer made the respondent hold the visual aids/did not show the visual aids	5
Explanation concerned with respondent's relationship with first interviewer	
Respondent did not like to stop the interviewer to rectify respondent's mistakes (2) / to get a term clarified (3)	5
Respondent did not like to keep on saying 'No' to the interviewer (1) / tried to impress the interviewer (1) / guessed the answer to help the interviewer (3)	5
Respondent did not trust the interviewer	3
Misunderstandings about what was what in the first interview	
Respondent thought purchases by others associated with respondent should be included (36) / thought items given to the respondent by others should be included (6)	42
Respondent thought products eaten (not necessarily bought by the respondent) should be included	7
Respondent thought products that the respondent had in the house should be included (irrespective of whether respondent purchased them or when)	11
Respondent thought products 'liked' or 'often purchased' should be included	2
Respondent did not realise that size/price mattered (18) / type of package mattered (3)	21
Respondent mistook one product for another	17
Explanations relating to usual pattern of buying	
Respondent answered in terms of *usual* buying behaviour	13
Respondent considered only the *usual* shopping days	1
Explanations relating to forgetting	
Forgot incidental purchases (outside of usual pattern)	3
Forgot purchase made for someone else	3
Forgot purchase because respondent did not eat it	1
Forgot because respondent changed mind at moment of purchase	1
Purchase simply not recalled at the first interview	13

*One respondent could give more than one explanation.

planations' of discrepancies between the two interviews that went far beyond erroneous interpretations of the qualifying time period. These 'explanations', which relate to all 12 products, are set out in Table 3.8.

Commentary on the reasons for error

Table 3.7 shows that only 6% of the 295 respondents considered a period which was entirely correct, that is, the full seven days prior to, but not including, the day of the interview. Nearly half (46%) of the respondents were found to have included the day of the interview in their reckoning, despite the fact that the printed instructions embodied an instruction not to do so. The period actually considered varied greatly from respondent to respondent. For some it was the qualifying period of seven days, but for many it was longer. Whereas, for nearly half of the respondents the considered period included 'today', for some it ended before 'yesterday'. On average, the period considered was in excess of the specified seven days.

The lengthening or shortening of the specified time period was very frequently claimed by respondents to have contributed to their errors in saying how much chocolate confectionery they had bought. The main reasons given for this time distortion are set out in Table 3.7, and the main indications of this table are:

1   Respondent included 'today' because the interviewer failed to say 'not counting today'/because he *wanted* to include some purchasing done that day.

2   The respondent counted only days or occasions when chocolate *was* bought, sometimes going back quite a period for this, sometimes considering only shopping days, sometimes considering only usual behaviour and ignoring incidental buying.

3   Another common tendency was for the respondent to convert 'last seven days' into last week and for that term to be interpreted according to a personal 'set' (for example, Monday to Friday, Friday to Friday, pay day to pay day, shopping day to shopping day).

4   The respondent said he just did not think in terms of any time period.

Although misinterpretation of time period by respondents was an important source of error in estimating numbers of purchases, there were other sources of error, as listed in Table 3.8.

1   Quite often the respondent was not aware that only his *own* purchasing was to be included in the count, so there was inclusion of

purchases by others, of bars given to the respondent, of chocolate confectionery stored in the house (irrespective of when purchased), of chocolate confectionery eaten in the last seven days but not necessarily bought then. The inclusion of family purchases sometimes arose, and of 'you' being interpreted to mean 'you or your family'.

2   Another cause of error given by respondents was confusion over which particular product was being asked about. The respondents sometimes got the product wrong and they sometimes thought in terms of the right product at the wrong price (for example, the 4d or 3d or 9d bar rather than the 6d bar actually asked about). This occurred in spite of the fact of the photographic visual used, in spite of the price being shown in the visual, and in spite of the interviewer being told to call out both the particular product being asked about and its price. At the same time, it is important to note that the differently priced versions of one product could have the same wrapping on them but with price given on the wrappings.

3   Especially noteworthy is the fairly frequent claim that the first interviewer failed in one way or another in conducting the interview: that she failed to say specifically 'not counting today'; that she did not specify 'in the last seven days'; that she encouraged the respondent to include other people's buying; that she misused the visual aids; that she made mistakes in writing down the respondent's replies. Since one or two of the interviews of most of the interviewers had been fully tape-recorded,* it was often possible to check respondent claims about interviewer failures against what actually happened. These recordings did in fact provide evidence of interviewers deviating from instructions, changing question wording (including omitting 'not counting today', asking leading questions, encouraging the inclusion of irrelevant purchases).

4   There were also cases of the respondent just plain forgetting.

To sum up

There appear to have been a considerable number of different factors making for errors by the respondents, some involving overclaiming, some underclaiming and some just errors. A somewhat fuller summary follows.

---

*A research worker had been introduced to each interviewer as a student studying response patterns in interviews. She accompanied the interviewers, making tape-recordings of the full exchange between respondent and interviewer.

Factors making for overclaiming

- Inclusion of purchases made outside of the specified seven day period
      by including the day of the interview
      by stretching the period of purchase to include known purchasing occasions
- Inclusion of purchases by others
- Inclusion of wrongly priced or sized products

Factors making for underclaiming

- Exclusion of purchases made in a specified period
      by forgetting them
      by failing to consider some of the purchasing days

Other factors producing error

- Respondent answered in terms of usual buying behaviour
- Interviewer made mistakes in recording replies

NEXT STEPS

It is expected that any modification of the first interview procedure will involve:

1   Reshaping of all aspects of the procedure that are involved in error production.

2   The testing of the modified procedure *as a whole* (through the intensive interview method) and the securement of evidence about its remaining sources of error.

3   A further stage of overall modification in line with the evidence of error, followed by testing through the intensive interview method.

4   And so on until the procedure has reached an acceptable level of accuracy for each of the products asked about.

It would be quite wrong simply to patch up the present form of the procedure on the basis of the evidence of error presented here and to consider the modification complete.

Similarly, it would be quite wrong to submit just one or two parts of the survey method to progressive modification and to cease the correction procedure when that one aspect or those several aspects of the method were found to be satisfactory in their own right. To do this is to ignore the very likely possibility that one feature of the method will influence another and that accuracy is wholly dependent upon a balance of over- and underclaiming tendencies from different parts of the total procedure. All modification and testing must involve the whole procedure.

APPENDICES

* see microfiche supplement

APPENDIX 3.1

INSTRUCTIONS FOR INTENSIVE INTERVIEWERS

A. THE PURPOSE OF THE ENQUIRY

1 To find out the exact quantity of specified chocolate lines bought *by* the respondent (for herself *or for others*) in the last seven days, not counting the day on which the first interview was made.

2 If there is a difference between this amount and the quantity stated by respondent to the first interviewer, to find out how and why the difference occurred.

B. THE SEVERAL SECTIONS OF THE INTERVIEW

SECTION I

> The *purpose* of this section of the interview is to secure the intensive interview and to establish a co-operative state of mind in the respondent.
>
> The first interviewer will have made your appointment for you and explained that you want to ask a few more questions and that you will be paying for the interview.

TELL RESPONDENT THAT YOU ARE FROM THE UNIVERSITY AND GO INSIDE THE HOME FOR THE INTERVIEW. DON'T PAY THE FIVE SHILLINGS TILL YOU FINISH THE INTERVIEW.

AFTER A *BRIEF* EXCHANGE OF TALK ON ANYTHING OF INTEREST TO THE RESPONDENT, TELL RESPONDENT WHAT YOUR PURPOSE IS. SAY (SLOWLY AND DISTINCTLY):

'At the University we are trying to find out how people's *memory* works . . . *especially* our memory for the little things we *do* and *buy* each day. Our *memory* for those little things we do and buy each day.'

ADD:

'We've been doing quite a lot of this *memory* work and people everywhere have been wonderful in the way they have helped . . . *but* it has meant they had to *think hard* in trying to remember for us.'

SAY:

'Some of my questions are about the things that happened in the first interview. Think back to the first interview.'

NOW PROCEED TO SECTION II. AT THIS STAGE, *DON'T* MAKE ANY REFERENCE TO 7 DAYS.

SECTION II

> *Your purpose* is to find out if, *in the first interview*, respondent was in fact thinking of the 'last 7 days *ex*cluding today'. If not, what *was* the period she thought of? When did it start? Exactly what days were included? Was *today ex*cluded?
>
> (We tackle this issue first because the respondent's memory of the period she actually used might be confused by the other processing yet to be done.)

SAY (SLOWLY):

'When you were telling the first interviewer about any chocolates you bought, *what period* were you thinking of?'

FOLLOW THIS WITH:

'Exactly when was the start of the period you were actually thinking of?'

AND:

'Which were the days you counted when you answered the first interviewer?'

PURSUE IN THIS WAY AND PROBE AS NECESSARY IN ORDER TO MEET THE PURPOSE OF THIS SECTION. (NOTE THAT PEOPLE SOMETIMES LEAVE OUT SOME PARTICULAR DAY.)

SECTION III

> *Your purpose* in this Section is to establish in the respondent's mind the particular 7 days about which the first interviewer was asking. This 7 day period, properly established, is an essential context for the rest of the interview.
>
> *Your method* of doing this must be to get the respondent to identify the days of this period, particularly the boundary days, by helping her to think of things that happened on these particular days.

SAY SLOWLY:

'Now the period the interviewer should have asked about was the 7 days which started on the morning of . . . and which ended last night — that is, on . . . night. It was the 7 days that started on the morning of . . . and ended last night.'

PAUSE AND SAY:

'Now I want to ask you about some of the things you did in that 7-day period. By the way, do you keep a diary . . . or a shopping list? (IF YES) Can you get them, please, because it may help if you can look at them.'
- -
IF SHE GOES TO GET THEM, START THIS SECTION AGAIN ON HER RETURN, STARTING RIGHT AT THE BEGINNING WITH:

'As I was saying, the period the interviewer *should* have asked you about was the 7 days which started on the morning of . . . and which ended last night. (REPEAT) It was the 7 days that started on the morning of . . . and which ended last night.'
- -

IF RESPONDENT DOES *NOT* HAVE A DIARY OR SHOPPING LIST TO FETCH, KEEP RIGHT ON AS FOLLOWS:

'Will you think hard about that 7-day period for me, please, and tell me anything at all that you remember doing in it . . . or that happened to you during it . . . .'

FOR EACH EVENT REFERRED TO, ASK: 'EXACTLY WHICH DAY WAS THAT ON?'

.HELP BY REFERRING TO A FEW PUBLIC EVENTS OF THE PERIOD.

THEN ASK RESPONDENT TO THINK SPECIALLY OF THE DAY AT THE START OF THIS PERIOD. SAY:

'Now I want you to think hard about all that happened on . . . , the very first day of the period we are interested in. It may help if I remind you of some of the things in the news that day.'

GIVE HER ALL THE PUBLIC LANDMARKS YOU CAN BEFORE YOU ASK HER TO TELL YOU SOME OF THE THINGS SHE DID THAT DAY. ALSO NAME A FEW OF THE PROGRAMMES THAT EVENING (BOTH BBC AND ITA). THEN SAY:

'Now can you think of anything at all you did that day . . . PAUSE . . . . Any place you went . . . PAUSE . . . . Anything that happened to you or your family that day . . . .'

LET HER THOUGHTS CONTINUE TO COME OUT WITHOUT INTERRUPTING THEM BUT MAKE A NOTE OF WHAT THEY ARE. AS SOON AS THE FLOW OF MEMORIES STOPS, TAKE THE HAPPENINGS SHE HAS GIVEN YOU AND ASK OF EACH:

'How can you be sure you did this (or that this happened) on that particular day? That particular day . . . .' (NAME THE DAY).

CHECK AGAINST OR RELATE TO OTHER THINGS WHICH ARE SAID TO HAVE HAPPENED THAT DAY. CHALLENGE RESPONDENT'S IDEA THAT IT WAS *THAT* DAY. IN THE PROCESS, ASK FOR ANYTHING ELSE THAT MAY HAVE HAPPENED THAT DAY.

NOW TURN YOUR EFFORTS TO GETTING THE RESPONDENT TO IDENTIFY *YESTERDAY* IN THE SAME WAY.

HERE, TOO, USE YOUR KNOWLEDGE OF CURRENT EVENTS AND OF TV PROGRAMMES TO HELP THE RESPONDENT. CHECK AND CHALLENGE HER STATEMENTS.

AT THE END OF THIS SECTION, BE PREPARED TO GO STRAIGHT INTO SECTION IV, BEGINNING WITH THE REMINDER TO THE RESPONDENT OF WHAT SHE HAS TOLD YOU ABOUT WHAT SHE DID ON THE FIRST AND LAST DAY OF THE 7-DAY PERIOD AND SOME OF THE THINGS THAT HAPPENED IN BETWEEN. SEE SECTION IV.

> The *purpose* of this section is to ask respondent if she has bought any of the five items (which you are checking) in this 7-day period. Another and more detailed check will be made, day by day, later on in this interview.
>
> The *present* check on buying is an overall one meant as an insurance against missing some element of buying when we work day by day through the week — as in Sections V and VI below.
>
> Remember that it is *buying* we are asking about and *not* eating. Whether or not they eat it is beside the point.

SAY, STRAIGHT AFTER SECTION III:

'So the period we are asking about started with . . . (NAME THE DAY). That was the day on which you . . . (REMIND HER OF HER OWN ACTIVITIES). And it ended yesterday . . . (NAME IT). That was the day when you . . . (REMIND OF HER OWN ACTIVITIES). Is that right?'

THEN SAY (*AND THIS IS YOUR PAYOFF*):

'Now in that 7-day period did you buy *any* of these?'

SPREAD OUT THE FIVE VISUAL AIDS AND REPEAT THE QUESTION. IF YES, SAY:

'Which ones?'

PUT ANY 'YES' CARDS TO ONE SIDE AND ASK RESPONDENT TO SAY YES OR NO TO EACH OF THE REMAINING CARDS, TAKING THEM ONE AT A TIME.

FOR ALL LEFT OVER AS NOT BOUGHT, SAY:

'Look once more at these (POINT TO AIDS). Think back over every possible opportunity you had for buying sweets in the 7 days we are asking about. Every opportunity. Did you happen to buy any of these (POINT TO AIDS) in the 7 day period we have been asking about?'

THEN SAY (AND STRESS):

'It counts even if you bought them for someone else . . . . Does that make any difference?'

WHEN THIS HAS BEEN DONE, PROCEED AS FOLLOWS FOR THE FIRST OF THOSE SELECTED.

'How can you be sure that it was *that* brand . . . (SAY IT) . . . at *that* price (SAY THE PRICE)? Could it have been a different one?'

'Are you quite sure it was during the 7 days we are asking about — that is, between . . . and yesterday?'

IF RESPONDENT STICKS TO CLAIM THAT SHE *DID* BUY THE SELECTED ONE IN THE 7 DAY PERIOD, ASK:

'Exactly *how many* of these did you buy in the last 7 days . . . the 7 days we have been talking about? Think carefully first and then say *exactly* how many.'

THEN CHALLENGE WITH:

'How can you be sure it was *exactly* that number? Were *all* of them bought in that 7 day period or just some of them?'

AND:

'Did *you* yourself buy the . . . (SAY THE NUMBER) or did someone *else* buy some of them?'

NOW DO THE SAME FOR EACH OF THE OTHER CLAIMED BRANDS OR ITEMS AMONGST THE FIVE.

SECTION V

> The *purpose* of this part of the interview is to take the respondent through each day of the past 7, checking for each one of them any buying of the test five that may have occurred. This is meant to be a major step in getting the exact amount bought.
>
> For each day, we help to recreate the day in respondent's memory, to get her to reveal the opportunities she had for sweet buying that day and then to examine what *was* bought at those opportunities.

START WITH YESTERDAY. SAY:

'Now I want to ask you about what you did *yesterday*. First of all let me remind you . . . .'

REMIND RESPONDENT OF WHAT LATTER TOLD YOU HE/SHE DID THAT DAY. REMIND ALSO OF ANY PUBLIC MARKERS OF THAT DAY. THEN ASK:

'Apart from those things, did anything special happen yesterday? Anything to remind you specially of yesterday?'

NOW GET RESPONDENT TO TELL YOU ABOUT ALL HE/SHE DID THAT DAY.

'Now I want to go through all the different things you did yesterday, starting from the morning when you got up.'

*ADD (AND BE VERY CLEAR AND EMPHATIC ABOUT THIS):

'And I am particularly interested in any opportunities there might have been for you to buy any sweets during the day . . . any place . . . any time. *In fact that's why I'm going through your day in such detail.* So let's work through the day and find out together what you did and where you went. *I'll ask you to be very patient about this even if you feel you couldn't possibly have bought any sweets that day.*'

NOW GO THROUGH THE DAY WITH THE RESPONDENT, HELPING WITH PROMPTS SUCH AS 'AND AFTER THAT?' . . . GET RESPONDENT TO USE DIARY AND SHOPPING LISTS IF SHE HAS THESE.

WATCH PARTICULARLY FOR ANY OPPORTUNITIES TO BUY SWEETS AND EACH TIME YOU FIND SUCH AN OPPORTUNITY, ASK RESPONDENT IF SHE/HE DID IN FACT BUY ANY SWEETS THEN/THERE. E.g.:

'So you went into a shop on the way to work. Did you buy sweets of any kind there?'

DON'T GIVE UP WHEN YOU FIND ONE OPPORTUNITY OR ONE BUY. GO ON LOOKING FOR OTHER BUYING OPPORTUNITIES.

WHEN RESPONDENT HAS GONE THROUGH THE DAY, CHECK ON OTHER POSSIBILITIES SUCH AS WORKS CANTEEN, SLOT MACHINE ON STATION OR ELSEWHERE, KIOSK, TOBACCONIST, ETC.

IF RESPONDENT DENIES GOING OUT OF HOUSE ALL DAY, OR DOESN'T REMEMBER DOING SO, CHALLENGE:

'Not out of the house at all . . . all day? Not once?'

FOLLOW UP IF 'YES'.

FOR ALL RESPONDENTS, CHECK ALSO ON ANY BUYING THAT MIGHT HAVE OCCURRED AT HOME (i.e. FROM SOMEONE WHO CALLED). DO THIS FOR PEOPLE WHO SAY THEY DID NOT GO OUT AT ALL AND ALSO FOR PEOPLE WHO SPENT *SOME* TIME AT HOME THAT DAY. DON'T PUSH THIS TOO HARD, BUT CHECK ALL THE SAME:

'Could anyone have come to the house to sell sweets?'

IF NO, ASK:

'Has this ever happened to you? In the last month or two?'

IF NO, DROP IT FOR THE OTHER DAYS OF THE SEVEN.

REMEMBER AT ALL TIMES THAT IT COUNTS IF RESPONDENT BOUGHT THE SWEETS FOR SOMEONE ELSE. IT DOES *NOT* COUNT IF SOMEONE *GAVE* THEM TO RESPONDENT. THE ALL-IMPORTANT AND *ONLY* CRITERION IN YOUR SEARCH IS THE *BUYING OF THE SWEETS BY THE RESPONDENT.*

ON EACH AND EVERY OCCASION WHEN RESPONDENT SAYS HE/SHE BOUGHT SWEETS, PROCEED AS FOLLOWS:

POINT TO THE FIVE VISUAL AIDS AND SAY:

'Look very carefully at each of these.' PAUSE WHILE RESPONDENT LOOKS.

'Did you buy any of these? Any at all?'

IF 'YES', ASK WHICH AND PUT THE CHOSEN ONE ASIDE. THEN PICK UP EACH OF THE OTHERS IN TURN AND PUT IT IN FRONT OF RESPONDENT. SAY ITS NAME AND ITS PRICE. ASK RESPONDENT IF HE COULD POSSIBLY HAVE BOUGHT THAT ONE TOO? PUT IT INTO 'YES' PILE IF RESPONDENT SAYS 'YES'. REMIND THAT IT COUNTS *EVEN IF IT WAS BOUGHT FOR SOMEONE ELSE.*

DO THIS FOR ALL FIVE IF RESPONDENT SAYS 'NO' TO YOUR FIRST QUESTION (THE QUESTION IN QUOTES IMMEDIATELY ABOVE).

HAVING JUST OVER-ENCOURAGED RESPONDENT TO TELL YOU OF ANY SHE OR HE MAY HAVE BOUGHT ON THAT SWEET-BUYING OCCASION, PROCEED NOW TO *CHALLENGE* EACH CLAIM.

PICK UP FIRST OF THE CLAIMED ITEMS (THE VISUAL AID).

'You said you bought *this* one. Could you possibly be mixing it up with another one that just *looks* like it or *sounds* like it? Some people *do* mix them up.'

ADD

'This is the one that costs . . . (SAY PRICE). Did the one you bought cost . . . (SAY THE PRICE) or is it the one that costs . . . or . . . or . . . (SAY THE OTHER PRICES IF THERE ARE ANY OTHERS)?'

IF RESPONDENT STILL STICKS TO CLAIM, SAY:

'Exactly how many did you buy? *Exactly* how many?'

IF MORE THAN ONE, SAY:

'Were they *all* at this price . . . (SAY THE PRICE)?'

GET MODIFIED NUMBER IF HE SAYS 'NO'

ASK ALSO (IF MORE THAN ONE):

'Did you buy all of them yourself?' MODIFY NUMBER IF 'NO'.

ENTER THE FINAL NUMBER *TENTATIVELY* IN YOUR REPORT FORM IN APPRO-PRIATE PLACE, BEING FULLY PREPARED TO MODIFY IT IF FURTHER PURCHASES OF THIS ITEM WERE MADE THE SAME DAY (AS SHOWN BY YOUR CONTINUED SEARCH OF RESPONDENT'S DAY).

NOW DO THE SAME FOR EACH OF THE OTHER VISUAL AIDS IN THE 'YES' PILE FOR THIS SWEET-BUYING OCCASION.

WHEN YOU HAVE DEALT WITH ALL BUYING POSSIBILITIES FOR YESTERDAY, ASK:

'Have I missed any sweet buying for that day?'

IF 'NO', GO BACK TO THE DAY BEFORE YESTERDAY AND DEAL WITH IT IN THE SAME WAY. THEN DEAL IN THE SAME WAY WITH EACH OF THE OTHER DAYS IN THE 7-DAY PERIOD.

NOW PROCEED AS ABOVE FOR EACH OTHER DAY OF THE 7, WORKING BACK-WARDS DAY BY DAY.

FOR EACH DAY, ESTABLISH WHAT THE RESPONDENT DID, HELPING HER WITH HER EARLIER RECALLS OF HER ACTIVITIES THAT DAY (IF SHE OFFERED ANY), WITH ANYTHING AVAILABLE ABOUT THE NEWS THAT DAY, AND WITH INFORMATION ABOUT TV SHOWS THAT DAY. ASK FOR HER OWN PERSONAL ACTIVITIES THAT DAY, PARTICULARLY ANY *SHOPPING ACTIVITIES*.

DON'T FORGET TO CHASE BUYING FOR OTHER PEOPLE, SWEETS DELIVERED TO THE HOME, SWEETS BOUGHT ON CREDIT.

BE ALERT FOR THE REPORTING OF THE ONE DAY'S ACTIVITIES ON EACH OF TWO DAYS.

SECTION VI

> The *purpose* in this Section is to get respondent to look at her claims for the whole week and to correct any overclaims or underclaims if this overview seems wrong to her in any way.

SAY:

'Let's see how all that information looks, now that we've brought it together.'

ALL CLAIMS DAY BY DAY WILL HAVE BEEN ENTERED ON A SINGLE (MASTER) SHEET, ONE COLUMN FOR EACH OF THE TEST ITEMS AND ONE ROW FOR EACH OF THE DAYS OF THE 7-DAY PERIOD.

SEPARATELY FOR EACH TEST ITEM, GO DOWN EACH COLUMN, SAYING:

'. . . yesterday, . . . on Wednesday, . . . on Tuesday, . . . on Monday, . . . on Sunday, . . . on Saturday, . . . on Friday. Is that absolutely right? Anything counted twice? Anything left out? . . . .'

CORRECT AS NECESSARY, ENTERING CORRECTIONS IN NEXT COLUMN (CENTRE, UNDER VI). THEN ADD THEM UP AND SAY:

'That makes . . . (GIVE THE TOTAL FOR THE SEVEN DAYS).'

'Are you sure that's exactly right?'

'Does it include everything . . . the ones you bought for the children . . . for others . . . ?'

'Does the number seem a bit too high to you? A bit too low?'

CORRECT AS NECESSARY, TRACING THE ERROR BACK TO THE DAY CONCERNED.

NOW DO THE SAME FOR EACH OF THE OTHER TEST ITEMS.

SECTION VII

The *purpose* of this section is to confront the respondent with two other figures, namely her overall estimates of Section IV, and her estimate to the first interviewer. The purpose of the first confrontation is to *trigger off further corrections in the intensive estimate* along with explanations of what seems to have produced any differences found between the two estimates.

The purpose of the second confrontation is to get respondent's explanation of any difference between the estimate to the first interviewer and the final intensive estimate.

(a) NEXT COMPARE THE SECTION IV ESTIMATE WITH THE ESTIMATE OF SECTION VI. DO THIS SEPARATELY FOR EACH OF THE FIVE TEST ITEMS.

IF THE TWO ESTIMATES ARE EXACTLY THE SAME, SIMPLY NOTE IT AND GO TO THE NEXT OF THE FIVE TEST ITEMS. IF THEY ARE DIFFERENT, POINT THIS OUT TO THE RESPONDENT AND ASK FOR HER HELP IN TRYING TO UNDERSTAND HOW THE DIFFERENCE OCCURRED. WORK TOWARDS A CORRECTED ESTIMATE IF THERE IS GROUND FOR DOING SO. OTHERWISE SAY THAT A RESOLUTION CANNOT BE MADE. IF YOU MAKE A FINAL ESTIMATE, DO NOT CHANGE ANY OF THE EARLIER ENTRIES. SIMPLY ENTER YOUR FINAL ESTIMATE IN THE NEW SPACE PROVIDED FOR IT.

(b) NOW OPEN THE ENVELOPE CONTAINING THE QUESTIONNAIRE OF THE FIRST INTERVIEW, SAYING (ONTO THE TAPE):

'I am now going to open up the form the first interviewer used.'

COMPARE THE ESTIMATES ON THIS FORM WITH THOSE YOU HAVE NOW DERIVED FROM RESPONDENT. IF THEY ARE THE SAME, SAY SO TO THE RESPONDENT. IF THEY ARE DIFFERENT, ASK THE RESPONDENT TO HELP YOU UNDERSTAND HOW THE DIFFERENCE OCCURRED.

EXPLAIN THAT RESPONDENT IS NOT BEING CRITICISED . . . ONLY THE WAY WE HAD THE FIRST INTERVIEWER ASK THE QUESTION.

RECORD RESPONDENT'S EXPLANATIONS.

GET EXPLANATIONS SEPARATELY FOR EACH OF THE FIVE TEST ITEMS. RECORD THEM SEPARATELY.

---

4 Testing the accuracy of survey-based claims about publication readership: the accuracy of the National Readership Survey of the United Kingdom in the survey's 1960 form

A STATEMENT BY WILLIAM BELSON BASED CLOSELY UPON
PART I OF HIS *STUDIES IN READERSHIP*, 1962

ORIGINAL RESEARCH BY

W.A. Belson, BA, PhD (Design, direction and participation)
C. McNaughton, BA (Team leader and later C. Collis)

*WORKING PARTY MEMBERS**

W.A. Belson, BA, PhD, London School of Economics and
    Political Science
T. Corlett, MA, British Market Research Bureau
A.S.C. Ehrenberg, BSc, Research Services Ltd

*ADVISORY COMMITTEE**

M. Abrams, BSc, PhD, FIPA, The London Press Exchange Ltd
H. Henry, BSc (Econ), FIPA, McCann-Erickson Advertising Ltd
Professor M.G. Kendall, MA, ScD, London School of Economics
    and Political Science
J.A.P. Treasure, BA, PhD, MIPA, J. Walter Thompson Co. Ltd

*As in 1962.

CONTENTS OF CHAPTER

The study reported in this chapter is concerned with the accuracy of the 1960 form of the National Readership Survey (NRS) of the United Kingdom. For reasons that are not to the credit of readership research, the reported study is just as relevant to current readership research practice in the United Kingdom as it was then.

The purpose of the National Readership Survey at the time of the enquiry was to determine the number of readers of various publications. The readership survey was conducted by a research agency for the Institute of Practitioners in Advertising (IPA), as a service to advertising agencies, the Press, advertisers and others. It dealt with over 90 publications, consisting of groups of monthlies, weeklies, Sundays and dailies. For the purposes of the NRS of that period, a reader of a given publication was someone who had 'looked at' that publication in a given qualifying period: yesterday for dailies; the last seven days for Sundays and weeklies; and the last four weeks for monthlies. If that person had looked at publication X in the qualifying period, he was regarded as having had the opportunity to see the content of the publication, and it was this that made the NRS results of considerable interest to advertisers and their agencies. On the basis of such information, they decided which publications to use in their advertising campaigns. Indeed, very large sums of money were invested on the basis of the results of the NRS.

The methods of research used at that time in the NRS are described fully in a manual held by the IPA. However, in very broad terms, the method was as follows (the full NRS questionnaire is given in Appendix 4.2E).

1   The National Readership Survey, involving a 20–30 minute interview, was conducted throughout the United Kingdom on a continuing basis, with approximately 15200 interviews in the course of 1960.

2   In the first stage of the interview, the interviewer was to say to the respondent:

> 'I want you to go through this booklet with me, and tell me, for each paper, whether you happen to have looked at any copy of it in the past three months, it doesn't matter where.'

The interviewer was required to explain the terms: 'looked at' 'any copy', 'past three months', 'it doesn't matter where'.

The booklet was a set of 91 'mastheads' or 'logos' presenting the titles of each publication to the respondent. Examples of mastheads are given in Figure 4.1.

THE OBSERVER

DAILY EXPRESS

Figure 4.1 Examples of mastheads included in the booklet used by the NRS interviewers

The booklet was to be passed to the respondent for her/him to run through. As the respondent went through the booklet, the interviewer recorded in her questionnaire all the publications claimed by the respondent to have been looked at in the past three months.

3   At the end of this stage the interviewer took the respondent back over all the publications claimed by her (as having been 'looked at'). She was instructed to ask, for each of them:

'When was the last time you "looked at a copy of . . . ?"'

If the respondent answered 'today', the interviewer was to say:

'When did you last look at a copy apart from today?'

These replies were to be coded to indicate whether the respondent had or had not looked at the publication in the qualifying period ('yesterday' for dailies; 'within the last seven days' for Sundays and weekly publications; 'within the last four weeks' for monthlies).

It had become clear in various ways that the accuracy of the NRS results of 1960 were open to doubt: (i) over the years the readership figures had altered with changes in the readership methods used; (ii) the order of presentation of the publications (in the sequence of 91) clearly had an effect upon the results obtained;* (iii) an enquiry by the Survey Research Centre during 1959 had produced evidence of considerable error with respect to monthly publications.† Against this background, the Centre was asked to conduct a full-scale investigation into the accuracy of the NRS. The request to the Centre and the funding for the study came from the Institute of Practitioners in Advertising, through its National Readership Survey Controlling Committee and its Technical Sub-Committee.‡

Following the completion of the accuracy study, *with its evidence of substantial error in certain of the readership figures*, the Centre was asked to develop a modified procedure based on the evidence of the validity study (see Chapter 8 for the report of this part of the investigation).

The aims of the total enquiry were thus as follows:

Part I: To examine the adequacy of the NRS procedure with special reference to:

1 the accuracy of the NRS readership figures for daily, Sunday, weekly and monthly publications, and for a range of publications within each of those four groups;

*See page 111, with figures based upon the 1958 readership survey (approximately 15000 cases).
†A considerable under-estimate.
‡An advisory committee and a working party were set up to facilitate the conduct of the Centre's work. The members of these two committees are named on the title page to this chapter.

2 the extent to which respondent error is associated with the different features of the survey procedure and with the background and the characteristics of respondents;

3 possible reasons for respondent error.

Part II: To design, on an empirical basis, such modifications to the current procedure as seemed to be necessitated by the results of the accuracy check.

The two-part study was geared to the United Kingdom system of readership research and not to the methods then current in the USA, for example, the 'through the book method' of Simmonds. However, it will be argued that the findings do in fact have much relevance for the validity of the Simmonds procedure and to the other methods that are currently in use in the USA. Certainly the validating procedures of the Centre's study are of considerable relevance to current USA practices and difficulties.

This chapter will be concentrated solely upon Part I of the investigation and it is presented here as an example of an investigation of the accuracy of a major research procedure.

THE METHODS OF ENQUIRY INTO THE ACCURACY OF THE NATIONAL READERSHIP SURVEY

In this report, great emphasis has been placed upon the methods of investigation. This is because they are specialist in character and because that specialism is vital to the success of the operation. The statement of methods starts with a summary giving the overall rationale of the study and its principal features. *This summary is essential reading for understanding the details of methodology that follow.*

SUMMARY OF METHODS

The accuracy check was a two-step operation. In the first step, NRS interviewers working on this project* conducted their readership interviews in the normal way. Very shortly after this, intensive interviewers called on each respondent and conducted a detective-like probing procedure designed to test the accuracy of the respondent's first interview

---

*NRS interviewers were supplied by the research agency conducting the NRS on contract at that time.

claims. The appointments for the intensive interviews were made by the NRS interviewers without the latter knowing the true purpose of the second interview. There were 963 completed intensive interviews, each lasting for over an hour and together constituting 71% of the completed NRS interviews. The intensive interviews were concentrated upon each of 28 publications (four to each respondent) amongst the 91 dealt with in the NRS. For these 28 publications, a comparison could then be made between the NRS result and the result from the intensive check. Where differences occurred, the respondents were asked which result was the nearer to being correct and to explain how the difference had occurred. The intensive interviewers were trained in the intensive interview method and were subject to continuing quality control and to re-training throughout the enquiry. They worked from local centres set up in each of the sampling areas. The investigation was based upon Greater London. Fieldwork was carried out during the first half of 1960.

METHODS IN DETAIL

The sampling methods used

It was planned that the first or NRS-type interviews should be conducted through two equivalent sample surveys (A and B), run one after the other. Interviews in the first sample survey would be followed on the same day by an intensive interview dealing with four claims made by the respondent in relation to two daily papers and two Sunday papers. The interviews in the second of the sample surveys would likewise be followed by an intensive interview dealing with four claims made by the respondent. However in this case the intensive interview would be conducted *next day* and the four claims would relate to two weekly publications and two monthly publications. The reason for splitting the NRS-type survey in this way was (i) to limit as much as possible the qualifying periods dealt with in the *one* intensive interview (with all the essential build-up of time awareness, that is, yesterday and last seven days in one survey, and last seven days and last four weeks in the other); and (ii) to allow the management team to focus one major effort in getting intensive interviewers to respondents on the same day as the NRS interviews (this being unnecessary for the tests of NRS items about weeklies and monthlies, but vital for the details of NRS claims about dailies).

Drawing the two samples for the NRS-type interview

Sampling was conducted within Greater London only. For certain practical reasons, these two samples were based upon a limited number of sub-areas, in fact six polling districts for NRS Survey A and six polling districts for NRS Survey B. The practical reasons were compelling: thus the planned testing operation required that each week a fresh office be found and set up in the heart of a new interviewing area. Moreover, that office had to be sufficient to accommodate a fairly complicated operational process.

Random sampling methods were used. More specifically, the primary sampling units were the polling districts of Greater London. With stratification control over geographic location and economic level,* 12 polling districts were drawn through random sampling with probability proportional to size. The 12 polling districts were sorted into two sets of six, equated as nearly as possible for location and economic level. From each of these polling districts, 50 names were drawn through systematic random sampling. Of these, some 15 (systematically drawn) were designated as potential substitutes, for use only when a sampled respondent was unavailable and then only with local office clearance.

The NRS survey yielded completed interviews with 1362 respondents, this being 69% of the 1984† potential contacts attempted. Details are shown in Table 4.1.

Table 4.1
Showing interviewing success rates in the NRS-type survey

	Original sample (1,300) %		Reserves (684) %	All (1,984) %
First interview completed	71		64	69
First interview not completed	29		36	31
		%	%	%
Moved/not known		7	5	6
Gone away long period		2	2	2
Ill		3	3	2
Dead		*	*	*
Not at home:				
after 1 call		1	10	4
after 2 calls		4	7	5
after 3 or more calls		6	2	5
Refusal		6	7	6

*As indicated by 'juror percentage level'. See Gray, Corlett and Jones (1951).
†For most weeks, there were three NRS interviewers at work. Each week they were replaced by a new set of three. Each interviewer was issued with 50 names per week, 15 of which were potential substitutes. Throughout the survey period reserve interviewers (NRS) were available and on occasions one was brought into the survey and given a randomly drawn set of names to help out the requirements for the intensive interviews and of the overall sampling of publications for testing. This arrangement lifted the NRS totals to the levels shown in Table 4.1.

Success level in securing the intensive (follow-up) interview

Appointments for a second interview were sought with people who had completed the NRS interview. These appointments had to be geared to the sampling requirements for testing the 28 test publications.

Second interviews were secured and completed with 71% (=963 individuals) of those who had completed the NRS-type interview. Details of the response rate are given in Table 4.2.

Table 4.2
Showing success level in getting second interviews

	Daily and Sunday survey		Weekly and monthly survey		Both surveys	
		(%)		(%)		(%)
Number of NRS interviews completed	665	100	697	100	1362	100
Appointment made for second interview	542	82	613	88	1155	85
Appointment with second interviewer completed	463	70	500	72	963	71
		(%)		(%)		(%)
'Reason' reported by intensive interviewer when appointment not effective	79	100	113	100	192	100
Respondent refused/possibly refused		18		29		24
Respondent said time not suitable		10		4		7
Respondent not there		25		48		38
Respondent ill		5		3		4
Intensive interviewer did not keep appointment or was late		5		2		3
Other reasons		12		5		8
Reason not stated		25		9		16

DETERMINING WHICH PUBLICATIONS SHOULD BE TESTED

At the time of the enquiry, the NRS dealt with 91 publications. In view of the character of the proposed accuracy testing procedure, it was out of the question to try to test all 91 publications. A selection had to be made.

Several requirements conditioned the choice of publications for testing. In the first place, the enquiry should not only provide a comparison of accuracy levels of the four main groups of publications (that is, dailies, Sundays, weeklies, monthlies), but should also tell us if the error level within publication groups was of a constant or a variable kind. This meant that the number of publications tested in each of the four publication groups should be as high as possible and should be well spread across the publications in each group. On the other hand, the more publications that were tested, the smaller would be the numerical basis of the results for each publication. In fact, the selection of publications for test was limited to 28 as follows:

- *Daily Mirror, Daily Express, Daily Herald, Daily Sketch, The Evening News, The Daily Telegraph, The Times* (that is, seven dailies including one evening paper)
- *News of the World, Sunday Pictorial, The People, Sunday Express, Sunday Despatch, The Observer, The Sunday Times* (that is, seven Sunday papers)
- *Woman's Own, Woman, TV Times, Radio Times, Reveille* (that is, five weeklies)
- *Ideal Home, True Romances, Good Housekeeping, Woman and Home, True Story, Practical Householder, Reader's Digest, Vogue, Do It Yourself* (that is, nine monthlies)

ALLOCATING READERSHIP CLAIMS FOR TESTING

It was desirable to spread the tests of readership claims as evenly as possible over the 28 test publications. What had to be avoided was the large readership publications getting a large share of the accuracy tests allotted to them — to the statistical disadvantage of the smaller circulation publications. The following allocation control was therefore used. This system is described in terms of what was done for the group of *daily* papers.

For the intensive interviews following the Survey A interviews, each intensive interviewer had two claims about dailies to test (as well as two about Sundays) — one a claim that one of the seven test dailies was looked at yesterday and the other that another of the seven test dailies was *not* looked at yesterday. If only one of the seven was claimed as looked at yesterday, that was the claim that would be tested. However, if two of the seven were claimed as looked at yesterday, the one that was allocated for test was that which, at that point in the investigation, had been tested the less often of the two. This practice damped down the tendency of the big circulation dailies (amongst the seven) to go ahead numerically and the tendency of the small circulation dailies to fall behind. For the negative claims, the same principle was employed: the allocation of claims for testing (among the seven dailies) was kept as equal as possible.

Using the foregoing system for all four groups of publications, the final allocation of claims for testing was as shown in Table 4.3 below.

Table 4.3
The NRS claims tested

Publications	NRS claims tested		
	Positive	Negative	All
Daily Mirror	91	70	161
Daily Express	76	120	197
Daily Herald	35	84	119
Daily Sketch	49	76	125
The Daily Telegraph	38	42	80
The Times	14	47	61
The Evening News	79	78	157
News of the World	80	75	155
Sunday Pictorial	96	64	160
The People	67	79	146
Sunday Express	83	74	157
Sunday Dispatch	29	66	95
The Observer	24	48	72
The Sunday Times	32	38	70
Woman's Own	70	103	173
Woman	82	103	185
TV Times	93	113	206
Radio Times	130	67	197
Reveille	34	134	168
Ideal Home	30	71	101
True Romances	10	63	73
Good Housekeeping	36	74	110
Woman and Home	15	73	88
True Story	11	68	79
Practical Householder	37	83	120
Reader's Digest	70	80	150
Vogue	52	63	115
Do It Yourself	43	69	112

THE FIRST INTERVIEW (NRS)

Getting a normal performance of the NRS interview

Since it was the normal NRS procedure that was to be tested for validity, it was essential that its normality be preserved in spite of its immersion in what clearly was going to be a complex research procedure. The steps taken to ensure this normality were numerous and sometimes devious. They are detailed in the following description of the first interview.

The interviewers taking part in the first (NRS-type) interview

The NRS interviews were carried out from the Centre by interviewers currently or recently working on the National Readership Survey. They had been selected by the representatives of the involved research agencies (on the Working Party) as broadly representative of the members of the NRS interviewer force. They had been through standard training, briefing and experience in relation to the NRS and were re-briefed by their agencies before coming to the Centre for the present enquiry.* Each week three of them were brought into the project, to be replaced by another three in the following week and so on for each of the 12 weeks of the accuracy study.

The special briefing of the NRS interviewers

The three NRS interviewers came to the local centre each Monday morning for briefing on those aspects of the accuracy study which went beyond their normal NRS instruction and procedures. At this briefing, the interviewers were given a 'reason' (not the correct one) for conducting the enquiry, were given sampling instructions, were told of the requirement that they arrange appointments for a second interviewer to call, were given detailed instructions for making and reporting those appointments, were told of a student recordist who would accompany them on certain of their interviewing days. These arrangements were vital to the enquiry and are given in some detail hereunder.

The NRS interviewers were told that a university group† was conducting the NRS interviews (through them) because it wanted readership details (for certain parts of London) that were strictly comparable with those produced by the NRS.

One important feature of these first-stage interviews was that it was the job of the interviewer to secure an appointment with respondents for a second interview either the same day or next day (according to whether it was Survey A or Survey B). Obviously this arrangement could set the NRS interviewers wondering what was going on. Accordingly they were told that the purpose of the follow-up interview was to facilitate a study of the characteristics of the respondents according to reading patterns, to provide information about the reasons for public preference of certain kinds of publication. These reasons they were to pass on to respondents in securing appointments.

---

*Without any reference to the true nature of the project within which they were to work.
†The centre was such a group.

The NRS interview and associated arrangements

The general form of the NRS interview was set out briefly under 'Background and Aims'. Further details are available in the original report of the accuracy check[2] and the full interviewing manual is available through the library of the Institute of Practitioners in Advertising.*

In delivering the NRS interview, the interviewer arrived on the respondent's doorstep with or without the 'student' recordist,† delivered the 20 to 25 minute interview and then set about securing an appointment for the intensive interview.

Making the appointments   The NRS interviewers were given extensive instructions for securing from respondents appointments for the second interviewer to call.

1   The appointment was to be sought only at the end of the NRS-type interview.

2   To prevent the first (NRS) interview being regarded as important only as a lead to the second interview, interviewers were told that the NRS results were extremely important, that if they (the interviewers) failed for some reason to get one of their requested appointments, 'we' would fully understand and that under no circumstance should they allow the appointment-making to interfere with the conduct of the interview. Conducting that interview in a normal way was absolutely vital. Whatever else happened, it was their own interview that was wanted. The second interview, though important, was, as it were, just 'tacked on'.

3   Nonetheless, the interviewers were given full and helpful instructions for *securing appointments for follow-up interviews.*

4   Respondents were to be told that the second interviewer was from the university and that she would be asking more questions about the respondent's reading and reading interests. The respondent was also to be told that the second interview was to be paid for and that the enquiry was an important one.

5   The interviewer was to give the respondent an appointment card specifying the agreed time for the second interview and thanking the respondent for the appointment. She was to thank and re-thank the respondent for her promise and to tell her that the second interviewer would be there at the time arranged. She was

*Institute of Practitioners in Advertising, 44 Belgrave Square, London, SW1.
†A given interviewer was accompanied by the recordist on one day in three.

to leave a letter from the London School of Economics thanking the respondent for the promised interview.

6   The appointments for second interviews had to be made at certain times to enable the intensive interviewers to work efficiently. In the first of the two NRS surveys the appointment for a second interview had to be made for the same day as the second interview.* In Survey B leading to the testing of claims about weeklies and monthlies, the appointments were made for the following day. In the first case, the appointments were reported as soon as possible after being made. In the second, they were reported at the end of the interviewing day.

The tape-recording of interviews   The NRS interviewer was told that a tape-recordist would be accompanying her one day in each of three worked. She was told that the tape-recordist was a student studying respondent behaviour in the interviewing situation. The reason for this deception was to allow the recording of performances by NRS interviewers without alarming them. The accompaniments were arranged on a rotation system, and followed arrangements made for them at the beginning of the week. The resulting recordings provided detailed information about the faithfulness of interviewers' deliveries of the NRS procedure and allowed a partial check to be made of respondents' explanations of errors.

Lists of names for interviews   Each interviewer was given a list of 50 names for interview. Of these, 15 were starred as potential substitutes. These were to be used only when a sample member could not be contacted and only then after specific clearance from the local office.

THE INTENSIVE INTERVIEW

The intensive interview was the central element in the research design for Part I. It was a detective-type procedure designed to provide information, at as accurate a level as possible, about a respondent's reading behaviour in relation to four publications about which the respondent had made claims (positive or negative) in the NRS interview. The intensive method has been described in general terms in Chapter 2. In the present case it can be thought of as an interrogation process aimed at providing a web of evidence about a respondent's last exposure to a specified publication. As a method, it was designed to overcome the

---

*Each of Survey A and Survey B was normal and dealt with all 91 publications. It was only the intensive follow-up that was limited in its coverage (to just four publication claims).

known weaknesses of the ordinary survey interview method. The result of the intensive interview for that respondent could then be compared with the first interview result. Where a difference occurred, the respondent would be challenged to say which reply was the nearer to being correct. He was required to 'explain' the difference.

The intensive interview as a substitute for an objective criterion of truth

The intensive interview was clearly a substitute for an objective criterion of whatever readership of a given publication had in fact occurred. If such a criterion had itself been available, it would immediately have been adopted for this enquiry. But no such criterion was available. A respondent's reading behaviour may on some occasions be objectively reported by a reliable witness available to research staff. However, in the majority of instances reading occurs in situations that are beyond the observational range of reliable witnesses available to the researchers within any viable data collection system. Thus reading may occur in public transport, at place of work, at the hairdressers and in various waiting rooms, or at home when nobody else is in the reader's immediate presence.

During the planning of the study, various suggestions were made to secure firm evidence. One was that the study be limited to people to whom specific publications are regularly delivered. Another was that a particular publication be delivered to a sample of householders, each publication being sealed in such a way (including the use of a glue spot) that a reader would leave behind her evidence in the form of a broken seal. There was also a suggestion that a sample of household observers be recruited and be prepared for reporting on the reading of one target respondent (in the household). The limitations of these and other simulation techniques are fairly easily seen and in the end the research team faced the fact that the required evidence of reading existed only in the 'memory traces' of respondents and that techniques for getting that evidence from that source would have to be developed. Other available evidence or pointers in a given case would never be ignored, but in the end a high grade extraction procedure based upon respondent memory would have to be the central source of evidence.

The gathering of such evidence would call for the development of specialised procedures and a great deal of thought and effort would have to go into the development of these. They would not yield certainty, but it was expected that they could be made to go a long way towards it.

A global outline of the testing tactics actually used

The method that was used was based upon one developed by the writer a year previously in his exploratory studies of error in readership results for monthly publications. As a technique it combined the probing tactics of the psychologist and various devices of the detective. The testing tactics actually used are described in detail on pages 103—8. However, it may help the reader to see them first in the form of a skeletal list. They included the following:

1   Right from the beginning, an explanation to the respondent of precisely what the interview was to be about.

2   The gathering of information about the respondent's background and behaviour, especially in relation to her/his opportunities for looking at publications.

3   The use of familiarisation processes designed to concentrate the respondent's mind upon the particular publication then being asked about.

4   An intensive search for 'looking at' occasions, against the background of opportunity for these.

5   The filling in of circumstances or events surrounding some claimed last reading occasion; the cross-checking of these different circumstances or events; the dating of the instances/events to produce an estimate of when the last 'looking at' behaviour occurred.

6   The use throughout the interview of probing and challenging techniques in relation to any clues that showed up.

7   The confrontation of the respondent with any differences between intensive and NRS claims and the respondent's explanations of these.

The application of these procedures is described below in the context of the intensive interview.*

The claims to be tested

Staff at the local centre told each intensive interviewer which publication claims she was to test.† There were always four of these claims, either two dailies and two Sundays, or two weeklies and two monthlies, according to whether it was NRS Survey A or NRS Survey B that was being followed up. The particular publications involved were deter-

*See full procedure in the appendix to *Studies in Readership*, 1962.[4]
†But not whether it was a positive or a negative claim.

mined by the system described under 'the sampling of publications', on pages 95, 96.

An intensive interviewer was given the first interview questionnaire (of the respondent she was to see) in a sealed envelope with the instruction not to open this until the last stage of the interview (see later). Thus, on going out to an interview, the intensive interviewer knew which four publications she was to test, but she did not know if the NRS claim made about any one of them was positive or negative. She would have to complete the intensive interview through to the end of the challenging stage without knowing this.

The stages of the intensive interview

The various stages of the intensive interview, already summarised on page 102, are set out in detail on pages 103–8. To recap, the NRS Survey A led on to the investigation of claims about daily and Sunday papers and the NRS Survey B led on to the investigation of claims about weekly and monthly publications. The following description of the stages of the intensive interview is limited to the checking of claims about daily and Sunday papers, but it may be taken that this description applies equally in principle to the investigation of claims about weekly and monthly papers.

Explanation of the purposes of the second interview   Right at the beginning of the interview, the intensive interviewer explained quite openly what its purposes were. It was to be described as a university-based study of how well people can remember when they are asked for information on the doorstep. They were told the method was designed to reveal the sorts of errors that people make in that situation. The respondent was to be assured that this was not a test of her, but of the research methods 'we' had used in the first interview.

The purpose of this open explanation was to produce in the respondent the sort of co-operation that would accommodate and be sympathetic towards the rigorous and ranging questioning that was to come. The respondent also knew by now that her time would be paid for.

The intensive interview was always conducted within the home and lasted, on average, a little over an hour.

Establishing the respondent's usual behaviour in relation to reading publications of the kind being investigated   After the explanation of 'purpose', there came a series of simple questions about the respondent's usual pattern of reading. This was meant (i) to give the intensive interviewer a vantage point from which to carry out her subsequent questioning (just as a detective seeks general background information which may sharpen his later pursuit of details); (ii) to get her usual behaviour 'out of her system' so that, when later asked about what *actually* happened in a given time period, the respondent would answer in those terms rather than in terms of what she *usually* did; and (iii) to help the intensive interviewer establish an effective frame of reference in the questioning yet to come.

The 'usual' details sought related to: publications usually read; where and when this reading is usually done; how these publications usually come into the reader's hands. In addition, details were collected about exceptions to the usual with respect to where and when read.

Beyond the rather general 'background data' questions, the intensive interview dealt with one publication at a time.

Initial sorting of publications On going to her appointment, the intensive interviewer had with her the three latest issues of each of the four publications she was due to deal with. Her first step was to get the four publications tentatively sorted into two groups, those the respondent said she *never* looks at and the others.*

The order of testing indicated by the preliminary sorting of the four publications The 'never' claims were tested ahead of the 'yes' claims. In both cases, claims about Sunday publications were tested ahead of claims about dailies. However, for purposes of exposition, I have here tied my description of the intensive interviewing process to a test of a positive claim about a Sunday publication.

The familiarisation phase (geared in this illustration to a positive claim about a Sunday publication). The respondent was asked to turn through the latest issue of that publication, then the second last and then the third last. She was asked to do this to see if she recognised anything in it. If she protested that she had never seen it, she was told, 'See if there is anything in it that especially interests you.'

Now it is vital to understand that this process was *not* meant to get evidence of readership. Rather it was meant to do certain other things. In the first place, it was meant to impress upon the respondent precisely which publication was being asked about. Secondly, it was meant to fill the respondent's mind with 'this publication' as the focus of attention during the test now entered upon. It was also expected that the comments of the respondent as she turned through the publication would throw up clues that the intensive interviewer could use at the right time later on in the interrogation (for example, 'Oh, I

*This was an early unchallenged sorting, used for management purposes, that could very easily be reversed by the processes that would follow.

remember talking with my husband about that'/'My daughter gets this one').

At the end of the familiarisation process for a given publication, the respondent was asked:

'Have you ever looked at *any* copies of that paper/publication before (I mean *any* copy of it)?'

If the respondent said 'No' she was challenged at length, in terms of any earlier claim that she had 'looked at' it, in terms of the different situations in which she usually sees publications, in terms of the exceptional situations in which she sometimes sees publications. If still 'No', that response was subjected to specialised challenging as set out on pages 167, 168.

If the respondent said 'Yes', she was taken into the next phase of the intensive interview.

Challenging the 'Yes' replies and establishing the circumstances of the last 'looking at' event If the respondent said 'Yes' at the end of the 'familiarisation' process, that reply was challenged (for example, 'How can you be sure of that?'). If still 'Yes', the respondent was asked to think back to the very last occasion when she had looked at the publication.

'I want you to go back to the very latest occasion when you looked at any copy of this paper. The very latest that you looked at *any* copy of it.'

In this context the intensive interviewer asked the respondent where she was then and, after that, 'Just when it was'. However, before getting further involved with this detail, the intensive interviewer tried to find out if there was an even *later* occasion. She asked 'What about since then?' and encouraged the respondent to think in terms of her own background and opportunities as revealed in the introductory stages of the interview.

Whatever now emerged as the very last occasion, the respondent was interrogated to try to fix the circumstances (not yet the date) of that last occasion: *what the 'looking at' actually was or entailed, where she was at the time, the time of day, who was with her, what else was going on at the time, what it was she looked at, how she came to be looking at it.* These details would later be used to help her fix or date the 'looking at' event.

Dating the last 'looking at' occasion These details of the last occasion were cross-checked with each other and with all the information that could be gathered about the respondent's pattern of access to the publication and her opportunities to look at it. *At the end of this process, the respondent was asked to date the circumstances of that last 'looking at' event.*

In handling this vital stage of the interview, the interviewers had been warned against respondents who substituted the 'usual' for what actually happened and had been given devices for coping with it. They had been alerted to look for anything special or unusual about the claimed circumstances of the last 'looking at' event, in order to increase the chances of dating that event. They had been asked to draw on the respondent's diary if she kept one. The respondent had been told (and re-told) that just 'noticing it on a bookshelf' or 'seeing a headline over someone's shoulder' did *not* qualify as reading, whereas 'turning through it' or 'reading just a little' or 'studying the pictures or advertisements' *did* count as of course did more deliberate and extensive reading of the publication.

Interviewers were told to challenge all statements and to check them wherever possible. The basic feature of this approach to respondent testimony was to be one of scepticism.

In due course, this process led the interviewer to enter (on her report form) a date or an approximate date of the last occasion of looking at the test publication.

The testing of claims about dailies   The same general procedure was used in dealing with a daily that had been tentatively claimed as seen.

Dealing with marginal versus non-marginal cases   Intensive interviewers were required to get a 'last time' estimate for each publication. However, where a marginal situation occurred (for example, 'a daily publication just might have been looked at yesterday' or 'a Sunday publication just might have been looked at seven days ago'), the interviewer was to be especially rigorous and persistent in determining whether the 'looking at' was in or out of the qualifying period. By contrast, when the last reading event for a Sunday paper was clearly between five and eight weeks ago, the effort to determine precisely *when* (in that period) was relaxed. Similarly for someone whose last 'looking at' of a given daily newspaper was clearly over five days ago.

Dealing with publications that the respondent had regarded as 'never' seen (see initial sorting of publications)   In cases where the respondent claimed 'never seen' in the initial searching stage of the intensive interview, the interviewer was warned to go warily. This was because experience had shown that after 'never' claims, the respondents seemed specially prone to take offence if that sweeping statement was doubted.

The interviewer was told to start by stating that it was necessary for her to go through a full questioning procedure for *all* publications and by asking for their patience whilst doing this. She might if necessary go further, trying to get the respondent to see that whilst *she* (the respondent) *knows* various things about her reading behaviour, she (the interviewer) does not, and that the nature of memory research requires that she (the interviewer) should look at *all* the evidence – just to make absolutely sure.

The intensive procedure then proceeded in this way.

1   The respondent was put through the familiarisation process and was asked to watch out for anything of interest or anything that she had seen in another paper (as a means of increasing attention to the publication). The intensive interviewer was to watch specially for evidence that the respondent just might be *pretending* never to have seen (for example, a down market paper seen by an upmarket respondent, a leftist publication seen by a rightist respondent).

2   The interviewer was to try to find out if the respondent's family or friends or associates ever read it and, in that case, if the respondent had been in their company in the qualifying period. She was then to probe for incidental or forgotten exposure to the publication concerned.

3   The interviewer was to find out if the respondent had *opportunity* to see it, exploring fully the respondent's background details about usual (and occasional) reading behaviour and experiences.

4   Where a 'never' reply persisted, the interviewer was to find out *why* the respondent 'never' looked at the publication. This device conceivably could reveal an attitude of relevance or could point to lack of opportunity.

If any of these steps produced a 'Yes' response, then the questioning procedure was continued along the lines already detailed under 'The familiarisation phase'.

The confrontation phase   After all four publications claims had been processed to the point of yielding an estimate of 'when last looked at', a confrontation stage was started. The intensive interviewer said, on tape:

> 'I am now going to open this envelope. The results of your first interview are in it. Be my witness that I am doing this now.'

(This statement was meant to guard against premature opening of the envelope by the intensive interviewer.)

The estimates from the NRS and the intensive interview were then put side by side and the respondent and the interviewer went through them together to find any pairs that were different in terms of whether the respondent qualified as a reader. For each such difference, the interviewer tried to find out from the respondent how the difference had come about. It was not expected that this would provide a final or satisfactory explanation of the difference in anything like all cases. Obviously the respondent might try to defend herself. However, it *was* expected that these explanations would provide a great deal of insight into the error-making process.

The intensive interviewer was also required to use this situation to get a short statement from the respondent about how the first interview was conducted and to seek both criticisms and praise of that interview. Had the NRS interviewer's instructions been clear enough? Did the interviewer make it clear that she wanted *actual* reading behaviour and not just what *usually* happened? Did the respondent think the NRS interview was too rushed? Also, how did the respondent think she herself performed in the interview? Did she, the respondent, try hard, and if not why not? Did she understand what was wanted? These additional approaches were meant to increase insight into how the NRS interview went and into its strengths and weaknesses. Some third of the sampled NRS interviews had, of course, been tape-recorded and this evidence was expected to be brought into the appraisal of the NRS interviewers' performances.

The selection and training of the intensive interviewers

The intensive interviewing technique cannot be properly understood without at least some comment on the selection and training of the intensive interviewers. The team of intensive interviewers did not at any time exceed ten. These people were in the first instance some of those selected from approximately 220 applicants for this sort of work. The first selection was in terms of interviewing experience and of university training. For those passing this check came a test in the field in which each applicant was required to interrogate a respondent concerning her reading behaviour, this interview being witnessed and tape-recorded. Selection at this point was in terms of ability to interrogate intelligently, purposefully and with tact. Preference was given to people who were capable of seeing a relevant lead and following it.

Those passing this test joined a team for training and final selection. Over a period of several weeks, they took part in the following operations.

1   After extensive briefing each interviewer conducted several (morning) interrogations, which were fully tape-recorded.

2   During the afternoon, interviewers took part in a group hearing and criticism of the tapes of several members of the team. The pattern of criticism was that all members of the team concentrated upon spotting weak patches in the recorded interview, asking the interviewer concerned why she had not followed such and such a lead. With as many as 12 of them in the group, not many failures went unnoticed. This process also made it clear which were the alert members of the team, which of them were prone to follow irrelevant leads, and what elements in the interrogation procedure required emphasis or change.

Each interviewer-trainee faced this scrutiny of her own performance a number of times and had frequent opportunity to criticise the work of others. The result of this was that: (i) weak members were weeded out; (ii) the people directing the operation got ample chance to illustrate inadequate performances and to drive home the fact that extreme scepticism on the part of the interviewer was required. Also, and most important, the procedure underwent a certain amount of modification in the course of the training period.

The tape-recording of the intensive interviews

Throughout the survey proper (that is, beyond the training period) the intensive interviewers continued to tape-record their own performances and these were subject to re-play by both a 'Quality Control' officer and team members themselves. The purpose of this was to keep a constant watch on interview performance and to provide evidence which might bear tellingly upon error-making processes and on recall behaviour.

THE LOCAL OFFICES

An integral part of the validity operation described in this report was the *local office* system referred to in earlier pages. A local office was set up in the heart of each survey sector, usually in an hotel. It was from here that the intensive interviewers operated, completing their reports between calls, being subjected to quality control, discussing interrogation procedure. The NRS interviewers reported here with their appointments, though steps were taken to limit any contact between the two teams of interviewers. The local office was in the charge of a research officer responsible for receiving appointments from NRS interviewers, for the allocation of appointments to intensive interviewers, for seeing that intensive interviewers took out recording machines with them and for general office management duties.

In the course of the survey the local office was moved each Sunday to a new interviewing area. There were 12 such moves in the course of the two surveys.

THE CHOICE (FOR THE NRS INTERVIEW) OF ONE PARTICULAR ORDER OF PRESENTATION OF PUBLICATION GROUPS AS A BASIS FOR THIS ENQUIRY (WITH SPECIAL REFERENCE TO THE ROTATION EFFECT)

This enquiry was based upon one particular order of presentation of publication groups in the two NRS surveys, namely: dailies, Sundays, weeklies and monthlies. Obviously other orders are feasible and, since it is known that order of presentation can make a difference to the results,* one may reasonably enquire why other orders were not tried out as well, or why this particular order was chosen for study.

1   The point of first importance is that the funds available would not have supported a thorough-going study of more than one order-position. To have split these resources between several orders of presentation would have meant that the statistical basis of each would have been too small to say much about that order-position in its own right. Some sort of recombination might, of course, have been possible, for certain sub-analyses, but this would have introduced an unfortunate element of ambiguity into the interpretation of the findings. (See 3 below for the reasons for choosing one order-position rather than another.)

2   In fact, the concentration of effort on one order-position *so that results coming from that position are statistically meaningful*, has considerable advantages if we wish to calculate results for any other order-position at all. We know enough about order-position to make this calculation, the main facts for the 1958 readership survey (16000 cases) being as set out in Table 4.4.

---

*In 1955 Henry compared the yield of readership claims when publication groups were presented in the order (i) dailies, Sundays, weeklies, monthlies and (ii) monthlies, weeklies, Sundays, dailies. The second order showed increases of 75%, 10%, 3% and 12% over the first order for monthlies, weeklies, Sundays, dailies, respectively. Gales in 1959 produced further evidence of an order effect when re-analysing IPA data for 1956/58. Order effects were also detected in an analysis of the readership data for the 1958 survey and it is on this that Table 4.4 in this report is based. Both Henry and Gales detected a further order effect *within* publication groups.

Table 4.4

Showing the effect upon the level of the readership figure,
of changing the order of presentation of publications

| Publication group | Order of presentation | | | |
	First	Second	Third	Fourth
Dailies (less evening papers)	1.00*	1.07	1.02	1.03
Sundays	1.00	1.05	1.06	1.07
Weeklies	1.00	0.99	0.93	0.88
Monthlies	1.00	0.83	0.77	0.74

*The average when the group is in first position is given as 1.00, while the averages for other positions are expressed as multiples of this. Thus the average for dailies in second position is 1.07 times the average for dailies in first position.

Suppose that the average readership figure for the 29 monthlies on which it is based was 5.3% when monthlies are presented in fourth position. Then the figure for monthlies when tested in *first* position should approximate to

$$\frac{1.00}{0.74} \times 5.3 \ (\doteqdot 7.2).$$

The same sort of conversion data can, of course, be developed for each of the 28 publications to be tested in this enquiry. Some details of such conversions are given under 'Recommendations' and in Appendix 4.4. What this means is that a study which is soundly based on one order-position can take us a long way towards a realistic estimate of what *other* order-positions would have given us — or, most important, what the result would have been when using a rotation of order positions. However, this type of calculation demands that the results for the single order on which it is based be firmly established.

3   This enquiry was intended to yield something more than an assessment of the amount of error in the NRS survey. It was meant to help us to understand how it was that errors were made — to give us insight into the process of error-making itself. It seemed reasonable to concentrate the enquiry upon that order-position which was suspected as being most sharply associated with error, namely, when monthlies were last in order of presentation. Certainly it would have been pointless to seek insight into this process by concentrating upon an order-position where error was least suspected. The grounds for suspecting that error was greatest when monthlies were last in order of presentation were (i) the evidence in Table 4.4 above (though this is by no means enough in itself) and (ii) the evidence from the LSE enquiry in 1958 in which readership figures for monthlies in fourth position

were found to be subject to considerable error at the individual level.

4   One other aspect of order-position should be presented here. As I see it, the main function of order-position (also called 'rotation effect') is to highlight the instability of the IPA testing procedure as applied to weeklies and monthlies — especially monthlies. Table 4.4 tells us that the research method used in the readership enquiry is unstable to the extent that a mere change in the order of presentation of weeklies/monthlies can make a considerable difference to the results.

There are two ways of reacting to this evidence. One is to concentrate research effort on error level as different positions are used; the other is to turn to the research procedure itself (preferably in its worst order-position) and to try to understand what it is about the procedure that makes it unstable. I consider that the first of these reactions — studying the rotation effect in its own right — is relatively sterile in this context, but that the second opens the way to specific remedial action.

FINDINGS OF THE INVESTIGATION

METHODS OF ANALYSIS AND PRESENTATION

Table 4.5 gives discrepancies between NRS and intensive estimates for each of the publications tested. I have referred throughout this statement of the findings to these discrepancies as 'errors'. I have done this as a useful but also meaningful shorthand for both the lengthier phrase of 'discrepancy between NRS and intensive estimates' *and* for the rationale of the intensive technique as explained at length in the Methods section of this report. I do not suggest that the term 'error' is entirely satisfactory as a substitute for 'discrepancy between NRS and intensive estimates'; but there is a very good case for assuming that the intensive interviewing technique makes the terms approximately interchangeable.

The means of developing these tables from the raw material must be explained. Survey results concerning the *Daily Mirror* are given as an example in Table 4.5. For this paper, 161 NRS claims were tested, 91 of them to the effect that the respondent looked at the *Daily Mirror* yesterday and 70 that it was *not* looked at 'yesterday'.

Obviously these figures (91 : 70) are unlikely to reflect accurately the actual ratios found in the National Readership Survey, for the simple reason that the number of positive and negative claims tested

Table 4.5
Showing the re-weighting of results to give a measure of
error in the NRS survey

| | | (a) Before Weighting | | | | | | (b) After Weighting* | | | |
| | | Intensive result | | | | | | Intensive result | | | |
		No	Yes	?	All			No	Yes	?	All
NRS Claim	No	58	12	0	70	NRS Claim	No	82	17	0	99
NRS Claim	Yes	15	75	1	91	NRS Claim	Yes	15	75	1	91
NRS Claim	All	73	87	1	161	NRS Claim	All	97	92	1	190

*Re-weighting is by multiplication rather than replication of cards.

was a function of survey convenience. But a simple process of re-weighting (by multiplication) can readjust the balance. Thus, the 91 positive claims were given a weight of 48%, this being the NRS readership figure for the *Daily Mirror* in Greater London (mid-1959 to mid-1960). From this it followed that the 52% of NRS negative claims ought to be represented by 99 cases instead of the 70 actually tested (i.e. 52/48 x 91). This was done with appropriate weighting-up of the figures which emerged from the intensive testing of the 70 negative claims. Thus, the number of the NRS claims which should appear as negative in the intensive check is 58/70 x 99 = 82.

As can be seen from the above example, the result of this re-weighting was to give greater weight to the number of NRS negative claims subsequently found to be in error (that is, 12 before weighting and 17 after).

THE ACCURACY OF THE READERSHIP FIGURES

The dailies

Tables 4.6 and 4.7 *(a—g)* give the main results for the seven dailies. From these two tables, several things stand out fairly clearly.

1   *There is a marked agreement between the NRS and the intensive estimates;* in view of the special character of the intensive interview, this agreement strongly implies that the NRS results for the dailies are accurate.

Table 4.6

Table 4.6
Showing extent of error for daily papers

	% NRS Yes	% Intensive Yes	Difference
Daily Mirror	48	48	0
The Evening News	37	40	−3
Daily Express	29	30	−1
Daily Sketch	18	19	−1
The Daily Telegraph	14	13	+1
Daily Herald	12	11	+1
The Times	5	5	0

2   This outcome depends in part upon compensating error in the NRS interview. Once again the *Daily Mirror* can be taken as an example (Table 4.7(a)). Some 8% of the NRS responses for that paper were overclaims in the sense that the respondent indicated he looked at the paper yesterday when in fact he did not; but a further 9% underclaimed in the sense that they indicated that they

Table 4.7
Showing compensating error for the daily papers

(a) Daily Mirror

		Intensive survey				Error (%)
		No	Yes	?	All	
NRS Claim	No	43	9	0	52	17
NRS Claim	Yes	8	39	1	48	17
	All	51	48	1	100	

(b) Daily Express

		Intensive survey				Error (%)
		No	Yes	?	All	
NRS Claim	No	62	8	1	71	11
NRS Claim	Yes	7	22	0	29	24
	All	69	30	1	100	

(c) The Evening News

		Intensive survey				Error (%)
		No	Yes	?	All	
NRS Claim	No	51	11	1	63	17
NRS Claim	Yes	8	29	0	37	22
	All	59	40	1	100	

(d) Daily Sketch

		Intensive survey				Error (%)
		No	Yes	?	All	
NRS Claim	No	77	4	1	82	5
NRS Claim	Yes	3	15	0	18	17
	All	80	19	1	100	

(e) Daily Telegraph

		Intensive survey				Error (%)
		No	Yes	?	All	
NRS Claim	No	84	2	0	86	2
NRS Claim	Yes	3	11	0	14	21
	All	87	13	0	100	

(f) Daily Herald

		Intensive survey				Error (%)
		No	Yes	?	All	
NRS Claim	No	86	1	1	88	1
NRS Claim	Yes	2	10	0	12	17
	All	88	11	1	100	

(g) The Times

		Intensive survey				Error (%)
		No	Yes	?	All	
NRS Claim	No	93	2	0	95	2
NRS Claim	Yes	2	3	0	5	40
	All	95	5	0	100	

did *not* look at it yesterday when in fact they did. It is partly because underclaims and overclaims happen almost to balance that the final figure is accurate. However, it must be noted too that the margin or scope for imbalance was rendered small for the simple reason that so many of the individual claims were apparently correct:* in the case of the *Daily Mirror*, 82%; for the *Daily Express*, 84%; for the *Daily Herald*, 96%.

3   The balancing-out of error is of course quite common in research, particularly in the social sciences, and it is hard to imagine a measuring process where it does not apply to at least some extent. However, Table 4.7 *(a—g)* brings out several of its special features in this situation. In the first place there appears to be more variation in the proportion of NRS *negative* claims which were in error than can be accounted for solely by sampling error (17% of those for the *Daily Mirror* and 2% of those for *The Daily Telegraph*); positive NRS claims, on the other hand, were subject to much the same error rate — it ranges from 17% to 24% except for *The Times*, where the numbers are too small for the calculation of such a figure. At the same time the positive claims seem more prone to error than the negative claims, and the fact that a balancing out *has* occurred is due simply to the fact that there tend also to be more negative claims than positive claims. This point is stressed because it does suggest an element of luck in the balance achieved for dailies. There will be further comment on this point in relation to the other groups of publications — where the same element of luck does not occur. However, having said this, let me re-state that the balancing out of errors affects only a small minority of the claims made. In fact, the position of the 'average' daily paper is that 89% of the NRS claims made were substantiated in the intensive interview. (See Table 4.15(a).)

Sunday papers

Tables 4.8 and 4.9 *(a—g)* give the main results for the seven Sunday papers.

1   For two of the Sunday papers tested, *News of the World* and the *Sunday Pictorial*, there is marked accuracy in the NRS results. For the rest, however, there is error, some of it quite large.

2   In all cases the error takes the form of an under-estimate in the NRS interview.

---

*Because so many of the NRS and the intensive claims were in agreement, that is, both 'yes' or 'no'.

Table 4.8
Showing extent of error for Sunday papers

	% NRS Yes	% Intensive Yes	% Difference	Difference intensive
News of the World	49	51	−2	−0.03*
Sunday Pictorial	45	47	−2	−0.03
The People	36	41	−5	−0.11
Sunday Express	26	33	−7	−0.20
Sunday Dispatch	13	19	−6	−0.29
The Sunday Times	10	17	−7	−0.39
The Observer	9	14	−5	−0.35

*These proportions are based upon the raw figures and not upon the rounded percentages in the second and third columns.

Table 4.9
Showing compensating error for the Sunday papers

(a) *News of the World*

		Intensive survey				Error (%)
		No	Yes	?	All	
NRS Claim	No	41	10	0	51	20
NRS Claim	Yes	8	41	0	49	16
	All	49	51	0	100	

(b) *Sunday Pictorial*

		Intensive survey				Error (%)
		No	Yes	?	All	
NRS Claim	No	46	9	0	55	16
NRS Claim	Yes	7	38	0	45	16
	All	53	47	0	100	

(c) *The People*

		Intensive survey				Error (%)
		No	Yes	?	All	
NRS Claim	No	54	10	0	64	16
NRS Claim	Yes	5	31	0	36	14
	All	59	41	0	100	

(d) *Sunday Express*

		Intensive survey				Error (%)
		No	Yes	?	All	
NRS Claim	No	62	11	1	74	15
NRS Claim	Yes	4	22	0	26	15
	All	66	33	1	100	

(e) *Sunday Dispatch*

		Intensive survey				Error (%)
		No	Yes	?	All	
NRS Claim	No	80	7	0	87	8
NRS Claim	Yes	1	12	0	13	8
	All	81	19	0	100	

(f) *The Observer*

		Intensive survey				Error (%)
		No	Yes	?	All	
NRS Claim	No	85	6	0	91	7
NRS Claim	Yes	1	8	0	9	11
	All	86	14	0	100	

(g) *The Sunday Times*

		Intensive survey				Error (%)
		No	Yes	?	All	
NRS Claim	No	80	10	0	90	11
NRS Claim	Yes	3	7	0	10	30
	All	83	17	0	100	

3   Where the amount of error is expressed as a proportion of the intensive interview figure, we find an increase in error with movement down the scale in terms of the NRS readership figure — from an under-estimating tendency of 0.03 for *News of the World*, to one of 0.39 for *The Sunday Times*.

4   Here, as with the dailies, we find a balancing-out process, the over-claims being set against the underclaims. However, in this case, the process does not always produce a close balance: underclaims outweigh overclaims. The fact that the imbalance increases as we come down the readership scale (Table 4.8) is an outcome of the fact that the error tendency affecting NRS *negative* claims is similar in size to that affecting NRS *positive* claims. Accordingly, a falling readership figure means that negative claims constitute more and more of the total error. Of course errors for NRS *negative* claims must all, by the nature of things, be *under*-estimates.

The weekly publications

Tables 4.10 and 4.11 *(a—e)* give the main results for the five weeklies tested.

Table 4.10
Showing extent of error for weekly papers

	NRS % Yes	Intensive % Yes	Difference %	Difference intensive
Radio Times	55	59	−4	0.06*
TV Times	43	46	−3	0.06
Woman	38	42	−4	0.10
Woman's Own	34	41	−7	0.18
Reveille	18	24	−6	0.24

*These proportions are based upon the raw figures and not upon the rounded percentages in the second and third columns.

1   Expressed as decimal fractions of the intensive interview figure (see last column in Table 4.10), the errors affecting *Radio Times* and *Television Times* are relatively small; they are somewhat greater for *Woman* and are quite large for *Woman's Own* and for *Reveille*.

2   We find here the same tendency as was apparent for Sunday papers, namely an increase in the error ratio in going from the

Table 4.11
Showing compensating error for the weekly papers

(a) Radio Times

		Intensive survey				Error (%)
		No	Yes	?	All	
NRS Claim	No	37	7	1	45	16
NRS Claim	Yes	3	52	0	55	5
	All	40	59	1	100	

(b) TV Times

		Intensive survey				Error (%)
		No	Yes	?	All	
NRS Claim	No	47	9	1	57	16
NRS Claim	Yes	6	37	0	43	14
	All	53	46	1	100	

(c) Woman

		Intensive survey				Error (%)
		No	Yes	?	All	
NRS Claim	No	50	12	0	62	19
NRS Claim	Yes	7	30	1	38	18
	All	57	42	1	100	

(d) Woman's Own

		Intensive survey				Error (%)
		No	Yes	?	All	
NRS Claim	No	50	13	3	66	20
NRS Claim	Yes	5	28	1	34	15
	All	55	41	4	100	

(e) Reveille

		Intensive survey				Error (%)
		No	Yes	?	All	
NRS Claim	No	72	10	0	82	12
NRS Claim	Yes	4	14	0	18	22
	All	76	24	0	100	

paper with the largest readership figure to that with the smallest. If this trend is maintained beyond the range of these five papers, the implications are serious because the papers not tested tend to have smaller readership figures than these, many of them much smaller.

3   The mechanics of this trend are very similar to those operating for the Sunday papers: it is largely a question of the degree to which *negative* NRS claims outweigh *positive* NRS claims.

The monthly publications

Detailed results for the nine monthly publications tested are given in Tables 4.12 and 4.13 (a—i).

1   On this evidence, four of the nine NRS estimates were seriously in error: *Do It Yourself, Ideal Home, Woman and Home, True Romances*. All nine were involved in error to at least some degree.

2   Eight of the nine errors are under-estimates. Here, however, there is little of the tendency (found for Sunday and weekly publications) for the proportionate size of the error to increase as readership figures become smaller. In fact what we have is evidence of sharp variability (on no obvious pattern) in the level of

Table 4.12
Showing extent of errors for monthly papers

	NRS % Yes	Intensive % Yes	Difference %	Difference intensive
Readers Digest	23	26	−3	−0.15*
Do It Yourself	12	19	−7	−0.37
Practical Householder	10	13	−3	−0.23
Vogue	10	12	−2	−0.16
Good Housekeeping	9	8	+1	+0.13
Ideal Home	7	22	−15	−0.68
Woman and Home	6	21	−15	−0.71
True Story	4	5	−1	−0.25
True Romances	2	7	−5	−0.71

*These proportions are based upon the raw figures and not upon the rounded percentages in the second and third columns.

Table 4.13
Showing compensating errors for the monthly publications

(a) Readers Digest

		Intensive survey				Error (%)
		No	Yes	?	All	
NRS Claim	No	61	13	3	77	17
NRS Claim	Yes	9	13	1	23	39
	All	70	26	4	100	

(b) Do It Yourself

		Intensive survey				Error (%)
		No	Yes	?	All	
NRS Claim	No	77	10	1	88	11
NRS Claim	Yes	3	9	0	12	(25)*
	All	80	19	1	100	

(c) Practical Householder

		Intensive survey				Error (%)
		No	Yes	?	All	
NRS Claim	No	81	8	1	90	9
NRS Claim	Yes	4	5	1	10	(40)
	All	85	13	2	100	

(d) Vogue

		Intensive survey				Error (%)
		No	Yes	?	All	
NRS Claim	No	80	6	4	90	7
NRS Claim	Yes	4	6	0	10	40
	All	84	12	4	100	

(e) Good Housekeeping

		Intensive survey				Error (%)
		No	Yes	?	All	
NRS Claim	No	86	4	1	91	4
NRS Claim	Yes	4	4	1	9	(44)
	All	90	8	2	100	

(f) Ideal Home

		Intensive survey				Error (%)
		No	Yes	?	All	
NRS Claim	No	75	17	1	93	18
NRS Claim	Yes	2	5	0	7	(29)
	All	77	22	1	100	

(g) Woman and Home

		Intensive survey				Error (%)
		No	Yes	?	All	
NRS Claim	No	71	18	5	94	19
NRS Claim	Yes	2	3	1	6	(33)
	All	73	21	6	100	

(h) True Story

		Intensive survey				Error (%)
		No	Yes	?	All	
NRS Claim	No	92	4	0	96	4
NRS Claim	Yes	3	1	0	4	75
	All	95	5	0	100	

(i) True Romances

		Intensive survey				Error (%)
		No	Yes	?	All	
NRS Claim	No	90	6	2	98	6
NRS Claim	Yes	1	1	0	2	(−)
	All	91	7	2	100	

*Percentages are shown in brackets when the number of cases on which they are based is less than 45.

− Base number only 10.

error in going from one monthly publication to another. It is always possible that this variability springs from sampling error* and this should not be forgotten. On the other hand we cannot preclude other causes. Thus, it could stem from the greater difficulty of recalling for the monthlies.† Greater difficulty of this kind would render the NRS estimates more open to certain other influences which can vary from one publication to another (for example, regularity of looking at the publication; pattern of delivery; interviewer effects). See pages 134—40 for an analysis of the association of these (and other factors) with error in broad publication groups. Whatever the precise cause (and we have no way in the present context of knowing this for sure), it is noteworthy that the percentage wrong among NRS negative claims varies greatly from one to another publication, and that this might inject variability into the error rate for the positive and negative claims combined (because the NRS *negative* claims count for the great majority of claims for monthly publications).

Comparing the four groups of publications for accuracy

Tables 4.14 and 4.15 *(a—d)* compare the results for the four groups of publications (dailies, Sundays, weeklies, monthlies).‡ It must be remembered however that the five publications in the weekly group were drawn from those with the higher readership figures and that the findings suggested some increase in error (relative to readership level) for those with smaller readership figures (that is, many of the weeklies).

1   For the average daily (of the seven dailies tested) the error in readership level is practically zero; for the Sundays and weeklies it is a small under-estimate and for the monthlies a large under-estimate.

2   These error tendencies are a function of a number of factors: (i) the proportion of the NRS negative claims which are in error (these are all underclaims); (ii) the proportion of the NRS positive claims which are in error (these are all overclaims); (iii) the size of the readership figure. (Tendencies (i) and (ii) will of course tend to balance each other out.) However, in going from one group of publications to another, there is variation in the power of these

*The sample sizes vary from 150 for *Readers Digest* to 73 for *True Romances*. At the same time it is worth noticing that the discrepancy between NRS and intensive estimates is almost always in the one direction.
†The work of the intensive interviewers and the relatively greater size of the discrepancy for the monthlies support this point.
‡This comparison is of averages. Thus the details about dailies are based on the averages of all entries in the seven units of Table 4.7 *(a—g).*

Table 4.14
Comparing the four groups of publications for accuracy

	NRS (%)	Intensive (%)	Difference (%)	Difference intensive*
Dailies	23.2	23.7	–0.5	–0.02
Sundays	26.9	31.7	–4.8	–0.15
Weeklies	37.6	42.4	–4.8	–0.11
Monthlies	9.2	14.8	–5.6	–0.38

*These percentages are based upon the figures shown in the second and third columns.

Table 4.15
Comparing the four groups of publications

(a) Dailies

		Intensive				Error (%)
		No	Yes	?	All	
NRS	No	70.9	5.3	0.6	76.8	7
NRS	Yes	4.7	18.4	0.1	23.2	20
	All	75.6	23.7	0.7	100.0	

(b) Sundays

		Intensive				Error (%)
		No	Yes	?	All	
NRS	No	64.0	9.0	0.1	73.1	12
NRS	Yes	4.2	22.7	0.0	26.9	16
	All	68.2	31.7	0.1	100.0	

(c) Weeklies

		Intensive				Error (%)
		No	Yes	?	All	
NRS	No	51.2	10.2	1.0	62.4	16
NRS	Yes	5.0	32.2	0.4	37.6	13
	All	56.2	42.4	1.4	100.0	

(d) Monthlies

		Intensive				Error (%)
		No	Yes	?	All	
NRS	No	79.2	9.6	2.0	90.8	11
NRS	Yes	3.6	5.2	0.4	9.2	39
	All	82.8	14.8	2.4	100.0	

Table 4.16
Showing the percentage of responses in error

	%
Dailies	10.0 (5.3% under-estimate + 4.7% over-estimate)
Sundays	13.2 (9.0% under-estimate + 4.2% over-estimate)
Weeklies	15.2 (10.2% under-estimate + 5.0% over-estimate)
Monthlies	13.2 (9.6% under-estimate + 3.6% over-estimate)

three factors to account for error tendencies. For daily papers the errors among negative claims balance out the errors amongst positive claims. For monthlies however this does not occur; the negative claims are in a great majority (91%) and the error ratio among them is somewhat larger than that for the dailies (11% compared with 7%). Weekly and Sunday papers taken together have a higher rate of error among the negative claims than do the monthlies, but the total number of negative claims for each of these two groups is smaller than that for monthlies (73% for Sundays, 62% for weeklies and 91% for monthlies) and it is this and this alone which keeps their final error levels down below that of the monthlies. *There is, then, an element of fortuitousness about the comparative results from the four groups of publications, particularly with respect to Sundays, weeklies and monthlies — namely the size of the readership figure.*

In line with this type of result, we show in Table 4.16 the distribution with respect to the total amount of error (whether it cancels out or not) in the four publication groups.

3   Having said this it is still important to look at the various levels of error affecting NRS positive and negative claims as such. These are in Table 4.15 *(a–d)*. The outstanding figure is the 39% error in respect of NRS positive claims about monthlies, representing a sharp tendency to bring that reading event forward in time (paradoxically the effect of this — an over-estimating tendency — is to cut down somewhat on the total amount of error, in that it reduces the effect of the under-estimating tendency for monthlies). It is the dailies, not the weeklies or Sundays, that have the next highest ratio of error among the positive claims (20%). Nonetheless, the other two figures for error in NRS positive claims are both appreciable (16% for Sundays and 13% for weeklies).

4   Returning to errors in NRS negative claims (and this is a vital group because of its size) the largest error tendency (16%) occurs among the weeklies. Then come Sunday papers (12%), monthlies (11%) and dailies (7%).

5   The process of identifying sources of error can lead to the results themselves being seen out of perspective. It is well, therefore, to remind ourselves of the actual proportion of NRS estimates that *did* agree with the intensive estimates: 89% for the average of the dailies tested; 87% for the average of the Sunday papers tested; 83% for the average of the five weeklies tested; 84% for the average of the nine monthlies tested.

THE CORRELATES OF ERROR

(The extent to which respondent error is associated with the different features of the survey procedure and with the characteristics of the respondent)

Error associated with the filter system incorporated in questions 1 and 2

The form of the questions used in the NRS readership survey affects the pattern or character of the error. It will be remembered that respondents were asked (of a particular publication) if they looked at it in the past three months. This is done for all 91 publications. After this, respondents were questioned further in respect of those of the publications which they have just said *were* 'looked at in the last three months'. The aim of this questioning was to find out if the past occasion of looking at the publication was in the NRS qualifying period (that is, the last four weeks for monthlies, the last seven days for weeklies and Sundays, and yesterday for dailies).

As a direct consequence of this a number of things can happen.

1   The first question may exclude reading events which actually took place in the qualifying period. These represent *under*-estimates.

2   Some of those qualifying events which are included by the first question may be excluded by the second. These are also *under*-estimates.

3   Non-qualifying events, rightly or wrongly passing the first question, may also pass the second question and so be recorded as qualifying. These are *over*-estimates.

The point of special importance about this trio of error possibilities is that the use of the first question as a general screening device leaves us with the possibility that, on this question alone, qualifying events may be lost without any chance of a second check on them as happens with claims that wrongly *pass* the 'first question' screen. The effect of this is to build into the procedure a permanent potential for under-estimating. Whether or not it operates this way will be seen from the following analysis of over- and under-estimating tendencies.

The three-month question

Table 4.17 gives details of the accuracy or otherwise of claims that publications were not looked at *in the past three months*. These findings are expressed as averages for the four groups of papers tested. In calculating them, each publication was given the weight of 100, hence the following figures represent an 'average' paper, as it were.*

Table 4.17
Level of accuracy of NRS claims that a publication
was not looked at in past three months

| | Estimates based on the intensive interview | | | | | Total cases tested |
| | More than 3 months ago | Between 3 months and qualifying period | In qualifying period | | | |
Publication group	(%)	(%)	Yes (%)	? (%)	(%)	(Raw numbers)
Dailies	59	33	7	1	100	379
Sundays	73	18	9	0	100	369
Weeklies	52	33	13	2	100	396
Monthlies	77	12	9	2	100	547

1   The point of first importance in Table 4.17 is that for all publication groups, there is an appreciable exclusion of qualifying publications through the three-month question: 7% for the dailies, 9% for the Sunday papers, 13% for the weeklies and 9% for the monthlies. These averages mask considerable variability among individual papers. The important point, however, is that *the three-month question provides a considerable loophole for the loss of reading events which qualify.*

2   The reasons for these errors are, on analysis, simple enough and more will be said about them later on. Briefly, however, the three-month question: (i) is frequently not understood by respondents; (ii) is sometimes omitted altogether in the interview because the *respondent* has the book of mastheads and turns more than one of them at a time.

3   The three-month question also excludes a great many reading events which occurred less than three months ago but not in the qualifying period. These exclusions do not in fact matter, but any understanding of the character of the process involved here makes it essential that we be aware of this particular occurrence. This error is 33% for dailies and weeklies, 12% for monthlies and 18% for Sunday papers.

4   Notice that the total error affecting monthlies at this stage of the

---

*This giving of equal weight to each of the publications departs from the real-life situation and, in so doing, under-represents the contribution of 'yes' claims made in respect of the larger circulation publications. The point of equalising them, however, is to develop a picture of what happens 'on average'.

testing procedure is proportionately smaller than the error for the other three groups of publications and that the weeklies are more error-prone than any of the others.

NRS claims that the reading event occurred between
three months ago and the qualifying period

Table 4.18 gives details of the accuracy or otherwise of respondent claims in the NRS survey that publications were looked at between three months ago and the qualifying period. Figures are based on analyses for the four groups of papers tested (each paper being given the weight of 100 for the calculation of this average).*

1   We see from this table that the sieving-out achieved through the second question does three things:

(a) It gets rid of a considerable number of claims that should not have passed the three-month question;

(b) It correctly identifies a considerable number of reading events which fell between three months and the qualifying period;

(c) *It excludes an appreciable number of reading events which in fact should have qualified for readership in the NRS survey.*

Process (a) is as it should be, but process (c) certainly is not. Actually the magnitude of error resulting from (c) is greater than is suggested by the aggregate of cases in Table 4.18 (for example, 139 for monthlies); the reason for this is that the negative NRS claims were under-represented (deliberately) in the testing operation. Properly weighted, the 139 dailies would nearly equal the level for *positive* NRS claims tested in that group of publications.

Table 4.18
Level of accuracy of NRS claims that the paper was looked at between the qualifying period and three months ago

	Estimates based on the intensive interview			Total cases tested
Publication group	More than 3 months ago (%)	Between 3 months and qualifying period (%)	In qualifying period (%)	(Number)
Dailies	12	78	10	139
Sundays	18	53	29	75
Weeklies	14	57	28	124
Monthlies	48	33	17	97

*See footnote on page 124.

2　It is noteworthy (i) that about half of the claims for monthlies which are sieved out through the second question *should* have been eliminated through the three-month question (question 1) and (ii) that Sunday and weekly papers lose proportionately more qualifiers through question 2 than do either the dailies or the monthlies.

NRS claims that the reading event
occurred in the qualifying period

Table 4.19 gives details of the accuracy or otherwise of respondent claims (in the NRS-type survey) that publications were looked at in the qualifying period. Here, too, the averages shown are based on an equal weighting of the individual publications in the groups concerned.*

Just as the sieving function of question 2 above led to errors in the form of casting out reading events which actually qualified for readership (Table 4.18), so it allows to qualify many reading events which occurred *outside* the qualifying period, some of them even more than three months ago. The monthly publications are particularly prone to this sort of error: 22% of the 304 reading events rated in the NRS survey as qualifying occurred over three months ago and a further 18% were outside the qualifying period. In fact only 53% of the 304 reading events rated as qualifying by NRS interviewers appear to have *warranted* such a rating. By comparison, NRS estimates for daily, weekly and Sunday publications fare much better: very few of those allowed to qualify occurred more than three months ago. At the same time only about 80% of these were correct.

Table 4.19
Showing level of accuracy of claims that a publication
was looked at in the qualifying period

	Estimates based on the intensive interview				Total cases tested
	More than 3 months ago	Between 3 months and qualifying period	In qualifying period		
Publication group	(%)	(%)	Yes (%)	? (%)	
Dailies	2	20	78	0	382
Sundays	4	11	84	1	411
Weeklies	1	14	84	1	409
Monthlies	22	18	53	7	304

*See footnote on page 124.

The non-balance of the
over- and the underclaims

The evidence in Tables 4.17—4.19 strongly suggests that a considerable number of errors occur: some of these do not matter (there are many errors of this kind) and others do. Confining ourselves to errors which matter, we find these taking three different forms. (i) Between 7% and 13% of the events classified in the NRS interview as occurring more than three months ago actually occurred in the qualifying period. (ii) To these under-estimates we must add a further group of under-estimates, namely events said to occur between three months ago and the qualifying period but actually occurring within the qualifying period; between 10% and 29% of such cases were of this kind. (iii) The third group of errors, all of them representing overclaims, were reading events described by the NRS interviewers as qualifying but in fact occurring outside the qualifying period.

Of these three groups of errors (errors that matter), the first constitutes a major threat because the great majority of all responses in the readership survey take the form of 'no' to the 'three-month' question, and for any publication with a small circulation an error at this point (that is, an under-estimate) is likely to do much more than swamp out such compensating effects as are produced by later overclaims. The implication of this particular point is extremely important: it means that *any attempt to modify this technique within the limits of its present form must involve the closing of the loophole (for qualifying readers) provided by the three-month question.*

Comparing the four publication
groups for filter-linked errors

The four different groups of publications fare somewhat differently in the degree to which they are involved in these three sorts of error (that is, errors that matter). It is well to compare them in this respect because the comparison bears upon what we must do to correct error tendencies generally. The dailies have the least loss through the three-month question (much the least when *The Evening News* is excluded), and through negative claims on the second question; but they are not much different from weeklies and Sundays in respect of positive claims to the second question. It is the difference in the weight of the negative claims they get which produces the final difference in the error tendencies in going from dailies, on the one hand, to weekly and Sunday publications on the other. The monthly publications appear to be subject to *less* error than Sunday and weekly publications in respect of the negative claims (through questions 1 and 2 considered together), being closer to the dailies in this respect; but they are subject to much greater error than any of the other publication groups in respect of the third sort of error (namely incorrect positive claims to the second question).

Summing up about filter-linked errors

There is an appreciable degree of error in the responses of individuals in this survey, some of them representing overclaims and some under-claims. There is a considerable amount of balancing out of overclaims and underclaims. Whether or not a near balance is achieved is largely a matter of circumstances depending upon the size of the readership figure for the publication and partly upon the actual size of the different sorts of errors involved (that is underclaims and overclaims). Moreover the evidence gives no discernible support to the hope of achieving a balance of error by some form of re-weighting of positive and negative claims, or through some other form of readjustment or manipulation.

Table 4.20
Rank orders in terms of source of error

| Publication group | Qualifying reading events discarded | | Non-qualifying reading events included |
	Through the 3-month question	Through the second question	Through the second question
Dailies	1*	1	3
Sundays	2	4	1
Weeklies	4	3	1
Monthlies	2	2	4

*= least error; 4 = most error.

Accordingly, in any consideration of the nature of the remedial steps to be taken, it appears that we must turn our attention directly to the *reduction* (and not just to balancing out) of each of the three sorts of error which matter: underclaims through the three-month question; underclaims through the second question; overclaims through the second question. Of course, it is quite clear that the most important of them is the first — the exclusion of qualifying events through the first question ('Have you looked at . . . in the past three months?'). At the same time it must be clear that (i) no *full* elimination of error can occur and that (ii) in that case we may find ourselves in the odd position of having to preserve enough error of one kind (for example overclaims) to balance out irreducible error of another kind (underclaims). Any attempt to improve the general accuracy level of the survey must have incorporated into it a consideration of this requirement. Otherwise reduction of error (of one kind) may automatically produce greater error in the final estimate.

ERRORS ASSOCIATED WITH THE SPECIAL NATURE OF RESPONDENT READING BEHAVIOUR

Variations in response error by recency of respondent's last 'reading' of the test publication

Tables 4.21 to 4.24 give details, for each publication group, of error tendency as date of the last occurrence of reading ranges from yesterday to more than twelve months ago or 'never'.

The dailies

Table 4.21 presents such information with respect to the seven daily papers which were tested. Its main indications are as follows.

1   The reading events which *last* occurred yesterday greatly outnumber the events which last occurred on any other single day and accordingly any systematic errors by respondents in saying when these occurred will have a major bearing on the total result. There is little scope for their being brought forward in time, but they can go back in time. In fact, 27% of them are said (by the respondents) to have occurred *before* yesterday and 16% as far back as 'more than three months ago'.*

2   When the last event occurred two or three or even more days ago, there is scope for bringing it forward as well as for pushing back. In fact, 37% of the events which last occurred two days ago, and 20% of those last occurring three days ago, were brought forward to yesterday. This 'bringing forward to yesterday' is thus fairly marked and in fact it appears to extend back as far as 'about three weeks ago', that is, when the last reading event of the kind being asked about took place as long ago as that. For last reading events which occurred more than three weeks ago, many are no doubt brought forward to some degree but not as far forward as 'yesterday'.

---

*Claims that the event occurred more than three months ago arose not as positive statements in answer to question 2 ('When did you last look at a copy of . . . ?') but as denials that the publication concerned had been looked at in the last three months (question 1).

3   As the last occurrence of a reading event goes back from 1 to 2 to 3 to 4 to 5 days ago there is a disproportionate increase in the percentage of the events claimed to have occurred more than three months ago (that is, 16% of yesterday's events and over 30% if the last event was three to four days ago). By the time the last events are two to three weeks old, over 50% are credited with occurring more than three months ago.

Table 4.21
Showing errors in estimates (NRS) as the last reading event
becomes more and more remote in time: dailies

| | Distribution of NRS responses* for each time period | | | | | | | |
Last reading event actually occurred	Last event estimated as yesterday		Last event estimated as between yesterday and 3 months ago		Last event estimated as more than 3 months ago		All cases	
	No.	%	No.	%	No.	%	No.	%
Yesterday	304	73	46	11	69	16	419	100
2 days ago	32	37	33	38	22	25	87	100
3 days ago	20	20	43	44	35	36	98	100
4 days ago	6	13	26	54	16	33	48	100
5–7 days ago	5	5	41	41	54	54	100	100
1–2 weeks ago	5	5	41	39	60	56	106	100
2–3 weeks ago	6	8	20	26	50	66	76	100
3–4 weeks ago	0	0	31	50	31	50	62	100
4–8 weeks ago	1	2	15	29	35	69	51	100
8–12 weeks ago	2	3	23	35	41	62	66	100
3–6 months ago	0	0	26	23	88	77	114	100
7–12 months ago	1	1	10	8	107	91	118	100
12+ months ago	0	0	0	0	207	100	207	100
Never	1	0	0	0	233	100	234	100
All	383	21	355	20	1048	59	1786	100

*Negative claims (NRS interview) have been weighted so that the negative and the positive claims have that numerical relationship found in the IPA survey itself as it applies for the Greater London area.

Sunday papers

Table 4.22 gives the same type of detail for Sunday papers. Very much the same pattern emerged here as did for the dailies.

1   Some 33% of the 523 reading events which last occurred in the 'present' week were set back in time, 20% of them as far back as three months ago.

2   For reading events which last occurred in the recent past there was scope for bringing certain of these events forward in time and this occurred to an appreciable extent: 22% of the (last) events of the

130

Table 4.22
Showing errors in estimate (NRS) as the last reading event becomes more and more remote in time: Sunday papers

Distribution of NRS responses* for each time period

Last reading event actually occurred	Last event estimated as in last 7 days		Last event estimated as between 1 week and 3 months ago		Last event estimated as more than 3 months ago		All cases	
	No.	%	No.	%	No.	%	No.	%
Yesterday	60	70	14	16	12	14	86	100
2 days ago	69	73	12	13	14	15	95	100
3 days ago	60	66	14	15	17	19	91	100
4 days ago	63	69	14	15	14	15	91	100
5 days ago	41	59	6	8	23	33	70	100
6 days ago	53	62	9	11	23	27	85	100
7 days ago	2	–	0	–	3	–	5	100
(subtotal)	348	67	69	13	106	20	523	100
8 days ago	10		3		6		19	100
9 days ago	0		12		12		24	100
10 days ago	3		9		3		15	100
11 days ago	2		3		6		11	100
12 days ago	3		0		9		12	100
13 days ago	6		14		0		20	100
14 days ago	0		3		3		6	100
(subtotal)	24	22	44	41	39	37	107	100
2–3 weeks ago	8	16	20	39	23	45	51	100
3–4 weeks ago	4	11	14	40	17	49	35	100
4–8 weeks ago	10	12	26	32	46	56	82	100
8–12 weeks ago	1	1	9	15	52	84	62	100
3–6 months ago	3	3	20	23	64	74	87	100
6–12 months ago	3	2	3	2	127	96	133	100
over 12 months ago	5	2	9	3	272	95	286	100
never	3	1	0	0	321	99	324	100
	409	24	214	13	1067	63	1690	100

*See footnote to Table 4.21.

Table 4.23
Showing errors in estimates (NRS) as the last reading event becomes more and more remote in time: weekly papers

Last reading event actually occurred	Distribution of NRS responses* for each time period							All cases	
	Last event estimated as in last 7 days			Last event estimated as between 7 days and 3 months ago		Last event estimated as more than 3 months ago			
	No.	%	%	No.	%	No.	%	No.	%
Yesterday	168	88		7		15	14	190	100
2 days ago	60	78		7		10		77	100
3 days ago	32	65		8		9		49	100
4 days ago	33 (351)	60	75	8 (49)	11	14 (67)	14	55	100
5 days ago	21	62		7		6		34	100
6 days ago	18	64		5		5		28	100
7 days ago	19	56		7		8		34	100
1–2 weeks ago	22	25		31	35	36	40	89	100
2–3 weeks ago	13	23		16	28	28	49	57	100
3–4 weeks ago	7	19		14	38	16	43	37	100
4–8 weeks ago	18	20		21	24	50	56	89	100
8–12 weeks ago	2	5		9	21	31	74	42	100
3–6 months ago	3	3		14	16	71	81	88	100
6–12 months ago	0	0		1	2	41	98	42	100
over 12 months ago	2	2		1	1	80	97	83	100
never	1	1		3	4	74	95	78	100
All	419	39		159	15	494	46	1072	100

*See footnote to Table 4.21.

week before last, and 16% of those occurring the week before that were brought forward to the present week. Bringing forward to the present week did not appear to cut out entirely until the last reading event was about eight weeks ago.

3   As the last reading event went back in time to one to two weeks ago there was a disproportionate increase in the percentage of events claimed to have occurred more than three months ago.

Weekly and monthly papers

Much the same type of conclusion may be drawn for weekly and monthly publications (see Tables 4.23 and 4.24). With the weeklies, the tendency to bring (last) events forward to the current week appears to extend back as far as eight weeks ago, while for monthlies appreciable numbers of last events were brought forward to the current month from as far back as six months ago.

Table 4.24

Showing errors in estimate (NRS) as the last reading event becomes more and more remote in time: monthly publications

Distribution of NRS responses* for each time period

Last reading event actually occurred	Last event estimated as in last 4 weeks No.	%	Last event estimated as between 4 weeks and 3 months ago No.	%	Last event estimated as more than 3 months ago No.	%	All cases No.	%
During the present week	78	38	28		102		208	100
1–2 weeks ago	41	36	19		53		113	100
2–3 weeks ago	34	33	19		49		102	100
3–4 weeks ago	32	26	28		63		123	100
4–5 weeks ago	10	12	23		49		82	100
5–6 weeks ago	11	20	19		24		54	100
6–7 weeks ago	7	14	19		24		50	100
7–8 weeks ago	7	11	9		49		65	100
8–12 weeks ago	27	10	65	24	175	66	267	100
3–6 months ago	31	7	121	27	301	66	453	100
6–12 months ago	10	4	42	15	223	81	275	100
over 12 months ago	7	2	51	13	335	85	393	100
never	10	1	9	1	1195	98	1214	100
All	305	9	452	13	2642	78	3399	100

Grouped subtotals (braces):
- Present week – 3–4 weeks ago: in last 4 weeks No. 185 (34%); between 4 weeks and 3 months No. 94 (17%); more than 3 months No. 267 (49%); All cases No. 541 (100%)
- 4–5 weeks ago – 7–8 weeks ago: in last 4 weeks No. 35 (14%); between 4 weeks and 3 months No. 70 (28%); more than 3 months No. 146 (58%); All cases No. 251 (100%)

*See footnote to Table 4.21.

133

Variations in response error by frequency of respondent's reading of the test publication

This section of the chapter deals with the association between respondent error and frequency of reading for the test publications.

To assess *frequency* of reading a test publication, the respondent was asked, in the intensive interview, to say how often he had looked at issues of that publication. He was given plenty of time and was pressed to be accurate in choosing a reply from the following scale: read every copy, read most copies, read a copy now and then, hardly ever read a copy, never read a copy. Response error, on the other hand, was to be represented by each of three indices; namely: percentage of NRS claims (about the test publications) that turned out to be erroneous; the percentage of the NRS claims that turned out to be *over*claims; the percentage of the NRS claims that turned out to be *under*claims.

The association between response error and frequency of reading was examined separately for each of the four publication groups and the results are set out in Table 4.25.

The principal indications of Table 4.25 are as follows.

1　For each of the five groups of publications, the percentage of responses that were in error (column 3) is closely related to the frequency with which such publications were claimed to have been read fully: it is relatively low where the respondent claimed to have read 'every copy'; high where the respondent claimed he saw 'most copies' or saw a copy 'now and then'; very low where the respondent claimed he 'never sees a copy'. Possible reasons for these findings are not hard to suggest: when people 'never' see a publication, there is little scope for error in the NRS replies — it is as if they cannot help being right; when they read 'most copies' of a publication or read it 'now and then', the error potential is clearly much higher; that potential should fall again for those who say they read 'every' copy. (These possible reasons are purely speculative of course.)

2　Interpretation of the data in the overclaiming and the underclaiming columns must be done with great care because the two columns are not comparable quantitatively. *Within* each column, however, the trends are broadly meaningful.

Table 4.25 indicates that the percentage who overclaim in the NRS *falls off* with reading frequency for the publication concerned, whereas the percentage who underclaim in the NRS *increases* with reading frequency.

Table 4.25
Relating response error to frequency of reading

Frequency of reading	Percentage of estimates which are overclaims		Percentage of estimates which are underclaims		Bias tendency* $= \frac{\% O}{\% U}$	Percentages of all estimates which are in error †
	%	(n)	%	(n)		%
Dailies						
Every copy	5.7	(227)	37.5	(16)	0.15	11
Most copies	31.6	(95)	46.7	(30)	0.68	39
Now and then	51.3	(37)	8.1	(149)	6.35	12
Hardly ever	100.0	(7)	5.0	(160)	20.00	7
Never	100.0	(2)	1.0	(110)	100.00	2
Sundays						
Every copy	5.0	(258)	75.0	(30)	0.07	17
Most copies	19.5	(77)	58.0	(19)	0.34	34
Now and then	51.3	(39)	24.3	(74)	2.11	29
Hardly ever	73.0	(11)	7.7	(144)	9.50	10
Never	60.0	(10)	0.0	(170)	‡	1
Weeklies						
Every copy	2.9	(273)	87.5	(16)	0.03	9
Most copies	25.8	(70)	47.5	(61)	0.54	37
Now and then	56.0	(34)	18.3	(164)	3.06	23
Hardly ever	60.0	(10)	5.6	(162)	10.70	8
Never	25.0	(4)	0.0	(101)	‡	1
Monthlies						
Every copy	8.1	(62)	55.5	(9)	0.15	27
Most copies	24.1	(58)	55.0	(20)	0.44	43
Now and then	42.5	(118)	27.7	(134)	1.54	31
Hardly ever	65.0	(46)	8.3	(168)	7.85	14
Never	100.0	(9)	0.0	(283)	‡	1
All publication groups						
Every copy	4.8	(820)	65.7	(61)	0.07	16
Most copies	25.6	(300)	50.0	(130)	0.51	38
Now and then	49.6	(218)	19.0	(511)	2.62	24
Hardly ever	69.0	(74)	6.6	(634)	10.41	10
Never	72.0	(25)	0.2	(663)	481.00	1

*Bias tendency = proportion of estimates which are overclaims: proportion of which are underclaims.
†Irrespective of whether over- or underclaim.
‡Very large.

At the purely speculative level, it is perhaps not surprising that the people who testify* that they 'never' read a given publication should turn out to be mostly wrong *if they claim readership* of that publication in the period of the NRS. Nor is it surprising that those who testify that they read every copy of a given publication should turn out to be mostly right when they claim readership of it in the NRS.

The results relating to *under*claiming seem equally predictable. A denial of readership in the NRS situation is more likely to be correct for those who 'never' read the publication concerned than for those who testify they read 'every copy'.

Variation in response error by other aspects of respondent behaviour in relation to publications

A study was also made of error tendency in relation to a number of other aspects of the respondent's behaviour in relation to publications.

1   There is a slight tendency for the percentage of NRS errors to be greater: where the publication concerned is delivered; where it is kept around the house for a while; where its reading by the respondent is spread over a number of days; and where the respondent cares about reading it.

2   Overclaiming is more common where the publication is not delivered to the respondent and where the respondent does *not* care if he reads it or not. *Under*claiming is less common for those two groups. For monthly publications, overclaiming is much greater when the respondent reads the publication 'all in the one day' than when his reading is more spread out.

For publications generally, underclaiming is more likely to occur amongst those who do their reading of the one publication on different days than amongst those who do all their reading of it on the one day.

Error associated with the respondents' personal characteristics

The data collected in the enquiry makes it possible to analyse error tendency in each population group according to a range of personal

---

*'Testify' in the sense that this claim was made in the challenging section of the intensive interview.

Table 4.26
Relating response error to various aspects of reading behaviour

	Percentage of estimates which are overclaims O		Percentage of estimates which are underclaims U		Bias tendency = %O / %U	Percentage of of total in error*
	%	n	%	n		
(a) Delivered to home or not?						
Yes	7.6	(658)	53.7	(67)	0.14	20
No	29.2	(710)	12.4	(1575)	2.35	15
Not applicable or varies	40.6	(96)	4.8	(396)	8.46	8
(b) Is it retained in the house? (All publications)						
Yes, kept round the house	16.4	(648)	28.0	(407)	0.59	22
No, get rid of it quickly	15.1	(449)	18.3	(246)	0.83	17
Not applicable	45.9	(270)	6.7	(1389)	6.85	9
(c) Does respondent care if she does not see it?						
Yes	9.7	(735)	37.8	(164)	0.26	20
No	30.6	(640)	11.6	(1488)	2.64	14
(d) How soon is it read?						
Dailies						
All in the one day	18.6	(323)	11.9	(236)	1.56	14
On different days	20.6	(34)	15.4	(26)	1.34	17
Not applicable or varies	33.3	(21)	4.4	(205)	7.57	5
Sundays						
All in the one day	14.4	(271)	20.6	(165)	0.70	18
On different days	8.7	(104)	32.5	(40)	0.27	20
Not applicable or varies	48.5	(33)	4.7	(234)	10.32	7
Weeklies						
All in the one day	11.1	(45)	16.9	(148)	0.66	16
On different days	9.7	(318)	31.3	(166)	0.31	19
Not applicable or varies	44.4	(36)	4.1	(197)	10.83	9
Monthlies						
All in the one day	54.5	(55)	16.7	(96)	3.26	21
On different days	26.4	(178)	25.3	(154)	1.04	26
Not applicable or varies	63.0	(54)	3.5	(374)	18.00	5
All publications						
All in the one day	19.3	(694)	16.0	(645)	1.21	17
On different days	14.8	(634)	28.0	(386)	0.51	21
Not applicable or varies	50.7	(144)	4.1	(1010)	12.35	7

*Percentage based upon equal weighting of the four publication groups.

characteristics. The results are set out in Tables 4.27 to 4.30.*

There is little evidence in these tables to suggest trends that are both substantial and common to the different publication groups. This situation is in marked contrast with the error trends associated with reading frequencies (see Table 4.25). Nonetheless, it is noteworthy that the error level tends to be higher: where there are many adults (four or more) in the respondent's household; where the number of household members in full-time jobs is large (four or more); where the respondent has not had any further education; for the Sunday and weekly publications for both those who finished full-time education aged 15 years or less and for those in social class groups C2, D, E; for the Sunday papers where the respondent is in a less skilled job; for the more frequent watchers of television.

The reader will also notice several sub-groups scattered through Tables 4.27 to 4.30 for which the error level is especially low/high.

---

*In developing these figures, the negative NRS claims were weighted so that the negative and the positive claims had that numerical relationship found in the NRS survey itself as it applies for the Greater London area. This weighting was done by publication groups (that is, dailies, Sundays, weeklies, monthlies) on the basis of the figures in Table 4.15. The following point should also be noted. Under this system, the weighted figure could be expected to reflect, to some degree, the fact that the sampling techniques used in the enquiry meant that small circulation papers were given slightly greater representation among 'yes' claims than did larger circulation papers. However, a careful examination of the extent and the character of this bias made it clear (see Tables 4.7, 4.9 and 4.11 and Appendices 4.1A−2) that the extra cost of eliminating it could lead to no appreciable variation in the pattern of results reported in Tables 4.27 to 4.29.

Table 4.27
Showing proportion of estimates in error
according to composition of respondent's household*

	Percentage of estimates in error				
Number of adults in household	Dailies (%)	Sundays (%)	Weeklies (%)	Monthlies (%)	Average (%)
1	7	11	13	15	12
2	11	13	16	15	14
3	12	15	17	17	15
4+	14	18	22	17	18
Number in full-time jobs	Dailies (%)	Sundays (%)	Weeklies (%)	Monthlies (%)	Average (%)
0	5	9	20	11	11
1	10	13	14	13	13
2	14	15	16	14	15
3	20	21	11	14	17
4+	17	26	35	33	28
Total number in household	Dailies (%)	Sundays (%)	Weeklies (%)	Monthlies (%)	Average (%)
1	4	10	10	14	10
2	10	13	19	14	14
3	13	12	18	10	13
4	11	11	10	16	12
5	17	27	12	13	17
6+	6	21	27	20	19

*See footnote on previous page.

Table 4.28
Showing percentage of estimates in error
according to respondent's educational background*

Any further education?	Dailies (%)	Sundays (%)	Weeklies (%)	Monthlies (%)	Average (%)
Yes	9	9	15	15	12
No	13	18	16	18	16
Age of ceasing full-time school	Dailies (%)	Sundays (%)	Weeklies (%)	Monthlies (%)	Average (%)
18+	10	6	15	14	11
17	13	15	8	10	12
16	12	14	11	15	13
15	11	20	17	14	16
14	11	14	16	14	14
13–	11	15	27	11	16

* See footnote on previous page.

Table 4.29
Showing percentage of estimates in error
according to respondent's social and occupational background

Social class	Dailies (%)	Sundays (%)	Weeklies (%)	Monthlies (%)	Average (%)
A	7	10	8	13	10
B	9	6	11	15	10
C^1	11	14	11	13	12
C^2	15	18	20	16	17
D	8	17	19	11	14
E	2	11	25	14	13
Job level now or in last job	Dailies (%)	Sundays (%)	Weeklies (%)	Monthlies (%)	Average (%)
Professional	7	4	12	5	7
Semi-professional	17	9	11	13	13
Highly skilled	6	10	17	17	13
Skilled	10	14	14	17	14
Moderately skilled	12	19	17	11	15
Semi-skilled	13	17	9	10	12
Unskilled	14	19	20	11	16

Table 4.30
Showing percentage of estimates in error
according to respondent's viewing of ITV programmes

Watches on . . . days per week	Dailies (%)	Sundays (%)	Weeklies (%)	Monthlies (%)	Average (%)
3—7 days	13	16	17	15	15
Less	7	11	16	13	12

LOOKING FOR THE CAUSES OF ERROR IN THE
FINDINGS OF THE NATIONAL READERSHIP SURVEY

Although the enquiry was directed primarily at determining the extent of error in the NRS figures, it was hoped that it would also yield a certain amount of information about the *causes* of such error as occurred. Information of this sort was clearly necessary for the projected second phase of the enquiry, possibly involving modification of the NRS technique to give increased accuracy.

Tacking the search for causes onto an enquiry aimed at doing something else raised obvious difficulties and did in effect put a practical limit upon the search for causes. In particular it was essential that the search for possible causes should not interfere with the error-estimating operation.

In the circumstances, the search for causes of error was made in three ways: (i) through the confrontation phase of the intensive interview in which the intensive interviewer asked the respondent to explain any discrepancies found between her first and her second estimates; (ii) through tape-recordings of NRS-type interviews by NRS interviewers actually carrying these out in the context of the present enquiry; (iii) through the reports of NRS interviewers themselves and of members of the research team in a position to observe interviewers at work, especially tape-recordists who accompanied the NRS interviewers.

One must treat the implications of this information with care: the information can provide *leads* but not hard facts. Thus, the respondent's 'reasons' for error may well be influenced by some tendency to put the blame on the interviewer rather than carry it herself. Again, evidence of certain deviations from instructions (on the part of the NRS interviewers) collected through analysis of the tape-recordings and through the testimony of the tape-recordists, does not necessarily imply error. Indeed it may well be that certain deviations were impossible to avoid in certain situations and may on occasions have had the opposite effect to producing error. *The fact of the matter is that over 80% of the NRS estimates were correct.*

It is of the utmost importance that this point be kept in mind while reading this section, because the search for possible causes of error means concentrating upon unfavourable rather than favourable aspects of the NRS interviewer's performance.

What I have done in my analysis of possible causes of error is to study the different strands of evidence in combination, starting with the respondent's own statement about causes, and checking this against the evidence of what actually happened and against the observations of tape-recordists. Further I am regarding the indications of this as essentially tentative and as providing leads or ideas, but not hard facts. Table 4.32 at the end of this section gives the main body of evidence about alleged causes of error.

SOME IDEAS ABOUT THE CAUSES OF ERROR

The overlooking of isolated events and the tendency to answer in terms of the usual

The most frequently-given reason for error, sometimes partly interpreted by the intensive interviewer, was that an isolated event was overlooked or was remembered only when the respondent was questioned in detail (227 of the 562 errors received this as at least a partial explanation). Probably allied to this reason is another which was also given fairly frequently: that the respondent answered in terms of what he *usually* did (96/562), or that the respondent thought the interviewer meant 'looked at regularly or actually bought it' (122/562). See Table 4.32.

Now to some extent, errors of this sort appear to spring out of a fairly basic human process not easily thwarted or diverted by the activities of an interviewer. Thus, intensive interviewers reported strong tendencies, frequently encountered, for the *usual* pattern of behaviour to override or to swamp out deviations from it. This, of course, is nothing new in the literature of psychology. Indeed, intensive interviewers reported that many events of the incidental and of the isolated kind were recalled only after the usual pattern of reading had been expressed and as interrogation became focused on the day-to-day details of the respondent's behaviour and on her *slightest opportunity* to look at any papers or magazines.

On the other hand, there was evidence to suggest that the alleged tendency to forget the isolated event (and to answer in terms of the usual) appears to have been less guarded against or thwarted than was intended in the NRS interview. Thus, we find some respondents saying that the interviewer actually asked about 'papers looked at *regularly*'. This may well be imagination on the part of the respondent, but on turning to the tape-recordings of interviews there is evidence of considerable departure from certain instructions which may reasonably be regarded as attempts to guard against such tendencies.

Thus interviewers, in their first statement of Question 1, tended to omit the terms 'any copy' and 'it doesn't matter where', Moreover, there was frequent failure to explain or to re-emphasise in the course of the interview: that the interviewer was asking about 'any copy' and not necessarily the most recent one; that she was asking about any time in the last three months; that seeing it in a dentist's waiting-room, at work, at home, were equally valid. In asking Question 2 ('When was the last time you looked at a copy of . . . ?'), there was frequent omission of the terms 'last time' and 'a copy of'. Further, it is worth noting that there was very little repetition of these key terms in the course of asking about the 91 publications, or about those of them that passed the Question 1 sieve.

Now it is quite possible to argue that the results would not necessarily have been different had these omissions not occurred; and in this connection we must remember that the total number of errors was not large (over 80% of the estimates were correct). Nonetheless, if we are seeking modification in the direction of safety, that is, to reduce the forgetting of isolated events and to reduce answering in terms of the usual, then this combination of findings does seem to suggest that two precautions be taken:

1   that further devices be brought into the interviewing procedure to restrict the overlooking tendency of the respondent and the tendency to answer in terms of the usual (for example, the explanation of key concepts or instructions and their repetition at chosen points in the interview);

2   that such steps as are necessary be taken to prevent the interviewer from deviation from such instructions of this kind as are found to be necessary, at the same time taking care not to make the procedure so rigid that an able and intelligent interviewer cannot use her discretion about dropping a specific instruction in special circumstances.

Misunderstanding of the meaning of 'looked at'

Some 91 of the 562 erroneous estimates (see Table 4.32) were said by respondents to have been caused (at least in part) by failure to understand what was meant by 'looked at', some of them interpreting it as 'read', some as 'seen' and some counting 'noticing it on bookstalls'. This could well be a point of importance, for misunderstanding of this key term could lead to the wrongful omission or inclusion of 'looking at' behaviour as defined in the NRS survey. Testimony of intensive interviewers on this point has suggested that about one in five of their respondents was still having difficulty in grasping this concept after careful explanation and questioning in the course of the early stages of that intensive interview. The trouble appears to be that people frequently have their own ideas about what the interviewer is after (for example, what they *usually see*, what they *read*) and consequently take that part of the instruction for granted rather than giving much attention to the special definition of it. In other words, the scales appear to be weighted somewhat against any easy intake of the interviewer's definition of this term.

This appears to put special emphasis on the need for carefully communicating this term to the respondent. A study of the tape-recordings does not, however, suggest that this has occurred to the extent asked for in that interview. Thus for the tape-recorded interview: (1) the term 'looked at' was quite often omitted from the initial statement of Question 1, usually with one or another of the terms 'read', 'seen', 'looked through' substituted for it; (2) there was a marked tendency for interviewers to omit the required explanation (a) that the term 'looked at' included anything from idly turning pages to reading it completely and (b) that it was not necessary to have actually *read* any part of it, only that it was consciously looked at; (3) there was relatively little repetition of the term 'looked at' after its first application in Question 1.

Here again we cannot by any means conclude that omissions of this sort or misunderstanding of the term 'looked at' will necessarily produce error (obviously it has not done so in a great many cases) but the evidence suggests that two steps be taken:

1   that the instructions to interviewers should include more 'hammering in' of the term 'looked at' and its special meaning than is at present called for; and

2   that special devices be used to force the interviewer to do this.

Misunderstanding of the term 'past three months'

Misunderstanding of the term 'the past three months' came up but little as an alleged 'cause' of error. Moreover analysis of the 38 tape-recordings indicated that the term was used in Question 1 in practically all interviews. At the same time, intensive interviewers reckoned that for at least one case in ten, this reference was seriously lacking in meaning or failed to get across to the respondent. The upshot of this was that some relatively recent 'looking at' events were being 'counted out' and some very old ones 'counted in'. Intensive interviewers reported the term to be interpreted by some as 'ever', by some as 'regularly' and by others as 'take'. Others appeared to have very little idea of how long ago 'three months' actually was. It was largely to give the three-month question the character of a time marker that the interviewers were required (by the NRS instructions) to put a date to the beginning of the three-month period. This, however, was by no means always carried out in the interviews which were tape-recorded.

Here again, the evidence suggests that the term 'past three months' may not automatically produce the intended meaning and that if it is to be retained as a sieving device (and this is one of its main purposes at present) certain further steps may have to be taken, including the imposition of the necessary interviewer control.

Other failures to get the respondent thinking in the right terms

While dealing with communication failures it is worth noting that a few of the errors (20/562) were said to occur: through the respondent saying 'no' because it was someone else's copy; through the respondent saying 'yes' because it was in the house though not looked at. See Table 4.32.

Confusion of papers and allied reasons

Another sizeable group of 'reasons' implied some degree of confusion of papers. Thus, there were 74 claims that the respondent had mis-understood which one was being asked about and 22 that the respondent saw too many papers to be accurate.

Now there can be little doubt that with the presentation of some 91 publications in the course of a short interview, some sort of confusion can arise, particularly when many of the publications have names which sound alike: *TV Times, TV Guide, Radio Times; Picturegoer, Picture Show; Woman's Day, Woman's Realm, Woman's Mirror, Woman, Woman's Companion, Woman's Weekly, Woman's Own, Woman's Illustrated; Red Star, Red Letter; True Romances, True Story.*

Now this sort of situation may be thought sufficient to explain most of the errors which appear to have occurred through 'confusion' of publications. The other evidence available does, however, suggest that this situation may not be the sole condition contributing to such errors. This additional evidence concerns the degree to which the respondent obtained full benefit from the visual aids provided. The instructions to the NRS interviewers require that the respondent should turn through the book of aids and call out 'yes' or 'no' for each one of them. If the respondent cannot or will not do this, the interviewer may read out the names from the booklet, at the same time showing the visual aids to the respondent. In fact what frequently happened was this: the respondent held the booklet (this was so in the great majority of interviews), the interviewer read out the names of the publications from the questionnaire (at least half of them appear to have done this with respect to the recorded interviews) getting and coding a 'yes' or 'no' from the respondent for each one. The reasons for this are fairly compelling and I will turn to them shortly. The consequence, however, is that it is all too easy for the interviewer and the respondent to be out of phase — for the respondent to be looking at one publication while the interviewer calls out the name of another. The tape-recordists present at interviews were not in a position to get precise frequencies, but their statements are to the effect that this happened to at least some degree in most interviews where the interviewer read the publication from her questionnaire and that in some cases it happened to a marked degree. Whatever the precise frequency of this sort of confusion, the situation is fairly clearly one where there can be a conflict of visual and verbal stimuli, and hence a possibility of confusion about which publication was being referred to.

The apparent reason for this situation is illuminating and simple enough. Respondents left to turn the pages of the booklet themselves *and* to call out their answers may well turn several pages at once, particularly when they are in a hurry (and many apparently were — see Table 4.32). This is not uncommon in the experience of interviewers and of tape-recordists. If the respondent is calling out for *each* publication she considers, the interviewer will pick up omissions of this sort, but if the respondent calls out only those that warrant a 'yes', the interviewer is in difficulty and has either to insist that everything be called out or take over the calling out herself. When the respondent is in a hurry insistence may not be very profitable and may (in the mind of the interviewer) involve a risk of losing the interview. Now when the interviewer decides to do the reading out herself, it may be very difficult to do so from the booklet. Consider her position: she has to hold her interviewing board in one hand, her pencil in the other and at the same time either hold and turn the booklet of mastheads herself or point to the appropriate page in the booklet as the respondent does the turning. In the circumstances the interviewer is really in a very difficult position and deviation of some sort must be expected. At the same time it is relevant to any attempt to improve the NRS technique that some interviewers appear to make a practice of calling out the names themselves *without attempting* to get the respondent to do so.

From the point of view of improving the technique, I think that the implications of this section of evidence are clear enough. They appear to me to be that several precautions be taken:

1   The presentation of the visual aids must be put fully under the control of the interviewer in a manner which allows delivery of verbal and visual stimuli to be properly synchronised, without making the task in any way difficult for the interviewer;

2　　This arrangement must be such that the interviewer cannot easily depart from it or get into the *habit* of departing from it.

The length (and the difficulty)
of the questioning procedure

One of the outstanding facts about the NRS interview is that it called for questioning about 91 publications in the course of 15—20 minutes. In view of this, questions have been raised about whether or not it is too long or too difficult. A certain amount of evidence about respondent reaction on these scores is available, but I must point out straight away that much of it is indirect and tenuous.

It is well to start with a brief outline of the questioning procedure. It is in two stages. In the first stage, the interviewer takes the respondent through 91 publications, the respondent being required to say of each whether or not he looked at it in the past three months. In the second phase, a further question is asked about each of them claimed to have been looked at in that period, namely, 'When was the last time you looked at a copy of . . . ?' In asking this question, the interviewer is not allowed to question in terms of the specific periods in terms of which responses are to be coded as qualifying or not. Where the answer leaves the code vague or ambiguous, special questioning (probing) is required. Stage 1 is to be completed before Stage 2 is started, and Stage 2 is described to the interviewer as a vital part of the interview.

An analysis was made of the time spent, per publication, in the first phase of this interview. It was based upon 50 cases. Details follow.

	Dailies	Sundays	Weeklies	Monthlies
Seconds per publication	3.2	2.9	2.6	2.2

On average, it was 2—3 seconds. This interval included time spent on page-turning, and occasional breaks in the interview, so that, in practice, the time actually spent on the recall operation was somewhat less than 2—3 seconds. In this period, the respondent has to do the following things: recognise the publication named by the interviewer; link this to the last occasion he looked at it; decide whether or not this was in the last three months. Now for a single publication (that is, one judgement taken in isolation), this process should be swift and practically automatic — provided of course that the respondent thinks automatically in terms of the working concepts ('past three months' and 'looked at'), and does not have to ponder about them. For this, an average of 2—3 seconds ought to be enough.

However, with one such process following another at fair speed, we must expect neural interference and fatigue to set in and to build up to at least some degree as the process goes on. On the basis of what is known, one could expect such interference and fatigue to take the form of a weakening distinction between stimuli (that is, names of different publications), a growing vagueness about the several criteria, and some slowing of the thought process. The onset of an allied condition, boredom, may well accentuate such effects.

Now one cannot say for sure that any such effects, stemming from the length of the questionnaire, actually lead to errors. Nonetheless, the evidence in Tables 4.17—4.19 indicates that for one reason or another a considerable error *did* occur in the course of giving 91 answers. It is clear that a large majority of these would not necessarily affect the accuracy of the survey and were in fact picked up in the second stage of the interview. But about one in ten of the claims that a 'last reading event' occurred over three months ago appears to have occurred in reality *within* the qualifying period and the interviewing procedure provides no chance to correct such errors. Accordingly it is reasonable to think further about the possibility that some of the errors occurring in this first stage of the interview may be related to fatigue/boredom effects. Several things are worth noting in this connection.

1   There was some degree of speeding up as the first stage of the interview progressed from dailies to monthlies (3.2 seconds, 2.9, 2.6, 2.2 seconds).

2   While fatigue and boredom effects might have been reduced by breaking and re-emphasising the procedure in going from one publication group to another, this tended not to occur.

The observations of tape-recordists and of interviewers themselves suggest that the cause lies in part in the length of the interview. Thus, while many respondents showed no sign of impatience with the procedure, others did. This impatience may be limited to verbal expression ('Why go through all these? I know what I read. Do I have to do all this?'). On the other hand, it may take the form of one or more of the following: rapid movement through the booklet; the calling-out of only 'yes' responses; the turning of several visual aids at once, particularly towards the end of the 91; the making of long series of snap judgements. In these circumstances, the interviewer may quite rightly feel that any attempt to slow down the process would only irritate the respondent and perhaps lose the interview. The interviewer has an additional problem in such situations. She knows that the second stage of the interview is described as 'vital' and that if she does not get the respondent to this and through it, the interview is useless. Some interviewers have openly expressed this view.

For a great many publications a rapid and automatic response, perhaps accentuated by the length of the questionnaire, will probably be quite safe; these are cases where the publication is 'never' looked at or where it is looked at quite regularly. These are very large groups of cases and this gives the procedure a considerably safety. It is with 'looking at' events which occur with a frequency between these extremes that dangers related to the length of the interview seem most likely to arise.

The question of the length of the interview must be considered also in terms of its second phase, where the interviewer asks the question: 'When was the last time you looked at a copy of . . . ?'. The first thing to note about this phase of the interview is that it follows directly on phase 1 and so stands some chance of being affected by whatever build-up of impatience, fatigue or boredom has been generated by that phase. Here too the evidence is of an ambiguous kind. Although it is consistent with a suggestion that the length of the interview has some unfortunate consequences, the evidence could conceivably point to something quite different. This must be kept fully in mind. This evidence is based largely on the recorded interviews. We find that in most of these interviews the second phase was entered without any real pause, without setting it up, and without a *precise* statement of Question 2 (indeed, frequently one or another of the key terms was dropped). Some of the interviewers did not appear to do this deliberately, but several have explained that after the long first stage, the introduction of an apparently fresh stage seemed to them to be risky, and that they preferred to get the respondent into it before the respondent realised it had happened. In addition, there is a certain amount of corner-cutting in relation to probing, and the tape-recordings and observation of the interview can all too easily convey an impression of haste in this part of some of the interviews. Finally, it may or may not be relevant that about 40 of the 562 errors were 'explained' as being due to the second part of the interview not taking place.

What, then, are the implications with respect to the length of the interview? Even though the evidence is indirect, I think it cannot help but sharpen concern at anything in the interview that necessarily adds to its length or which reduces effort and motivation where it is necessary, particularly in the vital second phase of the interview. One move which has been suggested is a halving of the list of publications to be tested. This may or may not help. However, it has such major disadvantages with respect to cost and the cross-referencing of information that it seems too drastic a move to make, particularly in view of the indirect and tenuous character of the evidence at present available. I think it may be better to consider certain other modifications. However, what one must remember in making suggestions is that the problem here is not one solely of length, but of length in conjunction with conditions that appear to produce fatigue and some reduction in motivation.

1   We might, for instance, consider making the first stage of the interview easier, so that length served less to fatigue (for example, 'Have you *ever* looked at . . . ?'). This might mean that the first phase could be retained as a sieve for the second process with less danger of its producing fatigue ahead of the vital phase 2 of the interview or of its wasting qualifying cases in the process. The workability of such a device depends very much on the number of publications which the sieve lets through, for this in turn controls the amount of work to be done in the second phase of the interview.

2   Another possibility is to do away with the first phase altogether. There are difficulties and dangers about this, resolvable only through experimental work, and of course any such proposal would call first for very careful consideration of the case for introducing phase 1 in the first place.

Some difficulties in the second phase of the interview

Some of these have already been referred to in the context of the length of the interview (that is, an element of corner-cutting), others in dealing with the overlooking of isolated events (that is, infrequent use of the terms 'any copy' and 'last time'). However, one of them seems to call for comment in its own right. This concerns the way in which the tape-recorded interviews showed the *probing system* working. According to the instructions, the respondent is first asked: 'When was the last time you looked at a copy of . . . ?'. If this produces an unambiguous reply, the response is coded and no further action is called for. Where the reply does not make the coding action clear, or where the reply is ambiguous, further questioning is required. In doing this, the actual qualifying time periods must not be mentioned but only the date or the day defining the period or its further extremity. One of the aims of this sort of probing system is to make the respondent *think* rather than easily accept one or other of two alternatives.

Now as it turns out, the great majority of responses did not call for this extra questioning (that is, according to the instructions). Where they did, however, there was usually some degree of breakdown in one or another aspect of the probing technique.

1   In some cases the actual qualifying period was given in the very first application of Question 2, and in a majority of the tape-

recorded interviews was offered in the course of the interview. Moreover, once given, there was some tendency for the respondent to couch her replies in terms of it.

2   We find too that there was little systematic use of the device of asking in terms of the borderline day or date.

3   In some cases the probing system was not used at all when, on the evidence of the tape-recordings, it should have been.

Now in reacting to this information one should not under-estimate the difficulties of the interviewer. She must slip in, at the right time and sometimes under situational pressure, the appropriate day or date. She knows too that the offering of the name of yesterday is not very different from saying 'yesterday' directly. Much the same applies to the name of a day seven days ago, particularly if one has to say something like 'Wednesday last week'. Whatever one may say on this score, however, the fact remains that there is some breakdown in the rigour of the probing system, and, to the extent that the thinking behind the system is sound, this implies some reduction in the amount of thought which the respondent gives to his reply.

'The interview was conducted in a hurry'

Some 147 of the 562 errors were attributed, in part at least: to the respondent being in a hurry at the time of the interview; to the interviewer proceeding in spite of inconvenience to the respondent; to the respondent being distracted at the time. There were also 26 claims that error arose out of the *interviewer* being in a hurry.

In view of the special character of this interview, we must, I think, regard its completion under hurried conditions as something to be avoided if at all possible, presumably by conducting the interview at a time convenient to the respondent.

Table 4.31 gives the distribution of what respondents say they were doing when the interviewer called. From this it is clear that the dominant activities were (1) cooking, preparing a meal, eating a meal; (2) relaxing; (3) housework. In addition, many respondents had just come in or were just going out, and a further large group was involved in either gardening or car-cleaning or sewing. Table 4.31 also gives the rate of error in these different groups, the highest rate being for those who were 'about to go out'. The latter situation is clearly one to be avoided, though this must not be taken to mean that the other situations are automatically safe: hurry or distraction can occur in most of them and it is this which, on respondent evidence, has to be avoided.

Table 4.31
Showing distribution of respondent activity at the time of the interview, and error level according to the character of the activity

Type of activity	No. of estimates tested	Percentage of these in error
Cooking/Preparing meal/Eating meal	734	15
Looking after children	96	11
Bathing/Washing/Shaving/Dressing	122	12
About to go out	157	25
Housework	647	16
Decorating/Carpentry	99	21
Working at full-time job/at work	151	18
Gardening/Cleaning car/Sewing	176	13
Just came in	209	17
Relaxing	884	17
Watching TV/Listening to radio	239	13
Social activities	101	10

The numbers relate to the NRS claims tested, and these can be taken as being four per respondent.

The respondent did not make any real effort

Some 161 of the errors were attributed by respondents to a lack of real effort on their own part though in some cases this judgement is compounded with the interpretations of the intensive interviewer. A few of these respondents went further and claimed that the interviewer did not make it clear that an effort was needed. A further 60 errors were attributed by respondents to their estimates being guesses.

For many of the publications, it is clear enough that not much effort *is* in fact needed, particularly in those many cases where the respondent looks at the publication either 'never' or quite regularly. However, for cases between these extremes some effort is necessary and quite often a great deal of it. The experience of intensive interviewers leaves no doubt at all about this. In this connection it is well to note that Table 4.32 shows 213 of the 562 errors blamed (in part at least) upon one or another aspect of bad memory and 62 more upon the respondent's being confused over dates.

While it is impossible to be quite certain about this, the evidence available has created among those gathering and analysing it a strong impression of a lack of real effort on the part of many respondents. Thus one may find the respondent giving the interviewer quick-fire strings of replies not only in the first but also in the second stage of the interview and in extreme cases this can take the form: 'about two weeks ago . . . two weeks ago . . . two weeks ago . . . ', or 'less than a month . . . the same . . . about the same'. This situation can contrast quite strongly with the hesitancy and the uncertainty which is frequently brought out in the intensive interview.

Relative lack of effort appears to arise out of a number of things. One seems to be the length of the interview itself — there is a great deal to do and both parties just have to get on with it. Moreover, one does not find in the interview, as prescribed, any appreciable stress to the respondent on the need *really to try.* I think it is to the point to add that on top of this some of the interviewers feel that it helps in securing their interviews to tell the respondent that it won't take long or that it is fairly easy or straightforward. I think that in addition there is a case for asking if the interviewers themselves fully realise the need to inspire effort.

Of course, any systematic effort to make the respondent *try* is up against certain difficulties. One is that for the great majority of the 91 publications not much effort is needed. The respondent knows quite well that he has never looked at such and such a publication or that he looked at it yesterday, and it will only irritate him to insist that he should think carefully before replying. The trouble, however, is that non-effort of this sort all too easily spreads to situations where effort *is* necessary. This makes any *general* instruction 'to try' of doubtful value. The second difficulty is that to get special effort from people, it is necessary to convince them that it is worthwhile to make the effort and that there is some sense in it.

In the circumstances several things seem called for:

1   special instruction to interviewers doing this sort of work to alert them to the difficulties of certain recall processes;

2   the development of a challenging or checking system which automatically and effectively forces a thought process;

3   the taking of steps to make the whole interviewing process less monotonous, more meaningful and more interesting (for example, handling cards, perhaps with a posting system*; breaking the interview in going from monthly to weekly to Sunday to daily publications);

4   ensuring that the interview takes place in a period when there is time to stress the need for effort and to probe fully and carefully whenever necessary. In addition, it may well be that the section about 'when the publication was last looked at' is placed too far on in the interview for this to be given the effort which I am suggesting it sometimes warrants.

*This involves sorting cards into 'pockets' in a sorting folder to indicate when last looked at.

Poor memory of respondents

A large number of the errors — 213/562 — were blamed by respondents (in part at least) upon 'poor memory' on their own part. After all that has been said, I think that the only comment necessary here is that this underlines the case I have been making for increasing the efficiency of the memory aids being used and for sharpening respondent effort.

Some remaining 'reasons'

Among the other 'reasons' for error offered by respondents, we find a medley of things, most of them getting some degree of support from other evidence. These include suggestions that the book of visual aids was occasionally not used, and that interviewers sometimes misheard or miscoded replies. There were 75 references of the latter kind. With respect to miscoding — and the tape-recordings make it clear that this occasionally occurs — it is possible that the layout of the questionnaire is partly responsible: the publications are printed close together but are relatively distant from the codes. It might help to move the code numbers closer to the publications or to link them with dots.

SEEING THESE COMMENTS IN PERSPECTIVE

It is all too easy, when concentrating upon the causes of such errors as occurred to give an impression that there was a great deal of error, or possibly that every deviation from instructions produced error. Neither is true. The fact of the matter is that on the evidence of this enquiry over 80% of the NRS estimates are correct: what I have been doing is focusing attention on that minority of responses which appear to be wrong, in the hope that we may find means of reducing their proportions still further. Another point is well worth making. Although at times the task of getting an accurate response is a distinctly demanding one, it happens that in the great majority of cases it is simple and that for these an automatic reply is not likely to be wrong — for example: the respondent hardly ever or never looks at the publication and automatically says 'no'; the publication is delivered to his home every day or every week and his unthinking or automatic answers cause him to be classified as a reader. In such situations the effortless response will in all probability be right and considerably more deviation than occurred in the interviews studied would be needed to disturb this basic stability of the questioning system. However, in seeking greater accuracy we appear to be dealing with reading events of a less stable kind and it is here that certain deviations from instructions, but not all, could assume

Table 4.32
Alleged reasons for error given by respondents*
in the course of the intensive interview
(Based on 562 erroneous NRS estimates)

Reasons given for error	Dailies 117	Sundays 125	Weeklies 138	Monthlies 182	All 562
Poor memory/mind wanders/vague/un- reliable memory/forgot/too long ago	45	39	61	68	213
Confused over dates	1	6	18	37	62
Occasion borderline	6	2	10	17	35
Respondent sees too many papers to be accurate	4	5	5	8	22
Confused papers/misunderstood which paper asked about	13	12	19	30	74
Paper not cared for/not admitted	3	5	7	4	19
Wrong interpretation of 'looked at'	27	19	22	23	91
Thought interviewer meant looked at regularly/bought or ordered	21 }	22 }	35 }	15 }	93 }
Says interviewer *said* regularly seen/ bought or ordered	6 }	5 }	12 }	6 }	29 }
Misunderstood question/misheard	8	13	8	4	33
Said 'no' because it was someone else's copy/ said 'yes' because it was in the house though not looked at	4	7	5	10	26
Answered in terms of the usual/inter- viewer asked for ones usually read	33 }	17 }	22 }	18 }	90 }
	2 }	1 }	0 }	3 }	6 }
Isolated event overlooked	49 }	41 }	72 }	65 }	227 }
No real effort by respondent/interviewer did not make it clear effort was needed	26	33	37	62	161
Easier to say 'yes' than 'no'	2	1	1	5	9
Original estimate was a guess	5	6	19	30	60
Respondent was in a hurry at first interview/ interviewer insisted in spite of incon- venience to respondent/respondent was distracted at first interview	24	21	52	50	147
Other respondent failures	3	4	17	12	36
Interviewer allowed two respondents to answer together/lack of control over respondent	2	3	5	5	15
Book of mastheads not used at all	11	3	7	12	33
Book not properly used	5	3	10	7	25
Interviewer did not deal with all publications	3	8	14	8	33
The 'when' question not asked	9	5	12	15	41
Interviewer did not date the start of the three-month period	1	4	6	10	21
Interviewer asked specifically about qualifying period	2	2	2	4	10
Interviewer in a hurry	6	7	7	6	26
Interviewer misheard reply/misrecorded reply	20	20	20	15	75
Interviewer decided when respondent was doubtful	4	2	2	8	16
Other failings of interviewer	13	21	22	17	73

*These 'reasons' were compounded to some degree with the observations and the reporting procedure of the intensive interviewers. Thus, 'reasons' are reported in the third person and obvious points of reference were added by intensive interviewers. Again it was inevitable that intensive interviewers would from time to time lean on something of the evidence collected in the course of the intensive interview in interpreting what the respondent gave as his 'reason' (for example, with reference to the claim that an isolated event had been overlooked). However, intensive interviewers had instructions to regard this section of the report as presenting the respondent's reasons and not their own, and they were, in fact, given a separate space in which to record any such personal opinions or interpretations.

some importance. It should also be clear that whatever we do about eliminating deviations from instructions, the present aim of further improvement will probably call for at least some modification of the technique itself, including some of the requirements which at present give the thoughtful interviewer little alternative to deviating to some extent.

RECOMMENDATIONS

The recommendations set out here are necessarily brief and tentative. They are brief because they are to be developed more fully in Part II of this report. They are tentative because to be put into action they must first pass the rigours of examination against available evidence, and then of empirical test.

These recommendations are influenced by three conditions, each of them emerging quite strongly from the work reported in this volume.

1   One is that although many of the recall tasks to be performed by the respondent are quite easy, others are not. Yet, on the evidence available, at least some of the improvement sought will have to come through the more difficult recall situation. Further, the difficult and the easy tasks are inextricably mixed. This seems to mean that if further improvement of any appreciable degree is to be made, the whole questioning procedure will have to be put upon a more rigorous and searching basis.

2   If rigorous and searching procedures are to be employed, they must be such that interviewers of the right calibre are both able and willing to carry them out. The point is important because qualitative aspects of the work reported here point both to deviating tendencies on the part of the interviewers and to features of the interviewing procedure which virtually force deviations.

3   We cannot expect that a respondent will automatically make the necessary effort for a task of this kind. In many cases the necessary effort will have to be systematically evoked.

A series of tentative recommendations follow.

THE ORDER OF PRESENTATION OF DIFFERENT GROUPS OF PUBLICATIONS

The most promising order of presentation of the main groups of publications is: monthly, weekly, Sunday and daily. Estimating on the evidence in Table 4.4, this change should give us NRS averages of the level shown in row 2 of Table 4.33. Comparing these with the intensive estimates in row 3, it will be seen that the main effect of the change would be to give a somewhat improved degree of accuracy to the average for monthly publications (that is, a reduction of the underestimate by about a third).

Table 4.33

Showing expected errors using the presentation order:
monthlies, weeklies, Sundays, dailies

		Average readership figure by publication group*			
Condition of testing or of estimating		Daily	Sunday	Weekly	Monthly
(1)	When NRS-tested in the order DSWM	23.2	26.9	37.6	9.2
(2)	Estimated values when† NRS-tested in order MWSD	23.7	26.9	38.3	10.9
(3)	When intensive-tested without order effect	23.7	31.7	42.4	14.8

*For the 28 publications tested in this enquiry (seven dailies, seven Sundays, five weeklies and nine monthlies).
†These estimates are based upon certain 'rotation data' as they apply to the 28 publications concerned in this enquiry. These 'rotation data' are those developed from the analysis of the results of the 1958 readership survey and presented in the NRS tabulation, PSI 58/141.

We see too that this order of presentation: produced some increase in accuracy for the average of the five *weeklies* tested; closed altogether the small gap for the dailies; left the average for the Sundays unchanged. If nothing else were done to the present research procedure, this device alone should bring about a worthwhile improvement in the general level of accuracy — perhaps more so for the monthlies with relatively small readership figures (compare Tables 4.4 and 4.33 for order effect on monthlies).

At the same time it must be made quite clear that what we are dealing with here are *averages* or *groups* of publications and that even if the improvement in the average figure went much further than it does, we could not conclude that the accuracy level for *individual* publications would be improved to the same degree. In fact, the estimates for individual publications in this new order of presentation (that is, monthlies, weeklies, Sundays, dailies) are given in the appendix to Chapter 8 (see microfiche section).

From these it appears that the effect of the change is by no means even: for some publications accuracy is improved, for others it is not.

In the end, the point that matters is that for quite a lot of publications (particularly the monthlies) the margin of error remains appreciable and that the extent of error varies from one paper to another. It follows that though the best order of presentation (for accuracy) is 'monthly, weekly, Sunday, daily', the goal of accuracy for all publications calls for further measures.

QUESTION ORDER

The opening stages of the interview might with advantage be devoted to straightforward, easy, questions — possibly some of those at the end of the present procedure. The presentation of vital instructions for the recall procedure should come only *after* the respondent has settled into the situation and has a reasonable chance of taking them in.

REPETITION OF KEY INSTRUCTIONS

All important instructions should be repeated at required intervals and the interviewer's tendency to forget about such repetitions should be constrained — possibly through writing the repetition on additional cards in planned positions within the book of mastheads.

ENSURING COMMUNICATION OF KEY INSTRUCTIONS

Steps should be taken early in the interview both to *force* an explanation of basic instructions and concepts, and to find out if the respondent has taken them in. Here again, instruction cards integrated into the book of mastheads at planned intervals might be effective. It should also be possible to require the interviewer to write down on her questionnaire the respondent's reply to her questions about what is meant by 'looked at' and other important terms. Such questions would probably be asked shortly after the explanation had been made.

DROPPING THE FIRST PHASE OF THE INTERVIEW

In view of the evidence offered in this report, it might well be desirable to do away with the present two-phase character of the NRS interview. Various one-phase substitutes might be considered. Conceivably these might be to ask the respondent directly if he has looked at the publication within some specific period — that is, by offering the present qualifying periods directly. Part of the case for doing this is the apparent difficulty of preventing many of the respondents from thinking in terms of qualifying periods in any case, either because the interviewer starts to offer these or because a respondent works out a qualifying period (or thinks he has) in the course of the questioning procedure. In using any such method (that is, directly offering the qualifying periods), special devices would of course have to be employed to guard against sloppy and careless responses.

Whether or not the present first stage of the interview could so be done away with must depend upon a consideration of the functions it is *supposed* to serve and whether or not it does serve those functions. Were it in fact possible to drop it, it would mean that the efforts of the respondent could be brought fresh to this vital phase of the interview, that is, without respondents having first to go through the long and demotivating first stage of the interview. Even if the first stage is not dropped it certainly *will* have to be reshaped to reduce its present error-proneness, so that it does not serve as a source of loss of qualifying readership.

SYNCHRONISING VERBAL AND VISUAL AIDS

Techniques of presentation must be devised to give the interviewer full control over the synchronised presentation of questions and of visual aids, and which at the same time discourage the interviewer from *relinquishing* such control.

PAUSES BETWEEN GROUPS OF PUBLICATIONS

A definite pause between publication groups should be ensured and steps taken, in these pauses, to change the respondent's mental set (for example, from *monthly* to *weekly* publications).

TRAINING OF INTERVIEWERS

A special type of training of interviewers for this special task seems necessary. First and foremost, the interviewer must understand what the difficulties are in getting accurate recall, under survey conditions, in relation to incidental or irregular reading. This will probably involve nothing less than an explanation of the memory process from a psychological point of view. I think this is essential if interviewers are to understand why it is necessary to generate a special memory effort (and they won't if they don't) and why a simple question-and-answer approach is not enough. They must also understand and accept the problems of communicating instructions to ordinary people under survey conditions. Examples of communication failure — perhaps drawn from this report — might well help. The rejection of interviewers not able to cope with this sort of work is also vital and can be achieved readily enough through the tape-recording system used in this enquiry. The use of tape-recordings can also add considerably to the efficiency of the training process itself.

GEARING THE TECHNIQUE TO THE INTERVIEWING SITUATION

Finally, I consider it necessary to regard the development of a revised technique as a type of engineering problem — one in which the technique is built round the known difficulties of the situation. One cannot force interviewers to do what they dislike doing or what they consider to be inadequate. Interviewers work too much on their own for that to be possible. Nor can one expect respondents to *try* unless they can be shown a good reason for trying. Nor can we expect respondents to achieve an automatic intake or understanding of new or difficult instructions; nor to achieve easy recall of something about which they are simply vague. The technique to be developed must be built round the limitations and the difficulties of the real situation.

APPENDICES

*see microfiche supplement

161

APPENDIX 4.1A

INSTRUCTIONS FOR INTENSIVE INTERVIEWERS ON THE DAILY/SUNDAY SURVEY*

YOUR PURPOSE IN THE INTERVIEW

1   *Your Aims*

(a) *Your purpose in the intensive interview is to find out when the respondent last 'looked at' certain publications. You will be dealing in this way with two daily papers and two Sunday papers. Throughout your work you will have two related aims:*

(i) To determine, for each *daily* paper, whether or not respondent looked at it *yesterday*; to determine, for each *Sunday* paper, whether or not respondent looked at it *in the last seven days;*

(ii) to put a precise date and a precise time to the last occasion on which the respondent looked at the specific publications with which you are dealing.

(b) Each of these two aims is of extreme importance, but it is clear that aim (i) could temper aim (ii). Thus, where the respondent's reading of a Sunday paper occurred about a week ago, it is extremely important that the exact day be pinned down rigorously. In other words, there comes a point in time at which your estimate of when it occurred makes all the difference between the reading event being *in* the last seven days and *not* in the last seven days. It is at this borderline that extreme care is needed. For the same reason, it would be wasteful to go *on and on* trying to get the exact day when the last reading of the Sunday paper clearly occurred over four weeks ago. I don't mean that the precise day is unimportant as you get back that far: all I am saying is that when the circumstances are specially difficult or when the respondent is extremely vague, a little inaccuracy about a day four or more weeks ago is not something over which you should 'go to the stake'.

(c) In just the same way, when you are dealing with dailies, vagueness about whether or not it was *yesterday* must be penetrated or cleared up. *Whether it was yesterday or the day before is absolutely vital.* On the other hand, we can live with a vagueness about whether or not it was three or four days ago. The point of all this is that yesterday is the borderline point and so calls for rigorous pinning down.

(d) This general directive about key periods is no invitation for slackness over other periods. I have given it simply to alert you to the fact that there are certain periods about which precision is even more important than usual. All the care and accuracy in the world would be wasted (i) if the last reading of a daily was *not* accurately tied to either 'yesterday' or 'not yesterday'; (ii) if the last reading of a Sunday paper was not accurately tied to either 'in the last seven days' or '*not* in the last seven days'.

2   *The difficulty of your task*

(a) Your task is to establish facts about an event which is very likely indeed to be hazy and of little importance to the respondent. You will get nowhere by a passive writing-down of what the respondent deigns to tell you. Your only hope of success is to probe, to encourage, to challenge and to test. Nonetheless, all this must be done politely and with a clear realisation that your informant is doing us a favour. Partly because of this, you have a very difficult task; you must focus all your own attention and that of the respondent upon the single purpose of finding out when respondent last looked at certain publications. By far the most difficult part of your task is to cause the respondent to *think* — to make a real effort on our behalf. In this sense you are interrogating with the co-operation of the respondent. It is only through developing co-operation of this sort that you can break the respondent's habit of answering in terms of what she *usually* does or what she *probably* did. This tendency is likely to be the main barrier to your getting worthwhile and reliable information from your respondent. This point gets lengthy comment in a later part of your instructions.

*Closely similar instructions were issued for the weekly/monthly survey.

(b) We have set out here various ways and means of going about your interrogation. The methods we have set out have been tried and are workable and you must stick to them. Within the broad structure of your outline, there is scope — and necessity — for sharp intelligence and rigorous cross-checking.

STARTING THE INTERVIEW AND TELLING RESPONDENT WHAT IT'S ABOUT

You should start the interview with easy conversation in order to set up a friendly co-operative situation. Various topics of conversation are possible, but one that immediately suggests itself is how they got on in the first interview, and about being interviewed in general. This has the advantage of giving you a certain amount of insight into the situation at the first interview. This phase of your own interview should not last for much more than a minute or two.

You should be quite frank with the respondent about what you are doing. Thus, you should make it clear that you are carrying out a study of how well people can remember things when they are asked for information on the doorstep. You should explain that your part of the job is to learn as much as possible about the sort of errors that people make under these conditions. Obviously you must do this without 'putting people's backs up' or making them in any way defensive. It is undesirable to come out with all this at the beginning. Feel your way, giving out a little extra as the circumstances call for it. Thus, any full statement about the need for a special memory effort should come only at that part of the interview where this is necessary. Looking at it from another point of view, some people will want to know much more about the reason for their interview than will others, and here your job is to be quite frank about what you are doing.

The point of all this is that the nature of our questions is such that it would be all too easy for an uninformed respondent to say to himself: 'What is the point of all this questioning? I don't see the sense of all this'. The distinct advantage of letting people know what you are doing is that they can actively co-operate with you. Our experience in the past has been that this is what happens.

GETTING THE RESPONDENT'S USUAL PATTERN OF READING

This, the second part of your questioning takes you into the enquiry proper. In it you are to question the respondent about usual patterns of reading. The questions themselves appear on your questionnaire. Your questioning about the respondent's usual pattern of reading is meant to give you a vantage point from which to carry out your subsequent questioning. It is also meant to help the respondent establish an effective frame of reference for what is to come, i.e. to get him thinking along the right lines. One special advantage of knowing about the usual pattern of reading is that it allows you to pick or to look for departures from the usual. Departures from the usual are likely to be a special source of error. The precise questioning procedure to be used here is as set out in your report form. You will notice from this that it calls for (i) which daily and Sunday papers they usually read, (ii) where do they do their reading of these, (iii) how these papers come into their hands, (iv) any special circumstances connected with their reading of any of them, (v) whether or not they ever read Sunday or daily papers in waiting rooms, at friends' houses, etc., (vi) whether or not they ever pick them up while travelling. You should, however, fill out these details with anything else that you happen to learn about the respondent's usual reading behaviour.

GETTING THE RESPONDENT TO CONSIDER SPECIFIC PAPERS: WHETHER OR NOT HE HAS EVER LOOKED AT THESE

Sorting by 'Never' or by 'Yes'

Your subsequent questioning procedure is designed to find out whether or not your respondent has looked at certain publications within a specified time period. The first step in this is a sorting process in which the papers being tested in this way are put into two heaps. In one heap are papers which respondent says he never looks at and in the other are papers which he says he does look at. Go forward as follows, *dealing with each test paper quite separately.*

Pass respondent the last copy of the test paper, getting respondent to look at the cover page. Say:

'Here is a copy of . . . . Have you *ever* looked at a copy of . . . .?'

If 'no', say:

'I mean *any* copy of it — not just *this* one.'

If still 'no', say:

'Never?'

If still 'never' put it (and the other copies of it) to one side (you will be coming back to it shortly).

If respondent says 'yes' to any of these questions put the paper (and the other copies of it) on the other side (you will be coming back to it).

Do just the same for all four papers to be tested, putting the 'never's' on one side and the 'yes's' on the other.

MAKING SURE OF THE 'NEVER'S

You should deal with the 'Never's *before* the 'Yes's. But for the purpose of effective explanation I am leaving details of this procedure until after telling you how to cope with the 'yes' publications. Full details for dealing with the 'never's are given on pages 167, 168.

FINDING OUT ABOUT THE 'YES' PAPERS: SUNDAY PAPERS

Our basic task is to find out if specific Sunday papers were looked at in the last seven days and if dailies were looked at yesterday. We will of course be striving hard for actual date of the last 'looking at' event, but 'yesterday' for dailies and 'the last seven days' for Sundays are vital points of reference and must condition your pursuit of dates (see 1 (a)—(d) under 'Your Purpose in the Interview').

Because of the difference in the two reference systems, it is necessary to deal with Sunday papers before daily papers. More particularly this is because it seems reasonable to expect recall over the last seven days to be more difficult than recall over yesterday: accordingly we start with the harder task (Sunday papers), leaving the easier one until later.

Start this operation by asking respondent to turn through each of the three latest copies of this paper. Then ask:

'Have you ever looked at *any* copy of that paper before (I mean any copy of it)?'

If 'no', make it clear that you mean *any* copy of it — even six months back. Also make it clear that 'looked at' has the same meaning as given above. If still 'no', ask respondent how he came to make his first error in this particular interview (I am not referring to any errors in the first-stage interview). Also, ask respondent if there is any reason *why* he has never looked at it before. Record all these answers on your questionnaire.

If 'yes' to any of these questions proceed as follows:

Fixing on the Last Occasion

The next question is the 64,000 dollar one. See that it registers good and well.

'I want you to go back to the VERY LATEST OCCASION when you looked at ANY copy of this paper. THE VERY LATEST OCCASION that you looked at ANY copy of it.'

The point of this question is that you want the respondent to think about it and so be in a position to answer the next question in a thoughtful fashion. Then say:

'Can you tell me where you were then?'

164

Record this, and then ask:

'And just when was it?'

Record this.

Before going ahead with examining the accuracy of this claim, try respondent for a *later* occasion. Do this through the following question.

'What about since then? What about in the last week or so?'

Then add:

'What about in a waiting room? Or in a bus or train? At work? At a friend's place? Perhaps you just glanced through it?'

If the last occasion was *within* the last seven days, proceed as detailed below in order to detect error and to examine all the evidence in support of or in contradiction of the claim.

If *before* the last seven days, your main purpose must be to make sure that it didn't in fact occur *during* the last seven days. You do this in an oblique way. You examine evidence for the claimed occasion and you give a date to the last reading event. But you must use all the evidence as a means of studying the possibility of there having been reading in the last seven days in order to pounce on this as it shows. *There is a detailed section on this process* later in your instructions.

The cross-examination to fix the date of the last 'Looked At' occasion

Start your study of the last occasion by telling the respondent that your job is to get all possible details of that reading occasion. *You should regard this as a rigorous cross-examination to establish the consistency of all claims about other reading events.* Use the following lines of search.

1   Find out *where* the respondent was on that last occasion, getting him to fill in all possible details. This will give you leads which may be easier to date than the reading event itself. A possible form of words for this is as follows:

'I want you to tell me just *where you were* on that *last occasion*, and anything else you can remember about it.'

Use the following prompt system as necessary:

'In a bus or train? In a waiting room? At a hairdresser's? At work? At lunch? At a friend's? At home in the evening? In between TV programmes?'

2   Find out what the respondent was reading on that last occasion. Don't let respondent look it up except as a last resort. Check what he says against the paper itself to see if he is right or wrong. Don't regard a failure on his part to tell you what it was as disproof of his claim — though that might in fact be what it means. Regard a failure of this kind as a signal to find out why it has occurred. In the final event be prepared to let respondent find what it was he looked at, even if this means going back over several papers. The outcome of this may well be to indicate that the respondent either looked at an old copy on the occasion he claimed or was incorrect in his claim. Pursue the indications of this to a conclusion.

3   Find out what time of day it was that respondent read it (on that last occasion). Be specially on your guard here against a reply in terms of what respondent *usually* does. Challenge or test any generalisations of this kind with something like the following:

'Yes, but *on this particular occasion* what time was it? How can you be sure of that?'

The main point of this lead is to make the event come alive more in the respondent's mind and to give *you* extra leads. It should also serve to *break generalising tendencies*.

4   Find out what was going on at the time of that reading occasion. In addition get the events that occurred that same day. Use these events, etc., as extra fixes on the reading event, trying in all cases to link this to a date or time.

5   Find out how the paper came into the respondent's hands, or what led up to the respondent's reading of it. *Use this to check and challenge other statements*. In the same way, find out what happened to the copy afterwards. If still in the home, ask to see it. *If passed on, find out when and to whom*. This may well put a limit to the respondent's chances of seeing it after a certain date. It will also give you an extra clue to dodginess on the part of the respondent.

6   Find out how the last occasion differed from what *usually* happens. *Pursue the unusual elements in the event in order to date them*.

7   Get all the details of regular or semi-regular deliveries of this paper (including cases when it is passed on by a friend). *Use this to establish limits to respondent's chances of seeing it before certain dates*.

8   Ask for exact day of the reading event. Don't press for this too soon as this may lead the respondent to defend a less considered estimate. *Ask respondent how he can be sure it was that day . . .* or what makes him think it might be that day. *Check these claims against other evidence*.

9   Study respondent's motives and his opportunity to read it. OPPORTUNITY IS OBVIOUSLY AN IMPORTANT CONSIDERATION IN FIXING THE TIME OF THE ACT OF READING.

Be prepared to use all these leads, but above all keep the following principles clearly in mind.

1   You are an interrogator. You are not a passive writer-down of answers. You must use all your wits to pick up clues, to cross-check on all replies, and finish up with a reliable estimate of *when* the last reading occurred.

2   Don't let respondent evade any of your questions.

3   Break any tendency by respondent to generalise or to say what he usually does. *This is probably the most important of all your instructions*.

4   *Check and challenge all the way*. The technique you are employing is that of the police investigator (a polite one) who is not put off by confident statements or evasive replies. Every statement by the respondent should be tested or challenged: 'How can you be sure of that?' . . . 'If you get it on order, how was it you didn't see it last week?' . . . 'But if it was lying around the house all week, how was it you didn't look at it again?' . . . 'Could it have been the evening when you looked at it?' Check even the simplest of statements. Make a practice of it. Think of yourself as in a courtroom trying to get at the truth. Go into the interview *on guard* against simply believing what you are told. Watch specially for any inconsistencies or vaguenesses.

5   The interview must be on *your* terms — it is no good at all to have your respondent deciding on the rules of the exchange or dodging questions or rambling on. Clearly state what the conditions are when you start the interview and stick to them. This may even involve getting other members of the household to leave the room — especially children and budgerigars.

6   Use any lead available to you — a diary kept by a respondent, a copy of the paper still around the house, a statement that a neighbour or another member of the family could help fix the date, your knowledge of the respondent's usual pattern of reading.

7   After every interview look back over your performance to see what you missed and where you fell down in checking and challenging.

FINDING OUT ABOUT THE 'YES' PUBLICATIONS: DAILY PAPERS

If there is a daily paper in the 'yes' group (see pages 163–4 for description of early sort into 'yes' and 'never' groups) proceed on the same lines as for Sunday papers.

If respondent's estimate of when he last looked at this daily takes you beyond yesterday, use your interrogation procedure both to get the actual time of reading *and* to double check that reading didn't in fact occur yesterday. To a large extent this will involve you in finding out *why* and *how* it didn't occur yesterday. See the special instruction on this important process.

In dealing with dailies, an important frame of reference is in terms of 'yesterday' versus 'not yesterday'. (This is in contrast with Sunday papers, where the frame of reference was 'last seven days' versus 'before that'.) This automatically makes a difference to the exact form of wording used in several of your questions. This, however, should become obvious as you go through the procedure described in the section concerned.

WHEN RESPONDENT SAYS THAT THE SUNDAY PAPER WAS LAST LOOKED AT *MORE THAN* SEVEN DAYS AGO

AND

WHEN RESPONDENT SAYS THAT THE DAILY PAPER WAS LAST LOOKED AT *BEFORE* YESTERDAY

In both these situations you have a special sort of procedure. It calls for an oblique type of approach. You go right ahead with trying to find out *when* that last occasion actually was. But all the time you are doing this you must also be looking for leads which can be used to check that there was in fact *no* reading in the crucial period ('last seven days' for Sundays and 'yesterday' for dailies). Most of the leads we have given you provide this sort of opportunity, but some which are specially fruitful for this sort of operation are the following:

1   Establish respondent's usual routine for looking at the publication and then find out *why* this pattern (if one exists) did not apply in the last seven days/yesterday.

2   Put respondent very carefully through the test copies of the paper concerned, looking for recognition of anything and pursuing this.

3   Establish the channels or means whereby respondent gets this paper (or got it on the last occasion) and find out why this did not bring her to it in the last week/yesterday. When she gets it in order, this can be easy enough. If she sees it at work, at a friend's place, in a library, etc., it will be harder for you to pick up the necessary evidence. But pick it up you must and then it is a matter of seeing why it didn't happen this way in the last seven days/yesterday.

4   Find out *where the respondent was and what she was doing* yesterday/last seven days and study the events in that week/day as possibly providing an opportunity for reading or 'looking at'.

WHEN RESPONDENT SAYS THAT THE SUNDAY/DAILY PAPER IS NEVER READ (OR HAS NOT BEEN SEEN IN YEARS)

This section describes a process which must come ahead of your check on publications which the respondent said he had looked at some time (you will have this information from your early sorting process). I have held over describing it until now because it rests very much on the rationale set out on pages 163–6.

In cases like these (the 'never' papers) you have to go warily because people who say they never look at certain publications seem specially prone to take offence if their sweeping statement is doubted. Start by making it clear that you have to go through a questioning procedure and by asking for their patience even when they feel you are wasting time. This appeal for patience is usually met by the respondent. You can go further if the situation is right, and try to get the respondent to see that while *she* knows various things about her reading behaviour, *you* don't, and that the nature of your work on memory means that you have to start by looking at all the evidence — you have to make absolutely sure. Ask for patience as you do this.

Your leads, in cases where respondent denies ever reading a publication are as follows.

1   Put respondent carefully through the familiarisation process, asking him to look for anything at all he remembers seeing *even in another paper*. (The latter point may well give you a means of making the respondent look seriously at the content of your test copies of the

paper.) Watch constantly for evidence that they may be pretending they don't look at this paper.

2 Find out if any of their friends or associates read it. This includes: members of own family, workmates or colleagues, friends or relations. There may be others. If so, find out if respondent has been in their company at all, particularly in the test period (yesterday/in the last seven days) and probe for incidental or forgotten exposure to the publications concerned.

3 Find out if respondent has been in any waiting room, common rooms, libraries, etc., in the test period (yesterday/in the last seven days) and probe for incidental or forgotten exposure to the publication.

4 Find out if respondent happened to see it as wrapping paper or if he picked it up in the train and glanced through it, or if he came by it in any other such way. Link this specially to yesterday/last seven days, but don't rule out admissions about earlier occasions.

5 Get reasons why respondent never looks at it. This may reveal an attitude or it may point to lack of opportunity. Pursue both.

CONFRONTING THE RESPONDENT
WITH THE RESULTS OF THE FIRST INTERVIEW

This happens with all the four publications you test. You do it *after* coping with all four (and *not* after each one of them). You will have with you a sealed envelope in which is the first questionnaire. *You must not open this until you are quite through with your interrogation*, and with your final estimate of *when* respondent last saw the four publications. You must say to respondent:

> 'I am now going to open this envelope. The results of your first interview are in it. Be my witness that I am doing this now.'

(This statement is tape-recorded along with the rest of the interview.)

Then put this questionnaire and your own results side by side and look for any differences in respect of the publications you have tested. Where differences occur, ask respondent directly for his explanation of how these differences occurred. Write down the answers and probe for anything extra.

Use this situation to get a short statement about how the first interview was undertaken. Get criticism of it and points of praise: Did the interviewer say exactly what was wanted? Did the interviewer make it clear that what we wanted was what actually happened and not what *usually* happened? Did respondent think the interview took too long? And so on. Then get respondent's statement of how he, himself, performed in the interview: Did he really try hard in it? What stopped him trying hard? Did he clearly understand what was wanted? Did he learn what it was all about and what was wanted as he went through the interview, or did he know right at the start?

This is our one chance of getting insight into sources of error. We depend upon you to make the most of it.

APPENDIX 4.1B

REPORT FORM USED BY INTENSIVE INTERVIEWERS ON THE DAILY/SUNDAY SURVEY*

Serial No. . . . .

REPORT FORM

1   *Name and address of informant* . . . .

. . . .

2   *Papers for Test*

(1) . . . .

(2) . . . .

(3) . . . .

(4) . . . .

3   *Appointment fixed:*   Date . . . .   Time . . . .

(Complete filling in details on return to office)

4   Date first interview . . . .   Date second interview . . . .

5   Was second interview carried out? Yes/no/?

6   If 'yes', when?

(a)   Date . . . .   (b)   Time . . . .

(c)   Length of interview . . . .

7   If 'no', why not? . . . .

8   Number of tape . . . .

STAGE I. USUAL PATTERN OF READING

Ask the following questions exactly as written and as in the order shown.

1   (a)   What daily newspapers do you read? . . . .

. . . .

(b)   Prompt with 'What about evening papers?' Add these to the above list.

(c)   Which of these do you read regularly? Underline those of above so named.

*A closely similar report form was used in the weekly/monthly Survey.

2   (a)   What about Sunday papers? Which Sunday papers do you read? . . . .

. . . .

     (b)   Which of these do you read regularly? Underline those of above so named.

3   Will you try to tell me the usual places where you do your reading of newspapers? Daily and Sunday newspapers. *When* you usually read them and at what *times* you usually read them.

     (a)   . . . .

     (b)   . . . .

     (c)   . . . .

     (d)   . . . .

     (e)   . . . .

4   That's what you *usually* do. Now I want you to think about any exceptions. Do you ever read it at any other place or time? Give me a list of the exceptions — any other places or times you ever read a newspaper.

     (a)   . . . .

     (b)   . . . .

     (c)   . . . .

5   How do you usually come by the different papers you read? How do you come by them — get them — in what ways do they come into your hands?

. . . .

Prompt with: Any that are passed on to you? Any you see at work? Any that are brought home by others in the house? What about waiting rooms? Or libraries? Do you see them in trains? Or at a friend's place?

6   Do you ever look at papers over someone else's shoulder when you are travelling? Yes/no/?

STAGE II. SORTING BY 'YES' AND 'NEVER'

(Do this on the basis of the latest copy of each of your four publications)

1   Names of 'Never' papers . . . .

2   Names of 'Yes' papers . . . .

3   Comments on sorting process.

STAGE III. INTERROGATION TO ESTABLISH FACTS ABOUT
LAST OCCASION OF 'LOOKING AT'

— Use *all three copies* of each paper in the familiarisation process.
— Start with 'nevers'. Then all the 'yes's'. Test on all four, one after the other, *before* doing *any* of Stage IV.
— While it is O.K. to enter *some* of the following details on return to the office, you MUST enter the four estimates at the time you estimated them (i.e. at respondent's home). Ditto 'Results of familiarisation'.

First paper . . . . (Name it)

(a)   Results of familiarisation:

  Which of the three issues did respondent recognise as having seen before?

  . . . .

(b) | Final estimate of *when* respondent last looked at it

  . . . .

(c)   *Where* was respondent on this last occasion? . . . .

  Source of the paper looked at on this last occasion? . . . .

  . . . .

(d)   Evidence leading you to doubt the above estimate . . . .

  . . . .

  . . . .

  . . . .

(e)   Evidence giving you confidence in the above estimate . . . .

  . . . .

  . . . .

  . . . .

Second paper . . . . (Name it)

(a)   Results of familiarisation:

  Which of the three issues did respondent recognise as having seen before?

  . . . .

(b) | Final estimate of *when* respondent last looked at it

  . . . .

(c)   *Where* was respondent on this last occasion? . . . .

  Source of the paper looked at on this last occasion? . . . .

  . . . .

(d)   Evidence leading you to doubt the above estimate . . . .

  . . . .

  . . . .

  . . . .

(e)   Evidence giving you confidence in the above estimate . . . .

  . . . .

  . . . .

  . . . .

Third paper . . . . (Name it)

(a)   Results of familiarisation:
     Which of the three issues did respondent recognise as having seen before?
     . . . .

(b) | Final estimate of *when* respondent last looked at it
     . . . .

(c)   *Where* was respondent on this last occasion? . . . .
     Source of the paper looked at on this last occasion? . . . .
     . . . .

(d)   Evidence leading you to doubt the above estimate . . . .
     . . . .
     . . . .
     . . . .

(e)   Evidence giving you confidence in the above estimate . . . .
     . . . .
     . . . .
     . . . .

Fourth paper . . . . (Name it)

(a)   Results of familiarisation:
     Which of the three issues did respondent recognise as having seen before?
     . . . .

(b) | Final estimate of *when* respondent last looked at it
     . . . .

(c)   *Where* was respondent on this last occasion? . . . .
     Source of the paper looked at on this last occasion? . . . .
     . . . .

(d)   Evidence leading you to doubt the above estimate . . . .
     . . . .
     . . . .
     . . . .

(e)   Evidence giving you confidence in the above estimate . . . .
     . . . .
     . . . .
     . . . .

STAGE IV. CONFRONTING RESPONDENT WITH RESULTS
OF FIRST INTERVIEW

This is done after all four papers have been tested by you. Once you open the envelope containing the first interview questionnaire you *cannot* alter any of your estimates of when 'last looked at'.

Paper 1 . . . . (Name it)

(a) Nature of discrepancy . . . .

(b) Respondent's explanation of discrepancy . . . .

. . . .

(c) Your own explanation of discrepancy . . . .

. . . .

Paper 2 . . . . (Name it)

(a) Nature of discrepancy . . . .

(b) Respondent's explanation of discrepancy . . . .

. . . .

(c) Your own explanation of discrepancy . . . .

. . . .

Paper 3 . . . . (Name it)

(a) Nature of discrepancy . . . .

(b) Respondent's explanation of discrepancy . . . .

. . . .

(c) Your own explanation of discrepancy . . . .

. . . .

Paper 4 . . . . (Name it)

(a) Nature of discrepancy . . . .

(b) Respondent's explanation of discrepancy . . . .

. . . .

(c) Your own explanation of discrepancy . . . .

. . . .

STAGE V. CONDITIONS OF TAKING THE PAPER

*These questions come *after* the confronting stage and you must ask them exactly as here. Tell respondent what the choice of answers is and prevent respondent from evading a choice of one or another of them. Write in the name of the paper to which each set of questions is addressed.
    *Repeat these questions even if you already have the information.

Paper 1 . . . . (Name it)

(a) How often do you see this paper?
    SEE EVERY COPY/MOST COPIES/SEE NOW AND THEN/HARDLY EVER/NEVER.
(b) Is it delivered to your home? YES/NO/?
(c) Do you read it all in one day or do you look at it on different days? ALL ONE DAY/
    DIFFERENT DAYS.
(d) Do you keep it round the house for a long time or do you get rid of it quickly? KEEP IT
    ROUND/GET RID OF IT QUICKLY.
(e) If you could not see a copy of this paper, would you care much? YES/NO/?

Paper 2 . . . . (Name it)

(a) How often do you see this paper?
    SEE EVERY COPY/MOST COPIES/SEE NOW AND THEN/HARDLY EVER/NEVER.
(b) Is it delivered to your home? YES/NO/?
(c) Do you read it all in one day or do you look at it on different days? ALL ONE DAY/
    DIFFERENT DAYS.
(d) Do you keep it round the house for a long time or do you get rid of it quickly? KEEP IT
    ROUND/GET RID OF IT QUICKLY.
(e) If you could not see a copy of this paper, would you care much? YES/NO/?

Paper 3 . . . . (Name it)

(a) How often do you see this paper?
    SEE EVERY COPY/MOST COPIES/SEE NOW AND THEN/HARDLY EVER/NEVER.
(b) Is it delivered to your home? YES/NO/?
(c) Do you read it all in one day or do you look at it on different days? ALL ONE DAY/
    DIFFERENT DAYS.
(d) Do you keep it round the house for a long time or do you get rid of it quickly? KEEP IT
    ROUND/GET RID OF IT QUICKLY.
(e) If you could not see a copy of this paper, would you care much? YES/NO/?

Paper 4 . . . . (Name it)

(a) How often do you see this paper?
    SEE EVERY COPY/MOST COPIES/SEE NOW AND THEN/HARDLY EVER/NEVER.
(b) Is it delivered to your home? YES/NO/?
(c) Do you read it all in one day or do you look at it on different days? ALL ONE DAY/
    DIFFERENT DAYS.
(d) Do you keep it round the house for a long time or do you get rid of it quickly? KEEP IT
    ROUND/GET RID OF IT QUICKLY.
(e) If you could not see a copy of this paper, would you care much? YES/NO/?

STAGE VI. PERSONAL DETAILS, ETC.

1   Age . . . . Sex . . . . Marital state . . . .

2   Occupational state: Full-time job/Part-time job/Retired/Self-employed/Housewife/
                         Student.
                         (Underline *all* that apply.)

3   Job held (if not in a job, get last full-time job before marriage or before retirement)
    . . . .

4   At what age did you finish full-time school? . . . .

5   Did you have any further education *after* that? . . . .

6   Ages of all young people and children in the home (up to age of 21 years) . . . .
    . . . .

7   Is there a TV set in the home? . . . .

8   (a) Exactly what were you doing at the time the first interviewer called? . . . .
        . . . .

    (b) Was there anything to distract you at your first interview? What? . . . .
        . . . .

    (c) Did you have to try hard or make a big effort to remember *at your first interview?*
        YES/NO/?

    (d) Did you enjoy the first interview? YES/NO/?

    (e) Were you in a hurry to get that interview finished? YES/NO/?

174

9   Have you ever been interviewed before — not counting the other one today? YES/NO/?

10   How do you feel about giving an interview to people doing market research? (Underline choice)
A BIT OF A NUISANCE/NO TROUBLE AT ALL/?

11   Which of the following applies to you? (Underline *all* that apply.) Would you say you are:
VERY PATIENT/VERY EASY GOING/VERY BUSY/A BIT UNTIDY/LEAD A VERY VARIED SORT OF LIFE/MOSTLY DO WHAT OTHERS WANT OF YOU/A BIT ABSENT MINDED/OFTEN FORGET THINGS.

12   Does your mind wander from one subject to another/or do you concentrate on just the one thing for a long time? (Tick the one chosen.)

STAGE VII. INSIGHT GAINED INTO THE NATURE OF THE FIRST INTERVIEW

Complete this when you get back to the office. This is essentially *your opinion*, based on your appraisal of the evidence. (It is quite possible that your opinion will be in sharp disagreement with the respondent's actual statements about the first interview.)

1   Conditions of first interview (e.g. respondent in a hurry, tired, baby crying, on doorstep, etc.)
. . . .

2   Did respondent really try to remember (i.e. in the first interview)?
TRIED VERY HARD/FAIRLY HARD/JUST A LITTLE/NOT AT ALL.

3   If respondent didn't try to remember (in the first interview) why? . . . .
. . . .

4   How do you think that the respondent felt about the first interviewer? . . . .
. . . .

175

APPENDIX 4.2A

ADDITIONAL INSTRUCTIONS TO NRS INTERVIEWERS
(see also Appendix 4.3)

INTERVIEWERS' INSTRUCTIONS (NRS)

1 What we want you to do

Your task is to carry out a series of interviews on precisely the lines now employed in the IPA National Readership Surveys. In other words, all interviewers will be using the method (and the equipment) now employed by the British Market Research Bureau. For interviewers working with Research Services, this involves certain changes from the methods formerly used by them, but they will already have been briefed on the difference and will have practised the modified procedure.

Apart from this, we don't want you to depart from normal procedure or normal practice. We want you to carry on with the questioning procedure just as usual.

There are several reasons for this particular enquiry. One is that we want readership data in specific areas (in London) in which we are specially interested; it is vital that our results are directly comparable with those from the National Readership Surveys; in other words, your questioning procedure must be *as usual*. Another reason is that we want to follow your interview with a further interview designed to tell us quite a lot about the informants' interests and the behavioural background of people in various readership groups.

2 The follow up interview

The second of our aims is important and it involves you in fixing an appointment for a second interviewer to call on your informant. This must be done only after you have completed the interview. This appointment has to be fixed *for the day following your own interview*, except on Saturdays when you fix appointments for a second interview for the *Monday*. There is a special way of fixing this appointment.

(i) We want you to fix this appointment with everyone you interview. For this, you will have a set of appointment times and it will be your task to get the informant to accept one of these. These appointment times are allocated to fit the availability of a small team of people conducting the second interview.

(ii) It is extremely important that we get this second interview with *all* members of the survey sample. You may tell your informant that its purpose is to ask more questions about their reading, about what they are interested in and about the sort of things they would like to have more of in their papers. Make it clear that the second interviewer comes from the London School of Economics. Our experience has been that very few people indeed will refuse it if the appointment is well made. In some areas we are offering payment for the second interview (the more depressed areas) and in all of them you should make it clear that the second interview will be an extremely interesting and worthwhile one.

(iii) You have an appointment card on which to write the time of the appointment and this should be left with the respondent, along with your thanks for co-operation and a repetition of the fact that the second interview will serve a very useful purpose and that it will be specially interesting.

(iv) The appointment you make should be a *firm* one. Don't leave it that the respondent just *might* be in at the time arranged. Make every effort to fix all appointments firmly. Naturally, there will be occasions when you fail, and in that case a loose appointment is better than no appointment at all. But regard a loose appointment as a last resort.

(v) You must write the following information on your questionnaire (in the space at the bottom right-hand corner under 'Notes')

— *Respondent's name and address*
— *Time of appointment*
— *Reason, if appointment is refused*

3 Where to report with your appointments

We are working from a local office. This office is very close to your interviewing area. You are to go to this office at the end of each working day in order to hand in your appointments and your completed questionnaires. The address of the local office will be given to you at briefing.

4 Times of work

Briefing is at 10 a.m. on Monday. After this we want you to go out to your interviewing area. There will be an agreed day off each week. Saturday, however, is a working day for all. On your week-days, you will be free to choose your own times of work, though the sampling requirements, (i.e. equal males and females each day) mean that you will have to do a lot of your work in the evenings.

5 Your list of names

You will have a list of fifty names and addresses. Of these, fifteen have a star against them. These are reserves and should be used only when the person listed above or below it proves unavailable. A person can be considered unavailable only if he or she:

- is ill or deceased
- has moved or is away for a long period
- is not at home after three calls on three separate days
- refuses to grant a second interview.

You cannot use a reserve name without first getting permission to do so at the local office.

6 In case of illness

This is a team operation and it depends very much upon our having a full team operating on each working day. Thus, if you become ill your own organisation should know about it straight away so that they can try to fill the gap.

APPENDIX 4.2E

QUESTIONNAIRE USED BY THE NRS INTERVIEWERS

ASK Q.1 ABOUT *ALL* PUBLICATIONS IN BOOKLET BEFORE GOING TO Q.2.

1. I want you to go through this booklet with me, and tell me, for each paper, whether you happen to have looked at any copy of it in the past three months, it doesn't matter where.

NOW EXPLAIN: 'looked at', 'any copy',
                     'past 3 months' (i.e. since . . . . ').
                     'doesn't matter where'.

AFTER *ALL* PUBLICATIONS HAVE BEEN DEALT WITH UNDER Q.1, ASK Q.2 FOR EACH PUBLICATION 'LOOKED AT IN PAST 3 MONTHS' (Code A). TAKE *GROUPS* IN THE SAME ORDER AS IN THE BOOKLET.

2. When was the last time you looked at a copy of . . . . ?

DISREGARD ANY READING ON THE DAY OF INTERVIEW:

If the answer is 'to-day' ask:

    When did you last look at a copy, apart from to-day?

	Order:

DAILY MORNING AND EVENING NEWSPAPERS

PUBLICATION	Q.1 (in last 3 months)		Q.2 (If Code A) When last looked at:	
	Looked at	Not looked at	Before yesterday	Yesterday (include Saturday for Monday interviews)
ALL REGIONS				39.
News Chronicle and Daily Dispatch	A	B	C	1
Daily Express	A	B	C	2
Daily Mirror	A	B	C	3
Daily Sketch	A	B	C	4
Daily Mail	A	B	C	5
Daily Herald	A	B	C	6
The Times	A	B	C	7
Daily Telegraph	A	B	C	8
The Guardian	A	B	C	0
LONDON, SOUTH EAST, EAST, AND SOUTHERN REGIONS ONLY				40.
Evening Standard	A	B	C	1
Evening News	A	B	C	2
Star	A	B	C	3

178

SUNDAY NEWSPAPERS

PUBLICATION	Q.1 (in last 3 months)		Q.2 (If Code A) When last looked at:	
	Looked at	Not looked at	Over 7 days ago	Within the last 7 days
ALL REGIONS				41.
News of the World	A	B	C	1
Empire News and Sunday Chronicle	A	B	C	2
Sunday Times	A	B	C	3
Sunday Express	A	B	C	4
Sunday Pictorial	A	B	C	5
Sunday Graphic	A	B	C	6
Observer	A	B	C	7
People	A	B	C	8
Sunday Dispatch	A	B	C	9
Reynolds News	A	B	C	0
Glasgow Sunday Post	A	B	C	X
Glasgow Sunday Mail	A	B	C	Y

WEEKLY MAGAZINES

PUBLICATION	Q.1 (in last 3 months)		Q.2 (If Code A) When last looked at:	
	Looked at	Not looked at	Over 7 days ago	Within the last 7 days
GENERAL WEEKLY MAGAZINES				42.
Punch	A	B	C	1
Reveille	A	B	C	3
Today — The New John Bull	A	B	C	4
Universe	A	B	C	5
Christian Herald	A	B	C	8
TV Times	A	B	C	9
TV Guide/TV Weekly/The Viewer	A	B	C	2
Tit-Bits	A	B	C	X
Weekly News (Glasgow Weekly News in Scotland)	A	B	C	Y
				43.
Listener	A	B	C	1
Weekend	A	B	C	2
Parade and Blighty	A	B	C	3
Radio Times	A	B	C	4
Picturegoer	A	B	C	6
Picture Show	A	B	C	7
WOMEN'S WEEKLY MAGAZINES				
Woman's Day	A	B	C	8
Woman's Realm	A	B	C	9
Roxy	A	B	C	0
				44.
Secrets	A	B	C	3
Family Star	A	B	C	5
Marilyn	A	B	C	6
Woman's Mirror	A	B	C	7
Woman	A	B	C	8
Woman's Companion	A	B	C	9
Woman's Weekly	A	B	C	0
Silver Star and Lucky Star	A	B	C	X
Woman's Own	A	B	C	Y
				45.
Woman's Illustrated	A	B	C	1
Red Star	A	B	C	3
Red Letter	A	B	C	4
People's Friend	A	B	C	5
Mirabelle	A	B	C	8
Valentine	A	B	C	9
My Weekly and Welcome	A	B	C	0
Boyfriend	A	B	C	7
Romeo	A	B	C	X
				48.
Marty	A	B	C	0

MONTHLY MAGAZINES

PUBLICATION	Q.1 (in last 3 months)		Q.2 (If Code A) When last looked at:	
	Looked at	Not looked at	Over 4 weeks ago	Within the last 4 weeks
GENERAL MONTHLY MAGAZINES				46.
Lilliput	A	B	C	1
Practical Householder	A	B	C	2
Argosy	A	B	C	3
Reader's Digest	A	B	C	4
Ideal Home	A	B	C	5
House Beautiful	A	B	C	6
Homes and Gardens	A	B	C	7
Wide World	A	B	C	8
Men Only	A	B	C	9
Photoplay	A	B	C	0
Practical Motorist	A	B	C	X
Do It Yourself	A	B	C	Y
				48.
Homemaker	A	B	C	8
Car Mechanics	A	B	C	X
WOMEN'S MONTHLY MAGAZINES				47.
Woman and Beauty	A	B	C	1
Vogue	A	B	C	2
My Home and Wife and Home	A	B	C	3
True Romances	A	B	C	4
Modern Woman	A	B	C	5
She	A	B	C	6
Good Housekeeping	A	B	C	7
Home	A	B	C	8
Vanity Fair	A	B	C	9
True Magazine	A	B	C	0
Woman and Home	A	B	C	X
				48.
True Story	A	B	C	1
Woman's Journal	A	B	C	3
Everywoman	A	B	C	4
Housewife	A	B	C	5
Sincerely	A	B	C	7

NOTES

3.	How often these days do you go to the cinema?			
	Twice a week or more often		49.	1
	Once a week			2
	Once a fortnight			3
	Once a month			4
	Less often			5
	Never go these days			0

4.	How many times have you been in the last week?	50

5 *(a)*	Do you have a television set at home yet?	Yes		A
		No	51.	0

IF 'YES'

(b)	Can you get both the BBC and the Independent TV station on it, or not?	BBC only		1
		BBC and ITV		2

ASK ALL

6 How often these days do you watch BBC television?
. . . and what about Independent TV?

	BBC	ITV
5 or more days a week	52. 1	6
3 or 4 days a week	2	7
Once or twice a week	3	8
Less often	4	9
Never view these days	5	0

7.	Did you view either station yesterday?		
	Neither	53.	0
	BBC		1
	ITV		2
	(ring 2 codes if necessary)		

8.	About how often these days do you listen to Radio Luxembourg?	
	5 or more days a week	4
	3 or 4 days a week	5
	Once or twice a week	6
	Less often	7
	Never listen these days	8

9.	How many times have you listened to Radio Luxembourg in the last week?	54

10.	Do you have a washing machine at home?	Yes	55.	2
		No		A

11 *(a)*	Do you have a car at home?	Yes	56.	1
		No		0

IF 'YES'

(b)	Are you the person who buys most of the petrol?	Yes	2
		No	3

		57/58
(c)	Year of car?	19

(d)	Is the car used for:		
	Business only?	59.	0
	Business and pleasure?		X
OR	Pleasure only?		Y

NOTES

12. Do you or your family rent or own the place you live in?

Private Households only	Rent	60.	1
	Own (or are buying)		2
	Live rent free		3
Institution	.. .. ..	..	4

13. Do you smoke?

Cigarettes only	61.	1
Pipe only		2
Cigs. and pipe		3
Neither		4

14. How often do you have a drink of:

		Beer?	Spirits?	Wine?
Once a week or more often	61.	5	7	9
Less often		6	8	0
Never	62.	9	0	X

ASK ALL WOMEN

15. Which of the following have you used in the last 7 days?

(Note: Cleansing Preparations include cleansing cream/milk/lotion only: NOT cold cream)

Lipstick	62.	1
Face powder		2
Nail varnish		3
Cleansing preparations		4
Rouge		5
Mascara		6
Eye shadow		7
None of the above		8

ASK ALL

16 (a) Have you in the last 12 months taken part in any painting or decorating of any part of your house?

Yes	63.	X
No		Y

IF YES (b)   What?

17. Have you any of the following pets at home? State number:

Dogs	None		A
	1	65.	1
	2		2
	3 or more		3
Cats	None		B
	1		4
	2		5
	3 or more		6
Cage Birds	None		C
	1		7
	2		8
	3 or more		9

OFFICE USE ONLY			66	67	68	69	70	71
72	73	74	75	76	77	78 4	79 2	80 4

Quarter	Serial No.		Informant is:			Identification of informant
2 X6	3	4	Elector 5.	1	6	
			Non-elector	2		
			Living at			
			Institution	3		

	R	Cons.		PD	TS
	7	8	9	10	11

Sampling Area Code:

	C/L			J	
	12	13	14	15	16

OFFICE USE ONLY

Constituency: _____

Polling District: _____
Name of informant: Mr./Mrs./Miss

Full Postal Address: _____

Day of interview:			Month of interview:		
Monday	17.	1	January	20.	1
Tuesday		2	February		2
Wednesday		3	March		3
Thursday		4	April		4
Friday		5	May		5
Saturday		6	June		6
			July		7
			August		8
			September		9
			October		0
	18/19		November		X
Day of month:			December		Y

Booklet used for interview: 21

Sex and household status of informant:

	Informant is Male	Informant is Female
Head of Household	22.	
Informant is H. of H.	1	A
Informant is NOT H. of H.	2	B
Housewife		
Informant is solely/mainly responsible	C	3
Other person is solely/mainly responsible	D	4
Informant shares equally with:	E	3/5

Sex	
Age	

Interviewer's Number: 23/24/25

OFFICE USE ONLY	26

Marital Status of informant:	Married	27. X
	Single/widowed/divorced	Y

184

Edition X

		28/29

Age of informant:

Exact age:

Age group	16—24	30.	1
	25—34		2
	35—44		3
	45—64		4
	65 or over		5

How old were you when you finished your **full time** education?

	15 or under		6
	16—18		7
	19—23		8
	24 or over		9
	Still at school or college		0

Composition of Household:

Number of adults 21+		31
Number of adults 16—20		
Number of children 5—15		32
Number of infants 2—4		33
Number of infants under 2		
Total (check with informant)		34
OFFICE USE ONLY		35
How many of them have full-time jobs?		36

OCCUPATION AND INDUSTRY OF:

Head of Household	Informant (if not H. of H.)

Social Grade:	A	37.	1
	B		2
	C1		3
	C2		4
	D		5
	E		6

Informant is occupied:

Full-time	38.	1
Part-time		4
Retired		2
Unoccupied		3

Length of Interview:	Interviewer:
_____ mins.	Supervisor:

185

APPENDIX 4.3

EXTRACT FROM THE INSTRUCTIONS TO
NRS INTERVIEWERS
(From Pages 13—17 of BMRB Instructions
Part 3: 'THE INTERVIEW')

THE QUESTIONNAIRE

Introduction

The questionnaire has been printed on a single sheet of paper which can be folded down the middle to form a sort of booklet.

It has been pre-coded as far as possible and there is a minimum of actual writing for you to do. It will usually be sufficient for you to put a ring round the appropriate code or to enter a figure in one of the boxes provided, but whenever you are in doubt about the correct answer to a question you should write all of the relevant information on the questionnaire.

The questionnaire is divided into two main parts:

(i) The questions about readership which all appear on one side of the sheet (the inside pages when the questionnaire is folded)

(ii) The remaining questions which are about the informants themselves (their characteristics and their habits) all appear on the other side of the sheet (the outside pages when the questionnaire is folded).

A specimen questionnaire is included at the end of this section.

THE READERSHIP QUESTIONS

This section of the questionnaire is designed to establish whether or not the informant can be counted as a reader of any particular newspaper or magazine. There are four separate groups of publications in which we are interested:

Daily newspapers
Sunday newspapers
Weekly magazines (general and women's)
Monthly magazines (general and women's)

Each of these groups of publications is listed separately on the questionnaire.

Question 1: Publications looked at in the last three months

After you have introduced the survey to the informant you should show him the booklet and say Question 1.

'I want you to go through this booklet with me and tell me, for each paper, whether you happen to have looked at any copy of it in the past three months, it doesn't matter where.'

You should then *explain* to the informant that we want him to go through the booklet page by page (*starting at the beginning of the book*) and to say, for each publication, whether or not he has looked at *any copy* (not necessarily the most recent issue) *at any time* during the past three months. You should explain 'the past three months' as 'that is, since about . . . .' (mentioning the date three months ago). You should also explain that it does not matter where the publication was looked at; in a dentist's waiting room, at work or at home are equally valid. 'Looked at' includes anything from idly turning the pages of the publication to reading it completely; it is not necessary that the informant should have actually read any part of it, only that he has consciously *looked* at it. The fact that a household 'always has' a particular publication does not mean that the informant will necessarily have looked at it.

You should make every effort to get the informant actually to go through the booklet turning the pages himself. If this is impossible because the informant cannot or will not do it, you may actually read out the names of the publications and at the same time show him (if this is possible) the pages of the booklet you are reading. Please remember in these cases to read from the booklet and *not* from the questionnaire as the publications may not be in the same order on each. If you do have to read out the names, you should make a note on the questionnaire to this effect and give the reason.

As the informant goes through the booklet you should record on the questionnaire the answer for *each* publication. It is important therefore that you control the speed with which the informant goes through the booklet in order that you may keep up with him. You should also keep an eye open for publications missed out (perhaps because two pages are turned at one time). We want the informant to say FOR EACH publication whether or not he has looked at a copy within the last three months. The answers should be recorded by ringing either the code (A) (for 'looked at') or the code (B) (for 'not looked at') opposite the publication on the questionnaire.

It is important to remember here that the publications may not appear in the booklet in the same order as they do on the questionnaire. This means that you may have to record the answers to the different *groups* of publications in any order, and you may have to read the lists within each group either from the top down or from the bottom up. There are boxes at the top of each group of publications on the questionnaire labelled 'Order'. Before you commence interviewing in any district it would be a good idea if you entered on each questionnaire the order in which the groups of publications appear in the booklet you will be using. You can do this by writing '1' in the box at the top of the group of publications which appear first, '2' in the box at the top of the group of publications which appear second, and so on. In any one booklet the publications within all the groups will appear either all in the same order as on the questionnaire or all in the reverse order.

Question 2: recent readership

After the informant has been through the booklet you can put it away. For each of the publications which the informant claims to have looked in the last three months (coded (A)) you should then ask question 2.

In asking question 2 you should take the *groups* of publications in the order in which you have numbered them on the questionnaire (i.e. the order in which the groups appear in the booklet); but you should always start reading from the *top* of each list (i.e. ignore the fact that in the booklet the order within groups may have been reversed).

The question must be asked in the form: '*When was the last time you looked at a copy of* ....?' Do not mention the time periods we are interested in.

This is the most important question on the survey; it is also the most difficult from the informant's point of view. Answering the question will involve a considerable memory effort on the part of the informant and you should therefore be extremely tactful when dealing with it. However, in view of the importance of this part of the questionnaire you must also be persistent.

For each group of publications we want to know which of the informants looked at a copy of the publications within certain time-periods, as follows:

Daily newspapers — yesterday
Sunday newspapers — within the last week
Weekly magazines — within the last week
Monthly magazines — within the last four weeks

If therefore you get an answer which does not tell you quite clearly whether or not a publication has been looked at within the appropriate time-period you should enquire further in order to make a firm classification. *Do not mention the time-period at all.* If you have to probe in order to get an answer say, 'Would you say that you looked at it before . . . . . or was it after that?' mentioning the first day of the period in question. (e.g. if you are interviewing on a Wednesday and you are talking about a weekly magazine which the informant says he last looked at 'about a week ago', you would say, 'Would you say that the last time you looked at it was before last Wednesday or was it after that?' 'If you were talking about a monthly magazine you would mention the date four weeks before the date on which you are interviewing.) Never accept ambiguous answers; if the informant says 'about a month ago' to a monthly magazine or 'about a week ago' to a weekly magazine you should probe further to find out whether it was really within the last week or four weeks.

You should also be careful of the informant who says 'Oh! Yes — we always have that'. This does not necessarily mean that he has actually looked at it.

You must always ignore any reading on the day on which you are interviewing. If an informant claims to have looked at a publication 'today' you should then ask when was the last time it was looked at 'before today' and classify according to this.

When you are interviewing on a Monday you should count people who last looked at a daily newspaper on *Saturday* as having looked at it 'yesterday', as well as those who say 'yesterday' (i.e. Sunday). (You will note that at the top of the coding column of the Daily Newspapers, Saturday reading is specifically included for Monday interviews. This is because no interviewing is carried out on Sundays.)

You must get an answer for each publication claimed as looked at within the last three months. You should code (C) if it was looked at outside the appropriate time period or the figure in the last column if it was looked at within the given period.

In the BMRB instructions there follow details relating to provincial newspapers which have very similar sounding titles to the national newspapers being studied.

Table 4A.1

Cumulative table showing error tendencies for all daily and Sunday papers tested, showing transition from raw to weighted figures

		Numerical distribution of test results														% Distribution (weighted)								
		Unweighted results							Weighted results														
		NRS No			NRS Yes			All tested	NRS No			NRS Yes			NRS No			NRS Yes			NRS % with yes claims	Int. % with yes claims	NRS % - Int. %
Publications		Int. No	Int. Yes	Int. ?	Int. No	Int. Yes	Int. ?		Int. No	Int. Yes	Int. ?	Int. No	Int. Yes	Int. ?	Int. No	Int. Yes	Int. ?	Int. No	Int. Yes	Int. ?			
Daily Mirror	(48%)	58	12	0	15	75	1	161	81	17	0	15	75	1	43	9	0	8	39	1	48	48	0
The Evening News	(37%)	64	13	1	16	63	0	157	111	22	2	16	63	0	51	11	1	8	29	0	37	40	-3
Daily Express	(29%)	106	14	1	18	58	0	197	163	21	2	18	58	0	62	8	1	7	22	0	29	30	-1
Daily Sketch	(18%)	71	4	1	8	41	0	125	209	12	3	8	41	0	77	4	1	3	15	0	18	19	-1
The Daily Telegraph	(14%)	41	1	0	8	30	0	80	227	6	0	8	30	0	84	2	0	3	11	0	14	13	-1
Daily Herald	(12%)	82	1	1	6	29	0	119	250	3	3	6	29	0	86	1	1	2	10	0	12	11	-1
The Times	(5%)	46	1	0	5	9	0	61	260	6	0	5	9	0	93	2	0	2	3	0	5	5	0
News of the World	(49%)	60	15	0	13	67	0	155	66	17	0	13	67	0	41	10	0	8	41	0	49	51	-2
Sunday Pictorial	(45%)	54	10	0	15	81	0	160	99	18	0	15	81	0	46	9	0	7	38	0	45	47	-2
The People	(36%)	67	12	0	10	57	0	146	101	18	0	10	57	0	54	11	0	5	31	0	36	41	-5
Sunday Express	(26%)	62	11	1	13	69	1	157	199	35	3	13	69	1	62	11	1	4	22	0	26	33	-7
Sunday Dispatch	(13%)	61	5	0	3	26	0	95	179	15	0	3	26	0	80	7	0	1	12	0	13	19	-6
The Observer	(9%)	45	3	0	2	22	0	72	228	15	0	2	22	0	85	6	0	1	8	0	9	14	-5
The Sunday Times	(10%)	34	4	0	9	22	1	70	257	31	0	9	22	0	80	10	0	3	7	0	10	17	-7

Table 4A.2
Cumulative table showing error tendencies for all weekly and monthly papers tested, showing transition from raw to weighted figures

Publications		Numerical distribution of test results						Weighted results								% Distribution (weighted)								
		Unweighted results							Weighted results							% Distribution (weighted)								
		NRS No			NRS Yes			All tested	NRS No			NRS Yes			NRS No			NRS Yes			NRS % with yes claims	Int. % with yes claims	NRS % - Int. %
		Int. No	Int. Yes	Int. ?	Int. No	Int. Yes	Int. ?		Int. No	Int. Yes	Int. ?	Int. No	Int. Yes	Int. ?	Int. No	Int. Yes	Int. ?	Int. No	Int. Yes	Int. ?			
Radio Times	(55%)	55	11	1	8	121	1	197	87	17	2	8	121	1	37	7	1	3	52	0	55	59	-4
TV Times	(43%)	94	17	2	12	80	1	206	102	19	2	12	80	1	47	9	1	6	37	0	43	46	-3
Woman	(38%)	83	20	0	14	65	3	185	108	26	0	14	65	3	50	12	0	7	30	1	38	42	-4
Woman's Own	(34%)	77	21	5	11	58	1	173	102	28	6	11	58	1	50	13	3	5	28	1	34	41	-7
Reveille	(18%)	118	16	0	8	26	0	168	136	19	0	8	26	0	72	10	0	4	14	0	18	24	-6
Reader's Digest	(23%)	63	14	3	27	41	2	150	184	41	9	27	41	2	61	13	3	9	13	1	23	26	-3
Do It Yourself	(12%)	60	8	1	11	32	0	112	234	37	4	11	32	0	77	10	0	3	9	0	12	19	-7
Practical Householder	(10%)	75	7	1	14	20	3	120	301	28	4	14	20	3	81	8	1	4	5	1	10	13	-3
Vogue	(10%)	56	4	3	18	32	2	115	416	30	22	18	32	2	80	6	4	4	6	0	10	12	-2
Good Housekeeping	(9%)	70	3	1	17	17	2	110	344	15	5	17	17	2	86	4	1	4	4	0	9	8	+1
Ideal Home	(7%)	57	13	1	9	21	0	101	321	73	6	9	21	0	75	17	1	2	5	0	7	22	-15
Woman and Home	(6%)	55	14	4	5	7	3	88	177	45	13	5	7	3	71	18	5	2	3	1	6	21	-15
True Story	(4%)	65	3	0	8	3	0	79	252	12	0	8	3	0	92	4	0	3	1	0	4	5	-1
True Romances	(2%)	58	4	1	4	4	2	73	451	31	8	4	4	2	90	6	2	1	1	0	2	7	-5

5 Testing the accuracy of survey-based statements of opinion: the accuracy of the 'Semantic Differential scaling' technique

IN THE CONTEXT OF
OPINIONS ABOUT HEADACHE REMEDIES

A STATEMENT BY WILLIAM BELSON BASED UPON
A REPORT BY W.A. BELSON AND V.R. YULE
OF THE SURVEY RESEARCH CENTRE

ORIGINAL RESEARCH BY

W.A. Belson, BA, PhD (Design and direction)
V.R. Yule, BA (General execution of the enquiry)
D.W. Osborne, BSc
S.B. Quinn, BA
V.R. Thompson (Analysis)

---

*This term is a mis-application of Osgood's terminology as used in his *Measurement of Meaning*[37] and other publications. Nonetheless it is the term used in market research circles for the technique investigated in this study.

CONTENTS OF CHAPTER

During the summer of 1967, the Survey Research Centre began a series of studies that was broadly concerned with the accuracy of the Semantic Differential[3,7,38,39,40] scaling technique as used in market research. This particular series was prompted largely by the requests of Survey Research Centre subscribers that such work be conducted. This suggestion was of particular interest to the Centre because it provided an opportunity to assess the accuracy of *attitudinal* data — a class of validity checking that was thought by many to pose special methodological problems. Indeed, there were some who felt that such work was impossible. For reasons that will be given later, the present check on the Semantic Differential technique was geared to the study of headache remedies.

THE NATURE OF THE SEMANTIC DIFFERENTIAL SCALING METHOD AS USED IN MARKET RESEARCH

The Semantic Differential scaling system* is one of the techniques used by market researchers for measuring consumer attitudes. In its market research application, it has the following features.

1   The basic element in the Semantic Differential scaling system (as used in commerce) is a rating scale, usually divided into five or seven separate scale positions. This scale is designed to represent one aspect or 'dimension' of the brand or product being studied. It expresses a continuum ranging from one extreme to the other. The two extremes of the scale are defined by adjectives or phrases written beside each end of the scale. For example, if the objective was to elicit consumers' opinions concerning the *speed of action* of a branded headache remedy, the scale might look like this:

QUICK ACTING   ⌊___⌐___⌐___⌐___⌐___⌐___⌐___⌋   SLOW ACTING

Figure 5.1   A Semantic Differential rating scale

*Semantic Differential scaling, as used by market research practitioners in Britain, appears to have developed out of the Semantic Differential technique designed by the American psychologist, C.E. Osgood.[40] The commercial application is, however, substantially different from the original technique and does some violence to the meaning of the term Semantic Differential. A description of the method as used by Osgood is available in texts by Osgood[41] and Sellitz.[42]

The respondent indicates how he feels about this aspect of the brand by marking one of the positions along the scale. The interviewer tells the respondent how to use the scale, usually on the following lines:

> If the respondent thinks the specified brand of headache remedy is *very* quick acting, he should put a mark in the left-hand end position on the scale, right next to the term 'QUICK ACTING'. If he thinks it is *fairly* quick acting, the mark would go in the next position along; if he thinks it is only *slightly* quick acting, the mark would go in the *next* one along. In the same way, he is told that the position next to 'SLOW ACTING' should be marked to indicate *very* slow acting, the next one on for *fairly* slow acting and the next one on for only *slightly* slow acting. The middle position should be marked if the respondent feels that the brand concerned is just *half-way between* quick acting and slow acting.

2　Ordinarily there is not just one Semantic Differential scale, but as many as 12 scales (sometimes more), each of them dealing with a seemingly different but relevant attribute of the product concerned and each with opposite terms at its ends. For example:

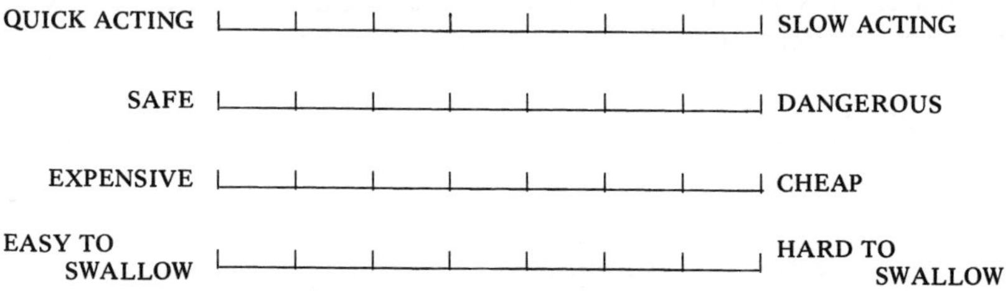

Figure 5.2　Semantic Differential rating scales
dealing with attributes of a product

3　In applying the Semantic Differential scaling system in market research, the respondent is typically required to rate first one brand on all the scales in the set, then a competing brand on all scales, then another competing brand on all of them and so on for possibly five or six brands in all. Supposing that there were five brands being rated on each of 12 scales, the respondent would have to deal with five sets of scales (60 ratings in all), the five sets of scales making up the Semantic Differential questionnaire.

4　The result of this use of the system is typically a 'profile' of reactions for each of the brands rated. These may then be studied *comparatively.*

5　Some of the following technicalities of Semantic Differential scaling are important both for an understanding of the system and for understanding this report.

(a) Each of the 'scales' used within the system is meant to have opposites at its two ends. Such scales are referred to as 'bipolar' scales, in the sense that they feature both 'poles' or 'extremes' of a single dimension. In fact some of those in use are unipolar, in the sense that they run from one extreme to zero (for example: habit-forming versus not habit-forming; unpleasant side effects versus no unpleasant side effects).

(b) The decision as to which 'scales' or 'dimensions' to include in a Semantic Differential set should be guided by strictly purposive and empirical considerations. Thus it would be wasteful if two scales in the full set (for example, of 12) measured much the same thing (that is, tended to duplicate each other); and from a marketing viewpoint it would be highly desirable to ascertain at the outset that each of the scaled dimensions was relevant, to at least some extent, to the making of marketing decisions. Relevance and non-duplication are both requirements of any efficient use of the Semantic Differential scaling system.

PROBLEMS OVER THE USE OF THE SEMANTIC DIFFERENTIAL SCALING SYSTEM

As with many other types of rating procedure, the Semantic Differential technique presents certain problems to those who wish to use it in sample survey questionnaires. Among these problems are the following.

1 The respondents may not fully understand how to use the scale to express their opinions. They may not grasp that it has opposites at its two ends, each representing a scale extreme; that the scale is graduated outwards from its centre; that the centre point is exactly halfway between the two extreme positions on the scale.

2 Associated with the above problem is the possibility that the interviewers may not deliver the set instructions as intended.

3 When a respondent has no opinion at all, does he nonetheless enter a tick somewhere on the rating scale? The usual absence of a special position for DK responses leaves some research practitioners uneasy on this particular score. It is often suggested that the centre point of the Semantic Differential scale is especially open to misuse in this way.

4   Another concern is that the *ordinal* position of the brand in the questionnaire may affect the responses given with respect to the attributes of that brand. In other words, it is asked if there may not be an order effect, perhaps produced by fatigue or boredom or diminished effort on the part of the respondent as he works through 60 or so scales, or by other factors such as 'learning', 'privacy' or 'recency'?

It is because of problems or concerns such as these that research practitioners have asked to what extent the ratings obtained through a battery of Semantic Differential rating scales provide a true picture of what respondents actually felt about the brand characteristics rated by them.

THREE LINKED STUDIES AND THE AIMS OF THIS ONE

It was against this background that three linked enquiries (including the present one) were launched. These three were concerned with:

A   The extent and nature of order effects in using the Semantic Differential scaling system

B   The faithfulness of the interviewers in delivering the Semantic Differential system to respondents

C   The accuracy of respondents' ratings

This chapter deals with the third of these three projects. Project C had the following aims or purposes.

1   To determine the ways in which respondents understand the basic instructions for using the Semantic Differential scales, with special reference to any misunderstandings that occur.

2   To find out to what extent the responses registered on Semantic Differential scales properly reflect the respondent's opinions and to identify the sources of any detected errors. In this sense, are the Semantic Differential ratings accurate?

3   To determine the accuracy levels of response distributions and means based upon the Semantic Differential scaling system.

4   To determine the effects of error by individuals in terms of ratings, means and the *comparison* of brands.

Projects A, B and C shared the one overall sample. Each of them has been reported in full in Survey Research Centre documents.[38-40] The present chapter is a shortened version of the report of Project C.

SUMMARY OF METHODS

See page 254 for a summary of the methods of research — as a necessary frame of reference for studying the details set out below.

THE RESEARCH STRATEGY

The research strategy used in this enquiry was a form of *double interview*. Thus the procedure under investigation was administered in the normal way through market research interviewers. Immediately after this, intensive interviewers put a subsample of the respondents through a further interview, intensive and probing in character, which was designed as a check on the responses given in the first interview. The two interviews are described in detail in this statement of methods used.

The interpretation of any difference between the two results must remain open to some degree of uncertainty, but the nature of the intensive interview is such that there is a very strong case for regarding the latter as approximating to a test of the accuracy of the ratings made in the first interview.

The particular way in which the first and the intensive interviews were linked, so that one followed immediately upon the other, is described in detail in a later part of the description of methods.

SELECTING THE SUBJECT MATTER ON WHICH TO BASE THE ENQUIRY

It was important that the product field selected should be one which the research practitioner would regard as warranting the use of the Semantic Differential scaling technique. Thus: there should be within it a number of competing brands; the product must have a range of attributes or characteristics which the consumer quite conceivably can regard as relevant to his choice of one or another brand of it; it would have to prove possible to identify such attributes and to derive meaningful Semantic Differential scales for rating brands in terms of them.

Some of these requirements called for empirical checks, and so it was necessary to start with a number of *possibly* suitable products in case some one or more proved unsuitable. The products considered in this way were: refrigerators; analgesics; instant coffee; toilet soaps; cigarettes; paint; toothpaste.

Each of these seven products was then subjected to the following procedure. Forty members of the public, not atypical of the population of Greater London in terms of age, sex and social class, were brought together as a group under test room conditions. They were asked to enumerate those aspects of the product which they felt would influence their choice of one or another brand of it (for example, silent running in a refrigerator, quick action in an analgesic). They did this in writing, separately for each product. The purpose of this operation was to derive for each respondent a list of attributes which might possibly be relevant to brand choice.

Several of the product fields tested in this way were eliminated because they appeared to have very few attributes which respondents could offer (as associated with brand choice) with any frequency. Each of the others was then dealt with as follows. A list of its more frequently enumerated attributes was drawn up and presented to a further (not atypical) group of 40 people, who were asked to write against each attribute its *opposite*. The purpose of this step was to derive 'opposites' as conceived by members of the public rather than by members of the research team. For some of the products tested in this way, the 'opposites' were widely dispersed and for some there was evidence of confusion as to the meaning of various of the listed attributes.

On the basis of this total body of evidence, several of the original products were picked out as suitable for Semantic Differential testing. Of these, analgesics was selected as the most suitable choice. The whole of the present report is thus based upon analgesics.

GEARING TOGETHER THE INTENSIVE INTERVIEW AND THE ORDINARY SURVEY INTERVIEW

An important objective in this enquiry was to carry out the first interviews under conditions as nearly normal as possible, but at the same time to conduct the follow-up (that is, intensive) interviews immediately. To achieve this end, a fairly complicated procedure was adopted.

At their briefing the ordinary market research interviewers were given normal instructions for delivering the questionnaire. They were also told, however, that many of their interviews would be followed up immediately by a depth interviewer who would be seeking additional information about the headache remedies actually used by the respondents concerned.* They were told that for this reason each of them would be working 'in harness' with a 'depth' interviewer. At this point the six intensive interviewers were brought into the briefing room and pairings arranged. Instructions were then given concerning the way in which they were to work together.

Each pair would meet in the interviewing area at the beginning of the interviewing day. They would call together at the home of each listed contact until the first interview had been successfully completed. At this point the intensive interviewer would stay on for an intensive interview while the market research interviewer went on alone to secure her next interview. The latter's potential contacts were, in fact, spaced out along each of a limited number of streets, and this made it possible for the intensive interviewer to find and re-join the market research interviewer† as soon as the intensive interview had been completed. The two of them then proceeded together as before until the completion of the next market research interview, whereupon the previous arrangement was repeated. In the course of an interviewing day, the intensive interviewer completed two to three intensive interviews and the market research interviewer five to seven (including the two to three that were conducted in the presence of the intensive interviewer and that led to intensive follow-up).

The device of having the market research interviewer continue interviewing (alone) while the intensive interviewer stayed on at the last interviewee's home had the advantage of (i) allowing the ordinary interviewing habits and tactics of the market research interviewer to develop and consolidate in the absence of an onlooker; (ii) keeping her usefully active during the whole of the interviewing day; (iii) providing interviewers for the 'order effects' project (Project A).

It is most important that the market research interviewer should not become aware at any time of the true purpose of the intensive interview — that she should continue to think of the latter as being about some further (but different) aspect of headache remedies. Otherwise the normality of her performance would have been endangered. According to the intensive interviewers and according to the comments of the market research interviewers, there was no leak or breakdown of this kind. The six market research interviewers were, of course, replaced by a new six in the following week, six more in the week after that, and so on for the full five weeks of interviewing, making 30 market research interviewers in all. This arrangement served not only to introduce a

---

*In fact, the real purpose was to conduct methodological checks of the kind indicated under 'Aims'.
†With the aid of chalk marking on the pavement by the market research interviewer.

realistic range of interviewer behaviour into the project, but also to guard against any possible leak becoming really serious.

Another feature of the double interview was that the intensive interviewer tape-recorded each of the market research interviews immediately preceding her own intensive interview. It had been 'explained' to the market research interviewers that some of the things that the respondents said in the interview might possibly be relevant to product usage — which was to be the subject of the 'depth' interview — and that it would help if the intensive interviewer could record what was said by the respondent in the first interview. The market research interviewers were all agreeable to this, and the intensive interviewer was therefore able to say to the respondent (at the point of being introduced to her): 'I hope you don't mind my using this — it saves such a lot of writing down'. The purpose of tape-recording the first interview was, of course, to determine precisely what was actually said to the respondent in the first interview — information which was most relevant in any study of the respondent's understanding of interviewer instructions.

SAMPLING METHODS

Sampling for the accuracy study (Project C) was done in the context of sampling for all three proposed projects as outlined on page 202. This was because data collection for all three projects was to be done through the one sequence of interviewing — partly for economy reasons and partly because there would be some degree of interlinking of the results from the three enquiries. For the order effects study (Project A), a total of at least 1000 cases was needed. For the 'faithfulness of interviewer delivery of instructions' enquiry (Project B) the required total was 300. For the accuracy check, a total of approximately 300 (double interviews) was financially feasible and would be sufficient.

Below is a description of sampling designed to meet the needs of the study when considered jointly (that is, all three projects), and this leads on to a short statement about the subsampling done to meet the special needs of Project C (the accuracy check).

The overall sample

The area sampled was Greater London.* In the first stage of sampling, 30 wards were drawn with a control over geographic locations. From

---

*Excluding the outer districts — because they were too far out from the town centre for economical interviewing.

each of these 30 wards, a polling district was then drawn randomly. From each polling district a sample of streets was drawn and from these streets 100 names were drawn (using systematic random sampling) from the then current electoral registers.* That process yielded 3000 names. Of these, half (every second name, polling district by polling district), constituted the primary sample. The others were to be used as substitutes where primary sample members could not be interviewed.

The total number of interviews attempted out of the potential 3000 was 2536 adults (consisting of 1496 primary sampling members and 1040 substitutes). Of the 2536, some 1069† were interviewed, that is 42% of the target sample and 57% if 'away' cases and 'incapacitated' cases are excluded.‡

*Probability sampling with preliminary stratification by geographic location, with multi-stage random sampling, with probability proportional to size and with systematic random sampling in the final stage of sampling.

†Sample losses and achieved sample size were as follows:

	Primary sample	Substitute	Total	%
Refusals, including unusable questionnaires	230	159	389	15‡
Moved away from the district	154	127	281	11
Away (for duration of the survey)	147	86	233	9
Dead/ill/senile/mentally incompetent	83	74	160	6
Not available after so many calls				
− 4 or more calls	86	49	135	6
− 3 or more calls	35	39	74	3
− 2 calls	32	54	86	3
− 1 call	26	83	109	4
Interview obtained	700	369	1069	42

‡The success level is low for the following reasons.

(a)   Interviewers had been instructed not to abandon any primary contacts until they had made at least four calls without success or had established a reason for non-interviewability such as illness, death, removal from the district. Nonetheless, the knowledge that there *was* a 'substitute' list, plus the fact that the intensive interviewer with whom the 'first' interviewer was working would be thought of as needing fruitful calls (to enable her to obtain her 'follow-up' interviews) seems likely to have pushed some of the first interviewers into using the 'substitute' list prematurely. In fact 7% of the total sample (that is, *including* 'substitutes') were abandoned after only one or two calls and 3% more after only three calls.

(b)   The survey was carried out during the holiday season (July, August and September), so that many people (up to 9%) were away during the whole week when interviewing was taking place in their area.

(c)   The survey was conducted in London and the sample included a number of notoriously low-contact districts. Also, the current Electoral Registers were 'aging' when used, so that losses through 'moving' could be expected.

(d)   The questionnaire took respondents straight into the rating of specific brands of head-ache remedy and this appears to have led some respondents to opt out on the grounds that they didn't know anything about the branded product(s) concerned. This difficulty appears to have helped to swell the refusal rate to its 15% level. Certainly it is something to note as perhaps intrinsic to the use of the survey method for delivering Semantic Differential rating scales.

The Project C sample

For the reasons given above, the total 1069 achieved survey interviews went far beyond the needs of the accuracy check (Project C). For the latter check, it was desirable that 300 of the survey interviews should be followed by an intensive checking interview. On the basis of piloting, the sampling procedure described above was expected to yield the required 300 double interviews without selective bias.

In fact, the procedure led to 391 requests being made for a second interview and to 280 of these being successfully carried out. There were thus 280 double interviews, with full tape-recording of each of them.

THE FIRST OR SURVEY INTERVIEW

The first interview was a simulation of a normal market research interview involving the use of Semantic Differential rating scales. That is to say, all the circumstances of the first interview, including the questionnaire, the sample and the interviewers, were intended to reproduce as closely as possible the normal survey situation in which such rating scales are delivered to respondents.

Developing the first interview questionnaire

The questionnaire procedure used in the first stage of this study was the result of considerable preparatory work.

In the first instance, it was necessary to select a product which would be suitable for the enquiry. That selected was 'headache remedies' and the procedure for making that selection has already been described (see pages 197, 198). That procedure had also led to: the identification of a provisional set of 12 product attributes in terms of which the Semantic Differential ratings would be made (for example, speed of action, cost, effectiveness, and so on); the development of pairs of 'opposites' for each of the scalar attributes (for example, quick acting versus slow acting). There still remained the task of developing the verbal instructions, for the respondent, for completing the scaling task.

Developing instructions for respondents concerning the use of the Semantic Differential rating scale

If the proposed enquiry was to be meaningful, the instructions used would have to be similar to those used in practice. Various currently used forms of instruction were therefore examined, and from this material was derived a set of instructions which included the more common and basic features of the former. This new form of instruction was then modified to rid it of any obvious weaknesses and was then pre-tested on a survey sample. The pre-test included a form of semi-intensive follow-up aimed at detecting points of failure in the instructions. The instructions were then modified as necessary and then tested, and then modified once more. They are set out in full in the Appendix to this chapter.

Pre-testing the 'end items' derived through the test room groups

The pre-testing procedure described above and on page 202 was extended to include pre-tests of the 12 scales which were to be included in the enquiry. It became apparent that some of the pairs of opposites were open to misunderstanding by respondents when delivered under survey conditions. Accordingly modifications were made to various of these terms. A further pre-test tended to confirm the suitability of these modifications, and the final scales are shown below.

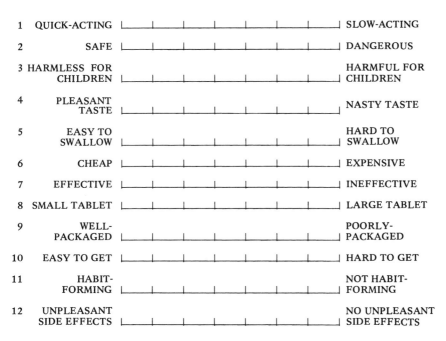

Figure 5.3   The 12 scales to be used in the
Semantic Differential questions

Certain features of three of the 12 constituent Semantic Differential scales must be noted.

1 Scales 11 and 12 are not bipolar in character. They are unipolar in that they go from the complete absence of something to a great deal of it (for example, not habit-forming . . . very habit-forming). Strictly speaking, such scales would not form part of the Semantic Differential battery. However, unipolar attributes are frequently included in Semantic Differential batteries in spite of the peculiarities of the rating task (for example, very habit-forming/ fairly habit-forming/slightly habit-forming/halfway between habit-forming and not habit-forming/slightly non habit-forming/fairly non habit-forming/very non habit-forming). Just how respondents manage to use such nonsensical scales is a matter for some wonderment.

2 Scale 4 raised problems because some practitioners argued that people who really felt the brand had 'no taste at all' would be forced to register that opinion by endorsing the 'halfway' scaler position and that, in testing the scale, a special effort would therefore have to be made to find out what respondents actually did about such an opinion. Such steps were in fact taken in the testing programme.

The final form of the Semantic Differential questionnaire

The Semantic Differential questionnaire as finally developed for use in the survey interview consisted of: (i) an introductory page to demonstrate to the respondent, by means of an actual example, what the scales meant and how to fill them in; (ii) a page presenting the 12 Semantic Differential scales, each referring to the one brand of headache remedy (for example, Aspro); four more identical pages, each referring to another headache remedy (for example, Phensic, Asprin); (iv) a final page for entering personal details. The page of instructions, the first page of Semantic Differential rating scales and the personal detail page are set out in the Appendix. The five headache remedies dealt with were: Aspro, Anadin, Asprin, Disprin, Phensic. The name of the brand to be rated on a given page was printed in capitals at the top of the rating page.

Rotation arrangements

It will be remembered that Project A was to deal with 'order effects' in delivering the Semantic Differential scales. And the latter enquiry was tied into the present one. The order effects study had required systematic rotation of the order of presentation of the five brands (of headache remedies) in the Semantic Differential questionnaire. This rotation was however a necessary feature of the 'accuracy' check as well: it was intended to equalise brand differences in the comparison of 'accuracy' levels achieved for the different rating scales.

There were then five *versions* of the questionnaire. In each version the same five brands were presented but in a different order, namely:

Version 1 (brand order 1): Anadin, Asprin, Disprin, Phensic, Aspro
Version 2 (brand order 2): Asprin, Disprin, Phensic, Aspro, Anadin
Version 3 (brand order 3): Disprin, Phensic, Aspro, Anadin, Asprin
Version 4 (brand order 4): Phensic, Aspro, Anadin, Asprin, Disprin
Version 5 (brand order 5): Aspro, Anadin, Asprin, Disprin, Phensic

The questionnaire with brand order 1 was to be administered to one-fifth of the sample, the brand order 2 questionnaire to another fifth, and so on.

The interviewers and their briefing

The interviewers who were to administer the Semantic Differential questionnaire in the first interview were purposely chosen so as to bring into the enquiry a wide and not atypical range of interviewer experience, training and ability. Some were freelance interviewers who normally worked for a variety of firms, but the majority were members of the interviewing staffs of market research agencies or of the market research departments of large manufacturing companies. There were 30 interviewers in all, one for each of the 30 polling districts of the sample, and each of these worked for one week in her given area. The fieldwork was carried out over a five-week period, starting in mid-July.

Each Monday morning, the interviewers who were to work that week were given a two-hour personal briefing at the Survey Research Centre. At the end of the briefing, each interviewer was given 50 questionnaires, consisting of ten of each of the five brand-order versions. Each interviewer had 50 substitute names as well. Each batch of 50 questionnaires had previously been shuffled, to randomise the position of the different brand orders.

As stated already, the six intensive interviewers joined the market research interviewers at the end of the briefing session and were paired off with the six market research interviewers.

The purposes of the intensive interview

The purposes of the intensive interview were as follows:

1 To find out how the respondent had understood the instruction to use the Semantic Differential scales, her grasp of what the different intervals along the scale meant to her (including the central or neutral interval) and what the respondent did about any 'don't know' responses that she wanted to voice.

2 To determine the accuracy of at least 14* of the first interview ratings.

The scales selected for testing

The particular scales selected for testing on each respondent were spread through the Semantic Differential questionnaire on the following pattern.

	Brand A	Brand B	Brand C	Brand D	Brand E
Scale 1	⌊_⌋ *	⌊_⌋	⌊_⌋	⌊_⌋	⌊_⌋ *
2	⌊_⌋	⌊_⌋ *	⌊_⌋	⌊_⌋	⌊_⌋
3	⌊_⌋	⌊_⌋	⌊_⌋ *	⌊_⌋	⌊_⌋
4	⌊_⌋	⌊_⌋	⌊_⌋	⌊_⌋ *	⌊_⌋
5	⌊_⌋	⌊_⌋	⌊_⌋	⌊_⌋	⌊_⌋ *
6	⌊_⌋	⌊_⌋ *	⌊_⌋	⌊_⌋	⌊_⌋
7	⌊_⌋	⌊_⌋	⌊_⌋	⌊_⌋ *	⌊_⌋
8	⌊_⌋ *	⌊_⌋	⌊_⌋ *	⌊_⌋	⌊_⌋
9	⌊_⌋	⌊_⌋ *	⌊_⌋	⌊_⌋	⌊_⌋
10	⌊_⌋	⌊_⌋	⌊_⌋ *	⌊_⌋	⌊_⌋
11	⌊_⌋	⌊_⌋	⌊_⌋	⌊_⌋ *	⌊_⌋
12	⌊_⌋	⌊_⌋	⌊_⌋	⌊_⌋	⌊_⌋ *

Figure 5.4 The particular scales selected for testing *

*Project A.

This pattern was partly determined by the requirements of the order-effect study in that it was intended to study variation in 'accuracy level' according to scale order. It will be seen, however, that the particular pattern used served also to spread the 14 chosen over all 12 scales and distributed them about two to three to each brand (the system of brand rotation used did of course ensure that each of the test scales was equally spread over the five brands).

The general form of the intensive interview

The second interview was an intensive probing procedure in which the intensive interviewer, although working within a highly structured framework, was specially trained to apply probing and challenging techniques at certain points in the interview. The intensive interview was focused upon only certain parts of the first interview and lasted for between one and one-and-a-half hours.

The intensive interview is presented in full in the Appendix to this chapter. It consisted of several stages with the following functions or purposes. Stage I was intended to introduce the respondent to the intensive interview and, above all, to get the respondent co-operating with her. Stage II consisted of a series of questions about the meaning of the different parts of the rating scales. Stage III, which was the central part of the intensive interview, was a very careful assessment of the accuracy of the respondent's first interview rating on at least 14 of the Semantic Differential scales.* Stage IV was a confrontation process in which the respondent was asked to explain any differences between her first and her intensive interview ratings on those tested scales.

The intensive interview in detail

Securing the intensive interview

On being briefly introduced to the respondent by the first interviewer ('This is . . . who is working with me.'), the intensive interviewer had asked if she could use her tape-recorder. Thereafter she had stood, in silence, just back from the first interviewer. At the end of the inter-view, the first interviewer thanked the respondent and then told her that her colleague was from the university and would like to ask her a few more questions. The first interviewer then moved off to continue interviewing in homes further along the street while the intensive inter-viewer took the necessary steps to secure an extra interview with the respondent then and there. She offered a small fee for the interview and

---

*See pages 206, 207 for the rationale of the selection of ratings for validity checking.

asked to carry it out inside the house (if not there already). Having obtained the respondent's agreement to go through the second interview (there was a 72% success rate in doing this), she explained that its purpose was to find out if the questions asked in the first interview were as clear as they should be and were making sense to the people who were asked them. She explained that this would mean asking the respondent what she thought those questions meant, and she repeated that she would be paying the respondent a fee for the time spent doing this. She said again to the respondent that she hoped it would be alright if she used her tape-recorder, explaining that it saved 'such a lot of writing down'.

Testing the respondent's understanding
of the Semantic Differential instructions

The interviewer then began a series of questions designed to find out if the respondent had grasped the first interviewer's instructions as to the meaning of the different parts of the Semantic Differential rating scale. Her instructions for this part of the questioning procedure began as follows.

SLOW ACTING |⌐ T T T T T T ⌐| QUICK ACTING

SAY:
'Now I'd like you to think back to the other interviewer's explanation to you of how to mark your opinions. She used this line as an example.'
SHOW EXAMPLE LINE AS ABOVE.

SAY:
'Do you remember?' I'd like to find out what sort of impression you got from what she said.'

SAY:
(a) 'If someone put their tick *there* (POINT TO SCALE CENTRE)
what would *that* mean?' |⌐ T T T √T T T ⌐|
'According to the first interviewer, what would *that* mean?'

. . . .

(b) 'And if they put it *there* (|⌐ T T T T √T T ⌐|) what would it mean?'
(Point to the space where the √ is shown). 'Anything else?'

. . . .

The interviewer systematically worked through the seven points of the scale in this way, tape-recording each response in full. She then asked:

> 'What do you think the interviewer wanted you to do if you had no opinion at all about a brand being quick acting or slow acting?' (REPLY TAPE-RECORDED)
>
> And what did the interviewer want you to do if you had no opinion of any kind about a *brand*?' (REPLY TAPE-RECORDED)

Where the interviewer had any doubts about the respondent's grasp of first interviewer instructions, she was required to ask the following additional questions to clarify the matter:

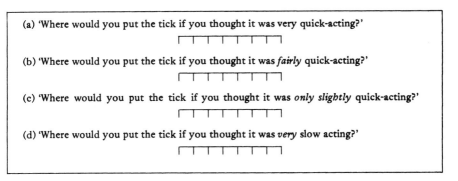

Finally, a check was made to find out if the respondent had grasped the fact that the words at the end of the scales were meant to be opposites. The respondent was shown a scale at one end of which was the word 'HOT' and was asked:

> 'Now look at this line. If you were putting your tick on this line (POINT *ALONG* IT) and you saw this word *here* (POINT TO THE WORD "HOT"), what word would you expect to see *here* (POINT TO THE BLANK END OF THE SCALE)?'
>
> (ENTER REPLY)

Testing the accuracy of the first interview ratings

The central part of the interview then followed. The respondent had made up to 60 ratings in her first interview, 12 for each of five branded headache remedies. For each of at least 14 of these, the interviewer took the respondent through a special process of re-rating (see below) with a view to assessing the extent to which her *first* rating *properly* reflected her opinion.

The tactics in this central process were designed to remove as much as possible the error-making conditions that might have entered into the first interview ratings, namely: non-involvement; confusion over *what* brand and *what* attitude were being asked about; failure to understand the rating instructions and the names of the different rating positions; forgetting about some aspect of the lengthy rating instructions; carelessness in making the ratings.

In other words, in this accuracy checking operation, we sought to get the respondent interested in the rating task, to get her thinking clearly about the brand and the scalar dimensions being dealt with; to get her clearly understanding what she was to do; to get her working conscientiously at each rating. It was assumed that this approach to the rating task would produce responses that approximated to what the respondent really felt. (This approach would not defeat deliberate lying, but there seems to be no good reason for thinking that lying would be present to any substantial degree.)

This central part of the intensive questionnaire is presented in full in the Appendix. The present description is geared to just one of the 14 (or so) rating checks, the others being done in just the same way.

1   The interviewer reminded the respondent that in the first interview she had been asked to put a tick on each of 60 different lines. She then explained that she (the interviewer) would like to go through a few of those again.

2   To get the respondent thinking about the relevant brand for the first rating check (for example, Aspro), the interviewer asked the respondent to talk out about what she thought of that brand. The question was subject to probing for a full reply. The name of the brand, in large letters was placed before the respondent for this operation.

3   To make a careful check of the 14 first interview ratings (for example, the quick acting . . . slow acting rating for Aspro), steps (i) to (iv) were taken:

(i)   Rating boxes were placed before the respondent (see Figure 5.5). This arrangement was meant to correspond with the seven-point Semantic Differential scale presented in the first interview. Here, however, the values of each scale position were printed in the scale boxes — whereas in the first interview the respondent was required to *remember*, on the basis of verbal instruction, that they had these particular

VERY	FAIRLY	SLIGHTLY	HALF-WAY BETWEEN QUICK AND	SLIGHTLY	FAIRLY	VERY
QUICK ACTING	QUICK ACTING	QUICK ACTING	SLOW ACTING	SLOW ACTING	SLOW ACTING	SLOW ACTING

ABSOLUTELY NO IDEA *AT ALL* ABOUT HOW QUICK OR SLOW ACTING IT IS

Figure 5.5   The rating boxes

values or meanings. By printing them on the scale in the way shown above, it was expected that we would eliminate *one* possible source of mis-rating in the first interview, that is, mis-rating through forgetting what the different points on the scale actually meant. It seemed also that this device might reduce the difficulty of another feature of the Semantic Differential scale, namely the placing of a term like 'quick acting' right against the Semantic Differential scale position which was meant to signify '*very* quick acting'.

Another feature of the arrangement presented above was the addition of a special box for those who had 'no idea at all' about the speed of action of this brand. Here, again, we were trying to eliminate a possible source of trouble in the ordinary Semantic Differential scale — where respondents were simply *told* to put DK at the side of the scale concerned if they had no opinion — and where forgetting can therefore occur. Certainly there is ground for concern on this point, because preliminary work had shown that the *centre* point of the scale could be used as a sort of 'dumping ground' for such cases.

(ii)   The respondent was then asked to read out aloud for the interviewer all the entries in the eight boxes. After this she was asked to take ten seconds to decide which applied to

ASPRO as far as she, herself, was concerned. Only after ten seconds was she handed a coloured marker card to put onto the chosen square.

> 'Now I want you to look at these boxes for me. They're all about (NAME THE BRAND). I want you to read out aloud for me what's in each box.'
>
> SEE THAT RESPONDENT READS THE ENTRIES OUT ALOUD — ALL OF THEM. AFTER THIS, SAY:
>
> 'So you see that they are all about (NAME THE BRAND). Also they are all about how QUICK ACTING or how SLOW ACTING it is.'
>
> Now take about ten seconds to work out which one of them is true for you personally. Look at them all and then pick the one that is true for you.'
> IF SHE RUSHES, SAY: 'Take your time and think about it.'
>
> THEN SAY:
>
> 'Put this card into the square you have chosen.' (PASS THE BRANDED MARKER CARD)

We hoped in this way (a) to make the respondent consider *all* the boxes; (b) to prevent a hasty choice of any one box.

(iii) This choice was now *challenged* in case it did in some way fail to represent what the respondent actually felt. Thus she was asked to say *why* she put the disc *in that particular square*; could it possibly go into another square?

> 'Tell me why you put it in that particular square?' PAUSE:
>
> 'Could it possibly go in any of the other squares?'
>
> IF SHE IS DOUBTFUL AT ALL, *URGE HER TO THINK HARD AND PUT THE CARD WHERE SHE REALLY THINKS IT SHOULD GO.*
>
> FINALLY, RECORD RESPONDENT'S PLACEMENT OF CARD (√) IN CHOSEN SQUARE.

(iv) As a further check — this time against the possibility that the respondent is misinterpreting the wording in the square chosen — the respondent is asked to say in her own words just *how* quick acting or *how* slow acting she consider this brand to be.

> 'Instead of the words in the box you chose, tell me *in your own words* exactly *how* quick acting or *how* slow acting you think (NAME THE BRAND) is.'
>
> . . . .
>
> . . . .
>
> IF THIS IS NOT IN LINE WITH WHAT THE RESPONDENT HAS CHOSEN IN THE BOX SYSTEM, CHALLENGE TO FIND OUT *WHICH SHE REALLY MEANS. PURSUE THIS UNTIL YOU GET A CLARIFICATION. IF SHE DECIDES HER EARLIER CHOICE OF BOXES WAS WRONG, PUT A LINE THROUGH THE FIRST TICK (√) AND PUT A NEW TICK IN THE FINAL CHOICE OF BOX.*

212

The interviewer now proceeded in just the same way with each of the other first interview ratings that had been designated for testing.

Respondent usage of centre points on the rating scale

The research team had a special interest in determining what particular use the respondents made of the centre points in the Semantic Differential scales. Were they, for example, using the centre point as a dumping place for 'no opinion' reactions or for 'I can't be bothered formulating a reply' reactions? For many of the respondents, there were cases of centre point usage amongst the 14 scales set for checking. Where there were less than two such cases for an individual, additional checks were made, namely the first and the last instance of the respondent's centre point usages.

A confrontation stage

After the various re-ratings had been made, 'confrontation' tests were carried out. Thus for each scale for which there was any difference between the first and the intensive ratings made on them, the respondent was asked to explain that difference.

The interviewer also attempted to find out *which* of the two ratings the interviewer now thought was correct (if neither, which other box she thought would be the right one and why this one was not chosen before).

The purpose of the confrontation stage was to provide material for hypothesis development about sources of error in the first interview, though it was recognised that it could serve also as a form of healthy challenge to the validity of this application of the intensive interviewing technique.

Finding out what the respondent meant
when he replied with a 'don't know'

Finally, a check was also made on the first and the last scales marked by the respondent as 'don't know' or the equivalent (if this had not already been done through the set 14 test scales). In each case, the interviewer said to the respondent:

'You marked this line as "don't know". Exactly what did you mean by that?' (Probe for a full reply.)

SELECTING AND TRAINING THE
INTENSIVE INTERVIEWERS *

Six people were employed as intensive interviewers. It was necessary that such people be of above average intelligence, well educated and acceptable to all types of respondents. They had also to have a certain detective mentality and to be flexible enough both to accept criticism and to learn from it.

Out of about 100 applicants, nine were taken on for training, all of them graduates. Training lasted for a week and consisted mainly of trial interviews which were followed by group criticism sessions. In such sessions, the tapes from the trial interviews were played back to the group of trainees who, under the guidance of an instructor, critically analysed the whole recorded performance. The interviewer concerned was always invited to lead off with the criticisms. The instructor offered guidance and advice throughout and re-briefed the trainees at the end of the day in preparation for the next day's trial interviewing.

Once the survey started, a Quality Controller was appointed. His job was to listen regularly to the tapes of the interviewers throughout the survey, to correct inadequate performance and generally to maintain a high quality of interviewing. In other words, training was a continuing process.

FINDINGS: SETTING THE SCENE

(The reader should start with the
summary of findings on pages 254—6.)

The findings of the enquiry are presented in three parts, I, II and III. Part I deals with respondent understanding of the instructions of the first interviewer concerning the nature and the use of the Semantic Differential scaling system, with special reference to the meaning of the different scale positions and to what to do when one has no opinion of any kind about a brand as a whole or about some particular aspect of a brand. Part II deals with the degree to which the ratings actually made in the first interview are a proper reflection of the respondent's views on the matters concerned. Part III reports on the validity of a Semantic Differential finding that one brand is better than another brand with respect to a given product attribute.

---

*Project C in the Semantic Differential series.

214

The relationship of these three parts of the report calls for special comment. The respondent who fully grasps the instructions is doubtless in a much better position to use the Semantic Differential scales for the accurate expression of her or his opinions. However, factors additional to 'understanding of the instructions' are also likely to be operative in the Semantic Differential interview: respondent confusion of one brand with another; a desire to give a brand the benefit of some doubt; hurried endorsement of the scale; carelessness; deliberate falsification; guessing in the absence of personal knowledge or experience; and so on. In other words, error in presenting one's opinions through the Semantic Differential scaling system can occur in spite of the respondent having a clear grasp of the Semantic Differential instructions. Of course a respondent can still be right on a given occasion *in spite* of a defective understanding of *some part of* the instructions. For example (i) the respondent does not know what to do if she has no opinions about a specific attribute of a specific brand, but she *does* have an opinion on it; (ii) the respondent does not know what the centre section of a Semantic Differential scale means, but in rating Aspro she thinks (and says) that Aspro is 'very quick acting'.

Again, it is possible for a considerable number of respondents to misrepresent what they feel about a particular attribute of a brand and yet for the overall sample to yield a distribution of ratings or a mean rating of the attitude that is largely correct. This is because of a tendency for over- and under-statements by sampled individuals to partly balance each other out. Occasionally they do so almost totally.

Finally, it is possible for the indicated superiority of A over B on a given product attribute to be correct in spite of both the A and the B ratings being wrong (that is, they may be subject to a common level of error).

In the circumstances, we might have gone straight to Part III. However, the view is taken here that each sort of error is of importance and interest in its own right.

FINDINGS: PART I

RESPONDENT UNDERSTANDING OF THE
FIRST INTERVIEW INSTRUCTIONS

The extent of respondent grasp of instructions is given with reference to: the seven scale positions; instances where the respondent has no opinion at all; the 'opposites' concept; different sections of the population.

UNDERSTANDING OF THE MEANING
OF THE SEVEN SCALE POSITIONS

The extent and variability of misunderstanding

For each of the seven positions on one of the 12 scales (in fact the first of them, dealing with 'speed of action' of the brand), the respondent had been asked to offer a verbal meaning. For example, respondents were asked of the following diagram:

QUICK ACTING |⎽⎽⎽⎽⎽|⎽⎽⎽⎽⎽ ✓ ⎽⎽⎽⎽⎽|⎽⎽⎽⎽⎽|⎽⎽⎽⎽⎽|⎽⎽⎽⎽⎽|⎽⎽⎽⎽⎽| SLOW ACTING

'If someone put their tick *there* (POINT TO SPACE WHERE THE TICK IS SHOWN), what would that mean?'

This question was asked in turn of all seven of the scale positions. However, for some of the verbal definitions offered by the respondent, it would be difficult to say that they were really equivalent, in the respondent's mind, to the terms originally used by the market research interviewer. Can we be sure, for instance, that the term 'rather' (quick acting) means the same as the term 'fairly' (quick acting). If the respondent defined the positions *on either side* of that term just as given by the interviewer, the ambiguity of the term 'rather' would of course be much more limited. However, if the definition of either of these two positions was doubtful, the ambiguity of the term 'rather' would remain or perhaps even increase. In view of this kind of difficulty in interpreting some respondent replies, a marking system was used which was both generous and imprecise. Thus, responses were rated as one or another of the following:

- Correct or very probably correct
- More likely correct than incorrect
- More likely incorrect than correct
- Incorrect or very probably incorrect*
- Don't know (that is, the respondent simply had no idea what an endorsement of the signified scale position would mean)

For the seven positions in the 'speed of action' scale† respondent understanding was as set out in Table 5.1. The main indications of

---

*For example, the following were judged either incorrect or very probably incorrect as definitions of the *first* scale position: I've never used anything else; slower still; average; very slow; not too bad; slow until it took effect on you. Similarly the following were judged incorrect or very probably incorrect as definitions of the *centre* position on the scale: on the slow side; very slow acting; quick acting; between medium and slow; good; not too effective; takes about five and a half hours to act.
†This particular scale was chosen because it was this one that the 'first' interviewer used to explain the rating system.

216

Table 5.1
Respondent understanding of the meanings of individual scale positions

QUICK ACTING   SLOW ACTING

'If someone put their tick there, what would it mean?'

Scale position indicated:

Percentage of respondents who gave an answer which indicated that their understanding was:	1	2	3	4	5	6	7	All scales
	%	%	%	%	%	%	%	%
Correct (or very probably correct)	88*	67	58	65	33	53	78	63
More likely correct than incorrect	6	15	18	7	25	19	12	15
More likely incorrect than correct	2	5	7	5	8	8	4	6
Incorrect (or very probably incorrect)	3	9	12	18	28	17	5	13
Don't know	1	4	5	5	6	3	1	3

*Percentages for each scale position based on 280 cases.

217

Table 5.1 are as follows.

1   Taking an average over the seven scale positions, the percentage of respondents who were 'incorrect' or 'very probably incorrect', or who did not know what a particular position meant, was 16%. If we take into account those who were 'more likely incorrect than correct', the 16% figure would rise to 22%.

2   On the other hand, there was considerable variability, from one scale position to another, in respondent understanding of what the scale positions meant; thus the range for 'correct or very probably correct' was from 88% to 33%.

3   The first and last scale positions were *least* subject to misunderstanding and the fifth scale position *most* subject to misunderstanding.

The nature of the misunderstandings

Since respondents offered interpretations of each scale position, it is possible to see something of the direction and the nature of the misinterpretations that occurred, and these are set out below for certain of the scale positions.

The mid-position on the scale (|___|___|___|___√|___|___|___|) Of the 280 persons who were asked what this position meant, 14 simply did not know and there were 64 more who were either incorrect or more likely incorrect than correct. Of the 64: 11 thought that the centre point was to be used for a non-committal response or for 'don't know' or 'not sure'; 21 appeared to interpret it as 'slow acting' and 11 as 'quick acting'. Further evidence about the interpretation of the centre point, with particular reference to those who had no opinion at all, will be presented in later sections of this report.

Positions 5 and 6 on the scale (|___|___|___|___|___√|√|___|) Position 5 on the scale fared worse than any other in terms of respondent understanding. Some (17 of the 280) could not say what this position meant, but there were approximately 100 more who were either wrong or possibly wrong. Of these, there were several (8) who interpreted it as 'slow' in a general sense and without differentiating it in any noticeable way from the two 'slower' positions, 6 and 7. A surprisingly large number of respondents (over 30) interpreted this position as meaning that the brand concerned was quite markedly slow (for example, slowest, very slow, extremely slow, practically standstill, particularly slow) — almost as if they had reversed the slow section of the scale so

218

that movement from right to left along it signified a progression in slowness! Indeed there were 14 who explained it as 'slower still' (that is, than position 6). There were, on the other hand, some who interpreted the position either as quick acting to some degree or as in the middle of the speed of action range.

Misunderstanding of scale position 6, also quite appreciable, seemed to be broadly similar in kind to that found for position 5 — namely a lack of differentiation between it and its neighbouring scale positions and some degree of reversal of the gradient of this part of the scale. Here again there was evidence of several of the respondents giving this scale position a 'quick acting' connotation.

Positions 2 and 3 on the scale (|___|_✓_|_✓_|___|___|___|) The forms of misunderstanding featuring respondent interpretations of the *left-hand* intermediate scale positions (that is, positions 2 and 3), although lesser in degree, tend to be similar in kind to those observed in respect of positions 5 and 6, the *right-hand* intermediate positions. In other words, there was for some a lack of differentiation in terms of speed of action along this part of the scale and for a few there was evidence even of a reversal of the intended gradient of this part of the scale. Over and above this, there were several respondents who appeared to have completely reversed the scale in that positions 2 and 3 were interpreted by them as having 'slow acting' connotations.

Positions 1 and 7 on the scale (|✓_|___|___|___|___|_✓|) The most common form of misunderstanding for these two extreme scale positions was a form of under-rating — that is, a less extreme interpretation than that intended. There were also several cases of complete reversal — that is, of scale position 1 being regarded as 'very slow' and scale position 7 being regarded as 'very fast'.

RESPONDENTS' UNDERSTANDING OF WHAT TO DO IF THEY HAD NO OPINION ABOUT A BRAND'S RATING ON A PARTICULAR SCALE

The market research interviewers had the following instructions regarding those respondents who made it clear that they had no opinion at all about some specified aspect of a brand. In other words this instruction was not automatically delivered to *all* respondents.

'If a respondent has no opinion at all with regard to a particular scale within a brand being rated, this scale should be marked DK. It is very important that you do not allow respondents to use the *middle space* for 'don't know', 'no opinion', or 'not sure'. The middle space is *only* for a definite opinion halfway between the two extremes.'

In Stage II of the testing procedure, the respondent was asked of the 'speed of action' scale:

'What do you think that the (first) interviewer wanted you to do if you had no opinion at all about a brand being quick acting or slow acting?'

The distribution of responses to this question is set out in Table 5.2.

Table 5.2
Respondent explanation of what to do when she did not have any opinion about a specified attribute of a brand

	%
Mark it as 'don't know' or DK	49
Ask for guidance	1
Go by any impression I have/use my imagination or intuition	13
Put something somewhere rather than nothing at all/guess at it	6
Put a √ in the middle position	8
Put a √ on the quick acting side of the scale	2
Put a √ on the slow acting side of the scale	1
Respondent did not know what to do in such a circumstance	13
Answer not clear or no evidence	7
	100

From this table it appears that there is a serious problem over the 'don't know' reactions, with 6% saying that they would guess or mark at random, 8% saying they would use the centre point of the scale and 13% being simply unaware of what to do. A further 13% simply said they would go by whatever impression they had — a statement which would be wrong if they were really replying to a question about what to do *if they had no opinion at all* and which in that case would be a form of guess.*

---

*In estimating the importance of this finding, one must note that many respondents gave the interviewer no evidence of 'having no opinion' and that the interviewer was *not* under instruction to tell such people what to do with regard to DKs. This may explain at least part of the ignorance demonstrated in Table 5.2. On the other hand, it is possible that up to 30% of the respondents might, on the evidence of that table, have given no sign to the interviewer of 'not knowing', but might simply have entered a mark upon the scale.

The respondent was also asked, in Stage II of the intensive interview:

'What did the (first) interviewer want you to do if you had no opinion of any kind about a brand?'

This covered the situation where the respondent's 'no opinion' went wider than some particular attribute of a brand and concerned all aspects of that brand.

The distribution of responses is set out in Table 5.3.

Table 5.3
Respondent explanation of what to do when she did not have
any opinion about a brand

	%
Mark the whole page as 'don't know' or DK	59
Ask for help or guidance	0
Go by any impression I had/use my imagination or intuition/report someone else's impression	14
Put the ticks somewhere (eg at random) rather than nowhere at all	5
Put the ticks in the middle	1
Put ticks on the good side/presume it is OK	1
Ask for interviewer's opinions and enter these	1
Respondent did not know *what* to do	10
Answer not clear or no evidence	9
	100

Whereas the position here is somewhat better than that for 'don't know' with respect to specific attributes, a problem clearly does exist.* Thus there were 5% who said they would tick the scales more or less at random rather than nowhere at all ('have a guess'/'she was happy as long as I filled it in') and 10% who simply did not know what to do. In addition there were some who said they'd go by an impression, use their imagination, go by hearsay — in spite of their answer being to the proposition that they had 'no opinion of any kind' about the brand — a reaction which may in some cases be very close to guessing. There were still several who would settle for a series of ticks in the middle of each scale, but by no means as many as showed up in Table 5.2 (dealing with 'no opinion' about *single* dimensions).

*See footnote on previous page.

RESPONDENTS' GRASP OF
THE CONCEPT OF OPPOSITES

In the last part of Stage II, respondents were questioned to find out if they had grasped the idea that the words at the two ends of scales were meant to be opposites in meaning. The respondent was shown a Semantic Differential scale with the word HOT at one end and was asked what word she would expect to see at the other end.

Of the 280 respondents, only ten did not give the required word (that is, COLD). This could hardly be called a rigorous or crucial test of grasp of the system, but its result is consistent with an assumption of fairly successful communication of the concept of 'opposites'.

GRASP OF INSTRUCTIONS ANALYSED
BY RESPONDENT CHARACTERISTICS

For the purposes of comparing different population sections with respect to grasp of instructions, each of the 280 respondents was scored on the ten questions asked in this section of the intensive interview. One mark was given for each 'incorrect or very probably incorrect' response, the maximum score being 10 and the total score being regarded as an index of respondent misunderstanding. Comparisons (of 'misunderstanding score') were then made in terms of social class, occupational level, size of household, occupational state, terminal school age, sex, present age. These are all presented in Table 5.4.

As general background to the comparisons in Table 5.4 we should note that 25% of the total sample appear to have been involved in no misunderstandings at all, 45% had a score of one to two misunderstandings and 30% had three or more misunderstandings.

The principal difference in level of misunderstanding was in terms of age of leaving school: those who left at 15 or less were involved in much more misunderstanding of the instructions than were the others. This educational difference was significant at the 1% level. Differences were also apparent, though to a much smaller degree, in the analysis by class, occupational level and age.

Table 5.4
Number of 'misunderstandings' out of ten, classified by respondent characteristics

Characteristics*	Percentage distribution of misunderstandings			Average score per respondent	Number of cases
	None†	1–2 mis-understandings†	3 or more misunder-standings†		
	%	%	%		n
Social class					
Upper 29% of population	25	55	20	1.8	65
Lower 71%	24	45	31	2.1	170
Occupational level					
Professional, managerial and highly skilled (19%)	30	49	21	1.8	67
Skilled (26%)	21	54	25	1.9	77
Moderately skilled or less (55%)	24	39	37	2.2	129
Occupational state					
Full-time job	21	50	29	2.0	160
Housewife not in full-time job	28	41	31	2.1	94
Others	36	27	36	2.1	22
Terminal school age					
15 years or less	20	47	33	2.2	208
16 years or more	38	42	20	1.3	66
Number in household					
1–2	24	41	33	2.1	115
3–4	27	47	26	1.8	123
5 or more	17	58	25	2.0	40
Sex					
Male	22	45	33	2.1	130
Female	27	47	27	1.9	150
Age					
21–40	24	49	27	1.9	106
41–60	25	48	27	2.0	119
61 or over	26	33	41	2.4	54
All respondents	25%	45%	30%	2.0	280

*Excluding cases which could not be classified.
†That is, number of misunderstandings out of ten.

THE EXTENT AND NATURE OF THE DIFFERENCES BETWEEN THE FIRST AND THE INTENSIVE INTERVIEW RESPONSES

A reminder of the special function of the intensive interview — a criterion of accuracy

The principal aim of this study was to assess the extent to which the ratings made during the first interview were a true reflection of the opinions of the respondents. This assessment is based upon a comparison of each first interview rating with a re-rating made through a second interview of a specialised and intensive kind. This second interview was designed so that the re-ratings made through it would be protected from the various sources of error suspected of entering into the first interview ratings. These design elements were detailed in the Methods section of this report (pages 206—15) but are summarised here because of their importance to the rationale of the enquiry.

1 To guard against the respondent forgetting what the different scale positions meant, the meanings of these subpositions were written into each position on the scale (see pages 210—11).

2 To reduce the possibility of a careless rating being made, the respondent was required to read out all the scale positions before being asked to choose, to spend 10 seconds deciding which scale position was right for her and was not offered the marking disc until that 10 seconds was up. Her rating, once made, was then subjected to immediate and extended challenging (see pages 211—12).

3 The use of seven boxes, each with its scalar meaning written into it, made it unnecessary for the respondent to grasp the concept of opposites and also ruled out whatever traps there were in the contradictory placement of a term such as 'quick acting' right against a scale position which really meant *very* quick acting' (see page 211).

4 To guard against a 'don't know' reaction being registered somewhere *on* the scale itself, a special box was provided for such ratings, and a full verbal description of what it meant was written into it (see page 211).

5 Steps were also taken: to set the respondent thinking about the relevant brand before the introduction of the rating scale; to reduce the likelihood of the respondent confusing the brand

actually asked about with some other brand; to reduce the likelihood of the respondent making token ratings of a brand about which he had 'no opinions at all' (see page 210).

Because the intensive interview had these features, re-ratings made through it were regarded as approximating to the ratings which the respondent would have made in the first interview if he had fully understood the instructions and if he had given each rating his full and careful attention. It is in this special sense that the ratings made through the intensive interview are here regarded as criteria against which to assess the accuracy of the ratings made in the first interview. Putting the matter another way: it is in this special sense that the difference between comparable ratings from the first and second interviews is being regarded here as approximating to error in the first interview rating.

The two sections of Part II

The comparison of the first and the intensive ratings is presented in two sections, A and B. Section A deals with the 'accuracy' of the first interview ratings of individual respondents, whereas Section B deals with the 'accuracy' of sample distributions and averages.

Before proceeding with these two sections, it is important to note that their coverage still leaves for consideration the question of the degree to which the first interview ratings provide a valid basis for comparing brands on specific dimensions or scales. This matter is really vital because the main *legitimate* use of the Semantic Differential scaling system in market research is to provide such comparisons. This aspect of the findings is presented in Part III starting on page 248.

SECTION A: 'ACCURACY' OF RESPONSES
BY INDIVIDUAL RESPONDENTS

Several anomalous scales

In turning to the comparison of the first interview and the intensive interview ratings for the 12 test scales, we should first take note of certain features of scales 4, 11 and 12 (see page 231 for a listing of the 12).

1   Scales 11 and 12 are *unipolar* in character and *not* bipolar as are the other ten scales. Thus each of them runs from an absence of some attribute to a lot of that attribute, for example: 'No unpleasant side effects' to 'Very unpleasant side effects'. Strictly

speaking, unipolar scales should not be included in Semantic Differential batteries, for they require the respondent to make ratings that may be nonsensical, for example:

> very unpleasant side effects/fairly unpleasant side effects/ slightly unpleasant side effects/halfway between pleasant side effects and 'no unpleasant side effects'/slightly 'no unpleasant side effects'/fairly 'no unpleasant side effects'/very 'no unpleasant side effects'

Nonetheless, some unipolar scales *are*, in practice, included in many Semantic Differential batteries. It was planned that this study should be made to reveal how respondents dealt with such scales. At the same time, it would be misleading to include the results from double interview checks on them in aggregate findings meant to bring out general tendencies in Semantic Differential scale usage. They must be kept out of such aggregates and reported separately.

2   Scale 4 also raised problems. Research practitioners who were consulted took the view that many people who feel that a given brand could have no taste at all would, with the absence of specific instructions, enter such reactions as centre point ratings. Any testing of the first interview usage of that scale should include (they suggested) opportunity for the respondent to give that particular response. This suggestion was accepted. However this in turn rendered that scale unsuitable for inclusion in any aggregate of findings for bipolar scales. Scale 4 results are therefore kept out of any aggregate (but are presented separately).

**The accuracy of individual respondents:
all nine (comparable) scales aggregated**

The incidence of frequency of error by individuals

The details in Table 5.5 allow a comparison to be made of first and intensive interviewer ratings for scales 1 to 3 and 5 to 10 considered together.

It is quite clear from Table 5.5 that many of the first interview ratings were not upheld by the intensive check. Table 5.6 brings out more clearly the nature of the discrepancies.

About half the first interview ratings (51%) did not stand up to the intensive challenge to them. Of those 1573 discrepant responses in the first interview, 1381 were actual ratings, of which 495 were discrepant by two or more scalar positions and at least 133 became 'don't know'.

Table 5.5
Comparing the results from first and intensive interviews;
scales 1 to 10 (less 4) combined*

First interview responses

Intensive interview responses	First interview responses							Don't know for given scale	Don't know for brand	No information	Total
	1	2	3	4	5	6	7				
Scale position											
1	26.5% (817† cases)	2.9% (89)	0.9% (29)	1.0% (31)	0.3% (9)	0.2% (6)	0.4% (12)	0.2% (7)	1.1% (35)	0.1% (2)	33.7% (1037)
2	9.9% (306)	7.4% (227)	3.3% (102)	1.6% (49)	0.5% (16)	0.4% (13)	0.7% (21)	0.8% (26)	1.6% (49)	0.1% (3)	26.4% (812)
3	1.2% (38)	1.0% (30)	1.9% (59)	0.7% (23)	0.2% (6)	0.1% (4)	0.2% (7)	0.1% (2)	0.2% (6)	0.0% (0)	5.7% (175)
4	1.9% (58)	1.3% (39)	1.1% (34)	2.3% (70)	0.3% (9)	0.2% (5)	0.4% (13)	0.2% (6)	0.4% (11)	0.0% (1)	8.0% (246)
5	0.5% (16)	0.3% (10)	0.4% (13)	0.7% (23)	0.7% (22)	0.4% (11)	0.4% (11)	0.1% (4)	0.1% (2)	0.0% (1)	3.7% (113)
6	0.5% (14)	0.3% (10)	0.5% (15)	0.5% (15)	0.4% (12)	0.8% (26)	0.6% (19)	0.1% (4)	0.2% (6)	0.1% (2)	4.0% (123)
7	0.2% (7)	0.2% (5)	0.4% (11)	0.2% (7)	0.2% (5)	0.1% (3)	1.2% (36)	0.1% (3)	0.1% (2)	0.0% (0)	2.6% (79)
Don't know for given scale	1.6% (50)	1.1% (34)	0.4% (11)	0.6% (19)	0.2% (6)	0.1% (4)	0.3% (9)	1.8% (54)	3.1% (96)	0.1% (3)	9.3% (286)
Don't know for brand	0.0% (0)	0.0% (0)	0.0% (0)	0.0% (0)	0.0% (0)	0.0% (0)	0.0% (0)	0.0% (0)	3.1% (97)	0.0% (0)	3.1% (97)
No information	1.7% (52)	0.4% (13)	0.3% (10)	0.1% (3)	0.1% (4)	0.1% (2)	0.3% (8)	0.1% (2)	0.5% (15)	0.1% (3)	3.6% (112)
Total	44.1% (1358)	14.8% (457)	9.2% (284)	7.8% (240)	2.9% (89)	2.4% (74)	4.4% (136)	3.5% (108)	10.4% (319)	0.5% (15)	(3080)

*Scales 4, 11 and 12 were sufficiently different in character from the other nine for them to be kept out of this aggregate. They are presented separately in the Appendix.
†In each cell is shown the percentage distribution of responses and, underneath this in brackets, the raw number on which that percentage is based. All percentages are taken out against the overall base of 3080 responses.

Table 5.6
Summing up on the nature and direction of the discrepancies between first and intensive interviews

		Cases	%
1	*First interview responses upheld by intensive check*	1507	49
	Same scalar rating	1257	41
	'Don't know' response in first and intensive interview	247	8
	No information* each time	3	–
2	*First interview responses not upheld by intensive check*	1573	51
	First interview rating changed:		
	by one scale position	661	21
	by two scale positions	210	7
	by three scale positions	154	5
	by four scale positions	66	2
	by five scale positions	46	1
	by six scale positions	19	1
	First interview rating changed to 'don't know'	133	4
	First interview rating changed to 'no information'*	92	3
	'Don't know' changed to a rating	163	5
	'Don't know' changed to 'no information'*	17	1
	'No information'* changed to a rating	9	–
	'No information'* changed to 'don't know'	3	–

*No information means no information secured.
– Means less than 0.5%.

Of the 427 first interview 'don't knows', 247 remained 'don't know' but 163 became scalar ratings (17 becoming 'no information').

Full results for each of the nine constituent scales were prepared separately and are presented in the Appendix to this chapter. Despite differences in degree, their individual indications are broadly similar to those set out in Table 5.6 and summarised above. In the Appendix with them are tables of similar format for scales 4, 11 and 12, and these tables are reported on separately.

The direction of inaccuracy and 'scale reversal'

Table 5.7, also based on Table 5.5, provides evidence of the degree to which respondents used the wrong half of the Semantic Differential scale in making their ratings.

228

Table 5.7
Degree to which respondents used the wrong half of the
Semantic Differential scale in making their ratings

Nature of shift		Number of cases
First interview	Intensive interview	
1st position →	position 5, 6 or 7	37
2nd position →	position 5, 6 or 7	25
3rd position →	position 5, 6 or 7	39
5th position →	position 1, 2 or 3	31
6th position →	position 1, 2 or 3	23
7th position →	position 1, 2 or 3	40
All		195

Some 2638 scalar ratings* were made by the 280 respondents in the first interview. Of these, 195 (7%) shifted from one side of the scale to the other under the challenge of the intensive interview. The phenomenon of 'scale reversal' thus did occur, but it was by no means a major feature of Semantic Differential scaling in this particular check.

Inaccuracy associated with the first interview usage of the centre positions of scales

Table 5.8, column (a) provides evidence about respondent use or misuse, in the first interview, of the centre points of scales.

About a quarter of these 453 Semantic Differential scale responses (that is, centre point ratings in the first interview) appear to have involved quite proper use of the centre point of the scale concerned. If we allow for a limited marginal error in its usage (that is, one scale point out), the figure for acceptable use of the centre point rises to 45%. This still leaves us with 46% of the centre point ratings which should in fact have been entered towards one or the other half of the scale rather than at its centre, and 14% which should have been entered at one or the other of the scale's extremities.

What is particularly noteworthy is that only 9% of these 453 centre point ratings should have been registered as 'don't know'. In other words, misuse of the centre point more frequently represents an erroneous placement of an opinion than the use of it to register 'don't know'. This, of course, still leaves us with the related question of what proportion of an interviewer's DK entries should have been registered as centre point responses (see next section).

*For scales 1 to 3 and 5 to 10 considered together.

Table 5.8
The use in the first interview of (a) the centre point in the
Semantic Differential scale and (b) the DK response

(Data based on scales 1 to 3 and 5 to 10 combined)

		Percentage distribution of responses	
Response derived from intensive interview		(a)* Centre point ratings in first interview (all = 453)	(b)† DK responses in first interview (all = 530)
		%	%
Scale position	1	11	8
	2	25	15
	3	9	2
	4	27	5
	5	9	2
	6	7	2
	7	3	1
Don't know		9	61
No information		0	4

*In fact some 625 centre point ratings were checked through the intensive interview, only 453 of which were found in the nine scales involved in Table 5.5. Table 5.8 is based on the latter 453, but the other scales are dealt with in a later section of this report. They do not, however, provide appreciably different findings about centre point usage of Semantic Differential scales.
†Shown in this table for convenience and dealt with in the next section of the report.

The meaning of respondents' 'don't know' responses

The (b) column in Table 5.8 provides evidence about the meaning of respondents' 'don't know' answers in the first interview. Over half the original 'don't know' responses remained 'don't know' when challenged through the intensive interview, *only 5% converting to the centre point ratings*. On the other hand, 35% of them converted into ratings on either side of the centre point. The more frequent 'explanations' of this sort of error tended to be: respondent was in a hurry or was hurried by the interviewer and said 'don't know' to get rid of the interviewer; respondent confused one brand with another; respondent thought harder the second time; respondent was not sure about how to use the scale to register an opinion.

The 'accuracy' of individual respondent ratings, scale by scale

Table 5.9, which is modelled on Table 5.6, presents results for each of nine rating scales that were accumulated in Table 5.5 for the discovery of general tendencies. It also provides results for scales 4, 11 and 12.

There is a lot of variability in going from one scale to another with respect to the number of ratings which were the same in each inter-

Table 5.9
Showing the degree to which the first interview response was changed in the second interview
Details for each of the 12 scales (all brands combined)

Scale	First interview response maintained		First interview response not maintained								Others*	Total ratings tested
	DK each time	Same rating	Rating 1 space different	Rating 2 spaces different	Rating 3 spaces different	Rating 4 spaces different	Rating 5 spaces different	Rating 6 spaces different	Rating becomes DK	DK becomes a rating		No.
	%	%	%	%	%	%	%	%	%	%	%	No.
1 Quick acting/slow acting	7.3	36.1	24.8	8.0	4.1	2.7	2.0	0.7	6.3	3.2	4.8	560
2 Safe/dangerous	5.7	47.9	23.9	4.3	3.9	2.1	1.8	1.1	2.9	5.4	1.1	280
3 Harmless for children/ harmful for children	14.6	29.6	14.6	4.3	9.3	1.8	2.1	2.1	5.7	9.6	6.1	280
4 Pleasant taste/nasty taste	9.6	16.8	20.3	8.2	5.4	4.6	0.7	0.4	10.0	2.5	21.4†	280
5 Easy to swallow/hard to swallow	8.2	44.3	18.9	5.7	2.9	3.6	2.1	1.1	3.9	2.5	6.8	280
6 Cheap/expensive	8.9	36.8	26.1	6.4	4.6	2.5	1.8	0.0	6.8	4.3	1.8	280
7 Effective/ineffective	7.9	45.7	19.6	6.1	4.6	1.8	1.1	0.4	4.3	3.9	4.6	560
8 Small tablet/large tablet	7.5	29.3	25.5	12.5	8.4	2.1	2.5	0.7	3.6	6.4	3.2	280
9 Well packaged/poorly packaged	7.1	52.5	22.1	5.0	2.5	0.4	0.4	0.4	3.2	4.6	1.8	280
10 Easy to get/hard to get	6.1	61.1	10.0	2.1	2.5	1.4	0.7	0.0	1.1	8.6	6.1	280
11 Habit forming/not habit forming‡	10.0	57.0	10.0	4.3	4.6	§	§	§	4.6	3.2	6.4	280
12 Unpleasant side effects/ No unpleasant side effects‡	7.5	56.1	9.3	2.9	3.6	§	§	§	9.6	1.4	9.6	280

*Others = with the exception of scale 4, these are all cases where there was no evidence of whether the ratings were the same or different (that is, no information about one or both the responses).

†Made up of: 28 for which there was no information on one or both occasions; 38 for which the rating became 'no taste at all'; four where DK became 'no taste at all'.

‡The intensive interview allowed for only four working scale positions, the fourth (= 'not habit forming' [scale 11] or 'no unpleasant side effects' [scale 12]) being regarded as equivalent to 4, 5, 6, 7 in the first interview (see later).

§Only four positions in the scale used in the intensive interview (see later).

view: from 61% for the 'easy to get' scale to 46% for the 'effectiveness' scale; to 29% for the 'size of tablet' scale to 17% for the 'taste' scale. There is also a lot of variability, scale by scale, with respect to the proportion of ratings which became 'DK' in the intensive interview and the number of 'DKs' that became ratings.

However, in spite of this variability in the apparent accuracy of the responses associated with the different Semantic Differential scales, the average picture presented in Table 5.6 appears generally to apply to the nine different scales on which it is based. Thus for most of these, there are many instances of ratings for the first interview being two to three scale points different from those derived through the intensive interview; there is a small but noteworthy number of cases where the first and the intensive ratings are four to six spaces apart; for each of the scales there is a small but noteworthy incidence of 'DKs' being changed to ratings in the intensive interview, and vice versa.

RESPONDENT'S EXPLANATIONS OF THEIR 'ERRORS' WHEN CONFRONTED WITH DIFFERENCES BETWEEN THEIR FIRST AND THEIR INTENSIVE INTERVIEW RESPONSES

How the explanations were elicited

In Stage V of the intensive interview, the interviewer challenged the respondent with respect to all the differences found between first and second ratings. The intensive interviewer had the following instructions:

SAY:

'Now I am going to get you to look over what you did in the first interview. I want to put it side by side with what you have just told me.'

TAKE THE PAIRS OF RATINGS ONE AT A TIME. IF NO DIFFERENCE BETWEEN THEM, SAY SO TO THE RESPONDENT.

'These two are the same in both interviews.'

IF A DIFFERENCE OCCURS, NOTE THE BRAND AND THE PAGE NUMBER OF THE INTENSIVE INTERVIEW AND SAY:

'These two are in different positions. This is what you marked for the first interviewer and this is the one you just marked for me.'

PAUSE.

'Can you help me to understand why the two are in different positions?'

PROBE AND DO NOT STOP PROBING UNTIL YOU GET A CLEAR, MEANINGFUL EXPLANATION. THEN ENTER REASONS AT FOOT OF APPROPRIATE PAGE.

'Now that you've thought about it, which would you say was correct?'

'*This* (POINT) or *this* (POINT) or *neither*?'

CIRCLE CHOSEN ANSWER. IF NEITHER, ASK:

'What would you say is your *correct* answer?'

ENTER IT. SAY:

'Why were they *both* wrong?'

ENTER REPLY AT FOOT OF APPROPRIATE PAGE.

The respondents' 'explanations' should of course be regarded warily because it would be all too easy for the explanations to take the form of face-saving excuses. Nonetheless it would be a mistake simply to discount such 'explanations', and the position is taken here that the respondents' 'explanations' could provide valuable insights into the factors and conditions which make for 'error' in the ordinary market research use of the Semantic Differential rating system. We therefore present them, warily of course, with this in mind. They are set out in Table 5.10 in groups.

THE DIFFERENT TYPES OF 'EXPLANATION' GIVEN*

One major class of reasons was to the effect that the respondent's first interview rating was based upon a misunderstanding of what he or she was required to do. Some 36% of those making 'errors' claimed this as a causal factor. Table 5.10 lists the kinds of misunderstanding to which they laid claim: a tendency on the part of the respondent to think or judge only in terms of the end positions of the scale; mistaken usage of the middle position on the scale; confusion over how to register a DK response; and so on. Along with this broad class of 'reasons' must be grouped those (from 28% of the respondents) to the effect that the respondent was conscious of confusion over what he or she was supposed to be doing, most of them to the effect that they were unsure about the meanings of the different positions on the scales.

Another large group of 'reasons' (from 31%) attributed 'error' to hurried or careless completion of the first interview ratings, most of them to the effect that the respondent did not have enough time for making the rating and/or had to make a quick or snap decision. Other noteworthy 'reasons' in this group included: guessed; pressed by the interviewer to get *something* marked; desire by the respondent to get the interview over.

Some of the first interview 'errors' appear to have sprung, not from a misunderstanding of the instructions, but from the respondent originating mistakes of her own: a tendency to give an opinion other than her own; a tendency to consider different ways of taking the drug in going from the first to the second interview (for example without

---

*After the confrontation, the respondent was asked which she now considered was the correct response in her own case — the first, the second or neither. If 'neither', she was asked to say what *would* be a correct response in her case. It was this final choice of response (that is, first or second or a fresh one) which was regarded as the 'correct' one in the analysis reported in this document.

Table 5.10

Percentage distribution of respondent explanations of differences between their first and intensive interviews

The explanation(s) given	All scales	Individual scales									
Total number of explanations given (= numerical base for %)	1922	1: 336	2: 146	3: 186	4: 251	5: 123	6: 164	7: 135	8: 383	9: 109	10: 59
	%	%	%	%	%	%	%	%	%	%	%
Completed first rating hurriedly or with lack of seriousness	30.7	33.9	30.0	27.7	34.0	28.1	27.5	34.4	27.8	28.4	31.5
R* did not have enough time to make up mind in first interview/had to make a quick or snap decision/had more time to think in second interview	21.4	23.8	21.5	22.3	22.6	19.9	19.6	20.6	18.2	19.8	22.4
R rushed through it to avoid standing at the door/to get rid of the interviewer/said DK to get interview over	1.9	2.4	1.9	0.8	2.9	2.3	1.6	2.0	0.7	1.2	6.1
R guessed/marked the scale at random/R claimed the interviewer pressed him to put a tick *somewhere*	6.2	6.5	6.6	3.8	6.8	3.5	4.7	9.8	7.4	7.4	2.0
R regarded the first interview as a joke/took it lightly/lacked interest in the first interview	1.2	1.2	0.0	0.8	1.7	2.4	1.6	2.0	1.5	0.0	0.0
The respondent felt, at the time of using the scales, that he did not properly understand the instructions	28.3	35.5	20.5	21.2	23.1	33.7	25.2	25.6	37.1	27.1	19.1
The interviewer didn't explain it fully/R didn't understand the instructions/it was explained to R more fully in second interview	4.0	9.8	3.7	4.6	3.4	2.3	4.0	5.9	4.4	0.0	2.0
R didn't get the idea of there being different grades along the line	2.0	1.2	0.0	0.8	1.1	4.7	3.9	0.0	3.7	2.5	2.0
The meaning of the different spaces was not marked/R didn't realise what the different spaces meant/forgot what the different spaces meant/found it easier having the words in the boxes/the actual words were given in the second interview/R was given a choice of clearly presented statements in the second interview	22.3										
Respondent misunderstood (in first interview) what he was to do	22.3	24.5	16.8	15.8	18.6	26.7	17.3	19.7	29.0	24.6	14.1
There was no DK space/R used the middle space for DK/R said DK if not one of the extremes	36.0	24.9	29.7	53.6	40.3	26.7	46.4	37.2	37.2	32.0	24.5
There was no halfway space/R didn't realise what the middle space meant/R used the middle space for when he had 'no opinion'/R thought the middle space meant 'good' or 'best' or 'most satisfactory'	6.4	4.5	5.6	15.1	8.4	2.3	9.4	8.8	3.0	3.7	6.1
R thought the words at the end of the line described the last and the first positions on the scale	6.9	4.5	5.5	11.3	9.6	3.5	9.5	10.7	5.6	3.7	4.1
R thought only in terms of ends or extremes of scale/tended to go for end spaces/thought the choice was only between end	2.3	1.2	2.8	1.5	2.3	1.2	0.8	3.9	3.0	3.7	4.1

R thought only in terms of end position and 'in between'	1.7	0.8	0.9	3.0	1.1	2.3	3.9	—	1.5	3.7	0.0
R thought he had to answer only if he used it himself	1.7	0.4	1.9	2.3	1.7	—	1.6	2.0	2.6	1.2	4.1
Other misinterpretations of the scale/instructions	5.6	4.5	4.7	8.3	7.3	7.0	5.5	3.9	7.0	—	2.0
Various errors by the respondent	15.5	15.8	23.2	21.2	18.7	21.1	8.7	11.8	9.6	19.7	10.2
I gave something other than my own opinion in the first interview (e.g. what the advertisements say, what others say)/I included the opinions of others (in the first interview)/I gave my personal opinion in the second interview	6.2	8.5	8.3	3.8	7.9	10.5	4.0	7.9	2.9	6.2	6.1
R confused one brand with another	1.6	3.7	—	—	1.7	1.2	—	—	1.9	4.9	—
R was 'drawn' by position of her previous tick	0.4	—	—	0.8	—	1.2	—	—	—	1.2	4.1
R didn't want to condemn the brand so gave it a favourable rating/gave it the benefit of the doubt	1.0	0.8	—	—	3.4	—	0.8	1.0	1.1	1.2	—
R made a 'mistake'	2.3	1.6	0.9	2.3	3.4	3.5	1.6	2.9	2.6	2.5	—
R thought about it differently on the two occasions (e.g. without water first time and with water the second; considered 'overdose' in first interview and described dose in the second)	4.0	1.2	14.0	14.3	2.3	4.7	2.3	—	1.1	3.7	—
Other 'reasons' for error in the first interview	16.7	19.2	15.8	15.0	20.4	14.0	12.5	13.8	16.3	12.3	28.6
R had 'second thoughts'/changed mind between first and second interview	5.8	9.0	1.8	3.0	4.6	3.5	6.2	2.0	5.9	7.4	18.4
R accepted the advice of interviewer in first interview	0.4	0.4	—	—	1.1	—	0.8	—	0.4	—	2.0
Miscellaneous 'reasons'	10.5	9.8	14.0	12.0	14.7	10.5	5.5	11.8	10.0	4.9	8.2
NOT CLEAR WHETHER RESPONDENT WRONG IN FIRST OR IN SECOND INTERVIEW											
R noticed no difference/little difference between meanings given to the scale positions by the interviewer	7.8	10.2	10.3	3.8	5.1	9.3	8.6	4.9	9.6	7.4	4.1
R did not know how the difference occurred/R's views not understandable or ambiguous/no information	6.6	7.4	8.4	4.5	4.6	7.0	8.6	8.8	5.2	11.1	4.1
RESPONDENT(S) WRONG IN SECOND INTERVIEW											
R gave his personal opinion in the first interview but included the views of others in the second interview	1.8	2.9	1.9	2.3	1.1	5.8	—	2.0	0.4	1.2	4.1

* R = respondent.

water in first interviews but *with* water in the second); confusion between brands; giving the brand the benefit of any doubt or avoiding being hard on a brand.

Table 5.10 deals also with 'causes of error' in the intensive interview* and noteworthy here is the substitution (by 2%) of the views of *others* for their own opinions.

Variation, between scales, in the volunteered 'explanations of error'

All the scales appear to have been subject to most of the difficulties outlined above. However, some of these are outstanding in the sense that their use was more featured by certain of these difficulties and less by others. Some examples follow.

1   In the use of scales 2 and 3, respondents frequently explained 'error' as due to their 'thinking about the rating differently on the two occasions'. Thus, in making a rating along scale 3 (in terms of 'harmless/safe for children'), some respondents thought, *in the first interview*, in terms of the use of an adult dose for children, but in terms of a *child dosage* in the second interview. Similarly, in making a rating on scale 2 (safe/dangerous), some initially thought in terms of overdose and subsequently in terms of prescribed dose. The same sort of difficulty arose for other scales, though to a lesser degree. Thus a few respondents, in rating a brand for 'easy/hard to swallow', thought in the first interview in terms of 'without water' . . . but in terms of 'with water' in the intensive interview.

2   'Errors' in the use of scale 3 (harmless/harmful for children) were also blamed (more than were errors in other scales) upon a misunderstanding of what the respondent was supposed to do, respondents quite frequently being in difficulty over how to register a DK and over the proper use of the midpoint on the scale. This appears to have been partly because the use of this scale called for much greater use of the 'DK' and the 'halfway' responses than did the other scales.

3   Table 5.10 presents variability of other kinds with respect to reasons given for first interview 'error'. What lies behind this variability is by no means clear, but we have presented it in full as

---

*Whenever there was a difference between the first and the intensive ratings, the respondent was asked to explain that difference and *then* was asked to consider which of the two ratings, *if either*, was correct. If the *first* interview was considered to be correct, the explanation of error was linked to the intensive interview. (If the respondent thought that neither was correct, he was asked to do the rating job once more and this last rating was regarded as 'correct' for the purposes of this analysis.)

a basis for constructive hypothesising of relevance to the communication process. It should serve in the meantime to point out the variability and the complexity of the response processes in Semantic Differential scaling.

'Error' in the first interview, analysed
by respondent characteristics

An analysis was made of the degree to which 'error' in the first interview varied with the characteristics of respondents, in this case: age of leaving school; social class; occupational level; occupational state; number in household; age; sex; use of product. Details are given in Table 5.11.

Table 5.11
Percentage of first interview responses
upheld by the intensive interview

Characteristics	Number of ratings	%	Characteristics	Number of ratings	%
Age of leaving school			*Occupational state*		
14 or less	(1650)	51.9	Housewife	(1034)	49.2
Over 14	(1430)	49.6	Others	(2046)	48.7
Social class			*Occupational level*		
$ABC_1 C_2$	(1780)	46.8	Grades 1–4	(1584)	49.5
DE	(1300)	51.6	Grades 5–7	(1496)	48.0
Product usage			*Sex*		
R* uses it	(1695)	50.8	Male	(1430)	49.1
R not but family			Female	(1650)	48.6
does	(169)	45.0			
Neither R nor family	(1216)	46.7	*Age*		
			21–50	(1848)	48.6
Number in household			51 and over	(1232)	29.1
1–2	(1265)	51.7			
3 or more	(1815)	46.9			

*R = respondent.

This table suggests that there is a marked tendency for 'error level' to be much the same in the different subgroups examined.

Results for three anomalous scales

The accuracy of individual responses to scales 11 and 12

Whereas scales 1—10 in the Semantic Differential battery are bipolar in character, scales 11 and 12 are unipolar. The view has already been advanced that there is an inherent nonsense about asking respondents to make ratings on unipolar scales set in the instructional context of a battery of bipolar scales. This is because the instructions for using bipolar scales postulate an equal distance between the zero point on a scale and its either end — whereas for a unipolar scale one of the end points corresponds to the zero or midpoint of the bipolar scale.

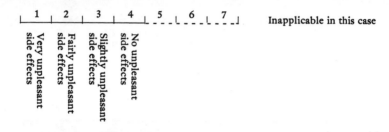

Figure 5.6   Showing the meanings of scale
positions for unipolar scales

Nonetheless, it was the team's intention to find out what respondents actually did when faced with the unipolar scale in the midst of the Semantic Differential battery.

A modified form of checking

For each of scales 11 and 12, the full intensive interview, as detailed in the Methods section of this chapter, was applied to test the accuracy of the first interview ratings. However, instead of the usual seven-box testing system (with a DK box), the following criterion system was used in the intensive interview.

Very unpleasant side effects	Fairly unpleasant side effects	Slightly unpleasant side effects	No unpleasant side effects

Absolutely no idea at all about any unpleasant side effects

Figure 5.7   The five-box criteria system . . . in
testing ratings on Unipolar scales

238

The results of such checks, for each of the unipolar scales, are given in full in Appendix Tables 5A.11 and 5A.12, but are summarised in Tables 5.12 and 5.13.

Table 5.12
Comparing first interview distributions for unipolar and bipolar scales

	First interview ratings							
	1	2	3	4	5	6	7	DK/NI
Scale 11	10.0	7.5	6.1	7.1	3.2	8.2	43.2	14.7
Scale 12	7.5	3.9	4.6	7.1	4.6	9.6	50.7	11.4
All bipolars (1—3, 5—10)	44.1	14.8	9.2	7.8	2.9	2.4	4.4	14.4

On the positive front (i) the evidence does not suggest that the inclusion of the two unipolar scales amongst the bipolars has increased the frequency of 'DK' and 'no information' cases (for the unipolars — see Table 5.12); (ii) at least two-thirds of the first interview responses (for the unipolars) were upheld by the intensive interview — a higher proportion than for the aggregated bipolars (Table 5.13); (iii) the mean rating for scale 12 had a high level of accuracy. On the other hand, (i) the weighted average for scale 11 was more in error than the weighted average for the aggregated bipolar scales (though less than for some of the individual bipolars — Table 5.19); (ii) at least 11% of the sample endorsed nonsense ratings (5 and 6) on scale 11 and at least 14% on scale 12.

So on balance, there is nothing to show that the inclusion of the two unipolars was especially unfortunate. However clearly those two scales raise problems of face validity.

Table 5.13
Accuracy check for scales 11 and 12

	Scale 11	Scale 12	Agg. of 1—5, 5—10
	%	%	%
First interview responses upheld by intensive interview			
Same scalar rating	57	56	41
'DK' or 'no information' upheld	10	8	8
First interviewer response not upheld			
Rating out by 1 position	10	9	21
Rating out by 2 positions	4	3	7
Rating out by 3 positions	5	4	5
Rating out by > 3 positions	NA	NA	4
Other changes	14	20	14
Weighted ratings based on four point scale			
First interview	3.40	3.59	2.25
Intensive interview	3.67	3.62	2.33

It had been suggested by several research practitioners that the proposed rating system for dealing with the pleasantness or unpleasantness of taste of headache remedies was incomplete: it did not offer scope for the reply 'no taste at all'. To find out if this view of the product did occur and, if so, what respondents did about it, an extra response box was included in the intensive testing procedure for scale 4.

Very pleasant taste	Fairly pleasant taste	Slightly pleasant taste	Half-way between pleasant and nasty taste	Slightly nasty taste	Fairly nasty taste	Very nasty taste

| | | | Don't know if it has pleasant or nasty taste | | No taste at all | |

Figure 5.8   Rating boxes used in the intensive testing procedure for scale 4

This feature of the testing operation made it unrealistic to group the results for this scale with the other bipolar results. The results relating to it have therefore been presented separately and are shown in Tables 5.14, 5.15 and 5.16.

Table 5.14
Comparing results for scale 4 and those for
bipolar scales considered in aggregate

	Scale positions									
	1	2	3	4	5	6	7	DK/ NI*	No taste	Average
	%	%	%	%	%	%	%	%	%	%
Scale 4										
First interview	27.9	13.6	11.1	11.4	6.8	5.0	9.6	14.7	N/A	3.10
Check interview	5.7	13.6	3.9	8.6	15.4	5.4	6.4	25.7	15.4	3.95
Scales 1–3, 5–10										
First interview	44.1	14.8	9.2	7.8	2.9	2.4	4.4	14.4	–	2.25
Check interview	33.7	26.4	5.7	8.0	3.7	4.0	2.6	16.0	–	2.33

*Don't know/No information available.

Table 5.15
Showing per cent of first interview responses
upheld by the intensive interview

	%		%
Scale 1	43.4	Scale 7	53.6
Scale 2	53.4	Scale 8	36.8
Scale 3	44.2	Scale 9	59.6
Scale 4	26.4	Scale 10	67.2
Scale 5	52.5	Scale 11	67.0
Scale 6	45.7	Scale 12	63.6
		Average	48.9

Table 5.16
Showing where respondents placed their
'no taste' reactions to the product

Pleasant taste			Halfway	Unpleasant taste			
Very n	Fairly n	Slightly n	n	Slightly n	Fairly n	Very n	All n
17	4	5	7	1	1	3	38

1   The first interview endorsement of scale position 1 (very pleasant taste) is much lower than is the average position for the nine standard bipolar scales grouped together (28% : 44%).

2   Position 1 on scale 4, though giving relatively low endorsement is especially prone to *over*-endorsement, dropping from 28% to 6% in the accuracy check. This compares with a drop for the nine standard scales from 44% to 34%.

3   Only 26.4% of the first interview responses were upheld by the intensive interview, compared with an all-in average of 48.9% for the aggregate of scales 1 to 3 and 5 to 10.

4   In the intensive interview, 38 of the first interview ratings were converted to 'no taste at all'. Only seven of these came from the halfway scalar slot (4), indicating that there had been no whole-sale dumping of the 'no taste' reaction into the scalar midpoint. These reactions had been distributed or spread over the whole scale, with half of them lodging in the 'very pleasant taste' scalar position.

Clearly scale 4 is of a type that calls for special attention in Semantic

Differential scaling questionnaires. What happens with it in Part II of this report should be carefully noted.

SECTION B: 'ACCURACY' OF SAMPLE DISTRIBUTIONS AND SAMPLE MEANS

It is quite possible to have a situation where many individuals give erroneous responses in a survey interview *but* where the errors of the different individuals cancel out to some appreciable degree. Indeed, cancelling out or 'compensating error' enters in a beneficial way into the results of virtually all sample research. On the other hand, there is no guarantee at all that anything like a *complete* balancing out will occur, for the simple reason that error in one direction may be more frequent or more substantial than error in the other direction.

For the market researcher involved in sample research, it is of course the result for the whole sample or for specified sections of the sample that is of importance.

The accuracy of sample distributions and means

(All nine comparable scales aggregated)

In order to obtain an *overall* impression of the *sample* differences between first and intensive interviews, the results for all the comparable scales (that is, scales 1 to 3 and 5 to 10) were combined. These are shown in Figure 5.9 and Table 5.17.*

Scales 11 and 12 were kept out of this combination because they (alone) were unipolar in character. Scale 4 was also left out because of peculiarities connected with it and already described. The results for the three scales are given separately in Table 5.18.

The principal indications of Figure 5.9 and Table 5.17 are as follows.

1   There was a tendency, in the intensive interview, for respondents to endorse scale positions 1 and 3 *less* frequently than in the first interview and scale position 2 *more* frequently. The differences were particularly marked for scale positions 1 and 2. In other words, it appears that in the first interview scale position 2 was under-endorsed and scale positions 1 and 3 over-endorsed.

2   The same kind of thing occurred at the other end of the scale, though to a smaller degree: thus it appears that in the first interview scale position 7 was somewhat over-endorsed and scale

---

*Figure 5.9 and Table 5.17 give principally the same information — in graphic and numerical forms, respectively.

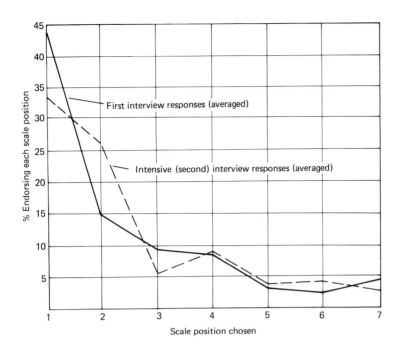

Figure 5.9 Diagrammatic presentation of the data in Table 5.17

Table 5.17
Comparing rating distributions from the
first and the intensive interviews
(Aggregate trends based on scales 1 to 3 and 5 to 10)

Scale position	First interview	Intensive interview
	%	%
1	44.1	33.7
2	14.8	26.4
3	9.2	5.7
4	7.8	8.0
5	2.9	3.7
6	2.4	4.0
7	4.4	2.6
Weighted rating	2.25	2.33
Don't know	13.9	12.4
No information	0.5	3.6

Table 5.18

Comparing percentage* distributions of endorsements in the first and the intensive interviews, shown separately for each scale

Type of response made	Scale 1 1st int. %	Scale 1 Intensive int. %	Scale 2 1st int. %	Scale 2 Intensive int. %	Scale 3 1st int. %	Scale 3 Intensive int. %	Scale 4 1st int. %	Scale 4 Intensive int. %	Scale 5 1st int. %	Scale 5 Intensive int. %	Scale 6 1st int. %	Scale 6 Intensive int. %	Scale 7 1st int. %	Scale 7 Intensive int. %	Scale 8 1st int. %	Scale 8 Intensive int. %	Scale 9 1st int. %	Scale 9 Intensive int. %	Scale 10 1st int. %	Scale 10 Intensive int. %	Scale 11 1st int. %	Scale 11 Intensive int. %	Scale 12 1st int. %	Scale 12 Intensive int. %
Scale position																								
1	30.4	22.1	57.5	51.4	27.1	27.9	27.9	5.7	53.9	45.4	38.2	20.4	45.0	37.1	37.1	9.8	61.4	53.6	66.8	70.7	10.0	3.2	7.9	4.3
2	21.6	32.5	13.6	32.1	9.6	19.2	13.6	13.6	11.8	21.4	16.4	28.2	15.7	26.8	16.3	30.7	11.8	23.6	8.6	12.1	7.5	5.0	3.9	3.6
3	16.1	8.2	6.8	2.5	7.1	5.7	11.1	3.9	6.1	2.5	8.2	5.7	10.4	6.8	10.2	9.1	6.4	3.6	3.9	1.1	6.1	6.4	4.6	7.9
4	8.8	7.3	4.3	0.7	7.9	5.7	11.4	8.6	7.1	2.1	11.1	11.8	7.9	3.9	11.8	22.3	3.9	3.6	2.5	0.7	7.1	7.1	7.1	
5	3.6	2.1	1.8	2.9	6.1	5.4	6.8	15.4	2.5	1.8	4.6	7.9	2.5	2.1	2.3	6.8	1.1	1.4	1.4	1.1	3.2	—	4.6	58.2‡
6	2.1	5.2	1.8	0.7	3.2	5.7	5.0	5.4	2.9	3.9	3.2	7.5	2.1	2.1	3.8	5.5	1.1	1.4	0.4	1.1	8.2	64.6‡	9.6	—
7	5.5	4.6	3.2	0.0	11.8	4.6	9.6	6.4	3.9	4.3	4.3	1.4	3.9	4.3	3.8	1.6	2.5	0.7	0.4	0.4	43.2	—	50.7	—
Don't know	10.9	13.9	11.0	8.6	26.1	20.7	14.3	19.6	11.4	12.1	13.5	15.8	12.1	12.1	14.5	11.1	11.8	10.4	15.7	7.2	13.6	15.0	10.0	17.5
No information	1.1	3.9	0.0	1.1	1.1	5.0	0.4	6.1 / 15.4†	0.4	6.4	0.4	1.4	0.4	4.6	0.4	3.0	0.0	1.8	0.4	5.7	1.1	5.7	1.4	8.6
Average scalar rating	2.57	2.62	1.85	1.60	3.18	2.69	3.10	3.95	2.06	2.05	2.47	2.84	2.19	2.17	2.44	3.08	1.69	1.67	1.40	1.32	3.40	3.67	3.59	3.62

*Sometimes the 'rounding process' has meant that the total is a point or two over 100.0% and sometimes a point or two below 100.0%.
†15.4% of the responses were 'no taste at all'.
‡In the intensive interview, there were only four scale positions (see later).

position 6 somewhat under-endorsed. However, scale position 5 was *also* (slightly) under-endorsed (in the first interview).

3 The overall indication of points (1) and (2) above is that the Semantic Differential scaling process leads to under-use of some of the intermediate scale positions and an over-use of the extreme positions.

4 The number of endorsements of the centre position of the scale was, for this composite of nine scales, much the same in the intensive interview as it was in the first interview.

5 There was no substantial difference in the total number of 'don't know' responses in going from the first to the intensive interview — in spite of the fact that some first interview ratings changed to DKs and vice versa. The increase in the 'no information' category arose out of the intensive interviewers occasionally failing to get through all the scales assigned to them for intensive checking.

The total picture presented by Figure 5.9 and Table 5.17 is consistent with respondents giving more attention to certain of the intermediate parts of the scale when taken through it more slowly and more carefully in the intensive interview. Put another way, the results are consistent with an over-use of the end positions in the first interview.

So much, then, for a comparison based upon a composite of nine bipolar scales. This comparison has been useful in providing a broad indication of the nature and the extent of error involved in the first interview. However, it leaves us needing answers to the following important questions.

1 Do these results apply separately to each of the nine scales on which the composite was based? And what about scales 4, 11 and 12? If not, how much variability is there in going from one to another scale?

2 Does the picture presented by Figure 5.9 apply for each of the different population subgroups in which the research practitioner is likely to be interested?

Over and above these matters, we do of course still have to consider the very important question of the degree to which the first interview findings lead to the ranking of brands on any one scale *in the same order* as do the intensive interview findings. After all, it is mainly for the *ranking* of brands that the market research practitioner uses the Semantic Differential scaling system. This question is dealt with on pages 248—53 of this report.

Accuracy of scale distributions and means: scale by scale (12 in all)

Rating distributions

The results for all 12 scales are presented in detail in Tables 5A.1–5A.12 in the Appendix and are summarised in Table 5.18. Generally speaking, the result based on the nine scales taken in combination (Table 5.16) provides a fair indication of the kind of thing that happened with the individual scales, though there are a few noteworthy exceptions, as shown in Table 5.18. Thus for scale 3 ('harmless for children/harmful for children'), the first position in the scale was given virtually the same proportion of endorsements in the first and the intensive interviews. For scale 10 ('easy to get/hard to get'), the position 1 ratings of the intensive interview somewhat exceeded the position 1 ratings of the first interview. Any explanation as to why these scales should be exceptions must be in the nature of speculation. However at that level, it seems worth considering that a particular scale may be such as to *invite* a search for an alternative position to the extreme one, as when the latter raises problems of interpretation or of ready acceptability.

Means

Many research practitioners will be more interested in weighted *averages* computed from the distributions than in the distributions themselves. This is simply because they want in the end to have simple indices of how any one brand compares with the others. The question which therefore arises is whether the differences in distribution, which showed up in the Appendix Tables 5A.1–5A.12 and in Table 5.18, produce any differences in weighted averages. In Table 5.19 these averages are set out for each scale. In computing these averages, scale points 1 to 7 were given weights of one to seven respectively (so that the lower the average, the more positive is the sample response). While six pairs of averages are closely similar, some of the other pairs are not,* and quite conceivably these discrepancies could lead to misguided decision-making when the latter is based upon the first interview results. The situation is made the more complex by the fact that there

---

*The biggest difference was for scale 4 — where a large number of respondents reported, in the intensive interview, that the brand had 'no taste at all' — having tended to rate it in the first interview as 'pleasant'. Another large change concerned the scale 'harmless for children/harmful for children'. The change seems to have been due in part to the clearing up, in the intensive interview, of a respondent confusion to the effect that it was the *adult* dose that was being considered.

Table 5.19
Comparing weighted averages in the first and the intensive interviews

Number and nature of the scale	Weighted averages		Difference (=(a) − (b))
	First interview (a)	Intensive interview (b)	
1 Quick acting/slow acting	2.57	2.62	−0.05
2 Safe/dangerous	1.85	1.60	+0.25
3 Harmless for children/harmful for children	3.18	2.69	+0.49
4 Pleasant taste/unpleasant taste	3.10	3.95	−0.85
5 Easy to swallow/hard to swallow	2.06	2.05	+0.01
6 Cheap/expensive	2.47	2.84	−0.37
7 Effective/ineffective	2.19	2.17	+0.02
8 Small tablet/large tablet	2.44	3.10	−0.66
9 Well packaged/poorly packaged	1.69	1.67	+0.02
10 Easy to get/hard to get	1.40	1.32	+0.08
11 Habit forming/not habit forming	3.40	3.67	−0.27
12 Unpleasant side effects/no unpleasant side effects	3.59	3.62	−0.03

is no regular relationship between the averages for the two interviews: sometimes the intensive figure is greater than that from the first interview and sometimes it is less. It can be a *great deal* less or a *great deal* more.

We do not yet know just how this sort of 'error' in the first interview results will distort the comparison of one brand with another, because in the results presented so far the various brands have been grouped together. To this comparison we will be coming in Part III. Irrespective of this, however, the findings so far presented do seem to constitute a case for wariness in using the Semantic Differential system.

The 'accuracy' of sample means in different population subgroups

First and intensive averages (nine bipolar scales combined) were calculated for each of the subgroups shown in Table 5.20. This table indicates that all the subgroup averages erred on the favourable side. It also indicates that the subgroups more involved in first interview error were (in order of error level): housewives; those aged over 51 years; the less skilled. The position is, however, more one of similarity than one of difference.

Table 5.20
Comparing first and intensive averages in various subgroups
(Nine scales combined)

Characteristics of respondents	Average of ratings		
	First interview (a)	Intensive interview (b)	Difference (a–b)
Age of leaving school			
14 or less	2.14	2.26	−0.12
15 or more	2.33	2.39	−0.06
Social class			
A–C$_2$	2.31	2.39	−0.08
D, E	2.11	2.22	−0.11
Product usage			
R* uses/d it	2.12	2.23	−0.11
R's family (but not R) uses/d it	2.46	2.53	−0.07
Neither R nor family uses/d it	2.42	2.46	−0.04
Number in household			
1–2	2.14	2.24	−0.10
3 or more	2.27	2.37	−0.10
Occupational status			
Housewife	2.15	2.35	−0.20
Others	2.26	2.30	−0.04
Occupational level			
Skilled and upwards	2.31	2.36	−0.05
Moderately skilled and down	2.14	2.27	−0.13
Sex			
Male	2.18	2.25	−0.07
Female	2.27	2.38	−0.11
Age			
21–50 years	2.30	2.36	−0.06
51 and over	2.10	2.24	−0.14

*R = respondent.

FINDINGS: PART III

THE VALIDITY OF SEMANTIC SCALES
AS BASES FOR COMPARING BRANDS

NATURE OF THE ISSUE

So far we have examined respondent error both at the level of individual ratings and at the level of distributions of broad averages based on
those ratings. This examination has provided evidence of error at each
level, some of it substantial, and such findings call for wariness on the
part of the research practitioner who plans to use the Semantic Differential scaling technique in market research. However, it may be

argued that what matters to the practitioner is not individual error or distribution error or even error in averages. What matters to him is the *comparison*, in terms of scalar averages, of the different brands being rated through the Semantic Differential questionnaire. What this practitioner tends to do with the results is to compare the different brands in terms of the weighted averages of their ratings. Such comparisons would be made separately for each of the 12 dimensions or scales, and in each case the basis of the comparison would be the weighted average of ratings with respect to the dimension and brand concerned. For scale 1, the rank order of the five brands would in fact be as follows:

Table 5.21
Rank order of the five brands

Brand	Weighted average of ratings	Rank order of averages
A	2.08	1
C	2.46	2
D	2.48	3
E	2.78	4
B	3.04	5

If the difference between Brands B and E proved to be statistically significant at some acceptable level, then the research practitioner would ordinarily feel safe in concluding that E did in fact have a higher rating level for 'speed of action' than did Brand B.

However, what really matters is whether such findings would be supported by a comparison of the intensively derived means. Part III of Findings presents an analysis of the results in these terms.

DETERMINING THE ACCURACY OF THE RANK ORDERS OF THE DIFFERENT BRANDS FOR EACH OF THE 12 RATING SCALES

The check proposed through Part III involved, first of all, the calculation for each of the 60 rating scales of two averages — the average or mean of respondent ratings based on the ordinary survey interview and the mean based on the intensive interview. In calculating the means, the weights one to seven were given to the Semantic Differential ratings. The results are shown in Table 5.22. It makes possible a comparison of first interview and intensive interview rank orders for each brand, scale by scale. The intensive rank orders have been interpreted as what

Table 5.22
Indicating the accuracy of the brand comparisons emerging from the survey interview

All 12 rating scales		Rank order of brands				
		1	2	3	4	5
Scale 1	First interview	A/ 2.08	C/ 2.46	D/ 2.48	E/ 2.78	B/ 3.04
	Intensive interview	A/ 2.17	D/ 2.37	C/ 2.43	E/ 2.83	B/ 3.05
Scale 2	First interview	C/ 1.44	A/ 1.72	E/ 1.85	D/ 2.05	B/ 2.17
	Intensive interview	A/ 1.34	C/ 1.55	E/ 1.60	D/ 1.76	B/ 1.77
Scale 3	First interview	C/ 2.85	E/ 2.94	B/ 2.95	D/ 3.39	A/ 3.84
	Intensive interview	E/ 2.14	C/ 2.23	B/ 2.40	D/ 3.13	A/ 3.74
Scale 4	First interview	D/ 2.33	C/ 2.62	A/ 3.34	E/ 3.37	B/ 3.65
	Intensive interview	D/ 2.95	C/ 3.23	B/ 4.22	E/ 4.23	A/ 4.53
Scale 5	First interview	E/ 1.77	B/ 1.91	C/ 1.96	A/ 2.31	D/ 2.38
	Intensive interview	C/ 1.90	B/ 1.94	A/ 1.98	D/ 2.21	E/ 2.23
Scale 6	First interview	B/ 1.62	E/ 1.88	D/ 2.79	C/ 2.98	A/ 3.22
	Intensive interview	E/ 1.93	B/ 1.98	A/ 3.41	D/ 3.43	C/ 3.57
Scale 7	First interview	A/ 1.43	C/ 1.89	D/ 2.13	E/ 2.51	B/ 2.98
	Intensive interview	A/ 1.45	C/ 1.89	D/ 2.00	E/ 2.58	B/ 2.85
Scale 8	First interview	A/ 2.03	D/ 2.35	B/ 2.43	E/ 2.45	C/ 2.84
	Intensive interview	A/ 2.84	B/ 2.81	E/ 2.96	D/ 3.08	C/ 3.84
Scale 9	First interview	A/ 1.32	C/ 1.43	D/ 1.71	E/ 1.80	B/ 2.20
	Intensive interview	A/ 1.44	C/ 1.57	E/ 1.67	D/ 1.71	B/ 1.94
Scale 10	First interview	E/ 1.15	B/ 1.36	A/ 1.38	C/ 1.40	D/ 1.67
	Intensive interview	E/ 1.04	B/ 1.05	A/ 1.44	C/ 1.52	D/ 1.61
Scale 11	First interview	E/ 3.22	C/ 3.33	B/ 3.37	D/ 3.47	A/ 3.63
	Intensive interview	B/ 3.42	E/ 3.66	D/ 3.66	C/ 3.77	A/ 3.84
Scale 12	First interview	E/ 3.45	B/ 3.47	A/ 3.64	D/ 3.73	C/ 3.80
	Intensive interview	E/ 3.52	B/ 3.59	A/ 3.64	D/ 3.70	C/ 3.71

Table 5.23
The accuracy of first interview rank ordering of brands

Extent of difference in rank order	The scales concerned
No difference at all	7, 10, 12
2 differences in rank ordering	1, 2, 3, 4, 9
3 differences in rank ordering	8
4 differences in rank ordering	5, 11
5 differences in rank ordering	6

should have emerged from the first interview had the latter been free of respondent error.

It can be seen from Table 5.23 that whereas the two rank orders are the same for scales 7, 10 and 12, they are different *to at least some degree* for the remaining nine scales. So, at this level, the rank ordering of brands through the Semantic Differential method leaves us with trouble.

Comparing one brand with another

A more detailed and probably more relevant comparison of rank order is in terms of one brand with any one other, scale by scale. Thus the user of research findings of this kind will probably be asking: 'How does Brand A compare with Brand B with respect to "speed of action"?' 'How does Brand C compare with Brand E with respect to "safety"?' And so on. For any one scale there are, in fact, ten such comparisons available through the relative positioning of the five brands — and hence 120 (comparisons) over the whole 12 scales. Table 5.24 shows that for 98 of these comparisons, the superiority (or inferiority) of one brand over another was the same in the first and the intensive interviews, but that for 22 of the comparisons a first interview superiority (or inferiority) of one brand compared with another was *reversed* in the intensive interview.

Table 5.24
The frequency with which the superiority of one scale over another was reversed in the intensive interview

Brands compared	Number of scales (out of 12) for which the first interview relationship of two brands was		For which scales did a reversal of the first interview comparison occur?
	Maintained	Reversed	
	Yes	No	
A : B	11	1	4
A : C	10	2	2, 6
A : D	11	1	6
A : E	10	2	4, 5
B : C	10	2	5, 11
B : D	10	2	8, 11
B : E	8	4	4, 5, 6, 11
C : D	10	2	1, 11
C : E	10	2	3, 5
D : E	8	4	5, 8, 9, 11
All	98	22	—

Assessing the statistical significance of erroneous first interview differences

Of course it is not at all surprising that some reversals should occur. For example, it is hardly surprising that for scale 1, the first interview superiority of D over C should not be maintained in the intensive interview — because the first interview averages for these two brands are virtually the same (2.48 : 2.46). The knowledgeable user of research findings will want a significance test applied to first interview differences before he takes them seriously. The question which we must now face, therefore, is how many of the 22 reversals shown in the above table involve first interview differences of a statistically significant kind. An analysis of this type is given in Table 5.25.

Table 5.25
The statistical significance of the differences which were reversed in the intensive interview

Scale number	The first interview comparison which was reversed in the intensive interview		Significance of the first interview difference*
	Brands	Averages	
1	C : D	=	2.46 : 2.48	.47
2	A : C	=	1.72 : 1.44	.10
3	C : E	=	2.85 : 2.94	.43
4	A : B	=	3.34 : 3.65	.24
4	A : E	=	3.34 : 3.37	.47
4	B : E	=	3.65 : 3.37	.25
5	A : E	=	2.31 : 1.77	.04
5	B : C	=	1.91 : 1.96	.44
5	B : E	=	1.91 : 1.77	.33
5	C : E	=	1.96 : 1.77	.30
5	D : E	=	2.38 : 1.77	.05
6	A : C	=	3.22 : 2.98	.27
6	A : D	=	3.22 : 2.79	.14
6	B : E	=	1.62 : 1.88	.17
8	B : D	=	2.43 : 2.35	.37
8	D : E	=	2.35 : 2.45	.34
9	D : E	=	1.71 : 1.80	.38
11	B : C	=	3.37 : 3.33	.43
11	B : D	=	3.37 : 3.47	.33
11	B : E	=	3.37 : 3.22	.25
11	C : D	=	3.33 : 3.47	.29
11	D : E	=	3.47 : 3.22	.13

*Three test, one tail.

In fact, only two of the 22 reversals involved first interview differences that were statistically significant at the 0.05 level — and none at the 0.01 level. In other words, it appears that when we work at the level of means, the kinds of response error that enter so markedly into individual assessments are not sufficient to upset the meaningfulness of any highly significant *differences* derived through the ordinary market research interview. This is not the same as saying that brand averages derived through the ordinary market research interview are correct. Indeed, many of them were markedly incorrect. All that is being said is that *in spite of all the response error involved at the individual level*, a highly significant advantage of the weighted means of one brand over another (as indicated by the Semantic Differential technique when administered by ordinary market research interviewers) may be taken seriously provided that advantage is statistically significant at the 0.01 level.

Since a very common use of the findings from Semantic Differential scaling operations is to compare weighted means for competing brands, the present finding seems to be a very important one. At the same time, it would be wise to replicate the enquiry reported here in other product or subject matters.

SUMMARY

AIMS OF THE INVESTIGATION

The study had four aims.

1   To determine the ways in which respondents understood the basic instructions, as commonly formulated, for using the Semantic Differential scaling system.

2   To determine to what extent the ratings of individuals on Semantic Differential scales properly reflected their true opinions, and the reasons for such inaccuracies as occurred.

3   To determine the accuracy of response distributions and means based upon the Semantic Differential scaling system.

4   To determine the effects of errors by individuals upon the *comparison* of brands in terms of rating means.

METHODS OF ENQUIRY

In this study, a battery of 12 Semantic Differential rating scales was used to assess reactions to each of five different brands of headache remedies (making 60 scales in all). These were delivered by ordinary market research interviewers to a sample of London adults. For a systematically derived proportion of these interviews (280) there followed immediately an intensive interview. The intensive interview was conducted by investigators especially trained for this purpose and it was designed to find out how the respondent interpreted the instructions of the first interviewer and to get re-ratings on 14 to 18 of the 60 scales used in the first interview. The methods employed in getting these re-ratings were intensive in character and were designed to eliminate as much as possible the different sources of error to which the first interview ratings may possibly have been subject (see pages 209—13 for references to such possible sources of error). In this particular sense the re-ratings were meant to constitute a test of the accuracy of the corresponding first interview ratings.

The double interview was conducted with 280 adult Londoners and both interviews with each of the respondents were fully tape-recorded. The enquiry was spread over a five-week period, and each week six new market research interviewers were brought into the team to administer the Semantic Differential questionnaire. This rotation of the market research interviewers was intended to introduce into the enquiry a meaningful range and mix of interviewer tendencies, but it also contributed to the special efforts made to prevent the market research interviewers becoming aware of the true purpose of the enquiry and of the purpose of the second interviewer in particular.

At the end of the intensive interview the respondent was confronted with any discrepancies between her first and second ratings and was asked to help the interviewer understand how these had come about. The explanations so derived were then regarded as hypotheses as to possible sources of error in the first interview ratings.

FINDINGS

In spite of appreciable misunderstanding of instructions, appreciable error at the level of individual ratings, the Semantic Differential scaling system tended to provide *brand comparisons* which were substantiated by the intensive or checking interview. Behind this finding lies a considerable amount of 'balancing out of errors'.

At a more specific level, but still in the context of a summary, the findings were as follows.

Concerning respondent understanding of instructions about how to use the scales

1   There was considerable variation, in going from one scale position to another, in the proportion of respondents who correctly understood what the scale positions meant. The first and the last scale positions were *least* subject to misunderstanding and the fifth scale position *most* subject to misunderstanding. Taking an average over the seven scale positions, the proportion not grasping the meaning of a scale position was at least 16%.

2   Some respondents had not properly grasped the gradient character of the scale, in that they failed to distinguish between neighbouring positions on the scale.

3   Most respondents appeared to grasp the idea that the two ends of the Semantic Differential scale had *opposites* against them.

Concerning the accuracy of individual ratings

The main check on the accuracy of the Semantic Differential scaling system was based upon 3080 first interview responses (that is, an average of 11 each for the 280 respondents involved in this study). Of these responses, 2546 were scalar ratings and 410 were 'don't know' responses.

1   Of the 2546 first interview ratings, 49% were maintained in the intensive interview and a total of 75% of them were subject to no greater error than one scale position. On the other hand, 5% of them changed in the intensive interview by four to six scale positions and a further 5% became 'don't know'.

2   Of the 2546 first interview ratings, 8% appear to have been entered on the wrong half of the scale.

3   Of the 3080 first interview responses, at least 410 were 'don't know's and of these 40% became specific ratings in the intensive interview.

4   A special check was made on the use of the scalar *centre* point in the first interview: (i) about a quarter of these were maintained in the intensive interview and a total of about half were no more than one scalar point in error; (ii) about one in seven of them should in fact have been entered at one or the other scalar extreme; (iii) about one in ten were really cases of 'don't know'.

5   Of the first interview 'don't know' responses, over half remained

'Don't know' in the intensive interview, 5% converted to centre point ratings and the rest converted to scalar ratings.

Concerning the accuracy of sample distributions and sample averages

1   A comparison of rating distributions in the first and the intensive interviews was made. Any such comparison is likely to be featured by a certain amount of 'balancing out' of individual errors. Nonetheless, substantial differences in distributions occurred. The findings indicated that the Semantic Differential scaling process involves under-use of the intermediate scale points and an over-use of the extreme points. This applies for most, but not all, of the 12 scales.

2   Weighted averages were calculated for each scale. Further 'balancing out of error' occurred, with the result that, for six of the scales, the weighted averages from first and intensive interviews were very similar; for three of the others, the difference remained large.

Concerning the validity of comparison of brands made on the basis of first interview findings

The main use of the Semantic Differential scaling system by the research practitioner is for the *comparison* of brands in terms of specific characteristics (or dimensions). Such comparisons are usually based upon the weighted mean of the distribution of ratings. The present study provided a basis for 120 such comparisons of pairs of brands. For 98 of these, the superiority of one or other of the pairs, as indicated by the first interview, was maintained in the intensive interview. That finding suggests that, for similar uses, the Semantic Differential scaling system tends quite substantially to yield valid brand comparisons. It is noteworthy also that for the remaining 22 brand comparisons (the unsound ones) none of the first interview differences was statistically significant at the 1% level. In other words, a finding that one brand is superior to another in terms of a given dimension may be regarded as sound if that difference between them is statistically significant at the 1% level or better. The 1% significance criterion is a conservative test of the results from the Semantic Differential method when the latter is used comparatively.

RECOMMENDATIONS

1   In its present form (as exemplified in this enquiry) the Semantic Differential scaling system must be limited to *comparative* usage, that is, for comparing the average ratings for one brand with the average ratings for another brand (with respect to a given dimension or attribute). Even for this limited usage, differences between brands should first be challenged to ensure that they are significant at the 1% level or better.

2   In its present form, the Semantic Differential scaling system should not be used to develop respondent ratings of single brands for use in evaluating that brand in its own right. The error level for such purposes is too high. Such ratings tend to involve over-use of the end items of the scale and under-use of the intermediate items.

3   If the Semantic Differential rating system is, nonetheless, to be used for evaluating individual brands in their own right, then steps will have to be taken to modify the Semantic Differential system towards accuracy for that purpose. Those steps should be closely guided by the findings of this enquiry about the nature and the causes of error in the Semantic Differential scaling system. The modification process would have to be progressive in character, being guided at each modification stage by an intensive check on its accuracy level at that stage.

APPENDICES

*see microfiche supplement

258

APPENDIX 5.1

FIRST INTERVIEW QUESTIONNAIRE

HEADACHE REMEDIES SURVEY

(THESE INSTRUCTIONS ARE TO BE DELIVERED WORD FOR WORD, DO NOT DEVIATE. *DO NOT RUSH THROUGH THEM*)

'We are carrying out a survey on headache remedies. I'd like to get your views on some of them. There's a special way of doing this. You put a tick in one of the spaces along this line.' (POINT TO LINE BELOW)

STEP 1   'Let's take . . . *JUST AS AN EXAMPLE.*' (WRITE IN BRAND SHOWN ON FIRST RATING SHEET)

QUICK ACTING |____|____|____|____|____|____|____| SLOW ACTING

STEP 2   'You see at this end of the line we've got the words "QUICK ACTING" (POINT AND PAUSE), and at the other end of the line we've got the opposite, "SLOW ACTING" (POINT AND PAUSE).

STEP 3   'If you think it is *VERY* quick acting, you put a tick in this space (POINT) nearest to the words "QUICK ACTING".
If you think it is *FAIRLY* quick acting, you put a tick in the next space, here (POINT).
And if you think it is only *SLIGHTLY* quick acting, you put your tick in the next one along, here (POINT).

STEP 4   'In just the same way, if you think it is *VERY* slow acting you put your tick in the space nearest the words "SLOW ACTING" (POINT).
If you think it is *FAIRLY* slow acting, you put a tick in the next space, here (POINT).
And if you think it is only *SLIGHTLY* slow acting, you put your tick in the next one along, here (POINT).

STEP 5   (SAY SLOWLY) 'Now if you think it is *EXACTLY HALF-WAY BETWEEN* quick acting and slow acting, you put your tick in this middle space, here (POINT).

STEP 6   'If there's anything at all that's not quite clear, ask me and I'll try and sort it out.'

TURN TO FIRST RATING SHEET AND SHOW RESPONDENT.

STEP 7   'Now here's the brand we've been talking about, and there are some other pairs of words as well. They're all about . . . (NAME BRAND).
So where exactly would you put your tick on this line? (POINT TO TOP LINE. THEN TAKE RESPONDENT THROUGH THE REST).

AT THE END OF FIRST RATING SHEET, TURN TO THE NEXT ONE AND SAY:
'Right, now the same thing but this time for . . . (NAME NEXT BRAND).'

CONTINUE IN THE SAME WAY UNTIL ALL FIVE BRANDS HAVE BEEN RATED.

ASPRO*

QUICK ACTING |___|___|___|___|___|___|___| SLOW ACTING

SAFE |___|___|___|___|___|___|___| DANGEROUS

HARMLESS FOR
CHILDREN |___|___|___|___|___|___|___| HARMFUL FOR
CHILDREN

PLEASANT TASTE |___|___|___|___|___|___|___| NASTY TASTE

EASY TO SWALLOW |___|___|___|___|___|___|___| HARD TO SWALLOW

CHEAP |___|___|___|___|___|___|___| EXPENSIVE

EFFECTIVE |___|___|___|___|___|___|___| INEFFECTIVE

SMALL TABLET |___|___|___|___|___|___|___| LARGE TABLET

WELL-PACKAGED |___|___|___|___|___|___|___| POORLY-PACKAGED

EASY TO GET |___|___|___|___|___|___|___| HARD TO GET

HABIT-FORMING |___|___|___|___|___|___|___| NOT HABIT
FORMING

UNPLEASANT
SIDE EFFECTS |___|___|___|___|___|___|___| NO UNPLEASANT
SIDE EFFECTS

*There was a similar set of rating scales under the page heading ANADIN, another for ASPIRIN, another for DISPRIN, and another for PHENSIC.

Figure 5A.1   Rating Sheet

PERSONAL DETAILS

1   NAME — Mr / Mrs / Miss . . . .
       (ring as necessary)

2   ADDRESS — . . . .

       . . . .

3   SEX — Male / Female (ring as necessary)

4   JOB —

       Ask ALL:
              'Are you in a full-time job?' — YES / NO

       IF YES, ask:
              'Exactly what is your job?' . . . .

       IF NO, find out if housewife / unemployed / retired / student

         If housewife:
              'What is your husband's job?' . . . .

         If student:
              'What is your father's job?' . . . .

         If retired or unemployed:
              'What was your last full-time job?' . . . .

5   AGE — 'What is your age?' . . . .

6   EDUCATION — 'At what age did you finish your full-time education?' . . . .

7   HOUSEHOLD COMPOSITION — 'How many people are there in your household?' . . .
       (Check that respondent *is* including him/herself)

              'How many of them are under the age of 21?' . . . .

         If any
              'What are their ages?' . . . . / . . . . / . . . . / . . . .
              (Check that babies are included)

8   SOCIAL CLASS — AB / C1 / C2 / DE

9   INTERVIEW OBTAINED AT: 1st call / 2nd / 3rd / 4th / 4+ calls

                   INTERVIEWER'S SIGNATURE . . . .

                   DATE . . . .

APPENDIX 5.2

THE INTENSIVE INTERVIEW

Int. Int. . . . . Date . . . . Code No. of Int. . . . . Resp's Name . . . .

INSTRUCTIONS FOR INTENSIVE INTERVIEWERS

The purposes of the interview

The purpose of this *intensive interview* is to find out if the respondent understood and *applied* what the (first) interviewer told her about how to use the scales. More specifically, we want to know:

1   What did the respondent *actually* understand the first interviewer to be telling her to do (see Stage II)?

2   How accurate or otherwise are 14 of the ratings made through the first interviewer (Stage IV)?

3   What use does the respondent make of the centre point of the scale and how does she interpret it in practice?

4   Exactly how does the respondent use the 'don't know' (DK) rating?

STAGE I	The purpose of this Stage is to introduce the respondent to the intensive interview and, above all, to get the respondent co-operating with you.

(a)   *Before you get inside the house*

The first interviewer will tell the respondent that you (the intensive interviewer) are from the University and that you would like to ask a few more questions. She should then thank the respondent and leave you (the intensive interviewer) to get on with your interview.

Tell the respondent that you are from the University and add that you would like to ask a few more questions. If necessary, add then and there that you would like to pay her for the extra time. Ask if you can go inside for the interview. *Don't let the first interviewer stay on while you get this interview started.* This is because you might *have* to tell the respondent just a little about your real purpose and this would alert the first interviewer to what you are really doing and this could well spoil the operation.

(b)   *When you get inside*

Once inside tell the respondent that this university study is meant to improve the way questions are asked. Explain that we want to find out if the questions asked are as clear as they should be. Are they really making sense to people? *You should add, at this point, that you hope the respondent will let you pay for her time.* It may well be necessary for you to do this on the doorstep *as well* (i.e. when you are getting the respondent involved in the continuation of the interview).

Tell the respondent that your job will mean asking her questions about what she thought the first interviewer meant. Tell her that this is the only way we can find out if our way of getting information is any good.

Remind the respondent that you'd like to use the tape-recorder to save writing things down.

Then get into your interview, with the tape-recorder going.

262

STAGE II   The purpose of this Stage is to find out if the respondent grasped
                  the first interviewer's instructions

SAY:

'Now I'd like you to think back to the other interviewer's explanation to you of how to
mark your opinions. She used this line as an example.'
SHOW EXAMPLE LINE.

SAY:

'Do you remember? I'd like to find out what sort of impression you got from what she
said.'

SAY:

(a)   'If someone put their tick *there* (POINT TO SCALE CENTRE) ⌐ ⌐ ⌐ ⌐√⌐ ⌐ ⌐ ⌐
      what would *that* mean?'
      'According to the first interviewer, what would *that* mean?'

      . . . .

(b)   'And if they put it *there* (⌐ ⌐ ⌐ ⌐ ⌐√⌐ ⌐ ⌐) what would it mean?'
      (Point to the space where the √ is shown). 'Anything else?'

      . . . .

(c)   'And if they put it *here* what would it mean?' (⌐ ⌐ ⌐ ⌐ ⌐ ⌐√⌐ ⌐)

      . . . .

(d)   'And here?' (⌐ ⌐ ⌐ ⌐ ⌐ ⌐ ⌐√⌐)

      . . . .

(e)   'And what would it mean if someone put their tick *here*?' (⌐√⌐ ⌐ ⌐ ⌐ ⌐ ⌐ ⌐ ⌐)

      . . . .

(f)   'And *here*?' (⌐ ⌐√⌐ ⌐ ⌐ ⌐ ⌐ ⌐)

      . . . .

(g)   'And here?' (⌐ ⌐ ⌐√⌐ ⌐ ⌐ ⌐ ⌐)

      . . . .

(h)   'What do you think the interviewer wanted you to do if you had no opinion at all
      about a brand *being QUICK ACTING or SLOW ACTING?*'

      . . . .

(i)   'What did the interviewer want you to do if you had no opinion *of any kind* about a
      brand?'

      . . . .

263

(a) 'Where would you put the tick if you thought it was very quick acting?'

┌─┬─┬─┬─┬─┬─┬─┐

(b) 'Where would you put the tick if you thought it was *fairly* quick acting?'

┌─┬─┬─┬─┬─┬─┬─┐

(c) 'Where would you put the tick if you thought it was *only slightly* quick acting?'

┌─┬─┬─┬─┬─┬─┬─┐

(d) 'Where would you put the tick if you thought it was *very slow* acting?'

┌─┬─┬─┬─┬─┬─┬─┐

┌───┬───┬───┬───┬───┬───┬───┐ .LOH

SHOW THE HOT / . . . SCALE. SAY:

'Now look at this line. If you were putting your tick on this line (POINT *ALONG* IT)
and you saw this word *here* (POINT TO THE WORD 'HOT'), what word would you
expect to see *here* (point to the BLANK END of the scale)?'

. . . .
(ENTER REPLY)

STAGE III

> The purpose of this stage is to find out exactly what rating the respondent *should* have given on the first of the 14 test scales (that is, if respondent had fully understood the instructions and had given her rating in the first interview with a lot of care.

1   *Explaining the next stage*

   SAY:

   'In the other interview you put ticks on about 60 different lines . . . (PAUSE). I'd like to go through a few of these with you again.'

2   *Setting the respondent thinking about the relevant brand*

   'First of all I want you to think about (NAME THE ABOVE BRAND). Can you give me, in your own words, any opinions or ideas at all that you yourself have about (NAME THE BRAND)?'

   . . . .

   . . . .

   . . . .

   PROBE, ENCOURAGE TO SAY MORE.
   THEN PROCEED TO 3 OR 4 BELOW, AS NECESSARY.

---

3   IF NO OPINION AT ALL, FIND OUT IF THIS IS BECAUSE RESPONDENT HAS *NEVER USED* THIS BRAND.
   IF THIS IS THE CASE, SAY:

   'Even so, you may have an opinion about it. People sometimes form personal opinions about things even if they don't use them' PAUSE.

   SAY:

   'So, for example, would you have any idea at all about whether (NAME THE BRAND) is QUICK ACTING or SLOW ACTING?' IF NO, SAY:

   'Or about whether (NAME THE BRAND) is in SMALL or LARGE tablets?'

   > *IF YES ON ANY OF THE ABOVE*, PROCEED, AS ON NEXT PAGE, TO THE FIRST TEST SCALE ON WHICH YOU GOT A 'YES'. *OTHERWISE GO TO NEXT BRAND (ON PAGE 8).*

---

4   IF RESPONDENT OFFERED AN OPINION IN 2 ABOVE, SAY:

   'Tell me how you formed your opinions about (NAME THE BRAND)?' PAUSE.
   'Where or how did you get your opinions of (NAME THE BRAND)?'

   . . . .

   . . . .

VERY QUICK ACTING	FAIRLY QUICK ACTING	SLIGHTLY QUICK ACTING	HALF-WAY BETWEEN QUICK AND SLOW ACTING	SLIGHTLY SLOW ACTING	FAIRLY SLOW ACTING	VERY SLOW ACTING

ABSOLUTELY NO IDEA AT ALL ABOUT HOW QUICK OR SLOW ACTING IT IS

---

4   *Getting respondent to re-rate on the first test scale*

'Now I want you to look at these boxes for me. They're all about (NAME THE BRAND). I want you to read out aloud for me what's in each box.'

SEE THAT RESPONDENT READS THE ENTRIES OUT ALOUD — ALL OF THEM. AFTER THIS, SAY:

'So you see that they are all about (NAME THE BRAND). Also, they are all about how QUICK ACTING or how SLOW ACTING it is.'

'Now take about 10 seconds to work out which one of them is true for you personally. Look at them all and then pick the one that is true for you.' IF SHE RUSHES, SAY: 'Take your time and think about it.'

THEN SAY:

'Put this card into the square you have chosen.' (PASS THE BRANDED MARKER CARD)

5   *Finding out if the respondent really meant the card to go where she has just put it*

'Tell me why you put it in that particular square?' PAUSE:

'Could it possibly go in any of the other squares?'

IF SHE IS DOUBTFUL AT ALL, *URGE HER TO THINK HARD AND PUT THE CARD WHERE SHE REALLY THINKS IT SHOULD GO.*

FINALLY, RECORD RESPONDENT'S PLACEMENT OF CARD (√) IN CHOSEN SQUARE.

6   *Getting respondent to say it in her own words*

'Instead of the words in the box you chose, tell me *in your own words* exactly *how* quick acting or *how* slow acting you think (NAME THE BRAND) is.'

. . . .

. . . .

IF THIS IS NOT IN LINE WITH WHAT THE RESPONDENT HAS CHOSEN IN THE BOX SYSTEM, CHALLENGE TO FIND OUT *WHICH* **SHE REALLY MEANS. PURSUE THIS TILL YOU GET A CLARIFICATION.** *IF SHE DECIDES HER EARLIER CHOICE OF BOXES WAS WRONG, PUT A LINE THROUGH THE FIRST TICK (✗) AND PUT A NEW TICK IN THE FINAL CHOICE OF BOX*

AFTER ALL OF STAGE IV **AND ONLY IF DIFFERENT FROM FIRST QUESTIONNAIRE**

1. What was the reason given for error? . . . .

2. Which does Respondent say is correct: 1st interview / 2nd interview / neither.

3. If neither right, (a) What was the *correct* box/rating? . . . .

    (b) Why was this not chosen at first or second interview? . . . .

    . . . .

ABSOLUTELY NO IDEA AT ALL ABOUT HOW SMALL OR LARGE IT IS

VERY SMALL TABLET	FAIRLY SMALL TABLET	SLIGHTLY SMALL TABLET	HALF-WAY BETWEEN SMALL AND LARGE	SLIGHTLY LARGE TABLET	FAIRLY LARGE TABLET	VERY LARGE TABLET

ASPRO

STAGE IV/1	Your purpose is to deal wih each of the other test scales for this brand in a manner similar to that outlined on the previous page

7   *Getting the respondent to re-rate on the second test scale*

NOW DEAL WITH THE SECOND TEST SCALE FOR THIS PARTICULAR BRAND. IF RESPONDENT MADE IT CLEAR IN 1–2 ON PAGE 5 THAT SHE REALLY HAD *NO OPINION OF ANY KIND* ABOUT THAT BRAND, GO ON TO THE NEXT BRAND AS DESCRIBED ON PAGE 8. OTHERWISE, PROCEED AS FOLLOWS.

'Now let's take *this* one. It's also about (NAME THE ABOVE BRAND).'

'Just as before, will you please read through each of the boxes. Read out for me please what's in each of the boxes.' AFTER THIS, SAY:

'So you see they're all about (NAME THE BRAND). Also, they are all about how SMALL or how LARGE the tablet is.'

THEN SAY:

'Now take about 10 seconds to work out *which* one of them is true for you personally. Look at them all and then pick the one that's true *for you*.' IF SHE RUSHES, SAY: 'Take your time and think about it.'

THEN SAY:

'Put this card into the square you have chosen.' PASS THE BRANDED MARKER CARD.

8   *Finding out if the respondent really meant the card to go where she has just put it*

'Tell me why you put it in that particular square?' PAUSE:
'Could it possibly go in any of the other squares?'

IF SHE IS DOUBTFUL AT ALL, *URGE HER TO THINK HARD AND PUT THE CARD WHERE SHE REALLY THINKS IT SHOULD GO.*
FINALLY, RECORD RESPONDENT'S PLACEMENT OF THE CARD (√) IN APPROPRIATE SQUARE.

9   *Getting respondent to say it in her own words*

'Instead of the words in the box you chose, tell me, *in your own words*, exactly how small or *how* large you think (NAME THE BRAND) tablets are.' . . . .

. . . .

268

IF THIS IS NOT IN LINE WITH WHAT THE RESPONDENT HAS CHOSEN IN THE BOX SYSTEM, CHALLENGE TO FIND OUT *WHICH* SHE REALLY MEANS. PURSUE THIS TILL YOU GET A CLARIFICATION. *IF SHE DECIDES THAT HER EARLIER CHOICE OF BOXES WAS WRONG, THEN PUT A LINE THROUGH THE FIRST TICK (⫲), AND PUT A NEW TICK IN THE FINAL CHOICE OF BOX*

AFTER ALL OF STAGE IV AND ONLY IF DIFFERENT FROM FIRST QUESTIONNAIRE

1. What was the reason given for error? . . . .

2. Which does Respondent say is correct: 1st interview / 2nd interview / neither.

3. If neither right, (a) What was the *correct* box/rating? . . . .

    (b) Why was this not chosen at first or second interview? . . . .

    . . . .

STAGE IV/2	Your purpose in this stage is to deal in a closely similar way with the test scales for the *next* brand

1   *Introduction and getting the respondent to think about this particular brand*

SAY:

'Now I want to go over three of the lines for the *next* brand. This brand was (NAME THE BRAND). We'll do this in just the same way as we did the others.'

SAY:

'First of all, tell me exactly what you think of (NAME THE ABOVE BRAND). Tell me all your opinions about it.'

· ·

· ·

PROBE. ENCOURAGE RESPONDENT TO SAY MORE.
THEN PROCEED TO 2 or 3 BELOW AS NECESSARY.

---

2   *IF NO OPINION AT ALL*, FIND OUT IF THIS IS BECAUSE RESPONDENT HAS NEVER USED THIS BRAND. IF THIS IS THE CASE, SAY:

'Even so, you may have an opinion about it. People sometimes form personal opinions about things even if they don't use them.' PAUSE.

SAY:

'So, for example, would you have any idea at all about whether (NAME THE BRAND) is safe or dangerous?'

IF NO, SAY:

'Or about whether (NAME THE BRAND) is cheap or expensive?'

IF NO, SAY:

'Or whether (NAME THE BRAND) is well-packaged or poorly-packaged?'

IF NO, GO ON TO THE NEXT BRAND, ON PAGE 12.

IF *YES* ON *ANY* OF THE ABOVE, PROCEED AS ON NEXT PAGE FOR THE FIRST TEST SCALE ON WHICH YOU GOT A 'YES'.

---

3   *IF RESPONDENT OFFERED AN OPINION IN 2 ABOVE, SAY:*

'Tell me how you formed your opinions about (NAME THE BRAND)?' PAUSE.
'Where or how did you get your opinions of (NAME THE BRAND)?'

· ·

· ·

270

VERY DANGEROUS	FAIRLY DANGEROUS	SLIGHTLY DANGEROUS	HALF-WAY BETWEEN SAFE AND DANGEROUS	SLIGHTLY SAFE	FAIRLY SAFE	VERY SAFE

ABSOLUTELY NO OPINION ABOUT HOW SAFE OR DANGEROUS IT IS

---

2   *Getting the respondent to re-rate on the first test scale*

'Right. Now let's get your opinion on *this* one. It's about (NAME THE BRAND).'
'It's done the same way as the others.' SAY:

'Please read them out carefully, one at a time.' AFTER THIS, SAY:

'Now take 10 seconds to decide which one of these is true for you personally.'
THEN PASS RESPONDENT THE MARKER CARD AND SAY:

'Put this card into the square you have chosen.'

3   *Find out if the respondent really meant the card to go where she has put it*

'Why did you put it in that particular square?' PAUSE.

'Could it possibly go in any of the other squares?'

> IF RESPONDENT IS DOUBTFUL AT ALL, *URGE HER TO THINK HARD AND PUT THE CARD WHERE SHE REALLY THINKS IT SHOULD GO.*
>
> FINALLY, RECORD RESPONDENT'S PLACEMENT OF CARD (√) IN CHOSEN BOX

4   *Getting respondent to say it in her own words*

'Instead of the words in the box you chose, tell me *in your own words* exactly how SAFE or *how* DANGEROUS you think (NAME THE BRAND) is.'

. . . .

. . . .

> IF THIS IS NOT IN LINE WITH WHAT THE RESPONDENT HAS CHOSEN IN THE BOX SYSTEM, CHALLENGE TO FIND OUT WHICH SHE REALLY MEANS. PURSUE THIS TILL YOU GET A CLARIFICATION. *IF RESPONDENT DECIDES THAT HER EARLIER CHOICE OF BOXES WAS WRONG, THEN PUT A LINE THROUGH THE FIRST TICK (⅄) AND PUT A NEW TICK IN THE FINAL CHOICE OF BOX*

1.   What was the reason given for error? . . . .

2.   Which does Respondent say is correct: 1st interview / 2nd interview / neither.

3.   If neither right, (a) What was the *correct* box/rating? . . . .

   (b) Why was this not chosen at first or second interview? . . . .

   . . . .

ABSOLUTELY NO OPINION ABOUT HOW CHEAP OR EXPENSIVE IT IS

VERY EXPENSIVE	FAIRLY EXPENSIVE	SLIGHTLY EXPENSIVE	HALF-WAY BETWEEN CHEAP AND EXPENSIVE	SLIGHTLY CHEAP	FAIRLY CHEAP	VERY CHEAP

ANADIN

---

5   *Getting respondent to re-rate on the second scale for this brand*

'Now let's do this one. It's also about (NAME THE ABOVE BRAND).'
POINT TO THE TEST SCALE FOR CHEAP:EXPENSIVE. SAY:

'Please read them out carefully, one at a time.' THEN SAY:

'Now take about ten seconds to decide which of those is true for *you personally.*'
THEN PASS RESPONDENT THE MARKER CARD AND SAY:

'Put this card into the square you have chosen.'

6   *Finding out if the respondent really meant the card to go where she put it*

'Tell me why you put it into that particular square?' PAUSE:

'Could it possibly go in any of the other squares?'

        IF RESPONDENT IS DOUBTFUL AT ALL, *URGE HER TO THINK HARD AND PUT THE CARD WHERE SHE REALLY THINKS IT SHOULD GO.*

        FINALLY, RECORD RESPONDENT'S PLACEMENT OF CARD (√) IN CHOSEN BOX.

7   *Getting the respondent to say it in her own words*

'Instead of the words in the box you chose, tell me in *your own words*, exactly *how* CHEAP or *how* EXPENSIVE you think (NAME THE BRAND) is.'

. . . .

. . . .

        IF THIS IS NOT IN LINE WITH WHAT THE RESPONDENT HAS CHOSEN IN THE BOX SYSTEM, CHALLENGE TO FIND OUT WHICH SHE REALLY MEANS. PURSUE THIS TILL YOU GET A CLARIFICATION. *IF RESPONDENT DECIDES THAT HER EARLIER CHOICE OF BOXES WAS WRONG, THEN PUT A LINE THROUGH THE FIRST TICK (⨉) AND PUT A NEW TICK IN THE FINAL CHOICE OF BOX*

VERY POORLY PACKAGED	FAIRLY POORLY PACKAGED	SLIGHTLY POORLY PACKAGED	HALF-WAY BETWEEN WELL AND POORLY PACKAGED	SLIGHTLY WELL PACKAGED	FAIRLY WELL PACKAGED	VERY WELL PACKAGED

ANADIN

8 *Getting respondent to re-rate on the second scale for this brand*

'Now let's do this one. It's also about (NAME THE ABOVE BRAND).'
POINT TO THE TEST SCALE FOR WELL PACKAGED:POORLY PACKAGED. SAY:

'Please read them out carefully, one at a time.' THEN SAY:

'Now take about ten seconds to decide which of those is true for *you personally*.'
THEN PASS RESPONDENT THE MARKER CARD AND SAY:

'Put this card into the square you have chosen.'

9 *Finding out if the respondent really meant the card to go where she put it*

'Tell me why you put it into that particular square?' PAUSE:

'Could it possibly go in any of the other squares?'

> IF RESPONDENT IS DOUBTFUL AT ALL, *URGE HER TO THINK HARD AND PUT THE CARD WHERE SHE REALLY THINKS IT SHOULD GO.*

> FINALLY, RECORD RESPONDENT'S PLACEMENT OF CARD (√) IN CHOSEN BOX.

10 *Getting the respondent to say it in her own words*

'Instead of the words in the box you chose, tell me in *your own words*, exactly *how* WELL PACKAGED or *how* POORLY PACKAGED you think (NAME THE BRAND) is.'

. . . .

. . . .

> IF THIS IS NOT IN LINE WITH WHAT THE RESPONDENT HAS CHOSEN IN THE BOX SYSTEM, CHALLENGE TO FIND OUT *WHICH* SHE REALLY MEANS. PURSUE THIS TILL YOU GET A CLARIFICATION. *IF RESPONDENT DECIDES THAT HER EARLIER CHOICE OF BOXES WAS WRONG, THEN PUT A LINE THROUGH THE FIRST TICK (√) AND PUT A NEW TICK IN THE FINAL CHOICE OF BOX*

1. What was the reason given for error? . . . .

2. Which does Respondent say is correct: 1st interview / 2nd interview / neither.

3. If neither right, (a) What was the *correct* box/rating? . . . .

   (b) Why was this not chosen at first or second interview? . . . .

   . . . .

In the questionnaire,

pages 12—15   dealt with ASPIRIN in the same way as ANADIN was dealt with

pages 16—19   dealt with DISPRIN in the same way as ANADIN was dealt with

pages 20—23   dealt with PHENSIC in the same way as ANADIN was dealt with

page 25   dealt with the accuracy of a centre point rating (made in the first interview) — in the same way as did page 24

page 27   dealt with the accuracy of a centre point rating made on a unipolar scale — in the same way as did page 26

ABSOLUTELY NO OPINION

VERY	FAIRLY	SLIGHTLY	HALF-WAY BETWEEN	SLIGHTLY	FAIRLY	VERY

---

1 *Getting the respondent to re-rate on the first scale which has a centre tick in the 1st interview*

PLACE THE APPROPRIATE MARKER SCALE OVER THE BOXES AND WRITE IN THE BRAND NAME BELOW. NAME THE BRAND AND POINT TO THE TEST SCALE. SAY:

'Right. Now let's get your opinion on *this* one. It's about (NAME THE BRAND). It's done the same way as the others.' SAY:

'Please read them out carefully, one at a time.' AFTER THIS, SAY:

'Now take 10 seconds to decide which one of these is true for you personally.'
THEN PASS RESPONDENT THE MARKER CARD AND SAY:

'Put this card into the square you have chosen.'

2 *Find out if the respondent really meant the card to go where she has put it*

'Why did you put it in that particular square?' PAUSE:

'Could it possibly go in any of the other squares?'

IF RESPONDENT IS DOUBTFUL AT ALL, *URGE HER TO THINK HARD AND PUT THE CARD WHERE SHE REALLY THINKS IT SHOULD GO*

FINALLY, RECORD RESPONDENT'S PLACEMENT OF CARD (√) IN CHOSEN BOX AND WRITE IN THE SCALE NAME

3 *Getting respondent to say it in her own words*

'Instead of the words in the box you chose, tell me in your own words, exactly *how* (NAME ONE END OF SCALE) or *how* (NAME OTHER END OF SCALE) you think (NAME THE BRAND) is.'

. . . .

. . . .

IF THIS IS NOT IN LINE WITH WHAT THE RESPONDENT HAS CHOSEN IN THE BOX SYSTEM, CHALLENGE TO FIND OUT WHICH SHE REALLY MEANS. PURSUE THIS TILL YOU GET A CLARIFICATION. *IF RESPONDENT DECIDES THAT HER EARLIER CHOICE OF BOXES WAS WRONG, THEN PUT A LINE THROUGH THE FIRST TICK (✗) AND PUT A NEW TICK IN THE FINAL CHOICE OF BOX*

AFTER ALL OF STAGE IV AND ONLY IF DIFFERENT FROM FIRST QUESTIONNAIRE

1. What was the reason given for error? . . . .

2. Which does Respondent say is correct: 1st interview / 2nd interview / neither.

3. If neither right, (a) What was the *correct* box/rating? . . . .

   (b) Why was this not chosen at first or second interview? . . . .

   . . . .

VERY HABIT FORMING	FAIRLY HABIT FORMING	SLIGHTLY HABIT FORMING	NOT HABIT FORMING

ABSOLUTELY NO OPINION ABOUT IT. BEING HABIT-FORMING OR NOT.

---

1 *Getting the respondent to re-rate on the first/last (indicate which) scale which has a centre tick in the 1st interview*

WRITE IN THE APPROPRIATE BRAND NAME AND POINT TO THE TEST SCALE. SAY:

'Right. Now let's get your opinion on *this* one. It's about (NAME THE BRAND). It's done the same way as the others.' SAY:

'Please read them out carefully, one at a time.' AFTER THIS, SAY:

'Now take 10 seconds to decide which one of these is true for you personally.' THEN PASS RESPONDENT THE MARKER CARD AND SAY:

'Put this card into the square you have chosen.'

2 *Find out if the respondent really meant the card to go where she has put it*

'Why did you put it in that particular square?' PAUSE:

'Could it possibly go in any of the other squares?'

IF RESPONDENT IS DOUBTFUL AT ALL, *URGE HER TO THINK HARD AND PUT THE CARD WHERE SHE REALLY THINKS IT SHOULD GO*

FINALLY, RECORD RESPONDENT'S PLACEMENT OF CARD (√) IN CHOSEN SQUARE.

3 *Getting respondent to say it in her own words*

'Instead of the words in the box you chose, tell me in your own words, exactly how HABIT FORMING or NOT you think (NAME THE BRAND) is.'

. . . .

. . . .

IF THIS IS NOT IN LINE WITH WHAT THE RESPONDENT HAS CHOSEN IN THE BOX SYSTEM, CHALLENGE TO FIND OUT WHICH SHE REALLY MEANS. PURSUE THIS TILL YOU GET A CLARIFICATION. *IF RESPONDENT DECIDES THAT HER EARLIER CHOICE OF BOXES WAS WRONG, THEN PUT A LINE THROUGH THE FIRST TICK (✗) AND PUT A NEW TICK IN THE FINAL CHOICE OF BOX*

See over for Confrontation

LEARN THIS SECTION WORD FOR WORD

The purpose of this stage is to confront the respondent with any differences between her first ratings and her ratings in the intensive interview, to learn the reasons for the difference and to get a final estimate from the respondent as to which of two ratings is correct.

SAY:

'Now I am going to get you to look over what you did in the first interview. I want to put it side by side with what you have just told me.'

TAKE THE PAIRS OF RATINGS ONE AT A TIME. IF NO DIFFERENCE BETWEEN THEM, SAY SO TO THE RESPONDENT.

'These two are the same in both interviews.'

IF A DIFFERENCE OCCURS, NOTE BRAND AND PAGE NUMBER (OF INTENSIVE), AND SAY:

'These two are in different positions. This is what you marked for the first interviewer and this is the one you just marked for me.' PAUSE.

'Can you help me to understand why the two are in different positions?'

PROBE AND DO NOT STOP PROBING TILL YOU GET A CLEAR, MEANINGFUL EXPLANATION.
THEN ENTER REASONS AT FOOT OF APPROPRIATE PAGE.

'Now that you've thought about it, which would you say was correct?' *'This* or this or *neither?'*

CIRCLE CHOSEN ANSWER. IF NEITHER, ASK:

'What would you say is your *correct* answer?'

ENTER IT. SAY:

'Why were they *both* wrong?'

ENTER REPLY AT FOOT OF APPROPRIATE PAGE.

The purpose of this stage is to find out *what* the respondent meant by her DK entries against specific scales (as distinct from a whole page). The check will be based on the first and the last of these entries

LOCATE THE FIRST SCALE MARKED DK. IF YOU HAVE NOT TESTED IT ALREADY, TEST IT NOW AS FOLLOWS. SAY:

'You marked this line as DK. Exactly what did you mean by that?'

PROBE TO FIND OUT.

1. IF SHE REALLY HAD NO IDEA OR NO OPINION WITH REFERENCE TO THAT SCALE

2. IF SHE WAS SAYING DK *SIMPLY* BECAUSE SHE HAD NEVER USED THE BRAND (BUT IN REALITY HAD AN OPINION BASED ON SOMETHING SHE HAD HEARD OR SEEN SOMEWHERE)

. . . .

. . . .

. . . .

NOW DO THE SAME FOR THE RESPONDENT'S *LAST* DK ENTRY (FOR A SINGLE SCALE) UNLESS YOU HAVE DEALT WITH THIS ONE ALREADY.

. . . .

. . . .

. . . .

> The purpose of this stage is to get data about the respondent's experience of the five branded products

PASS RESPONDENT THE FREQUENCY CARD. SAY:

(1)   'Finally, and just to remind me, how often do *you yourself* use (NAME EACH BRAND IN TURN AND ENTER REPLY)?'

ASPIRIN . . . .

DISPRIN . . . .

ASPRO . . . .

ANADIN . . . .

PHENSIC . . . .

(2)   'Do *any other members* of your household, apart from yourself, ever take:—

    (a)   ASPIRIN   —   Yes/No

                If Yes, SHOW CARD AND ASK:

                'How often is it used?' . . . . (ENTER REPLY)

    (b)   DISPRIN   —   Yes/No

                If Yes, SHOW CARD AND ASK:

                'How often is it used?' . . . . (ENTER REPLY)

    (c)   ASPRO   —   Yes/No

                If Yes, SHOW CARD AND ASK:

                'How often is it used?' . . . . (ENTER REPLY)

    (d)   ANADIN   —   Yes/No

                If Yes, SHOW CARD AND ASK:

                'How often is it used?' . . . . (ENTER REPLY)

    (e)   PHENSIC   —   Yes/No

                If Yes, SHOW CARD AND ASK:

                'How often is it used?' . . . . (ENTER REPLY)

NOW CHECK BACK TO THE PERSONAL DETAILS PAGE OF THE FIRST QUESTIONNAIRE TO SEE IF ALL DETAILS HAVE BEEN ADEQUATELY ENTERED. IF NOT GET THE NECESSARY INFORMATION YOURSELF.

6 A note about another major study of accuracy: petrol buying

A STATEMENT BY WILLIAM BELSON BASED UPON
A REPORT BY S.B. QUINN AND W.A. BELSON[43]

ORIGINAL RESEARCH BY

S.B. Quinn, BA
W.A. Belson, BA, PhD

CONTENTS OF CHAPTER

INTRODUCTION TO THE SUMMARY

Originally, the petrol buying report was to have been included in this book. However, the sheer size of the total volume, had this been done, argued against the inclusion of anything more than a summary of it. This summary briefly presents the background and aims of the enquiry, the methods of research used, and the principal findings. Those wanting to examine the full report may do so by contacting William Belson.

BACKGROUND AND AIMS

This enquiry was another in a series of accuracy checking studies by the Survey Research Centre. The series was concerned with detecting error in the results from survey investigations of population behaviour.

All studies in this series were set in that majority situation where there is no available direct criterion of accuracy or truth against which to compare the survey findings. This particular study moves the area or subject of research on to the purchase of petrol.

It must be stressed that this series was in no way designed as a challenge to the use of sample surveys at the quantitative level. The series was undertaken first and foremost as an aid for the design of questions about matters the measurement of which seems fraught with difficulties. If we can somehow assess the *accuracy* of some proposed measuring technique, then we will know if modification of it is necessary. If in the latter case we are able to collect evidence about the *causes* of inaccuracy in a measuring technique, then we are in a strong position to modify that technique towards greater accuracy. *However, both accuracy checking and the detection of reasons for inaccuracy are demanding processes calling for intensive techniques of investigation.*

Against this background the aims of this enquiry were as follows.

1   To determine the degree to which a particular survey procedure provides accurate information about: (a) the amount of petrol purchased in 'the last seven days excluding today', and (b) the amount of petrol purchased in 'the average week'.

2   To identify the different sources of respondent error in going from the interviewer's question to the respondent's reply, with special reference to:

   (a) failings in the respondent's understanding of the key terms in the question asked;

(b) respondent failings in going from the perceived question to the reply given to the interviewer.

METHODS IN BRIEF

The research strategy employed consisted of a specialised form of double interview on the subject of quantities of petrol purchased (a) in the 'last seven days excluding today' and (b) in an 'average week' over the last three months. As a result of discussions with researchers in the petroleum industry and exploratory interviews with petrol buyers, a questioning procedure was devised as a realistic first approximation to a quantity-measuring survey procedure. (This would also provide a realistic basis for studying the factors and processes which enter into the eliciting of a quantity estimate.) This procedure was administered to respondents as in a normal survey interview. The second interview was an intensive and prolonged detective-like procedure principally involving probing and challenging techniques designed to find out: (i) how accurately the quantity questions had been answered; (ii) how the answers to these questions were arrived at, with special reference to sources of error and to those factors that either hindered or facilitated the giving of accurate replies. The same interviewers administered the first and second interviews. All intensive interviewers had a background of university education and were trained specifically for this project by the Survey Research Centre. In all, 199 double interviews were carried out with petrol buyers in the Greater London area.

SUMMARY OF FINDINGS

In this summary, the findings are set out under the two aims of the enquiry.

Aim 1: To determine the degree to which a survey procedure provides accurate information about petrol purchases

(a) Quantity of petrol purchased in the last seven days excluding today

(i) *Amount in gallons*   The first interview claims of 146 of the 199 (73%) respondents were supported by the intensive interview. Of the others, 31 offered under-estimates and 22 offered over-estimates. However, the over- and the under-claims virtually balanced each other out, and the first interview average of 5.99 gallons per person compared with 5.95 gallons from the intensive interview.

(ii) *Brands purchased*   Twenty-five brands were covered by the enquiry. For some of them, the sample average was largely correct (for example, Regent, BP, Conoco, Esso, Shell), but for others it was appreciably wrong (sometimes an over-statement and sometimes an understatement).

(iii) *Grade of petrol purchased*   Lower grades of petrol were over-estimated and higher grades under-estimated.

(iv) *Amount, brand and grade taken together*   Two out of five respondents estimated wrongly in terms of one or more of these elements of their replies.

(b) *Quantity of petrol purchased in the average week over the last three months*

(i) *Amount in gallons*   The first interview produced an appreciable overstatement of quantity — 6.21 gallons per person versus 5.55 gallons through the intensive interview.

(ii) *Classification by heaviness of purchase*   The purpose of the 'purchases in average week' question was to provide a basis for classifying respondents by heaviness of purchase. With a five-group system, 72% of the classifications based upon the first interview data were supported by the intensive interview results. With a three-group system (light, medium, heavy), 85% of the classifications based upon the first interview were supported by the intensive interview. With a two-group system, 90% of the first interview descriptions were so supported.

Aim 2: Concerning sources of respondent error in arriving at a quantity answer

In this study, a considerable amount of work went into identifying the different sources of error in the quantity answers of respondents. (a) The respondent's interpretations of the quantity questions were examined for error. (b) The respondent's first interview thought processes in arriving at an answer were examined to find out if they accommodated the facts of the respondent's actual buying behaviour (as established through the intensive interview); where they did *not* accommodate them, this was regarded as identifying a possible source of error. (c) Also, the respondent was eventually asked to help explain any errors in his first interview replies, and these explanations were regarded as pointing to possible sources of error. The different possible sources of error are detailed in sections 1 and 2 below.

1 Purchases in the last seven days excluding today

The first of the quantity questions dealt with the amount, brand and grade of petrol purchased by the respondent in the last seven days (not counting today).

(a) *Interpretation of terms* The term 'you yourself' was correctly identified by the great majority of respondents (93%), as excluding the purchases of others. However, of the 9% who bought petrol for some other car, about half did not regard this buying as requiring inclusion in the estimate given. The term 'seven days' was misinterpreted to an appreciable degree, with only 29% of respondents basing their seven-day estimates upon all seven days and no more than seven days. Though specifically asked to exclude 'today's' purchases, 5% of respondents included 'today' in calculating buying occasions.

(b) *Other sources of possible error* Apart from misinterpretation of key terms in the question, major sources of respondent error included the following: thinking in terms of what usually happens, with the resultant omission of unusual purchasing behaviour; forgetting specific occasions (especially by heavy buyers); failing to try to give an exact answer; thinking of petrol *used* rather than of petrol bought; poor recall of (and confusion over) where, when, what amount of petrol was bought.

2 Purchases in the 'average week during the last three months'

The second quantity question was 'Taking an average over the last three months or so, how much petrol have you yourself been buying each week?'

(a) *Interpretation of terms* The term 'average' was interpreted in its true mathematical sense (that is, total amount of petrol bought in a given period divided by the number of weeks in that period) by about one in four of the respondents (22%). Other interpretations included: normal, usual, regular, midpoint between high and low extremes, rough estimate based on 'usual' plus any extras. The term 'you yourself' was correctly interpreted by 92%, the principal misinterpretation being the inclusion of the buying of a spouse. The term 'last three months or so' was interpreted as intended by about a quarter of the respondents, with the majority thinking in terms of a longer period, many extending it to over a year. The term 'week' was correctly interpreted by 95% of the respondents.

(b) *Other sources of possible error*   Apart from misinterpretation of key terms, the principal sources of respondent error in formulating answers (about amount bought in the average week) were:

- Discounting non-buying interludes during the basic three months or so (as when ill or away or car being repaired); discounting any deviation from normality or usualness in that period; thinking of some normal three months; discounting any basic changes in habitual petrol buying behaviour during the three month period; excluding *extra* petrol bought for trips or extra trips
- Thinking in terms of a normal week
- Excluding petrol bought for car(s) other than *own* car/through account or credit card; including petrol bought by others
- Just went for some recent week
- Worked from mileage and was wrong
- Answered in terms of petrol used rather than bought
- Basing average on period over or under three months
- Amount given was for a period other than a week
- Went by some *recent* week
- Just over- or under-estimated the amount or the frequency of purchase
- Just forgot
- Didn't try to be exact

3   Thought processes

The examination of the thought processes of respondents in going from question to answer held clues for the question designer. They indicated the different types of mental behaviour to which respondents are prone in the present question and answer situation. The question designer who wants to succeed in getting accurate information should not disregard them. Some he may fruitfully exploit and others he must circumvent. These thought processes are detailed in the full report.

PART II
MODIFYING AN INACCURATE
MEASURE TOWARDS
GREATER ACCURACY

7 The case and methods for modifying inaccurate measures towards greater accuracy, with special reference to the method of Progressive Modification

Once a research procedure has been found to be inaccurate, a reasonable expectation is that one or other of two steps will then be taken. One of them is to throw out the defective method and design a new one. I think a reasonable case for doing this would be evidence that the defective method was so far from accuracy that mere adjustments to its basic procedure would be hopeless. Something quite drastic would have to be done — a total new approach would have to be devised. For example, the partly-aided recall method that was used in the United Kingdom and elsewhere to secure size of audience measurements for television output was so enmeshed in error for certain kinds of programmes that a quite different approach was required. In fact a meter system took over* — though its dependence upon a diary to identify *who* in the household was actually viewing left us with a new source of error. Similarly the use of a single direct question about whether the respondent would buy a specified new product will almost certainly be involved in serious error. Perhaps a multi-variable indicator system (built up through correlational work) may have to be tried instead. Nor, perhaps, should we persevere with direct questioning of respondents about involvement in illegal behaviour of some specified kind.

---

*The meter system has potential for providing accurate information about the percentage of sets tuned to a given station at any one time. However, this leaves open the question of which members of the household are actually viewing.

The use of a hopeless method may indicate an initial poor and unrealistic approach in setting up the defective measure. Perhaps the method was conceived in ignorance of the problems standing in the way of securing the kinds of data sought after. Or perhaps it was only in the course of intensive investigation that some unbeatable problem showed up. However, if the deficiency is serious and appears to be unbeatable, then the sensible course may well be to try a new approach altogether.

The other course of action, following the discovery of error in a survey method, is to *modify* the faulty method towards greater accuracy. The case for adopting this course of action is simply that the cause of the inaccuracy is considered to be amenable to corrective measures. If for example it turns out that error is occurring because the respondent has misunderstood some element in the questioning system, then the obvious thing to do is to try to take steps to achieve accurate understanding by the respondent. If it turns out that a particular visual aid is being misinterpreted (for example, *True Romances* confused with *True Story* or *Radio Times* confused with *TV Times*), then the obvious remedy is to take steps to see that this confusion of the visual aids is remedied. This way, steady progress can be made towards the development of a more effective measuring device.

Each of those two approaches does of course depend upon our finding out if there *is* error and then ferreting out the causes. This takes us back to the intensive interviewing method, which was described and illustrated in Part I.

There is, of course, another sort of reaction to evidence that the measuring system is producing error. It is to decide, without finding out what caused the error, to make a hunch-type judgement about the cause of the trouble and to make a change on the basis of that alone. This sort of behaviour can be at its worst when a committee does the modifying, especially if the members of that committee have vested interests in the results of the measuring procedure. Worse still is a situation where a method is changed on the basis of hunch or vested interest without even there being evidence that it is producing error!

Modification of an error-producing measure is best carried through on the basis of evidence about *what* in particular is going wrong with the research method and then through a process of modification, test of modification, modification, test of modification and so on to some final form. Here I am referring to the rationale of the progressive modification technique.

The method of progressive modification starts with evidence of error in a given measuring procedure. The intensive interviewing method as already described can provide such evidence along with the vital extra information about what sorts of problems are occurring or are helping to cause that error. The next step is to modify the defective technique, in line with good research practice, with a view to overcoming its known defects. This first modification is then tested through the intensive interview method and then modified again in line with the test results. This cyclical procedure is continued until the intensive interview check indicates that the procedure has reached a level of accuracy sufficient for safe decision-making.

This system is obviously one of well-grounded (that is, evidence-based) modification. It is not likely to work in the hands of some person or committee ignorant of the principles of question design or of people who do not care about such principles. However, in the hands of an experienced and diligent question designer, rapid progress towards accuracy can be made.

This procedure is, of course, quite separate from one in which the different elements in a proposed method are developed and tested separately and then put together as a finished technique. I have seen that going on in a major South African enquiry, with unfortunate results. For adequate development, the research technique must be tested as a whole, with all its interactions going on, and it must be modified and re-tested as a whole.

Ordinarily, and in experienced hands, the progressive modification method will need no more than four cycles of progressive modification, though occasionally more are needed, as when there are major problems in the measurement situation.

The details in Chapter 8 illustrate the method in use in the modification of a very demanding measuring technique, where a set of over 90 measurements, all carried within the one survey, had to be made. In this case, there were five different cycles of progressive modification, and a sixth could with advantage have been added.

One of the specially trying features of the progressive modification method is that it has to be carried through at speed, without loss of quality of performance. The point is that if the modification trails on and on for a long period of time, the potential users of the modified technique will lose patience or, in anticipation of long delay, will not agree to the modification of the procedure. A long drawn-out process also adds to the cost of the modification operation and to the danger of the specially trained team of intensive interviewers drifting away between cycles. In fact, in the study reported in Chapter 8, the five cycles of modification were completed in a six to seven week period, with a great deal of night work and weekend work going into the analysis and modification stages between the testing sequences.

Another requirement of the progressive modification tactic is that one must be on guard at all times against sloppiness and short-cutting. Above all the process must be protected against damage by those who are looking for a snap decision or who are hostile to the modification process. In the study reported in Chapter 8, we had the great benefit of a very hard-working and conscientious research team and of a working party that gave the project its full support.*

I have used the progressive modification method on a range of different projects. One of them is presented in Chapter 8. The study concerned was originally published in 1962 but has been out of print for many years.[2] Another project was concerned with the modification of a programme-appreciation diary being used by the Independent Broadcasting Authority. A third involved the modification of a radio diary being used by the Bureau of Broadcasting Measurement in Canada[44] and it is presented in summary form in Chapter 9. In the second and third cases, the modified method went into use just as re-designed. In the case illustrated in Chapter 8, this did not happen — for reasons that do not make for confidence in those then responsible for the technical adequacy of the National Readership Survey. There has been much eulogistic comment on the study but no discernible action.

I have one last — but very important — introductory point to make. I do not think that the demanding process of progressive modification (and, for that matter, of the intensive interview in testing a method) should be contemplated unless one is really sure that the call for it is sincere and likely to lead to modification.

---

*I am not referring to research team or working party in the comment in my next paragraph — rather I refer to those responsible for the adequacy of the NRS survey and its modification towards greater accuracy.

8 Modifying the 1960 National Readership Survey method toward greater accuracy: the method of progressive modification in action

A STATEMENT BY WILLIAM BELSON BASED CLOSELY UPON
PART II OF HIS REPORT 'STUDIES IN READERSHIP', 1962[2]

ORIGINAL RESEARCH BY

W.A. Belson, BA, PhD (Design, direction and participation)
C.M. McNaughton, BA (Team leader; later C. Collis)

WORKING PARTY MEMBERS

W.A. Belson, BA, PhD, London School of Economics and
Political Science
T. Corlett, MA, British Market Research Bureau
A.S.C. Ehrenberg, BSc, Research Services Ltd

ADVISORY COMMITTEE

M. Abrams, DSc, PhD, FIPA, The London Press Exchange Ltd
H. Henry, BSc (Econ), FIPA, McCann Ericksen Advertising Ltd
Professor M.G. Kendall, MA, ScD, London School of Economics
and Political Science
J.A.P. Treasure, BA, PhD, MPA, J. Walter Thompson Co. Ltd

The work reported in Chapter 4, Part I, indicated that an *improved* level of accuracy for monthlies could be achieved through the research procedure being used in the current National Readership Survey, provided that the monthlies were presented first (with weeklies, Sundays and dailies following in that order). At the same time, there was clearly room for further improvement in accuracy and reliability not only for monthlies but for other publications as well. It was to investigate the possibility of achieving such improvements that the present enquiry was conducted. It was envisaged as probably producing a modification of the existing research procedure.

Having said this, let me make it quite clear that a great many research activities which work quite well and are serving very useful purposes are still open to improvement of one sort or another. A technique is rarely so good that it cannot be improved. What is being attempted here is the improvement of a technique which is already capable of working fairly well for many of the publications tested — but not for others.

It was expected that the development of a modified technique might also be made to throw up further information about human processes which ordinarily shape or condition the information obtained, and which, because of this, are likely to have a permanent bearing upon the form and the tactics of questioning procedures as they apply to the sort of readership survey with which this enquiry is concerned.

THE PRINCIPLES GOVERNING THE RESHAPING OF THE SURVEY PROCEDURE USED IN THE NATIONAL READERSHIP SURVEYS (NRS)

The first step towards the required modification of the existing NRS technique must be to make tentative changes based on the detailed findings of the work described in Part I of this chapter. The changed procedure must then be tested to find out if it does what it is intended to do; if not, it must be re-modified and tested again. This process must be continued until the final modification gives accurate results.

The first modification is necessarily a most important one: if it is based upon a realistic appraisal of the difficulties of the interviewing situation, each subsequent modification should represent a refining process; if it is not so based, there is every likelihood that one major change will follow another with something of the character of 'shots in the dark'. Accordingly, I propose to integrate into that first modification every scrap of evidence available from the earlier part of this enquiry. This evidence springs from (i) the quantitative analysis of error and (ii) the study which we made of the interview itself — through tape-recorded evidence, through the respondent's 'explanation' of her errors, and through interviewer statements.

This evidence has already been presented in detail in Part I, and there is no real point in re-presenting it in full here. What *is* necessary, however, is that the changes which it appears to warrant should be enumerated, along with a clear statement of the case for making them. Some of these changes are fairly obvious, while others are not. Thus, a failure to understand what is meant by 'looked at' calls for at least a clear statement of what *is*, in fact, meant by it. On the other hand, although we have learned that the present probing system is subject to breakdown, it is not clear on the available evidence *what* should be substituted for it. It is with respect to the latter type of change that the major hazards of modifying the method are likely to arise.

The detailed character of the various modifications made in the course of developing an accurate procedure are described in appropriate sections after the outline of methods.

THE METHODS AND THE RESULTS OF THE ENQUIRY

A SUMMARY OF METHODS AND RESULTS

This operation was carried out in the London constituencies of Baron's Court and Fulham. This area was chosen because it offered a considerable variety of people in terms of economic level, all within approximately 10 minutes (walking) of an available local office. Just as in the work described in Part I, there were two waves of interviews. Ordinary market research interviewers drawn from a market research agency carried out the first wave of interviews after a period of training with the appropriate method. Either the same day or next day, second interviewers put the same respondents through *intensive* checks on all or part of their testimony to the first interviewer. Thus each respondent went through two interviews with two different people, either on the same day or on two consecutive days. This type of testing procedure was carried out anew for each revision of the interviewing procedure.

A running tally or record was kept day by day of: the differences between the two sets of estimates; the respondent's (and the intensive interviewer's) 'reasons' for such differences; the comments of the interviewers about the procedure they were using. Tape-recordings were made of a sample of the interviews based upon each new revision, and

these tape-recordings were listened to for deviations from instructions.
The first modification was tested for three weeks. After this the interviewing technique was modified in line with the growing body of evidence on the way it worked. This fresh modification then went through the same testing process and there were two more modifications in the course of the next two weeks. A final modification was developed and tested in the course of the next three weeks. After this we were satisfied with the way the method was now working but subjected it to a further and more intensive test.

The team of intensive interviewers and office staff worked on a shift basis (from 9 am to 10 pm) in order to maintain a high level of success in securing second interviews. The daily programme at the local office included periods of retraining for intensive interviewers and late evening discussions by the Survey Research Unit, of the case for further modifications. The team was based in a local office in the heart of the interviewing area.

A DETAILED DESCRIPTION OF METHODS AND RESULTS

The sampling methods

The sample was drawn from the constituencies of Baron's Court (wards: Baron's Court, Lillie, Margravine) and Fulham (ward: Munster), being spread over seven polling districts with a totalled electorate of approximately 26000. In the course of the enquiry, an adult was interviewed in each of 845 homes, 610 of them undergoing a second interview (the intensive one) as well.

Five separate and (approximately) equivalent samples were drawn, one for each of five expected phases of the modifying procedure. Beyond these, the area provided scope for several further samples of an equivalent kind. In order to get this equivalence, the total area was split into a large number of small units (that is, adjoining streets) and each of them was given an economic rating in terms of the percentage of their residents eligible for juror service. With a strict control over this index (of economic level) and over geographic location *within* the total area, random methods were used to sort these small units into five groups. Names were drawn at equal intervals from the electoral registers.

The first stage interviewers secured interviews with 63% of the total sample, and a study of these people in terms of occupational and of educational background, age and sex indicated a satisfactory level of similarity between the five samples in this respect; it was also clear from the analysis that they were not seriously atypical of the general population *in these terms*.

Approximately 72% of the people who went through the first stage interview (that is, one or another modification of the National Readership Survey) were put through the intensive follow-up interview either on the same day or the next day.

The interviewing success rates are given in the Appendix.

The strategy of two-stage interviewing

Just as in Chapter 4, there were two waves of interviewing. In the first wave, the modified NRS technique was administered. In the second wave, intensive interviewers checked on the accuracy of the information gathered in the first wave. The first wave interviewer completed her interview and then (and not before) sought an appointment for the second interviewer to call. The second interviewer came at the appointed time, spent about an hour on the interview, and then returned to a local office to write her report. The first stage interviewers also reported to the local office (with their list of appointments) but were kept away from the second stage interviewers — they had their own rest room.

One in three of the first stage interviews was tape-recorded by an accompanying recordist; practically all the intensive interviewers were tape-recorded by the intensive interviewer herself.

Briefing, instruction and control of the first stage interviewers

The first stage interviewers were deliberately selected as people who had *not* before worked as NRS interviewers. This was because the latter were bound to bring to this operation — the modified procedure — many of the habits which they had developed in the course of delivering the current procedure. It was undesirable from another point of view: regular NRS interviewers might well carry some element of such training back into the current NRS method when they returned to it.

The interviewers selected for the work went through an initial three-day briefing and training process. They were first given a general outline of what they would be doing. This led on to an introduction to the booklet of visual aids/instructions *and* an introduction to the relevant aspects of the psychology of recall and of communication. This was closely linked to the questioning procedure which they were being asked to administer, and it was meant to help them to understand *why* certain things were being asked of them in carrying out this interview. They then interviewed each other in the conference room under supervision. Next day, after a preliminary briefing, they went out to a test area to practise the technique. They were accompanied by a supervisor who also tape-recorded each of them in action. During the afternoon period they returned to the briefing room and their tape-recordings were made the basis of discussion and general comment. The same thing happened next day and after this the interviewers were regarded as ready to take part in the experimental work. The printed instructions which were issued to them are given in Appendix 8.1. The book of visual aids is held by the Institute of Practitioners in Advertising (IPA).

As each modification was made, there were special briefings intended to break down habit-patterns previously built up and also to 'drive in' the various new modifications. When the modifications were of a major kind, the whole experimental procedure was broken off for up to a week, so that the adequate retraining of interviewers could take place.

As the work proceeded there was a deliberate rotation of these first stage interviewers (that is, those administering the various modifications of the NRS method), so that the operation would be exposed to a variety of interviewer-performances. This rotation was also meant to prevent too great a build-up of experimental effects in the individual interviewers. When new interviewers were brought in they were put through the basic briefing/training referred to above, this being done while the existing team continued with its work.

The intensive interviewers, most of whom had worked in the earlier phase of this operation (see Chapter 4, Part I), went through a much longer preparatory briefing and training. This was on the same general pattern as before. The details of what they were doing did, however, vary with the different modifications being tested: thus, in the culminating test of the final modification they used the full intensive interview technique as employed in the earlier validation of the current NRS technique (see Part I). However, for the preceding tests of all five modifications, they used a shortened method in order to extend their check to a large number of respondent claims to readership. Full details of these two different techniques are given in the appropriate sections of this report and in Appendices 8.1 and 8.2.

The intensive interviewers tape-recorded all their interviews, and they were subject to continuous control in the form of: (i) an examination of their tape-recordings and reports; (ii) frequent discussions with the Quality Control Officer concerning the weaknesses brought out in this way; (iii) periodic re-briefing (as a group) under the Quality Control Officer and the Research Director. One additional feature of the local centre was a form of indoctrination for intensive interviewers. All the wall-space in the briefing/report-writing room was hung with large cards reminding the intensive interviewers of the basic rules of their procedure.

- Don't forget that people may answer in terms of the *usual*
- Always use the term LOOKED AT
- LOOKED AT can mean . . . (list follows)
- Don't forget the isolated occasions . . . (list follows)

It was virtually impossible to escape them completely and interviewer comments made it clear that, whilst they felt sometimes like talking about 'Big Brother', the messages went home. Moreover, the cards automatically answered many of the queries (about technical points) raised in them through day-to-day experiences in interviewing.

Keeping the tally of results

Records were kept up-to-date day by day. These included: (i) a comparison of the *results* of the two interviews; (ii) the 'reasons' for error derived from the confrontation phase of the intensive interview; (iii) the statements of the first stage interviewers (that is, those carrying out the modified NRS procedure). These records were the subject of a daily report to the research director.

The point of this close contact with what was happening was that it allowed us to make changes, at short notice, in any part of the readership interview which was obviously producing trouble — rather than let the procedure run on until the next planned modification.

The first modification and the results of testing it

The nature of the changes made

The work reported in Chapter 4 was made the basis of initial changes in the NRS interviewing procedure. These changes were to be tested, and it was expected that they would be subject to further modification before the end of the enquiry. Even so, the principles behind the initial modification are given at some length here because, as principles, they did in fact withstand the testing procedure. Accordingly, a clear statement now of what the changes were, along with the reasons for making them, will properly set the scene for what is to come.

The number of publications to be tested   The current NRS procedure deals with over 90 publications. No reduction in the number of these publications was proposed. An important aspect of the National Readership Survey report is the detail it provides about *overlapping readership*. To split the list (say, into two groups) would seriously limit the range of overlapping figures available. It is obvious, of course, that the large number of publications to be dealt with in the one interview increases the likelihood that the interview will be too long either to hold the respondent's interest or to command his efforts. However, it is equally clear that there are other conditions which contribute to a loss of interest and effort, and that length as such cannot be regarded as inevitably leading to that sort of effect. Accordingly, I would regard a reduction in length as a last resort, to be applied only if other changes were ineffective.

The order of presentation of the four main groups of publications   On that part of the evidence of Chapter 4 (see pages 110 and 156, 157 and Tables 4.4 and 4.32) that deals with the measured effect of rotating the order of presentation of publications, it appears that the best order of presentation is: monthlies, weeklies, Sundays and dailies. The main effect of this re-ordering would be to reduce error for the monthlies, leaving the averages for the other groups relatively unchanged. Table 4.4 gives order effects for *all* four publication groups, while Table 4.33 gives the effects, for the 28 publications actually tested, in going from order DSWM to order MWSD.

The mental and physical counterparts of this change as they apply to monthlies are likely to be as follows:

1   There should be some reduction of the tendency to skip publications as the interview proceeds — for, on the evidence of intensive interviewers and respondents, publication-skipping in its present form appears to be a joint product of fatigue *and* a well-founded expectation that the list of publications represented by the mastheads will include very few publications that the respondent has looked at.

2   The respondent's mind would be focused *at its freshest* on the most difficult part of the recall task, namely recall about monthlies; the nearer to the end we put the monthlies the more likely the respondent is to be fatigued when he gets to them.

Telling the respondent what she is to do   A considerable improvement must be made in the means at present used for communicating to the respondents what is required of them. In the tape-recorded interviews there was evidence of recurrent failure to use and explain key terms and a great deal to suggest that this contributed to erroneous statements by respondents (see pages 141—54 and Table 4.32). The modifications required to meet this difficulty appear to be as follows:

1   There should be an introductory phase in the interview devoted to the administration of simple questions, preferably some of those asked at the *end* of the current NRS interview. The purpose of this

would be to fill that early part of the interview when the respondent's mind is too busy with wondering 'what it's all about' to be able to take in important instructions. These should come only after that short initial phase.

2 Basic instruction must be given in a standardised form, and early steps must be taken to see that they have been understood and to correct any *mis*understandings. This applies particularly to concepts like 'looked at', 'last occasion', 'any copy'. They are frequently *not* understood,* and this is one of the reasons for the *loss* of qualifying reading, the most important case of this being the loss through the 'three-month' question. Further, the basic instruction must be repeated at appropriate intervals. It is entirely divorced from psychological knowledge to expect one or two utterances of a complicated instruction (even if understood at the time) to carry through for over 90 publications. Progressive resurgence of the respondent's original ideas of what was wanted, or his interpretation of key terms, must be expected.

Breaking the procedure at certain points   There should be a pause in the procedure in going from one group of publications to the next. At these points there should be a statement to the effect: 'The next lot come out . . .' (for example, weekly for weekly papers), with reminders of the basic instructions and such additional or changed instructions as are appropriate (see later for these). This measure is intended to meet the objection that respondents, many of whom come quickly to thinking in terms of the qualifying period, are often unaware that a *new* qualifying period has been started. It is important also to give shape or form to the interview, so that the respondent gets some feeling of 'getting somewhere'.

The probing system   The present probing system is a source of overclaiming. As such, it warrants close scrutiny. This scrutiny indicates that it is subject to breakdown.† When it breaks down, it tends to take the form of the respondent answering (or thinking) directly in terms of the qualifying periods (the last four weeks/seven days/yesterday). Sometimes the interviewer offers these directly, but the breakdown can be accelerated by the respondent *learning* to answer or to think in terms of them on the basis of the probing being done by the interviewer. Either way, this breakdown leads to the loss of the special

---

*Statement based upon evidence of intensive interviews, tape-recordings (that is, key terms omitted), explanations of error by respondents. Note also that difficulty in grasping such terms was strongly in evidence in the course of the experimental work reported in this Part (II).
†On the evidence of tape-recordings and of intensive interviews.

challenging function of the probe — a loss of its power to produce effort and thought in the respondent. Moreover, when this happens, there is no prescribed technique or device which the interviewer can fall back on in order to challenge the respondent or to make her think.

In these circumstances, it seems only realistic: (i) to *start out* with what tends to happen anyway, that is, to ask the respondent directly if she looked at publication X 'in the last seven days' or 'yesterday' or 'in the last four weeks' (whichever is appropriate); *and* (ii) to follow this with certain additional devices for challenging the respondent on all 'yes' answers, all 'not sure's and a proportion of 'no's.

In addition to this, the probing system must leave room for a final failure to pin down the respondent to a qualifying or a non-qualifying estimate (that is, there must be a 'not sure' category). Details of the technique actually adopted in the first modification are given in 'Interviewers' instructions' in Appendix 8.2.

The form of the interview   There is a very strong case for changing the present two-phase character of the interview, making it a single-phase system. The phase which would be dropped would be that linked to the 'three-month' question. It would be dropped because on all the evidence it has several serious weaknesses which do harm to the interview as a whole (see later). What would remain would be the system described in the preceding two paragraphs: the interviewer would ask, of publication X, if it was looked at 'in the last seven days' (or whatever the qualifying period for publication X happened to be); she would apply the challenging system in selected cases and would then do the same with the next publication, dealing with the whole 90+ in this way. There would of course be periodic breaks in the process as already described.

Clearly this is an important issue and, in making any tentative decision about it, it is well to look closely at the reasons both for establishing the two-phase system in the first place and for dropping it now. Let me deal first with the case for *dropping it*:

1   First and foremost, the first stage of the current NRS interview takes so long that the second and final phase gets inadequate attention from either the interviewer or the respondent or from both. All too often the respondent is losing interest at this stage, so that the interviewer is practically forced to go too rapidly into the final phase and to get through it quickly. This works against an adequate communication of what is wanted and it can reduce the respondent's effort at that very point in the interview where effort is necessary.

2   Secondly, it is wasteful, in terms both of the respondent's co-

operation and of effort, to get the respondent's attention fixed on a particular publication, to draw her away from it and then to bring her back to it again.

3   The first of the two phases of the current two-phase system has led to a considerable loss of qualifying cases. True, some of the causes of this could be eliminated by improving the system of instructions to the respondent. However, this extra phase constitutes just one more process into which the interviewer must introduce rigour and control.

The reasons put forward in support of the two-phase system at the time it was introduced were several:

1   Phase one (the three-month question) was felt by some to satisfy an element of prestige-seeking by the respondent, thereby rendering the second and final question less open to such effects.

2   Phase one was felt by some to work as a trapping device: people innocently say 'yes' to the first question without realising that every 'yes' lets them in for a further question about the publication concerned. If they knew that was coming, they would, it was argued, learn to say 'no' as a simple means of avoiding further questions about that publication.

Although the evidence collected so far raises some doubts about the efficacy of these two arguments* (that is, *in the present context*), any modification which does away with the first phase of the current NRS method must take these two suggested processes into account as possible threats to accuracy. On the first modification, described in

---

*While it could never be thought of as final, it is true that intensive interviewers watching for prestige effects found only occasional instances of people making incorrect statements about specific publications on the basis of a feeling that they should or should not have looked at that particular publication at some time or other. Moreover, the LSE pilot enquiry, which included an analysis specially devoted to this issue, provided very little in the way of numerical evidence to support this particular notion of prestige seeking. What *was* found, however, both in the LSE pilot study and in the work of the intensive interviewers in the enquiry reported in Chapter 4, was a tendency to get in a few 'yes's here and there.

Many respondents *wanted* to score. Sometimes this was because they felt they would be letting the interviewer down if they said 'no' all the time. Sometimes it was to save face: they would appear ignorant if they had not looked at anything. However, this tendency to say 'yes' did not appear to be linked to specific publications, but simply came out now and then after a run of 'no's.

This type of effect does, of course, seem to work in the opposite direction to the suggested 'escaping' process. Moreover, on this particular process it is worth noticing that intensive interviewers reported that whilst there *were* some people who said 'no . . . no . . . no . . .' to rid themselves of the interviewer as soon as possible, it was far more usual for people to steadfastly lay claim to reading if they had in fact done so *and* knew what was being asked for.

In the final count, however, these are but pointers and for safety in the modification process we must go on regarding 'prestige seeking' and 'escaping' as threats to accuracy which any modified system must take into account.

this section, the proposed safeguards were constituted as follows:

1   Periodic checks and challenges were made with respect to a claim that the respondent had *not* looked at publication X in the qualifying period, the checking and challenging system being that referred to under 'probing system'.

2   The same device was used on *all* 'yes' claims.

Tactic (1) was meant to discourage the use of 'no' as an escape device, and (2) to discourage overclaiming. It was expected that in subsequent testing of this first modification we would learn whether or not further checking and challenging devices were necessary.

The book of visual aids   The present device of using visual aids should, on all the evidence, be retained; but manipulation of the cards must remain entirely in the hands of the interviewer. More specifically, it is proposed that the masthead or logo cards be mounted on rings at the end of the interviewer's board. The interviewer flips each of these cards over to reveal the next publication only as she finishes with the previous one. Projecting beyond the bottom of the cards, also mounted on the rings (and part of the book of mastheads), is a large-lettered statement of the qualifying period with respect to the publication group being asked about (Figure 8.1). The respondent is required to answer 'yes' or 'no'. At the end of each publication group, the new card is flipped over showing the new qualifying period.

The book of visual aids is made the centre-piece of the whole operation, largely in line with the principles set out below.

Controlling both interviewer and respondent   All instructions are written on the backs of the masthead cards so that the interviewer may read them out while the relevant masthead card faces the respondent. Specific instructions can thus be built into the pack of visual aids at planned points or intervals. The same applies for the spaced repetition of important instructions. (For example, 'Remember. Any issue of it counts – old or new, so long as you looked at it in the period shown on the card.') There is also a carded instruction which requires the *respondent* to say what *she* understands by 'looked at'. The interviewer then corrects as necessary.

The case for this sort of control is a very strong one. In the first place, if interviewers are given the chance to forget about delivering an instruction, they are very likely to do so. Second, the instructions needed for a detailed operation of this sort are so numerous and call for such careful placement, that an interviewer could not reasonably be expected to remember how and where to use them simply from her

Figure 8.1   The book of visual aids

standard instructions: such instructions are normally left at home. Third, this system puts the control of the interview as much as possible into the hand of the interviewer, a control which is vital for an operation of this sort.

These, then, are the changes which were made to give us the first modification of the NRS technique. To repeat the point I made at the beginning of this section, the principles behind the first modification are given fully because, as principles, they stood up to the series of tests which were levelled against them. They thus serve as a background to the progressive modification described in this report.

Interviewing techniques used in the study of the adequacy of the first modification of the NRS procedure

The modified procedure   The principles behind the first modification have been described fully in the preceding section. The book of masthead cards is available (though it must be remembered always that this is the first of five such books developed on the way towards an acceptable one). The full text of instructions to interviewers is given in Appendix 8.1. There remain several points of detail which it is essential to present here.

1   Perhaps the central feature of this technique was that we built into the old book of mastheads a detailed verbal procedure. The verbal procedure was an integral part of the exposure process, the interviewer being directly confronted with what she had to say about publication X the moment she showed the respondent the masthead for that publication. She did not have to remember what she had to say at certain points in the interview, or when to issue reminders of certain instructions, or when to probe or challenge a response. Of course, her instructions could not easily be read by the respondent (because the respondent faced the interviewer). Granted that the interviewer was not irritated by this, it allowed for a considerable control over both the interviewer's procedure and the respondent's thought processes (Figure 8.2).

2   All mastheads flipped down and automatically came to rest just over a coloured card, showing the qualifying period for that set of publications. (Only the card was in colour, the mastheads being in black-and-white.) The respondent was asked to say whether or not she had looked at publication X in this period. She selected her answers from 'yes' or 'no' or 'not sure'. What the booklet did *not* include at this stage however, was the detail of the probing or challenging system that followed a specific reply. In this first modification this was given in the duplicated instructions for interviewers and at briefing. Details follow.

For 'yes' responses, the interviewer was to ask the respondent how he could be sure it was, in fact, in the last . . . , and had to go on to ask for details of what the respondent was doing on the last occasion. The interviewer was asked to try to put a date upon any such accompanying behaviour or events; the interviewer was generally to check and challenge the statements of the respondent.

For selected publications, 'no' responses were to be probed by asking the respondent if he could have looked at the publi-

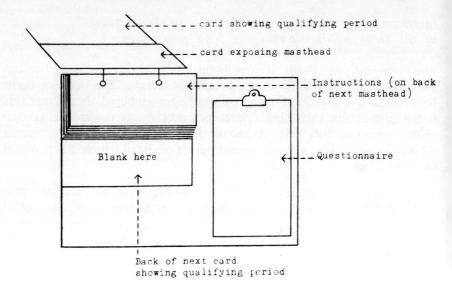

Figure 8.2 The modified system for presenting its visual aids

cation on some isolated occasion in the qualifying period; the interviewer was to prompt with a list of occasions such as: 'in a doctor's waiting room'; 'in the train'. Where the respondent was definite about his 'no', the interviewer was to pass on to the next publication.

I have given this detail about the character and the application of the probing system because as it turned out it was *a point of failure* in the first modification. More will be said about this after the presentation of the results of using this modification.

3 The duplicated instructions gave to the interviewer an overall view of what the survey was about, described the general shape of the interview, harped on the necessity of sticking to instruction, emphasised terms such as 'looked at' and alerted the interviewer to the more common failures in this sort of interview.

4 The interviewer's questionnaire (for recording responses) was 5 in. by 8 in. in size, and was clipped on to the interviewer's board at the side of the book of aids (Figure 8.2).

Any adequate survey technique developed out of this work would have to give an accurate result for *each* of the 91* publications involved in the National Readership Surveys; it is not enough to get an accurate average for broad publication groups. *After all, that can be achieved to a reasonable degree through the simple device of presenting the publications in the order monthlies, weeklies, Sundays and dailies* (using the current NRS technique). The need to study accuracy for *each* publication demands a change in the intensive interviewing technique described in Chapter 4. It has to be much more widely based than that method, that is, deal with more publications. In these circumstances, we concentrated upon rapid but tough treatment of each publication. Details of the procedure are given in the Appendix, but its main features were as follows.

1 Intensive interviewers used a book of mastheads (with certain instructions and with reminders built into it).

2 Intensive interviewers asked of each publication: 'When was the very last time you looked at any copy of . . . ?'

3 On getting a reply, the intensive interviewer asked 'What about since then?' and went through a range of possible occasions to draw out forgotten occasions of more recent occurrence.

4 On getting the respondent to think of the last occasion (and only then) the intensive interviewer set about trying to date that occasion. She tried linking that occasion to the events in the midst of which it happened and tried to date these, cross-checking them wherever possible.

5 When the respondent denied having looked at it at all an alternative technique was used.

6 The intensive interviewer was instructed to make no reference at all to the qualifying time period as such.

Findings: quantitative

A summary   Let me first summarise the outcome of the modification. The principal result was a sharp reduction in the proportion of replies that were underclaims with no overall reduction of overclaims. The upshot of this change was to reverse the NRS dominance of underclaims : overclaims. This happened for each publication group. The next step would have to be a drive to reduce the *over*claims.

---

*The numbers will, of course, vary with time: there were 91+ at the start of the work reported in this chapter.

Overclaiming and underclaiming tendencies   Table 8.1 compares the results using: (i) the current NRS technique employing the presentation order: dailies, Sundays, weeklies, monthlies; and (ii) the first modification of the NRS technique (a modification which employs the presentation order: MWSD). This comparison is necessarily based upon just those 28 publications for which estimates of accuracy are available (see Chapter 4), namely those tested in the study of NRS accuracy. Results for all 91 (but only as they apply to the first modification) are given in the Appendix.

Table 8.1
Comparing the current NRS method
(order 'daily, Sunday, weekly, monthly') and the
first modification with respect to overclaiming and underclaiming
(based on 28 selected publications)*

	Survey estimate Yes				Survey estimate No				Survey estimate ?		
	Int. Yes	Int. No	Int. ?	% Not Yes	Int. Yes	Int. No	Int. ?	% Not No	Int. Yes	Int. No	Int. ?
Monthly (nine)											
NRS method	177	113	14	41.8	312	2,680	71	12.5	0	0	0
1st Modn	220	122	38	42.1	53	1,072	24	6.7	6	24	7
Weekly (five)											
NRS method	350	53	6	14.4	109	535	10	18.2	0	0	0
1st Modn	311	72	15	21.9	19	420	9	6.3	4	9	1
Sunday (seven)											
NRS method	344	65	1	16.1	149	1,129	3	11.9	0	0	0
1st Modn	423	68	5	14.7	16	659	4	2.9	5	6	1
Daily (seven)											
NRS method	305	76	1	20.2	87	1,301	10	6.9	0	0	0
1st Modn	262	71	2	21.8	16	830	5	2.5	3	3	0
All (28)											
NRS method	1,176	307	22	21.9	657	5,645	94	11.7	0	0	0
1st Modn	1,216	333	60	24.4	104	2,981	42	4.7	18	42	9

*For comparability, these figures are based on the same publications (namely, nine monthly, five weekly, seven Sunday and seven daily publications) as were tested in the earlier study of the NRS technique.

It is vital, in considering this table, that we see that the NRS figures are based upon the order: 'daily, Sunday, weekly, monthly', while the first modification figures are based upon the order 'monthly, weekly, Sunday, daily'. This automatically puts the NRS figures for monthlies *out of phase* with the monthly figures with which they were compared in Table 8.1. The hard fact of the matter is that we do not have evidence, of the sort given in Table 8.1, for the NRS presentation-order MWSD (already referred to here as the 'best' for overall accuracy). We can of course estimate *readership* figures for any given position: but the details in Table 8.1 concern overclaiming and under-claiming tendencies, and there is no way of estimating these (for position MWSD) from the data available. Accordingly, it is not possible to present in Table 8.1 what is obviously the most relevant comparison. At the same time, the various facts about rotation effects strongly suggest that the ideal comparison would also support the *limited con-clusions* which I have drawn (see below) from the available material.*

The indications of Table 8.1, both for the comparison actually made in it and for the ideal comparison, appear to be as set out below.

1   The main effect of the first modification appears to be to reduce substantially the percentage of underclaims (that is, 'no' replies that were really 'yes's). This applies for each of the four publication groups. When we consider that underclaiming is the major source of error in the current NRS technique, this result represents a useful step forward.

2   At the same time, the modification did little or nothing to cut down the *overclaiming* which was also a source of error in the current NRS technique.†

Table 8A.2 in Appendix 8.3 gives the overclaiming and the under-claiming tendencies, expressed as averages, for the four main groups of publications, when the averages are based upon the whole 91 publi-cations dealt with in testing the accuracy of the first modification. Its

---

*My reasons for this interpretation of the situation are as follows.
1   The effect on accuracy of changing from DSWM to MWSD is very small or negligible for the daily, Sunday and weekly papers, and calls for no supposition of appreciable changes in the overclaiming and underclaiming tendencies (which do, of course, determine the final estimates of accuracy).
2   The change in accuracy level for the monthlies is also small (9.2% : 10.9%) — small enough to be explained by a very small reduction in the underclaiming tendency or a small increase in the overclaiming tendency (or both).

Having said this, I must add that 'no change' or 'a small increase' in *accuracy level* could pos-sibly follow from an appreciable increase in each tendency or an appreciable reduction in each tendency, provided that in each case the under- and overclaiming tendencies happened to produce a near-balance. *We cannot ignore this as a possibility.* At the same time, on the evi-dence available, it would seem unrealistic to *assume* it. This evidence consists of (a) the relative stability of accuracy levels, using the NRS method, for the 28 papers tested (see Table 8A.7 in Appendix 8.3) — its stability, that is, in going from presentation order DSWM (tested) to MWSD (estimated); (b) the comparative difficulty experienced in shifting either tendency by experimental changes in method; (c) the absence, in the evidence relating to 'causes of error', of anything which both suggests appreciable order-effects with respect to overclaiming/under-claiming *and* is in conformity with the estimated changes in accuracy level.
†The level of overclaiming for monthlies (order MWSD) conceivably may have been somewhat higher than 41.8% (see footnote above). However, even so, the amount of overclaiming for the first modification (42.1%) is unsatisfactory, and this is the main point of conclusion (2) above.

detail is much the same in character as that presented in Table 8.1, for it too reflects a low error rate amongst the negative claims and a very high error rate amongst the positive claims.

The total number of errors made   Another aim of the first modification was to reduce the total number of errors made — whether they balance out or not — thereby increasing the reliability of the research technique. Details of the degree to which this was achieved are given in Table 8A.6 in Appendix 8.3. In this table, a comparison is made of error rates, using the two systems with respect to the 28 publications available for such comparisons.

Here again, the comparison is in terms of the first modification and NRS results using the presentation order DSWM. The error rate using the best (for accuracy) NRS order is not available. However, on the grounds already advanced* in relation to the interpretation of the evidence in Table 8.1, there is a very good case for assuming that the 'best order' error level would equally support the limited conclusions being drawn from Table 8A.6. These follow.

1   For several of the nine monthly publications tested (see Chapter 4), there was some sign of reduction in the error rate as the first modification was used. On average, however, this modification failed to produce the required reduction in the total number of errors made.

2   Turning to the five weeklies tested (see Chapter 4), there is evidence of a reduction in error rate for two of them, but there is no appreciable change for the other three.

3   For both Sunday and daily papers, the evidence suggests an appreciable reduction in error level.

The accuracy of the final readership figures   Tables 8A.4 and 8A.5 in Appendix 8.3 give evidence about the effects of the first modification on the final readership figure. In this case, it is possible to present for comparison not only the NRS figure based upon the DSWM presentation order, but also the estimates for the 'best' (for accuracy) presentation order (MWSD). The indications of these tables are as follows.

1   The joint effect of overclaiming and underclaiming tendencies in the first modification was to inflate the actual readership figure. This applies not only to the averages for each of the four publication groups, but also to the great majority of the 91 publications

*See footnote on previous page.

considered individually (see Tables 8A.4 and 8A.5 in Appendix 8.3).

2   The inflating tendency of the first modification is greater for some publications than for others, and is particularly noticeable with various of the monthly publications for women (Table 8A.5 in Appendix 8.3). The import of this is that these may well call for special attention in the further modifications to come.

3   This inflating tendency contrasts with the under-estimating tendency of the NRS technique (whichever order of presentation is used).

In appraising the revised technique in terms of this evidence, we must of course remember that what has happened is precisely what we predicted *would* happen if the previous imbalance of overclaiming and underclaiming (using the current NRS method) was disturbed by an elimination or an appreciable reduction of just *one* of these two sources of error. *The obvious next move must be to turn the research effort to the elimination or reduction of the second source of error — the tendency to say 'yes' when the answer is 'no'.*

Findings: qualitative

Evidence of a qualitative kind, bearing on the way the modified technique worked, was also available. Some of it was in the form of tape-recordings, some came from the confrontation phase of the interview and some consisted of the remarks of interviewers themselves. Broadly speaking, the technique appeared to be administratively workable: the series of verbal/visual stimuli appeared to bring the respondent under control, instructions appeared to get home, and respondents appeared to be taking the interview seriously. At the same time, there was clear evidence of difficulties of various kinds.

1   The most serious difficulty in the method was the failure of the probing system. Quite often interviewers did not use it, or did so only infrequently. This was partly because they had to refer back to their printed instructions to remind themselves how to use it (and these instructions were, of course, usually left at home). When it *was* used, it frequently led to the conversion of correct 'not sure's and 'no's to 'yes' responses. The intensive interview frequently re-converted these back to 'not sure' or 'no'. To some extent this was because the interviewer used it in a way which stood a good chance of being interpreted as 'Surely you must have looked at it since then . . . surely there was some other occasion when you looked at it'. Ordinarily this sort of suggestion

might not have been so readily accepted, but it was becoming increasingly apparent that the respondents *wanted to score* and would do so if given reasonable encouragement in connection with publications that they saw 'often' or 'now and then'. This and the associated evidence suggested: (a) the dropping of the probe on the 'not sure's and 'no' claims; (b) the development of a simply worded, standardised probe printed on the book of aids itself; (c) the adoption of a more rigorous probe system in dealing with positive claims.

2   The confrontation technique led intensive interviewers to the conclusion that respondents were without a clear 'fix' in their minds about *when* the qualifying period started. Thus, 'Wednesday last' was as much seven days ago as 'Tuesday last': the respondent's desire to score appears to have led him to take advantage of his own vagueness about this borderline period.

3   There was frequent evidence of deviation from instructions by interviewers. When they disliked the wording of the instruction, they altered it and, moreover, felt that this was quite reasonable in spite of lengthy emphasis (both at briefing and afterwards) upon sticking to the printed wording. They particularly disliked repeating instructions and they felt it was unnecessary and unreasonable to ask the respondent to say what *she* thought was meant by 'looking at'. This is particularly important as the intensive interview made it clear that the necessary instructions were still not getting across to the degree required.

4   Interviewers reported that the respondents sometimes did not appear to see the visual aids or the printed statement about the qualifying period.

Various other difficulties arose, some linked with the turning of the pages of the book of aids, some with the wording of the instructions, some with what in fact constituted 'looking at' (the most frequent of these interpretations being a tendency to count 'just seeing the cover'). These and the objections listed above led to the series of alterations described in the next section of this report.

The second modification and the results of testing it

Changes made

Under these and related circumstances, various modifications were made, the chief of them being an increase in the pressure exerted against spurious 'yes' claims, with the aim of reducing this sort of error and with the additional aim of reducing the incidence of error of any kind.

1 The probing system was changed so that it took the form of instructions to the interviewer to say specific words in given situations:

(a) 'If 'yes', say:

(i) 'What makes you sure it was *this one* you looked at?' (Enter reply.)

(ii) 'Could you possibly be mixing it up with another one?' (Enter reply.)

If still 'yes', say:

(iii) 'Are you really sure it was since . . . ' (Enter reply.)

(b) 'Not sure' responses were encouraged but not probed, the evidence being that such replies usually represented a nonqualifying event and that probing by an interviewer tended to convert them into 'yes's.

(c) 'No' replies were probed only occasionally (though at stipulated points in the interview), the evidence being that, with the modifications already made, people tended to mean 'no' if they so answered. In these selected 'no' probes, the following questions were used:

(i) (If 'no') 'Would you recognise that one if you saw it?' (Drop the probe if 'no'.)

(ii) (If 'yes' to (i), say) 'How long ago was it that you last looked at a copy of . . . ?' (Recode if this reply indicates qualification.)

2 An attempt was made to give a meaning to the time period in terms of which the respondent had to reply. Thus, in starting with a new group of publications (for example, weeklies) the interviewer told the respondent what day or date it was which marked the start of the period concerned. Thereafter the interviewer referred to this 'marker date' at planned points in the procedure (these references being printed in the book of aids, on the backs of mastheads as illustrated in Figure 8.2):

'Have you looked at . . . in the last seven days? That would be since . . . '.

3 The term 'looked at' was explained more clearly and there were several reminders of its meaning in addition to the existing question about what the respondent thought was meant by 'looked at' (this being retained for the time being in the expec-

tation that some solution would be found to make interviewers ask it).

4 Respondents were reminded quite frequently (through printed statements in the book of aids) that 'just seeing the cover' did not count (in the modification just tested, this had been a frequent cause of an overclaim).

5 Respondents were reminded that the 'looking at' event could have been anywhere and that it could be *any*one's copy at all. Though this went against the policy of discouraging 'yes' claims, it was still necessary to guard against a growth in underclaims through a misunderstanding of the instructions. Such a misunderstanding had in fact been one of the causes of such underclaiming as still occurred.

6 There was no change in the form of the questionnaire itself.

Methods of testing the second modification

The revised technique was administered by market research interviewers after appropriate briefing. As before, these interviews were followed, on the same day, by a second interview — this time conducted by an intensive interviewer. The intensive interview was focused on monthlies only on the grounds that *these* publications were the principal source of error and that a solution for these publications would probably be a partial solution for other groups of publications as well. Later on, the intensive interview would be extended again to the full range of publications.

It was planned to test this modification for a week, provided of course that the daily record of results indicated it was profitable to continue. In the event, it was modified further after a trial of two days, by which time 28 double interviews had been completed.

Findings

The main effect of this change in method was to reduce the proportion of spurious 'yes' claims (the proportion of spurious 'no' claims remaining at the low level established by the first modification). Details are given in Tables 8A.2 and 8A.3 in Appendix 8.3.

This represents a further step in the intended direction — a reduction in the number of spurious 'yes' claims. The effect of this on the readership figure is indicated by Table 8.2 which is based on all 30 monthly publications and is derived from Table 8A.2 in Appendix 8.3: the ratio of the survey and the intensive readership figure is 1.28 as compared with 1.52 using the previous modification.

Table 8.2
Comparing first and second modifications
(with respect to all 30 monthlies)

Survey method	Survey result			Intensive result			Ratio of survey to intensive result
	Yes	No	?	Yes	No	?	
1st Modn	*808	4,315	113	532	4,540	164	1.52
2nd Modn	115	705	20	90	729	21	1.28

*The figure 808 is the total number of tests made with respect to monthly publications. It is an aggregate for all 30 monthly publications tested.

Though this was an improvement, these figures indicated that even greater pressure would have to be exerted against the occurrence of spurious 'yes' replies if the ratio 1.28 was to be reduced to the required level of approximately 1.00.

An analysis of tape-recordings, interviewer testimony and of respondent's 'reasons' for error indicated that some of the interviewers were still deviating from the probing system to an important degree and that both the system itself and various of the instructions were contributing unnecessarily to this deviating tendency. The direction of these deviations is brought out more fully through the following statement of what further modifications were then made and of the reasons for these.

The third modification and the results of testing it

Changes made

The main changes now introduced were: an increase in the pressure against spurious 'yes' responses; a very slight relaxation in such pressure as was being exerted against spurious 'no' responses; an encouragement of the 'not sure' response — on the grounds that 'not sure' tended to mean 'no' (on being tested through intensive methods).

Given in greater detail, these changes were as follows.

1 The probe was applied only to 'yes' responses and it consisted of two questions.

   (i)   Could you possibly be mixing it up with another one?'
      ('yes' or 'no'.)

   (ii) (If 'yes', discontinue and count as '?'; if 'no', ask)
      'When was the very last time you looked at it?'
      (Enter how long ago it was.)

The request for 'how long ago' made a memory effort necessary, an effort which could not, in these circumstances, be easily deflected into a response in terms of the qualifying period — for the *original answer* had been in such terms and now something else was being asked for. The response was recoded if this double probe warranted it.

2   The questionnaire had a space for these replies *to be entered as given*, this being a necessary step against a persistent — one might almost say 'determined' — attempt on the part of the interviewer to avoid probing in certain circumstances.

3   There was a fairly frequent encouragement to the respondent to say 'not sure'.

4   The warning not to mix publications was taken off most of the reminder cards and put into the probe (see above) because the analysis of 'reasons' for error indicated that it was associated primarily with 'yes' responses — also because interviewers felt that its various placements in the book of aids were quite often inappropriate and tended, because of this, to miss it out fairly often.

5   There was somewhat greater emphasis on 'just seeing the cover does not count' because people were still making this the basis of a 'yes' reply.

6   There was more repetition of the fact that what was wanted was what actually happened and *not* just what *usually* happened because response in terms of the usual continued to be a source of overclaiming.

7   There was increased reference to 'we really mean the last four weeks/seven days/yesterday' because people continued to say 'yes' without really thinking of the qualifying period.

8   There was less reference to 'any copy anywhere' because this seemed to be undermining the effort to suppress spurious 'yes' claims.

9   There was a special warning to the respondent when she was being asked about certain publications which were subject to special types of response errors. Thus, for *Vogue*, the respondent was told: 'We don't mean just the pattern book'.

Methods of testing the third modification

This technique was employed for three days, using the same double interview tactics to get a form of validation of the modified survey methods. This process led to 30 double interviews.

Findings

Table 8A.2 in Appendix 8.3 supports the conclusion that this further modification (called the third modification):

1 reduced still further the proportion of 'yes' responses which were wrong: 27% on this method and 37% on the previous method;
2 left the small proportion of spurious 'no' claims much as it was (3.5% on the previous method, and 4.8% on this one).

Table 8.3 below shows the effect of this further change on the accuracy of the readership figure.

Table 8.3
Comparing the first three modifications
(Based on 30 monthlies)

Survey method	Survey result*			Intensive result			Ratio of survey 'yes's to intensive 'yes's
	Yes	No	?	Yes	No	?	
1st Modn	808	4,315	113	532	4,540	164	1.52
2nd Modn	115	705	20	90	729	21	1.28
3rd Modn	102	776	21	102	776	21	1.00

*Monthly publications only (aggregate of 30 publications).

Although the number of cases double-tested on the second modification was small, the above table of results is suggestive of an acceptable degree of accuracy (for groups of publications) in the technique in its present form. Moreover, the combined results of modifications 2 and 3 as shown in Table 8A.5 in Appendix 8.3 suggest that there was now quite a lot of stability in the results being produced for individual publications — that is, with due consideration of the fact that only 58 cases were involved. Accordingly, effort now went into what had been a serious problem throughout the process of developing a new technique. This was the tendency of interviewers to deviate from instructions, a tendency which in the end must have its remedy in a form of words and a procedure which are *acceptable* to the interviewer, which are easy to grasp and which are *hard to alter*. Modifications 4 and 5 were directed to this end.

The fourth modification and the results of testing it

Changes made

The fourth modification was directed to producing a smooth, more acceptable procedure. It entailed the following changes.

1   The probe was modified to include a further question (placed ahead of the other two) namely:

'Did you look inside it?' (yes/no).

This allowed us to drop the repeated instructions 'Remember just seeing the cover does not count', and to focus attention on those few publications to which the respondent said 'yes'.

2   The probe question: 'Could you possibly be mixing it up with another one?' was replaced by: 'Are you absolutely certain it was . . . ?' This was done because confrontation evidence suggested that people were still mixing publications to an appreciable degree. This change in wording allowed us to repeat the name of the publication in the probe.

3   There was somewhat less verbal reference to the qualifying period, the interviewers saying that in their opinion it was given far too often (and in fact dropping it to the frequency which they considered appropriate).

Methods of testing the fourth modification

This technique was delivered as a questioning procedure for a week, in which double interviews were conducted with 53 respondents. As with the second and third modifications, this modification was concentrated on the monthlies, on the grounds that these were the major source of trouble and that a solution for these should work with the others.

Findings

Table 8A.2 in Appendix 8.3 points to about 24% of the 'yes' responses being overclaims, and 6% of the 'no' responses being underclaims. The effect of this was to produce a slight under-estimate in the readership figure (12.5/12.8 = 0.98). (See Table 8A.4 in Appendix 8.2.) More important, however, interviewers reported that they were happier with the method and an analysis of tape-recordings of the reports of the intensive interviewers indicated a workable adherence to instructions. The probe, so important, was now being used fairly systematically. Where it was still failing was in its second question, for there was still an appreciable tendency, by respondents, to confuse publications.

The fifth modification and the results of testing it

The question now was whether to go on trying to reduce the margin of error still affecting the monthly publication group, or to extend the fourth modification to the rest of the publications (63 more of them) to make sure that what worked for the monthlies worked for the Sunday, daily and weekly publications too. With an eye on time limits and resources, the latter course was taken.

Changes made

The following modifications were made with respect to the three additional groups of publications, namely the weekly, Sunday and daily groups.

1   The three-item probe was applied throughout, though there was some modification in wording appropriate to the different publication groups.

2   Just as with the monthlies, publications with similar sounding names were grouped together and a warning issued to respondents about the possibility of confusing them.

3   Before the introduction of each new group (that is, weeklies, Sundays, dailies) there was an instruction designed to *rest* the respondent and to change the old frame of reference to the *new* qualifying period. This went along with establishing *when* the period actually started and what the respondent was doing at the time.

4   There were special warnings just before all publications found on the earlier check to be specially prone to certain kinds of error (for example, *TV Times* and all publications with the word 'Woman' in them).

5   The meaning of 'looked at' was stressed at the beginning of each new section.

Over and above this extension of the general principles (so far developed) to the rest of the publications, one general change was made.

The probe system was built into the booklet itself so that it extended beyond the bottom of the publication to which it referred and was thus squarely in front of the interviewer when she was dealing with that publication. There was a *separate* probe sheet or card for each publication *group*. When, at the end of the monthlies, the probe sheet itself was turned over, the new card carrying the details for the probe on weeklies was exposed (under and below the weeklies). The same applied for the dailies. The instructions for probing were changed in this way to allow for the necessary slight change in the wording in going from one group to the next — the experience of the research team being that one could *not* rely on the interviewers to make this change themselves.

Full details of the fifth modification are given in Appendix 8.4.

Methods of testing the fifth modification

This procedure was administered by ordinary interviewers (after appropriate briefing) for a period of two weeks. As before, the first interview was followed by an intensive interview (also of the more extended kind). The two-week operation produced double interviews with 172 respondents, well distributed in terms of age, sex and occupational level.

Findings: relative accuracy of the fifth modification

The results achieved by this method were compared with those derived from the first modification and also from the current NRS method. The process of comparison is rendered a little unwieldy by two facts. One is that the check on the accuracy of the current NRS method was based on just 28 publications, while the first and fifth modification checks included 63 others as well (that is, 91 in all). The other fact is that only the DSWM presentation order was actually tested, statements about its best order (that is, MWSD) being available through the estimating process described in detail in Table 8A.7 in Appendix 8.3. This fact is important. Its implications have already been referred to in the detailed footnote on page 313. It (and the footnote) will be referred to whenever appropriate in the following statement of the findings.

Overclaiming and underclaiming tendencies in the first and fifth modifications   Tables 8.4 and 8.5 and Tables 8A.2 and 8A.4 in Appendix 8.3 compare the first and the fifth modifications with respect to overclaiming and underclaiming tendencies (Tables 8.4 and 8A.2) and with respect to accuracy levels (Tables 8.5 and 8A.4). They present *averages* for the four main publication groups (dailies, Sundays, weeklies, monthlies), these averages being based upon all 91 publications.

Between them, these tables indicate: (a) that the fifth modification leads to a substantial reduction in the overclaiming tendency which

Table 8.4
Comparing overclaiming and underclaiming tendencies for the first and fifth modifications
(Data based on the presentation order MWSD)

Survey method	Mod. survey: Yes				Mod. survey: No				Mod. survey: ?			No. publications†	No. cases tested
	Int. Yes*	Int. No	Int. ?	% Wrong or ?	Int. Yes	Int. No	Int. ?	% Wrong or ?	Int. Yes	Int. No	Int. ?		
Monthlies				§				§					
1st Modn	399	330	79‡	50.6	115	4,121	63	4.1	18	72	22	30	174
5th Modn	196	82	22	34.7	109	4,617	80	3.9	11	32	11	30	172
Weeklies													
1st Modn	504	228	26	33.5	72	5,976	26	1.6	8	30	6	40	174
5th Modn	401	779	25	20.6	116	6,076	35	2.4	8	16	5	40	172
Sundays													
1st Modn	473	90	7	17.0	21	1,422	11	2.2	5	7	1	12	174
5th Modn	375	35	8	10.3	49	1,549	9	3.6	0	2	1	12	172
Dailies													
1st Modn	318	97	2	23.7	28	1,411	5	2.3	4	6	1	9	174
5th Modn	249	51	2	17.5	32	1,520	3	2.3	0	2	0	9	172
All Pubs.													
1st Modn	1,694	745	114	33.6	236	12,930	105	2.6	35	116	30	91	174
5th Modn	1,221	247	57	19.9	306	13,762	127	3.1	19	52	17	91	172

*Int. Yes = qualified when testing by means of the intensive interview.

†No. Ps. = number of publications in this group and hence used to give the aggregates in this table.

‡399 + 330 + 79 = all 'yes' claims yielded through the 174 respondents on the 30 monthly publications.

§In this survey process, the readership of monthly publications was lower than that for any of the other surveys, *though the intensive check gave the same low figure.* That the overclaiming ratio should have risen in the last modification (it was previously 24%) is thus not surprising, for this is what happens with smaller circulation publications.

Table 8.5
Comparing accuracy levels on the first and the fifth modifications
(Data based upon 91 publications in the presentation order MWSD)

	Survey result			Intensive result			Ratio of survey 'yes's to intensive 'yes's
	Yes	No	?	Yes	No	?	
Monthly							
1st Modn	808	4,315	113	532	4,540	164	1.52
Final Modn	300	4,806	54	316	4,731	113	0.95
Weekly							
1st Modn	758	6,074	44	584	6,234	58	1.30
Final Modn	505	6,227	29	525	6,171	65	0.96
Sunday							
1st Modn	570	1,454	13	499	1,519	19	1.14
Final Modn	418	1,607	3	424	1,586	18	0.99
Daily							
1st Modn	417	1,444	11	350	1,514	8	1.19
Final Modn	302	1,555	2	281	1,573	5	1.07

was characteristic of the first modification; and (b) that the fifth modification produces averages of a fairly high degree of accuracy. Expressed as ratios of the estimated correct average, the fifth modification ratios are: 0.95 (monthlies), 0.96 (weeklies), 0.99 (Sundays), 1.07 (dailies). These compare with first modification ratios of 1.52, 1.30, 1.14, 1.19.

Comparing accuracy levels for the fifth modification and the NRS method Tables 8.6, 8A.3 and 8A.4 allow us to compare the fifth modification (order MWSD) with the current NRS method. In each case the comparison is based upon the 28 publications on which the NRS method was tested.*

Tables 8.6 and 8A.4 in Appendix 8.3 deal with the accuracy of *average* readership figures, the NRS method being tested on the presentation order DSWM but allowing also the calculation of *estimates* for the order MWSD (that is, 'best order' as established in Chapter 4, referred to on page 303 and tabulated in Table 8A.7 of Appendix 8.3.

---

*Nine monthlies: *Reader's Digest, Do It Yourself, True Story, True Romances, Practical Householder, Ideal Home, Good Housekeeping, Woman and Home, Vogue.* Five weeklies: *Radio Times, TV Times, Reveille, Woman's Own, Woman.* Seven Sundays: *News of the World, Sunday Pictorial, The People, Sunday Express, Sunday Dispatch, The Observer, The Sunday Times.* Seven dailies: *Daily Mirror, The Evening News, Daily Express, Daily Sketch, The Daily Telegraph, Daily Herald, The Times.*

Table 8.6
Comparing accuracy levels on the fifth modification
and the NRS technique
(28 publications)

	Survey result			Intensive result			Ratio of survey 'yes's and intensive 'yes's
	Yes	No	?	Yes	No	?	
Monthly							
NRS order							
DSWM	304	3,063	0	489	2,793	85	0.62
NRS *estimated*							
MSWD							0.74
Final modn							
MWSD	171	1,353	27	169	1,328	54	1.01
Weekly							
NRS order							
DSWM	409	654	0	459	588	16	0.89
NRS *estimated*							
MWSD							0.90
Final modn							
MWSD	292	542	12	298	521	27	0.98
Sunday							
NRS order							
DSWM	410	1,281	0	493	1,194	4	0.83
NRS *estimated*							
MWSD							0.85
Final modn							
MWSD	376	805	2	377	794	12	1.00
Daily							
NRS order							
DSWM	382	1,398	0	392	1,377	11	0.98
NRS *estimated*							
MWSD							1.00
Final modn							
MWSD	267	917	0	239	940	5	1.12

These data indicate that the fifth modification gives *averages* which are more accurate with respect to monthlies, weeklies and Sundays: (a) than those derived from the current NRS method when the latter is used in the order DSWM; (b) than the *estimated* averages for the NRS method in its best order of presentation (that is, best for accuracy), namely 'monthlies, weeklies, Sundays, dailies'. The improvement for the monthlies is considerable. For the dailies, the result of using the fifth modification is a small reduction in the accuracy of the average (whether the presentation order in the NRS method be DSWM or MWSD).

Comparing overclaiming and underclaiming tendencies of the fifth modification and the NRS method   Table 8A.3 in Appendix 8.3 compares the overclaiming and underclaiming tendencies of the two techniques when the NRS method is based on the DSWM order. It is clear from Table 8A.3 that the fifth modification offers an appreciable reduction in both these tendencies as they affect the DSWM presentation order of the NRS method.

We do not have direct evidence on the extent of overclaiming and of underclaiming when the MWSD presentation order of the NRS method is used. Nonetheless the combined evidence of this enquiry* including the extent of the effect of rotation upon accuracy levels (see Table 8A.7 in Appendix 8.3) makes it rather unlikely that the presentation order MWSD produces overclaiming or underclaiming tendencies sufficiently different from those for order DSWM to invalidate the conclusion that the fifth modification reduces these two tendencies, whichever order is used in the existing NRS method.

Accuracy of readership figures for individual publications   Table 8A.5 in Appendix 8.3 and Table 8.7 below deal with accuracy levels for individual publications. Table 8A.5 compares the accuracy of the fifth modification with that for the NRS method, orders DSWM (tested) and MWSD (estimated). The comparison indicates that the fifth modification gives more accurate readership figures than does the NRS method with respect to the individual publication in the monthly, weekly, and Sunday categories. It is somewhat less accurate however for the individual dailies. Looking at the fifth modification in its own right we see that the different readership figures in the monthly, weekly and Sunday categories tend to be fairly accurate and that in all four categories they tend to be without consistent bias above or below the true figure.

Table 8.7 gives the readership figures for the 30 monthlies as developed through the fifth modification and based on the combined sample for the fourth and fifth modification (giving us 225 cases). They show a reasonable degree of accuracy.

The number of erroneous estimates   A reasonably accurate readership figure may yet involve a considerable number of errors (by individual respondents) which happen to balance out each other. Table 8A.6 in Appendix 8.3 gives the percentages of all estimates which were in error (that is, irrespective of the degree to which they cancel out each other). It gives these percentages both for the modified technique and for the NRS method in presentation order DSWM. Such percentages are direct indices of the reliability of the method concerned. For the great majority of publications, the modified technique leads to a lower

*See detailed footnote, page 313.

Table 8.7
Showing accuracy levels for 30 monthly publications,*
using the fifth modification, MWSD

	% Yes			% Yes	
	Survey	Int.		Survey	Int.
Reader's Digest	21	22	Homes and Gardens	6	6
Do It Yourself	11	12	Home Maker	2	4
True Story	11	9	Home Beautiful	4	5
True Romance	5	6	Woman and Home	14	13
True Magazine	2	3	Sincerely	†	†
Practical Householder	8	8	Photoplay	7	10
Practical Motorist	7	6	Everywoman	9	9
Car Mechanics	2	2	Woman and Beauty	6	8
Ideal Home	13	12	Modern Woman	5	4
My Home	4	5	Woman's Journal	6	7
Home	4	4	Argosy	4	5
Men Only	4	5	Vogue	21	22
Wide World	4	2	She	8	8
Good Housekeeping	17	15	Vanity Fair	6	7
Housewife	5	8	Honey	2	3

*See Table 8A.5 for details about all 91 publications.
†Less than 1%.

percentage of erroneous estimates. This applies as much to the dailies as to any other group of publications. (It will be remembered that the *accuracy* of the final readership figure for the dailies was *less* on the modified method, so that what is now indicated is a relative failure of overclaims and underclaims to balance out.)

Here, as of the statement about overclaiming and underclaiming tendencies, we cannot develop numerical estimates of the percentage of erroneous estimates arising out of the use of the *NRS method in presentation order MWSD*. However, the same argument applies here as did for that statement,* and it seems reasonable to conclude generally that the modified technique offers a higher degree of reliability for individual publications than does the NRS technique.

Summing up on the quantitative
aspects of the fifth modification

Accuracy level   The fifth modification provides more accurate readership figures than the NRS method in its best order, with respect to the following:

1   the *averages* for the nine monthlies, five weeklies and seven Sunday papers for which a comparison of accuracy was available;

*See the detailed footnote, page 313.

2   the individual publications in the monthly, weekly and Sunday groups.

The accuracy level for dailies — both the *average* figure and the figures for the individual publications — tends to be somewhat less in the fifth modification than in the NRS method in presentation order MWSD.

Overclaiming, underclaiming and reliability   The fifth modification has lower rates of overclaiming and of underclaiming and higher reliability for individual publications than does the NRS method in the presentation order DSWM.

Although we do not have comparable information or estimates for the *best order* of the NRS method, the body of evidence available indicates that here, too, the fifth modification has the higher rate of reliability for the individual publications and that its overclaiming and underclaiming tendencies are smaller.

The fifth modification in its own right   The fifth modification considered in its own right appears to provide reasonably accurate readership figures at the individual level as well as in terms of averages. It is somewhat less accurate for dailies than for the other groups of publications.

Other fifth modification findings:
the probing system

The probe used in this modification consisted of three questions:

(a) 'Did you actually look inside it/*look* at it?'

(b) 'Are you *absolutely* certain it was . . . ?'

(c) 'When was the *very last* time you looked at any copy of . . . ?'

If the reply to (a) was 'yes', question (b) was asked; if the reply to (b) was 'yes', (c) was asked. Thus each of the three questions was a knock-out question in its own right. The process stopped as soon as a 'yes' was not forthcoming.

An analysis was made of the more visible effects of using this probing system — which, it will be remembered, was applied only to the 'yes' replies. Combining the test results for modifications 4 and 5, we get the pattern shown in Table 8.8.

Reclassification on the basis of the probe (as above) almost always withstood the intensive check when this was later applied.

In evaluating the probe in terms of its effectiveness, it is most important to realise that the following table presents only the more

Table 8.8
Probing system

The three questions of the probe	'Yes' became		
	Yes	No	?
On first question (a)	–	11	3
On second question (b)	–	6	5
On third question (c)	2,173	73	11
Total	2,173	90	19

visible effects of using it. The probe was meant, as much as anything else, to drive home three basic rules: that just seeing the cover is not counted; that we really mean the publication named on the visual aid; that the time of the last 'looking at' event *is* important. The subjective evidence available (in the form of confrontation testimony and the post-interview questioning of interviewers) strongly suggested that the probe was driving home the first and the third of these rules and, generally speaking, was tending to make the respondent more responsible in his replies. This point is of course subjective in character, but it is clear that the relatively small yield reported in the above table could not in itself account for the major increase in accuracy which followed the introduction of this particular probe. Where the probe/rule teacher was still breaking down, however, was with respect to the aim embodied in its second question: 'Are you absolutely certain it was . . . ?' This was to make respondents think more about the paper they were supposed to be reporting on. It was working well enough for 'yes' claims (when it was used as a direct reminder or probe), but many of the errors amongst 'no' responses continued to be associated with a confusion of publication in the mind of the respondent. In other words, this part of the three-question probe was not doing the *full* teaching job we expected of it. At the same time, because the technique was now producing a workable balance of over- and underclaims, we left it alone.

Findings: other sources of error   A study of the evidence from the confrontation stage of the enquiry indicated that a major source of error still remaining was what the respondent (and the intensive interviewer) called 'poor memory' or 'vague' or 'mind wanders'. There was also a certain amount of reference, still, to: 'the forgetting of isolated events'; 'the misunderstanding of what was meant by "looked at"'; misreporting by the interviewer; hurried conditions in the interview. The first of these was probably irreducible within the context of a survey interview; with an eye on the balance of errors already achieved, the other sources of trouble were left as being relatively small-scale and as being under control.

A further check on the fifth modification

Methods Finally, it seemed desirable to subject the fifth modification to a further check, *small-scale but rigorous*, to help pick up any serious failure of the validity technique used (namely the semi-intensive interview). This method had, it will be remembered, been used to give us a quick running-check, widely based in character, on the adequacy of changes as we made them.

For this final purpose we re-introduced the intensive technique employed in the earlier check on the current NRS method. Its full detail is to be found in Chapter 4 and in the Instructions to intensive interviewers in the Appendix to that chapter. At this point I must restrict myself to repeating that it principally involves: (a) the use of recent issues of the publications concerned (that is, those to be tested) solely for *familiarisation* purposes; (b) the filling-in of the circumstances surrounding the reading event; (c) the persistent cross-checking of all circumstances linked to the reading event. The intensive interviewer went through a week's re-training before the survey was launched.

The use of this technique inevitably cut down on the number of claims which could be tested in the one intensive interview (not more than four), and this brought us back to a concentration of these tests upon a smaller number of publications; it seemed desirable that these should be the 28 included in the earlier study of the current NRS technique. These were: *Reader's Digest, Do It Yourself, True Story, True Romance, Practical Householder, Ideal Home, Good Housekeeping, Woman and Home, Vogue* (= nine monthly magazines); *Radio Times, TV Times, Woman, Woman's Own, Reveille* (= five weekly publications); *Sunday Pictorial, The Sunday Times, News of the World, Sunday Dispatch, People, The Observer, Sunday Express* (= seven Sunday publications); *Daily Express, Daily Mirror, Daily Sketch, Daily Herald, The Times, The Evening News, The Daily Telegraph* (= seven daily papers).

The sample of people tested was essentially small — 153 in double interviews. The scale of this part of the operation was dictated by the limits of time and resources, but its smallness meant that the results for the *individual* publications included in the test could never be meaningful, and that meaningful comparisons could be made only in terms of aggregates (for example, all dailies, all Sundays, all weeklies, all monthlies). The briefing of interviewers was extended in time and included a considerable number of warnings about the pitfalls which the enquiry had revealed. The survey took place over a two-week period, the second interview being completed with 74% of the people who went through the first interview.

Findings: group averages   This small-scale check tended to confirm the results of the tests already made of the accuracy of the fifth modification. Details are given in Tables 8.9 and 8.10.

1   Overclaiming and underclaiming tendencies are at much the same level on each of the two tests of the final modification (see Table 8.9).

2   The total number of wrong estimates given in response to the modified technique (neglecting whether they are over- or under-claims) is much the same on each test, and this applies separately to each of the four groups of publications (Table 8.9).

3   The accuracy of the final readership figure (that is, after over- and underclaiming have been balanced out) is at the same fairly satisfactory level in each case (see Table 8.10).

Table 8.9
The final modification tested by semi- and full-intensive interviews, showing over- and underclaim ratios
(28 publications)

	Survey estimate: Yes				Survey estimate: No				Survey estimate: ?			%* in error,
Modification tested by	Int. Yes	Int. No	Int. ?	% Wrong or ?	Int. Yes	Int. No	Int. ?	% Wrong or ?	Int. Yes	Int. No	Int. ?	or ?
Monthly (nine)												
Semi-intensive	114	42	15	33.3	49	1,271	33	6.1	6	15	6	10.3
Full-intensive	75	22	3	25.0	30	731	29	7.5	0	0	11	9.3
Weekly (five)												
Semi-intensive	252	31	9	13.7	43	484	15	10.7	3	6	3	12.6
Full-intensive	134	19	0	12.4	29	301	0	8.8	3	14	0	13.0
Sunday (seven)												
Semi-intensive	339	31	6	9.8	38	762	5	5.3	0	1	1	6.8
Full-intensive	208	13	2	6.7	20	437	7	5.8	0	13	0	7.9
Daily (seven)												
Semi-intensive	218	47	2	18.4	21	893	3	2.6	0	0	0	6.2
Full-intensive	140	26	5	18.0	18	511	0	3.4	0	0	0	7.0

*These are the total errors, irrespective of whether or not they balance each other out. (See columns 4 and 8 for percentage of over- and underclaiming.)

The qualitative evidence gathered in the intensive test of the fifth modification closely parallels that gathered in the previous test of it. Here again it indicated that the interviewers found the method workable and that the main groups of 'reasons' given for errors were: (i) poor or vague memory; and (ii) confusion of publications.

Table 8.10

Final modification tested by the semi- and the full-intensive interview, showing relative accuracy levels
(28 publications)

Modification tested by	Survey estimates			Intensive results			% Yes		Survey %* Intensive %
	Yes	No	?	Yes	No	?	Survey	Intensive	
Monthly (nine)									
Semi-intensive	171	1,353	27	169	1,328	54	11.0	10.9	1.01
Full-intensive	100	790	11	105	753	43	11.1	11.7	0.95
Weekly (five)									
Semi-intensive	292	542	12	298	521	27	34.0	34.7	0.98
Full-intensive	153	330	17	166	334	0	30.6	33.2	0.92
Sunday (seven)									
Semi-intensive	376	805	2	377	794	12	31.2	31.3	1.00
Full-intensive	223	464	13	228	463	9	31.9	32.6	0.98
Daily (seven)									
Semi-intensive	267	917	0	239	940	5	22.2	19.9	1.12
Full-intensive	171	529	0	158	537	5	24.4	22.6	1.08

*The testing of 'no' responses, using the full-intensive method, was based upon about as many 'no's as 'yes's. In this table, the 'no's have been weighted so that they contribute in their due proportion to the final result. The actual weight allotted depended upon the average readership figure for the publication concerned in the survey area itself, this being established through the administration of the modified method by the first stage interviewers. Thus, the method used for weighting was just the same as that used in Chapter 4 (see pp. 318, 319).

SEEING THE MODIFICATION PROCESS AS A WHOLE

In the preceding pages, I have described, step by step, the development of a questioning procedure, dealing with each step in detail. This present section is meant to bring it together to allow the reader to see the method and the results as a whole. Reference to summary tables in the Appendix is vital in what follows.

A reminder about the general character of the new method

There is a full description of the technique in the Appendix to the original report and key illustrative material is given in Appendix 8.4. What follows is meant to do no more than set the scene for a summing up at the quantitative level.

1   The technique is specially designed to meet the inadequacies of the respondents' recalling processes and at the same time to increase the likelihood that the interviewer will carry out the instructions necessary for dealing with these inadequacies in the respondent. Each of these two *aims* or *targets* of the designing process is firmly based on detailed experience with the behaviour of respondents and interviewers engaged in the readership survey.

2   Instead of the original two-phase interview, this modified version has only *one* phase. The interviewer asks the respondent if she looked at publication X during the last four weeks/seven days/ yesterday (whichever is appropriate), and probes all 'yes' replies as they come. (She does *not* go back to do this separately.) The probe consists of three questions designed to convert spurious 'yes' replies into 'no' replies. There are various blocks against the occurrence of spurious 'no' replies.

3   Synchronised visual and verbal stimuli of a particular kind are built into a book of aids, *to be used by the interviewer*. It is so constructed as to minimise the likelihood that the interviewer will fail to use it as required. With regard to verbal and physical procedures it is designed to be independent of detailed instructions ordinarily presented in the Interviewer's Manual (and ordinarily left at home). The book of aids is built on to the interviewer's book and the questionnaire itself is clipped beside the book of cards, on to the base board itself. These and other devices reduce the likelihood that the interviewer will do without her book of aids or pass it to the respondent to deal with (see Figure 8.1 on page 310).

TRACING THE EFFECT OF THE MODIFICATION STAGE BY STAGE*

Quantitative evidence   Seen in total, the effect of the series of modifications made was to increase the level of accuracy of readership figures. This was achieved by reducing the incidence: (i) of spurious 'no' replies (that is, underclaims) and (ii) of spurious 'yes' claims (that is, overclaims). Neither was eliminated entirely — or could be, for that matter — but what *was* done was to achieve a fairly good balance of

*See Tables 8A.2–8A.4 in Appendix 8.3.

what still remained of these two sorts of error. In other words, it proved possible to get a reliable balancing-out of the spurious 'yes' claims and spurious 'no' claims which could not be eliminated.

Each of the five modifications which we made took us a step towards this final situation. The *first* modification achieved a substantial reduction in the number of spurious 'no' replies (that is, compared with the current NRS method). However, it produced no such reduction in the number of spurious 'yes' replies (see Table 8.11). The result of this was a final over-estimate of the readership figure.

The next modification (which was focused upon the monthly publications) led to a reduction in the number of spurious 'yes' claims (at the same time maintaining the earlier reduction in spurious 'no' replies), while the third/fourth modifications reduced the number of spurious 'yes' replies still further. At this stage, the proportion of spurious 'no' replies (for monthlies) had fallen from approximately 13% to approximately 8% (see Table 8A.3), while the proportion of spurious 'yes's had fallen from 42% (on the current NRS method) to approximately 21%. The result of this sequence of changes was to produce a fairly complete balancing out of these two sources of error.

The fifth (final) modification extended the changes made for monthlies to all four publication groups. Two tests of this final modification were made, the second more intensive than the first. These produced closely similar results, and each indicated that the fifth modification had produced a workable level of accuracy in all four publication groups. Thus, on the first of the two tests of the fifth modification, the average for monthlies was 0.95 of its estimated true value, while the equivalent figures for weekly, Sunday and daily publications were 0.96, 0.99 and 1.08 (Table 8A.4 in Appendix 8.3, based on all 91 publications). On the second (full interview) check, the results were as given in the same table.

Table 8.11
The effects of the first modification

	Proportion of 'no's which were spurious		Proportion of 'yes's which were spurious	
	Current NRS (DSWM) (%)	First modification (%)	Current NRS (DSWM) (%)	First modification (%)
Monthly	12.5	6.7	41.8	42.1
Weekly	18.2	6.3	14.4	21.9
Sunday	11.9	2.9	16.1	14.7
Daily	6.9	2.5	20.2	21.8

The modification process had also produced an increase in the accuracy and in the reliability of readership figures for *individual* publications and, in these respects, the fifth modification was superior to the current NRS method.

Qualitative evidence   These changes were paralleled by: (i) a reduction in the frequency of certain types of error amongst respondents; and (ii) a reduction in the tendency of interviewers to deviate from their instructions. The evidence for this statement comes from tape-recordings of interviews and from the respondent's excuses or 'reasons' when confronted with evidence of her own errors.

1   The study of the current NRS technique indicated that this procedure was subject to: recurrent failure to communicate to the respondent what she was required to do, particularly with respect to terms like 'looked at', 'any copy', 'last occasion'; breakdown of the probing system; some degree of failure of the visual aids to help in focusing the respondent's attention (including a skipping of publications when the respondent held the book of mastheads in her own hands); loose control over the respondent; general lack of real effort by the respondent; some failure by the respondent to report isolated reading events.

2   The first modification, designed to correct various of these tendencies, did so on a large number of counts. It led to a better communication of basic instructions; tighter control by the interviewer over the respondent; more efficient use of the visual aids; greater responsibility and effort on the part of the respondent; also, the tendency to skip publications was reduced substantially. It is the correction of certain of these failures in the technique which appears to have led to the reduction (provided by the first modification) in the number of spurious 'no' replies. At the same time, the new method was still failing on various counts: the probing system was still weak; some respondents were still answering in terms of the usual; frequently the respondent did not have much sense of time so that, say, 'seven days ago' did not mean much. Moreover, interviewers did not like the extra control which this technique exercised over their own activities, and at times responded to this by omitting or modifying various of their instructions — to the detriment of communication.

3   The second, third and fourth modifications were aimed at correcting these faults and particularly those associated with spurious 'yes' replies. The changes made included: an alteration in the probing system; the use of wording more favoured by the inter-

viewers; a reduction in the number of repetitions of certain instructions — by the device of including them in the probe putting a day/date to the beginning of the qualifying period. These devices led to greater use of the probing system, considerably more adherence to instructions (by interviewers), and a reduction in the number of spurious 'yes' replies. One effect of this sequence of changes was that certain sources of error were now assuming greater *relative* importance than formerly. Chief amongst these at this stage were: confusion of one publication with another; confusion over dates.

4   The fifth modification was primarily an extension of the principles of the fourth modification to all four publication groups (the second, third and fourth modifications had, quite deliberately, been based on monthlies only). Interviewers reacted to the fifth modification much as they had to the fourth — they carried it out much as required, but disliked the 'strait-jacket' which it put upon them and continued to deviate to some extent in line with their objections to the procedure. The detail of the results of using it — and some of its residual points of failure — are given in the next section.

THE REMAINING WEAKNESSES OF THE METHOD

The technique in its final form has a number of weaknesses. These were, for the most part, recognised at the time the fifth modification was made. They were regarded then as irreducible within the context of this survey. To understand them more fully, however, an intensive analysis of interviewer performance was made in the course of, and after, the final check on the technique. The following statement is based in part upon this information, but also upon the excuses/'reasons' for error given in the confrontation part of the intensive interview.

Communicating instructions to the respondent   There is still an appreciable degree of failure on this count. Thus, the term 'looking at' can still take one or another of the following meanings: read it; read it properly; handled it, saw the cover; take it regularly; see it now and then; usually see it; it comes into the house; I know it, I recognised the cover. The terms 'any copy' and 'last occasion' are also involved in certain of these interpretations and include the following as well: ones I take myself; ones that come into the house (that is, looking at publications, for example, at work or at a hairdresser, may well be excluded when this interpretation is adopted).
    These failures in communication come about in several ways.

1   One of them is rather basic: these terms have special meanings, and they may have to get across to the respondent in the face of his expectation of what the interviewer is asking about *and* the meanings he would himself attribute to such terms. This is a major barrier to communication; even if the special meaning of our terms are hammered in, there is every likelihood that the old pattern will reassert itself before the interview is much advanced. It is, therefore, specially dangerous when the interviewer follows a tendency to skip reminders about the meaning of our terms 'because they might embarrass the respondent'. Interviewers *do* skip some of these from time to time. More frequently, however, they slur them over, blending them (as it were) into a chatty conversational flow and thereby taking out of the instructions the sharpness and the discreteness which is essential if the respondent's attention is to be focused on what is said. Whereas the interviewers rarely skip the question to the respondent, asking the latter what she thinks we mean by 'looking at', it often happens that the interviewer does not check an incorrect reply. We have evidence, too, of interviewers ignoring clues, thrown up in the course of the interview, which indicate that the respondent has missed our meaning. It also happens from time to time that interviewers themselves drift into saying 'read' and 'take', with the possibility that these will stimulate a resurgence of a respondent's expectations and assumptions.

   One can correct a certain amount of misunderstanding of this sort through the probe, and the probe itself is a hidden 'repetition of instruction'. However, certain of these misinterpretations produce a 'no', and there is simply no way of picking this up later on — there are far too many 'no's to be probed.

2   Some respondents fail to grasp the time periods in terms of which they are being asked to reply. With respect to the monthlies it could be four weeks or six weeks as far as they are concerned. Others, knowing that the time period is seven days, can't 'feel' the difference between four days and eight days and don't have, in their lives, many special events to use as guides or reference points. Some interviewers were found to be aggravating this tendency by failing to give the respondent the date on which the qualifying period started. In several cases, we found that the interviewer had not entered the starting day or date on the questionnaire before going out and was subsequently 'caught out' in the interview itself. The probe can rectify some of the results of this difficulty in so far as it is related to 'yes' replies — but it cannot help with incorrect 'no's.

3   The probe was usually delivered fairly well. Nonetheless, we found it undermined in certain cases by the following practices: (i) the running together of the first two questions* ('And you're absolutely certain it was *Good Housekeeping*, and you're not mixing it up with any other?') with a resulting loss of most of the probing or challenging power of these two questions; (ii) the reversing of one or another part of it in a positive form ('You're absolutely sure it was . . . ?'); (iii) the delivery of the three-question probe in a mechanical way, with the result that the questions lost their challenging power. There were instances, too, of one or another of the probe questions not being asked but yet being reported as asked in the questionnaire. In addition, many rather loose replies were accepted in delivering the third probe ('I see that every night'). The third probe for monthlies was sometimes applied to the dailies instead of the special probe designed for the latter group of publications (thus, in dealing with the dailies, interviewers may have said 'When was the very last time you looked at . . . ?' instead of 'Are you quite certain it was yesterday?').

4   Quite often respondents said (in giving their 'reasons' for error) that they had mixed up one publication with another. This occurred with both 'yes' and 'no' replies, though more with the latter. Under the conditions of the intensive interview, confusion of this sort is constantly encountered and it is doubtful if there is any way, in the context of an ordinary survey interview, of overcoming it. This is, in fact, the largest single category of 'reasons' given for error, and it must, therefore, be regarded seriously. Having said this, I must add that it is certainly to the point that respondent testimony suggests that on some occasions at least interviewers were making it very difficult for the respondent to *see* the masthead: in some cases an interviewer sat down side by side with the respondent, making it necessary for the respondent to crane his head sideways to see the masthead; in others the interviewer sat at the other side of the room from the respondent!

5   Interviewers varied in their treatment of uncertain replies by respondents. Some of them missed either the tone or the words of uncertainty. ('Well, I *think* it was in the last four weeks') and coded 'yes' or 'no' without any check or challenge at all. Others recognised uncertainty, but failed to turn the respondent's attention back to the choice of responses offered ('Yes'/'No'/'Don't know'). In fact, the 'Don't know' classification was used

*For the wording of these questions, see page 330.

but rarely, in spite of the fact that the intensive interviews brought out a great deal of evidence of vagueness and plain uncertainty.

6   On the evidence of tape-recordings and completed questionnaires, miscoding was not infrequent. This was obviously aggravated by the crowded nature of the questionnaire, though on the evidence this cannot have been the only cause of the trouble.

These, then, are the points of weakness in a technique which, nonetheless, gave evidence of working reasonably well. Neither its success in this instance nor its points of weakness should be underestimated. I say this because the conditions under which the method is administered are going to have a great deal to do with whether its success or its weaknesses become its dominant feature. It is this particular point which is dealt with in the next and final section of this report.

The full working details of the modified technique, card by card, are given in Appendix 8.4.

DECIDING WHETHER TO USE THE
MODIFIED NATIONAL READERSHIP SURVEY TECHNIQUE*

Whether or not to use this modification does, of course, turn upon such further validation of it as seems required. However, apart from this, the advisability of using it depends upon one vital issue: the technique as we have developed it calls for a high level of performance on the part of the interviewers and on the part of those who *control* the interviewers. If this cannot be guaranteed, then it may well be better, in my opinion, not to use the new but to stay instead with the old NRS technique, provided:

What any method must overcome

- that the order of presentation is monthlies first, then weeklies, then Sundays and then dailies;
- that the first phase of it be made more efficient with respect to the communication of basic instructions and the use of visual aids.

Having made this point, let me say more about the requirements for administering any effective readership survey technique.

---

*Some minor re-writing of this section of the report has been done, solely to clarify the points made in the original statement. The meaning of the section has remained the same.

1 A number of respondent-based difficulties normally stand in the way of getting accurate information about anything as complex as the readership of over 90 publications.

(a) The first of these is that the *communication* of the instructions to the respondent is intrinsically hazardous. All too easily, some part of the message does not get across. Effective communication calls for both repetition of difficult and key points *and* a considerable alertness on the part of the interviewer. The interviewer must *watch for* misconceptions and correct them; she must have a sufficient understanding of what the difficulties are if she is to be willing to repeat certain instructions in the face of a basic feeling that 'repetition should not be necessary and will offend the respondent'. The respondent is so often the focus of preconceptions about what is wanted, of distractions which mean that some instructions are not heard at all, of periodic 'mental blanks', and so on. With simple, straightforward instructions, these difficulties might not matter very much. However, the instructions required for increased efficiency in this particular survey are by no means simple and they depend upon concepts like: 'looked at'; 'any copy' (that is, including an old one, someone else's copy); 'last time'.

(b) Another difficulty is that even if the respondent *does* understand, there is no good reason why she should really *try* to recall what happened — why should she do more than offer some rough idea of when it was — particularly when so many publications are involved. Even if she *does* try all the time, there are isolated occasions when she will simply not remember, or which a strong habitual pattern of behaviour may all but blot out.

(c) There are other tendencies to which many respondents are prone: a tendency to bring some 'last events' nearer in time and to push others well back; a tendency to want to score; an expectation that the interviewer *wants* a positive score; a tendency to get the interview finished as soon as possible.

2 Over and above these problems are difficulties which characterise the interviewers themselves. We have found a marked tendency for interviewers to deviate from instructions. They do this even when their performance as interviewers is being witnessed and tape-recorded. They may deviate under the impulse of different motives. With some, it is plain laziness or cussedness or dimness. For many, however, it springs out of reasons such as: a basic respect for the respondent which takes the form of an exaggerated

342

view of what the respondent is capable of; an awareness that in certain situations a particular repetition just does *not* make sense; a feeling that the respondent will get irritated ('you can't keep on at them like that'); a desire to have a nice rounded way of saying things, so that one statement flows easily into another like a good essay; a dislike of certain expressions or a tendency to think in terms of certain words.

The new method can work if properly administered

Now, in the course of our experimental work we slowly developed techniques which appeared to correct certain of the error-producing tendencies of respondents. However, these had to be administered by interviewers, and we succeeded in getting interviewers to do this only by modifying the technique to counter their own divergent tendencies *and* by giving them special training.

This training is, in my opinion, extremely important. It means getting the interviewers to understand the traps and the difficulties of the operation on which they are engaged. They must know a certain amount of the psychology of recall and of communication and they must have drummed into them the case for doing what they are told.

Even after this we found strong evidence of a periodic breakdown in the indoctrinated procedure. This had to be discovered and corrected. *Nothing short of careful and continuing supervision can pick it up as it happens and systematic re-training became essential.*

However, even granted a spirited adherence to instructions, there is still another difficulty, which itself calls for certain qualities in an interviewer. Briefly, no standardised technique can ever be adequate for *all* interviews. From time to time some form of deviation, big or small, is, in fact, necessary. It takes an intelligent interviewer to know when to do this and when not, and it calls for something special in the interviewer to resist general and continuing deviation once she finds a case in which deviation is, in fact, needed. A desire to do things one's own way is very strong, and it re-asserts itself given just a small opportunity.

What this comes to, then, is that if respondent inadequacies in the recalling process are to be countered, then the interviewer responsible for doing this *through the modified technique* must be specially trained, well supervised, and must be bright without being irresponsible. By normally operative standards these are demanding requirements. *In actual fact* we satisfied them in our experimental work and I am convinced that a competent survey organisation can also do so on a continuing basis, if it undertakes that task with dedication. However, if that dedicated approach cannot be guaranteed then, I say again, it might well be better not to use the new method at all.

POSTSCRIPT — 1985

The advice I gave about using or not using the modified procedure may seem to some to have been over-strong. However, in order for the modified technique to work it was necessary that it be competently administered. After all, it had the necessary controls built into it *and* it had worked well with the quite ordinary interviewers who had administered it. We did of course specially train and control them, but they were ordinary material from a middle range research agency and our training and control procedures were highly effective with them.

By contrast, we had earlier found clear evidence of major failings in the work of the interviewers who ordinarily carried out the National Readership Survey of that time. The extent of that failure is detailed in Chapter 4. To some degree, those interviewer failures were precipitated by faults in the NRS procedure. But they were also the result of sloppy and poorly controlled interviewing and in my considered opinion that sloppiness and lack of control resulted largely from the common tendency of that time for research personnel to regard the special training and the firm control of interviewers as being uneconomical. The fact of the matter was that the NRS interviewers were doing poor work and were not up to the standard called for by the very demanding (though faulty) research procedure they were administering.

It was for this reason that I strongly recommended 'special training and control' of the interviewers as a necessary condition for the adoption and the administration of the modified procedure. I had hoped that this recommendation would be adopted and would be seen to be a reasonable price to pay for more accurate results.

In the event, that hope was not realised.

APPENDICES

APPENDIX 8.1

INSTRUCTIONS TO INTERVIEWERS CARRYING OUT THE FIRST MODIFICATION OF THE NRS TECHNIQUE

INTERVIEWER'S INSTRUCTIONS

Nature of your work

Your task is to conduct an interview aimed at finding out if your respondent looked at certain publications during time periods which will be specified.

Publications about which you are to ask include monthly, weekly, Sunday and daily papers:

- for each monthly paper you are to find out if it was looked at *in the last four weeks* (*not counting* 'today');
- for each weekly paper, *in the last seven days* (*not* 'today');
- for each Sunday paper, *in the last seven days* (*not* 'today');
- for each daily paper, *yesterday* (*not* 'today').

The difficulties you face

This is not an easy task for you or for the respondent. It is difficult because memory about a trifle such as when a paper was looked at may be very vague indeed. Certainly you cannot expect people to give you a quick answer which is also accurate. They cannot give you an accurate answer unless they really try to remember — and it is your very special task to make them try. If you fail in this, the answers you get will not be worth very much.

The technique you are to use

We have developed a technique for this sort of work which will make it possible to succeed in your task but which must be adhered to very carefully indeed.

1   You will have a book of visual aids and of instructions. The visual aids are photos of the captions of each of the publications, and the respondent is shown each of them in turn. Your instructions will tell you precisely what questioning procedure to use throughout the interview, where to repeat important instructions, and so on. *Your instructions are in fact written into your book of aids.*

2   While there will be variations in going from one paper to another the basic procedure is as follows:

(a)   You show a visual aid (e.g. *Reader's Digest*) to the respondent and at the same time call out the name of the publication concerned. (Point to it at the same time.)

(b)   You ask the respondent if she has looked at the publication any time at all *in the last four weeks* (or seven days or yesterday as the case may be.) She will have in front of her (as part of your visual aid system) a choice of answers: Yes definitely/No definitely/Not sure.

(c)   The respondent is encouraged to answer 'Not sure' if that is the case for her, but all such responses (i.e. 'Not sure') you must probe carefully to find out if the last occasion of looking at the publication was in fact in the last four weeks (or whatever the qualifying period is). See later for details of *how* to probe.

3   There will be deivations from this simple pattern from time to time. Thus, for specific publications you will be asked to probe for the answer 'No definitely' (as well as for 'Not sure'). For others you will be instructed to probe any reply you get. This is because we do not want the respondent to feel that 'Not sure' brings her a lot of work, and hence is to be avoided. It is also to prevent the respondent getting into lazy habits in her choice of answers.

4   The mastheads (i.e. the captions of papers) are shown first, the weeklies next, the Sunday papers third and the dailies last. Between each of these blocks you will tell the respondent of the change, using the words set out in your book of aids. The presentation of this is done in this particular order on the basis of a considerable amount of research. One of the reasons behind the decision is that memory of 'having

346

looked at publications' *in the last four weeks* is considerably harder — and more open to error — than memory of looking at newspapers *yesterday*. We therefore give respondents the hardest part first so that if fatigue sets in, what remains will be the *easier* part of the task. There are other reasons for this and you should feel free to ask about them on or after your briefing.

5   Your instructions require you: to present all the rules very clearly; to test the respondent for her understanding of certain terms (such as 'looked at'); to repeat your instructions at specified times throughout the interview. The first of the visual aids or mastheads is used for *driving your instructions home and for testing that this has occurred*. You may wonder why a simple instruction given once is not enough. A great deal of research has been done on this particular issue and it is abundantly clear that one of the main sorts of error in this sort of readership survey has been the failure of the respondent to understand what was wanted of her. Respondents make all sorts of mistakes, generally in line with what they *expect* interviewers to ask them about. So it is not just a matter of telling the respondent what you want, but of doing so in the face of her own expectations. The work we have done also shows quite clearly that the intelligent people in your sample are *just as likely* to misunderstand what you want as are the duller ones. *So the driving home of instructions, the repeating of them, and the testing of them are absolutely vital*. Your book of aids tells you just what to do: stick to it rigidly.

The meaning of LOOKED AT

In all your questions you must ask the respondent if she LOOKED AT the publications concerned in a specified period. LOOKED AT has a definite meaning, and you *must* get this clearly and firmly into the respondent's head. LOOKED AT includes both careful reading and glancing through. If the respondent simply saw the cover of a monthly magazine, that is *not* 'looking at' it. But if she looked at *pictures* in the magazine, or flipped through it, that would qualify as LOOKING AT it. If she read just a little bit of it, that too would qualify.

You must use the term LOOKED AT throughout your interview and *never* drop into using terms like 'read' or 'take' or 'like to see'. Both you and the respondent must at all times think in terms of LOOKED AT as I have defined it. Our work has so far pointed to deviations from instructions as another serious source of error, hence keep your ears wide open for any hint at all that your respondent has forgotten what we are after.

Does it matter WHERE the respondent was at the time of looking at the publication?

It does not matter WHERE the respondent was when she *looked at* it. She might have been in the train or bus, in a doctor's or dentist's waiting-room, at a hairdresser's, at work, at a library, at a launderette, whilst on holiday, and so on. The respondent might simply have picked it up in the train and glanced through it or she might have read it after unwrapping groceries or food of some sort.

As a matter of fact LOOKING AT the paper in places like the ones I have mentioned is constantly forgotten. *Respondents tend to forget anything at all which is not regular or part of the usual pattern.*

Your printed instructions in the book of aids refer to this part of the definition of LOOKED AT, but be alert at all times for any hint that your instructions have not got across. Repeat them if necessary and always be ready to ask a question of the respondent — just to make sure.

Introducing yourself to the respondent

You are to represent yourself as working for your own firm. Carry your pass-card for this. Tell your respondent that you want to ask her about the newspapers or magazines she has looked at. Explain that you have a special way of going about this and go straight ahead. If the respondent wants to know more, you can explain that the publishers need to know about *who* looks at *what*, so that they can design the paper more to suit its actual readers. (This explanation should not however be necessary.)

The people you are to call on and other details about contacting your respondent

You will have a list of the people on whom you are to call. You must make at least three different calls to find them at home. The three calls to be on three different days.

You will have a list of reserves or substitutes for use when your respondent has moved or is away for a long period, is ill or dead, refuses to be interviewed. These reserves are typed in red and the one to use is that nearest to the name of the person who could not be seen or who refused.

Keeping your record sheet

Ring the answer given by the respondent (Yes/No/Not sure). If 'Not sure' enter the result of your probing. Do this as well as your original 'Not sure' entry. If the respondent is still 'Not sure' after your probe, that is what you must enter (again) in your record sheet. The greater part of your record sheet is given up to the question about when the publication was LOOKED AT. You will need also to enter the respondent's age, sex, marital status and various other details as indicated.

The method to be used for probing

There is a special probing technique. If the respondent is 'Not sure' say:

'Try to think of where you were on the very last occasion you LOOKED AT it. And do not forget the odd occasion — in the train, at work, in a library, at the launderette, in the doctor's or dentist's waiting-room, at the hairdresser's — or *any place at all*.'

If from this question you get a rough indication of when it was, *do not* pursue it straight away. Say:

'What about since then? Is there any chance of your having looked at it *since* then?'

Once you get your respondent thinking of the *very last occasion* try to pin down *when* that was. Do this by trying to link LOOKING AT it with what was happening on that occasion, because often enough *this* will be linked to *time*, whereas the LOOKING AT event may not. Thus, if your respondent looked at the paper concerned while in a train and going on holiday, it should not be hard to fix the time. If, on the other hand, we have her thinking only of what it was she looked at or simply of the fact that she had looked at it, it may be very hard indeed to find when it was.

If the respondent had said 'never look at it' (and where this is one of your required probes) ask respondent if she could possibly have LOOKED AT it on some odd occasion.

'Could you possibly have looked at it by chance somewhere, or because it was lying around somewhere — at a dentist's or doctor's, hairdresser's, or at a launderette, at work, in a friend's place, in a library, on holiday, or on any odd occasion like that?'

If the respondent is definite that she has *never even heard of it* pass on to the next card.

If respondent said 'Yes' (and if this is one of the occasions where you probe the 'yes' reply) ask respondent how she can be sure it *was* in the last . . . . Ask for details of what she was doing at the time, try to date these doings and generally check and challenge her statement.

Do not take this probing operation lightly. It is a vital part of the general strategy which keeps the respondent awake and trying. It should also be a constant reminder to you that you are doing a highly skilled job in trying to make people remember things like this.

MAKING OF APPOINTMENTS FOR A SECOND INTERVIEWER TO CALL

You have one other duty to perform. It is a most important duty. This is the making of appointments for a second interviewer to call. The purpose of this *is to learn more about reading habits of the respondent and to get a little more information about the way the method is working.*

1   How to get the appointment

When you finish your interview you must ask the respondent to allow a second interviewer to call. The interview must take place on the same day as your own. There is a special way of making the appointment for it.

(i)   We want you to fix this appointment with everyone you interview. For this, you will have a set of appointment times and it will be your task to get the informant to accept one of these. These appointment times are allocated to fit the availability of a small team of people conducting the second interview.

(ii)   It is extremely important that we get this second interview with *all* members of the survey sample. You may tell your informant that its purpose is to ask more questions about their reading, about what they are interested in and about the sort of things they would like to have more of in their papers. Make it clear that the second interviewer comes from the London School of Economics. Our experience has been that very few people indeed will refuse it if the appointment is well made. Make it clear that we are paying for the time given us in the second interview. Make it clear too that the second interview will be an extremely interesting and worthwhile one.

(iii)   You have an appointment card on which to write the time of the appointment and this should be left with the respondent, along with your thanks for co-operation and a repetition of the fact that the second interview will serve a very useful purpose and it will be specially interesting.

(iv)   You must write the following information on your questionnaire (in the space provided)
   —   *Respondent's name and address*
   —   *Date and time of appointment*

2   *Where to report with your appointments*

We are working from a local office. It is at 26 Charleville Street in Baron's Court (down basement stairs). This office is very close to your interviewing area. You are to return to this office at particular times, along with your appointments up to that time. Pass in these (and your completed questionnaires) at the local office and then go on out to the job again.

3   *Times of work*

The requirements of the appointment system mean that we have to conduct our interviews during set periods each day. Of the 4/5 interviewers on this job, one will be working from 9.30 a.m. to 4.30 p.m. and the others from 1.0 p.m. to 8.0 p.m. There are set periods for reporting to the local office.

(i)   Report there before you start work each day.
(ii)   Return to the local office to report your appointments. These calls at the local office are made at times set out on a sheet labelled Appointment Times. Make sure you have this and have studied it carefully.

There is a rest room at the centre and you will be able to get a cup of tea there.

APPENDIX 8.2

THE EXTENDED VALIDATION PROCEDURE*

INSTRUCTIONS FOR INTENSIVE INTERVIEWERS

What you are to do

1   You will be carrying out a series of intensive interviews dealing with readership. The results of these interviews will be compared with the results of a more conventional readership survey being carried out by ordinary interviewers.

2   The appointment for each of your interviews is, in fact, made by the people doing the ordinary interviewing. You will deal with their respondents on the same day as they did. BUT you will use a basically different method — a much more intensive and probing method. At the end of the interview you will compare your results with those from the first interview and seek reasons for any differences which occur.

Method of interviewing

3   *Basic procedure*   For each of ninety-plus papers, find out if your respondent LOOKED AT it within a certain qualifying period. There are different qualifying periods for different publications:

-    for monthly publications, it is 'the last four weeks' (not counting 'today');
-    for weekly publications it is 'the last seven days' (not counting 'today');
-    for Sunday publications it is 'the last seven days' (not counting 'today');
-    for daily papers it is 'yesterday' (i.e. 'today' does not count).

You must NOT mention these periods but must find out by rigorous probing whether or not the LAST occasion falls into the qualifying period concerned.

4   *You must use the following basic procedure*

(a)   Ask respondent: 'WHEN WAS THE VERY LAST TIME YOU LOOKED AT ANY COPY OF . . . . ?'

(b)   On getting a reply, immediately ask 'WHAT ABOUT SINCE THEN?'

(c)   Then establish exactly when the very last occasion actually was.

5   In applying this basic procedure, take careful note of the following points or sub-procedures:

(i)   In asking 'WHAT ABOUT SINCE THEN?', you must do so through reminding them of the many ODD OCCASIONS on which people happen to look at publications. These include the following:

-    at the doctors or dentists/hairdressers/other waiting rooms
-    at work/on way to work
-    at social club/library/common room
-    at friend's place/when visiting
-    on holiday/whilst travelling
-    on unwrapping the meat.

It is the ODD OCCASION which people forget to tell you about. What they do instead is to tell you what they *usually* do, leaving out any departure from the usual. Hence you MUST probe for the ODD OCCASION.

(ii)   When, and only when, you have located the very last occasion, try to fix its position (in time) with accuracy. There is a special way of doing this. Try to link the LOOKING AT to the events or conditions of the occasion. *These* may be time-linked, whereas it is very unlikely that the LOOKING AT is time-linked in its own right. (It

*See Part I for the less extended (= more intensive) technique

would be most wasteful to go very far with this process before satisfying yourself that you are, in fact, dealing with the *very last occasion*. Hence make a point of completing 4(b) above before going on with 4(c).)

6   The above procedure is, of course, linked to the case where you get a positive reply. But respondent might well answer that she has *never* looked at the publication. In that event, ask:

(a) Would you know the publication if you saw it?' (*If 'no', drop it and deal with the next publication.*)

(b) If 'yes', ask respondent if she might not have looked at it on some odd occasion — by chance, as it were. Lead into the ODD OCCASIONS, going as far as seems sensible.

(c) If no acceptance, drop it and go to next publication.

(d) If 'yes' seek very last occasion and then date it.

7   Since our purpose is to decide, for each publication, whether or not it was LOOKED AT in a certain qualifying period, there is no point in trying for an accurate time fix when the LAST OCCASION is hopelessly out of the qualifying period. Hence work by the following rules:

(a) For monthlies, try for a time fix if the event appears to be within the last three months (or seems to be). If, on trying for a fix, it becomes clear that the event was outside of the qualifying period, don't take it further. Nor, for monthlies, is it sensible to try to pin down whether it was *four* days ago as distinct from *five*. It would, however, be vital to find out if it was three weeks ago as distinct from five. In other words, an event near the border of the qualifying period has to be tightly tied down. But obviously you have to go some distance in fixing the time before you can decide if it is sensible to go on tightening up or not.

(b) For weeklies and Sunday papers, do the same sort of thing, keeping it in mind that your qualifying period for these is the LAST SEVEN DAYS (not counting 'to-day'). *Don't waste time and effort by seeking a distinction between dates which could not possibly make any difference to your coded record.*

8   *Some fundamental terms* The words LOOKED AT are absolutely *central* to this interview. It is hard enough to stick to them yourself, let alone train your respondent to think in terms of them.

9   Teach the respondent from the very beginning what you mean by LOOKED AT. It means any of the following:

   — reading the whole thing right through
   — reading just a little bit of it
   — looking at the picture in it
   — looking at the advertisements in it
   — flipping through it
   — reading it after unwrapping the meat

It does *not* include:

   — noticing a headline on a news-stand or on someone else's paper
   — seeing the cover of it on a book-stall.

You will find that respondent constantly forgets what you told her about this and slips back to common words like 'read' or 'take it' or 'usually see it', and so on.

10   We also use the words THE VERY LAST TIME. This is exactly what we mean, and you must get that point across to your respondent. Respondent will automatically think in terms of what she *usually* does. Indeed, she may often feel that she is doing herself and the survey harm if she answers in any other way. What she may feel is that what she *usually* does is a fairer representation of what happens than the atypical week when she misses out! *But as you know we really do want to know what ACTUALLY happened.* You have, therefore, to break down the tendency for respondent to answer in terms of the *usual*. Be alert for it at all times. Be prepared to explain our need again and again to the respondent. Punch the words *very last* again and again in phrasing your question to her.

11   *Your general attitude*   You must keep a tight control over the interview. At all times know exactly where you are taking it. You can do this by sticking to your basic strategy and keeping it always in mind. It is all too easy to get lost in an interesting but woolly conversation. You must aim at:

(a)   setting the question firmly in front of the respondent;

(b)   finding out when was the VERY LAST occasion of LOOKING AT the publication concerned (i.e. via probing for a 'later occasion' and tying the event to things which are time-linked);

(c)   cutting out any unnecessary questioning (see 6 and 7 above).

12   Quite apart from this, you must maintain a basically sceptical attitude towards all your respondent says. Obviously one can take this too far, and irritate the respondent. On the other hand, a statement that the last occasion was 'in the last week' is not to be taken at face value just because it is said emphatically or just because the respondent seems to you to be 'intelligent'. There is, in fact, no correlation between intelligence and accuracy level on this readership survey (i.e. according to work done so far). Conduct your interrogation politely but firmly, and with a well-hidden scepticism.

13   In the same vein, *don't* assume that one or two repetitions will be enough to teach your respondent what you want her to know. For most people it is necessary to say it again and again — and this applies to the intelligent *just as much* as to the dull. The trouble is that everyone has some sort of preconception of what is wanted and this gets in the way of learning what we do, in fact, want.

14   *Keeping your record*   Ring the appropriate answer for each paper. This includes the '?' which means 'not sure'. Notice carefully that the back of your questionnaire calls for a report on the quality of the interview and upon various aspects of respondent behaviour.

15   *The confrontation*   At the end of your questioning about the publications, you are to open a sealed envelope in which is the first interviewer's questionnaire. You must *not* open it until this point in your own interview. Then set the two questionnaires side by side and ask respondent to explain to you what she thinks are the causes of the discrepancies which exist between the two records.
    This is a very important part of the procedure and I want the reasons written in your questionnaire in the space shown.

16   *Introducing the interview*   You must make it clear at the beginning that:

— you are from the London School of Economics (in the University of London);
— you are making a special study of memory, particularly of their memory in the first interview;
— you'll be asking about the same papers as before, a few of your questions will be the same, but *most of them* will be different.

London School of Economics

W.A. BELSON,
24.8.60

352

APPENDIX 8.3

INTERVIEWING SUCCESS RATES

Table 8A.1
Success rates for each of the modifications

	Interview attempted, completed, etc. for the various modifications						
	First modifi- cation	Second	Third	Fourth	Fifth	Fifth re-tested	All
Cases named for first interview	390	50	64	120	340	374	1,346
First interview completed	246	35	39	71	226	228	845
Second interview granted	208	31	33	66	210	199	747
Second interview completed	174	28	30	53	172	153	610
	%	%	%	%	%	%	%
Percentage first interviews com- pleted	63	70	61	59	65	61	63
Percentage second interviews com- pleted:							
on basis of all first interviews completed	71	80	77	75	76	67	72
on basis of all appointments made for second inter- views	84	90	91	80	82	77	82

APPENDIX 8.4

TABLES SHOWING IN DETAIL THE RESULTS FROM THE VARIOUS MODIFICATIONS

Table 8A.2
Overclaiming and underclaiming tendencies using the different techniques: figures based on all 91 publications

	Survey estimate: Yes %				Survey estimate: No %				Survey estimate: ?		
	Int. Yes	Int. No	Int. ?	No* ?	Int. Yes	Int. No	Int. ?	Yes* ?	Int. Yes	Int. No	Int. ?
30 Monthlies†											
1st Modn.	399	330	79	50·6	115	4,121	63	4·1	18	73	22
2nd Modn.	73	36	6	36·5	15	680	10	3·5	2	13	5
3rd Modn.	75	23	4	26·5	22	739	15	4·8	5	14	2
4th Modn.	151	33	15	24·1	46	1,284	34	5·9	7	13	7
5th Modn.	196	82	22	34·7	109	4,617	80	3·9	11	32	11
40 Weeklies											
1st Modn.	504	228	26	33·5	72	5,976	26	1·6	8	30	6
2nd Modn.											
3rd Modn.											
4th Modn.											
5th Modn.	401	79	25	20·6	116	6,076	35	2·4	8	16	5
12 Sunday Papers											
1st Modn.	473	90	7	17·0	21	1,422	11	2·2	5	7	1
2nd Modn.											
3rd Modn.											
4th Modn.											
5th Modn.	375	35	8	10·3	49	1,549	9	3·6	0	2	1
9 Daily papers											
1st Modn.	318	97	2	23·7	28	1,411	5	2·3	4	6	1
2nd Modn.											
3rd Modn.											
4th Modn.											
5th Modn.	249	51	2	17·5	32	1,520	3	2·3	0	2	0
All											
1st Modn.	1,694	745	114	33·6	236	12,930	105	2·6	35	116	30
5th Modn.	1,221	247	57	19·9	306	13,762	127	3·1	19	52	17

*The full ninety-one publications tested in the current National Readership Survey. See also Table 8A.3 which gives details for a selected twenty-eight and which includes the current NRS technique in its comparison of results.

†The number of cases tested (through double interviews) varied with the modification used: 174 on first modification; 28 on the second; 30 on the third; 53 on the fourth; 172 on the fifth. For the first and last modifications there was a slight fall-off in cases in going from the monthly to the other publication groups.

Showing the overclaiming and underclaiming tendencies using the different techniques: figures based upon 28 selected publications*

	Survey estimate: Yes				Survey estimate: No				Survey estimate: ?		
	Int. Yes	Int. No	Int. ?	% Wrong or ?	Int. Yes	Int. No	Int. ?	% Wrong or ?	Int. Yes	Int. No	Int ?
9 Monthlies†											
N.R.S. Method (D.S.W.M.)	177	113	14	41·8	312	2,680	71	12·5	0	0	0
1st Modification M.S.W.D.‡	220	122	38	42·1	53	1,072	24	6·7	6	24	7
2nd Modn. M. only	37	18	2	35·1	8	174	3	5·9	1	6	3
3rd Modn. M. only	38	9	2	22·4	13	188	10	10·9	3	4	1
4th Modn. M. only	82	13	9	21·2	15	324	14	8·2	4	10	5
5th Modn. M.W.S.D.	114	42	15	33·3	49	1,271	33	6·1	6	15	6
5th re-tested M.W.S.D.	75	22	3	25·0	30	731	29	7·5	0	0	11
5 Weeklies†											
N.R.S. Method (D.S.W.M.)	350	53	6	14·4	109	535	10	18·2	0	0	0
1st Modification M.W.S.D.	311	72	15	21·9	19	420	9	6·3	4	9	1
5th Modn. M.W.S.D.	252	31	9	13·7	43	484	15	10·7	3	6	3
5th re-tested M.W.S.D.	134	19	0	12·4	29	301	0	8·8	3	14	0
7 Sunday Papers†											
N.R.S. Method (D.S.W.M.)	344	65	1	16·1	149	1,129	3	11·9	0	0	0
1st Modification M.W.S.D.	423	68	5	14·7	16	659	4	2·9	5	6	1
5th Modn. M.W.S.D.	339	31	6	9·8	38	762	5	5·3	0	1	1
5th Re-tested M.W.S.D.	208	13	2	6·7	20	437	7	5·8	0	13	0
7 Daily Papers†											
N.R.S. Method (D.S.W.M.)	305	76	1	20·2	87	1,301	10	6·9	0	0	0
1st Modification M.W.S.D.	262	71	2	21·8	16	830	5	2·5	3	3	0
5th Modn. M.W.S.D.	218	47	2	18·4	21	893	3	2·6	0	0	0
5th Re-tested M.W.S.D.	140	26	5	18·0	18	511	0	3·4	0	0	0

*These 28 were the publications tested in the original validation of the current National Readership Survey. See Table 8A.2 which gives comparable details for the full 91 publications tested in the National Readership Survey.

†Nine monthlies: Readers Digest, Practical Householder, Do It Yourself, Good Housekeeping, Vogue, Woman and Home, True Romances, True Story, Ideal Home.

Five weeklies: Woman, Woman's Own, TV Times, Radio Times, Reveille.

Seven Sunday papers: News of the World, The Sunday Times, The Observer, Sunday Express, Sunday Pictorial, The Sunday Dispatch, The People.

Seven daily papers: Daily Express, Daily Mirror, Daily Sketch, Daily Herald, The Times, The Daily Telegraph, The Evening News.

‡The number of cases tested (through double interviews) varied with the modification used: 174 on the first modification; 28 on the second; 30 on the third, 53 on the fourth; 172 on the fifth; 153 in the intensive re-test of the fifth. For the first and last modifications there was a slight fall-off in cases in going from the monthly to the other publication groups.

Comparing the accuracy of the different techniques:
(i) averages based on 28 selected publications;
(ii) averages based on all 91 publications

	Based on 28 publications*				Based on all 91 publications			
	Monthlies (9)	Weeklies (5)	Sundays (7)	Dailies (7)	Monthlies (30)	Weeklies (40)	Sundays (12)	Dailies (9)
N.R.S., order D.S.W.M.								
Survey (S)	9·2	37·6	26·9	23·3				
Intensive (I)	14·8	42·4	31·7	23·7				
Ratio: S/I	0·62	0·89	0·83	0·98				
N.R.S., estimated for four orders, rotated								
Survey (S)	9·5	37·1	27·3	23·4				
Intensive (I)	14·8	42·4	31·7	23·7				
Ratio: S/I	0·64	0·88	0·86	0·99				
N.R.S., estimated for order M.W.S.D.								
Survey (S)	10·9	38·3	26·9	23·7				
Intensive (I)	14·8	42·4	31·7	23·7				
Ratio: S/I	0·74	0·90	0·85	1·00				
1st Modification								
Survey (S)	24·3	45·7	40·7	27·5	15·5	10·9	27·3	21·8
Intensive (I)	17·8	38·4	36·5	23·1	10·2	8·4	23·9	18·3
Ratio: S/I	1·36	1·19	1·12	1·19	1·52	1·30	1·14	1·19
2nd Modification								
Survey (S)	22·6				13·7			
Intensive (I)	18·3				10·7			
Ratio: S/I	1·24				1·28			
3rd Modification								
Survey (S)	18·1†				11·3			
Intensive (I)	20·0				11·3			
Ratio: S/I	0·91				1·00			
4th Modification								
Survey (S)	21·8				12·5			
Intensive (I)	21·2				12·8			
Ratio: S/I	1·03				0·98			
5th Modification								
Survey (S)	11·0	34·0	31·2	22·2	5·8	7·3	20·3	16·0
Intensive (I)	10·9	34·7	31·3	19·9	6·1	7·6	20·5	14·9
Ratio: S/I	1·01	0·98	1·00	1·12	0·95	0·96	0·99	1·07
5th Modification								
Survey (S)	11·1	30·6	31·9	24·2				
Full-intensive (I)	11·7	33·2	32·6	22·6				
Ratio: S/I	0·95	0·92	0·98	1·08				

*That is, those tested in the study of the accuracy of the NRS figures. (See page 326.)
†Each modification was tested in a different survey area. Hence readership figures in the different modification can vary, even to a marked degree.

Table 8A.5 (i)
Comparing accuracy level for individual publication for each modification: 30 monthlies

Publications	On N.R.S. method († cases)				On first Mdn. 174 cases		On 2nd/3rd Mdn. 59 cases		On 4th Mdn. 53 cases		On final Mdn. 172 cases	
	Order D.S.W.M.	Estimated for all orders (full rotation)	Estimated for order M.W.S.D.	Intensive (I)	Survey (S)	Intensive (I)	Survey (S)	Intensive (I)	Survey (S)	Intensive (I)	Survey (S)	Intensive ( )
	%	%	%	%	%	%	%	%	%	%	%	%
Reader's Digest	23	24	25	26	41	35	39	37	28	32	19	19
Do It Yourself	12	11	14	19	13	15	24	24	15	23	9	9
True Story	4	4	5	5	10	7	20	14	4	8	13	10
True Romances	2	2	3	7	5	5	7	5	6	8	5	5
Practical Householder	10	9	9	13	17	13	17	19	8	6	9	9
Ideal Home	7	7	8	22	30	23	17	19	26	25	9	8
Good Housekeeping	9	10	11	8	39	20	12	17	40	32	10	9
Woman and Home	6	8	10	21	26	16	19	8	28	23	10	10
Vogue	10	11	13	12	37	25	15	27	42	34	15	17
True Magazine					5	3	7	3	0	0	2	3
Practical Motorist					11	10	14	15	6	8	7	5
Car Mechanics					6	3	8	7	2	0	2	2
My Home					11	8	3	2	9	15	3	2
Home					9	6	5	5	13	8	2	3
Men Only and Lilliput					14	9	8	8	9	9	3	3
Wide World					6	5	12	7	6	2	3	2
Housewife					17	10	8	7	13	6	3	6
Homes and Gardens					16	9	8	8	13	1	4	4
Homemaker					8	4	5	7	4	8	2	3
House Beautiful					7	5	8	3	6	8	3	4
Sincerely					1	1	2	2	0	0	1	1
Photoplay					10	6	12	10	9	13	6	9
Everywoman					22	11	20	14	15	11	8	8
Woman and Beauty					18	8	15	12	9	13	5	6
Modern Woman					14	9	7	7	4	6	5	4
Woman's Journal					18	9	10	10	15	15	3	4
Argosy					16	10	12	10	11	16	2	2
She					19	10	8	5	16	16	5	5
Vanity Fair					14	7	10	10	11	11	5	5
Honey					2	2	3	3	6	6	1	2

* Each modification was tested in a different survey area. Hence these readership figures, if converted into percentages, may well be different.

† This varied from one publication to another: 150 for *Reader's Digest;* 120 for *Practical Householder;* 206 for *TV Times;* 168 for *Reveille;* 155 for *News of the World;* 161 for *Daily Mirror.*

357

Table 8A.5 (ii)
Showing results for individual publications for first and final modifications: 40 weekly publications

Publications	Percentage qualifying as readers*							
	On N.R.S. method survey/intensive († cases)				On first mdn.* survey/intensive (174 cases)		On final mdn.* survey/intensive (172 cases)	
	Order D.S.W.M.	Estimated for all orders (full rotation)	Estimated for order M.W.S.D.	Intensive (I)	Survey (S)	Intensive (I)	Survey (S)	Intensive (I)
	%	%	%	%	%	%	%	%
Radio Times	55	55	57	59	68	66	49	51
TV Times	43	42	41	46	49	45	41	44
Woman	38	37	38	42	43	32	32	34
Woman's Own	34	36	38	41	41	32	27	25
Reveille	18	17	18	24	28	17	21	20
Listener					6	5	2	1
The Viewer					0	0	0	0
Television Guide					0	0	1	1
TV Guide					2	0	1	1
Woman's Day					15	12	8	9
Woman's Realm					28	18	16	14
Woman's Companion					3	2	1	1
Woman's Mirror					17	14	23	20
Woman's Weekly					20	11	4	7
Woman's Illustrated					14	10	4	7
Weekend					15	11	15	16
My Weekly					1	1	0	0
The Weekly News					5	3	2	1
Date					3	1	2	2
Silver Star					1	1	2	1
Family Star					1	1	1	1
Red Star Weekly					1	1	0	1
Red Letter					1	2	2	1
Punch					17	13	3	3
Universe					5	3	2	3
The Christian Herald					1	0	0	0
Tit-Bits					10	6	8	8
Parade and Blighty					1	0	0	1
Roxy					3	2	3	4
Secrets					0	1	1	2
Marilyn					4	2	3	5
Marty					3	2	3	3
Mirabelle					3	2	2	2
Valentine					4	2	4	4
Boyfriend					2	2	2	1
Romeo					1	2	2	3
Picture Show					7	1	2	2
People's Friend					1	1	0	1
Today					13	9	5	8
Glasgow Weekly News					0	0	0	0

*These two modifications were tested in different parts of the survey area.
†As at foot of Table 8A.5 (i).

Table 8A.5 (iii)
Showing results for individual publications for first and final modifications: Sunday and dailies

Publications	N.R.S. method survey/intensive († cases)				First Mdn.* survey/intensive (174 cases)		Final Mdn.* survey/intensive (172 cases)	
	Order D.S.W.M.	Estimated for all orders (full rotation)	Estimated for order M.W.S.D.	Intensive (I)	Survey (S)	Intensive (I)	Survey (S)	Intensive (I)
	%	%	%	%	%	%	%	%
Sunday papers (12)								
News of the World	49	50	51	51	52	51	59	59
Sunday Pictorial	45	46	46	47	59	54	55	55
The People	36	37	35	41	45	41	46	45
Sunday Express	26	26	26	33	48	43	28	27
Sunday Dispatch	13	14	14	19	29	21	12	14
The Observer	9	10	9	15	24	19	10	8
The Sunday Times	10	9	8	17	28	25	9	10
Empire News					11	9	7	8
Reynolds News					7	6	5	5
Sunday Graphic					18	13	11	14
Glasgow Sunday Post					5	2	0	0
Glasgow Sunday Mail					1	1	0	0
Daily papers (9)								
Daily Mirror	48	48	48	48	41	39	52	45
The Evening News	37	34	36	40	49	41	47	40
Daily Express	29	29	29	30	38	32	21	22
Daily Sketch	18	21	22	19	16	12	12	11
The Daily Telegraph	14	13	13	13	25	18	6	5
Daily Herald	12	14	14	11	10	9	12	10
The Times	5	4	5	5	14	12	5	6
Daily Mail					16	12	7	9
Evening Standard					28	26	13	15

*These two modifications were carried out in different parts of the survey area.
†See footnote to Table 8A.5 (i).

Table 8A.6 (i)
Comparing NRS method and first and final modifications: monthly papers

Publications	Error+possible error as % of cases tested*		
	N.R.S. († cases) %	First modification (174 cases) %	Final modification (172 cases) %
Monthly publications			
Reader's Digest	26	15	6
Do It Yourself	14	10	5
True Story	7	6	9
True Romances	9	5	2
Practical Householder	14	16	9
Ideal Home	20	20	9
Good Housekeeping	10	26	13
Woman and Home	26	19	15
Vogue	14	22	13
Average	15·6%	15·4%	9·0%
True Magazine		6	2
Practical Motorist		8	5
Car Mechanics		6	2
My Home		12	5
Home		7	4
Men Only and Lilliput		9	2
Wide World		5	14
Housewife		16	6
Homes and Gardens		14	4
Homemaker		9	4
House Beautiful		7	2
Sincerely		1	1
Photoplay		11	5
Everywoman		19	10
Woman and Beauty		16	5
Modern Woman		16	5
Woman's Journal		16	7
Argosy		10	2
She		11	5
Vanity Fair		12	4
Honey		0	4
Average all monthly publications		11·7%	6·0%

*Excluding the cases classified as doubtful in the NRS or modified survey.
†The number varies for each publication: e.g. 206 for *TV Times*; 150 for *Practical Householder*; 88 for *Woman and Home*; see Appendix, Chapter 4, for the other numbers.

Table 8A.6 (ii)
Comparing NRS method and first and final modifications: weekly papers

Publications	Error × possible error as % of cases tested*		
	N.R.S. († cases) %	First modification (174 cases) %	Final modification (172 cases) %
Weekly publications			
Radio Times	11	4	8
TV Times	16	8	10
Woman	20	19	15
Woman's Own	22	20	18
Reveille	14	17	6
Average	16·6%	13·6%	11·4%
Listener		6	1
The Viewer		1	0
TV Weekly		1	1
TV Guide		2	1
Woman's Day		8	9
Woman's Realm		17	12
Woman's Companion		5	2
Woman's Mirror		6	8
Woman's Weekly		19	6
Woman's Illustrated		8	8
Weekend		9	11
My Weekly		2	0
Weekly News		4	1
Date		2	1
Silver Star		1	1
Family Star		1	0
Red Star Weekly		1	1
Red Letter		2	1
Punch		11	1
Universe		2	1
The Christian Herald		1	0
Tit-Bits		4	4
Parade and Blighty		1	1
Roxy		3	1
Secrets		1	1
Marilyn		3	3
Marty		1	2
Mirabelle		1	2
Valentine		2	2
Boyfriend		1	3
Romeo		1	2
Picture Show		6	2
People's Friend		0	1
Today		7	3
Glasgow Weekly News		0	0
Average of weekly publications		5·2%	3·8%

*Excluding the cases classified as doubtful in the NRS or modified survey.
†See footnote to Table 8A.6 (i).

Table 8A.6 (iii)
Comparing NRS method and first and final modifications: Sunday and daily papers

Publications	Error + possible error as % of cases tested*		
	N.R.S. († cases) %	First modification (174 cases) %	Final modification (172 cases) %
Sunday papers			
Sunday Pictorial	16	7	10
The Sunday Times	13	5	3
News of the World	18	3	10
Sunday Dispatch	8	13	6
The People	15	12	11
The Observer	7	6	2
Sunday Express	16	8	7
Average	13·3%	7·7%	7·0%
Empire News		3	3
Reynolds News		5	2
Sunday Graphic		10	8
Glasgow Sunday Post		2	0
Glasgow Sunday Mail		1	0
Average, all Sundays		6·3%	5·2%
Daily papers			
Daily Express	16	11	8
Daily Mirror	18	6	11
Daily Sketch	8	5	4
Daily Herald	4	4	4
The Times	4	7	2
The Evening News	20	14	11
The Daily Telegraph	5	8	4
Average	10·7%	7·9%	7·0%
Evening Standard		11	5
Daily Mail		10	4
Average, all dailies		8·4%	5·9%

*Excluding the cases classified as doubtful in the NRS or modified survey.
†See footnote to Table 8A.6 (i).

Table 8A.7
Showing process for estimating readership figures in other presentation orders

Publications	1958 figures for different order presentations			Conversion ratios		Present enquiry		
Dailies	First position (no reversal) (a)	Fourth position (with reversals) (b)	All four positions (with reversals) (c)	$\frac{b}{a}$	$\frac{c}{a}$	First position (no reversal) (d)	Estimated fourth position (with reversals) (b/a ×d)	Estimated all positions (with reversals) (c/a ×d)
	%	%	%			%	%	%
Daily Mirror	35·4	35·4	35·4	1·00	1·00	48	48·0	48·0
Daily Express	31·5	31·7	31·8	1·01	1·01	29	29·3	29·3
Daily Herald	12·1	13·9	14·2	1·15	1·17	12	13·8	14·0
Daily Sketch	10·2	12·2	11·6	1·22	1·14	18	21·6	20·5
The Daily Telegraph	7·7	6·9	7·3	0·90	0·95	14	12·6	13·3
The Times	3·1	2·8	2·6	0·90	0·84	5	4·5	4·2
The Evening News	12·1	11·7	11·3	0·97	0·93	37	35·9	34·4
Average all						23·3	23·7	23·4
Sundays	Second position (no reversal) (a)	Third position (with reversals) (b)	All four positions (with reversals) (c)	$\frac{b}{a}$	$\frac{c}{a}$	Second position (no reversal) (d)	Estimated third position (with reversals) (b/a ×d)	Estimated all positions (with reversals) (c/a ×d)
	%	%	%			%	%	%
News of the World	47·1	48·5	48·2	1·03	1·02	49	50·5	50·0
Sunday Pictorial	38·9	39·9	39·1	1·03	1·01	45	46·4	45·5
People	36·7	35·7	37·4	0·97	1·02	36	34·9	36·7
Sunday Express	25·7	25·3	25·2	0·98	0·98	26	25·5	25·5
Sunday Dispatch	13·1	13·7	13·9	1·05	1·06	13	13·7	13·8
The Sunday Times	6·4	5·4	6·0	0·84	0·94	10	8·4	9·4
The Observer	5·1	5·0	5·7	0·98	1·12	9	8·8	10·1
Average all						26·9	26·9	27·3

Table 8A.7 (cont.)

Publications	1958 figures for different order presentations			Conversion ratios		Present enquiry		
Weeklies	Third position (no reversal) (a)	Second position (with reversals) (b)	All four positions (with reversals) (c)	$\dfrac{b}{a}$	$\dfrac{c}{a}$	Third position (no reversal) (d)	Estimated second position (with reversals) (b/a×d)	Estimated all positions (with reversals) (c/a×d)
	%	%	%			%	%	%
Woman	29·1	29·1	28·0	1·00	0·96	38	38·0	36·5
Woman's Own	24·8	27·7	26·2	1·12	1·06	34	38·1	36·0
Radio Times	57·0	58·8	56·7	1·03	0·99	55	56·7	54·5
TV Times	27·7	26·7	26·9	0·96	0·97	43	41·3	41·7
Reveille	25·3	24·9	23·7	0·98	0·94	18	17·6	16·9
Average all						37·6	38·3	37·1
Monthlies	Fourth position (no reversal) (a)	First position (no reversal) (b)	All four positions (c)	$\dfrac{b}{a}$	$\dfrac{c}{a}$	Fourth position (no reversal) (d)	Estimated first position (with reversals) (b/a×d)	Estimated all positions (with reversals) (d/a×d)
	%	%	%			%	%	%
Readers Digest	20·6	22·2	21·7	1·08	1·05	23	24·8	24·2
Do It Yourself	10·6	12·4	9·9	1·17	0·93	12	14·0	11·2
Practical Householder	11·6	10·9	10·0	0·94	0·86	10	9·4	8·6
Ideal Home	8·9	10·4	8·7	1·17	0·98	7	8·2	6·9
Good Housekeeping	8·6	10·5	9·3	1·22	1·08	9	11·0	9·7
Vogue	7·3	9·4	8·2	1·29	1·12	10	12·9	11·2
Woman and Home	6·3	10·4	8·1	1·65	1·29	6	9·9	7·7
True Story	6·7	8·5	6·8	1·27	1·01	4	5·1	4·0
True Romances	6·6	8·5	6·8	1·29	1·03	2	2·6	2·1
Average all						9·2	10·9	9·5

APPENDIX 8.5

THE ACTUAL FORM OF THE FINAL MODIFICATION

Note: In the actual book of aids pages 376, 391 and 395 can be folded out, for continual reference.

Page 1 of the book·of aids is read by the interviewer as she faces
respondent on the doorstep. <u>No visual aids showing</u>. Page 1 measures
6" (deep) by 8" (wide). The page is semi-stiff board as are all the
pages in the book of aids. Page 1 is in light colour.

○   ○

* Do NOT depart from the instructions in this
  questionnaire. Stick to the wording completely.

* Pay special attention to getting the PROBE just
  right.
  ALL YES REPLIES MUST BE PROBED <u>FULLY</u>.

Establish the identity of your respondent. Then SAY:

I am working on a READERSHIP survey. I am asking people about the
newspapers and the magazines they have looked at.

I'd like to ask you some questions about what you have looked at
and what you have NOT looked at.

    As soon as you see you have a go-ahead on this, ASK
    RESPONDENT IF YOU CAN GO INSIDE THE HOUSE.

    If asked why you want to know about their reading,
    explain that it helps the publishers to know who
    their readers are, and that this can help them to
    design their papers for their <u>actual</u> readers.

Page 2, with back of page 1 (blank) shown to the respondent. Page
2 is on the back of the Reader's Digest mast-head. It measures
8" by 3",

○   <u>SAY SLOWLY</u>   ○

We want to ask you about the magazines and newspapers you have
looked at.

The first lot of magazines are monthlies and for each of them I
want to ask you if you looked at it in the last four weeks.

Now the last four weeks started on .... (give day and date).
Can you think of anything at all you were doing around that time?

<u>Enter this day and date on top of questionnaire</u>. Record what doing

I'm going to show you the names of each of these magazines. Then
I'll ask you if you actually looked at it in the LAST 4 WEEKS.

Page Three of book of aids. Whilst interviewers go through this page
the Reader's Digest mast-head is showing to the respondent. Page 3 of
the book of aids measures 6" (deep) by 8" (wide). Page 3 is in light
colour.

(SHOWING)
(READER'S DIGEST

○   ○

NEVER OMIT THIS

○   ○

SAY THIS SLOWLY

AND CLEARLY

I want to find out if you LOOKED AT any copy of READER'S DIGEST in
the LAST FOUR WEEKS - Don't hesitate to say NOT SURE.

Let respondent reply and then say, SLOWLY,

But let me tell you what I mean by LOOKED AT. It's got a special
meaning. By LOOKED AT I mean opening it and looking at what's
inside. It could be a lot or just a little - it might be just the
pictures of the adverts. We DON'T mean just seeing the cover.

Does that make any difference to your answer ?

Of course that includes looking at it in doctors' or dentists'
waiting-rooms, at work, at a friend's place, in a train, at a library,
.... anywhere at all.

Does that make a difference to your answer ?   RECORD FINAL REPLY.

If final reply is 'yes', PROBE as instructed.

The rest of the instructions for the monthlies follow each on the back
of a mast-head card, and each shown against the same setting. For
economy in presentation in this report, this common setting is given just
once, namely, on the fold-out page. But of course the relevant section
of it faces the respondent throughout, operating as a constant reminder
of certain important things.

This fold-out should be opened now. In the top half of the fold-out
page (shown upside down because it is meant to be in front of the
respondent), is the reference to the qualifying period (in this case
it reads:

ANY COPY IN

LAST 4 WEEKS)

The Respondent sees this particular statement just under the mast-
head being shown at that time. Each new mast-head flops down over
this continuing statement of the qualifying period.

At the bottom of this fold-out page is the probe to be used for all 'yes'
claims with respect to monthlies. This is showing all the time, the
mast-heads being set above it.

The following statements should be examined with page 376 extended, for they are all presented against this as a background or setting. What follows below is the content of each instruction page, just as it appears on the back of a masthead. In all cases the relative masthead was showing to the respondent at the time this instruction was being delivered. All cards are 3 inches deep and 8 inches wide, though they are shown in somewhat smaller dimensions in this document in order to fit as many as possible of them on one page.

O   O

The next one is DO IT YOURSELF

Did you look at any copy of DO IT YOURSELF in the LAST 4
WEEKS ?
Any copy ... (PAUSE) ... Anywhere ?

Probe if 'yes'

(No mast-head showing)

NEVER OMIT THIS
O   O

And of course for all these magazines, I mean ANY copy of it in
the last 4 weeks.

An OLD one or a NEW one, so long as it was in the last 4 weeks.

O   O

Have you looked at any copy of TRUE STORY in the last 4 weeks?

Probe 'yes'

NEVER OMIT THIS	Now could you just tell me what you think I mean by LOOKING AT so we can be sure we are both talking about the same thing. If in any way wrong, remind respondent that: + it does not include just seeing the cover + it means opening it and looking inside even if it was only the pictures or advertisements or only a small part of it. (If correct, say so/praise).

TRUE ROMANCES   (call it out)

Probe 'yes'

TRUE MAGAZINE   (call it out)

Probe 'yes'

PRACTICAL HOUSEHOLDER   (call it out)
Probe 'yes'

NEVER OMIT THIS

SAY SLOWLY AND CAREFULLY

Remember for every single magazine I ask you about, it would
be any place at all - at home, at work, in a doctor's or
dentist's waiting room, at the launderette, anywhere at all.
These all count. So don't forget that extra occasion.

Have you looked at

PRACTICAL MOTORIST in the last 4 weeks ?

Probe 'yes'

The next one is CAR MECHANICS

Probe 'yes'

IDEAL HOME in the last 4 weeks?

That would be since....(give DAY and DATE)

Probe if 'yes'

If 'no' say, "Could you possibly be mixing it up
with another one that sounds like it....a lot of
them do sound alike."

MY HOME   (call it out)

Probe 'yes'

Any copy of HOME in the last 4 weeks

Probe 'yes'

Remember: LOOKING AT means opening it and looking at what's inside.

MEN ONLY (and LILLIPUT)   Call it out.

Probe 'yes'

If 'yes', check that they mean the amalgamated publication and not
the original Lilliput or the original Men Only.   This is a common
source of error.

THE WIDE WORLD in the last 4 weeks.   Call it out.

Probe 'yes'

DON'T FORGET

Remember for every single one of these magazines, that it
could be any place at all - at home, at work, in a doctor's
or dentist's waiting-room, anywhere at all.   All these
places count, so don't forget that extra occasion.

Have you looked at GOOD HOUSEKEEPING in the last 4 weeks?

Probe if 'yes'

Now the next few sound a bit alike, so you'll need to be
especially careful with them.

HOUSEWIFE   (call it out)

Probe if 'yes'

Any copy of HOMES AND GARDENS in the last 4 weeks

Probe if 'yes'

HOMEMAKER   (call it out)

Probe if 'yes'

HOUSE BEAUTIFUL   (call it out)

Probe if 'yes'

Have you looked at any copy of

WOMAN AND HOME in the last 4 weeks ?

That will be since................(Give day and date).

DON'T FORGET

Probe if 'yes'

SINCERELY   (call it out)

Probe if 'yes'.

PHOTOPLAY   (call it out)

Probe if 'yes'

EVERYWOMAN   (call it out)

Probe if 'yes'

Have you looked at ANY copy of
WOMAN AND BEAUTY in the last 4 weeks ?

Probe if 'yes'

MODERN WOMAN   (call it out)

Probe if 'yes'

WOMAN'S JOURNAL   (call it out with stress on the word WOMAN'S)

Probe if 'yes'

ARGOSY..........(any copy at all)......in the last 4 weeks

Probe if 'yes'

VOGUE (call it out)   in the last 4 weeks - that will be since
                       (give day and date) ?

If you're NOT SURE, please say so.

If yes, say: We don't mean the pattern book - does that make any
             difference to your answer ?

Probe if still 'yes'

SHE   (call it out)

Probe if 'yes'.

Any copy of VANITY FAIR

Probe if 'yes'.

HONEY   (call it out)

Probe if 'yes'.

(NO MAST-HEAD SHOWING)

That is the end of the Monthly magazines.
The next lot come out WEEKLY.

This time I'll be asking you if you looked AT THEM IN THE
LAST 7 DAYS.

Now the last 7 days started on .... of last week.
Is that quite clear?

LAST 4 WEEKS

ANY COPY IN

(MASTHEADS)

○   ○

○   ○

(INSTRUCTIONS AS ON LEFT)

For monthly papers: If YES, PROBE as follows:

(a) DID YOU ACTUALLY LOOK INSIDE IT?   If 'yes', put ($\checkmark$) in Col. (a) and go
     on to (b).   If 'no' or 'not sure', put X in Col. (a) and drop the probe.

(b) ARE YOU ABSOLUTELY CERTAIN IT WAS ..... ?   If 'yes' put ($\checkmark$) in Col. (b)
     and go on to (c).   If 'no' or 'not sure' put X in Col. (b) and drop the
     probe.

(c) WHEN WAS THE VERY LAST TIME YOU LOOKED AT A COPY OF ..... ?   Record the
     time given.   If less than 4 weeks, ring 'yes' in final code.   If more
     than 4 weeks, ring 'no' in final code.   If '4 weeks' or 'month' given as
     time, ask: WOULD THAT BE MORE THAN 4 WEEKS OR LESS THAN 4 WEEKS?   If
     'less', ring 'yes' in final code.   If 'more' ring 'no' in final code.
     If doubtful ring (?) in final code.

The following instructions all deal with weekly publications. These are shown against the setting laid out on page 391. This page should now be folded out. It shows the continuing reference to the qualifying period (upside down in this document because it faces the respondent rather than the interviewer). On the lower part of the sheet are the probe questions as these apply to weekly and to Sunday publications, set on the backs of the mastheads measuring 8 inches by 3 inches.

O   O

The first one is RADIO TIMES.

Have you looked at RADIO TIMES in the LAST 7 DAYS?
It counts if you just looked up a programme in it.

Probe if 'yes'.

O   O

Now the next one is TV TIMES.

Did you look at any copy at all of this in the
last 7 days?

Probe if 'yes'.

O   O

THE LISTENER in the last 7 days.

Remember, even an old copy would count as long
as you looked at it in the last 7 days.

Probe if 'yes'.

THE VIEWER in the last 7 days.

Probe if 'yes'.

Remember, for all these papers, you could have looked at them at a friend's place, at work, on a train or bus, at the doctor's or dentist's - anywhere at all.

TELEVISION WEEKLY (call it out)

Probe if 'yes'.

TV GUIDE (call it out)

Probe if 'yes'.

SAY SLOWLY, AND GET RESPONDENT'S ATTENTION.

Now at this point we usually remind people what we mean by LOOKED AT.

It could mean reading a bit of it or just looking at the pictures or advertisements.

The next one is WOMAN'S DAY.

Did you look at that - in the last 7 days?

Probe if 'yes'.

STOP - SAY SLOWLY
The next few sound much the same - they all have the word WOMAN in them.
A lot of people get them mixed up.

Now have you looked at any copy of <u>WOMAN'S REALM</u> in the last 7 days?

That would go back to .... of last week.

Probe if 'yes'.

WOMAN'S <u>COMPANION</u> - call it out with stress on the word COMPANION.

Probe if 'yes'.

WOMAN (call it out)

Probe if 'yes'

WOMAN'S <u>MIRROR</u> - (call it out, stressing word MIRROR)

Probe if 'yes'.

WOMAN'S <u>WEEKLY</u> (call it out, stressing word WEEKLY)

Probe if 'yes'.

WOMAN'S <u>OWN</u> (call it out, stressing word OWN)

Probe if 'yes'.

WOMAN'S <u>ILLUSTRATED</u> (call it out, stressing word ILLUSTRATED)

Probe if 'yes'.

Now the next one is WEEKEND

Have you looked at WEEKEND in the last 7 days?

Probe if 'yes'.

MY WEEKLY (call it out)

Probe if 'yes'.

THE WEEKLY NEWS (call it out)

Probe if 'yes'.

Have you looked at any copy of <u>DATE</u> in the last 7 days?

Probe if 'yes'.

SILVER STAR (call it out)

Probe if 'yes'.

O   O

FAMILY STAR (call it out with stress on the word FAMILY)

Probe if 'yes'.

O   O

RED STAR (call it out)

Probe if 'yes'

O   O

RED LETTER (Call it out)

Probe if 'yes'.

Of course, for all these magazines it doesn't matter
where you were at the time or whose copy it was.

O   O

Have you looked at
PUNCH in the last 7 days ? That would be going back
to...... of last week.

Probe if 'yes'.

REVEILLE in the last 7 days ?

Probe if 'yes'

UNIVERSE in the last 7 days ?

Probe if 'yes'.

CHRISTIAN HERALD (Call it out)

Probe if 'yes'.

TIT-BITS

Probe if 'yes'.

PARADE (Call it out)

Probe if 'yes'.

ROXY in the last 7 days ?

Probe if 'yes'.

SECRETS   (Call it out)

Probe if 'yes'.

MARILYN (Call it out)

Probe if 'yes'.

MARTY   in the last 7 days.

Probe if 'yes'.

MIRABELLE   (call it out)

Probe if 'yes'.

VALENTINE - Did you look at any copy of that in the last 7 days ?

Probe if 'yes'.

BOYFRIEND   (Call it out)

Probe if 'yes'.

ROMEO   (Call it out)

Probe if 'yes'.

Any copy of PICTURE SHOW in the last 7 days ?

Probe if 'yes'.

THE PEOPLE'S FRIEND   (Call it out)

Probe if 'yes'.

TODAY   (Call it out)

Probe if 'yes'.

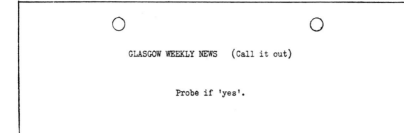

GLASGOW WEEKLY NEWS   (Call it out)

Probe if 'yes'.

This brings the interviewer to the end of the weeklies.   She introduces
the Sunday papers as set out on the next instructions sheet.   At this
point in the interview a blank·card covers the last mast-head, though
the general setting showing the qualifying period and the probe remain
visible (to the respondent and the interviewer respectively).

Now we come to the Sunday Papers..
The rules are just the same.

SAY
SLOWLY

1. It could be any copy of this paper
   so long as you yourself have looked
   at it in the last 7 days.

2. It doesn't matter where you were
   at the time.

The various Sunday mast-heads now follow

(SUNDAY PICTORIAL SHOWING)

Have you looked at any copy of SUNDAY PICTORIAL
in the last 7 days ?
That would be going back to.......of last week.

Probe if 'yes'.

DON'T OMIT

Now you will remember that it's only the last 7 days
we're interested in. If you looked at it before then,
it doesn't count.

SUNDAY   TIMES - in the last 7 days ?

Probe if 'yes'.

For all of these, it doesn't matter if it was an old
copy, so long as you looked at it in the last 7 days.

Now have you looked at
NEWS OF THE WORLD in the last 7 days ?

Probe if 'yes'.

REYNOLDS NEWS   (call it out)

Probe if 'yes'

SUNDAY DISPATCH   (call it out)

Probe if 'yes'

THE PEOPLE   (call it out)

Probe if 'yes'

Have you looked at any copy of
THE OBSERVER in the last 7 days ?

Probe if 'yes'

SUNDAY GRAPHIC   (call it out)

Probe if 'yes'

SUNDAY EXPRESS (Call it out)

Probe if 'yes'.

THE GLASGOW SUNDAY POST (Call it out)

Probe if 'yes'.

GLASGOW SUNDAY MAIL

Probe if 'yes'.

LAST 7 DAYS

ANY COPY IN

(MASTHEAD SHOWING)

◯   ◯

◯   ◯

(INSTRUCTIONS AS ON LEFT)

For weekly and Sunday papers.   If YES, PROBE as follows:

(a)   DID YOU ACTUALLY LOOK AT IT?   If yes, put (✓) in Col. (a) and go on to
      (b).   If 'no' or 'not sure' put X in Col. (a) and drop the probe.

(b)   ARE YOU ABSOLUTELY CERTAIN IT WAS .... ?   If 'yes' put (✓) in Col. (b)
      and go on to (c).   If 'no' or 'not sure' put X in Col. (b) and drop the
      probe.

(c)   WHEN WAS THE VERY LAST TIME YOU LOOKED AT A COPY OF .... ?   Write down
      the period given.   If less than 7 days, ring 'yes' in final code.   If
      more than 7 days, ring 'no' in final code.

      If respondent says 'today', say that TODAY does not count and ask respondent
      'WHEN WAS THE VERY LAST TIME BEFORE TODAY?'

      If respondent says 'a week'. or '7 days' enter this in Col. (c) but say
      'WOULD IT BE DURING THE LAST 7 DAYS OR BEFORE THAT?'   Ring final code as
      'yes' or 'no' or '?' according to reply.

The following instructions all deal with the daily publications. These are shown against the setting laid out on page 395. This should now be unfolded. It shows the continuing reference to the new qualifying period (yesterday): the special probe for dailies.

NO MAST-HEAD SHOWING

○   ○

Now, finally here are the DAILIES.
I want to know if you looked at the YESTERDAY.
It's just YESTERDAY I am asking about.

○   ○

Did you look at the   DAILY EXPRESS.......yesterday?

Probe if 'yes'

(If they say it was today, ask when was the last
occasion not counting today)

○   ○

Did you look at the   DAILY MIRROR.........YESTERDAY ?

Probe if 'yes'

1. Remember, for every single paper I ask you about
   it could be anywhere at all - at work, on a train
   or bus, at a friend's place, in a library.   Anywhere at all.

2. Also, an old copy counts so long as you looked at it
   YESTERDAY.

The DAILY SKETCH...........Yesterday ?

Probe if 'yes'

The DAILY MAIL.............YESTERDAY ?

Probe if 'yes'

The DAILY HERALD.........(call it out)

Probe if 'yes'

Did you look at any copy of

THE TIMES......... yesterday ?

Probe if 'yes'

The EVENING STANDARD   (Call it out)

Probe if 'yes'

The EVENING NEWS .... yesterday?

Probe if 'yes'.

The DAILY TELEGRAPH .... yesterday?

Probe if 'yes'.

THE GUARDIAN

Probe if 'yes'.

GLASGOW DAILY RECORD

Probe if 'yes'.

ХЕSTERDAY

ANY COPY

(MASTHEAD SHOWING)

○   ○

○   ○

(INSTRUCTIONS AS ON LEFT)

For Daily Papers.   If YES, PROBE as follows.

(a) DID YOU ACTUALLY LOOK AT IT?   If 'yes' put (✓) in Col. (a) and go on to
     (b).   If 'no' or 'not sure' put X in Col. (a) and drop the probe.

(b) ARE YOU ABSOLUTELY CERTAIN IT WAS .... ?   If 'yes' put (✓) in Col. (b)
     and go on to (c).   If 'no' or 'not sure' put X in Col. (b) and drop the
     probe.

(c) ARE YOU QUITE CERTAIN IT WAS YESTERDAY?
     Write down the period given.   If yesterday, ring 'yes' in final code.   If
     not yesterday, ring 'no' in final code.

     If respondent says TODAY, say that TODAY does not count, and ask 'When was
     the very last time before today?'

     If respondent can't say or is not sure, say 'DID YOU LOOK AT IT YESTERDAY?'
     Ring Yes/No/? in final code.

9 Modifying a radio diary towards greater effectiveness

A SUMMARY WITH EMPHASIS ON METHODS OF RESEARCH
AND THE FINAL FORM OF THE DIARY

DRAWN FROM A STUDY COMMISSIONED BY THE
BUREAU OF BROADCAST MEASUREMENT IN CANADA[44]

RESEARCH BY

William Belson, BA, PhD
Ken Purdye, BSc (Econ.)

Conducted in association with the Technical Research Committee of the Bureau of Broadcast Measurement (BBM) under the Chairmanship of Phil Jursek, BA, PhD.

Acknowledgement

The writer thanks Peter Jones, President of BBM, for facilitating the study and for the release of this summary of it.

CONTENTS OF CHAPTER

INTRODUCTION

The methods that had been used in modifying the National Readership Survey towards greater accuracy were later used in other studies. One of these concerned a radio diary developed by the Bureau of Broadcasting Measurement in Canada in 1973.

The background to this Canadian study was as follows. The Bureau of Broadcast Measurement (BBM) had since 1967 been administering a diary which collected information about both radio and television exposure. In 1973, in response to a request by members of the survey's Controlling Committee, the BBM conducted a comparative study of the results from a radio-only diary, a TV-only diary and from the existing radio-plus-TV diary. The results were published in 1974 and revealed that the single-medium diaries, especially the radio-only diary, yielded significantly higher 'size of audience' figures than did the dual-medium diary.[31]

Following the issue of the findings of the comparative study, the Controlling Committee agreed that a study be made of the validity of single-medium diaries, for completion by early 1975. The author was brought in by BBM to conduct the validity study and, following this, to use the method of progressive modification to modify the single-diary method towards greater validity.

In this chapter I am going to concentrate upon the use of the progressive modification method in the context of modifying the radio-only diary towards greater accuracy. The researcher who wants full details of the study will find them in the full report of the BBM.[32] More specifically, my outline will have the following coverage: (1) a short description of the methods used in the investigation; (2) a short statement of the findings as they relate to the accuracy of the radio diary, and the causes of such inaccuracy as was found; and (3) a more extended description of the ways in which the final form of the diary (after two stages of modification) differed from that of the original radio diary.

METHODS OF RESEARCH RELEVANT TO THE RADIO-ONLY DIARY

THE OVERALL STRATEGY OF RESEARCH

The method used was that of the intensive interview built into the progressive modification strategy. In other words, the original form of the radio-only diary was subjected to a test by the intensive interviewing method. The results of this test were studied for level of error and reasons for error. On the basis of such evidence, the form of the radio diary was modified. The modified form of the radio diary was then subjected to test through the intensive interviewing method and a further modification was made.

Cycle 1 of the progressive modification sequence was based upon 87 diarists, all in the Toronto area. Cycle 2 was based upon 64 Toronto diarists.

THE ARRANGEMENTS FOR DIARY KEEPING AND THE TIMES OF THE INTENSIVE INTERVIEWS

Diaries were posted in the usual way. For the intensive follow-up an appointment was made by telephone for an intensive interviewer to call on a given diarist. The reason for the call was not given at this point but a $5 fee was offered. The arrangements for the intensive interview were made by members of the intensive interviewing team themselves. Once in the respondent's home, the intensive interviewer explained that her purpose was to check the adequacy of the diary — not to test the respondent — and thereafter concentrated her attention on the diary entries for 'yesterday'. The 'yesterday's tested were spread over the whole week of the diary period.

THE NATURE OF THE INTENSIVE INTERVIEW

The intensive interview, which was fully tape-recorded, consisted of a number of steps, as follows (see also Figure 9.1).

1   A full explanation was given to the respondent of the purposes and nature of the interview (to get the respondent co-operating).

2   The interviewer then set out to establish the general background to the diarist's listening behaviour: the composition of the household; what the diarist usually listens to; who does the tuning in the household; *where* listening takes place including car listening; likes and dislikes with respect to radio programmes; number, type and location of sets available to the diarist; places other than home and car where radio is listened to.

3   The interviewer was required to find out if the diary for 'yesterday' was fully completed — getting the respondent to complete it if this had not been done already.

```
┌─────────────────────────────────────────────────────────────────────┐
│ INTRODUCTION:   A general orientation to the intensive interview      │
└─────────────────────────────────────────────────────────────────────┘

┌─────────────────────────────────────────────────────────────────────┐
│ STAGE A (1):   Securing background details relating to radio listening:│
│              • in what places respondent listens and to what          │
│              • stations listened to and program preferences           │
│              • tuning behaviour/number and location of sets           │
└─────────────────────────────────────────────────────────────────────┘

┌─────────────────────────────────────────────────────────────────────┐
│ STAGE A (2):   Screening out non-qualifying diarists                  │
└─────────────────────────────────────────────────────────────────────┘

┌─────────────────────────────────────────────────────────────────────┐
│ STAGE A (3):   The diarist's understanding of instructions and        │
│                of basic terms                                         │
└─────────────────────────────────────────────────────────────────────┘

┌─────────────────────────────────────────────────────────────────────┐
│ STAGE B:   Further preparation of the diarist for intensive interviewing│
│            about the details of his 'yesterday'                       │
└─────────────────────────────────────────────────────────────────────┘

┌─────────────────────────────────────────────────────────────────────┐
│ STAGE C:   A first step in getting details of the diarist's yesterday:│
│            his main events                                            │
└─────────────────────────────────────────────────────────────────────┘

┌─────────────────────────────────────────────────────────────────────┐
│ STAGE D:   Second (and final) step in filling in the diarist's 'yesterday',│
│            complete with quarter-hour record of activities, locations │
│            and listening behaviour — aided by rigorous challenging and│
│            by reference back to the details of Stage A (1)            │
└─────────────────────────────────────────────────────────────────────┘

┌─────────────────────────────────────────────────────────────────────┐
│ STAGE E:   Confrontation of diarist with a comparison of his diary entries│
│            and his evidence from Stage D, leading to a well-probed     │
│            explanation of any discrepancies                           │
└─────────────────────────────────────────────────────────────────────┘

┌─────────────────────────────────────────────────────────────────────┐
│ STAGE F:   Finding out how the diarist reacted to and coped with the diary│
└─────────────────────────────────────────────────────────────────────┘

     ► FURTHER MODIFICATION OF THE DIARY
```

Figure 9.1   The sequence of steps in the intensive interview
and the internal logic of that sequence

4   The intensive interviewer now focused the diarist's attention on 'yesterday' and stimulated the diarist's memory by going through a large number of public events of that day (that is, as reported in the Press).

5   The intensive interviewer then encouraged the respondent to think about his *private* events of 'yesterday' (using a checklist of ordinary household events as a preliminary aid).

6   The next step involved 'locating' the diarist throughout the day, going from before he arose, to the time of getting up, to first location after getting up, and so on. For each location during the day, he was asked where he was and (if the question was reasonable and discreet) what he was doing and who he was with. After this — *for each location* — he was asked about his listening, with the intensive interviewer making full use of his knowledge of the availability of working radio sets to each location. All claims *not* to have listened (when opportunity for this existed) were checked. Equally, all claims to *have* listened were challenged in terms of opportunity to listen and in terms of what was on at that time (on the station claimed). Station listened to was asked for and challenged.

7   At the end of this vital stage in the questioning, the diarist and the intensive interviewer worked together to discover any points of difference between the diary record of yesterday's listening and the intensive interview evidence. Where a difference occurred, the diarist was asked which statement was correct and what he felt lay behind that difference. This was the 'confrontation' stage of the interview.

8   Finally, the diarist was questioned to find out how he reacted to the diary and was asked to suggest ways in which the diary might be improved.

THE FORM OF THE RADIO DIARY THAT
WAS TO BE TESTED/MODIFIED

The diary in its initial (that is, pre-modification) form is illustrated in Figures 9.2–9.5.
    Its central features were as follows:

1   The original diary was printed in both English and French, with rotation of the use of each language.

2   The diary began with a 'General instructions' section and was followed by a section called 'How to keep your diary'. These two sections were illustrated with an example of a completed page of the diary (Figure 9.2).

3   Then came a section asking for various personal details, for example, age, sex, languages spoken, present occupation, and so on (see Figure 9.3).

4   After this came a small booklet built into the self-completion document and starting with the first page of the diary itself. It ran from Sunday through to Sunday. It requested 'stations listened to for each quarter-hour of the day', running from 5 am through to 1 am each day. For each quarter-hour sector information was sought about whether the listening was at home or away from home (that is, car/other) (see Figure 9.4). This kind of information was sought for each of eight days, Sunday to Sunday.

5   At the bottom of the page for each day, there was a box for the diarist to tick if he had not 'tuned in' at all that day.

6   At the end of the eight-day diary, there was a large space for the diarist to write his 'comments' on radio programmes (Figure 9.5).

Even without the aid of research, several features of this diary seemed to the writer to be error prone.

1   The 'General instructions' referred to 'listening' *and* to 'tuning' as if those two terms were synonymous.

2   The request for personal details came very early in the diary — something likely to be off-putting to diarists and something of a barrier to full completion of the diary.

3   The quarter-hour periods presented in the diary were in very small print — much smaller in fact than the code numbers that office staff would later use for processing the diary yield.

4   There was no *repetition* in the diary of the rules for diary keeping — one mention was all that each rule had.

5   The request for 'Comments' came at the *end* of the diary — whereas early placement of it would probably have 'tied' the diarist into completion of the rest of the diary — for the diarist would want his/her opinions about programmes to be noted.

COMMENT REMPLIR CE CAHIER D'ÉCOUTE

Seule, la oersonne à qui est adressée ce cahier doit y indiquer son écoute de la radio. Il

quer son ecoute de la radio. Il ne faut pas indiquer l' écoute des autres personnes. Pour chaque jour de la semaine, il y a deux pages.

Indiquer tous les moments pendant lesquels vous avez écouté la radio, à la maison, en automobile ou ailleurs même si vous êtes en vacances ou en voyage.

Il faut inscrire votre écoute de la radio pendant la semaine indiquée, même si ce n'est pas une semaine ordinaire; inscrivez les moments réels d' écoute et dans la page des commentaires à la fin du cahier, vous pouvez dire pourquoi ce n' est pas une semaine ordinaire.

Commencez à remplir ce cahier d' écoute la première journée du sandage.

FACON DE PROCEDER

1. Lorsque vous écoutez la radio, vous inscrivez les lettres d' appel de la station écoutée dans la colonne " station ".

2. Vous faites un crochet (√) dans l a colonne "à la maison" ou dans la colonne " en auto/ailleurs" pour indiquer à quel endroit vous étiez quand vous avez écouté.

3. Quand vous commencez à écouter la radio, vous faites une ligne horizontale, ou is vous en faites une autre, quand vous écoutez une autre station ou quand vous cessez d' écouter. (Voir l' exemple)

4. Il faut indiquer tous les ¼ d'heures pendant lesquels vous avez écouté la radio.

5. Si vous n'avez pas écoute la radio une journée donnée, n'oubliez pas de l'indiquer au bas de la page. Ceci est très important.

RADIO

TIME HEURE AM	STATION		AT HOME A LA MAISON	CAR OTHER AUTO AUTRE
5.00-5.15		1		
5.15-5.30		2		
5.30-5.45	CDXZ	3	√	
5.45-6.00		4	√	
6.00-6.15		5	√	
6.15-6.30		6		
6.30-6.45		7		
6.45-7.00		8		
7.00-7.15	CDXZ	9	√	
7.15-7.30		10	√	
7.30-7.45		11	√	
7.45-8.00	CLIP – FM	12	√	
8.00-8.15		13	√	
8.15-8.30		14	√	
8.30-8.45		15	√	
8.45-9.00		16		
9.00-9.15		17		
9.15-9.30		18		
9.30-9.45		19		
9.45-10.00		20		
10.00-10.15		21		
10.15-10.30		22		
10.30-10.45		23		
10.45-11.00		24		
11.00-11.15		25		
11.15-11.30	CSYT	26	√	
11.30-11.45		27	√	
11.45-12.00		28	√	
PM 12.00-12.15		29	√	
12.15-12.30	CSYT	30		√
12.30-12.45		31		√
12.45-1.00		32		√
1.00-1.15		33		
1.15-1.30		34		
1.30-1.45		35		
1-45-2.00		36		
2.00-2.15		37		
2.15- 2.30		38		
2.30-2.45		39		
2.45-3.00		40		

GENERAL INSTRUCTIONS

This is a personal diary. Enter only your own listening to radio.

There are two pages for each day of the week.

Please enter all your listening, including in car, at work, on holiday etc. If for any reason your listening is different from what it normally is, still record it but state this in the comments section at back of dira

section at back of diary.

Start recording your tuning the first day of the survey.

HOW TO KEEP YOUR DIARY

1. Write call letters of sta

1. Write call letters of station tuned .

2. Place check mark (√) in appropriate column to show whether you tuned "At Home" or "Car/ Other."

3. Check all quarter hours tuned .

4. Draw horizontal lines when you begin and end tuning and when you change stations.

5. If you do no listening for a specific day indicate in box at bottom of page.

Note: Shaded areas of **TIME** and **AT HOME** columns are blue. The **CAR/OTHER** column is yellow.

Figure 9.2   Opening spread of radio diary

IMPORTANT
PLEASE ANSWER THE FOLLOWING QUESTIONS FIRST

1. Sex
Check (√) one square
Male 1□
Female 2□

2. Age
Check (√) one square
Years
2-6 1□
7-11 2□
12-17 3□
18-24 4□
25-34 5□
35-49 6□
50-64 7□
65 and over 8□

3. Which of the following languages can You speak?
Check(√) one square
English only 1□
French only 2□
Both English and French 3□

4. What is your present occupation (work 0r job)
Check (√) one square only
Student (include pre-school children) 1□
Housewife (not doing any other whole time job) 2□
Retired 3□
Manager / Professional (include proprietors, executives, doctors, teachers, nurses, armed forces officers, etc.) 4□
Official / Sales (include bookkeepers, stenographers, all sales people 5□
Farmer / Farm Worker 6□
Unemployed 7□
All Other Workers not above included 8□
If in doubt, write your occupation below:

5. What was the last grade YOU completed in school?
Check (√) one square
No formal schooling 1□
Some grade school (grades1-7) 2□
Completed grade school (grade8) 3□
Some Vocational or High School (grades 9-11) 4□
Graduated from Vocational or High School (grade 12 or 13) 5□
Special or professional training without University education 6□
Some College or University 7□
Graduated from College or University 8□
Post graduate studies.

6. What language did you first learn in childhood and still understand?
English 1□
French 2□
If other, please specify

7. Which one of the following are you?
Check (√) one square only
Man of the house 1□
Woman of the house 2□
Son or Daughter 3□
Living with parents 4□
Other

8. Are there any children under 12 years in your home?
Yes 1□
No 2□

9. How many persons, including yourself, are living in your home, apartment or flat? (write number of persons)
Number

IMPORTANT
VEUILLEZ D'ABORD REPONDRE A CES QUESTIONS

1. Votre sexe
Masculin 1□
Feminin 2□

2. Votre âge
2-6 ans 1□
7-11 ans 2□
12-17 qns 3□
18-24 ans 4□
25-34 ans 5□
35-49 ans 6□
50-64 ans 7□
65 ans et plus 8□

3. Quelle langue parlez-vous?
Français seulement 1□
Français et Anglais 2□
Autre langue 3□

4. Quelle est votre occupation?
Ménagère 1□
Etudiant 2□
Enfant 2 à 6 ans 3□
Retraité 4□
Directeur / gérant / professionnel (incluant propriétaire d'entrept d'entreprises, administrateur, médecin, instituteur, contremaître) 5□
Employé de bureau / vendeur 6□
Ouvrier agricole / cultivateur 7□
Chômeurs 8□
Tout autre ouvrier 9□
Si en doute, indiquez votre occupation ci-dessous.

5. Combien d'années d'étude avez-vous complétées?
Aucune 1□
Ecole élémentaire (1 a 7 ans) 2□
Ecole secondaire (8 a 11 ans) 3□
Ecole technique ou école spécialisée 4□
Cours collégial 5□
Université 6□

6. Quelle est la première langue que vous avez apprise dans l'enfance?
Français 1□
Anglais 2□
Autre 3□

7. Etes-vous
Le chef de famille 1□
La maîtresse de maison 2□
Le fils ou la fille vivant avec ses parents 3□
Autre 4□

8. Y-a-t-il des enfants de 12 ans et moins dans votre foyer?
Oui 1□
Non 2□

9. Comien de personnes, en vous comptant, vivent dans votre logement? Inscrire le nombre de personne y compris vous-même

Figure 9.3 Section in radio diary requesting personal details

THURSDAY/JEUDI ④ RADIO

TIME HEURE ► A.M. ◄	STATION		AT HOME À LA MAISON	CAR OTHER AUTO AUTRE
5.00-5.15		1		
5.15-5.30		2		
5.30-5.45		3		
5.45-6.00		4		
6.00-6.15		5		
6.15-6.30		6		
6.30-6.45		7		
6.45-7.00		8		
7.00-7.15		9		
7.30		10		
7.30-7.45		11		
7.45-8.00		12		
8.00-8.15		13		
8.15-8.30		14		
8.30-8.45		15		
8.45-9.00		16		
9.00-9.15		17		
9.15-9.30		18		
9.30-9.45		19		
9.45-10.00		20		
10.00-10.15		21		
10.15-10.30		22		
10.30-10.45		23		
10.45-11.00		24		
11.00-11.15		25		
11.15-11.30		26		
11.30-11.45		27		
11.45-12.00		28		
► P.M. ◄ 12.00-12.15		29		
12.15-12.30		30		
12.45		31		
12.45-1.00		32		
1.00-1.15		33		
1.15-1.30		34		
1.30-1.45		35		
1.45-2.00		36		
2.00-2.15		37		
2.15-2.30		38		
2.30-2.45		39		
2.45-3.00		40		

Please check ☑ if you did not tune to Radio Thursday ☐

Reminder! Have you answered the questions in the front page?

7

JEUDI/THURSDAY ④ RADIO

HEURE TIME ► P.M. ◄	STATION		À LA MAISON AT HOME	AUTO AUTRE CAR OTHER
3.00-3.15		41		
3.15-3.30		42		
3.30-3.45		43		
3.45-4.00		44		
4.00-4.15		45		
4.15-4.30		46		
4.30-4.45		47		
4.45-5.00		48		
5.00-5.15		49		
5.15-5.30		50		
5.30-5.45		51		
5.45-6.00		52		
6.00-6.15		53		
6.15-6.30		54		
6.30-6.45		55		
6.45-7.00		56		
7.00-7.15		57		
7.15-7.30		58		
7.30-7.45		59		
7.45-8.00		60		
8.00-8.15		61		
8.15-8.30		62		
8.30-8.45		63		
8.45-9.00		64		
9.00-9.15		65		
9.15-9.30		66		
9.30-9.45		67		
9.45-10.00		68		
10.00-10.15		69		
10.15-10.30		70		
10.30-10.45		71		
10.45-11.00		72		
11.00-11.15		73		
11.15-11.30		74		
11.30-11.45		75		
11.45-12.00		76		
► A.M. ◄ 12.00-12.15		77		
12.15-12.30		78		
12.30-12.45		79		
12.45-1.00		80		

Cochez S.V.P. ☑ si vous n'avez pas écouté la Radio jeudi ☐

À noter! Avez-vous répondu aux questions sur la page couverture? 8

Note: Shaded area of TIME and AT HOME columns are blue.
The CAR/OTHER columns are yellow.

Figure 9.4 A typical diary page

405

FOLD THIS OVER THE FRONT PAGE AND SEAL — PLIEZ SUR LA COUVERTURE ET COLLEZ

COMMENTAIRES

Veuilles utiliser cet espace pour inscrire vos commentaires sur ce que vous aimez, ou n'aimez pas, vos reflexions et vos critiques sur les programmes, la musique et les annonces commerciales.
Vos commentaires sont tres importants et nous les apprecierons vivement

COMMENTS

Please use this space to comment about your likes and dislikes, your thoughts and criticisms of programs, music and commercials. Your comments are valuable and will be greatly appreciated

Figure 9.5   Section in radio diary requesting comments

FINDINGS

THE FIRST CYCLE OF THE TEST-MODIFICATION

The intensive interview (based on 87 cases) revealed a great many errors by diarists and the confrontation part of the interview produced the following explanations by respondents.

Table 9.1
Reasons for error yielded through the confrontation stage
of the intensive interview*

	n†
Did not count it because he was doing something else	8
Respondent counted it only if really interested in what was on	8
Respondent counted only the tuning he did himself	6
It was just a short period so he didn't enter it	1
Didn't know it was important to include the few odd minutes	2
Respondent listed only his car listening	2
Respondent listed only his home listening	1
Respondent listed only his 'getting up and going to bed' listening	1
Respondent answered in terms of what he usually or habitually does	8
Respondent got the time wrong	2
Respondent didn't really know the time of his listening	2
Respondent didn't enter his listening because he didn't know what station he was on	7
Radio listening is not all that important to the respondent	1
Respondent was in a hurry and so put off filling in some part of listening	2
Respondent didn't have time to make entry	2
Respondent didn't write it down straight away and so forgot	3
Diary not filled in yet	2
Didn't have diary with him in car	3
Car too bumpy to enter details in diary	1
Diary was filled in in advance of listening (which did not occur)	1
Someone other than the diarist filled it in	3
Respondent answered diary for his wife	1
Respondent made entries on wrong day of diary	1
Respondent was sleepy/it was late when diary filled in	5
Respondent was just guessing	1
Listening to traffic news was forgotten	1
Just forgot to enter it	38
Made a mistake in drawing horizontal line	1
Respondent does not know how many minutes qualify as 'listening'	4
Received the diary too late for accurate entries	1
All reasons	119
Total cases	87

*For 'he' read also 'she'.
†The number of mentions of the different reasons on this table must not be interpreted with numerical exactness and certainly must not be converted into population distributions. The numbers under 'n' represent no more than the number of times that certain reasons for error were volunteered by respondents. Sometimes the reason given by a respondent relates to a whole set of errors; sometimes the diarist could not offer a reason at all; occasionally a diarist gave two reasons for a single error.

'Forgot to enter' it (38 mentions) was usually explained by the diarist for example because:

- I am too old;
- I had something else on my mind;
- I was distracted by getting my car unparked;
- I had visitors;
- I forgot I had it on to wake me up;
- I made the entries next day and forgot certain of them;
- my listening was out of my usual schedule/don't usually have it on at that time;
- I was in another room;
- I got the wrong day;
- I had first to get home (and forgot by the time I got there).

In addition, there were complaints that:

- the small print in the diary was hard to read;
- the diary itself fell apart due to weak construction;
- listening which is done while on vacation is not catered for;
- instructions were unclear regarding a number of points (for example, aims of the study, definition of listening, means of filling out);
- the contact letter and introductory material was either vague or not understandable.

The various reasons for error and the complaints about the diary provided fairly clear indications for change in the form of the diary, for example:

- delete the word 'tuning' in the instructions;
- redefine listening to include whatever level of listening is regarded as relevant to the investigation;
- discourage diarists from answering in terms of what they *usually* do;
- stress the need to record *all* listening — not just car listening or just home listening;
- attempt to motivate the diarist so that the diary is taken seriously;
- remind the diarist of the rules for completion, with repeats of the rules throughout the diary.

THE SECOND CYCLE OF TEST-MODIFICATION

The diary was changed accordingly and then subjected to a second cycle of test-modification. In this cycle, 64 diarists were put through normal diary keeping (with the modified diary) and were then intensively interviewed. They were, as was the Cycle 1 sample, asked also to explain any discrepancies between diary and intensive interview results and to suggest changes that could be made in the diary. These findings were taken into close consideration in designing the second modification of the radio-only diary.

THE FORM OF THE SECOND MODIFICATION OF THE RADIO DIARY

The form of the radio-only diary had by this time changed substantially from its initial form. The main features of the second modification are shown in Figures 9.6 to 9.14, and the full diary is given in the Appendix to this chapter. The reader should note the following of its features, each determined by the tests made in Cycles 1 and 2 of the progressive modification system.

1   The section of the diary dealing with comments on programmes ('Your opinions of radio') was presented at the very beginning of the diary in order to encourage people to complete the diary (that is, to ensure that their comments were seen by the authorities). On this page the diarist was also asked to name his main interests, say whether that interest could be catered for on radio and whether or not he thought it *was* being catered for on radio (Figure 9.6).

2   Then came a set of 'General instructions' (Figure 9.7) through which an attempt was made to avoid the miscommunications of the original statement.

3   There was a box for ticking when the respondent had read *all* his instructions (and this was done for all instructions on all pages).

4   An example of a completed page of the diary followed (Figure 9.8) and then came a step-by-step instruction for keeping the diary (Figure 9.9).

5   Next came a diary page for Sunday (Figure 9.10) — in fact it was regarded by Head Office only as giving the diarist a practice run. On this diary page there was a repeat of two key rules under the heading 'May we remind you' (for example, 'The rules for completing this diary are most important. Go back to them on page 5 if you are in the slightest doubt about what to do . . . . Even if you don't have any doubts, go back and study the rules from time to time').

┌─────────────────────────────┐
│   **QUE PENSEZ-VOUS DE LA RADIO?**   │
└─────────────────────────────┘

Just before you start your diary, please give us your opinions about what you hear on radio. What do you think of the programs broadcast by the stations? ... the music? ... the news? ... the announcers etc.? Please give your views and your suggestions for improvement.

Avant de commencer à remplir votre cahier d'écoute, pouvez-vous nous donner votre opinion sur la radio? Que pensez-vous de ce qui est diffusé par les stations? de la musique? des nouvelles? etc. ... Quelles améliorations seraient souhaitables dans les émissions?

_____

_____

_____

_____

_____

_____

_____

_____

SPARE TIME INTERESTS AND ACTIVITIES

(a) What is your main spare time interest or activity (for example, a sport, cooking, music, theatre, reading, horse racing)?

ACTIVITÉS DE LOISIRS

(a) Quelle est votre principale activité de loisirs? (par exemple: un sport, la cuisine, la lecture, le cinéma, le théatre, etc. ...)

(b) Is this spare time interest or activity the sort that could be dealt with on radio? . . . .

yes ☐ oui
no ☐ non

(b) Est-ce que, selon vous, il est possible de traiter ce sujet à la radio? . . .

(c) If yes, do you find the radio coverage of it satisfactory?

yes ☐ oui
no ☐ non

(c) Actuellement est-ce que les stations de radio en parlent suffisamment à votre goût? . . .

2

Figure 9.6   Section in revised radio diary requesting opinions of radio

410

GENERAL INSTRUCTIONS.

(Please take a few minutes to read them).

1. This diary is for **you** personally. It is meant to tell us what **you yourself** listened to on the radio on the days in your diary. Enter in the diary everything that you yourself listened to, no matter who did the tuning.

2. We are asking about your radio listening on the 8 days named in the diary. It is those particular days we are interested in, even if your listening on them was different from what you usually do.

3. It counts as listening so long as you are taking notice of what is being broadcast.

4. We need to know about **all** your listening, even if it was for just a short time.

5. We need to know about your listening no matter **where** you did it or the time of day you did it.

6. Please be careful in filling in your diary. We need accurate information because important decisions are made on the basis of what we find out. Write in your listening as soon as possible after you do it. And at the end of each day check through your diary to make sure you have entered **all** your listening for that day.

7. We are just as interested in people who do **no** listening as we are in people who do a lot of it.

Remember: It counts as listening as long as you are paying some attention to what is being broadcast.

Please check (✓) this box when you have definitely read all these general instructions. ☐

COMMENT REMPLIR CE CAHIER D'ÉCOUTE.

(S.V.P. prenez quelques minutes pour lire cette page)

1. Ce cahier d'écoute est pour votre usage exclusif. Il nous permettra de connaître votre écoute de la radio pour chaque journée du sondage. Vous devez inscrire dans ce cahier tout ce que vous avez écouté à la radio, même si ce n'est pas vous qui avez ouvert l'appareil.

2. Les jours pour lesquels vous devez indiquer votre écoute de la radio sont inscrits sur la page couverture. Seules ces journées nous intéressent, même si ce n'est pas ce que vous faites habituellement.

3. Vous inscrivez que vous avez écouté la radio si vous entendez la radio et si vous prêtez un peu attention à ce qui est diffusé.

4. Il est important d'inscrire toute votre écoute même si c'est une courte période de temps.

5. Il est important d'inscrire votre écoute quel que soit l'endroit où vous avez écouté et quel que soit le moment de la journée.

6. Veuillez remplir votre cahier d'écoute avec soin. Les informations doivent être les plus précises possible: des décisions importantes peuvent être prises par la suite. A la fin de chaque jour, regardez votre cahier d'écoute afin de vérifier si vous avez bien inscrit toute votre écoute.

7. Nous sommes autant intéressés aux réponses des personnes qui n'écoutent pas la radio que de celles qui l'écoutent beaucoup.

N'oubliez pas: vous inscrivez que vous avez écouté la radio si vous entendez la radio **et** que vous prêtez un peu attention à ce qui est diffusé.

Cochez dès que vous avez terminé de lire ces instructions ☐

3

Figure 9.7   Section in revised radio diary giving general instructions

411

EXEMPLE/EXAMPLE

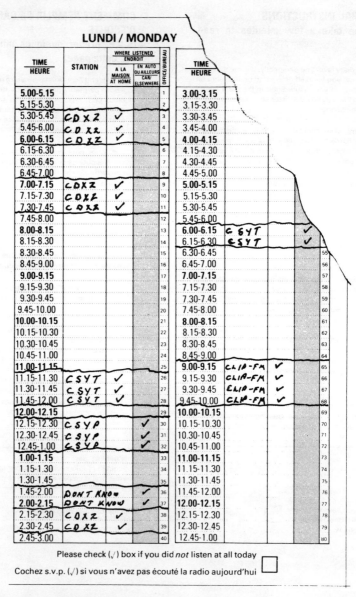

LUNDI / MONDAY									

LUNDI / MONDAY

TIME HEURE	STATION	WHERE LISTENED ENDROIT				TIME HEURE			
		A LA MAISON AT HOME	EN AUTO OU AILLEURS CAR/ ELSEWHERE	OFFICE/BUREAU					
5.00-5.15					1	3.00-3.15			
5.15-5.30					2	3.15-3.30			
5.30-5.45	CDXZ	✓			3	3.30-3.45			
5.45-6.00	CD XZ	✓			4	3.45-4.00			
6.00-6.15	CDXZ	✓			5	4.00-4.15			
6.15-6.30					6	4.15-4.30			
6.30-6.45					7	4.30-4.45			
6.45-7.00					8	4.45-5.00			
7.00-7.15	CDXZ	✓			9	5.00-5.15			
7.15-7.30	COXZ	✓			10	5.15-5.30			
7.30-7.45	CDXZ	✓			11	5.30-5.45			
7.45-8.00					12	5.45-6.00			
8.00-8.15					13	6.00-6.15	C 6YT		✓
8.15-8.30					14	6.15-6.30	CSYT		✓
8.30-8.45					15	6.30-6.45			55
8.45-9.00					16	6.45-7.00			56
9.00-9.15					17	7.00-7.15			57
9.15-9.30					18	7.15-7.30			58
9.30-9.45					19	7.30-7.45			59
9.45-10.00					20	7.45-8.00			60
10.00-10.15					21	8.00-8.15			61
10.15-10.30					22	8.15-8.30			62
10.30-10.45					23	8.30-8.45			63
10.45-11.00					24	8.45-9.00			64
11.00-11.15					25	9.00-9.15	CLIP-FM	✓	65
11.15-11.30	CSYT	✓			26	9.15-9.30	CLIP-FM	✓	66
11.30-11.45	C SYT	✓			27	9.30-9.45	ELIP-FM	✓	67
11.45-12.00	C SYT	✓			28	9.45-10.00	CLP-FM	✓	68
12.00-12.15					29	10.00-10.15			69
12.15-12.30	CSYP		✓		30	10.15-10.30			70
12.30-12.45	CSYP		✓		31	10.30-10.45			71
12.45-1.00	CSYP		✓		32	10.45-11.00			72
1.00-1.15					33	11.00-11.15			73
1.15-1.30					34	11.15-11.30			74
1.30-1.45					35	11.30-11.45			75
1.45-2.00	DONT KNOW		✓		36	11.45-12.00			76
2.00-2.15	DONT KNOW		✓		37	12.00-12.15			77
2.15-2.30	CDXZ	✓			38	12.15-12.30			78
2.30-2.45	CD XZ	✓			39	12.30-12.45			79
2.45-3.00					40	12.45-1.00			80

Please check (✓) box if you did *not* listen at all today ☐

Cochez s.v.p. (✓) si vous n'avez pas écouté la radio aujourd'hui ☐

Note: Shaded area of CAR/ELSEWHERE columns and bold numbers in TIME columns are pink.

Figure 9.8   Example of how to fill in revised radio diary

412

HOW TO KEEP YOUR DIARY (see the example).

1. If you did no listening at all on a particular diary day, just check (√) in the box at the bottom of that diary day.

2. If you were listening to a station, write down its call letters opposite each of the quarter hour periods when you did any listening to it. Do this even if your listening in any of those quarter hours was for only a few minutes.

3. If by any chance you listened to **two** stations in a particular quarter-hour period, write down the call letters of the station that got the greater part of your listening in that quarter-hour period.

4. For each station call letters you write in, show **where** you did that listening by putting a check (√) after it either in the 'at home' column or in the 'car or elsewhere' column. **We are interested in your listening no matter where you did it.**

5. Draw lines right across your diary day to show when you **began** to listen to any one station, the time you **stopped** listening to it and the time you changed from one station to another.

6. If you did some listening to a station but are not sure which one it was, write down 'DON'T KNOW' in the STATION column and put a check (√) to show where the listening was done.

7. If the station you listened to was an FM station, write FM after its call-letters.

Please check (√) this box when you have definitely read all these instructions.

FAÇON DE PROCÉDER (Voir l'exemple).

1. Si vous n'avez pas écouté la radio une journée donnée, n'oubliez pas de l'indiquer dans la case au bas de la page.

2. Lorsque vous écoutez la radio, vous inscrivez les lettres d'appel de la station écoutée dans la colonne "station" pour chacun des ¼ d'heure concernés. Vous inscrivez votre écoute, même s'il ne s'agit que de quelques minutes.

3. Si pendant un même ¼ d'heure, vous écoutez 2 stations, vous devez inscrire le nom de la station que vous avez écoutée le plus longtemps.

4. Pour chaque ¼ d'heure écouté, vous faites un crochet (√) dans la colonne "à la maison" ou dans la colonne "en auto/ailleurs" pour indiquer à quel endroit vous étiez quand vous avez écouté. Dans notre sondage, nous sommes intéressés à connaître votre écoute de la radio quel que soit l'endroit où vous avez écouté.

5. Quand vous commencez à écouter la radio, vous faites une ligne horizontale, puis vous en faites une autre quand vous écoutez une autre station ou quand vous cessez d'écouter.

6. Si vous ne connaissez pas le nom de la station que vous avez écoutée, vous inscrivez *ne sais pas* dans la colonne "station" et ensuite vous indiquez à quel endroit vous étiez.

7. Si vous écoutez une station FM, indiquez les lettres FM à la suite des lettres d'appel.

Indiquez ici que vous avez bien lu ces instructions

5

Figure 9.9   Section in revised radio diary on how to keep the diary

413

May we remind you	TIME HEURE	STATION	WHERE LISTENED ENDROIT		OFFICE/BUREAU	TIME HEURE	STATION	WHERE LISTENED ENDROIT		OFFICE/BUREAU
			A LA MAISON AT HOME	EN AUTO OU AILLEURS CAR/ ELSEWHERE				A LA MAISON AT HOME	EN AUTO OU AILLEURS CAR/ ELSEWHERE	
1. The rules for completing this diary are most important. Go back to them on page 5 if you are in the slightest doubt about what to do.	**5.00-5.15 AM**				1	**3.00-3.15 PM**				41
	5.15-5.30				2	3.15-3.30				42
	5.30-5.45				3	3.30-3.45				43
	5.45-6.00				4	3.45-4.00				44
	6.00-6.15				5	**4.00-4.15**				45
	6.15-6.30				6	4.15-4.30				46
	6.30-6.45				7	4.30-4.45				47
Even if you don't have any doubts, go back and study the rules from time to time.	6.45-7.00				8	4.45-5.00				48
	7.00-7.15				9	**5.00-5.15**				49
	7.15-7.30				10	5.15-5.30				50
	7.30-7.45				11	5.30-5.45				51
2. Please avoid getting behind with your entries in your diary. Try to keep it up to date.	7.45-8.00				12	5.45-6.00				52
	8.00-8.15				13	**6.00-6.15**				53
	8.15-8.30				14	6.15-6.30				54
	8.30-8.45				15	6.30-6.45				55
	8.45-9.00				16	6.45-7.00				56
	9.00-9.15				17	**7.00-7.15**				57
	9.15-9.30				18	7.15-7.30				58
	9.30-9.45				19	7.30-7.45				59
N'oubliez pas ...	9.45-10.00				20	7.45-8.00				60
	10.00-10.15				21	**8.00-8.15**				61
	10.15-10.30				22	8.15-8.30				62
	10.30-10.45				23	8.30-8.45				63
	10.45-11.00				24	8.45-9.00				64
1. Il est important de bien connaître la façon de procéder pour remplir ce cahier d'écoute. En cas de doute, relisez les instructions en page 5.	**11.00-11.15**				25	**9.00-9.15**				65
	11.15-11.30				26	9.15-9.30				66
	11.30-11.45				27	9.30-9.45				67
	11.45-12.00				28	9.45-10.00				68
	12.00-12.15 PM				29	**10.00-10.15**				69
2. Il est bon de relire les instructions de temps à autre, même si vous n'avez pas de difficultés.	12.15-12.30				30	10.15-10.30				70
	12.30-12.45				31	10.30-10.45				71
	12.45-1.00				32	10.45-11.00				72
	1.00-1.15				33	**11.00-11.15**				73
	1.15-1.30				34	11.15-11.30				74
3. N'attendez pas au lendemain pour remplir votre cahier d'écoute.	1.30-1.45				35	11.30-11.45				75
	1.45-2.00				36	11.45-12.00				76
	2.00-2.15				37	**12.00-12.15 AM**				77
	2.15-2.30				38	12.15-12.30				78
	2.30-2.45				39	12.30-12.45				79
	2.45-3.00				40	12.45-1.00				80

Please check (√) box if you did *not* listen at all today ☐

Cochez s.v.p. (√) si vous n'avez pas écouté la radio aujourd'hui

Note: Shaded area of CAR/ELSEWHERE columns and bold numbers in TIME columns are pink.

Figure 9.10 Section in revised radio diary showing the page for Sunday

Just before you continue

1. Suppose **someone else had selected a station** and you were listening to it. Should you enter this listening in your diary? (Answer: YES.)

2. Suppose a radio was left on in another room but that you could hear it and were listening to it. Should you enter that listening in your diary? (Answer: YES.)

3. Suppose you yourself do very little listening. Is it OK to pass your diary to someone else who does a lot of listening? (Answer: NO, NO, NO.)

4. Suppose that in a pàrticular quarter-hour period you listened to CDXZ for five minutes and then switched to CSYT for ten minutes. What call letters should you enter in that quarter-hour sector? (Answer: CSYT, because it got the longer period of listening in that quarter hour.)

5. Suppose you USUALLY listen to CDXZ each evening between 7 pm and 8 pm, but that on one of your diary days you did not listen to the radio at all in that period. What should you enter in the four quarter-hour periods for that particular diary day? (Answer: You make no entries at all.)

6. Suppose you are a passenger in a car and the driver tunes to a particular station and you listen to it. Suppose also that you didn't notice the name of this station. What should you enter in your diary? (Answer: For each quarter hour concerned, write DON'T KNOW and also a check to show you were in a car.)

7. Suppose you were in a car or in *someone else's* home, or at an office or waiting room and you did some listening there. Should this be entered in your diary? (Answer: yes in the car/elsewhere column.)

Now please go on with your entries for Monday

Avant de continuer

1. Si c'est quelqu'un d'autre qui a choisi la station et que vous l'écoutez, devez-vous indiquer que vous avez écouté la radio? (réponse: oui)

2. Vous pouvez entendre un appareil de radio ouvert dans une autre pièce et vous l'écoutez. Devez-vous inscrire votre écoute? (réponse: oui)

3. Vous-même vous écoutez très peu la radio. Pouvez-vous demander à quelqu'un d'autre de remplir votre cahier d'écoute? (réponse: non-non-non)

4. À un quart d'heure donné, vous écoutez la station CDXZ pendant 5 minutes. Dans le même quart d'heure vous changez l'appareil à la station CSYT et vous écoutez cette station pendant 10 minutes. Que devez-vous inscrire dans le cahier d'écoute pour ce quart d'heure? (réponse: CSYT parce que vous l'avez écoutée plus longtemps).

5. D'habitude vous écoutez la station CDXZ chaque matin entre 7 heures et 8 heures. Mais un quart donné, vous n'avez pas du tout écouté la radio. Que devez-vous inscrire entre 7 heures et 8 heures ce matin-là? (réponse: rien).

6. Vous êtes passager en automobile et le conducteur ouvre la radio et vous l'écoutez. Cependant vous n'avez pas remarqué à quelle station l'appareil était ouvert. Que devez-vous inscrire dans votre cahier d'écoute? (réponse: Pour chaque quart d'heure écouté, vous inscrivez N.S.P. dans la colonne "station" et vous indiquez que vous étiez en automobile).

7. Vous êtes en automobile ou chez un voisin ou dans une salle d'attente. A cet endroit vous écoutez la radio. Que devez-vous inscrire dans le cahier? (réponse: la station écoutée et un crochet dans la colonne en "auto/ailleurs").

Tournez la page pour le lundi

7

Figure 9.11 The 'check yourself' exercise in the revised radio diary

LUNDI / MONDAY ① **RADIO**

May we remind you

1. It counts as listening so long as you were paying some attention to what was being broadcast.

2. *It counts even if you were listening for just a few minutes.*

The questions over on the left are absolutely confidential and are very important for the survey.

Please answer them before going on with the rest of your diary.

N'oubliez pas ...

1. Si vous prêtez un peu attention à ce qui est diffusé à la radio, vous devez l'inscrire.

2. Inscrivez votre écoute même si vous n'avez écouté que quelques minutes.

3. Avant de continuer, veuillez répondre aux questions de la page 8. Ceci est très important pour le succès du sondage. Vos réponses sont confidentielles.

TIME HEURE	STATION	A LA MAISON AT HOME	EN AUTO OU AILLEURS CAR/ ELSEWHERE	OFFICE/BUREAU	
5.00-5.15AM					1
5.15-5.30					2
5.30-5.45					3
5.45-6.00					4
6.00-6.15					5
6.15-6.30					6
6.30-6.45					7
6.45-7.00					8
7.00-7.15					9
7.15-7.30					10
7.30-7.45					11
7.45-8.00					12
8.00-8.15					13
8.15-8.30					14
8.30-8.45					15
8.45-9.00					16
9.00-9.15					17
9.15-9.30					18
9.30-9.45					19
9.45-10.00					20
10.00-10.15					21
10.15-10.30					22
10.30-10.45					23
10.45-11.00					24
11.00-11.15					25
11.15-11.30					26
11.30-11.45					27
11.45-12.00					28
12.00-12.15PM					29
12.15-12.30					30
12.30-12.45					31
12.45-1.00					32
1.00-1.15					33
1.15-1.30					34
1.30-1.45					35
1.45-2.00					36
2.00-2.15					37
2.15-2.30					38
2.30-2.45					39
2.45-3.00					40

TIME HEURE	STATION	A LA MAISON AT HOME	EN AUTO OU AILLEURS CAR/ ELSEWHERE	OFFICE/BUREAU	
3.00-3.15PM					41
3.15-3.30					42
3.30-3.45					43
3.45-4.00					44
4.00-4.15					45
4.15-4.30					46
4.30-4.45					47
4.45-5.00					48
5.00-5.15					49
5.15-5.30					50
5.30-5.45					51
5.45-6.00					52
6.00-6.15					53
6.15-6.30					54
6.30-6.45					55
6.45-7.00					56
7.00-7.15					57
7.15-7.30					58
7.30-7.45					59
7.45-8.00					60
8.00-8.15					61
8.15-8.30					62
8.30-8.45					63
8.45-9.00					64
9.00-9.15					65
9.15-9.30					66
9.30-9.45					67
9.45-10.00					68
10.00-10.15					69
10.15-10.30					70
10.30-10.45					71
10.45-11.00					72
11.00-11.15					73
11.15-11.30					74
11.30-11.45					75
11.45-12.00					76
12.00-12.15AM					77
12.15-12.30					78
12.30-12.45					79
12.45-1.00					80

Please check (√) box if you did *not* listen at all today ☐

Cochez s.v.p. (√) si vous n'avez pas écouté la radio aujourd'hui ☐

Note: Shaded area of **CAR/ELSEWHERE** columns and bold numbers in **TIME** columns are pink.

Figure 9.12 A page in the revised radio diary needing to be completed

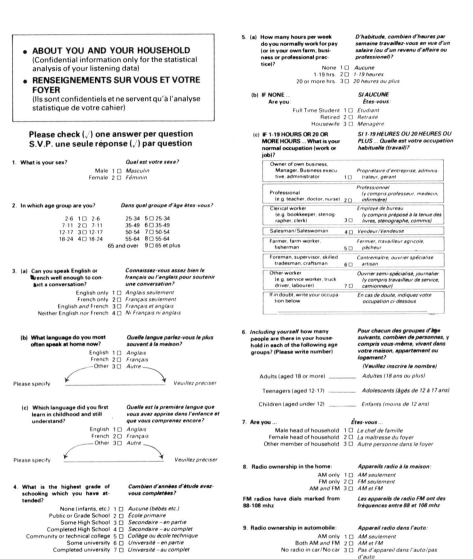

- **ABOUT YOU AND YOUR HOUSEHOLD**
  (Confidential information only for the statistical analysis of your listening data)
- **RENSEIGNEMENTS SUR VOUS ET VOTRE FOYER**
  (Ils sont confidentiels et ne servent qu'à l'analyse statistique de votre cahier)

Please check (√) one answer per question
S.V.P. une seule réponse (√) par question

1. What is your sex?   *Quel est votre sexe?*
   - Male   1 □   *Masculin*
   - Female   2 □   *Féminin*

2. In which age group are you?   *Dans quel groupe d'âge êtes-vous?*

2-6	1 □ 2-6	25-34	5 □ 25-34
7-11	2 □ 7-11	35-49	6 □ 35-49
12-17	3 □ 12-17	50-54	7 □ 50-54
18-24	4 □ 18-24	55-64	8 □ 55-64
		65 and over	9 □ 65 et plus

3. (a) Can you speak English or French well enough to conduct a conversation?   *Connaissez-vous assez bien le français ou l'anglais pour soutenir une conversation?*
   - English only   1 □   *Anglais seulement*
   - French only   2 □   *Français seulement*
   - English *and* French   3 □   *Français et anglais*
   - Neither English *nor* French   4 □   *Ni Français ni anglais*

   (b) What language do you most often speak at home now?   *Quelle langue parlez-vous le plus souvent à la maison?*
   - English   1 □   *Anglais*
   - French   2 □   *Français*
   - Other   3 □   *Autre*

   Please specify   *Veuillez préciser*

   (c) Which language did you first learn in childhood and still understand?   *Quelle est la première langue que vous avez apprise dans l'enfance et que vous comprenez encore?*
   - English   1 □   *Anglais*
   - French   2 □   *Français*
   - Other   3 □   *Autre*

   Please specify   *Veuillez préciser*

4. What is the highest grade of schooling which you have attended?   *Combien d'années d'étude avez-vous complétées?*
   - None (infants, etc.)   1 □   *Aucune (bébés etc.)*
   - Public or Grade School   2 □   *École primaire*
   - Some High School   3 □   *Secondaire – en partie*
   - Completed High School   4 □   *Secondaire – au complet*
   - Community or technical college   5 □   *Collège ou école technique*
   - Some university   6 □   *Université – en partie*
   - Completed university   7 □   *Université – au complet*

5. (a) How many hours per week do you normally work for pay (or in your own farm, business or professional practice)?   *D'habitude, combien d'heures par semaine travaillez-vous en vue d'un salaire (ou d'un revenu d'affaire ou professionel)?*
   - None   1 □   *Aucune*
   - 1-19 hrs.   2 □   *1-19 heures*
   - 20 or more hrs.   3 □   *20 heures ou plus*

   (b) IF NONE ... Are you: *SI AUCUNE Êtes-vous:*
   - Full Time Student   1 □   *Étudiant*
   - Retired   2 □   *Retraite*
   - Housewife   3 □   *Menagère*

   (c) IF 1-19 HOURS OR 20 OR MORE HOURS ... What is your normal occupation (work or job)?   *SI 1-19 HEURES OU 20 HEURES OU PLUS ... Quelle est votre occupation habituelle (travail)?*

Owner of own business, Manager, Business executive, administrator	1 □	*Propriétaire d'entreprise, administrateur, gérant*
Professional (e.g. teacher, doctor, nurse)	2 □	*Professionnel (y compris professeur, médecin, infirmière)*
Clerical worker (e.g. bookkeeper, stenographer, clerk)	3 □	*Employé de bureau (y compris préposé à la tenue des livres, sténographe, commis)*
Salesman/Saleswoman	4 □	*Vendeur/Vendeuse*
Farmer, farm-worker, fisherman	5 □	*Fermier, travailleur agricole, pêcheur*
Foreman, supervisor, skilled tradesman, craftsman	6 □	*Contremaître, ouvrier spécialise artisan*
Other worker (e.g. service worker, truck driver, labourer)	7 □	*Ouvrier semi-spécialisé, journalier (y compris travailleur de service, camionneur)*
If in doubt, write your occupation below		*En cas de doute, indiquez votre occupation ci-dessous*

6. *Including yourself* how many people are there in your household in each of the following age groups? (Please write number)   *Pour chacun des groupes d'âge suivants, combien de personnes, y compris vous-même, vivent dans votre maison, appartement ou logement?*

   (Veuillez inscrire le nombre)

   - Adults (aged 18 or more) _____   *Adultes (18 ans ou plus)*
   - Teenagers (aged 12-17) _____   *Adolescents (âgés de 12 à 17 ans)*
   - Children (aged under 12) _____   *Enfants (moins de 12 ans)*

7. Are you ...   *Êtes-vous ...*
   - Male head of household   1 □   *Le chef de famille*
   - Female head of household   2 □   *La maîtresse du foyer*
   - Other member of household   3 □   *Autre personne dans le foyer*

8. Radio ownership in the home: *Appareils radio à la maison:*
   - AM only   1 □   *AM seulement*
   - FM only   2 □   *FM seulement*
   - AM *and* FM   3 □   *AM et FM*

   FM radios have dials marked from 88-108 mhz   *Les appareils de radio FM ont des fréquences entre 88 et 108 mhz*

9. Radio ownership in automobile: *Appareil radio dans l'auto:*
   - AM only   1 □   *AM seulement*
   - Both AM *and* FM   2 □   *AM et FM*
   - No radio in car/No car   3 □   *Pas d'appareil dans l'auto/pas d'auto*

Figure 9.13   Section in revised radio diary requesting personal details

417

SATURDAY / SAMEDI ⑥ RADIO

May we remind you	TIME HEURE	STATION	WHERE LISTENED ENDROIT				TIME HEURE	STATION	WHERE LISTENED ENDROIT			
			A LA MAISON AT HOME	EN AUTO OU AILLEURS CAR/ELSEWHERE	OFFICE/BUREAU				A LA MAISON AT HOME	EN AUTO OU AILLEURS CAR/ELSEWHERE	OFFICE/BUREAU	
	5.00-5.15AM					1	3.00-3.15PM					41
The survey week ends	5.15-5.30					2	3.15-3.30					42
tomorrow – Sunday.	5.30-5.45					3	3.30-3.45					43
Please remember to	5.45-6.00					4	3.45-4.00					44
complete the Sunday	6.00-6.15					5	4.00-4.15					45
page tomorrow.	6.15-6.30					6	4.15-4.30					46
	6.30-6.45					7	4.30-4.45					47
	6.45-7.00					8	4.45-5.00					48
	7.00-7.15					9	5.00-5.15					49
	7.15-7.30					10	5.15-5.30					50
	7.30-7.45					11	5.30-5.45					51
	7.45-8.00					12	5.45-6.00					52
	8.00-8.15					13	6.00-6.15					53
	8.15-8.30					14	6.15-6.30					54
	8.30-8.45					15	6.30-6.45					55
	8.45-9.00					16	6.45-7.00					56
	9.00-9.15					17	7.00-7.15					57
	9.15-9.30					18	7.15-7.30					58
N'oubliez pas ...	9.30-9.45					19	7.30-7.45					59
	9.45-10.00					20	7.45-8.00					60
	10.00-10.15					21	8.00-8.15					61
	10.15-10.30					22	8.15-8.30					62
	10.30-10.45					23	8.30-8.45					63
Le sondage se termine	10.45-11.00					24	8.45-9.00					64
demain. N'oubliez pas	11.00-11.15					25	9.00-9.15					65
d'indiquer votre écoute	11.15-11.30					26	9.15-9.30					66
de cette dernière journée.	11.30-11.45					27	9.30-9.45					67
	11.45-12.00					28	9.45-10.00					68
	12.00-12.15PM					29	10.00-10.15					69
	12.15-12.30					30	10.15-10.30					70
	12.30-12.45					31	10.30-10.45					71
	12.45-1.00					32	10.45-11.00					72
	1.00-1.15					33	11.00-11.15					73
	1.15-1.30					34	11.15-11.30					74
	1.30-1.45					35	11.30-11.45					75
	1.45-2.00					36	11.45-12.00					76
	2.00-2.15					37	12.00-12.15AM					77
	2.15-2.30					38	12.15-12.30					78
	2.30-2.45					39	12.30-12.45					79
	2.45-3.00					40	12.45-1.00					80

Please check (√) box if you did *not* listen at all today ☐

Cochez s.v.p. (√) si vous n'avez pas écouté la radio aujourd'hui

14

Note: Shaded area of CAR/ELSEWHERE columns and bold numbers in TIME columns are pink.

Figure 9.14 A further page in the revised radio diary needing to be completed

6   On the next page (Figure 9.11) was a 'check yourself' exercise, the diarist being asked what he should do in each of a number of circumstances. The answer was given for each.

7   There then followed two pages of diary for completion (Monday and Tuesday) as in Figure 9.12. For each day there were reminders of rules under the column heading 'May we remind you'; for example, 'It counts as listening so long as you were paying some attention to what was being broadcast' . . . 'Don't leave anything out. Make sure you include all listening in cars and away from your home'.

8   Next came a page asking for personal details. It was expected that by this time the diarist would be sufficiently involved and 'in progress' to go through the personal details section without being disturbed by it (Figure 9.13).

9   Then came five more diary pages, one for each day of Wednesday through to Sunday (as in Figure 9.14). Repeats of rules were printed on each page under the heading 'May we remind you'.

10 Throughout the diary, the quarter-hours were printed in large figures, with the first quarter of each hour in colour. The coding numbers were in small letters under a column heading of 'office'. The 'listening in car/elsewhere' column was in colour to contrast it with the 'at home' column (see Figure 9.12).

11 At the bottom of each diary page was a box to tick if no listening was done that day (see Figure 9.12) — in order to indicate whether the diarist had done no listening that day as distinct from just forgetting to make a record of listening that had been done.

The modified diary (radio only) led to a marked reduction in the incidence of misuse of the diary.

THE WIDER ENQUIRY

In this short statement, I have dealt with only the radio diary. In fact the enquiry was broader in its coverage. It involved: a similar form of enquiry based upon a TV-only diary; a series of quite separate validity checks focused respectively on the radio-only diary, a TV-only diary, a TV and radio diary. In each of these validity checks, a comparison was made of the results from the modified diary method, administered in the usual way, and the results from a telephone survey in which a sample of the population was asked what programme if any they were listening to just before the telephone call.

On the basis of the validity checks, both the radio-only diary and the TV-only diary were accepted by the Bureau of Broadcasting Measurement as suitable for use in its radio and television surveys.

PART III
CONSTRUCTING A NEW
MEASURE FOR USE IN
SURVEY RESEARCH

10 Introduction to the construction of a new measure for use in survey research: problems and methods

Just as in Part I, I use the term 'measure' in a broad sense. Measurement is a procedure whereby we classify an individual into one or other of some set of categories or divisions. We may be classifying people simply as 'said yes or no', or as 'said true or false'. Or we may be sorting each of them into one of some four or five dimensions on a rating scale or on a frequency scale, and so on. Our measure may be a simple short question about some 'easy to answer' issue or it may be a set of questions dealing with a rather sensitive or complex matter.

Whatever the case, a very common response to the challenge of designing such a measure is simply to 'write the question(s)'. I think of people who do this as 'armchair operators'. Such a researcher may very well be bright. He is likely to believe that his careful judgement and grasp of words are quite sufficient to produce a question or a questioning system that will give him accurate information of the sort he needs.

Even with simple questions, that approach can very easily lead to error. I have illustrated this point fairly fully in Chapter 2. However consider these more complex cases:

- 'How many Mars Bars have you bought in the last seven days, not counting today?'
  (For many respondents, 'how many' becomes 'about how many'; 'you' is sometimes interpreted to include 'others who have bought them for you'; 'last seven days' can become a longer period allowing the respondent to include earlier buying; 'not counting today' can become 'counting today'; 'Mars Bars' can become 'bars of confectionery'.)
- When the respondent is asked about his reading of X yesterday, he may well answer in terms of his *usual* reading for 'yesterday'.
- A response to the question 'how many people are there in the household' can involve the respondent in omitting himself, in omitting very young people, in omitting boarders, in including family members who no longer live at home, and so on.
- 'Miles driven in the last seven days' is subject to error through the respondent not knowing whether to include miles travelled as a passenger, through sheer confusion and forgetting when the driving per day is irregular, through confusion with miles he *usually* drives per week.

The armchair operator will certainly be in trouble with questions of that kind. When it comes to matters as complex as the following, he is sure to go wrong:

- Obtaining household expenditure details through the diary method
- The use of a TV diary for converting meter-based data into information about *who* is watching
- Determining who will buy some new commodity
- Comprehension research
- The use of testing operations for pre-determining which of several advertisements would be the more effective if used

To sum up, the pitfalls that await the 'armchair operator' in question design are many and varied. This applies even for seemingly quite simple questions and measures. When it comes to more complex measurement, the dangers inherent in 'armchair construction' are much greater. I have illustrated these dangers through Part I of this book, in relation to the National Readership Survey procedure, the measurement of reaction through scalar methods, the assessment of chocolate confectionery purchasing over a seven day period.

FOR LACK OF AN AVAILABLE MEASURE, NOTHING GETS DONE

However, a demanding or challenging measuring task may well lead the more wary and experienced survey researcher to duck away from that particular task altogether — for the simple reason that the necessary measuring tools or procedures are not available.

When my research team and I set out to study causal factors in the development of stealing by London boys in a general population, we looked in vain for an adequate (existing) measure. Similarly for a measure of violent behaviour for a study of 'television and violence'. It was clear that we would have either to give up our planned research or to take the time and trouble to build the required measures as valid instruments.

It is not hard to think of other socially or commercially important variables, involving either an attitude or behaviour, for which measures suitable for survey application are unlikely to be found ready made. Here are a few.

Hard workingness	Frequency of acts of initiative
Ambition level	Imaginativeness
Conscientiousness	Improvidence
Laziness	Organised behaviour
Social behaviour in some specified recent period	Objectivity
	Frequency of acts of cruelty or unkindness
Incidence of acts of racial intolerance	Creativeness
Civilisation level	Shyness
Frequency of acts of dishonesty	Incidence and nature of family rows
Tax dodging	Willingness to buy
Social insecurity	Intention to buy
Extent of reading of pornography	Miles travelled by car in the last 7 days

Almost certainly valid measures of such variables, suitable for use in survey work, will not be available in ready-made form. Look for the survey measure you want and in all probability you won't find it. There is a simple reason for this situation. In the first place, the sorts of measures needed for thoroughgoing social or business research are many and varied and are specific to the situation under investigation. Secondly, the construction of measuring tools can be costly and time consuming. Thirdly, such work calls for considerable skills. Fourthly, it seems wasteful to build a measure that will be used just once and then abandoned. In these circumstances, problems that relate to such variables or issues are often avoided. When they *are* tackled, dubious measuring procedures may well be adopted or put together.

Whatever the reasons put forward for the neglect I have described, the overall outcome is very clear: studies that are dependent upon the construction of complex and demanding measuring techniques are not done; society does not receive the service it needs from social and business investigators in solving its many longstanding problems. I believe that social and business scientists must face up to the development of the quite complex measuring techniques that are often needed if they are to help solve the many problems of society and the business world.

THERE ARE WAYS TO GO ABOUT THE DEVELOPMENT OF A NEW MEASURING PROCEDURE

Against that background, I want to make it clear straight away that construction techniques do exist for dealing satisfactorily with the problems I have outlined. Questions do not have to depend for their validity upon some lucky formulation of an intuitive kind. There is no excuse for the purely armchair formulation of new measuring procedures; nor is there in general any excuse — beyond the unavailability of funds — for turning away from studies that require the construction of some new measuring technique. There are four well-established methods for constructing new measures of an essentially complex kind:

- The item analysis method
- The method of the scientific indicator
- The method of public judgements
- Barrier appraisal leading to progressive modification

The first three are described in full in a later part of this chapter. For the fourth, only the opening stages are detailed, the rest of it being the standard progressive modification method, which was presented very fully in Part II of the book.

SOME PRELIMINARY CONSIDERATIONS

Before going on to deal with the four construction methods, I wish to make several points, both to put the four into proper perspective and to prepare the way for their description.

General principles and tactics for question design

There are certain principles of question design that must be followed whether we are formulating a single question about some quite ordinary matter or constructing a complex eliciting technique. These principles do not ensure validity of the measure, but they are necessary conditions for validity.

Determining precisely what information is needed All question design must start with a clear determination of what it is that is to be measured or found out. We must have asked ourselves 'What will we do with this information when we get it?' If the answer to that question is not crystal clear and positive, then we must think again before entering the design work that would be required for formulating the proposed question or measure.

Sometimes we may know well enough the general character of what is wanted but not its working detail. For instance, a particular business house may want to know what are the opinions of its target market about its product. The business house can specify its broad need but, before any measurement can take place, we must discover what sorts of opinions the target market has. So exploratory work would be conducted to identify those different opinions. Only then would the researcher be able to define precisely what is to be measured. *Preliminary determination of what is to be measured or studied is an essential preliminary to the actual design of a question or measuring procedure.*

The strategy of design Once we have determined what it is we want to find out or measure, we must consider certain fundamental design strategies. In the first place, should we be asking open ended questions or fully structured ones? The function of the open ended question is to *explore the views* of respondents. However, if we have to count the number of people who think this or that, a fully structured question is essential. *We would be involved in measurement and classification and a fully structured question is intrinsic to that purpose.* In the second place, we have to decide whether the information required can be secured through just one question or a sequence of questions – perhaps in filter form. After all, it is essential that those who answer questions do understand what is being asked, and a long complex question will in all likelihood be misunderstood.

Turning the information wanted into a question   Once the above principles have been considered, the experienced and principle-guided researcher[8–15] will be in a position to write the questions. These may be single questions or they may be a composite of questions. The principles of question design are many and varied, and they have been summarised in Chapter 2. These principles apply both to the design of an answer system (a key element in any fully structured question) and to the design of the question itself. Chapter 2 had:

- Presented a series of DONT'S in design questions
- Presented principles for offering the respondent a choice of answer
- Provided warnings about interviewer deviation from question wording and instructions
- Offered well grounded hypotheses about how question understanding works
- Stressed the need for short, simple questions and for checks to establish how a particular question was understood/misunderstood.

These principles are also given in very considerable detail in *The design and understanding of survey questions.*[8]

The validity principle

Those question design principles hold whether we are constructing a single question or a complex measure of some kind. It is essential that they govern all question design. Unfortunately their application does not in itself guarantee validity. This is because other factors enter into the data collection process: the faithfulness of the interviewer's delivery of the question; the respondent's understanding of the question; the respondent's production of an accurate reply; and so on. Established validity in our measuring or questioning procedures calls for the application of good design principles, but is not guaranteed by this.

Nonetheless, for the great majority of ordinary survey questions, those principles and tactics are all the researcher practitioner is in a position to apply in his attempts to achieve validity. He may *want* to test those questions for validity but he will not have the time or the money to do so. In fact, if he applies those principles and tactics, with care and knowledgeability, to his design of questions about simple issues, he is not likely to go far wrong from a validity viewpoint.

However there is no guarantee of this in a given case. Moreover, as the complexity or the sensitivity of the issue increases, so does the likelihood of invalidity in the measure increase. The danger of invalidity can become considerable when the measuring technique involves factors such as multiple concept questions, a composite of questions, memory dependence, a sensitive issue. Adherence to basic design principles of the sort detailed in Chapter 2 is a necessary but not sufficient requirement of valid measurement.

If we want to guarantee the validity of a question or measure, we must be prepared to test it for accuracy against some criterion of truth or an acceptable substitute for such a criterion. If, as for the majority of survey questions, we are not in a position to do this, then we must be prepared to admit the possibility of error in our results. If we cannot afford validity testing of some complex measuring procedure on the results of which major decisions will be made, then this deficiency must be clearly recognised and declared.

Validity testing and the necessary 'criterion of truth'

The different methods for testing the validity of a measure have already been set out in Chapter 2. They involve the comparison of the results from some measure either with some 'criterion of truth' or with an acceptable substitute for that criterion. This 'criterion of truth' is obviously of key importance in validity testing and, at the risk of some repetition, I will comment on it here as well.

Occasionally a criterion of truth is available — usually in the form of records of some sort; for example: hospital records of visits and the reasons for them; sales records for some large durable; absentee records. However for most of the measuring devices we might want to make, such records would not exist or would not be available. We might also carry out observations of public behaviour, these to be used for checking on some questioning method we might ordinarily use for getting such information. However, this is not always easy to do and in any case it would be out of the question for the great bulk of the questions or measures we might want to validate.

In general, a direct criterion of truth for use in validity checks is hard to obtain. It is this situation that technique makers find so very frustrating and which sets them looking for substitute criteria of truth: the glue spot test in readership research; rubbish bin and pantry checks; collected testimony by others; an intensive interview focused long and searchingly on the matter being investigated.

Whatever the criterion of truth used, it is essential that we evaluate it for realism and general satisfactoriness. The evaluation is vital for those who subsequently use the measure or act upon the results of its use.

This applies all the way from the psychologist who uses the method of internal consistency and item analysis for constructing an intelligence test to the research practitioner conducting group discussions who simply asserts that his professional expertise makes his interpretations valid. Whenever anything is measured, we must be ready to ask for evidence about the validity of the measuring tool and to evaluate that evidence of validity. For the measurement specialist himself, validity is the 'stuff' of his professionalism. I would expect the validity issue to dominate his efforts throughout the construction procedure and to be a key consideration in his own evaluation of his completed technique.

That last point is important. Whereas Part I dealt with the validity of existing measuring procedures, in Part III we are dealing with the construction of *new* measures. It is important in making a new measure that the validity principle should guide us throughout the construction process rather than just at the end of it. That is why good practice in the construction of measuring techniques involves a form of progressive modification of the developing method . . . with accuracy testing built into the construction process itself.

FOUR MAJOR CONSTRUCTION STRATEGIES

As stated on page 426, these four construction tactics are:

- The method of item analysis
- The method of the scientific indicator
- The method of public judgements
- Barrier appraisal leading to progressive modification

The reader is urged to examine the description of each of these for evidence of a validity principle built into the method.

The method of item analysis

A construction procedure commonly used by those who make tests of ability is to develop a large pool of single item subtests* and then to

*In an intelligence test, such an item would probably be a particular test of the subject's ability to see a particular relationship in some set of figures or diagrams or items or words and to apply that relationship in solving some related problems. For example:

Write the missing word — onto toad adam . . . ends
Fill in the next two numbers — 5 6 11 17 . . ..
Mark the pair with the same relationship as the two in capitals —
      fry, bake, eat [HEAT : SOUP] turmoil, clay, pie

In a personality test of some kind, the subject might be asked to say true or false to each of many statements about her reactions to this or that, her views about this or that, and so on. These many statements would be the subtests referred to above.

reduce this large pool to some manageable smaller number by means of what is called 'item analysis'. In other words, for each item in the pool, a correlation index is calculated with a view to identifying those with the highest association with some 'criterion of truth'. These items tend to be the ones selected for inclusion in the measuring procedures. The process is almost always more complicated than this, but the underlying principle is as I have stated: the test maker is looking for some manageably small number of 'items' that are individually (and together) predictive of some criterion of truth. This approach has very considerable value for the measurement specialist in social and market research.

However, there are some features of this approach of the psychometrician that must be carefully scrutinised — as must be our own uses of his strategy. Let us take as an example the making of a test of intelligence. In the first place, our psychometrician is going to have major trouble in securing his criterion of truth. The common approach is to deliver the whole set or pool of trial subitems (say 200 of them) to the sorts of people on whom he will eventually use his test of intelligence. The test score of an individual on all 200 items is taken to be indicative of his *actual* intelligence. The subsequent test of each item in the pool is its correlation with that total score. This process leads to the identification of the items that have very low association with total score. These are thrown out of the pool, and the total score (on the remaining items) is recalculated. The correlation of the remaining pool items with this revised total score then follows. The modified criterion score is thought to be better — a more 'internally consistent' — criterion of true intelligence than was the original total.

The circularity of this process will be obvious. It is possibly defensible if each item in the pool is first challenged against a clear definition of what is meant by intelligence and of the type of intelligence that is being measured. However if the test maker has set up a dubious definition of intelligence to start with or if his interpretation of his own definition of intelligence is consistently twisted in some direction (that is, through his development of a pool of such dubious items) then his basic confusion would not be negated or put right by the item analysis itself.

Is there some other criterion of intelligence that might be used — something more objective? Well, another approach (more advocated than done) is to use as a criterion the intelligence ratings of individuals made by associates who know them well and are in a position to make an informed judgement or grading. In effect this usually means individuals with whom the psychologist-judge has had continuing close contact, so that an intelligence rating may be made with some safety. These ratings take the place of the 'score on all pool items' (involved in the internal consistency method). These rated people now complete the 200 or so items in the pool and the scene is set for calculating the association/correlation between specific items and the new 'criterion' score.

However, there are troubles here too. The overriding one is that the judging process is fallible, and the different judges may be fallible in different ways. Secondly, the people rated will tend to be persons known to the judges — so that a sampling problem exists. Thirdly, if the judges' ratings of specific persons has to start from 'scratch', a careful rating process can take a great deal of time. If the judges are not psychologists aware of the nature of intelligence, then they may be wrong in their rating of intelligence — indeed they may be judging in terms of something other than intelligence as conceived by the test constructor. For such reasons, the makers of intelligence tests tend not to use the rating system but to go instead for the method of internal consistency. The basic trouble is that intelligence is an hypothesised internal condition. We cannot *see it*. All we can see is what we think are the external signs of it and we could be mistaken in our conclusions from the signs we happen to see or to evoke in the individual.

There are some other problems about the item analysis approach and to these I will be coming. However, a point of prime importance is just how applicable this tactic or strategy of the psychometrician is to the development of measures for use in social and business research.

The tests made by the psychometrician tend to be for the measurement of ability and of personality. Moreover they are designed for administration under specified test room conditions. These two circumstances probably mean that the psychometrician's tests, as they stand, are of little use in survey work: the survey researcher will want methods that can be used under fieldwork conditions *and* he will frequently want measures of behaviour and of attitude.

However, with a little originality, the item analysis principle can be used for the development of tests or measuring systems for use in survey situations. All that is needed is the transfer of the whole construction system to the survey scene. The pool of items is administered in the survey situation. If the criterion is to be of the 'summation of all pool items' kind, then the field operation looks after this automatically. This is what Likert did in his construction of an attitude scale.[45] He amassed a large pool of about 150 statements and questions for delivery 'in the field'. He subsequently had a sample of 200 or so people (of a kind who would eventually be tested through his constructed measure) complete all 150 items, scored each sample member on all 150 to provide a total score. He then calculated the correlation between each of his 150 items and total score, and on that basis identified the 20 or so items with the highest correlations. These 20 or so were his test items, which he would then use instead of the full 150. He called his construction procedure the 'summation method'. In fact one of the problems about his system is that it tended to yield rather extreme statements — as it must do if his selection was based upon the correlational level of the different statements. Edwards[46] eventually improved the Likert method by combining it with that of Thurstone. Nonetheless the Likert approach could well be applied to the development of attitude measures of various kinds for use in the survey situation. Here, too, the method would be improved through Edwards's modification of it. If some criterion of truth *is* available, so much the better — so long as the testing of the items (through item analysis) is based upon delivery in the survey situation.

This same approach is usable for constructing measures going well beyond 'attitudes'. The writer used it in a study of 'initiative amongst adult Londoners'. A sample of London adults was asked to complete some 120 items, each of them designed to reflect initiative; for example: 'I went out of my way or made a special effort to get some information or to achieve something'/'I started up a conversation with someone I didn't know before'/'I used a dictionary'/'I did someone else's job for him or her without being told to do so'.

Correlational methods were used to discover some 20 key items in the total pool, these 20 being the more highly correlated with the total score for all 120 items in the pool. That method too would be improved by the addition of an Edwards-type curb to prevent all 20 plus items being drawn from the more extreme of the items in the pool.

Psychological, behavioural and attitudinal measures may be constructed using the item analysis system.

The method of the scientific indicator

The item analysis strategy takes us well into what is best called the method of the scientific indicator. This method is basically a correlational strategy. We aim through it to identify variables or questions that are predictive of whatever we really want to measure. We look for maximum joint-prediction power. The total composite of predictors is usually called an 'index' of such and such.

Here is an example. The author was asked whilst working at the BBC to put forward a measure of intelligence that could be used on the general population in the survey context. He pointed out that the existing tests were geared to test room delivery and could not be transferred into the field. An *index* would have to be developed. To this end, a sample of adults was brought to a BBC conference room and put through the intelligence test that it had been hoped might be delivered in the field. In the same session these people were also put

433

through some 15 or so questions about background abilities which the writer had built into the operation as *possible* indicators or correlates of intelligence. All 15 were of the sort that *could* be delivered under survey conditions; for example: age, age of ceasing full-time school-work, occupational details, reading behaviour.

It turned out that three of the variables put in as possible indicators or predictors of intelligence yielded between them a joint correlation with intelligence of about +0.80. These three were certain details about last job held/job of spouse; age (with a negative correlation with intelligence score); whether respondent claimed he/she had read a book in the last six months.[47]

This procedure differed from the usual item analysis strategy in that the pool of items from which the index was drawn did not consist of subtests that together made up a criterion score. Rather, the items in the pool could be anything at all — qualifications, past behaviour, personal values — all of them rather stable items for asking in the survey situation. Stability is of course vital for the index items used in the way intended. Also, the criterion of 'truth' was in fact performance on the very IQ test that the index was required to substitute for.

The index system tends to depend upon a criterion of truth being available or being developed. However, it has obvious relevance to the situation where the index is to be a substitute for an existing mental or personality test. It is also of great value for 'looking into the future', where one is seeking an index of some future event that can easily enough be measured later on but which is totally inaccessible at the time some decision has to be reached. One example of this concerns the development of indicators for use in pre-testing television advertisements. Another is an indicator of intention to buy, where much more is needed for prediction work than the statement of a respondent that he/she *will* buy this or that object. The writer is at present planning construction work on both projects.

The methodological basis for developing joint indicators has changed greatly since the time of the development of regression-type equations, which had been the principal tool for predictive and indicator work. For many years now, the system of progressive but asymmetrical empirical splitting[48] has been available and we can build the composite of indicators up to as many as 20 for one prediction or indication — with major gains in predictive or indicator power.*

*This technique was developed by the author during the 1950s and published in 1959.[48] At that time it was sent to J.N. Morgan at the Institute of Social Research in Michigan, USA, and in 1962 was personally discussed with him and Sonquist. In 1963, Morgan and Sonquist published a paper 'Problems in the analysis of survey data and a proposal', *Journal of the American Statistical Association*, vol.58 (302),[49] which was based on the principle set out in the Belson paper but did not attribute credit to the latter. In fact, Sonquist and Morgan did in that paper deny prior knowledge of the Belson method. The 1964 paper by Morgan and Sonquist,[50] setting out details of a computer program based on their 1963 paper, made no mention of the Belson method.

With modern indicator work, the criterion of truth must, as always, be developed to yield accurate results. However, the indicators in the pool need not do so. All that is necessary is that they be fairly stable and predictive. Thus it is even possible that a *lying* response to one of the indicator questions will be specially predictive. There are correlational systems available for calculating predictive power and the variables that thus emerge are the ones that are used.

The method of public judgements

Yet another construction strategy is one that is based upon public judgements. This is the technique used by Thurstone for constructing his attitude scales and called by him the method of 'equal appearing intervals'. What Thurstone did was to build up a large pool of statements, each of which he regarded as an opinion about some underlying attitude. Thurstone did not use any criterion of truth in the sense in which that term has been used in this chapter. All he did was to have a panel of people take each of his 150 or so statements of opinion and scale them, along an 11 point line, in terms of the degree to which they involved the existence, in the person putting the idea forward, of the attitude under investigation. Each opinion statement that received a wide scatter of ratings was thrown out and Thurstone kept only those about which the bulk of his raters were in agreement. He then selected some 20 or more of them, choosing them to be fairly evenly spaced along the 11 point scale in terms of their median values as established through the rating process. The raters were mostly academics and people he called 'experts', whereas the ratings should be made by members of the population on which the finished scale will be used. However that fault is easily overcome (by having all ratings made by members of that target population).

This method opens up an interesting line of attack when we do not have any 'criterion of truth' available but when the public is thought to have a good idea of what is meant by the variable that is to be measured.

Barrier appraisal leading to progressive modification

I turn now to a very common situation. It is one in which a sensitive or complex matter has to be subjected to measurement but where (a) there is available no evidence of the truth of the matter (and cannot be in the normal way); (b) what is wanted is a direct measure of an absolute kind; (c) where accuracy at an individual level is required. For such a situation the writer has been using a method which starts with preliminary identification of barriers and facilitating factors (with respect to getting at the truth) and then goes on to progressive modification geared to the intensive interviewing method.

1   First of all, a wide ranging exploratory study is made to identify: (a) the factors or conditions that operate against a respondent giving an honest and accurate reply with respect to the required information; (b) factors and conditions that facilitate the giving of an honest and accurate reply.

2   A first or trial form of the required eliciting procedure is then designed on the basis of the findings from the exploratory study, aided of course by the extensive knowledge that already exists about the principles of question design.

This is the end of the first stage of the construction procedure — a stage geared to the fact that no procedure (or at least no survey procedure) yet exists. Beyond this point, we would proceed with progressive modification geared to intensive interviewing as described in Part II. For the sake of completeness, these further steps are briefly outlined below.

3   That first or trial procedure is then subjected to test through the intensive interviewing method that has already been described in detail in Parts I and II of this volume. The intensive interview is intended to produce evidence not only of how accurate or inaccurate the first form of the method is, but to yield a great deal of information about where it is going wrong and how.

4   On the basis of this evidence, the first form of the procedure is then modified with a view to overcoming the detected faults in it.

5   The modified eliciting procedure is then subjected to intensive interviewing, just as in Step 3, and then modified as in Step 4.

6   This modifying and testing procedure is continued, cycle after cycle, until the technique appears to be giving information that is workably accurate or until no further progress towards accuracy can be made.

7   A larger scale intensive interview is then carried out. It involves a major effort to take the intensive interview to the limit with intensive challenging and cross examination.

Steps 1 and 2 as set out above are the new elements in this construction procedure as described in Part II. Step 1 is an extensive searching process that must take us to all promising sources of evidence about possible blocking and possible facilitating factors. These sources include: the views of the individuals about to be studied on what makes them hold back or otherwise hinder their making admissions; views of these people about anything that does or might facilitate the giving of an accurate reply; the views, with respect to blocking and facilitating factors, of people who are familiar with either the individuals or the situation that is to be studied; the available literature bearing on the subject, in the form either of findings or of opinion. The conduct of this exploratory work, where it involves illicit or sensitive behaviour, must be conducted not only with intensity but with tact and discretion. It may well be that anonymity would have to be guaranteed and this guarantee would have to be very convincing indeed.

Such information is a necessary insurance against the designer blundering into the formulation of a first or trial procedure that is really hopeless because it takes no account of some major blocking factor or takes no advantage of facilitating factors.

In Chapter 11 I have given an example of the method of 'barrier appraisal leading to progressive modification'. This example concerns the construction of a procedure for obtaining from boys information about the nature and extent of their stealing. I have limited this presentation to (a) the exploratory study, (b) the formulation of a first or trial procedure based on that exploratory work, (c) the first test of the trial method through intensive interviewing. Elements (a) and (b) are the parts of the theft study that are relevant to Part III of this book, but element (c) is presented to give continuity to the presentation.

11 Excerpts from 'The development of a procedure for eliciting information from boys about the nature of their stealing'

A STATEMENT BASED CLOSELY UPON A
SURVEY RESEARCH CENTRE REPORT[95] BY:

W.A. Belson, BA, PhD (Design and direction)
G.M. Millerson, BA, PhD
P.J. Didcott, BA, Dip.Crim.

CONTENTS OF CHAPTER

ORIGINS OF THE DEMAND FOR A MEASURE OF THEFT BEHAVIOUR AND A DEFINITION OF THEFT

During the late 1960s, it was agreed with the Home Office that the Survey Research Centre should use part of its Home Office grant in developing a technique for securing from boys information about the extent of such stealing as they had done.

This was to be a tool for research into theft behaviour – never for the prosecution of individuals – and it was at that stage understood that it would be designed for investigation of causal hypotheses about the origins and development of juvenile stealing.

The definition of theft had in this case to be as broad and inclusive as the law determined. It involved securing things and services through illegal means. It included small things as well as large; for example: stealing by finding; receiving stolen property; taking and driving; helping others to steal. Apparent justification did not somehow negate a theft. Whereas it was expected that the research tool would provide information about particular types of theft, the overall coverage of theft was as broad as the law defined.

THE NATURE OF THE STUDY FOR WHICH THE MEASURE OF THEFT WAS REQUIRED AND THE WAY IN WHICH THIS INFLUENCED THE CHARACTER OF THE MEASURE

The design of the theft measure was very much determined by the special character of the enquiry in which it was to be used. Accordingly I have set out below information about the character of the enquiry and I have gone on to specify what this implied regarding the form of the theft measure.

The technique for measuring boys' involvement in stealing was regarded as a central element in a major criminological study being conducted by the Survey Research Centre under the writer's direction. This study was in fact an investigation of a series of hypotheses about causal factors entering into the development of stealing by boys. It was funded by the Home Office and was to be based in London. It was to be concerned with boys generally and not just those who had been 'caught' by the police and placed in some form of custody.

The study began with a search for realistic hypotheses about the origins of stealing. This search included: long and intensive interviews with boys, some in custody and the rest in the general population; interviews with adults who worked with young people in youth clubs, in custody, in school; interviews with police officers and probation officers; a major search of the literature on criminology. From these beginnings 16 sets of causal hypotheses were developed, dealing with factors such as: desire for fun and excitement in the midst of an urban build-up; association with local thieves; breakdown of parental control/ discipline; miserable homes; broken homes; an expectation of 'getting away' with stealing; training in honesty; truancy; permissiveness in relation to the idea of stealing; and so on.

These causal hypotheses were to be investigated through a representative sample of boys (1425 in fact) in the age range 13 to 16 years. The method of investigation was complex and may be illustrated through the hypothesis that 'a desire for fun and excitement is a contributing factor to the initiation and maintenance of juvenile stealing'. The basic rationale of the investigatory procedure was the 'hypothetico-deductive' method – a method well suited to the situation where it is not possible to conduct a direct and crucial test of an hypothesis. Using this rationale, the researcher attempts to deduce from the hypothesis variable testable propositions that would be true if the hypothesis were true. He then proceeds to test these propositions. If they 'pass' the test, then the tenability of the hypothesis is increased. For the 'fun and excitement' hypothesis, there were ten deduced propositions, and these included the following:

1   When those wanting relatively little fun and excitement are massively matched (in terms of the correlates of stealing) to those wanting a lot of fun and excitement, there will remain a statistically meaningful difference between them in terms of the amount of stealing they have done.

2   Proposition 1 holds for each of a usable range of different types of theft.

3   Boys will volunteer/admit that they steal in order to get fun and excitement. The more fun and excitement they want, the more will they tend to volunteer/admit that they steal to get fun and excitement.

The testing of proposition 1 was a major operation, involving the use of the stable correlate technique,[48,51] with matching on a large composite of variables drawn from a very large pool of potential correlates of stealing.

The hypothetico-deductive method was applied to the investigation of each of the causal hypotheses dealt with in the enquiry. A detailed account of the investigatory procedure is set out in a report of the Survey Research Centre[51] and is summarised in the book *Juvenile theft: causal factors*.[52]

Whereas there were many hypotheses involved in this study, each of them was linked to 'amount of stealing' as the dependent variable. 'Amount of stealing' was thus a key variable in the whole enquiry, and one that therefore called for great care in its measurement.

THE CONDITIONS IMPOSED ON THE MEASURING TECHNIQUE BY THE SPECIAL CHARACTER OF THE AETIOLOGICAL INVESTIGATION

From the outset it was clear that the required measure of theft would have to be suitable for use on *ordinary boys* in the general population — as distinct from only those held in custodial institutions. In other words, there would be no ready-made pressure on boys to take part; as far as one might judge at this early stage, many of the boys would be relatively innocent and would be shocked at being asked about stealing; there would be serious problems about the confidentiality of the information being asked for; there would be problems over securing interviews with the busier and more evasive of the boys; there could well be problems over the desire of parents to be present at the interview. For it to work, these and related problems had to be overcome by the form of the administration of the measuring procedure. Furthermore, the aetiological study would have to be geared to the ages (13 to 16 years) of the boys, to their London values, their language, their availability, and to the London area itself.

The measuring tool would also have to provide information about boys' involvement in different *types* of theft — that is, to meet the requirements of the several hypotheses set up for testing. A single score for theft would not be enough.

The hypotheses all referred to stealing throughout the boy's life and to the operation of possibly causal factors for a lengthy period. This meant that the boys being interviewed would have to go back in time in reporting on their theft behaviour. That in turn meant that a serious memory problem was intruded into the tool-making task.

There would of course be other constraints upon the form of the required measuring technique. However, most of these were linked to the delicate character of the variable to be measured (that is, theft). These constraints showed up progressively as the construction process went on — and in each case something had to be done to the eliciting procedure to get it to work in spite of the difficulty. There were also occasions when special steps were taken to exploit some situation that was *helping* boys to make admissions (for example, an interviewer was short and boys concluded he could hardly be a policeman). However, these constraints and opportunities were different, in an operational sense, from the constraints that stemmed from the nature of the aetiological enquiry.

SEARCHING THE LITERATURE FOR
LEADS TO THE CONSTRUCTION OF THE REQUIRED MEASURE

An obvious first step to secure a measure of theft was to search the literature for a ready-made tool of a suitable kind or, failing that, a tool that might be modified towards suitability. If nothing like that was available, then we might at least expect that there would in the literature be clues and leads of value for the construction of a new procedure. Such a search was made, first of the criminological literature and then of the non-criminological literature on research methodology.

THE CRIMINOLOGICAL LITERATURE

The principal criminological texts that were examined are given at the end of this book.[53-71]

This search did not yield a ready-made measuring tool of the sort needed, or anything like it. The reader may think this a strange situation for a field of enquiry where criminologists had for decades been studying the incidence of stealing and the characteristics of thieves. Be that as it may, it did produce relevant details in the form of expected or real difficulties and steps that might be taken to deal with such difficulties. The more recurrently mentioned difficulties are set out below along with various of the steps suggested as solutions.

1 One of the more frequently expressed concerns was the obvious one that a boy could be expected to be uneasy about revealing his delinquencies, perhaps for the first time. The suggestions for meeting this difficulty included the following:

   - All possible threat should be removed from the interviewing situation
   - Questions should be administered anonymously and confidentially, possibly with the use of secret ballot boxes
   - The interviewer should avoid being associated with local agencies of any kind and should appear as a stranger in the district
   - The interviewer should adopt a permissive and understanding approach and suggest that it will do the boy good to talk

- Notetaking should be minimised or done unobtrusively — or should be done away with altogether (with the interviewer writing from memory after the interview)
- The interviewer should be free to modify his approach and practice according to the attitudes he finds in the boy respondent.

2　Another fairly obvious difficulty referred to in the literature is the possibility of boys lying or giving superficial or over-conforming replies. It was variously suggested that:

- Trick questions be used to detect liars and that these boys be excluded from the sample*
- Alternative sources of information be used to check the respondents' replies (for example, official records)
- Responses be probed and checked to detect mis-statements or over-conforming replies and to discourage the making of these
- The questions to boys be presented in the least expected order so that the 'setting in' of lying might be avoided

3　Another difficulty which was mentioned — but only occasionally — was misunderstanding by the boys of the questions put to them. One author suggested the use of standard piloting of proposed questions and another that the interviewer be allowed to rephrase a question if he thought a particular boy was misunderstanding it. The scarcity of reference to this sort of problem may for some be disconcerting — as may the fact that only one author suggested that continuing checks and probes be made throughout the interview to keep the boy trying.

4　Problems related to *interviewer* performance and control were also referred to and several authors advocated, between them:

- The selection of skilled and experienced interviewers
- Training to reduce subjective interpretation of replies and to reduce deviation from instruction
- The imposition of tight control over interviewer performance

5　Another broad area of difficulty raised in the literature concerned vagueness either in the definition of key terms in the interview or in the formulation of questions. Suggestions took various forms:

- Avoid the use of indefinite terms in the interview
- Use lists of thefts to define stealing rather than asking boys about their behaviour under the broad term 'stealing'
- See that questions define precisely what information is wanted

*A strange suggestion from anyone seeking a representative picture of theft 'behaviour'.

- Structure the questions and standardise the instructions to interviewers
- See that questions offer a specific choice of answers
- Use standardised procedures and forms for recording responses

Whereas we must take careful note of the foregoing enumeration of difficulties, we must bear in mind: (i) that at least some of them are intuitive in character; and (ii) that there is no guarantee that the enumeration relates to all the more serious sources of trouble standing in the way of the collection of data of the sensitive kind in which we are interested — especially where the boys concerned have never been caught. The *suggestions* put forward for meeting various of the alleged difficulties are in the same position: they include interesting and quite possibly useful suggestions, but almost all are as yet unvalidated.

At the time the elicitation project was being planned, several procedural contributions were available. The research team took special note of the following.[72-74]

1   The Institute for Social Research at the University of Michigan was carrying out a study of undetected delinquency in Flint, Michigan, at the time the elicitation project was being planned, and several aspects of this study influenced the form of our eliciting procedure in the preliminary stages of its development. These aspects of the Flint study were:

- Delinquent acts were defined by a series of statements, each printed on a card
- Each respondent sorted these into one of several boxes (stuck on to a screen), depending on whether he had 'never' done the act concerned or, if he had, the number of times he had done it
- The screen was positioned between the interviewer and the respondent
- Great stress was placed on confidentiality and anonymity, and respondents were interviewed at a centre (which provided a neutral meeting place)

2   Nye described a self-report study of delinquency in which a questionnaire listing various delinquent acts was administered anonymously and then placed in a sealed ballot box.

3   Robison, at the time the elicitation project was being planned, was carrying out a study popularly known as the Career Patterns Project. This was designed to test the hypothesis that 'youthful delinquency in various degrees characterises the adolescence of the majority of today's respectable male adults'. During the interview,

respondents were given a list of various kinds of delinquent behaviour and were asked to rate them according to how often they had been committed. For those acts committed more often, the respondent was asked, among other things: how old he was when each individual act was committed; how long he continued with that kind of act; how old he was when he stopped committing that kind of act.

4   The Mobilisation for Youth Study included the collection of data on delinquent activities. Questions relating to delinquent acts were put to respondents in a personal interview. The respondent was first asked whether he had ever committed a particular delinquent act; if he said he had, the interviewer asked for the frequency with which it had been committed.

Several enquiries, which have been reported since the construction of the Centre's elicitation procedure, are concerned with the technology of eliciting information about delinquency from boys.[eg 75] However, I have deliberately limited this review to work and reports that were available for study at the time we planned the elicitation project or during its execution.

THE NON-CRIMINOLOGICAL LITERATURE

The search of the (then) available literature was extended to relevant parts of that major body of literature that deal with the techniques of business and social research.*

A full statement about the relevant yield of the non-criminological literature is given in the detailed report of the construction of the eliciting procedure.[5] What follows is a summary statement giving the general thrust of that yield of evidence.

1   Survey questions are often misunderstood. Small changes in wording can on occasions produce substantial changes in the distribution of responses. The order of presentation of choice of answer items and of a series of questions can influence appreciably the distribution of responses.

2   Memory-dependent questions (about personal behaviour) are especially open to respondent error.

3   Interviewers can on occasions have an appreciable effect on the responses elicited. Such influence operates through:

  • Changes made by the interviewer in the wording of the question

*See references 2, 12, 17, 20, 26, 32, 33, 76–94.

- The attitude of the interviewer about the matter/issue asked about, especially when the replies are somewhat ambiguous or vague
- The tendency of some interviewers to form expectations about the replies that a respondent will give to some questions
- Cheating of various kinds.

4   A number of studies indicated a greater tendency for respondents to make admissions when working under conditions of anonymity.

SUMMING UP ON THE SEARCH OF THE LITERATURE

One function of the available literature must be to warn us about the existence of major problems standing in the way of the projected development of an elicitation procedure — problems concerning: respondent understanding of questions; respondent willingness to make admissions about sensitive matters; respondent memory failure; interviewer problems of various kinds. As warnings, various of the indications of the literature are most valuable. At the same time, these offerings from the literature do not necessarily tell us about *all* the difficulties. Moreover, most of them are too indirectly linked to our special problem (that is, the eliciting of information from boys about their own stealing) to allow us to identify the precise problems which have to be met and overcome. We are left with that particular task still to complete.

The literature also provided us with some valuable leads:

- The use of anonymity as a means of getting admissions of the delicate information involved in this case
- The use of a list of delinquencies as a means of defining what we want to know about
- *Bringing* the boys to an interviewing centre rather than going to boys in their homes or letting them make their own way to a centre
- The removal of threat from the interviewing situation
- The minimising of note-taking in the interview
- The use of trap questions to detect lying and of constant probing to keep boys alert and trying
- The training of interviewers into the necessary skills of the interview and the imposition of tight control over interviewer performance
- The testing of questions for comprehensibility

On the other hand, these suggestions do not themselves make up a procedure. Nor do they necessarily relate to all the problems likely to be met in the projected work. Nor are these leads as yet validated as eliciting devices in the present situation. We should bear them in mind and very likely draw upon them in appropriate contexts, but the construction work itself had still to be done.

THE SEQUENCE OF STEPS TAKEN IN CONSTRUCTING
THE REQUIRED MEASURE OF THEFT BEHAVIOUR

It was now clear that the required measure would have to be constructed as a new procedure. Construction work took off from the background I have presented of: (i) the findings, the ideas, the suggestions, the opportunities, and the dangers detailed in the literature; (ii) the constraints imposed by the very nature of the larger study for which the measure of theft was required.

The full sequence of steps was as follows.

1   The construction process began with a search of the relevant literature, details of which have already been presented.

2   An exploratory study, involving intensive interviews with boys, was launched in order: (i) to identify the principal barriers to boys giving accurate information about their own stealing; (ii) to identify any circumstances that seemed to facilitate the provision of such information. This is a vital step in the construction of any 'new measure' *and in this case it was the first step in the method of progressive modification.*

3   The information from steps 1 and 2 above was then used for the formulation of an initial form of the required eliciting procedure. It was fully expected that, despite whatever skills went into this formulation, one or another part of it would be found to be faulty when tested.

4   Testing of the initial form of the procedure was now carried out through a type of intensive interviewing. As is usual, the tentative procedure was found wanting in various ways. It was then modified in an attempt to eliminate its weaknesses. This ended Cycle 1 of the progressive modification construction system.

5   There then followed five more cycles of modification followed by test. At the end of this process the measure appeared to be providing information at an acceptably accurate level.

6   After minor further modifications, a final and substantial test of procedure was made. The test involved: (i) the application of the eliciting procedure to a sample of London boys; (ii) a fortnight later, a repeat application to the same boys, but on this occasion

with extensive and intensive challenging and checking of the testimony given in that second interview. This second interview was regarded as providing something between a reliability and a validity test. This test indicated a high degree of reliability/validity for the new measure.

As stated in Chapter 10, the purpose of this presentation is to illustrate the construction of a new procedure insofar as it differs from the processes of progressive modification applied to a procedure found to be faulty (see Part II for a full description of the progressive modification technique). Accordingly, this illustration has been focused upon the following construction stages:

- A full description of steps 1 to 3 above and of the testing part of step 4
- A short statement about the modification of the method based upon the test of it (with a reference to where the full description may be found)
- A summary statement about the next four cycles of 'test-modification' (with a reference to where the full description may be found)
- A brief statement about the final form of the method (with a reference to where the full description and the procedure itself may be found).

AN EXPLORATORY STUDY TO IDENTIFY PROBLEMS AND FACILITATING FACTORS

It is not unusual for researchers to go straight from a review of the literature to the formulation of a questioning procedure (for obtaining information of the sort they want). However, this can be a very dangerous practice, for it assumes a considerable degree of realism and empiricism on the part of those who 'write' the literature. *What was absolutely necessary for the present project was special exploratory work through the intensive interviewing of boys themselves.* Moreover, these boys would have to be drawn from the population on which the theft measure would eventually be used, namely the general population of London boys aged 13—16 years. Such a study was undertaken.[95]

The purposes of the exploratory study

The main purposes of the exploratory study were: to identify the principal factors and conditions that work against boys making accurate statements about the nature and extent of such stealing as they may have done; to identify the principal factors and conditions that *facilitate* the giving of accurate information of that kind. The exploratory work had two further purposes. The first concerned the sheer practicability of securing a meaningful sample of boys for the administration of the theft measure; the second involved identifying any administrative problems associated with getting the required information.

The case for identifying barriers or blocking factors is not hard to make. Only if we know what these are will we be in a position to direct our efforts to overcoming them. In the same way, if we know what circumstances facilitate the giving of accurate theft information, we will be better placed to exploit those circumstances — to make the most of them in seeking the information we want. Similarly, there is little point in developing the required measuring procedure unless we know that we can secure a meaningful sample of boys for its administration to them once it has been made. Finally, it seemed very likely that there would be major problems over the administration of the proposed measure. The exploratory study was meant to identify these problems as well.

HOW THE EXPLORATORY INTERVIEWS WERE CARRIED OUT

The sampling methods used

The exploratory interviewing was to be small scale but intensive in character. It was conducted in four polling districts in Greater London. There were originally seven polling districts, drawn with a view to their being well separated geographically and appreciably different in terms of socio-economic and cultural characteristics. Strict sampling methods for drawing these polling districts (in which interviews would be conducted) were not as important at this exploratory stage as ensuring a wide spread of boys and, presumably, the problems facing any eliciting technique. In any case, the sampling of small areas (from which respondents would later be randomly drawn) is a well-established procedure and not one that required exploratory study. (The sampling of boys *within* such small areas was another matter altogether — see later.)

The seven polling districts were reduced to four as the search for local interviewing centres proved ineffective in three of them (an outcome of importance for the planning of the eliciting procedure). The remainder were nonetheless different from each other in the ways intended.*

*The four were drawn respectively from: Tooting, Kensington, Kentish Town and St John's Wood.

The drawing of the names of boys from the four polling districts raised problems, principally because full lists of boys in any age group are not available ready-made. In the first of the four polling districts from which a sample of boys aged 13 to 16 years was to be drawn, several different sampling methods were tried out. However, by the time work started in the second polling district, an enumeration system[95] had been adopted as the only feasible sampling method. With the proper use of this method, all the addresses in each subarea are visited, and a list is prepared of all the relevant individuals living there. From this list, stratified by age and other characteristics, a random sample of those individuals may be drawn.

However, an enumeration system is very expensive to operate, and so for this *exploratory study* it was applied on only a very limited basis* — but nonetheless in such a way that the research team could gain experience in using it for our rather specialised purposes.

The enumeration system (and the recruitment of boys in the first area) led to the listing of 212 boys† in the age range 13 to 16 years,‡§ this being the range required for the projected aetiological enquiry and hence the range most relevant to the present exploratory study. Interviews were sought with each of these 212 boys.

In each of the four polling districts, the boys were split half and half between local centre and home interviews. Where a home interview seemed (or proved) to be impossible because of conditions there, the boy concerned was transferred to the subgroup to be interviewed at a local centre.¶

Arranging interviews with boys

Interviews were made by appointment, usually after talking with parents and boys and giving them some but not all the reasons for the interview.# The boy and his parents were told that the interview would

---

*Working from the electoral register for a given area, enumeration started with the homes nearest to the local centre in that area and was then extended outwards until sufficient boys in the appropriate age range had been 'found' for our interviewing purposes, namely approximately 50 in that area. In each of the remaining two areas the same system was applied, the total yield over the four areas being 212 boys aged 13 to 16 years. (In all future survey work, the full enumeration system was used.)

†The aetiological study was to be concerned only with boys because the evidence available clearly indicated that boys account for the great bulk of the class of crime to be studied, namely stealing. So the tool-making work was focused on boys alone.

‡The original lower age limit of 12 was raised because earlier work had indicated: (i) parental wariness and resistance to the interviewing of younger boys away from their homes; (ii) a tendency for younger boys to lose interest and to become fatigued in the course of the possibly long and tough interview which was to be conducted.

§An upper age limit of 16 had been adopted because this is the limit, according to the law, of the juvenile status.

¶See details of local centre arrangements later.

#For example: that it was a youth survey; that it involved some of the things boys do in their spare time.

last for about an hour and that the interviewer was from a university research group. Boys would be interviewed either at home or at a local centre manned by the Survey Research Centre staff. The local centre consisted of small rooms, set up for interviewing, in hired premises.

The time between the making of the appointment and the interview itself was kept fairly short. Where boys were not at home when the interviewer called back or where they did not arrive at the local centre for interview, a fresh appointment was made. For elusive boys, a small fee for the interview was offered.

Records were kept of the interviewing success rates and of the nature of the difficulties experienced in securing interviews and in getting boys to the local centre. Some 159 boys (out of the target of 212) were interviewed.

The selection and training of interviewers

The initial selection of interviewers was through tape-recorded tests. Those selected in this way then underwent a week of training in the proposed interviewing technique. Training took the following form: (i) in-house teaching of the required method; (ii) trainee interviewers conducting tape-recorded interviews each morning with boys (not those later interviewed in the exploratory study); (iii) these recordings being played back each afternoon to the whole group of trainees (and to the trainer) for criticism and re-instruction of the interviewer concerned.

Preparing the boy for the interview

Boys were to be interviewed alone (that is, no parents were to be allowed to sit in and there was always only *one* interviewer present). Each boy was told that he would be asked various questions and that the interviewer would then go back over the answers that he had given. The boy was assured that no name would be entered on any of the papers used in the interview, that 'we' had no interest at all in who he was and that he could regard the whole thing as strictly private.

The form of the interview

About 10 minutes were given over to an introductory process during which boys were asked fairly innocuous questions about themselves and their families. Apart from the information so secured, this process was expected to settle boys into the interview. After this, approximately 20 minutes was spent with the delicate process of asking boys about their own stealing, stealing by friends and related delicate matters. Then came approximately 30 minutes of intensive questioning designed to obtain from each boy admissions of any difficulties he had with the questions about stealing, any tendency to hold back information about stealing, his reasons for tending to hold back, anything at all that helped him to make admissions.

Directly after this three-stage interview, each interviewer prepared a report on: (i) the difficulties reported by the boys; (ii) anything that helped the boy to give the interviewer the information required; (iii) the difficulties that the interviewer experienced; (iv) any suggestions that the interviewer had for the further collection of such information.

FINDINGS RELATING TO SAMPLING*

It was clear from the outset that if the proposed measure of theft behaviour was to be effective in a general population study of boys, an adequate sample of boys would have to be available for measurement. Success level in securing a sample of boys was therefore a matter of great importance.

THE COMPLETENESS OF THE LIST FROM THE ENUMERATION PROCESS

The enumeration system appeared to work reasonably well, but approximately 10% more boys from the enumerated streets were subsequently identified through leads from other boys and through street contacts. The reasons for missing these boys in the first place appeared to include:

- Failure by the enumerator to account for all the houses in the streets being enumerated,† and the willingness of some interviewers to 'make do' with the statements of neighbours
- The provision by parents of inaccurate information about the number, the ages and the names of their children and (perhaps related to the provision of inaccurate information) parents' confusion of the enumerator with public officials (for example, housing officers, attendance officers) or with salesmen

---

*For the sake of brevity and relevance, only the information relating to boys' *stealing* is presented here. For full details of findings of the exploratory study, see the full report.[95]
†For example, by giving up after three calls.

453

- The out-of-dateness of the electoral registers as records of addresses
- The presence in the one home of several families.

A full enumeration system would have to be employed in the tool-making process (and its eventual use), but in any case greater than normal rigour in the administration of the enumeration survey would obviously be necessary and ways would have to be found for gaining the confidence of parents sufficiently for them to provide more accurate information.

THE PERCENTAGE OF THE SAMPLE OF BOYS WHO WERE INTERVIEWED

Interviews were sought with all 212 boys listed through the enumeration survey and 75% of these (159) were eventually interviewed. For 60% of the boys with whom an interview was sought, there was relatively little difficulty in the sense that the appointment for interview was made after one to three calls *and was kept*. The remaining 40% proved more difficult: for some, the first approach for an appointment resulted in a refusal, so that further approaches for appointment had to be made. For some, the appointment was not kept so that a further appointment had to be sought. Out of the difficult 40%, only 15% were interviewed.

The percentage success rate was somewhat lower for the 'centre' interviews than for the home interviews and for the older boys (80% for younger boys versus 71% for older boys). There was also variation in success rate according to the length of the period between the making of an appointment and the date of that appointment: the greater this period, the greater was the failure of boys to keep the appointment.

Table 11.1
Relating time gap between appointment and interview to success in securing the interview

Interval between making of the appointment and the interview	Percentage interviewed
Up to ¼ hour	100
¼ hour to 2 hours	95
2 hours to 1 day	73
1 day to 3 days	65
3 days and over	42

The trend apparent in Table 11.1 may have been due to the fact that the boys who were given appointments further ahead were those who were particularly busy or who perhaps were the more elusive of the boys approached. However, we cannot overlook the possibility that as the period gets longer boys lose interest in taking part or tend to forget about the arrangements made. It is noteworthy, too, that the rate of loss with increased interval was somewhat greater for the interviews conducted at the local centre than for the home interviews.

A check through the files of the Greater London Council's children's department revealed that, of the 159 boys interviewed, 9% had a Court Appearance Record and that for the 53 boys with whom we failed to secure an interview the Court Appearance figure was 11%. While this evidence is reassuring, we must remember that the base numbers are small.

SOME POSSIBLE CAUSES OF FAILURES IN APPOINTMENT MAKING AND IN SECURING INTERVIEWS

When boys refused an appointment on at least one occasion, they, or their parents, were asked to say why. While the 'reasons' given may on occasions be of doubtful validity, they may nonetheless be usefully suggestive:

- The boy was ill/had moved from the neighbourhood (since the enumeration survey)/was on holiday (5)
- The boy said he was not interested in taking part (14)
- The boy had better things to do with his time (3)
- The boy was busy/found the suggested appointment times in-convenient/was on shift-work (10)
- The boy or his parent was suspicious or doubtful about the purpose of the interview or the identity of the interviewer (3)
- 'If this was a responsible operation it would have been done through the schools' (1)
- The boy had heard about the interview from other boys and felt he wouldn't like it (3)
- The boy was fed up with being questioned at school and elsewhere (1)
- The boy would come only with his friend (who was on holiday) (1)
- It is an invasion of people's privacy (1)
- Parent said that the boy was in an emotional state/was not clever enough (2)

- Parent(s) said the boy needed no help/would not benefit from being interviewed/might suffer from it (3)
- Parent disliked the idea of the boy being interviewed alone (1).

'Reasons' were also sought from boys or parents for failure to keep an appointment:

- Forgot or mistook the time (9)
- Found himself busy or otherwise engaged at the time (for example, in one or another leisure-time activity/doing overtime work/on shift work) (22)
- Ill or visiting hospital (3)
- In an emotional state or mentally defective or shy (3)
- Forbidden to participate by parents (1)
- Had lost interest (3)
- Lost the way to the centre (1)
- Thought the interviewer looked like a teacher (1)
- Preferred to spend his spare time in his own way (1).

INDICATIONS FOR IMPROVE-MENTS IN THE SUCCESS RATE

This evidence indicates that there is room for improvement in the recruitment system and it seems also to point to several ways of achieving improvement:

1. The interval between the making of the appointment and the interview itself should be kept as brief as possible and along with this the person making the appointments should have available a greater variety of (short-term) appointment slots;

2. In approaching boys (and parents) for an appointment, a major effort should be made to impress him/them with the importance of the enquiry, to establish the operation as interesting, respectable and worthwhile;

3. A reward or inducement system might have to be established as a regular feature of appointment making (for example, a money payment for attendance).

FINDINGS RELATING TO THE IDEA OF BEING INTERVIEWED ABOUT STEALING

The following statement of findings is in two parts: (i) difficulties and facilitating factors relating to the idea of being interviewed about stealing; (ii) difficulties and facilitating factors that emerged in the process of trying to secure specific information from the boys.

DIFFICULTIES RELATING TO THE IDEA OF BEING INTERVIEWED ABOUT STEALING (TABLE 11.2)

These difficulties all go beyond reasons for refusing to be interviewed — they all come from boys who were in fact interviewed. They are set out in detail in Table 11.2 and are discussed below.

1   Many of the boys admitted being or were observed to be 'uneasy'. For some, this state set in at the very start of the interview and for others it developed as the interview became increasingly focused on the detail of theft behaviour. It is impossible to say what this state meant to the accuracy of boys' statements, but it was clear from the outset that the interview was for many a stressful one calling for the use of special tactics and care.

2   Another problem concerned the degree of a boy's capacity to give information of the sort here involved. Some of the boys seemed unable to understand what was wanted of them (because they were unintelligent or slow or used to thinking carefully). Others had difficulty making the *interviewer* understand *them*, apparently because of things like limited vocabulary or inarticulateness or accent or stammering or (occasionally) a foreign language difficulty. Interviewers also had trouble with boys who talked too much, for it gave them the task of distinguishing between relevant and irrelevant statements and of steering boys back to the point. Problems of memory for detail also shows up. On this point, it is well established that memory for one's own behaviour is frequently subject to error and that there is often a greater memory failure than the respondent himself is aware of.

3   Another quite commonly experienced problem was the unpreparedness of boys with respect to the purpose and the nature of the interview, often resulting in surprise at what it turned out to be. Some simply did not know what to expect, some expected something else (for example, that it would be about sex, that it would be about getting into college). Just where some of these mistaken expectations came from is impossible to say at this stage, but from general experience of survey research it is virtually impossible to prevent some at least from occurring. Clearly the type of mistaken expectation to avoid is the one that either leaves the

Table 11.2
Problems related to the interview as a whole

			Frequency of mention (159 cases)
1	General uneasiness		45
	(a)	*Nervousness*	25
		Nervousness	19
		Nervousness at the start of the interview	6
	(b)	*Shyness*	12
		Shy	8
		Shy at the start of the interview	4
	(c)	*Uneasy, tense, strange*	13
		Unrelaxed/uneasy/jumpy/ill-at-ease	8
		Tenseness	3
		Unsureness/strangeness	2
	(d)	*Fidgeting*	4
2	Limitations in the boy's capacity to give information		28
	(a)	*Difficulties in remembering*	5
	(b)	*Problems of thinking or understanding*	10
		Unintelligent/low IQ/ESN	5
		Difficulties due to boy's way of thinking/slow/thoughtless/ superficial thinking/unused to thinking	3
		Difficulties in boy's understanding/poor understanding/ failures to understand	3
	(c)	*Problems of the boy making himself understood*	12
		Small vocabulary/limited vocabulary	2
		Inarticulateness	5
		Uncommunicativeness/saying little	2
		Foreign language difficulties	2
		Boy difficult to understand/difficult accent/mumbling/ stammering	3
	(d)	*Talkativeness/garrulousness/talking excessively/talkative with long, involved illustrations*	6
3	Problems of the preparation of the boy with respect to the purpose, nature or content of the interview		24
	(a)	*Ignorance of the purpose of the interview*	11
		Ignorance of the purpose/puzzlement at why questions were asked	2
		Ignorance of what to expect/not knowing what to expect	8
		Purpose of the interview not communicated	1
	(b)	*Wrong ideas about the purpose of the interview*	9
		Wrong idea of the purpose of the interview/expected test or help in getting to college	2
		Expectation that sex would be the subject matter of the interview	3
		Misunderstanding of the purpose or nature of the interview/ thought it was about a Youth Club	3
		Boy felt tricked into participating	2
	(c)	*Surprised at the nature of the questions*	4
		Surprised by the questions	2
		Found the questions unusual/had never been asked such questions before	2

Table 11.2 (cont.)

		Frequency of mention (159 cases)
4	Doubts about the authenticity of the interview	
	(a) *Disbelief of the confidentiality of the interview*	12
	Doubts about confidentiality/disbelief of the confidentiality at the start or throughout the interview	9
	Fear of the interviewer being connected with the police/being a policeman	3
	(b) *Suspicion or doubt of the interviewer or the procedure*	9
	Suspicions of the interviewer or the procedure	7
	Dissatisfied about who the interviewer was	2
5	Evasion, with no reason indicated	
	Evasiveness/caginess/boy appeared to be hiding or withholding information	8
6	Embarrassment, questions too personal, dislike of interview	9
	Embarrassment	4
	Found questions personal/too personal	2
	Disliked interview/disliked being asked or answering questions	4
7	Afraid of parents (or others) cross-examining or overhearing	15
	Afraid of cross-examination by parents about the interview	2
	Afraid of being overheard/door open throughout interview at home	3
	Father sitting in on the interview/interruptions of the interview by others in the household	10
8	Lack of interest on the part of the boy or a dislike of the interview	14
	(a) *Poor rapport, disinterest, passivity*	13
	Rapport did not develop/rapport was perilous	4
	Disinterestedness/boredom/casualness/inattentiveness	7
	Passivity/vacancy/impossibility of catching boy's imagination	3
	(b) *Dislike of the interviewer or his manner*	2
9	Boy hurried the interview	
	Boy hurried/the interview had to be telescoped/interview cut short	10
10	Miscellaneous references	
	Tiredness/no response to the 'I've done that sort of thing myself' approach from the interviewer/boy was full of himself/swaggering/boy wanted the interview on his own terms/boy trusted himself to decide some things he should not say/boy felt questions should be asked with parents about so that if he was going wrong he could be prevented from doing so/thought questions implied criticism of parents and resented this/felt foolish at not having offered the interviewer a chair/afraid of interviewer adopting a moral line/boy afraid of interviewer getting wrong ideas about him/boy had never talked so long at one time before this/boy initially thought the interviewer might be easily shocked	12

respondent resentful (as was reported of several of these boys) or which retards their reorientation to the real purpose of the interview. *Ignorance* of the true purpose of the interview is, however, a rather different matter, for it is doubtful whether a full divulgence of aims would necessarily lead to a sufficiently high rate of success in securing the boys. On the other hand, it seems desirable to try to eliminate bewilderment (as to what will come next) on the part of the boys actually taking part.

4   Understandably, there were doubts about the authenticity of the interview (see 4 in Table 11.2) in the form both of disbelief in its confidentiality and of suspicion as to the real identity and purpose of the interviewer (including suspicion that the interviewer was somehow connected with the police).

Possibly relevant to these reactions are some of evasiveness and of withholding (see 5 in Table 11.2), of apparent dislike of being questioned and of apparent dislike of this interview (see 6 in Table 11.2). Certainly it is not hard to see how boys, asked such personal questions as were put to them, might begin the interview with doubts and wariness and maintain these attitudes throughout the interview, in spite of the interviewer's attempts to forestall and allay them. In a few cases these doubts appear to have been strengthened through the interviewer's appearance reminding them of a policeman (for example, by his tallness or by his wearing a blue shirt, or possibly by his occasional authoritarian manner).

5   With interviews conducted at home, there were occasional interruptions by other members of the household. These included instances where the boy stopped giving information when he thought he was being overheard; and cases where parents actually sat in on part of the interview. What we do not know is the extent of undetected wariness and withholding attributable to the presence or near-presence of family members. Centre interviews were of course free from such interruptions. Another and associated source of worry for some boys was that parents might later question them about the content of the interview.*

6   Another source of trouble, almost certainly affecting the adequacy of response, was an apparent disinterest, a passivity and a generally unsatisfactory level of rapport on the part of some of the boys. There were not many of these cases, though just as with those who had doubts about the genuineness and the safety of the interview, one cannot tell to what extent difficulties of this kind existed without being detected. Having said this, it is most im-

---

*Martin Gold, in an American study, had given boys a set of additional questions about which they *could* safely talk to parents. [72]

portant to add that often enough where doubt was initially present, it appeared to be reduced or even dispelled in the course of the interview. The apparent willingness of the boys to talk was in fact much greater than had been expected.

7   In a number of cases, the interview was partly spoiled by the boy being in a hurry (or becoming impatient), and therefore cutting it short.

8   A considerable number of other difficulties were encountered just once or twice each and these are set out under 'miscellaneous' in Table 11.2. However, they should be studied closely, initially at least, on the principle that it may be only on these several occasions that interviewers have happened to detect something of importance. Thus it may be well to note the following items amongst them: the boy wanted the interview on his own terms; he felt the questions implied criticism of parents and he resented this; he was afraid of the interviewer adopting a moral line; he was afraid of the interviewer getting the wrong ideas about him.

We would like to stress that the frequency with which problems of the more general kind were noted is not to be taken as the frequency with which they actually occurred. They are presented here as evidence only of the kinds of difficulties that emerged or showed up in dealing with the boys studied. As such, they can serve to alert us against dangerous oversights and against naïvety, when we come to formulating the questioning procedure and to the isolating of special problems for further study. The frequencies actually derived here must be treated as only relative, and we must have reservations even about this.

Finally, it is worth noting that there are indications of certain differences in the difficulties experienced by younger and older boys. Younger boys were often described as nervous. They also more often showed limitations in their capacity to give information. Older boys, on the other hand, were perhaps more often inclined to suggest that they felt unprepared with respect to the purpose, nature or content of the interview.

Boys interviewed at home tended somewhat more than those interviewed at the centre to be rated as nervous and somewhat less to be rated as showing difficulty in making themselves understood.

FACILITATING FACTORS RELATING TO THE IDEA OF BEING INTERVIEWED ABOUT STEALING

The remarks of boys suggested that certain conditions or processes or factors *helped them* to co-operate in this interview. These are as

Table 11.3
Facilitating factors and conditions in relation to the interview about theft

	Frequency
1 Boy assured that the enquiry was genuine	27
(a) By assurances of interviewer/confidentiality	12
(b) Boy satisfied with purposes of interview	2
(c) Boy approved of survey/believed in survey/used to idea of survey	4
(d) University backing for inquiry/interviewer a student	4
(e) Interviewer approached parents/sought parental approval	7
2 Interviewer's manner/appearance	29
(a) Interviewer's introductory/informal talk	3
(b) Boy's relief/boy being made to feel normal	5
(c) Boy liked interviewer's attitude/sense of humour/friendliness	3
(d) Interviewer impersonal/had man-to-man attitude/unshocked	3
(e) Interviewer looked young/did not look like a teacher	6
(f) Boy became used to interviewer/came to trust interviewer	4
(g) Boy enjoyed talking in the interview	6
3 Miscellaneous references	
Indications of genuine interest/officialness of use of hall/ interviewer's persistence in obtaining boy/interviewer carrying papers/interviewer taking notes	3

detailed in Table 11.3. A commentary on them follows below.

1 Boys' feelings of confidence that the interview was genuine and/ or safe appear to have been strengthened in some cases by such things as: the initial assurance as to its confidentiality; satisfaction with its stated purpose and approval of the idea of it; the statement that a university was responsible for the project and an *impression* that the interviewer was a student;* the initial approach being made to the boy's parents and the securing of parental approval of the interview. We must, of course, see these influences as applying to *some* boys and not necessarily to others.

2 In some cases, the interviewer's manner also seems to have inspired co-operation. Thus boys referred to: relief at being made to feel normal (that is, in spite of things they had done); liking the interviewer's attitude, sense of humour and his friendliness; the interviewer's impersonal, man-to-man attitude and the fact that he was unshocked by what he was told; getting used to the interviewer and learning to trust him.

*This work was carried out before the recent wave of student strife. But in fact no interviewer was a student.

Table 11.4
Problems encountered in getting the boy to give
specific information about his own stealing

	Frequency of mention
1 *Problems of understanding*	24
Did not seem to understand what the interviewer wanted to know	3
Misunderstanding of some of the words used in the question (eg, thought 'breaking in' referred to behaviour with girls or to being 'rowdy')	3
Apparent uncertainty about *what* to include under 'stealing' (eg, taking money from mother's purse, acting as 'look-out' for others, taking money from telephone boxes/some incidents seemed too ridiculous to mention or happened too long ago to be mentioned	19
2 *Problems of memory (according to boy)*	22
Forgetting of incidents altogether/forgetting about details including date, nature of objects stolen, whether or not others were involved	22
3 *Unprepared for this question*	12
Surprised at the question because he did not expect it/boy felt the question should have been preceded by something that helped him to be more confident about later questions/surprised because it was not an everyday question/surprised because his own theft had been so recent/awkward because he had never talked like this before	8
Could not see any reason for the question/wondered what the interviewer was getting at	4
4 *General uneasiness and fear*	17
Nervousness	2
Uneasiness/ill-at-ease/wary	4
Awkward/tense/frightened/strange/scarey	9
Distressed/in an emotional state	2
5 *Reactions of embarrassment, shame, guilt*	35
Embarrassment	17
Ashamed/felt shame/feeling of continuing shame because of the sort of victim he had stolen from (including parents)/felt shame because theft was petty	16
Guilty/felt guilty because of the recency of the theft	7
Wanted to forget what he had done/did not want to remember	7
6 *Fear that the interviewer would condemn him*	27
Fear the interviewer would get a poor opinion of him/think badly or disapprove of him/fear the interviewer might be shocked/did not want to admit to being a fool (for having stolen) or to look like one/afraid of giving the impression of boasting/worried that the interviewer would not believe him	17
Fear of the interviewer misinterpreting the situation/fear of giving the interviewer a false impression that his parents were mean or that the incident was worse than it was	3
Fear the interviewer might adopt a moral line/might preach at him/expected to be in disgrace/expected the interviewer to be too self-righteous like others who have questioned him	4
Felt he was suspected of being guilty/that the interviewer thought he was a thief	7

Table 11.4 (cont.)

	Frequency of mention
7 *Fear of admissions leading to trouble*	23

Fears that the interviewer was possibly associated with the police/fear of his being a policeman (because of blue shirt and type of question) — 4

Fear of disclosure to police or to others — 7

Fear of information getting out/fear of trouble/fear of a leak to parents and others/felt that keeping quiet would keep him out of trouble — 10

Worried at the use of notes/wanted to know what was going to be done with the notes — 3

Doubts about confidentiality of the interview — 2

Distrust, doubt and suspicion of the interviewer/did not know the interviewer well enough/disbelief as to who the interviewer was — 6

Felt the incident was too serious to mention — 1

8 *Loyalty to others* — 3

Loyalty to mates/a mutual arrangement with mates to refrain from talking/fear of showing himself unreliable to mates — 3

9 *Concealment or reluctance to answer (no particular reason given)* — 36

Refusal to answer/refusal to disclose recent incidents/refusal to give details of incidents — 5

Withholding until probing produced answers/admissions had to be dragged out/reluctance to mention incident or to give details/wished interviewer would drop the subject/tried to shy away from the question/did not want to answer — 26

Had to debate with himself whether or not to answer/took time to think about the question/hesitated in answering — 8

10 *Other problems*

The boy's statement was confused/he was proud of his innocence or of not having stolen anything bigger/he thought the question implied he was guilty and disliked the idea/he was disinterested or vacant/he wanted to get the interview over quickly or to get past this question quickly/bravado/hard to distinguish from the truth/the matter was too personal to talk about and was none of the interviewer's business/he was not satisfied about what was in the interview for him/afraid of being asked *why* he did these things/would not have talked about incidents when he did them because then they were big things to him/he disagreed with interviewer's attitude that stealing was unimportant/felt the question was not easy to answer on his own/had previously had an unsatisfactory experience in being interviewed/anxiety over answering wrongly/did not think in terms of stealing/fidgeting/disliked talking about stealing — 23

3   Some lads referred to the youth of the interviewer as being helpful to them, and others to the fact that the interviewer did not look like a teacher (although in at least one case an interviewer *was* thought to look like a teacher).

4   Some boys said that they enjoyed *talking* in their interview.

These are all points of which more could, possibly, be made in an interviewing procedure developed out of the present exploratory study.

FINDINGS RELATING TO PROVIDING INFORMATION ABOUT STEALING

The boy was asked if he had ever taken anything that did not belong to him, what sorts of things he took, from where he took these things, when was the last time he took anything, who was in on the theft with him, what happened after the theft took place, and so on. After this, the interviewer attempted to find out how the boy felt about being so questioned and the difficulties he experienced in giving a reply. An understanding of these reactions is most important for the development of an effective way of extracting information of this seemingly delicate kind.

DIFFICULTIES

The 'difficulties' brought out in this way are set out in Table 11.4. They are discussed below.

1   Some boys gave evidence of not understanding at least some aspect of this composite of questions, the most common difficulty being an uncertainty as to what should be included as 'stealing'.

It appeared that there was a variety of marginal types of theft which boys did not know whether to mention, or only mentioned them when the interviewer broadened the concept of stealing, for example, taking money from mother's purse, acting as lookout for others, taking money from a telephone box. Short of asking the interviewer for a better definition — which is unlikely — boys had to rely upon their own personal judgements.

It is difficult to see how this problem can be overcome except through detailed specification of what is in fact to be included. A card-sorting system of the kind used by Martin Gold[72] (where each relevant item of theft-behaviour is presented on a separate card) may well offer a partial solution, though there remain problems of definition and the difficulties of communication (see later) are likely to be increased with every extra card.

This basic problem was aggravated in some cases by a misunderstanding of certain words and of questions generally. Misunderstanding of questions is, in fact, very common in interviewing,* and it is quite possible for a respondent to have a wrong idea of what a question is about, without this becoming apparent to the interviewer (or perhaps even to the respondent himself).

2   The boy's recall task was a twofold one. First he had to recall all occasions on which he took things that did not belong to him. In addition, he had to recall certain circumstances of the incidents he remembered: when and with whom they occurred; what was taken; what happened afterwards. The first of these tasks called for relatively unaided recall of a potentially varied array of incidents, the possibility being that one or another broad category would be completely (and innocently) overlooked. Certainly some boys mentioned more incidents as the questioning went on — both in the first and second stages of the interview — and claimed that they had not remembered them at first.

In relation to the second task, there were boys who were unable to provide information about the *times* at which incidents occurred and other details of such incidents and who claimed that this was a question of memory. It may not have been so in all cases (for example, as when the provision of certain information might incriminate other boys). However, evidence from this exploratory study certainly indicated difficulty in such recall and in any case it would be unwise simply to dismiss the boys' claims to this effect. Over and above the evidence of Table 11.3, the literature of memory research[22-30] cannot but emphasise the fallibility of memory-dependent information and the need to introduce memory aids of one or another kind.

3   Some of the boys appear to have been unprepared for the close detail of the questions, being somewhat surprised by their nature and puzzled at why they were being asked. There were several suggestions that these questions should have been preceded by something to increase confidence in answering them.

4   There were numerous reactions of a kind that seemed liable to discourage the admission of thefts. Thus there were feelings of embarrassment or shame (that is, shame of the nature of what had been taken and from whom) or guilt on the part of the boy. For

*See references 8—14, 96—98.

some, there was a 'desire to forget'. Others felt that the interviewer might disapprove of him, or wrongly judge him or his parents, or adopt a moralising or preaching line. These kinds of reactions would have to be reduced or eliminated, and it seemed at this point in the project that their reduction called for moves such as the use of non-censuring interviewers, gentle handling, non-authoritarianism on the part of the interviewer, perhaps anonymity for the respondent.

5 A reaction of a different kind, but one possibly leading to the same result, was a fear that an admission could lead to trouble for the boy, or others. Some reactions seemed to be based upon doubt about the confidentiality of the interview, fear that the interviewer might be connected with the police in some way, fear that the information divulged might leak to parents and other people, concern at the use of notes in the interview. These boys and various others make up a sizeable group, who resisted giving information about thefts and from whom the information had sometimes to be 'dragged', or who revealed it only after appreciable hesitation.

We can hardly be surprised at reluctance of this sort. Presumably it is necessary to remove as much as possible of the boy's grounds for fearing the consequences of making admissions. Anonymity (with all the problems it raises) might help. It may also be that some types of interviewer and some kinds of interviewing manner might evoke fewer suspicions of a police connection, or might better lull such suspicions of this kind as actually arise when the subject of theft is mentioned. The dropping altogether of note taking and of tape-recording might also be desirable, but this raises major problems of record keeping because so much must then be left to the memory of the interviewer.

Formidable as may seem the task of getting admissions, it is most important to say here that boys did in fact admit a great deal, as indicated in Table 11.6. They told not only of thefts which had in fact been detected by the police, but also of undetected thieving. In other words, though there are serious grounds for a boy withholding information, many boys were surprisingly forthright — sufficiently so to suggest that more might be achieved in getting admissions. The fact that admissions were made does of course raise the problem of possible boasting and exaggeration. See below.

*See Chapter 1 for studies of error related to data being memory-dependent.

6   A feeling of loyalty to 'mates', or a fear of seeming to be un-reliable to 'mates', was also reported of/by several boys, the probable effect of such reactions being to retard admission of theft committed with others. It may well be of course that fear of the consequences of 'splitting on mates' lies behind some of the reluctance to talk reported in 5 above and in 7–9 of Table 11.4. Also, the question involved in this case was about admitting his *own* thefts, and so we cannot expect the probing of the question properly to reveal the possibly blocking function of loyalty to mates. Indeed, such loyalty was clearly operating when questions were asked about the stealing of mates. In other words, sparse reference here (to withholding because of loyalty to mates) does not necessarily indicate the actual frequency of the occurrence of this sort of blocking.

7   Quite a large number of boys (36/159) were involved in conceal-ment (of some aspect of their theft behaviour) or at least a marked reluctance to talk, without the reason for this being clear. Con-cealment and reluctance to talk stood out as major problems for the proposed eliciting technique.

8   In the large group of 'miscellaneous' problems at the end of Table 11.4, there are several which may be of special importance, despite the infrequency of their appearance: the boy was un-interested or vacant; he was not satisfied with what was in the interview *for him*; he did not think in terms of stealing; bravado; he would not have talked about incidents at the time he did them because they were big things to him.

9   Bravado *may* have involved overclaiming, but it is important to take note of the fact that *exaggeration* of theft behaviour did not show up through this exploratory work as a recurrent factor — whereas reluctance to make admissions certainly did. This is not to argue that exaggeration does not occur and in fact a watch was kept for it in each succeeding stage of the interview. Indeed, what later emerged was strong evidence that exaggeration tended to take place, not in the invention of types of theft that the boy did not normally commit, but sometimes as an overstatement of the *number of times* that some act was committed. Nonetheless, because of the view of many criminologists that exaggeration is a major problem, it was treated as such when it came to the formulation of the first form of the eliciting procedure. More later. In any case, concealment *was* a major problem.

The considerable yield of information about thefts by boys interviewed in this enquiry appears to have been facilitated by the factors detailed in Table 11.5, on which I would like to make the following comments.

1   A feeling that the interview was genuine was said by many boys to have helped them to talk out. The belief that the interviewer was genuine was supported by the following reasons and reactions: the interviewer's assurance that the information given was confidential; the readiness of the interviewer to see the boy's mother; the fact that the study was conducted by an organisation in the university; the boy's impression that the interviewer did not look like a policeman (for example, on the basis of his hair style or his manner); the fact that other boys in the district were taking part in the enquiry; the boy's satisfaction with the reasons given for asking the questions.

2   In addition to this, the following aspects of *manner* of at least some of the interviewers appear to have encouraged boys to talk: the way the interviewer made stealing seem normal or commonplace and the way he seemed to *expect* boys to have stolen; the straightforwardness, directness and confidence of the interviewers; the interviewer's own admissions of theft; the interviewer's understandingness and the fact that he did not seem shocked at what boys admitted; the boy became used to the interviewer and felt he could trust him; the interviewer was of the right age (that is, in his twenties).

3   Certain of the methods of the interview (in fact those which interviewers were instructed to use) appeared to help get admissions: the prompting and probing system used; the way the interviewer widened the boy's ideas about what was included as theft and the way he was shown that the interviewer was interested even in trivial theft; the interviewer's insistence and perseverance; the way the interviewer gave the boy enough time to think and talk.

4   It appears too that some boys found it a relief to talk about their thefts and felt better for talking.

5   Others appear to have talked because they felt it fairly safe to do so. Thus: the boy was satisfied that nothing could be done about his admissions; the interviewer was a stranger and would not be seen again; the theft occurred a long time ago, or too far away, or it seemed trivial; the boy had already been caught for the offence which he now admitted.

Table 11.5
Showing factors which helped the boy to admit his thefts

1 *Boy assured that inquiry was genuine*   34

    (a) By assurances of interviewer/confidentiality   26
    (b) Interviewer seeing mother/readiness to see mother   4
    (c) University backing for inquiry/interviewer a student   3
    (d) Boy satisfied by interviewer's explanation/reasons for asking questions   3
    (e) Interviewer unlike policeman/haircut suggested interviewer was not a policeman/interviewer's manner unlike police when questioning   3
    (f) Inclusion of other boys in inquiry   3

2 *Interviewer's manner encouraged boy to tell truth*   34

    (a) Interviewer made study seem normal/commonplace/interviewer seemed to expect that boy had stolen   9
    (b) Interviewer's straightforwardness/directness/self-confidence   3
    (c) Interviewer's own admissions   7
    (d) Interviewer's understanding   4
    (e) Interviewer impartiality/would not be shocked   2
    (f) Boy getting used to interviewer   4
    (g) Boy's trust in the interviewer   4
    (h) Interviewer's age suitable (ie, in his twenties)   2
    (i) Interviewer's tone of voice gave boy confidence   1

3 *The interviewer's technique*   11

    (a) Interviewer's probing/prompting   3
    (b) Interviewer's insistence/perseverance   4
    (c) Interviewer giving boy time to think/talk   2
    (d) Interviewer widening boy's ideas of what was included as theft/boy's discovery of interviewer's interest even in trivial thefts   2

4 *Boy found it a relief to talk*   10

    (a) Boy relieved/felt better for talking   7
    (b) Boy's desire to tell truth/need to get story out   3

5 *Boy felt safe to talk*   26

    (a) Boy satisfied that nothing could be made of admissions   2
    (b) Interviewer a stranger/not to be seen again   6
    (c) Incident mentioned by boy occurred in Ireland   1
    (d) Incidents mentioned by boy were trivial/insignificant   3
    (e) Incident mentioned by boy happened long time ago   2
    (f) Boy's earlier admissions about thefts   3
    (g) Boy had been caught/punished for offence mentioned   1

6 *Miscellaneous*

    Boy prepared to take a chance/boy's desire to help/boy instructed by mother not to tell lies   4

Table 11.6
The types of theft admitted
(121 boys = 76% of 159)

Nature of item stolen	No. of boys involved (out of 121)	No. of these boys whose theft led to Court proceedings*
Picking up property in the street	2	—
Going on to building sites to play/into yards for conkers/ acting as look-out for such activities	3	—
Scrumping (taking fruit from trees in other people's gardens)	12	—
Going into houses/factories for a lark/to get a book	8	1
Taking scrap from lorries/yards/empty buildings	3	—
Taking own money without permission	1	—
Taking things from brothers or sisters — bicycle lamp/ unspecified/from sister's cupboard	4	—
Taking things from companions by force or from their homes — comics/toys/money/pens	9	—
Taking things from own school — books/pencils/rulers/ paper/clothing/pens	13	—
Taking food from school kitchen	1	—
Taking notices as souvenirs/spoon from restaurant	2	—
Taking a penknife from a relative's house	1	—
Taking money from telephone boxes	1	—
Stealing by finding — money (up to £5)/watch	15	1
Taking money from home/from purses/from parents/ by fiddling change from errands	12	—
Shoplifting — sweets/cigarettes/books/toys/fruit/biscuits/ eggs/unspecified	53	1
Stealing from market or other stalls — fruit/books/money	7	—
Acting as a look-out for shoplifting	1	—
Taking things from work/employer — tubing/magazines/ money/chocolates/food/haircream/case of drinks	8	—
Taking things from cloakrooms/baths — money/watch/ clothing	4	—
Stealing a quantity of cigarettes from automatic machines and selling them	1	—
Taking milk money from doorsteps	1	—
Taking coppers from launderette	1	—
Stealing a sleeping-bag from a youth club	1	—
Stealing a box of chewing gum unguarded in street	1	—
Entered houses/factories for theft — gas meters/money/ cigarettes/clothing	8	4
Stealing from a car/attempting to do so — spirits and cigarettes/clothing/tools/mirror	3	1
Stealing bicycles	3	1
Stealing a motorcycle/scooter	2	1
Taking and driving away a car	1	1
Caught by police as passenger in stolen car	1	—
Stealing cigarettes in quantity (place not specified)	1	—
Acting as look-out for theft of a watch (place not specified)	1	—
Stealing unspecified	2	—
Receiving a stolen wireless/buying a stolen pen/ receiving unspecified	3	1
Forging signature on Post Office Book to obtain money	1	—

*According to the boy.

6   Finally, there were several other facilitating factors of quite different kinds: the boy was prepared to take a chance on talking; the boy wanted to help the enquiry along; the boy's mother had instructed him not to tell lies.

Of the many different facilitating factors, we should be wary about the interviewer giving a boy an impression that theft was acceptable — on the grounds that this might possibly encourage the making of false admissions. However, the other factors listed could be of considerable value for the construction of the eliciting procedure.

FINDINGS RELATING TO TYPES OF THEFT ADMITTED

In the course of the exploratory questioning, 76% of the 159 boys admitted to at least some stealing, 18% denied having stolen at all and 8% left their positions unclear. From the 76% (121 boys) came information about the kinds of things they had stolen and this information is presented in Table 11.6. This table indicates a very wide range of items stolen. It also suggests that a great many thefts did not lead to Court proceedings.

The detail in Table 11.6 is particularly important for the construction of the proposed eliciting technique, for it supplies a list of the types of things stolen and some of the circumstances of theft. If the lead of Martin Gold of the Institute of Social Research in Michigan is to be followed, then such items might provide a beginning to the development of sorting cards that between them both serve as memory aids and define the repertoire of juvenile stealing. The first form of such a list is presented on page 492 in the context of the construction of the first form of the eliciting procedure.

FINDINGS RELATING TO ADMINISTRATIVE PROBLEMS

In the course of the exploratory study there emerged various difficulties and problems relating to administrative matters of relevance to the development of the elicitation technique and to the proposed causal study. These included: problems in securing suitable local centres; problems in administering the work at the local centres; difficulties in administering interviews in homes; problems in controlling the quality of the interviewing. Discussion of them follows.

One feature of the exploratory study was that interviewing was to be conducted both in boys' homes and at some local centres. There was such a local centre in each of the four areas in which the exploratory interviewing was carried out.

However, finding suitable centres raised major difficulties. We searched originally in seven polling districts for local centres and located centres in only four of them. In the process we approached local authorities (educational, housing, cleaning, civil defence), estate agents, youth clubs, business firms, welfare agencies, community clubs, churches, museums, local agents of political parties. This search was featured by miscommunications of various kinds, by wrong and misleading assumptions on the part of people approached for help, by general confusion. Some organisations refused to help once they heard what the enquiry was about (for fear of trouble from the boys) and for others the short duration of the requested period of tenancy offered little commercial incentive.

Over and above the time-consuming process of searching for acommodation, it turned out that the premises actually found and used (four of the seven areas) were really unsuitable.*

What all this seemed to mean was that the finding of local centres raises a number of problems:

- Areas in which work is eventually done may be subject to selective bias in that only those with available and suitable accommodation in them can be sampled
- Finding local centres is likely to be very time consuming
- The centres found may be unfit for the class of work to be done there.

In the circumstances, consideration was given to:

- The use of a mobile centre (that is, a type of caravan)
- The setting up of a special centre in central London selected and equipped for interviewing boys
- The conducting of all interviews in the homes of the boys.

*One centre provided only partial use of two rooms of a house normally providing office and living accommodation for a welfare organisation and, as the work of the latter continued throughout the period of our use of the accommodation, there was conflict between the two organisations. On occasions survey material had to be shifted from one to another room because of dual occupation of some of the space. As money and confidential records were kept by the other organisation, strict supervision of the boys attending the centre was required by us. Another of the centres obtained was in a very large and gloomy building which functioned as a youth club. The two rooms offered us were a long way apart and were approached by dismal corridors. Movement around the building involved the locking and unlocking of doors. Boys complained about the place.

THE ADMINISTRATION OF THE CENTRES

Appointment making was carried out by the interviewers themselves so that their availability for interviewing at the centre was very much reduced. It also meant that it was very difficult to offer a boy anonymity. The storing of valuable recording equipment was also a problem. Boys were often boisterous on arrival at the centre and difficult to control. It was fairly clear to the researchers conducting the exploratory study that someone should be engaged solely in appointment making, and that a centre administrator would have to be present to oversee the making and the timing of appointments and to receive (and control) the boys as they arrived at the centre.

THE HOME INTERVIEWS

In the home interviews, a problem arose in satisfying parents that the considerable length of the interview (about an hour) was necessary. Some parents were suspicious and stayed around so that it was impossible to develop the necessary high degree of rapport with the boy — let alone obtain from him statements about his stealing. Indeed, the most serious weakness of the home interview was the difficulty of interviewing the boy completely away from the hearing and the influence of his parents. One can readily understand why a parent might stay near a room in which his son was being interviewed by a stranger, or why a parent might want to listen in to his son's interview in the family sitting room. However, the result was to reduce the likelihood that the boy would make full admissions about his stealing.

Another difficulty about the home interview was that it seemed more difficult to make a full tape-recording of the interview in the boy's home than at a centre — a situation which worked against the rigorous quality control of the interviewer's performance.

CONTROL OVER THE PERFORMANCE OF THE INTERVIEWERS

Even at the local centres, however, the quality control of interviewer performance (based upon the tape-recordings made of the centre interviews) had to be given second place to the demanding requirement of keeping the flow of an interview going. Indeed, it soon became clear that quality control could be maintained at a satisfactory level only if the research team included someone responsible solely for that task.

SOME COMMENTS ON THE ADMINISTRATIVE
PROBLEMS ENCOUNTERED

One of the most serious of the difficulties referred to in this section is the failure of both the home *and* the local centre as interviewing situations. This seemed to leave only two other possibilities: (i) the use of a mobile interviewing centre; (ii) the use of a single centre in mid-London designed and equipped for the job. The idea of using a mobile interviewing centre was dropped on two grounds: (i) the difficulty of getting anything big enough to allow the parallel interviewing of three or four boys and to provide also for reception space; (ii) the difficulty experienced in a contemporary survey in getting satisfactory parking space for an ordinary caravan.

This left the mid-city centre, with its basic problem of bringing boys to it with minimum loss from the sample. Because the Survey Research Centre had a London building suitable for use as an interviewing block, our attention and our main efforts were turned in that direction.

It had also become clear that the efficient running of an interviewing centre would call for the appointment of a receptionist, at least one appointment maker and someone responsible for quality control. In addition to the interviewers, there would of course have to be a centre administrator responsible for the general running of the interviewing system. Since boys were to be brought to the centre, facilities would also have to be provided for collecting them from their homes.

SUMMING UP ON THE FINDINGS OF THE
EXPLORATORY STUDY

THE SAMPLING SYSTEM

1   An enumeration system seemed practicable as a means of setting up a sampling frame. However, it would have to be rigorously supervised and special steps taken to convince parents that the enumerator and the enquiry generally were genuine and constituted no threat of any kind.

2   Over and above this, there seemed to be scope for improvement in the way appointments were arranged with the boys eventually drawn in the sample, namely:

    (a)   The interval between the making of the appointment and the interview itself should be kept as brief as possible and along with this the person making the appointment should have available a greater variety of (short-term) appointment slots;

(b) A major effort should be made (just as in the enumeration survey) to convince the boy and his parents of the genuineness and worthwhileness of the enquiry;

(c) Boys' interest in the enquiry could with advantage be more strongly aroused so that they will not have lost enthusiasm for it by the time that the interview was due to take place.

THE DIFFICULTIES AND THE FACILITATING FACTORS IN GETTING INFORMATION ABOUT STEALING

Difficulties

1 Boys were not always clear about what was meant by 'stealing'. Hence some sort of defining operation seemed necessary.

2 There was evidence of memory failure, sometimes because the boy just did not happen to think of something that was relevant to his reply and sometimes because the boy found a specific recall too much for him. The first of these difficulties seemed to call for the use of a stimulus system which covered all aspects of stealing.

3 Some boys were nervous and ill at ease in dealing with the questions about stealing. Some were puzzled at why such questions were being asked. An explanatory and preparatory phase to the interview seemed to be required.

4 Some boys felt embarrassed at the questions about theft, some seemed to have felt guilty and some feared that the interviewer might judge or moralise. Special attention would have to be given to reducing embarrassment and feelings of guilt and the non-judging role of the interviewers would have to be maintained and possibly strengthened.

5 Other boys were worried lest the information given to the interviewer would somehow leak to the authorities or to parents. Obviously methods would have to be found which reassured the boy on this vital issue.

6 There was evidence of strong concern lest the boy's admissions should 'put his mates in'. Since we were not planning (in the aetiological enquiry) to elicit information about stealing by the boy's mates, it should be possible to avoid this source of trouble by carefully avoiding any questions which might seem to ask for it.

Facilitating factors

1   The genuineness of the interview was indicated (to boys) by:

- The assurance of the interviewer that the interview was confidential
- The interviewer's readiness to see the boy's mother
- The fact that the study was connected with the university
- The interviewer did not look to the boy like a policeman
- The fact that other boys in the district had taken part and were satisfied with it
- The reasons given for asking the questions (that is, writing a book)

2   The interviewer seemed straightforward and direct/was understanding/seemed trustworthy/made the boy's behaviour seem commonplace and normal.

3   The interviewer was young.

4   The boy was helped by the prompting and probing system used by the interviewer/by his explanation of what was meant and what was wanted, by the interviewer's perseverance/by the way the interviewer gave him time to think.

5   For some boys it was a relief to be able to talk about this subject.

6   Boys saw the interviewer as a stranger and felt that the interview was safe.

These are all conditions or procedures which should be maintained in any final form of the eliciting procedure, and some of them may well be open to extension or intensification.

ADMINISTRATIVE PROBLEMS

1   Neither home interviewing nor the use of temporary local centres seems feasible for this class of enquiry. Some other setting is required, and it seemed that attention could usefully be given to the use of a single city centre specially equipped for the job. This would, however, raise the problem of how to transport boys to such a centre without introducing a sampling hazard.

2   At any such centre, certain tasks will have to be assigned to separate individuals, namely:

- Appointment making
- The collection of boys and their transport to the centre
- The reception of boys at the centre

- Interviewing
- Quality control of interviewers' work
- General administration of the centre

CONSTRUCTING THE FIRST VERSION OF THE ELICITING PROCEDURE

INTRODUCTION AND SCENE SETTING

Against the background of the search of the literature and the exploratory study, the construction process was now set going. It began with the design of a very tentative first approximation to the required eliciting procedure. Its overall design and its every element were intended to take advantage of the more viable suggestions in the literature, to exploit the facilitating factors discovered through the exploratory work and to counter the various blocking factors revealed through that exploratory work.

Thereafter the method of progressive approximation was used in the same way as it was in the reconstruction of the National Readership Survey methodology already described in Chapter 8. There were seven* cycles of modification test in all. In Cycle 1, the first form of the procedure was formulated on the lines set out above, and this was followed by test work to identify its points of weakness and failure. In Cycle 2, the procedure was modified in line with the results of testing it in its first form, and this modification was then tested. After this came further cycles of modification and test, there being seven cycles from start to finish. In this chapter, I have deliberately limited my account to Cycle 1 and the modification part of Cycle 2. This is because Cycle 1 is specific to building a measuring technique from 'scratch'. Thereafter, the construction process (through Cycles 2–7) is the same in principle as that described in earlier chapters. The modification stage of Cycle 2 has also been described in full in order to take the reader fully into standard progressive modification as a construction technique. The reader who wants a description of all seven cycles will find them in the full report of the construction procedure.[5]

This section begins with the construction or design of a sampling system and a survey situation in the context of which the eliciting procedure would have to operate. This is a vital lead-in because in the first place, getting a representative sample of London boys into a situation in which the eliciting procedure (with its concentration upon stealing) could be administered was seen as a tough assignment. Unless a very high proportion of boys in a random type sample could be brought

---

*Six cycles of modifications in text plus a final cycle involving a reliability–validity test.

478

into such a situation, the eliciting procedure would be ineffective, no matter how accurate it could be made for the individual respondent. These proposed sampling/administration arrangements were of course to be tested and modified in just the same way as the first (and subsequent) versions of the eliciting procedure itself.

Then came the first (tentative) form of the eliciting procedure. However, only the first two of its planned three parts were presented and tested in Cycle 1. This was primarily because we needed to be sure of those two parts before finalising the design of Part III. In addition, the testing of Parts I and II was likely to be lengthy and the omission of Part III at this stage left more time for the testing process. In fact, Part III was not introduced (and tested) until Cycle 3.

SAMPLING AND ADMINISTRATION

The sample

It was planned that in the aetiological study some 40 polling districts would be used as the penultimate* sampling units and that 40 boys would be drawn from each of them on a random basis following enumeration procedures. This plan also governed the sampling methods that would be used throughout the various cycles of the progressive modification construction. It would thus be tested and modified as a vital part of the planned research methodology.

In preparation for the final testing procedure, a single polling district† was drawn and within it enumeration methods were used to secure a list of all boys aged 13 to 16 years living there, along with various background details. On the basis of this background data, certain boys were excluded, namely:

• Those who were seriously ill
• Those who were mentally handicapped
• Those who lived away from home
• Those whose parents were quite unco-operative
• Those not likely to be available at the time/period at which the proposed testing work was to be carried out

Approximately 12% of the listed boys were eliminated from the

---

*That is, the units chosen in the last but one stage of sampling – in this case, polling districts.
†For each cycle in the construction sequence, a different polling district was used. As a set, the seven were widely distributed throughout London. However, to advance the relevance of the testing programme, each of the seven had a somewhat higher than average juvenile delinquency level (according to police records).

'universe' in this way. The remaining boys were grouped by age (13, 14, 15, 16 years) and 15 boys were drawn randomly from each of the four age groups. The interviewers were all women.

Appointment making

Once the sample in the polling district was drawn, appointment makers, selected for their ability to secure appointments, visited the homes of the boys in the drawn sample. In each of these homes, the appointment maker sought parental and the boy's agreement for the boy to take part. A small fee was offered and the provision of light refreshment. A book token or record token was provided at the end of the interview. The appointment maker arranged for the boy to be collected by car and for him to be taken to an interviewing centre. The boy and his parents were told that the interview was part of a youth study, and that it would include questioning about spare-time activities. Where possible the appointment was fixed for just a few days ahead. The appointment maker left the boy a card showing the time of his appointment and reminding him of the inducements to attend.

Getting boys to the town centre
and preparing them for interview

As arranged with the appointment makers, the boys were brought to the town centre by a collector, four boys to a car. Where boys had refused to accompany the collector, she was required to find out from the boy just why he had changed his mind. The collector asked the boys *not* to exchange names in the car, and she passed the boys over to the centre receptionist without identifying any of them by name. At the centre, the boys were asked to choose a false name from the set on offer (for example, Burt, George, Len, Fred, Charlie, John) and were asked not to reveal their real names. The receptionist explained to each boy that the false name would make it easier for him to talk to the interviewer and that no-one would know his real name either during or after the interview. Boys were offered light refreshment (for example, orange juice, Coca Cola, doughnuts, sandwiches). The receptionist was friendly, and the reception room was pleasant. After reception processes were completed, the boys were taken to their individual interviewing rooms where they met their interviewers. They were introduced by false name. The collector brought one set of boys in for 5 pm interviews and a second set for 7 pm interviews.

The place of interview

The interviewing centre was located in central London at an annexe of a university college. This building had in it a considerable number of small rooms which were very suitable for private individual interview. A reception room was added to the complex of rooms to be used. The decision to use such a (town) centre was taken in view of the unsatisfactoriness of trying to interview boys at home and in view of the major problems experienced in trying to get and use *local* centres. Each interviewing room was simply furnished so that there could be no likelihood of a boy thinking someone or something might be hidden there.

The selection and training of the interviewers

Because the interview was expected to be difficult and demanding, special selection and control of interviewers was essential. Thus the first form of the interview was complex for the interviewer to deliver; it called for the use of probing techniques and demanded intelligence in the interviewer. Other qualities demanded in the interviewer were:

- Friendliness coupled with firmness
- An unshockable outlook
- An air of dependability
- A lack of off-putting mannerisms or peculiarities (for example, stammer, twitch, sophisticated accent)
- A tendency to use simple language
- Ability to sieze quickly on points of relevance
- A youthful appearance

It was assumed that boys would be more willing to talk to male interviewers on personal matters such as stealing. Promising applicants, most of them university graduates, were given a week's 'selection course' designed to assess their abilities to become successful interviewers, with special reference to the requirement of rigorous and intensive interviewing.

They were given instructions in the required interviewing techniques and in the use of equipment necessary for the interview. The candidates practiced by interviewing each other and subsequently carried out a number of interviews with boys. These trial interviews were fully tape-recorded. On the following morning, each recording was played to the interviewers (as a group) for discussion and for corrective suggestions by the persons responsible for training and selection. This process was repeated throughout the week, and at the end of it there was little difficulty in identifying people who either lacked the necessary ability or who seemed unable or unwilling to learn.

The subsequent training period for the selected interviewers lasted for another two weeks. During it, the trainee interviewers continued the procedure started in the week concerned with selection. Thus during evening interviewing sessions, each trainee used the tentative form of the elicitation procedure *followed by the required testing process* (that is, the follow-up interview)[5] in interviews with each of two boys. The following day they listened, in groups, to tape-recordings of their interviews. They were constantly encouraged to criticise their own performances and the performances of other interviewers, and they were asked questions about the application of both the eliciting and the follow-up procedures. The person in charge of training corrected errors in procedure, pointed out interrogating opportunities that were missed and generally reinstructed the trainees as necessary.

The emphasis during training was on the avoidance of any deviation from the required elicitation procedure and on the exacting requirements of the probing and challenging techniques to be used in the follow-up testing process. Stress was placed on the latter as a process of detection, demanding flexibility and concentration. The interviewers had to learn to avoid leading questions which might indicate to the boy some kind of answer expected by a given interviewer. It was emphasised that whereas the follow-up interview had to be of a probing, checking and challenging kind, the questions through which that follow-up was conducted had to be expressed simply and directly. Every effort was made to impress upon interviewers the fact that their approach had at all times to be firm yet friendly and helpful, and that on no account should there be any tendency on their part to judge or even to *seem* to judge the boy's behaviour as right or wrong.

Quality control arrangements

The method of progressive modification relies heavily on the performance of the interviewers. Thus the process of modification could be undermined by faulty administration of the technique being tested out — *as, of course, could the testing procedure itself* (that is, the follow-up interview).

Interviewer failure is in fact a very common occurrence in survey interviewing and in work of the present kind it can take the form of deviation from instructions, the use of leading probes, failure to challenge and clarify any vague or ambiguous statements, the making of errors in writing down the replies of boys. These and other potential sources of error become of crucial importance in the context of the method of progressive modification because they could invalidate the technique. Consequently a fairly elaborate process of control was set up with the purpose of maintaining the necessary high quality of interviewer performance.

Quality control was in the hands of a full-time Quality Control Officer, whose task depended to a large degree upon there being available tape-recordings of each interview.* These tape-recordings were made for a number of reasons.

1   They were to be used as a basis for the writing of a detailed report, next day, of each interview, involving a considerable amount of verbatim transcribing;

2   The use of the tape-recorder allowed the interviewer to concentrate upon his interview — and concentration was essential in the probing follow-up — without being distracted by the task of writing down what was said;

3   The presence of such a recording would make it possible for a Quality Controller to study in detail the performance of each interviewer.

Each day, the Quality Control Officer listened to recorded material from each interviewer, sometimes making spot checks and sometimes listening to the tape-recording in full. In addition, he was required to check the adequacy of interviewers' transfer of information from tape-recordings to report forms. Each day the Quality Control Officer was required to inform each interviewer of any points of failure in his work and to instruct him as to what to do instead. That this contact be daily was regarded as essential, since the value of quality control lies not only in detecting errors, but in taking steps to prevent such errors occurring in subsequent interviews. In addition, a general meeting between interviewers and the Quality Control Officer was held each day. In these meetings, there was discussion of recurrent points of failure and of how to overcome such failures; interviewers were alerted to any new classes of failure that were starting to develop in the work of team members; selected tape-recordings were played back for group criticism and for re-instruction by the Quality Controller, *just as in the training period*.†

---

*This was done with the full knowledge of the boy, who knew that he could, if he so wished, *have the recording completely erased at the end of the interview*. Obviously, the boy's acceptance of a tape-recorder in the interviewing room was crucial, and the tactics used to secure his acceptance and to prevent its presence doing harm are described fully in the original report.[5]

†The joint listening session also provided opportunity for interviewers to identify and discuss with the Quality Control Officer aspects of the required procedure which they found difficult to administer or which they believed the boys found difficult. Such difficulties — and any suggestions by interviewers as to how to overcome them — were then available for consideration at the next modification stage.

THE FIRST OR TRIAL FORM
OF THE ELICITING PROCEDURE

The general form of the eliciting procedure

The eliciting procedure was to have three parts. The first part was to deal with boys' spare time activities (an orienting and scene setting part). The second part would involve the sorting of cards to find out which broad classes of stealing the boy had done. The third part would be aimed at getting details of all the thefts committed within each admitted broad category.

At the time of the first test of the eliciting procedure, only Parts I and II had been developed in working detail. As stated on page 479 this was mainly because it was expected that administering Parts I and II and testing them would use all the test room time available with a boy. In addition, there seemed to be little point in detailing Part III (with its heavy dependence upon Part II) until it was clear that Part II (as envisaged) was workable.

Part I: Spare time interests

Coverage and strategies

The first part of the (inital form of the) eliciting procedure dealt with the various spare time interests and hobbies of the boys. As a procedure, it was meant to meet certain of the difficulties revealed by the exploratory research, namely:

- To reduce initial uneasiness about the interview
- To provide a means of 'easing into' more delicate territory
- To get the boy used to answering questions about himself; to give the boy something to tell his parents about if he did not want to mention stealing
- To get the boy used to (and trusting) his interviewer before the sensitive questioning (about stealing) began

Part I would also be in line with the original cover story.

However, there was another purpose linked to Part I. The procedure for asking about interests had to be given the same general form as that planned for the study of theft (Part II). Thus it involved card sorting, the teaching of rules for card sorting, the use of a screen during the sorting process, full use of the boy's false name, and the use of a tape-recorder. The rules were the same as those that would be used in Part II. This arrangement meant that by the time the boy came to Part II, he would be familiar with such features of it. Moreover he would have gained familiarity with the procedure in a non-threatening situation.

Introducing the boy to the interview

On meeting the boy, the interviewer asked for his false name and told the boy he did not know his real name and did not want to know it. He told the boy that he would be starting off by asking about spare time activities and hobbies and that this information was needed for a book on young people. No name, or even false name, could be mentioned. The boy was shown a book with sets of tables to indicate the sort of book that was to be written. He was told a tape-recorder was being used to save note taking during the interview and the reasons for this were given.* Every effort was made to put the boy at ease.

Introducing Part I and its card sorting routine

The boy was told that there was a special way of getting his information about his spare time activities. He was shown a pack of cards. There were 20 of these, each with a spare time activity or hobby on it (for example, 'I have played billiards or snooker'/'I have borrowed books from a public library'). The boy was asked to sort these cards into the two boxes which were fixed to a wooden screen set up on a table. The boy sat on one side of the screen and the interviewer on the other. The screen† was a device intended to encourage a sense of privacy which, though not necessary at this stage, would be important when the interviewer turned to questions about stealing (in Part II). The boy was told that one of the boxes (labelled YES) was for cards describing activities which he *had* done at some time. The other box (labelled NEVER) was for activities he had never done. If he was unsure about where to put a card, he was to place it face down on the table in front of him. (The interviewer would deal with any such cards later in the interview.) The cards would be passed to the boy one at a time through a small opening at the bottom of the board. The boy was to put each card into the appropriate box. Partly as a reading test and partly to get boys to see what was on each card, the boy was required to read out aloud what was on each card before he sorted it.

---

*The tape-recorder was essential for these reasons: to let the interviewer concentrate upon his interviewing rather than on note taking; to allow the Quality Controller to check on the performance of the interviewer; to secure an accurate record of what was in fact said. Further reassurances would of course be necessary at the start of Part II.
†The idea of using the screen came from the work of Martin Gold of the Institute of Social Research in Michigan.[72]

Rule teaching

Six rules for sorting the cards had to be taught to the boy. These were as follows.

1 A card should be sorted as 'Yes' even if the boy has done the thing concerned *only once*.

2 Similarly, if he had done it only a long time ago.

3 Similarly, if it was only a very minor instance of the listed activity.

4 Similarly, if he was only 'trying it out' on the occasion he did it.

5 Similarly, if he did it only when he was very young.

6 If he was unsure about which box to put the card into, he should place it face down in front of him.

Each of these rules was, of course, to enter into the sorting of the theft cards in Part II of the interview, so that teaching them in Part I was an important element in the preparation for Part II.

The teaching of these rules was linked to the first six cards in a pack of 20 with the explanation to the boy that these cards were being used to teach him the rules and to give him practice. The method of teaching the rules can be illustrated through the teaching of the first of them.

SAY:

'I am going to get you to sort some cards for me. The first five of them will be just to learn the rules and to get practice.'

'Here is the first one.'

PASS CARD 1 (FISHING). HOLD YOUR END OF IT AND SAY:

'Please read it out to me.'

IF HE CAN'T READ, *YOU* MUST READ ALL CARDS FOR HIM. ASK HIM:

'Where would you put that one?'

'Where would you put it if you had been fishing only *once*?'

'Where would you put it if it was a very long time ago?'

'Where would you put it if you only had a string and bent pin when you went fishing?'

IF HE HAS THE SORTING RULES WRONG, CORRECT HIM.

FINALLY, TELL HIM TO SORT THE CARD.

The other rules were presented in the same way (i.e. through the questioning system) on each practice card and there were 13 'teachings' of the six rules, spread over the administration of the six practice cards.

After the sorting of the first six rule-teaching cards, the boy was given 14 more cards, one at a time, and asked to sort them in the same way. When all these cards had been passed to the boy, the interviewer asked him if he had any he was 'not sure' about. (These would have been placed face down in front of him instead of being sorted.) If there were any such cards, the interviewer attempted to resolve whatever the difficulty was. When all the cards had been sorted, the interviewer asked the boy to take them out of the boxes and to put them to one side in two bundles. This ended the introductory phase of the interview.

Throughout this phase, the interviewer had stressed the need for careful and serious sorting of the cards but had attempted to make a show of his disinterest in what was on the cards that went into either box. He did this in order to create in the boy's mind (in preparation for the theft section of the interview) an impression that the sorting procedure was *private*, as of course it was.

The physical form of the instructions

The verbal procedure followed by the interviewers was set out in the form of a booklet of instructions. The printed instructions were to be followed by the interviewer — right down to the words he was to use. The 20 cards for sorting were slipped in between the pages of this booklet, in appropriate places. This arrangement allowed the interviewer to read out the instructions about a card, turn that page and pass the inserted card to the boy through the opening at the bottom of the screen. The form of the booklet and of the screen can be seen in Figures 11.2 and 11.3.

This arrangement provided a basis for controlling and standardising the interviewer's administration of the procedure — though it was still thought necessary to check the tape-recording of the interview to make sure that the interviewer was not deviating from instructions.

A reminder of the purpose of the
introductory phase of the interview

It is worth reminding ourselves at this point of the purpose of Part I of the eliciting procedure. Firstly, it was hoped that it would get the boy used to the interviewing situation and dispel any initial nervousness about how to sort the Part II cards. Secondly, it introduced several concepts to the boy in a situation not likely to arouse anxiety; namely those of anonymity, privacy, the use of a tape-recorder, and the sorting of cards behind a screen. Thirdly, the sorting of cards bearing statements about spare time activities was meant to familiarise the boy with both the actual sorting of cards and with certain rules which would become important when the boy sorted cards bearing statements about thefts.

Part II: Getting information about types of theft behaviour by boys

The second broad phase of the interview consisted, firstly, of the teaching/reinforcing of the rules necessary for sorting cards and, secondly, of the sorting of 52 cards, each bearing a statement about a class of theft (for example, 'I have taken something from school'). The first seven of these cards were used in teaching the rules. The full set of 52 theft cards is set out on page 492.

Introducing the sorting of theft cards to the boy

After dealing with the spare time activity cards, the interviewer (still separated from the boy by the screen) told the boy that there were some more cards to be sorted in just the same way. Then, for the first time, the interviewer referred indirectly to stealing (with which the central part of the interview was to be concerned). This initial reference to stealing was made as unalarming as possible, being phrased as 'mischief that boys get up to in their spare time'. This was immediately followed by renewed assurances that the boy was anonymous, and the interview completely private.

The book of instructions and the sorting of cards

Just as in Part I, the instructions to the interviewer (including the actual words he was to say) were typed into a booklet. Between the pages of this booklet were the theft cards — all 52* of them. The booklet, with its sorting cards showing, is depicted in Figure 11.1.

It was at this stage of the interview that the sorting screen (see Figure 11.2) became important, and it is appropriate to describe it in detail here. It consisted of a large flat piece of hardboard approximately 3 feet wide and 2½ feet high, supported in an upright position on a table between the interviewer and the boy. On the side facing the boy, at the bottom of the board, were two boxes (about 9 inches long and 6 inches high). One was labelled YES, and the other NEVER, in printed block capitals 2 inches high. At the bottom of the board, between the two boxes, was a slit wide enough to allow cards 5 inches wide to be passed through.

---

*Later to be reduced to 44 on the basis of the construction procedures of the progressive modification technique.

Figure 11.1 The book of instructions

Figure 11.2 The sorting screen in position

A sorting screen was used for a number of reasons suggested by the exploratory study. Thus, when asked about stealing, many of the boys had felt wary, ashamed, embarrassed or nervous. The screen was used to give the boy a sense of privacy when sorting the theft cards.

Cards could be passed to the boy one at a time at a pace regulated jointly by the interviewer and the boy. Thus the interviewer could keep holding the end of the card until the boy had read out (aloud) what was on it. The interviewer usually knew when the card had been sorted because he could hear it drop into one of the two sorting boxes on the other side of the board.* The interviewer could try to speed up any very slow sorting by verbal encouragement to the boy and by pushing the next card through the slot at the bottom of the board as soon as the current card had been removed by the boy for sorting.

The fact that there were only two sorting boxes, and that these were labelled YES and NEVER, meant that at this stage the boy had a relatively simple series of decisions to make. Certainly he was spared, at this initial stage, the closer thinking and the greater recall effort which might have been imposed upon him by some finer grading of responses; such as, for example: 'yes, in the last six months', 'yes, between six months and one year ago'; 'yes, longer than a year ago'; 'never'. (Later in the interview he was, of course, to be asked about his thefts in more detail, but by then the conditions of involvement necessary for eliciting such detail should have been better established.)

The reasons for using cards

One of the barriers to boys admitting their thefts (brought out by the exploratory study) was that they frequently forgot to mention some classes of theft altogether; another was that they simply did not think of certain acts as constituting thefts. Accordingly, it seemed necessary to design a system which would both define the sorts of things that the research team meant by 'stealing' and constitute a memory aid for the boy. Moreover, the system would have to be such that the boy's attention could be focused upon one class of theft at a time. To meet these needs, the card system was used, with each card presenting just one class of theft and with just one card presented at a time.

Some important features of the card system

There were 52 cards in all. They were *not* meant to constitute an

---

*The interviewer could not, of course, know for sure into which of the two boxes it fell; this was desirable in terms of maintaining the privacy of the card sorting.

exhaustive list of thefts — that would call for an enormous number of cards. Instead, these 52 cards (on each of which was presented some broad class of theft) were designed to provide a web or *network of defining stimuli*. Some of these stimuli referred to theft *situations* (for example, 'I have stolen from a shop', 'I have stolen something from a changing room or a cloakroom'). Other cards referred to *objects* stolen (for example, 'I have stolen cigarettes', 'I have stolen money', 'I have stolen milk'). Others again referred to *motivations* for stealing (for example, 'I have stolen things just for fun', 'I have taken things just for a dare'). The full list is given in Table 11.7.

These 52 categories or stimuli had been developed out of: exploratory interviews with boys (see Table 11.6); study of lists used by other researchers for broadly similar purposes; preparatory work to find out if these different proposed 'classes of theft' conjured up in boys' minds the range of thefts to which we intended them to refer.* Inevitably there was overlap between these different broad groupings, but for the sorting operaton this was a step in the direction of safety rather than danger. Details of this aspect of the work are given in the full report of the enquiry.[5]

The rules for sorting the cards

Whereas the use of a card system was expected to reduce difficulties related to the *meaning* of the term 'theft' and to the *recall* of thefts, it was clear that the cards alone would not settle some aspects of definition (for example, 'that even small thefts counted', 'that even if the boy had done the thing concerned only once in his whole life it still counted', 'that an act counted even if it was done a long time ago'). It was also clear that boys would need special instructions to think hard about each of the classes of theft set out on the cards. Over and above these needs, however, there were other matters on which special instructions would be necessary (for example, that it counted even if the boy was only *helping* a friend who was stealing; what the boy was to do if he was in doubt about whether he qualified in terms of any one of the cards). Accordingly, rule teaching was necessary as a preliminary to the full card sorting operation. The full set of rules, expressed in summary form, was as follows. As intended, many are the same as the rules taught for completing Part I of the eliciting procedure.

---

*That preparatory work had also been used to test the comprehensibility of the statements on the theft cards and to provide a basis for amending them in the direction of greater simplicity.

Table 11.7
List of theft cards used in Cycles 1 and 2

1	I have kept things I have found.
2	I have kept money I have found.
3	I have stolen things just for fun.
4	I have taken things just for a dare.
5	I have taken junk or scrap without asking for it first.
6	I have stolen something from a stall or a barrow.
7	I have stolen from a shop.
8	I have pinched something as a souvenir.
9	I have stolen books or newspapers or magazines or comics.
10	I have taken something from home that I was not supposed to take.
11	I have pinched things from my family or relations.
12	I have stolen something when I was in someone else's home.
13	I have got away without paying the fare or the proper fare.
14	I have taken things belonging to children or teenagers.
15	I have got things from others by threatening them.
16	I have stolen sweets.
17	I have stolen cigarettes.
18	I have sneaked something through the customs.
19	I have stolen something from a changing room or a cloakroom.
20	I have stolen fruit or other kinds of food.
21	I have got into places and stolen.
22	I have taken things belonging to the school. (Don't forget the little things.)
23	I have stolen things from other people at school.
24	I have stolen something when I was on holidays.
25	I stole something when I was living away from my family.
26	I have stolen from parks or playgrounds.
27	I have stolen toys.
28	I have stolen from cafes.
29	I have stolen things from doorsteps or doorways.
30	I have stolen milk.
31	I have stolen coal or wood or paraffin or something else that is used for burning.
32	I have stolen from building sites.
33	I have stolen by stripping things from buildings.
34	I have stolen from a goods yard or from the yard of a factory.
35	I have stolen letters or parcels.
36	I have cheated people out of money.
37	I have stolen from work.
38	I have stolen *from people* at work.
39	I have had things that I knew were stolen. (Someone else did the stealing and passed them on to me.)
40	I have stolen something out of a garden or out of the yard of a house.
41	I have stolen a bike or a motor-bike.
42	I have stolen something *from* a bike or a motor-bike.
43	I have stolen a car or a lorry or a van.
44	I have stolen something *from* a car or a lorry or a van.
45	I have borrowed a bike or a motor-bike or a car without asking.
46	I have stolen from a club.
47	I have got into some place without paying.
48	I have stolen from a meter.
49	I have stolen from a telephone box.
50	I have stolen from a slot machine.
51	I have stolen money.
52	I have borrowed things and not given them back.

Rule 1 If the boy had *ever* done what was on the card at any time during his whole life, he was to count the card as YES.

Rule 2 If the boy had *never* done what was on the card at any time during his whole life, he was to count the card as NEVER.

Rule 3 If the boy did what was on the card a long time ago, or when he was very young, he was nonetheless to count the card as YES.

Rule 4 If the boy had done what was on the card just once in his whole life, he was nonetheless to count the card as YES.

Rule 5 If the boy was just trying out what was on the card to see what it was like, or just did it for fun, he was nonetheless to count the card as YES.

Rule 6 If what the boy stole or took was only very small, the card nonetheless counted as YES.

Rule 7 If the boy only *helped someone else* do what was on the card, without actually doing it himself, it still counted as YES.

Rule 8 If the boy was *not sure* about where to sort a card, or if he could not remember whether or not he had done what was on the card, he was to put the card face down on the table in front of him.

Rule 9 If the boy had any difficulty with any card, he was to ask the interviewer for help. If this did not solve his problem, he was to put the card face down on the table in front of him.

Rule 10 The boy was asked to think hard and seriously before sorting any card.

Rule 11 The boy was required to admit *all* his thefts (for otherwise his time and ours would be wasted).

The teaching of the rules

The exploratory work had indicated not only the nature of the rules that should be presented to the boy, but that many of these rules would have to be made to surmount contrary tendencies, dullness or inertia in many of the boys. Accordingly a major effort, already initiated through the sorting of the spare time activity cards, was made to ensure that even the dullest boys grasped the rules and that boys used the rules as active guiding principles throughout the sorting process. The following procedures were used.

1   After being introduced to the idea of sorting theft cards,* the boy was reminded that he had a false name, that the interviewer did

*'The only difference is that these cards are about things that boys pinch or steal — some of the mischief they get up to in their spare time. This is something a lot of boys do in their spare time. We want to know *how much* of it boys do. Remember we are writing a book about it.'

not want to know his real name and that the reason for the false name was to help the boy to tell *all* he had ever done. The need to know *all* was re-stated and stressed.*

The boy was then told that the rules were just the same as before but that before starting with the new cards we wanted to make sure he knew them. This led to his being *asked questions* about three of the rules.

- 'If you had done this thing only once in your whole life, what box would you put it in?'
- 'If it was a very long time ago when you did it, what box would you put it in?'
- 'If you didn't know what box to put it in, what would you do?'

Where he did not know the answer, the interviewer gave it to him. When he did know the answer, the interviewer praised the boy.

2   Next, the interviewer used the first seven cards in the pack of 52 to teach/reinforce six of the rules in the context of actual sorting. The teaching system employed through them was again the 'question and answer' system, though in a more extended form. Thus the rule, 'It counts even if the amount is very small' was introduced to the boys through Card 2 which had in it the statement, 'I have kept money I have found.' After being told this rule, he was shown the card and, before being allowed to sort it, was asked: 'Suppose a boy kept sixpence he had found, which box should he put this card in?' After getting the boy's answer and correcting it if it was wrong,† the interviewer reinforced the rule by saying 'So it counts even if the amount is very small.' The boy was then asked to sort the card.‡

3   After the sorting of the last of the seven practice cards, the interviewer used the question and answer system to 'review' some of the rules so far presented to the boy. This was done before any of the other cards were sorted, and the procedure took the following form (this particular presentation being on one of the pages of the interviewer's book of instructions).

---

*'We want to know *everything* you have ever done — every single thing — if you don't tell us everything it is really just a waste. So we need to know everything. OK?'
†. . . and praising the boy if he was correct.
‡He was told: 'Now look at this card again and decide whether or not you've *ever* done it *yourself*. Then put it in the box where it ought to go'.

INTERVIEWER SAY:

'That's the end of the practice. Let's just make sure we've got all the rules.'

'If it was *just a small thing* you took, what box would you put the card in?'
(PRAISE IF HE SAYS 'YES' BOX; CORRECT IF WRONG.)

PAUSE AND SAY:

'If it was *a long time ago* that you took something, what box would you put the card in?'
(PRAISE IF HE SAYS 'YES' BOX; CORRECT IF WRONG.)

PAUSE AND SAY:

'If you did the thing on the card *just once in your life*, what box would you put the card in?'
(PRAISE IF HE SAYS 'YES' BOX; CORRECT IF WRONG.)

PAUSE AND SAY:

'If you did the thing on the card *just for fun* or if you were *just trying it out*, what box would you put the card in?'
(PRAISE IF HE SAYS 'YES' BOX; CORRECT IF WRONG.)

PAUSE AND SAY:

'If you were just helping someone else to do what was on the card, where would you put the card?'
(PRAISE IF HE SAYS 'YES' BOX; CORRECT IF WRONG.)

PAUSE AND SAY:

'If you can't remember whether you did it or not, where would you put the card?'
(IF THE BOY IS WRONG, TELL HIM: 'You put the card face down in front of you.')

PAUSE AND SAY:

'Are you allowed to ask me any questions to help you sort the cards?'
(IF THE BOY IS WRONG, EXPLAIN: 'Yes, of course you are – ask me as much as you like. *But if that doesn't help you*, put the card face down in front of you.')

Just as in Part I of the eliciting procedure, rule teaching was subject to certain principles:

1   The teaching technique was primarily the 'question and answer' method. This particular procedure had the advantage of setting the boy thinking in the context of each rule, of alerting the interviewer to the existence of misunderstanding on the part of the boy, of allowing the interviewer to reward the boy (with praise) when he showed evidence of having grasped the rule concerned.

2   Much of the rule teaching was in the context of a specific card sorting operation. We expected this to give the rule greater meaning than it would have if stated to the boy more or less in the abstract.

3   Each rule was subject to at least one repetition later in the interview, and some rules had three or four repetitions. The repetitions of any rule were spaced out.

Sorting the theft cards

The first seven theft cards had been utilised in teaching the rules, although they were in fact part of the total set of 52 theft cards. After the rule teaching, the boy was asked, once more, not to hold anything back. The rest of the 52 cards were then passed to the boy in slow sequence through the slit in the board. However, at set points the interviewer stopped the sorting procedure to issue reminders, encouragements or extra explanations. Thus the boy was reminded several times to ask for help or explanation if he was in any difficulty, he was reminded that he had a false name, he was told to place cards face down if uncertain where to sort them. These and the other instructions were all printed in appropriate places in the interviewer's book of instructions.

At one point, before two cards mentioning school,* the interviewer alerted the boy to think of *all* the schools that he (the boy) had ever been to. After all the cards had been sorted, the interviewer helped the boy to deal with any cards that he was not sure about, trying if possible to get them sorted into one or the other of the two boxes. Finally, the interviewer handed the boy two coloured cards, one labelled 'Yes' to be put into the 'YES' box and the other labelled 'NO' to be put into the 'NEVER' box. This was to enable the interviewer to identify the two packs of cards later in the interview. With the boy's help, the interviewer took all the cards out of the two boxes and put them to one side in full view of the boy *and without trying to look at the contents of either pack*. It was hoped that this evidence of disinterest would encourage the boy to feel that, as with the cards relating to spare-time activities, his sorting of cards was private.

Part III: Obtaining the details relating to theft types sorted as 'Yes'

This part of the procedure was not involved in the testing operation until Cycle 3. Thus, though broadly designed at the start of Cycle 1, it was *not* at that stage delivered to the boys or involved in the testing operation. See page 479 for reasons for this. However, its form and detail are available in the full report of the construction of the eliciting procedure.

---

*Cards 22 and 23. See page 492 for full list of cards in the Cycle 1 version of the web of stimuli.

TESTING THE FIRST VERSION
OF THE ELICITING PROCEDURE

In this, the test of the first form of the eliciting procedure, the aims were necessarily numerous and varied, their common element being the detection of difficulty or failure in any aspect of the card sorting procedure. More specifically, the aims of testing were to answer the following questions.

1   Were the boys deliberately mis-sorting the cards and, if so, what were the beliefs, suspicions, attitudes, and so on, which lay behind this? Any such attitudes would have to be made non-operative in subsequent modifications.

2   Where boys *were* admitting thefts, what attitudes or ideas were helping them to do so? Any such attitudes should be identified in case they could be developed in other of the boys and for all thefts.

3   Were there any classes of theft which the boys tended to sort wrongly and, if so, what sorts of thefts were these? What was the position with respect to 'little things', recent thefts, thefts where the boy was 'just helping'?

4   What were the difficulties which led boys to place some cards face down (that is, to indicate they were not sure where to sort them)?

5   Were some of the cards more subject to difficulty and/or to mis-sorting than others?

6   Did the boy have difficulty understanding what was printed on the cards?

7   Did the boy take the sorting of cards seriously? Did he consider each card carefully before sorting it? How did he react to the long run of 52 cards?

8   What did the boy think of the sorting screen? Did it help him to admit his thefts?

9   Did the boy seem to have any trouble remembering what he had stolen?

10 What did the boy think of the idea of having a false name and did he feel it affected his own willingness to make admissions?

11 Did he think the interview was quite private?

12 Would the boy like to see anything in the interview changed?

Methods used for testing the procedure

The testing of Parts I and II of the eliciting procedure was carried through a number of different steps, which involved the following.

1   Various questions about different aspects of the interview and about boys' own reactions to these were put to the boy at the end of the administration of the procedure itself, their replies being automatically probed and challenged;

2   All cards sorted as 'Never' were re-sorted by the boy and, where these were now sorted as 'Yes', boys were questioned for the reasons for their initial mis-sorting of these cards;

3   A 'pretending game' was set up in which the boys were asked to *pretend* they had done certain things, and were asked if they would then sort them as 'Yes' or 'Never'; their reasons for so sorting them were then probed in order to secure evidence about any residual resistances in these boys to making admissions;

4   Interviewers asked boys why they were sorting cards as 'not sure' and generally observed boys throughout the interview.

The whole of the testing procedure (as well as the delivery of Parts I and II of the eliciting procedure) was tape-recorded, and this recording was available to the interviewer in making his report and to the Quality Controller. The tape-recording had originally been introduced to the boy (in Part I) with a statement to the effect: 'I hope you won't mind my using this. It saves such a lot of writing down. Everything is absolutely private and confidential. And remember you've got a false name'. Now the interviewer reiterated this 'reason' but went on to tell the boy that he was *free to wipe or destroy the tape at the end of the interview* if he wanted to do so — but we hoped he wouldn't. He was reminded not to mention his own name.

Results of testing the first version of the eliciting procedure

The results of testing the first (tentative) form of the eliciting procedure are set out under the following headings:

- The general efficiency of the sampling and secural procedures
- Evidence of difficulty or defect derived by the interviewers through direct observation during the sorting of cards
- Evidence of difficulty or defect derived through the re-sorting test
- Evidence of difficulty or defect derived through the 'pretending game'
- Evidence of difficulty or defect derived through direct questioning on specific aspects of the eliciting procedure

The general efficiency of the
sampling and securement procedures

Success in enumerating addresses was very high (over 90%) and 35 of the target sample of 60 boys were brought to the test room for processing. At this stage no special steps were taken to secure the missing 25 boys. It seemed to the research team that the number secured would be much increased by call-backs and possibly by the use of a 'trouble shooting team' of the sort used in an American study.[99] For an acceptable level of success, such measures would be necessary. However, the securement of the 35 out of 60 was relatively easy and the team saw no reason for changing the *basic* sampling and securement tactics at this stage (in fact, with the aid of 'call-backs' and of a trouble shooting team, the eventual success rate for the aetiological study was 86%).[51]

The work of the collector was complicated by certain boys not being quite ready for collection when called for (so that delays occurred in getting to the centre); by traffic problems; by boys exchanging names in the car. In addition, at reception there was some degree of breach of security for boys in that the receptionist did on one night at least ask for individual names.

Evidence of difficulty or defect derived by the
interviewers through direct observation during
the sorting of cards

Of the 35 boys to whom the first form of the eliciting procedure was administered, 22 asked for help of some kind, 13 put at least one card face down to indicate 'not sure' and five appeared to be in some sort of difficulty without asking for help. Allowing for overlap, this left only seven boys who were not necessarily in trouble. The evidence gathered through this procedure indicated the presence of several different kinds of difficulty.

What acts are included under statements on particular cards? Many of the boys (18) admitted difficulty of this kind, instances of such difficulty being spread over 27 of the 52 theft cards. Some examples of this sort of difficulty follow.

Of Card 7 ('I have stolen from a shop'), a boy asked: 'Does acting as a look-out count?'

Of Card 47 ('I have got into some place without paying'), a boy asked: 'Does that include cinemas?'

Of Card 36 ('I have cheated people out of money'), a boy asked: 'Would it count if you just forgot to pay the fare on the bus?'

Of Card 26 ('I have stolen from parks or playgrounds'), a boy asked: 'Does that mean picking flowers from a park?'

Specific difficulties of this kind were recurrent for certain of the cards, but these will be dealt with in their own right later on.

Failure in recalling activities   Some of the boys (12) directly admitted having trouble in remembering whether they had or had not done certain things, and interviewers suspected others were having the same sort of trouble.

Nervousness or puzzlement   Some of the boys (at least five) were thought by the interviewers to be troubled by nervousness or puzzlement over the situation in which they found themselves.

Other recurrent difficulties   For several of the cards, there was difficulty of a recurrent kind. Of the 52 cards, 32 of them were subject to admitted difficulty of some kind. For several of these cards, the number of instances of difficulty rose to three or four, possibly indicating that these cards might be trouble-prone, and indicating that a watch should be kept on them through future test-modification cycles. These cards were: 5, 7, 13, 18, 21, 26, 36, 37. Some of the difficulties raised by these cards are worth noting.

Of Card 5 ('I have taken junk or scrap without asking for it first'), queries were: 'Would taking it from home count?'/'What sort of thing would count as junk or scrap?'

Of Card 7 ('I have stolen from a shop'), queries were: 'If you were just acting as a look-out or just helping, why should it count as stealing?'/'The boys who did it gave me some of what they pinched — does that count?'

Of Card 13 ('I got away without paying the fare or proper fare'), problems were: 'fare' interpreted as 'fair'/'What if he didn't ask for it?'

Of Card 18 ('I have sneaked something through the Customs'), a query was: 'What do you mean by Customs?'

Of Card 21 ('I have got into places and stolen'), queries were: 'What do you mean by "getting into places"?'/'Does "breaking and entering" count as "getting into places and taking things"?'

Of Card 26 ('I have stolen things from parks or playgrounds'), queries were: 'Does it count if you picked the flowers in the park?'/'How can you steal from *parks*?'

Of Card 36 ('I have cheated people out of money'), queries were: 'What if you just forgot to pay on the bus?'/'What about cheating at a game of chance?'/'What if you forgot to bring back what you borrowed?'

Of Card 37 ('I have stolen from people at work'): Boy excluded evening and spare time work/'Does that include school work?'/ 'Does that mean only *paid* work?'

Evidence of difficulty or defect
derived through the re-sorting test

Purely as part of the checking procedure (and not as part of the eliciting technique being tried out) boys were asked to *re-sort* all the cards which they had put into the 'Never' box. Each boy was told, quite correctly, that we were asking him to do this in case he had forgotten something in the first sorting of the cards or in case there were things he didn't like to tell us about the first time. He was also told that his re-sorting the cards would tell us a lot about what was wrong with our questions and how to improve them. He was reassured that the interviewer did not want to see *which* cards he re-sorted as 'Yes' and that the re-sort was very private.* He was urged, just before starting the re-sort, to work carefully so that he could think about the difficulties he had the first time.† He was also urged to ask questions, if he wished, about the purpose and the method of re-sorting.

Of the 35 boys, 28 re-sorted at least one of their 'Never' cards into the 'Yes' box. These boys were then intensively questioned to find out *why* these cards had not been sorted as 'Yes' in the first place. When this was over, they were asked if there were still any cards in their 'Never' pack which should have been sorted as 'Yes'. They were told that we would not want to know *which* cards these were but only to understand why they still felt unable to put such cards into the 'Yes' box.

It was expected that these several devices would help to reveal some of the reasons for the initial mis-sorting of cards.

---

*

> STRESS TO BOY THAT YOU DON'T WANT TO SEE WHICH CARDS NOW GO INTO THE 'YES' BOX.
>
> 'I don't want to see the ones you put into the YES box. They're private, I won't look at them. Everything you say is private.'

†The interviewer was, of course, going to question him about these difficulties at the end of the re-sort.

The extent of re-sorting   Of the 35 boys, 28 re-sorted at least some of their 'Never' cards as 'Yes'. The total number of re-sorts derived from the 35 boys was 92 cards.* There could, of course, be many more 'Yes' cards still hidden amidst the remaining 'Never' cards, but even so the 92 changes constituted a sufficient yield to provide a basis for enquiring into *why* the 92 had originally been sorted as 'Never'.

Reasons for re-sorting 'NEVER' as 'YES'   The most frequently given reason for change (20 boys) was that the re-sort helped the boy to remember things that had slipped his memory the first time:

- 'Small things come back to you the second time.'
- 'I was unsure because I'd been in the 'phone box with a friend who'd tapped a meter. But on thinking back, I realised I'd tried it once myself, so put it in the "YES" box. I'd had a few drinks at the time and I don't take much notice of things when in that state.'
- 'It was a long time ago, in fact first or second year at Secondary school. I was in need of a football shirt so took one. It was an isolated incident but it came back to me when I looked at the card a second time.'
- 'Seeing it a second time helped my memory.'
- 'It happened a long time ago and so slipped my memory.'

Several boys (9) admitted to *carelessness* or over-rapid sorting in the original card sort.

- 'I think it was because I was putting so many in the "Never" box. I put these in, but when I thought about it say a couple of cards after, I suddenly thought "YES". I did not think about it when I actually had the card in my hand. I just didn't. I did not want to take too long a time over it. I was used to putting cards in the "Never" box and these just slipped through.'
- 'It's better going through the second time, you've got more time to think about it.'

*The distribution of the 92 changes suggested that some of the cards were more subject to such change than were others. The cards which were the more subject to change are identified in a separate footnote,† as are those where no changes occurred.‡ However, evidence of this sort would have to be allowed to accumulate over a number of modification cycles before constituting a basis for changing particular cards or for mounting a special effort to deal with them.
†'I have taken something from home that I was not supposed to take.' (Card 10); 'I have stolen toys.' (Card 27); 'I have had things that I knew were stolen.' (Card 39); 'I have stolen something out of a garden or out of the yard of a house.' (Card 40).
‡'I have kept things I have found.' (Card 1); 'I have kept money I have found.' (Card 2); 'I have taken junk or scrap without asking for it first.' (Card 5); 'I have stolen something from a stall or a barrow.' (Card 6); 'I have got away without paying the fare or the proper fare.' (Card 13); 'I have got things from others by threatening them.' (Card 15); 'I have stolen by stripping things from buildings.' (Card 33); 'I have stolen letters or parcels.' (Card 35); 'I have stolen something from a bike or a motor-bike.' (Card 42); 'I have stolen a car or a lorry or a van.' (Card 43); 'I have stolen something from a van or a lorry or a car.' (Card 44).

Another apparent cause of mis-sorting (14 boys) was the temporary forgetting of certain of the rules (for example, that it counts even if the theft was trivial (7 boys), happened a long time ago (7), had been done only once (4)).

- 'Some of the things there were when I was ever so small.'
- 'It was only a bar of chocolate and I haven't done it since.'
- 'Somehow I was not thinking back far enough. I didn't seem to go right back in my thinking.'

In addition, some boys (5) were worried that the interview might not be really confidential, so that they might land in trouble through making admissions.

- 'I did not feel so sure about you then. Didn't know whether to or not. It might be a trick or something. You might have told the police.'
- 'My headmaster might have found out. My mum might get to know.'
- 'It might lead to my mates getting into trouble.'

These boys had admitted *now* because of the reassurance before the re-sort and because they were now more familiar with the interviewer.

Several boys (6) explained that the original mis-sort was due (at least partly) to a feeling of shame or guilt.

- 'I was a bit ashamed. ' 'Felt a bit guilty.' 'I got found out for most of them as well.' 'I got found out by the police once or twice.' 'I got fined.' 'I was trying to hide it from you.' (In the first sort, the boy had not fully taken in the significance of having a false name. He said it struck him in the re-sort and helped him to make the admission.)
- 'I didn't want to think about it, so I put it in the "Never" box.'
- 'I don't think it's right really, stealing from your family.'

Other reasons given for mis-sorting in the first sorting operation were: the boy was tense or nervous (2 boys said this); the boy misunderstood what was on the card; the boy was not sure whether or not something he had done counted as what was on the card (4), or he felt it didn't (1); the boy found the theft statement too vague (1); he wrongly felt that some things he had done were *not* cases of stealing (for example, keeping a look-out for mates, receiving the proceeds of a theft) (2).

Residual mis-sorting   When asked if there were still some 'Yes' cards sorted in the 'Never' box, only one boy out of 35 said there were in spite of their responses being challenged. At the same time, interviewers reported that in a number of cases (6) they suspected boys were lying on this count.

Where boys maintained that they had not concealed any 'Yes' cards among their 'Never' cards in their re-sort of 'Never', they were taken through what we have called the 'pretending game'.

At random, the interviewer took three of the cards sorted by the boy as 'Never'. For the first card, the interviewer asked the boy to 'suppose' that he *had* done what was on the card. 'Just suppose that you *had* done this. Let's just pretend you had. Would you have told us that you had done it?' If the boy said 'Yes', he was to be asked why he would have admitted it. If he said 'No', he was to be asked what would have *stopped* him from admitting it and after this, 'Just supposing you did what is on this card, is there anything we might do to help you tell us about it?' The interviewer was required to probe for a detailed response. The second and the third cards were dealt with in just the same way.

The purpose of the 'pretending game' was of course to gain insight into the difficulties, weaknesses and the current strengths of the eliciting procedure with the intention of using such insights to help in developing the next version of the eliciting procedure.

Reasons given for being willing to admit   Thirty-four of the 35 boys were put through the 'pretending game'. Of these, 29 said of at least one of the three theft cards that they would be willing to make an admission. Many of the boys (20) explained that they were convinced that the interview was confidential. This impression appears to have been helped along by:

- The use of the false name and the fact that the interviewer didn't know the boy's real identity and wouldn't see him again (11 boys volunteered one or another of these reasons)
- The interview itself was conducted in privacy and secrecy (6)
- The boy felt he could trust the interviewer not to talk or to take action (9)
- The interviewer couldn't do much even if he wanted to (5), in that the boy had a false name.

Another reason for being willing to make an admission was a concern on the part of the boy with truth telling (11 boys said something to this effect): the interviewer wanted or needed the truth if he was to write his book or if the interview was not to be wasted (6); the boy would tell the truth because he was honest or because there was no point in lying (5). Additional reasons for being willing to make admissions were: that the boy desired to help the interviewer; to clear my conscience; because everybody does it anyhow.

Some of the things actually said by boys add usefully to the foregoing statement of reasons for being willing to make admissions: 'You've been straightforward with me, so I'll be straightforward with you.' 'Yes, because nobody else could find out and they couldn't call me a thief even if they thought I was. And if you came up to me in the street and said I was a thief, I'd sue you for libel.' 'If you have to write a book, you have to know the truth'.

Reasons given for being unwilling to admit   Sixteen of the 34 who went through the 'pretending game' said of at least one of the three cards that they would be unwilling to admit the thefts concerned. Six boys explained that they would be too embarrassed to tell ('If I had to look you in the face, I'd say "No".' 'It's the same with most people, they don't like mentioning what they've done'). Other barriers to making admissions were: fear that the police or their parents might find out (5 boys); because the thing concerned was such a big item; because it was so petty. Some of the actual comments of boys were: 'No, because I don't know where that tape is going.' 'No, because a man downstairs has my name and address.' 'I don't like admitting things unless they're done just for fun — not for personal gain'.

Means suggested by boys for helping them to admit   Only 12 of the boys had suggestions to offer. Of these, the more recurrent were: avoid or continue to avoid having boy face-to-face with the interviewer when the boy is sorting the cards (6 boys said this, one of them saying that sitting face-to-face with the interviewer had made him feel guilty); put greater emphasis on the security arrangements already entered into (2 boys); find ways for seeing that the person bringing in the boys does not know their names or addresses; get rid of the tape-recorder (1 boy). Several other suggestions by individuals are worth noting: by reassuring the boy that the interviewer will not take any particular attitude towards boys who admit stealing; by making the statements about thefts less direct; by printing pictures on the cards.

Evidence of difficulty or defect derived
through direct questioning on specific
aspects of the eliciting procedure

Towards the end of the follow-up (or testing) process, the boy was asked a number of direct questions about his reaction to the eliciting procedure. These questions related to matters such as: his belief or otherwise in the confidentiality of the interview; what he thought of the use of a false name; what he thought of the use of the screen in the interview; other matters as detailed below.

The confidentiality of the interview   The boy was asked if he believed that the interview was *quite* private and confidential. What (if anything) led him to believe this, what reduced his confidence that it was private?

The great majority of boys said that they believed the interview *was* quite private and confidential (29 out of 35) and only two said it was not. Factors named as supporting a belief in the confidentiality of the interview were:

- The use of the false name (11 boys said this)
- Being alone with the interviewer (8)
- The general atmosphere of privacy and confidentiality (3)
- The explanations and reassurances given by the interviewer (12)
- The presence of the board (3)
- The easy manner of the interviewer (2)
- The fact that he was used to the interviewer (1)
- The youth of the interviewer (1)

Factors working *against* an acceptance of the interview as private and confidential appear to have been:

- The presence of the tape-recorder (5 boys volunteered this)
- A belief that the boy's name could be found out if the research team really wanted to do so (4)*
- A belief that the interviewer might be connected with 'the authorities' (1)
- Disbelief in the story that the information was wanted for writing a book (1)
- 'Confidentiality not sufficiently stressed to boys' (1)

The use of a false name   The boys were asked what they thought of the idea of having a false name and if this helped them to admit their thefts. Of the 35, some 26 felt it helped them admit, four were not sure and five said it did not. Of the nine who did not reply that it *helped* to have the false name, three explained that *someone had asked for names at reception*† and one more that he didn't believe his real name was unknown; two had insisted on giving their real names to the inter-

---

*See further details in the next section.
†This strongly indicated that someone in reception was disregarding an important instruction. Enquiries showed that this was so and steps were taken to try to prevent repetitions. At the same time, it was obvious that the use of a whole team of people in appointment making, in the collection of boys and in reception work posed real security problems and in the long run would call for fairly rigorous self discipline on the part of all concerned.

viewer on arrival so that they did not feel they really had false names anyhow. Others amongst the nine explained that: there was nothing much to admit anyhow; that being confidential was enough.

Perhaps the most important indication of this evidence is that whereas a great many boys were helped by the use of the false names, none said that it hindered him.

The use of the sorting board   Boys were asked what they thought of the screen, and whether or not it helped them to admit their thefts. Some 25 of the 35 boys said it helped them to make admissions, explaining variously that:

- It stopped the interviewer seeing where the cards went (8 boys said this)
- It gave them a feeling of privacy and of confidentiality (7)
- It reduced tension and embarrassment in that you did not have the interviewer watching you (10)
- It helped concentration (4)
- The presence of *two* sorting boxes helped sorting (5) by keeping the two choices right in front of them/by limiting the choice to just two things/by making the sorting job simple.

Of the remaining ten boys, five did not think it helped them ('unnecessary'; 'the interviewer could see my cards at any time anyhow'; 'a bit like looking at a blank wall' (one boy)) and five were not sure ('not necessary for me but it might help others').

The most important indication of this evidence is that whereas the screen helped with the great majority, it did not appear to be a hindrance (except possibly in that one case where the boy felt that sitting on the other side of the screen was 'a bit like looking at a blank wall').

Did boys have any difficulty understanding anything on the cards? Boys were questioned for evidence that they had difficulty in understanding something on one or more cards. Ten of the 35 boys admitted this kind of difficulty. *Most of these difficulties had in fact been picked up already* (that is, during the card sort). These difficulties took the following forms.

- The boy didn't think of certain of his activities as 'stealing' (for example, 'keeping a lookout for mates', 'not paying his fare because not asked for it by the conductor')
- The statement on some cards was not sufficiently specific, so that the boy was left wondering whether or not some one of his acts was included by it (for example, 'Would picking flowers in the park

count as "stealing things from the park"'/'Would "getting into places without paying" include "cinemas"?'/'Would "stripping things from buildings" include a piece of piping?')

- The boy did not grasp the intended meaning of some word on a card (for example, 'What does "souvenir" mean?'/'fare' interpreted as 'fair'/'work' interpreted only as 'full-time work')

Did the boys have any difficulty remembering what they had done? When asked about this directly, only nine of the 35 boys denied having had difficulty of some kind. With many of the boys, the difficulty was not identifiable as anything more than vagueness, but with some the difficulty appeared to be associated with an unwillingness to go so far back in time or with the stolen item being so small.

Did boys include things pinched quite recently? Of the 35 boys, 19 answered that they *did* admit things pinched quite recently. Of the remaining 16, some explained that they had not pinched anything recently, and it seems probable that several more of them were in this position. However, there were also some boys who said that they had not admitted or would not admit recent thefts — explaining, for example, that 'I would not give *precise details* of any recent theft'.

Did boys mind the long run of cards? Whereas there were 21 boys who said they did not mind the long run of cards, three said they did and for the rest of the boys the position was mixed or uncertain. Objections were largely on the grounds that the long run of cards became monotonous to at least some degree (5 boys indicated this). Other objections were: 'that it made the boy feel like a criminal or feel ashamed' (2); 'that there were too many repetitions of the rules and of reminders' (1).

Did boys take the sorting job seriously? Thirty boys said that they took it seriously and only one that he did not (he explained that he had committed some serious acts of theft and was not sure that the interview was confidential). On the other hand, 12 boys made comments to the effect that they could have taken more care than they actually did in sorting the cards.

Suggestions by boys concerning possible changes in the procedure
Boys were asked whether there was anything in the interview they would like to see changed, *apart from things they had mentioned already*. Some of the boys (8) said they found the tape-recorder worrying, at least initially, and suggested that something be done about it — either that it be not used or that it be put out of sight. Other

suggestions tended not to be concentrated on any single feature of the procedure:

- Increase the security of the interview (the boy saying this explained that the interviewer had asked him where he came from!)
- Have coloured cards to make the long run of cards less boring (1)
- Use a *list* of thefts rather than cards (2)
- Give the boy a chance to explain that he did not think it was stealing (1) or that he did not mean to do it (1)
- Tell the boy more about the interview before he comes in for it (1)
- Have an armchair for the boy to help him feel more relaxed (1)
- One boy suggested that pretty girls should do the interviewing — though he added that this might not help to get admissions of theft!

Suggestions for change made by the interviewers   At the end of each report, the interviewer was requested to set down any comments and suggestions which he felt could be made about the interview just completed. Interviewers also reported verbally to the Quality Control Officer on how the interview went. From these classes of evidence, it appears that for the most part the interview went off quite well, though not infrequently the interviewer was short of time in the follow-up to the administration of the sorting technique. There was also evidence that whereas some boys seemed to be apprehensive in the interview, they seemed to move out of this state as the interview progressed. On the latter point, a suggestion was made that interviewers should be free to jolly along such boys in the early stages of the interview in order to secure their earlier relaxation.

Several interviewers reported difficulty in dealing with some of the brighter boys in that these sometimes found the repetition of instructions boring and seemed to regard the 'pretending game' as unnecessary. On this point, one of the interviewers suggested varying the form of the repetition of any instruction. Another interviewer suggested that another word be substituted wherever possible for the word 'stole': the reason was that some boys did not seem to want to think of themselves as 'stealing things' or did not consider that what they did on a particular occasion should be regarded as genuine 'stealing'.

Summary of results of testing the
first form of the eliciting procedure

The impressions conveyed to the research team by these checks and tests were: (i) that the form and the main features of the eliciting procedure were generally effective and generally acceptable to the boys;

509

(ii) that there were, nonetheless, certain weaknesses and defects in the procedure and a number of clear indications for its modification.

The more recurrent evidence of weaknesses and defects indicated the following.

1 Some boys were embarrassed at the prospect of admitting their thefts.

2 Some were not fully convinced as to the confidentiality of the interview (feeling that their identity *could* be established or just that there *might* be a leak).

3 A few wondered if the interview was completely genuine (that is, *was* it really to help write a book/could it perhaps be connected with 'the authorities').

4 There were objections by some to the presence of the tape-recorder.

5 Many of the boys failed to recall at least some of their thefts and this failure may have been accentuated by some degree of careless-ness or over-rapid sorting of the many cards.

6 The statements on some of the cards did not make sufficiently clear *what* acts they included.

7 Some boys had difficulty with the wording on some of the cards.

8 In some cases, certain of the rules were not followed (for example, that even very small things count; that just *helping* others steal is to be counted; that very recent thefts must be counted).

Most of these difficulties and defects appear to have facilitated to at least some degree the mis-sorting of some cards as 'Never'. Clearly such difficulties/defects would have to be given careful consideration in developing a *modification* of this first form of the eliciting procedure.

On the other hand, the following factors appeared, on the basis of the tests made, to have aided the boy in admitting his thefts and hence should be considered for retention/use in the first modification.

1 The 'pretending game' (itself part of the *testing* operation and not part of the eliciting procedure) gave the interviewers considerable insight into the reasons why individual boys felt reticent about making admissions.

2 The re-sorting of cards (itself part of the *testing* operation and not part of the eliciting procedure) led to the making of further admissions.

3 As the eliciting procedure went on and merged into the follow-up operation, boys became used to the interviewer and felt more able to trust him.

4   For some boys at least, it was particularly important that the interviewer established himself as not likely to judge the boy (that is, as good or bad) in the light of the boy's admissions.

5   For most boys, the privacy of the interview and the steps taken to make it so (that is, no-one else in the room, the use of the screen, the false name) were reassuring and important.

6   The sorting process was administratively smooth and with few exceptions was accepted by the boys.

An important implication of the test results

Once we are committed to the method of progressive modification — once we accept it as a procedure — we are apt to accept the fact that our first thoughtful attempt at putting a method together will be faulty in at least some respects. However, to the 'armchair constructor', the results of the testing operation just presented should have traumatic significance. They should tell him that even with preliminary exploratory interviews to work from, the procedure he first puts together can have in it all sorts of weaknesses and that 'progressive testing and modification' is a *must* if a valid measuring procedure is to emerge. *Without* preliminary exploratory work, the 'armchair constructor' is likely to make even more mistakes. No amount of brilliance will protect him from error. Indeed I would expect armchair brilliance to be especially dangerous.

CONTINUING THE PROCESS OF
PROGRESSIVE MODIFICATION

The scene was now set for modifying the first form of the eliciting procedure. This modification was geared very closely to the detected faults in the initial procedure and to the extension of its strengths. Then came a further phase of testing, further modification, and so on, as detailed on pages   . Part III of the eliciting procedure was introduced in Cycle 3 and testing was then focused upon it. The final form of the procedure is shown in working order in *Juvenile theft: causal factors*[52] and in *The development of a procedure for eliciting information from boys about the nature and extent of their stealing.*[5] Furthermore, the step by step description of the progressive modification operation is given in the second of those two texts and may be studied there by the interested reader.

For present purposes, I will limit my further description of the method to the first modification of the initial procedure. That should be sufficient to point the way for the completion of a construction procedure that begins with no existing method at all.

THE FIRST MODIFICATION OF THE INITIAL FORM OF THE ELICITING PROCEDURE

The principle of this modificaton was that those elements in the procedure that seemed to be working well were either left alone or developed in order to make more of their satisfactory features. For the time being, we left alone those elements of the procedure about which further information would have to be collected before they could be identified as needing change. Where parts of the procedure were clearly causing errors, changes were now made. These changes involved both alteration of the detail of some elements of the procedure and the addition of some new features.

Sampling, appointment making and collection tactics

In line with the findings, the following steps were taken.

1   The time for collection was moved forward somewhat and the appointment makers stressed to boys the importance of being ready for collection on time.

2   The collector was to go quickly between 'pickups' and to plan a return route to the centre in order to arrive there on time.

The basic strategy of sampling and securement of boys was left unchanged, for both sets of tactics were working well.

The personal treatment of boys with a view to making them more willing to make admissions

1   The importance of boys remaining anonymous was stressed and re-stressed to all staff, especially the collector and the receptionist. Collectors were told to instruct the collected boys *not* to swap names in the car — and that there was a very good reason for this. The purpose of this step was to safeguard the anonymity of the boys.

2   At reception, the four to five boys in the group were handed over without any attempt to tell the receptionist who was who, and the collector departed for the time being. The receptionist was friendly. There were easy chairs for them and a selection of magazines and comics likely to appeal to teenage boys. The boys

were offered light refreshment, sweets and chewing gum. The purpose of this development was to encourage in the boy a relaxed and co-operative attitude — and also to try to make him feel a little indebted to the research operation before the interview began.

3   In the interview itself, every effort was made to maintain the same friendly relationship with the boy. Further, the interviewer attempted to make it clear that he was *not judging* the boy in any way at all. There were breaks in the interview in which sweets, drinks and sandwiches were offered to the boy.

The sorting of the spare-time activity cards

For the time being at least, no changes were made in this part of the procedure.

The introduction of extra reminders and stresses into the sorting of the theft cards

The entries on the theft cards themselves were at this stage unchanged. This was because it seemed desirable to accumulate evidence about them, through further testing cycles, before changes were devised. This precaution arose out of the slow build-up of evidence about the 52 items (or cards). However, various changes were made in this cycle, to the interviewer's *administration* of the cards.

1   To the introduction to the sorting of theft cards was added a reminder of the confidentiality of the information sought:

> 'I don't know you, you don't know me (PAUSE) and I don't suppose we'll ever meet again.'
>
> PAUSE:
>
> 'And everything you say is absolutely private.'

This reminder did, in fact, take the general form of one of the reasons given frequently by boys themselves when, in the course of the 'pretending game', they had explained why they would be willing to make admissions to the interviewer. (This 'playing back' of positive reasons derived from boys themselves was in fact to become a regular feature of the eliciting procedure.)

The original point in stressing the confidentiality, privacy and safety of the interview had, of course, been to produce a reduction (for the time being at least) in the boy's resistance to making admissions. The additional stress on it now was an attempt to take this process further.

2   After this came the rule teaching process just as before, except that there was an *extra* repetition of the rule, 'So it would count even if you were just helping.' This was one of the rules which previous testing had shown some boys not to have taken in.

3   In summing up the rules at the end of rule teaching, stress was put upon the fact that an act counted even if the thing taken was small or unimportant, and boys were reminded again to ask questions any time they were not sure about what to do. The interviewer was asked to note the number of all cards occasioning such difficulties (with a view to using this information in a later stage of modification).

4   Just before the sorting of the rest of the cards started, the boy was reminded once more that, 'You've got a false name and everything is absolutely private'.

5   In the *first* form of the eliciting procedure, there were reminder/instruction cards spread out through the remaining theft cards. On some of these cards we now printed additional instructions and reminders:

   (a)   An additional instruction to the interviewer

   > INTERVIEWER TO NOTE THE NUMBERS OF ALL CARDS THAT THE RESPONDENT ASKS ABOUT SO THAT WE CAN CONNECT THESE WITH THE DIFFICULTIES REPORTED.

   (b)   Additional appeal to the boy to ask if in any difficulty

   > 'Now remember to ask me anything you want to. *Don't be frightened to ask.*'

The addition to the eliciting procedure of a 'pretending game' of a re-sorting technique

Both the 'pretending game' and the re-sorting of 'Never' cards had been important elements in the *testing* of the first form of the eliciting procedure. The value of the re-sorting of the 'Never' cards had lain partly in indicating that boys had withheld at least some information in the original sorting of cards into 'Yes' and 'Never'. Its value had lain also in providing information about *why* they had mis-sorted cards and about what helped them to make admissions. Clearly the re-sorting technique was of great value as a tool of progressive modification. *It was also clear, however, that its power to get boys to admit to what*

514

they had previously denied could make it a valuable addition to the eliciting procedure itself. To this point I will be returning shortly.

The value of the 'pretending game' as a testing procedure had lain in its power to reveal how well or badly the eliciting procedure was working with respect to overcoming boys' resistances to making admissions. However, it was now clear that it could be used as part of the eliciting procedure itself in order to inform the interviewer about the residual difficulties with which he would have to cope in dealing with any particular boy.

The strategy of those two additions

Accordingly, these two processes were now added to the eliciting procedure itself, in the context of the following strategy.

1   The 'pretending game' was to be added just after the end of the first sorting of the cards.

2   It was intended:

   (a)   to reveal to the interviewer the precise nature of the boy's remaining resistances to making admissions, hence allowing the interviewer to bring to bear upon the boy appropriate arguments and reassurances;
   (b)   to reveal to the interviewer the boy's reasons for feeling willing to make admissions, so that the interviewer could boost and encourage these reasons;
   (c)   to advance the boy's feeling of contact with and confidence in the interviewer.

3   After this (and against the background of the interviewer's reassurances to the boy and to his boosting of any reasons the boy had for feeling able to *make* admissions), the boy *re-sorted* the cards which previously he had placed in the 'Never' box.

This total strategy was based upon the expectation that the preparatory work associated with the 'pretending game' would have increased the already demonstrated power of the re-sorting technique to get boys to admit thefts which previously they had withheld.

The detail of the two additions

The full details of the 'pretending game' and of the re-sorting of 'Never's is given in the report of the investigation,[5] but several points of detail should be presented here.

1   The theft cards used as a basis for the 'pretending game' when it was part of the testing process had been taken *at random* from the

'Never' cards of the boy. *Now* three cards were introduced especially for this purpose. They were:

Card A   'I have stolen a £5 note.'

Card B   'I have stolen something when I was in someone else's home.'

Card C   'I have stolen a bike or a motorbike.'

These particular thefts had been formulated because they seemed likely to evoke some of the known resistances of boys to making admissions. For each of them, one at a time, the boy was asked to suppose that he had done it and was asked if, in that case, he would be willing to admit it. Whatever his reply, he was asked to explain it. If his reply indicated some form of resistance to making admissions, specific counter-arguments were used in an attempt to counter or reduce that resistance, and so to open the way for further admissions during the next step, namely the re-sorting of the cards originally sorted as 'Never'. Many of these counter-arguments were derived directly from the reasons given by boys (in Cycle 1) for feeling able to *make* an admission. Different counter-arguments, as indicated below, were to be used for different kinds of resistances. Examples from the interviewers' book of instructions are given below.

---

1   IF THE BOY INDICATED HE WOULD BE TOO ASHAMED TO ADMIT THE THEFT:

SAY

'I'm not judging you. I'm just finding out.'

AND

'You don't know me . . . I don't know you . . . and I don't suppose we'll ever meet again.

2   IF THE BOY SAYS HE FEARS YOU MIGHT TELL SOMEONE:

SAY

'Do you really think we'd do a thing like that?'

WHATEVER HE REPLIES, TELL HIM:

'If we did a thing like that, boys would not help us any more . . . we'd be finished. If we talked, other boys in your area would get to know and we'd be finished.'

ALSO SAY:

'Anyhow, there were four boys who came in together. I don't know their names. Even if I did, I wouldn't know which one you were.'

IF HE HAS DOUBTS STILL, SAY:

'I wouldn't do a thing like that. Anyhow, it would only be my word against yours . . . and you could deny the whole thing.'

3   IF THE BOY SAYS THAT THE INTERVIEWER REALLY KNOWS HIS NAME:

SAY:

'I don't know your name. There were four boys came in here this afternoon/tonight and I don't know any of their names. Even if I did, I wouldn't know which one *you* were. You've got a false name. I don't know who you are.'

The interviewer had to decide *which* of the standard counter-arguments to use and he was told that he should, in the course of the re-sort of the boy's 'Never' cards, repeat those relevant to the worries of the boy concerned — in much the same way as advertisements are repeated. The interviewer was also told to counter any misunderstandings which the 'pretending game' had revealed as existing in the boys.

2   Certain changes were also made in the 'Re-sorting of cards originally counted as "Never"'. Thus:

(a)   the privacy of the interview was stressed again, just before the start of the re-sorting;

(b)   the boy was reminded that 'helping others to steal' counted as a theft;

(c)   if, during the re-sort, a boy tended to speed up, he was reminded to sort the cards slowly and to think carefully about each of them;

(d)   the appropriate counter-argument was to be delivered to him whenever the interviewer deemed this to be necessary.

We were, of course, well aware that some boys were bored by the long run of cards. However, there was no obvious answer to this difficulty at this stage. We decided to risk, for the time being at least, a certain degree of boredom for the sake of accuracy.

The personal treatment of the boy with a view to making him more willing to make admissions

There was an increased effort to make boys comfortable and to treat them in a friendly, relaxed manner. The reception room was equipped with easy chairs and a selection of magazines and comics likely to appeal to teenage boys. The receptionist offered the boys light refreshments, sweets and chewing gum and adopted a more friendly attitude towards them. In the interview itself every effort was made to maintain the same friendly relationship with the boy. Further, the interviewer attempted to make it clear that he was *not judging* the boy in any way at all. There were breaks in the interview in which sweets, drinks and sandwiches were offered to the boy.

Summing up on the nature and the form of the interviewer's equipment

Up to the end of the sorting of the spare time activity cards, the eliciting procedure was just the same as in its first form (Cycle 1), and it was contained in a single booklet. After this, but in a second booklet, the boy was introduced to the part of the interview that was to deal with stealing. His introduction to it was just as before, as was the rule teaching (except that with Rule 7 there was greater stress on the fact that 'just helping' counted as stealing). Next (just as in the first version of the eliciting procedure) there was a summing up of the rules (plus an additional plea to the boy to ask for help if he needed it). Then came the card sorting with its reminders of rules and its stresses on points of importance. After this, but in a third booklet, came instructions for the 'pretending game' and then the instructions for re-sorting of cards previously sorted as 'Never'.

It will be remembered that the last part of the eliciting procedure was to be concerned with obtaining certain details about each of the classes of theft sorted as 'Yes'. However, this last part of the eliciting procedure was not to be tested in this, the second cycle, because the purpose of the second cycle was to test the modifications just made to the sorting process and because a proper administration of such tests would call for all the time that could possibly be spared within the interview. The last part, to be administered through a third booklet, is described in the context of Cycle 3 (see full report).[5]

FURTHER TESTS AND MODIFICATIONS

Beyond this first modification, the progressive modification sequence was continued on, to a total of seven cycles, just as in the examples given in previous chapters. The last of these was a full scale investigation of what was seen as a final form of the eliciting procedure. This investigation involved a comparison of two sets of scores. The first set was made up of the scores of 80 London boys to whom the final form of the eliciting procedure had been delivered in the prescribed way. The second set came from a follow-up interview in which the same boys were put through the eliciting procedure again but with extensive and intensive challenging of their claims and denials. The correlation indices between the two scores, for the dimensions on which the hypothesis testing was to be based, ranged from +0.85 to +0.93. This result was interpreted as indicating that the eliciting procedure was sufficiently sound for the purposes for which it had been constructed.

It is not proposed to go into detail about the intermediate or the final cycles, because the purpose of this chapter is simply to describe the way in which the construction of a new procedure is initiated. Those wanting the full detail will find it in the full report of the investigation.[5]

However, as a compromise, I have set out below a list of the principal features of the method in its final form.

1   An enumeration technique was used to identify all the boys living in the subareas drawn for the investigation through a process of stratified multi-stage random sampling. For each subarea list of boys, a random sample was drawn with a control over the numbers drawn from each age-group.

2   Appointment makers went into each subarea to secure appointments with boys (with parental permission/approval). Collectors followed within several days to bring the appointees, by car, to the central interviewing premises. Boys were asked not to mention names to each other during the car journey. On arrival at the interviewing centre, they were passed over to the receptionist with a list of all four to five of them, but with no identific ition of any one of them. The collector left them at the door of the centre and went away.

3   When boys failed to keep appointments, a 'trouble shooting team' went to work to secure their participation. (In the theft enquiry, in which the testing procedure was eventually used, the success rate in bringing boys to the centre was 86%.)

4   On arrival, the boys were made welcome, were given the choice of a false name and were offered refreshments. There was a choice of teenage magazines for the boys whilst waiting. Each boy was introduced to his interviewer by his false name and the interviewer asked him not to use his own name at any time. The interviewer explained that the information he was after was needed for writing a book. The interviewer said to the boy that he hoped he would not mind a tape-recorder being used to save a great deal of writing down. This phase of the interview was informal and conversational, with the interviewer trying to avoid anything like stuffiness or authoritarianism.

5   The interview itself began with an extended introduction phase designed to prepare the boy for the questioning about theft. The introduction dealt with 20 spare-time activities; for example: fishing; train spotting; looking after a pet. Each activity was entered on the card, and the boy sorted these cards to indicate whether he had ever done what was on them. To sort them, he used the standard sorting screen (see page 489). He was tested for reading ability through calling out what was on each card as it was passed to him through a slot at the bottom of the screen. He was taught

the necessary rules for sorting — rules that would also apply to his sorting of theft cards later on. His sorting of cards was kept private to the boy, the interviewer never asking *which* cards were sorted as 'Yes' or which were sorted as 'Never'. The interviewer simply bundled the two sets of cards into packs and put them to one side. 'Not sure' cards were investigated by having the boy ask for help in sorting them.

6   Then came the crucial part of the interview, consisting of two phases: a card sorting part and a detail-seeking part.

The interviewer introduced the subject of stealing, initially referring to it as 'mischief boys get up to in their spare time'. The boy was reminded that he had a false name, that the interview was private, that the boy would never meet his interviewer again, that it was essential for the boy to tell us everything that he had done, that the tape-recording would be wiped off at the end of the interview if he wanted this done.

The sorting screen was reinserted between boy and interviewer. The interviewer used a set of 44 cards (reduced on empirical grounds from the 52 of the first form of the eliciting procedure), on each of which was a theft category. Some of these were situations ('I have stolen from work'), some were motivational ('I have taken something just for a dare'), and some were classes of objects taken ('I have stolen money from a meter). The 44 constituted a 'web of stimuli' found to be sufficient to cover practically all the stealing a boy might have done. Each card had the theft category printed on it, one way up for the boy to read and the other way up for the interviewer to read. The cards were passed to the boy one at a time through a slot in the screen, and the boy was required to read aloud what was on each. He could sort a card as 'Yes' (that is, have done that at some time), 'No' (that is, I have never done that), or 'Not sure' (that is, if he was not sure for any reason). The 44 cards were inserted into a book of instructions which the interviewer was required to read, sticking to the specified wording throughout. The first seven cards were used to teach the rules for sorting — which were those given on page 493 in the description of the first form of the eliciting procedure. The other cards followed, many of them with special instructions to deal with ambiguities and other comprehension problems found through the testing procedure.

7   At the end of this sorting process, the interviewer asked the boy about those of which he was 'Not sure' and tried to clear up the ambiguities or problems that had led the boy to sort them as 'Not sure'.

8   The sorting screen was now taken down. The interviewer then told the boy about a 'pretending game'. The boy was asked to pretend/ imagine that he had committed a particular serious theft and was asked to say if he would have admitted such a theft. If the boy said 'Yes', he was asked to say why. Whatever reasons were given were fed back to the boy in order to consolidate them. If the boy said 'No', he was asked to say why and immediately the interviewer came back with a specially prepared counter-argument (for example, if the boy said 'You might put me in', the interviewer was to say: 'If I did that, would the boys in your district get to hear about it?' (The boy almost always said 'yes'.) 'And would anybody come to take part after that?' (The boy almost always said 'no'.) 'So I'd be a fool to tell anyone wouldn't I? We'd be finished. And in any case, I don't know who you are. I only know your false name.' There were different counter-arguments for different reasons given by the boys for being unwilling to talk.

    The boy was now asked to imagine that he had committed some other serious theft and the whole process was repeated. After this, the interviewer asked the boy to sort his 'Never' cards again, because he may have forgotten something the first time or because he didn't want to admit it before. The screen went back up and the 'Never' cards were re-sorted — usually with a considerable number of them now going into the 'Yes' box.

9   After re-sorting the 'Never' cards, the boy was taken into the final detail stage of the interview — a stage designed to gather certain details about each of the categories of theft (out of the 44) that the boy had sorted as 'Yes'. The information needed for each theft category was:

(a)   what was the biggest thing of this sort the boy had ever taken?

(b)   how many times had he committed the class of theft on the card?

(c)   how long ago was the last act of this kind?

(d)   how old was he when he first committed such an act?

For this detail stage, the sorting screen was taken down for the last time. (The construction procedure had indicated that boys wanted it down at this stage.) The detail stage started with the more 'innocent' of the theft categories sorted as 'Yes' (for example, 'I have kept something I have found.'). The boy was asked for the biggest thing of this sort he had done ('found' in the example given above) and this was recorded. Then came a process of probing, reassurance and reconditioning, designed to check any residual or resurgent worries on the part of the boy and to encourage him to include his more recent thefts when considering the biggest thing. After this, the boy was asked again for the biggest thing taken (within the theft category being asked about). The same question was asked about each 'Yes' card, but there was recurrent probing, challenging and checking designed to keep the boy alert and trying. This probing, challenging and checking was maintained throughout the detail stage of the interview.

10　The boy was then taken through his 'Yes' cards once more and the remaining three items of information extracted from him. The first theft card for which this was done was subject to rather special treatment because it was being used for rule teaching and for instructing the boy to do something new. Thus in relation to 'How many times that had been done', he was reminded: that the count must include the little things as well as the big things; that his recent thefts must be included in the count; that the count should include occasions when he 'just helped'. Whatever the boy replied, his reply was subjected to challenge, to check and to probing. The same principle governed the extraction of the boy's information about how old he was when he first committed the act and how long ago it was when he last committed it.

　　　The rest of the 'Yes' cards were then dealt with one at a time, but there was an instruction systematically to probe and challenge replies as specified in the book of instruction.

The full procedure is given in the microfiche supplement to this book.

APPENDICES

The final form of the procedure:

11.1   Booklet A: Spare time activities*

11.2   Booklet B: The initial sorting of the theft cards as 'Yes' or 'Never'*

11.3   Booklet C: The 'pretending game' and the re-sort of cards originally sorted as 'Never' . . . the eliciting of details for cards sorted as 'Yes'*

11.4   The 44 theft cards used in the final form of the eliciting procedure*

11.5   The counter-arguments used in the 'pretending game'*

*see microfiche supplement

12 A note about the construction of another major measuring procedure: violence by London boys

BASED ON CHAPTER 6 OF
'TELEVISION VIOLENCE AND THE ADOLESCENT BOY'[100]

BASED ON RESEARCH BY

W.A. Belson, BA, PhD (Design and direction)
M.R.J. Couzens, BSc
G.A. Hankinson, BA
R.B. Kitney, BA
P. Southgate, BA, MA
C.A. Wain, BA, MPhil
G.A. Williams, BA
L.D. Williams, BSBA, MBA

CONTENTS OF CHAPTER

BACKGROUND TO THE CONSTRUCTION WORK

In the early 1970s, the Columbia Broadcasting System of the USA invited the author to conduct an investigation into the effects on boys of long-term exposure to television violence. The project was generously funded and provision was made for substantial involvement in the development of the necessary measuring techniques and research strategies.

This developmental work included:

- The derivation of hypotheses about the possible nature of any effects of long-term exposure to television violence
- The construction of a measure of the extent of exposure to violent television during the years of boys' growing up
- The construction of a measure of the extent of exposure to violence on television
- The construction of measures of each of the variables hypothesised as influenced by exposure to television violence.

In fact there were 23 of these hypothesised effects and these included:

- Change in the level of boys' involvement in ordinary or normal forms of violence
- Change in the level of boys' involvement in serious violence
- Change in the level of boys' involvement in violent behaviour in sport or play
- Changes in various attitudes towards violence or being violent

Each of the variables on which the different hypotheses were focused involved the research team in the development of a measuring instrument. The measure featured in this summary is involvement in violent behaviour (at any level of seriousness).

THE CONSTRUCTION OF A MEASURE OF INVOLVEMENT IN VIOLENT BEHAVIOUR

THE GENERAL NATURE OF THE REQUIRED MEASURE

For this investigation, violence had been defined as *any form of behaviour of a kind that produces hurt or harm of any kind for the object on the receiving end; this object could be animate or inanimate and the hurt or harm could be physical or psychological.*

The boys to be studied were all Londoners in the age range of 13 to 16 years, though the measure of exposure to television violence was

525

stretched all the way from their early years to the present. The period of time on which their present-day violent behaviour was to be based was the 'last six months'. In other words, we were to be concerned with the present-day effects of long-term exposure to television violence.

The tool to be constructed was, then, a measure of violent behaviour, in the last six months, by London boys in the age range 13 to 16 years.

HOW THE MEASURE WAS CONSTRUCTED

The different steps taken in constructing the required tool were very similar to those taken in developing a measure of juvenile stealing.

1 A search was made of the literature for leads that might aid the construction process. In fact the principal body of data of this sort was the Centre's own report on its theft study. At this early stage there seemed to be no good reason why the measure of violence should not use many of the same tactics and ploys as were successfully developed for that other measuring tool. (Indeed this proved to be so.)

2 There followed the usual exploratory work to identify 'blocking' and 'facilitating' factors that would have to be taken into account in constructing the measuring procedure.

3 Against the background of (1) and (2), the construction procedure began. It involved each of three parts of the total method; namely:

- The development of an extensive 'web of stimuli' of the sort used in the theft study, these stimuli being 53 'types' of violence (each set out on a card);
- The development of a sorting procedure with rules and checking tactics for taking the boy through the 53 'types' of violence (a sophisticated card sorting system);
- The development of a probing and challenging procedure for taking the boy through each admitted type of violence and getting from him all the specific acts committed in that context.

Each of these three parts of the procedure was developed through the progressive modification method. In other words, each part was first formulated on the basis of evidence, was tested through the intensive interviewing method, was modified on the basis of the test results, was tested again, modified, and so on until an acceptable level of accuracy was achieved. Construction work on the measure took over a year.

A full description of the construction methods used is given in Chapter 6 of *Television violence and the adolescent boy*.[100]

The procedure in its final form was complex from the administrative point of view, though its every element was designed to make it easy for boys to provide accurate information about their violent behaviour. In the full report, the method is described first in descriptive summary form and then as an operating procedure. The descriptive summary follows.

1   Boys were interviewed on centre premises under conditions of stressed anonymity and privacy, with each boy having a fictitious name for the occasion. Prior to this they had already been through lengthy questioning on a quite innocuous issue with the same interviewer.

2   A central feature of the present procedure involved the sorting, by the boys, of many cards on each of which was a different statement about violence and which together made up what has been called a 'web of stimuli'. Many of the statements referred to a form of violent behaviour in general or in specific terms (for example: 'I have thrown something at someone'; 'I have given someone a head butt').

Others referred to *situations* in which violence occurred (for example: 'I have been violent at a football match') and others again referred to *reasons* for being violent (for example: 'I have done something to get my own back on somebody', 'I have been violent just for fun or for a laugh or for a dare'). These carded statements together constituted a 'web of stimuli', sufficiently comprehensive in coverage to refer to virtually the whole range or 'universe' of the behaviour defined as violent in this enquiry.

3   The basic requirement in sorting was that the boy should look at each card in turn and put it into a bag labelled 'Yes' if he had done what was on it in the last six months and into one labelled 'No' if he had *not* done so. The two bags were fixed to a screen which separated the boy from the interviewer in order to give the boy a sense of privacy, the cards being passed to the boy one at a time through a slot at the bottom of the screen.

4   The sorting requirement had been preceded by an introductory phase in which the boy was told what the next set of questions would be about, was told that it was essential that he be completely frank and was reminded that he had a false name. There

was then a reading test and a period of fairly intensive teaching of the rules for sorting. These rules were principally that:

- The period being asked about was 'the last six months' and anything done earlier than that would not count
- An act was to be counted even if the boy considered it was not serious/even if accidental/even if done in self-defence
- The boy was to ask the interviewer for help whenever he was uncertain about anything
- The boy should place face down in front of him any cards about which he was unable to make a decision (even after seeking clarification through the interviewer)

For marker purposes, the interviewer was to set the boy thinking of public and personal events six months ago. During sorting, there were spaced reminders of rules and especially of the requirement that the boy be completely frank. For some cards, there were special introductory or clarifying statements.

5   After the 53 carded statements (that is, constituting the 'web of stimuli') had been sorted, the interviewer came out from behind the screen and tried to help the boy to clear up any 'Don't know' cards. He then put the boy through what has been called the 'pretending game'. In this 'game' the interviewer was required to ask the respondent to imagine that he had used violence on some other boy and that this had damaged the boy very badly. He then asked the respondent if he would have admitted such an act to the interviewer.

If the boy said 'yes', the interviewer was required to ask 'why' and to reinforce the boy's willingness to tell all, by (a) repeating the boy's reasons back to him, (b) delivering certain additional arguments (for telling 'all') as detailed in the interviewer's instructions (for example, 'What you say is absolutely private'/ 'There's no name connected with it – in fact you've got a false name'). The interviewer then proceeded to seek certain details about each card sorted as 'Yes', using the system detailed in (6) below.

If the boy said 'no', in the 'pretending game', the interviewer was required to find out 'why' and to discuss with the boy his reasons for *not* being willing to admit that act – the interviewer's purpose being to identify any general or specific reticence about making admissions and the reasons for such reticence. The interviewer sought to overcome that reticence or resistance both by clearing up any basic misunderstanding on the part of the boy and by delivering certain standard 'counter-arguments' proposed for such purposes and presented in the interviewer's instructions. For example, if the boy had said he was ashamed to tell, the interviewer would say, amongst other things: 'I'm not *judging* anyone — I'm just finding out'/'You don't know me, I don't know you, and I don't suppose we will ever meet again'. After this, the boy was asked to re-sort all the cards previously sorted as 'No'.

6 The interview now proceeded into its final stage. The sorting screen was taken down and the boy was questioned with respect to each of the statements or acts he had sorted into the 'Yes' box. Thus for a given statement (for example, 'I have thrown something at someone'), the interviewer asked the boy for:

(a) the total number of times he had done what was on the card over the last six months;

(b) the different sorts of things he had done (in relation to what was on the card;

(c) for each of these different sorts of things:

   (i) the nature of the act (for example, kicked, punched, pushed, cut);

   (ii) the object of the act (for example, another boy, the cat);

   (iii) the implement if any (for example, knife, stick);

   (iv) what led him to do it (for example, the other boy was rude to him, for fun);

   (v) the circumstances of the act (for example, at football);

   (vi) how many times he had done that sort of thing in the last six months.

Responses to questions (i) to (vi) were entered on the cards themselves as part of the record of the interview and subsequently were used to derive 'violence scores' for the boys.

7 The whole of the extraction procedure was controlled by a booklet which detailed what the interviewer had to do and say throughout, with the exception of the discussional stage of the 'pretending game'. The 53 statements were interlaced with the pages of the instruction booklet, because many of the instructions were geared to what was written on specific cards. The booklet and the statements on the 53 cards are presented in diagrammatic and verbal form at the end of Chapter 6 in the full report.[100]

The reader may study the full eliciting procedure, as an operating sequence, in *Television violence and the adolescent boy*[100] (pages 222–38).

13 Validity and invalidity in the wider reaches of market and social research

This book is principally an illustrated presentation of two key procedures in the development of valid measuring instruments. The first is the intensive interview used for testing the accuracy of existing measuring techniques. The second is the progressive modification method, used in conjunction with intensive interviewing, for modifying defective measuring techniques and for developing new ones.

However their description must be set in the broader context of validity in both market and social research generally. To some extent this was done in Chapter 2 in which I stated that validity in survey research could not be taken for granted and in which I gave some major causes of invalidity. I referred to interviewers changing the wording of questions, respondents failing to interpret the questions as intended, order effects, careless replies, memory decay, an unwillingness of respondents to make admissions on certain matters.

I would like to go further now and deal with the validity issue in a wider array of the procedures of contemporary market and social research in the UK. In doing this I aim to illustrate that the validity issue arises in all aspects of survey research and that it is not limited to complex techniques of the sort dealt with in the main body of this document. I expect that this final presentation will emphasise my thesis that validity should never be, but often is, taken for granted. On the other hand, I would argue that the tactics and procedures already exist for building the validity principle into the data collection techniques that we use.

VALIDITY IN CONTEMPORARY MARKET
AND SOCIAL RESEARCH PROCEDURES

THE QUALITATIVE–QUANTITATIVE OPPOSITION

From a validity standpoint, perhaps the most lively issue in the market and social research scene today is bound up in the opposition of the qualitative and the quantitative researchers. Let me start by defining the two positions and saying how they relate to each other.

Qualitative researchers are, for the most part, concerned with evoking the ideas, the feelings, the reactions, the creative potential of people in relation to specified issues or stimuli or things. They tend to use the methods of group discussion and its variants and of the intensive open-ended interviewing of small numbers of people, to secure such yields.* They may work at (a) the creative level, using the rich yield from the qualitative techniques to stimulate in themselves and others various concepts and approaches for the development of promotional material. Or they may use those qualitative techniques (b) to develop an understanding of some target population or (c) to assess reactions to something being tested.

For the first of those approaches there will probably be no attempt at quantification at all. For (b) and (c), however, there is often an implicit quantification involved and this will be attacked by the quantitative researcher as being invalid or at least suspect. He will insist upon fully structured questioning of a meaningful sample of people as a necessary basis for quantification.

On the other hand, the qualitative researcher tends to see the opposition as stuck with the measurement of some limited set of ideas and reactions and as failing to discover and deal with anything like the full diversity and complexity of the matter under study or to exploit the creativity of the informants.

There is of course the in-between position where (1) exploratory methods (principally group discussion and probed open-ended questioning of individuals) are used to discover different ideas, feelings, reactions in some situation and (2) quantitative methods are thereafter used to quantify those of them that are regarded as relevant to decision making. However, some qualitative researchers would object to this approach on several different grounds: (1) the creative process may well

---

*The qualitative methods include also: extended group work, projective techniques, sensitivity panel work, interviewing of couples, friendship groups.

be a 'leap' from just one idea, mentioned once — i.e. it need not depend upon knowing *how many* had this idea or that; (2) the method of group discussion provides a basis for non-precise quantification and this level of quantification may well be sufficient for the kinds of decision that have to be made; (3) quantification is a slow process and holds up decision making; (4) the results available from quantitative research are sterile in the sense that they fail to present the real complexity and sensitivity of the respondent's position or to exploit his creativity.

Some comments from a validity viewpoint

This issue is a lively and enduring one, raising questions of the validity of each approach. Perhaps the biggest block to its resolution is a peculiar failure on the part of the research profession to find out to what extent group discussion and open ended questioning do in fact provide us with counts that are accurate within the limits required for decision making.

Surprisingly, information bearing on the accuracy of open response questioning has been available (but ignored) for a long time. Thus it is quite clear from a series of reported studies[93, 101, 103] that the open response question produces different numerical results — often markedly different — from the check list version of the question. This does not settle the issue of the accuracy of the open response results, but it certainly should have produced a flurry of anxious research activity to find out precisely what credence can be put upon open response counts — let alone open response counts based upon *small samples* of respondents. In fact it was left to the writer to initiate a series of such studies which are on-going at present.

It is even stranger that we have not yet seen undertaken systematic research to determine the extent to which group discussion, a most extensively used and productive qualitative procedure, generates accurate population distributions of views and reactions. While many qualitative researchers do not use group discussion to generate even rough quantities of this kind, others do. Even in the absence of such validity research, it is not hard to understand why some quantitative researchers question the safety of quantifications based on group discussion. Thus they may argue: (1) group discussion is an interaction technique and that interaction is likely to modify the opinions that group members had before the discussion started, or the way they report their reactions to material shown to them; (2) the group discussion situation is not conducive to getting each group member privately to consider specified matters and then give an independent reply or comment or opinion; (3) self selection enters strongly into the group recruitment process and on top of this even five groups (which is often the maximum used) make up a very small total of people from a sampling viewpoint. What all this means, they argue, is that the derivation of quantities from a set of group discussions can be a chancy process. The position is worse when, as does happen from time to time, the moderator does not report what the group members actually said, but reports instead her *interpretations* of what was said.

The results of the little that *has* been done in the way of methodological checking of the validity of the group discussion method is disquieting,[e.g.104] but by no means sufficient. A thorough-going investigation of the validity of quantitative uses of that method is long overdue. In the meantime, one thing is clear. The discussion group method is a discussional and interactive technique and those are two characteristics that many researchers try to avoid when gathering 'countable' information from a sample of individuals.

ORDINARY INTERVIEWING

Another source of error in market and social research is the interviewer. The interviewer it is who is required to deliver the set questions and accurately to report the responses they elicit. This applies both to the open ended question — where the respondent may answer at length — and to the choice-of-answer system of the fully structured question. The interviewer is, as it were, at the cutting edge of the information gathering procedure. In the face-to-face interviewing situation the interviewer operates alone and only her trained abilities and indirect control stand between a faithful and skilled performance and a flawed one.

And yet the circumstances of most interviewer teams militate against their thorough training and adequate control. Thus: many interviewers work for more than one research agency or firm, so that there exists a possibility that any special training that one does do will be spoiled by some other employer; interviewers shift around, taking with them any special training that some caring employer has built into them. Then again quite a lot of interviewer faults are not detectable by inspection of the completed questionnaire (though some are) and so the organisation that cuts costs by inadequate checking and control of interviewers is likely to remain ignorant of many of their interviewers' misdemeanours. On top of all this, many researchers appear to take interviewing for granted.

As things stand, any supervisor who is doing the job properly will meet abundant evidence of faults such as deviation from set question wording;[2] failure to record faithfully what the respondent replied;[6]

failure to get some of the respondents to answer an open ended question with more than a bare minimum of information; failure to get vague replies clarified sufficiently for coding purposes; corner cutting with regard to the sampling requirements; a certain element of cheating.

I am aware that it is easy to call for special training for interviewers and that it can be extremely difficult and costly to develop a team of keen craftspeople. But that nonetheless is what we should be aiming for. The problem is that the interviewer is a vital part of our data gathering procedure and that no questioning technique is going to be valid unless the interviewing is done competently and faithfully. Put another way, the interviewer is herself a vital research tool, and if she is a faulty or invalid tool, the information she reports is likely to be flawed.

The Interviewer Card Scheme* co-ordinated by the Market Research Society is no doubt a vital step in the right direction, for it requires that its research agency members agree to adhere to certain standards with respect to office procedures, training, supervision and control and survey administration and that these agreements be honoured. However I doubt that many buyers of research will consider that the present minimum set for training (two days at present) and control are anything like enough to build a competent and conscientious team of interviewers.

There is another party to the 'quality of interviewing' issue. It is the buyer of research. Some buyers are willing to pay the extra that is needed to support effective training and control of interviewers. But others buy the cheapest research that is available and in so doing they help to drive out the good interviewing and the careful control that the better researchers want very much to provide.

POSTAL SURVEYS

From a validity viewpoint, one of the weak spots in survey research procedures has long been the postal survey. With this system, questionnaires are sent by post to a sample of individuals or firms. A letter normally accompanies the questionnaire. At least one reminder may be sent. The response rate may on rare occasions and for some kinds of subject matter, be as high as 90%. But it is much more common to have response rates of the order of 30% or less. A response rate of even 60% raises the question of 'What would the distribution of replies to

*See Interviewer Card Scheme Fieldwork Standards, available from the Market Research Society at 15 Belgrave Square, London, SW1.

questions have been if all 100% had replied?' So what shall we s[...]
response rate of 30% or even less? Clearly there is a question of valid[...]
here.

Whereas a lot of methodological research on postal questionnaires was carried out in the two decades up to 1960,[105] it was concentrated very much more on how to increase response rate than on the validity issue as such. In that period and since, validity checking has been singularly sparse and certainly insufficient.

Validity of postal questionnaires can be seen from two viewpoints: whether respondents who complete the questionnaire do so accurately; whether those who do not return the questionnaire would have given the same distribution of answers as did the returnees (the 'volunteer bias' issue).

The means of checking the accuracy of an individual's reply has been dealt with fairly fully in earlier chapters. As stated there, the accuracy check can be carried out at different levels of thoroughness and at least one of those levels is likely to be financially feasible.

Checking on and controlling volunteer bias is also possible and it is financially feasible for a set postal questionnaire that is sent out on a continuing basis and also for postal questionnaires that deal with the *same product* each time. Testing for volunteer bias is in principle fairly straight forward: one has to find out how the non-respondents would have replied to the questions if they had completed the questionnaire. In practice, this involves follow-up contact with the non-respondents through interviewers trained to secure interviews with such people. I would expect this follow-up to lift the response level to at least 70% — which is the sort of figure that the ordinary sample survey involving personal interviews ordinarily produces. With greater funding and effort that figure could be lifted to 80%. A comparison of the replies of respondents to the postal questionnaire with those of the successfully contacted non-respondents could then be made. If in general there is no difference, then the use of a postal questionnaire system, *on the same subject matters*, would seem to be a relatively viable proposition. If there are serious differences, even for some of the questions, then we must either not use the postal method for the subject matter here involved, or we must take special steps to control out or match out the volunteer basis.

The simplest case for control is the questionnaire that is sent out on a continuing basis and which deals each time with the same marketing or social matters. Following a postal survey for the firm concerned, personal interviews would be sought with the respondents and with as many as possible of the non-respondents. The non-respondents would be put through the same questions as were on the postal questionnaire and both they and the respondents would also be asked a series of

had been hypothesised as possible correlates of both
: and (ii) the matters asked about in the postal question-
s, based on a readily available computer programme*
us to identify a composite of those variables that are in
es of the sort wanted. Armed with these variables, built
ning programme, the yield from future postal questionnaires
same series could rapidly be corrected for volunteer bias.
gular subject matters, but a constant mail-out strategy, one
would limit the matching variables to those found to be correlates
simply of whether recipients completed and returned the questionnaire.
That limited solution would still be very useful. Moreover it is one that
the writer has used in matching operations in other contexts.

What I am saying is that potential invalidity has for decades hung
over the postal questionnaire system and that there is virtually no
published research of the sort that would determine the practical
relevance of that potential bias or help us to correct it. The result has
been decades of suspect work and hence of potentially bad decision
making.

TELEPHONE SURVEYS

In the USA, following the spread of telephone ownership to the great
majority of homes and the availability of the WATS zoning system,†
the use of the telephone for conducting sample surveys became wide-
spread. There is a great number of telephone interviewing bureaux in
the USA and the number goes on increasing. In Britain, following a
belated but rapid growth in the proportion of homes that could be
contacted by telephone, telephone surveys have similarly been on the
increase and are now a major research facility. Their speed and their
economy make them highly attractive and it seems very likely that they
will increasingly compete with face-to-face survey interviewing.

Speed and cheapness seem admirable criteria for guiding change. But
they are not the only criteria. What matters above all is validity. At the
time when 60% or so of the UK population was said to have a telephone in the home, there was a frequent expression of concern about
the representativeness of the telephone public, just as there had been in
the USA. Indeed, in the USA, a great deal of research had gone into the
'representativeness' issue,[106-115] being focused upon: Who are the non-

*The Automatic Interaction Detector (AID). See footnote on page 539.
†The Wide Area Telephone System. A telephone survey company could hire 'lines' each of
which the hirer could use continuously without further charge. The WATS system was linked
to subscriber zones which together covered the whole of the USA. With this facility, the
research company could keep each line in constant use for all the hours during which the
people in the different zones were wakefully available.

subscribers? Who are the voluntarily unlisted subscribers? Who are the subscribers who are not yet listed but will be in the next issue of the telephone directory? Who are the subscribers who have moved house since the last issue of the directory?

In the UK, a paper by Miln[116] presented evidence that during the mid 1970s certain buying behaviour was much the same for subscribers and total population — in spite of demographic and other differences between them. However, some of those demographic and other background differences were large — socio-economic level, home ownership, use of heating systems. That left us with the situation that error through unrepresentativeness *could* arise when the matter under investigation was substantially correlated with the variables with respect to which the telephone public were unrepresentative.

With the continued penetration of telephone ownership to the present day, those differences too have lessened, though by the end of 1983, there were still major differences in the degree of penetration of the telephone into the homes of the AB's and the DE's (96%:59%). There were some differences too in terms of house tenure, of number of persons in the telephone household, in terminal education age of the head of the household.* However, as the penetration figure for the UK as a whole moved into the 80% level, it seems generally to have been assumed by survey practitioners that background differences between telephone and non-telephone population would have only marginal consequences for survey validity — and that the validity issue had been outgrown!

For several reasons I doubt that we can now simply accept that the telephone survey method is usually a valid procedure — any more than we can simply accept that the face-to-face survey method is usually valid. In the first place we still have a problem over the substantial number of unlisted telephones, over the 15% plus of households that cannot yet be reached directly by telephone, over the usually large losses through non-contact and refusals. In the second place, the issue of validity also concerns the accuracy of the responses of the individual telephone respondents.

A number of comparative studies of the results from telephone and face-to-face surveys have been made.[117–120] These indicate a broad similarity of results for the two methods, though there are some exceptions. But even when there is *agreement*, there is still a possibility that both methods are wrong in the studies concerned. A start has been made in the USA with genuine validity checking linked to specific subject matters. This is fine, but we must remember that we cannot generalise about the validity of the telephone survey method from a

---

*NRS data for July—December 1983, analysed by British Telecom.

few tests based upon specific subject matters — anymore than we can from tests of the validity of face-to-face interviewing in just one or in several contexts. What is necessary for the safe use of the telephone survey method is that validity testing of it be carried out on a wide range of subject matters and that this practice be continued over time — just as is necessary for assessing the validity of the face-to-face survey interview method. Such validity testing would have to take into account different subject matters, different question forms, different contact rates and different refusal rates.

COMPUTER PROCESSING

The constant evidence of computer revolution in the management of market research could easily produce an impression of sound development. These revolutions do in general contribute greatly to the proper goals of cheapness and speed. And they not only relieve drudgery but they reduce the likelihood of human error. They are exciting, vital, and we cannot be without them. But I think we should take care to see that certain of their uses do not land us in new sorts of error. Certainly computer assisted telephone interviewing (CATI) should be evaluated from a validity standpoint before it becomes fully and widely established in the UK. So too for the computerised analysis of open ended data.[122] We need the validation of such specific practices before the ease or the speed claimed for them lead to their unchallenged acceptance. Nor should the design of response systems for fully structured questions be dominated by computer considerations. Nor should we forget that behind some elegant computer print-out may be questions that have not been tested and interviewing that has not been subjected to adequate training and control.

Above all, I hope that the electronic speed and precision of our computerised processing systems do not produce the illusion that a computer technology automatically means validity.

SEGMENTATION, PREDICTION AND MATCHING

Computer technology has made an enormous difference to the application and the feasibility of another technology, namely the closely linked processes of empirical segmentation, empirical matching and empirical prediction.

Let me say a little about matching and prediction as validity based techniques. In the early 1950s, in revolt against the intuitive matching then in vogue, I began matching samples on the basis of a small composite of variables derived through the Wherry-Doolittle technique. This technique identifies that composite of variables that, taken together, maximises the multiple correlation (with some dependent variable) that is available from some large pool of possible correlates. These are normally the variables that would be built into a regression equation used for prediction purposes. In other words I was attempting to match samples in terms of variables that were usefully correlated with what was under study. This approach would allow me to answer the question: 'What would this sample have scored if it had been the same as the other sample (to which it is to be matched) in terms of relevant characteristics? That of course is very similar to the predictive question of 'What will be the buying level of a given population at a period when the variables in the composite of predictors take new values?'. From a validity standpoint, we were simply establishing valid predictive/ matching variables.

I might have left the matter there, with the comment that empirical matching based upon the well established Wherry-Doolittle technique did not go into wide usage at that time and that many matching operations continued to be based on intuitively derived variables. So too for many prediction operations, with protagonists arguing strongly for *theory* based variables. However, the Wherry-Doolittle method has two severe limitations. In the first place, it depends upon the discovery of variables that are predictive right across the sample, whereas some variables are strongly predictive for only some section of the population. I wanted to take advantage of situations where a given variable was highly predictive for only part of the sample. For instance, suppose that social class is the best overall predictor of purchase of commodity X. Then we would use social class as the first predictor or discriminator and would segment the sample into two parts: (a) those social classes with a positive association with purchase of X and (b) those with a negative association. Next, we would look *quite separately* within each of those two groupings for the best correlate of buying X. It is most unlikely that the same correlate would emerge for each of those two groups. Thus it might be that age would be the best correlate (of buying X) for one of the groups and family type for the other. This strategy is continued in an inverted tree formation and it may well be that with a four-level splitting operation, as many as sixteen variables would emerge as correlates or predictors.*

*See W.A. Belson (1959). Matching and prediction on the principle of biological classification, *Applied Statistics*, vol. 8(2). The author passed the paper to Morgan and Sonquist of the Institute of Social Research in Michigan, USA, and later discussed it with them personally. Subsequently, Sonquist and Morgan published papers based closely on the same principle, but gave no credit to the 1959 publication. The Sonquist and Morgan technique was called the Automatic Interaction Detector.[50]

With this system it is possible to engage in empirically based and large scale matching of sample to sample. The technique is usable also for market segmentation, for short term prediction and for equating an achieved sample to the population which it was intended to represent. The method is frequently employed now for market segmentation. But for sample matching it is but little used and many researchers still match samples on the basis of intuitively derived variables.

I regard empirically established composites of correlates as valid variables from the standpoint of matching and segmentation, and I see in current matching practice another failure to adopt a validity stance.

OTHER AREAS WHERE THERE HAS BEEN A FAILURE TO VALIDATE

Here, to finish my illustrations, are other areas of research activity where it seems to me that the validity principle is insufficiently in operation: question design and the design of measuring instruments generally (I have dealt with this key aspect of research already); the current form of the National Readership Survey — the underlying principle of the whole operation being based upon a largely unchecked assumption; the construction of social indicators; causal research; advertisement pre-testing; quota sampling. I will leave it to the perceptive reader to think of more.

TAKING ACTION

It is one thing to lament the neglect of the validity principle — and quite another to secure its wide implementation. But much can be done towards that end.

1   In the first place, I hope that this book will contribute in some small way to the demand for valid research tools in social and commercial investigations. I hope that in this respect what I have said will indicate not only a need for action but specific *kinds* of action that can be taken.

2   One very basic step in the establishment of a sound research methodology is to make that methodology a key subject in relevant courses of higher education. I have in mind both university and polytechnic courses in sociology, psychology, social studies, social and business administration, epidemiology, and in any other discipline where measurements of human outlook, conditions or

behaviour are intrinsically involved. On the positive side, there is some teaching of 'methods of research' in many of the polytechnics and in some of the universities. This development has still a distance to go. But there is a problem in that many of the teachers tend not to be experienced research practitioners, but academic staff often with very little practical experience in conducting market or social or industrial investigations. There are exceptions of course, but what is in general necessary is that very experienced professional researchers be brought in on a part-time basis to teach a 'methods of research' programme* and that these people be directed to integrate into their teaching the key principle of validity. Many such people would welcome the opportunity to pass on what they know.

Methods of research teaching is very important as a basic skill for those who will later engage in research. But it is also an essential part of the academic preparation of students, for without it those students cannot properly appraise or evaluate or challenge the theory and the research findings presented to them. To do this, they must be aware of the strengths and the weaknesses and the general suitability of the research methods that lie behind such theories and findings. In this context, 'validity thinking' is crucial.

I am suggesting that the present growth in the teaching of research methods in academic institutions be speeded up and that it be strengthened both by the extensive use of professional researchers in the teaching programme and by a deliberate emphasis, in all teaching, on the validity principle.

3   Another necessary step towards the development of a sound research methodology is the presence, in research and user organisations, of at least one staff member with competence to *evaluate* the research procedures that are used to produce decision-making information. Thus an organisation that is dependent upon panel or upon diary information would be well advised to have its specialists investigate the adequacy of those methods; an organisation that buys or produces advertisements would be well advised to investigate the relevance of the pre-test criteria that are used to establish the potential effectiveness of such advertisements – a manufacturer who makes estimates of future sales of his product ought to evaluate the criteria in terms of which that estimate is

---

*Another approach that has been advocated is to give teachers of social and business studies work experience placement in research organisations so that they bring that experience to the teaching of research methods. The reader should consider to what extent such placements are likely to occur and whether the experience so gained could compare with what the veteran professional could provide.

made; pharmaceutical producers and hospitals would do well to look closely at the validity of clinical tests and trials. An in-house methodology specialist could in each case look after this vital evaluative work. In a sense this is nothing more than a special sort of quality control. It is both vital and feasible. It may well call for special training and nurture of the staff members who would make the evaluations. There is a lot of scope for this sort of quality control.

Vested interests will often stand in the way of such evaluations, with organisations and individuals who are already committed professionally or financially to some procedure discouraging any challenge to its continued use. But the best answer to that situation is to encourage the self interests of those who stand to lose through misinformation.

4   Another element that services the development of a valid body of research procedures is the methodological research unit that occasionally springs up in some fertile setting. One of the best known of these settings is the Institute of Social Research within Michigan University in the USA. It has for many years contributed richly to the development and teaching of research techniques. In the UK the Division of Social Surveys, within the Office of Population Censuses and Surveys, produces occasional papers based on a wide range of methodological investigations. These are circulated within the OPCS and to relevant people beyond the department. The Survey Research Methods unit of Social and Community Planning Research currently conducts programmes of methodological research and teaches research methods. The Survey Research Centre, then operating within the London School of Economics and Political Science had, for many years, made major contributions to question design, segmentation and matching technology, validity testing, interviewing techniques and to the teaching of research methods.

Such units can contribute richly to the development of a sound research technology. They usually have to operate under difficulties, not the least of which is the financial one. But they are certainly viable and there is a need for more of them.

The writer is particularly interested in seeing established an institute of research techniques geared to the methodological interests of researchers in different countries. Such an institute should, I believe, be established and operate under a trustee system constituted to keep it working on methodological problems of practical importance and to protect it from vested interests. It should be funded by contributions mainly from users of market and social research.

The functions of the institute should, I think, be principally as follows:

(a) The institute would conduct a wide range of methodological research projects relevant to commercial, social and government investigations. The methodological work would involve not only the testing of existing methods but the construction of new methods where the need for them exists.

(b) To a limited extent the institute would construct tools for specific business or social investigations and then *use* them in those enquiries. However, there would be no competition with other bodies for projects of a non-methodological kind where the institute's specialised skills were not needed.

(c) There should be a facility for accepting experienced researchers from industry and elsewhere to work at the institute for a period on key methodological issues related to the work they normally do.

(d) The institute would provide practical training courses on the techniques of market and social research, with a strong lacing of scientific method and validity thinking. Students or trainees would come from industry, the civil and public services, educational bodies, charities, research organisations. I would expect them to come mainly from the United Kingdom, but from other countries as well.

An institute of the kind I have described could play a vital role in advancing the scientific status of business and social research so that these disciplines increasingly fulfil their roles as dependable intelligence services for aiding decision makers.

References

1   Belson, W.A. (1966), *The ability of respondents to recall their purchases of chocolate confectionery*, Survey Research Centre, London.

2   Belson, W.A. (1962), *Studies in readership*, Business Publications Limited, London.

3   Belson, W.A. (1969), *The semantic differential scaling system in market research: accuracy of ratings*, Survey Research Centre, London.

4   Bureau of Broadcasting Measurement (1975), *A review of the 1974—75 research programme of the BBM Bureau of Measurement*, BBM, Toronto, Canada.

5   Belson, W.A., Millerson, G.L. and Didcott, P.J. (1968), *The development of a procedure for eliciting information from boys about the nature and extent of their stealing*, Survey Research Centre, London.

6   Belson, W.A. (1983), *The accuracy of interviewer reporting of respondent replies to open and to fully structured questions*, Market Research Society Annual Conference, Brighton.

7   Belson, W.A. (1969), *The Semantic Differential scaling system in market research: (III) interviewer deviation from instructions*, Survey Research Centre, London.

8   Belson, W.A. (1981), *The design and understanding of survey questions*, Gower Publishing Company, London.

9   Cantril, H. and Fried, E. (1944), 'The meaning of questions' in Cantril, H. et al., *Gauging public opinion*, Princeton University Press, Princeton.

10   Cambell, A. (1946), 'Polling opinion interviewing, and the problem of interpretation', *Journal of Social Issues*, vol.2(4).
11   Klare, G.R. (1950), 'Understandability and indefinite answers to public opinion questions', *International Journal of Opinion and Attitude Research*, vol.4(1).
12   Nuchols, R.C. (1953), 'A note on pre-testing public opinion questions', *Journal of Applied Psychology*, vol.37(2).
13   Vernon, P.E. (1950), *An investigation into the intelligibility of forces educational broadcasting*, BBC, London.
14   Gordon, W.D. (1963), 'Double interview', in *New Developments in Research*, Market Research Society and Osborne Press, London.
15   Sudman, S. and Bradburn, N.M. (1982), *Asking Questions*, Josey-Bass, San Francisco.
16   Government Social Survey (1962), *The relations between the police and the public:* Appendix 4 to the minutes of evidence, Royal Commission on the Police, Her Majesty's Stationery Office.
17   Rugg, D. and Cantril, H. (1944), 'The wording of questions', in Cantril, H. et al., *Gauging public opinion*, Princeton University Press, Princeton, pp.23—50.
18   Belson, W.A. (1966), 'The effects of reversing the presentation order of verbal rating scales', *Journal of Advertising Research*, vol.6(4).
19   Quinn, S. and Belson, W.A. (1969), *The effects of reversing the order of presentation of verbal rating scales in survey interviews*, Survey Research Centre, London.
20   Metzner, H. and Mann, F. (1953), 'Effects of grouping related questions in questionnaires', *Public Opinion Quarterly*, vol.17(1).
21   Bradburn, N.M. and Mason, W.M. (1964), 'The effect of question order on responses', *Journal of Marketing*, vol.1(4).
22   Ebbinghaus, H. (1885; translated 1913), *Memory: a contribution to experimental psychology*.
23   McGeogh, J.A. (1932), 'Forgetting and the law of disuse', *Psychological Review*, vol.39.
24   Woodworth, R.S. and Schloshberg, H. (1955), *Experimental Psychology*, Holt, New York.
25   Hunter, I.M.L. (1957), *Memory*, Pelican, London.
26   Gray, P.G. (1955), 'The memory factor in social surveys', *Journal of the American Statistical Association*, vol.50(270).
27   Scott, C.D. (1959), *A three-way check on memory for letters sent*, Office of Censuses and Surveys, London.
28   Krugman, H.E. (1977), 'Memory without recall, exposure without perception', *Journal of Advertising Research*, vol.17(4).
29   Bettman, J.R. (1979), 'Memory factors in consumer choice: a review', *Journal of Marketing*, vol.43(2).

30   Joyce, T. (1982), 'Readership research: the relationship between recent reading and through the book', *Admap*, February.
31   McFarlane-Smith, J. (1972), *Interviewing in market and social research*, Routledge and Kegan Paul, London.
32   Smith, H.L. and Hyman, H. (1950), 'The biasing effect of interviewer expectations on survey results', *Public Opinion Quarterly*, vol.14(3).
33   Cahalan, D., Tamulonis, V. and Verner, H.W. (1947), 'Interviewer bias involved in certain types of opinion survey questions', *International Journal of Opinion and Attitude Research*, vol.1(1).
34   Clemens, J., Day, C. and Walter, D. (1980), *Direct access panel: the research mode for the eighties and beyond*, Esomar Congress, September.
35   Roslow, S., Wulfeck, W.H. and Corby, P.G. (1940), 'Consumer and opinion research: experimental studies on the form of the question', *Journal of Applied Psychology*, vol.24(3).
36   Jicnars (1968), *Developmental research for the 1968 National Readership Survey*, London. (For reference to glue spot and camera checks, see Appendix 2, page 11.)
37   Osgood, C.E., Suci, G.J. and Tannenbaum, P.H. (1957), *The measurement of meaning*, University of Illinois Press, Urbana.
38   Belson, W.A. (1967), *The semantic differential scaling system in market research: order effect*, Survey Research Centre, London.
39   Belson, W.A. (1969), *The semantic differential scaling system in market research: III interviewer deviation from instructions*, Survey Research Centre, London.
40   Belson, W.A. (1969), *The semantic differential scaling system in market research: accuracy of ratings*, Survey Research Centre, London.
41   Osgood, C.E. (1953), *Method and theory in experimental psychology*, New York.
42   Sellitz, C., Jahoda, M., Deutch, M. and Cook, S.W. (1959), *Research methods in social relations*.
43   Quinn, S.B. and Belson, W.A. (1970), *Thought processes and accuracy in the recall of purchases: petrol buying*, Survey Research Centre, London.
44   Bureau of Broadcasting Measurement (1974), *A report on the BBM tests of revised and single-media diaries*, BBM, Toronto, Canada.
45   Likert, R. (1932), 'A technique for the measurement of attitudes', *Archives of Psychology*, no.140.
46   Edwards, A.I. and Kilpatrick, F.P. (1948), 'A technique for the construction of attitude scales', *Journal of Applied Psychology*, vol.32(4).
47   Belson, W.A. (1952), 'The construction of an index of intelligence', *British Journal of Psychology*.

48   Belson, W.A. (1959), 'Matching and prediction on the principle of biological classification', *Applied Statistics*, vol.8(2).

49   Morgan, J.N. and Sonquist, J.A. (1963), 'Problems in the analysis of survey data and a proposal', *Journal of the American Statistical Association*, vol.58(302).

50   Sonquist, J.A. and Morgan, J.N. (1964), *The detection of interaction effects: a report on a computer program for the selection of optimal combinations of explanatory variables*, Survey Research Centre, Ann Arbor, Michigan.

51   Belson, W.A. (1969), *Causal factors in the development of stealing by London boys: part I — methods of enquiry*, Survey Research Centre, London.

52   Belson, W.A. (1975), *Juvenile theft: causal factors*, Harper and Row, London.

53   Hartshorne, H. and May, M.A. (1930), *Studies in the Nature of Character: vol.1: Studies in Deceit*, Macmillan, New York.

54   Michael, J. and Adler, M.J. (1933), *Crime, Law and Social Science*, Harcourt Brace, New York.

55   Carr-Saunders, A.M., Mannheim, H. and Rhodes, E.C. (1942), *Juvenile offenders: an enquiry into juvenile delinquency*, Cambridge University Press.

56   Bowlby, J. (1946), *Forty-four juvenile thieves*, Balliere, Tindall and Cox, London.

57   Portersfield, A.L. (1946), *Youth in trouble*, Leo Potishman Foundation, Fort Worth.

58   Glueck, S. and Glueck, E.T. (1950), *Unraveling juvenile delinquency*, Harvard University Press for the Commonwealth Fund, Cambridge, Mass.

59   Stott, D.H. (1950), *Delinquency and human nature*, Carnegie United Kingdom Trust, Dunfermline, Fife.

60   Ferguson, T. and Cunnison, J. (1951), *The young wage-earner: a study of Glasgow boys*, Oxford University Press.

61   Hathaway, S.R. and Monachesi, E.D. (eds) (1953), *Analysing and predicting juvenile delinquency with the MMPI*, University of Minnesota Press, Minneapolis.

62   Sprott, W.J.H., Jephcott, A.P. and Carter, M.P. (1954), *The social background of delinquency*, University of Nottingham, (mimeographed).

63   Gibbs, D.N. (1955), 'Some differentiating characteristics of delinquent and non-delinquent national servicemen in the British army' (PhD thesis), London.

64   Grygier, T. (1955), 'Leisure pursuits of juvenile delinquents: a study in methodology', *British Journal of Delinquency*, vol.5(3).

65 Nye, F.I. (1958), *Family relationships and delinquent behaviour*, Wiley, New York.

66 Wootton, B. (1959), *Social science and social pathology*, Allen and Unwin, London.

67 Andry, R.C. (1960), *Delinquency and parental pathology*, Methuen, London.

68 Bennett, I. (1960), *Delinquent and neurotic children*, Tavistock Publications, London.

69 Reiss, A.J., jr, (1960), 'Conforming and deviating behaviour and the problem of guilt', *Psychiatric Research Reports*.

70 Dentler, R.A. and Monroe, L.J. (1961), 'The family and early adolescent conformity and deviance', *Marriage and Family Living*, vol.23(3).

71 Nye, F.I. (1956), *Family relationships and delinquent behaviour*, Wiley, New York.

72 Gold, M. (1961), *Interview objectives of the undetected delinquency*, Flint Youth Study (Project G65-4/U, Institute for Social Research, University of Michigan, (mimeographed). Questionnaire and other procedural details from this study were made available to the Survey Research Centre.

73 Mobilisation for Youth Study (1962), *Code book vol.II, adolescent survey*, Research Center, New York School of Social Work, Columbia University.

74 Robison, S.N. (1962), *Career patterns project: questionnaire*, New York Institute of Behavioural and Social Sciences, Adelphi College.

75 Willcock, H.D. (1965), 'The dark figure', a talk given to the British Society of Criminology (18 May).

76 Zeigarnik, B. (1927), 'Memorising of completed and incomplete actions', *Psychologische Forschung*, vol.9.

77 Rice, S.A. (1929), 'Contagious bias in the interview', *American Journal of Sociology*, vol.35.

78 Cavan, R.S. (1933), 'The questionnaire in a sociological research project', *American Journal of Sociology*, vol.38.

79 Olson, W.C. (1936), 'The waiver of signature in personal reports', *Journal of Applied Psychology*, vol.20.

80 Corey, S.M. (1937), 'Signed versus unsigned questionnaires', *Journal of Educational Psychology*, vol.28.

81 Rugg, D. (1941), 'Experiments in wording questions (II)', *Public Opinion Quarterly*, vol.5.

82 Turnbull, W. (1944), 'Secret versus non-secret ballots', in Cantril, H. et al., *Gauging Public Opinion*, Princeton University Press, Princeton.

83 Alper, T.G. (1946), 'Memory for completed and uncompleted tasks as a function of personality: analysis of group data', *Journal of*

Abnormal and Social Psychology, vol.41.

84   Fischer, R.P. (1946), 'Signed versus unsigned personal question-naires', *Journal of Applied Psychology*, vol.30.

85   Sheatsley, P.B. (1949), 'The influence of sub-questions on inter-viewer performance', *Public Opinion Quarterly*, vol.13.

86   Stember, H. and Hyman, H. (1949—50), 'How interviewer effects operate through question form', *International Journal of Opinion and Attitude Research*, vol.3.

87   Keating, E., Paterson, D.G. and Stone, C.H. (1950), 'Validity of work histories obtained by interview', *Journal of Applied Psychology* vol.34.

88   Berg, I.A. and Rapaport, G.M. (1954), 'Response bias in an un-structured questionnaire', *Journal of Psychology*, vol.38.

89   Withey, S.B. (1954), 'Reliability of recall of income', *Public Opinion Quarterly*, vol.18.

90   Gales, K. and Kendall, M.G. (1957), 'An enquiry concerning inter-viewer variability', *Journal of the Royal Statistical Society*, series A, vol.120.

91   Hanson, R.H. and Marks, E.S. (1958), 'Influence of the inter-viewer on the accuracy of survey results', *Journal of the American Statistical Association*, vol.53.

92   Television Audience Measurement (1961), *Comparison survey of audience composition techniques*, TAM, London.

93   Belson, W.A. and Duncan, J.A. (1962), 'A comparison of the check list and open response questioning systems', *Applied Statistics*, vol.11(2).

94   Survey Research Centre (1968), *Interviewer deviation from instructions*, London.

95   Belson, W.A., Didcott, P.J. and Millerson, G.L. (1968), *Identifying difficulties and facilitating factors in getting information from boys about their stealing and about associated matters: an exploratory study*, Survey Research Centre, London.

96   Mass Observation Limited (1947), *The language of leadership*, Mass Observation Limited, London.

97   Terris, F. (1949), 'Are poll questions too difficult?', *Public Opinion Quarterly*, vol.13.

98   Belson, W.A. (1966), *Respondent understanding of questions in the survey interview*, Survey Research Centre, London. (Later pub-lished as *The design and understanding of survey questions* (1981), Gower Publishing Company, London.

99   Benson, S., Booman, W.P. and Clark, K.E. (1951), 'A study of interviewer refusals', *Journal of Applied Psychology*, vol.35(2).

100   Belson, W.A. (1978), *Television violence and the adolescent boy*, Saxon House, London.

101 Belson, W.A. (1982), 'A comparison of the open-ended and the check-list questioning systems', Market Research Society Annual Conference, Brighton.

102 Schuman, H. and Presser, S. (1982), *Questions and answers in attitude surveys*, Academic Press, London.

103 Collins, M. & Courtney, J. (1983), 'The effect of question form on survey data', Market Research Society Annual Conference, Brighton.

104 Twyman, T. (1973), 'Designing advertising research for marketing decisions', *Journal of the Market Research Society*, vol. 15 (2).

105 Scott, C. (1961), 'Research on mail surveys', *Journal of Royal Statistical Society,* series A, vol. 124, part 2.

106 Kildegaard, I.C. (1966), 'Telephone trends', *Journal of Advertising Research*, vol. 6(2).

107 Tull, D.S. and Albaum, G.S. (1977), 'Bias in random digit dialled surveys', *Public Opinion Quarterly*, vol. 41.

108 Blankenship, A.B. (1977), *Professional telephone surveys*, McGraw Hill, New York.

109 Dillman, D.A. (1978), *Mail and telephone surveys: the total design method*, John Wiley and Sons, New York.

110 Wolfe, L.M. (1979), 'Characteristics of persons with and without home telephones', *Journal of Marketing Research*, vol. 16.

111 Groves, R.M. and Kahn, R.L. (1979), *Surveys by telephone: a national comparison with personal interviews*, Academic Press, New York.

112 Roslow, S. and Roslow, L. (1972), 'Unlisted phone subscribers are different', *Journal of Advertising Research*, vol. 12.

113 Glasser, G.J. and Metzger, G.D. (1975), 'National estimates of non-listed telephone households and their characteristics', *Journal of Marketing Research*, vol. 12.

114 Blankenship, A.B. (1976), 'Listed versus unlisted numbers in telephone survey samples', *Journal of Advertising Research*, vol. 17.

115 Brunner, J.A. and Brunner, G.A. (1977), 'Are voluntarily unlisted telephone subscribers really different?', *Journal of Marketing Research*, vol. 8.

116 Miln, D. (1976), 'Telephone research does work', *Marketing*, December.

117 Colombotus, J. (1965), 'The effects of personal vs telephone interviews on socially acceptable responses', *Public Opinion Quarterly*, vol. 29.

118 Henson, R., Roth, A. and Cannell, C.F. (1974), *Personal vs telephone interviews and the effect of telephone reinterviews on reporting of psychiatric symptomatology*, Survey Research Centre, Institute for Social Research, University of Michigan.

119 Rogers, T.F. (1976), 'Interviews by telephone and in person: quality of responses and field performance', *Public Opinion Quarterly*, vol. 40.

120 Groves, R., Cannell, C., Miller, P. (1981), 'A methodological study of telephone and face-to-face interviewing', The 36th Annual AAPOR Conference.

121 Cannell, C.F. (1982), *An experimental comparison of telephone and personal health surveys*, Institute of Social Research, University of Michigan.

122 McDonald, C., 'Computer analysis of open response data', Market Research Society Annual Conference, Brighton.

Index

accuracy checks 23–38, 43–4, 51–5, 102–8, 209–13, 284–5, 304–5, 311, 318, 320, 399–401, 429–30, 498, 541–2

accuracy of survey results 64–9, 113–40, 223, 225–32, 238–53, 255–6, 285–6, 311–16, 318–19, 321, 322–3, 324–34, 354–64, 532–8

activities engaged in at time of interview 151–2

administrative problems 472–5, 477–8

aetiological investigation 440–3

age limits for respondents 451

anonymity for respondents 437, 445, 447, 467, 480, 485, 504, 506–7, 512, 527

appearance of interviewers 465, 469, 481

appointments for intensive interviews, making 49–50, 98–100, 451–2, 454–5, 474, 480, 512, 519

areas for surveys, selection of 50, 298, 299, 450

'armchair operators' 424–5, 511

attitude scales 432–3, 435

attitudes of respondents to interviews 498, 504–9

balancing errors 68–9, 116, 117, 118, 119, 127, 128, 215, 242

barrier appraisal method 435–7, 438–522, 524–9; *for detailed headings see* stealing by boys, violence by boys

barriers to honesty/accuracy 435–7, 448, 450, 457–61, 464–5, 476, 497–8, 499–504, 505, 506–7, 510

BBC 433

behaviour, respondent: subject to confusion/memory effort 4; surveillance of 33, 35, 43; usual 103–4, 142–3; visibly obvious 3–4

biased questions *see* leading/loaded questions

bipolar/unipolar scales 195, 204, 225—6, 242

blocking factors *see* barriers

book of instructions for interviewers 488—9

boredom in respondent 148, 517

bravado/exaggeration by respondents 468

briefing/training of interviewers 49—50, 55—6, 98—100, 108—9, 153, 159—60, 198—200, 205, 214, 300—2, 343, 452, 534; *see also* instructions to interviewers; training of intensive interviewers

Bureau of Broadcasting Measurement 294, 398, 420

buyer of research 534

camera checks on behaviour 35

Cantril, H. 17—18

card system in sensitive interviews 485—96, 514—17, 519—22, 527—8

careless replies by respondents 18—19, 502

CATI (computer assisted telephone interviewing) 538

centre point in scales 192, 213, 218, 229—30, 240—2

characteristics of respondents: and error 136—40, 237, 247—8; and grasp of instructions 222—3; and purchasing behaviour 61, 67—8; and Semantic Differential Scaling system study 222—3, 237, 247—8; non-controversial 4; subconscious 5; visibly obvious 3

chocolate confectionery purchasing study 39—86: accuracy checks 43—4, 51—5; causes of error 69—75; errors in

purchaser/non-purchaser classification 66—8; errors in purchasing totals 64—5, 68—9; findings 64—75; instructions for interviewers 78—86; modification of survey procedure 75—6; nature of intensive interview 51—5; reasons for 41—2; research methods 42—64; re-weighting of data 61—4; sampling methods 59—61; scope of intensive interview 51—3; survey form 46—7; survey procedure 45—50; time periods relating to replies 45, 53, 69—71, 73; training of intensive interviewers 55—6; use of mobile control centre 56—9

'choice of answer' cards 24—5

claims about purchases, accuracy of 64—9, 285—6

classification questions, common 14

collection of respondents for interviewing at centre 480, 499, 512, 519

communication with respondent, problems of 338—9, 342, 457; *see also* misunderstanding by respondents; wording of questions

comparison of brands 248—53, 256

compensating errors *see* balancing errors

computer processing of research data 536, 538

conditioning to reduce resistance to making admissions *see* facilitating factors for honesty/accuracy; persuasion of respondents to make dangerous admissions

intelligence tests 430, 431–2, 433–4

intensive interviews: and objective 'criterion of truth' 101; confrontation phase 38, 54–5, 105–6, 107–8, 213, 304–5, 309–10, 315–16, 317, 330–1, 340, 482, 521–2; eliciting real opinions 210–13, 224–5; explanation of purposes of 53, 103, 207–8, 485, 488; familiarisation phase 104–5; gearing together with survey interview 198–200; introduction to concept of 35–8; open-ended 531–2; purpose of 51, 206; quality control of 482–3; securing appointments for *see* appointments for intensive interviews, making; stages of 53–5, 103–8, 399–401, tactics of 36–7; testing accuracy of survey interview 208–13

interest from respondents, lack of 460–1

internal consistency in measures 430, 431, 432

International Information Department 205–6

interpretation of questions by respondent 13–16, 287–8, 338–9, 424, 500–1: determining 29–32; *see also* misunderstandings by respondent

Interviewer Card Scheme 534

interviewer-based problems 20, 27–9, 74, 149, 339–41, 344, 444, 446–7, 482–3, 533–4

interviewers: and mobile control centres 57–8; briefing/training of 49–50, 55–6, 98–100, 108–9, 153, 159–60, 198–

200, 205, 214, 300–2, 343, 452, 534; *see also* instructions to interviewers; training of intensive interviewers

deviation by 10–12, 25, 32, 141, 154–6, 316, 339, 342–3, 533–4; difficulties of 146, 148, 309, 509; ignorance of survey objectives 49–50, 98, 100, 199–200; qualities needed in 343, 462–5, 469, 481, 517; selection of 48–9, 55, 98, 108, 205, 214, 300, 481

interviewing centres 473, 481

interviews, form of 305–7, 452–3, 519–22; *see also under study headings*

isolated events, overlooking of 142–3

item analysis method 430–3, 433–5

judging process, fallibility of 432

leading/loaded questions 16–18

length of interviews 147–50, 158–9

Likert, R. 432–3

local offices 56–9, 109–100, 473

London School of Economics 100, 542

'looked at', meaning of 105–6, 143–4, 316, 317–18, 322, 338

loyalty problems in sensitive interviews 468, 476

lying responses 435, 444

Market Research Society 534: Conference 10

mastheads 89–91, 307, 309

measurement, concept of 2—3, 424

measures available: lack of 425—6; limitations of 3—5

memory problems in respondents 19, 105—6, 154, 466, 476, 490, 500, 502, 508

methodological research units 542

methods for checking accuracy *see* accuracy checks

Miln, 537

misunderstanding by respondents 287—8, 444, 465—6, 476, 497, 507—8: of Semantic Differential Scaling system 195, 210—11, 218—19

misunderstandings between interviewer and respondent 145—6

mobile control centres 56—9

Mobilisation for Youth Study 446

modifications of procedures, making/testing *see* progressive modification method, radio diary; prog. mod., readership study; prog. mod., stealing by boys study

monthly publications 118—20, 132—3, 357, 360

Morgan, J.N. 434

National Readership Survey (NRS) *see* readership study

'network of defining stimuli' 491, 520, 526, 528

News of the World 115, 117

'no opinion' responses 220—1

non-balance of over/underclaims 127; *see also* balancing errors

Nye, F.I. 445

objective data, comparison of survey measures with 32—4, 44; *see also* 'criterion of truth'

occupational background of respondents 140, 223, 248

office managers 58—9

Office of Population Censuses and Surveys 542

open-ended interviewing, intensive 531—2

opinion surveys: accuracy of 225—32, 238—53; political 15, 33; tactics for eliciting real opinions on products 210—13, 224—5; *see also* Semantic Differential Scaling system, study involving

opinions: non-controversial 4; subconscious 5

opposites, concept of 222

order effects 18, 110—12, 156—8, 196, 204—5, 303, 326—7

Osgood, C.E. 193

over/under-estimating tendencies 123—9, 136, 312—14, 324—6, 327—8

'past three months', meaning of 144—5

pauses in interviews 304

personal treatment of respondents 512—13, 517, 519

personality tests 430

persuasion of respondents to make dangerous admissions 516—17, 521, 528—9

petrol buying survey 283—8: accuracy of information obtained 285—6; aims of stud; 284—5; misinterpretation of questions 287—8; research methods 285; sources of error 286—8

piloting of questionnaires 27—9: and interviewer-based problems 27—9; and respondent-based problems 27, 29 polling districts 59, 94, 201, 450

positive v. zero claims 52–3, 62, 66–8, 106–7, 123–5

postal surveys 534–6

prestige effects 306

'pretending game' in sensitive interviews 504, 510, 514–17, 521, 528

principles of question design 23–6, 156–9, 427–8

privacy in sensitive interviews 485, 487, 488–90, 496, 497, 501, 507, 511, 519–20, 527

probability sampling 201

probing system in intensive interviewing 304–5, 309–10, 315–16, 317, 330–1, 340, 500–1, 521–2

product research: and validity of Semantic Differential Scaling system 248–53, 256: selection of products 198

profiles of purchasers see characteristics of respondents, and purchasing behaviour

progressive modification method 295–395: and barrier appraisal method 436–7, 438–522, 524–9; and causes of error 331–2, 337–41; briefing of interviewers in 300–2; control of interview in 307–8; dangers of short-cutting 293–4; deciding whether to use modified procedure 341–4; extended validation procedure in 350–2; instructions to interviewers in 346–9; instructions to respondents in 303–4; keeping records for 302; methods of 292–3; need for speed in 293; order effects in 326–7; over/under-claiming ten-dencies in 312–14, 324–6, 327–8; probing system in 304–5, 309–10, 315–16, 317, 330–1, 340; quality control of interviewers in 482–3;

radio diary, first version 401–8, revised version 408–19;

readership study, changes made 302–10, 316–18, 319–20, 322, 323–4; fifth modification 323–34, 365–95; final check 332–4; findings 311–16, 318–19, 321, 322–3, 324–34, 354–64; first modification 297–8, 302–16, 336; first v. fifth modifications 324–6; fourth modification 322–3; incidence of error 314–15, 324–30; NRS survey v. fifth modification 326–8; qualitative findings 315–16, 337–8; quantitative findings 311–15, 335–7; second modification 316–19; stage by stage effects 335–8; third modification 319–21

response rates in 353; sampling methods in 299–300; selection of area in 298, 299; stealing by boys study, first version of procedure 478–512; further modifications of procedure 518; second version of procedure 512–18

training of intensive interviewers in 301–2; two-stage interviewing technique in 300; visual aids in 307, 309–10

psychological measures 5

psychometricians 432

readership study (cont.)
future surveys 156—60; report form for intensive interviewers 169—75; research methods 92—112; response rates 353; re-weighting of data 113, 138; sampling methods 93—5; survey interview 97—100; testing methods used 102—8; three-month question 123—5, 144—5, 305—6; time periods for replies 123—6, 129—33, 144—5, 316, 317, 339; training of intensive interviewers 108—9

recency of behaviour, and survey errors 129—33

records of research procedure, importance of keeping 302

relevance of scales 195

reliability, concept of 9—10

repetition of key instructions to respondents 158, 415

research literature 446—7

research methods *see under study headings*

re-shaping a survey procedure, principles of 297—8

re-sorting test in sensitive interviews 501—3, 510, 514—15, 517, 521

respondent-based problems 27, 29, 73—4, 286—8, 342, 408

respondents *see under individual headings, e.g.* careless replies; memory problems; characteristics of respondents

response rates 60—1, 201, 353, 454—6, 534—5, 537: causes of failure to secure interviews 455—6; methods for improving 456

Reveille 117

reversal of scales 218—19, 228—9

re-weighting of data 61—4, 113, 246—7

Robison, S.N. 445—6

rotation arrangements 204—5

'rotation effect' 112

Rugg, D. 17—18

rule teaching to respondents 486, 491, 493—5, 514, 519—20

sample level, errors at 64—5, 68—9, 113—22, 127, 128, 242—8, 285—6

sampling methods 59—61, 93—5, 200—2, 299—300, 450—1, 453—4, 475—6, 479, 499, 512

scientific indicator method 433—5

screens in sensitive interviews 485, 488—90, 497, 507, 519—20, 527

securing intensive interviews *see* appointments for intensive interviews, making

selection of interviewers 48—9, 55, 98, 108, 205, 214, 300, 418

Semantic Differential Scaling system 12

Semantic Differential Scaling system, study involving 191—282: accuracy of sample distributions/means 242—8, 256; aims of present study 196, 253; bipolar/unipolar scales 195, 204, 225—6, 242; centre point usage 192, 213, 218, 229—30, 240—2; differences between survey and intensive interviews 224—48; 'don't know' responses 195, 211, 213, 219—21, 229—30, 245; eliminating misunderstandings of SDS system 210—11; incidence of error in survey

validity (cont.)

428—9; qualitative/quantitative opposition 531—3

vested interests and survey research 22, 542

violence by boys, construction of measure for 524—99: background to study 525; card system 527—8; confidentiality problems 528—9; definition of violence 525, 528; eliciting procedure 527—9; instructions to interviewers 529; introductory phase of interview 527; obtaining details of violence 529; 'pretending game' 528; privacy in card sorting 527; rules for card sorting 528; search for causal hypotheses of violence 525; steps in construction of procedure 526; stress on confidentiality by interviewer 528—9; 'web of stimuli' 526, 528

visual aids: for chocolate confectionery purchasing survey 48, 53—4; for readership study 146, 159, 307, 308, 309—10; misinterpretation of 292

'volunteer bias' issue 535—6

voting intention 33

WATS zoning system 536

'web of stimuli' see 'network of defining stimuli'

weekly publications 117—18, 132, 358, 361

weighting of data 138 see also re-weighting of data

Wherry-Doolittle technique 539

Woman 117

Woman and Home 118

Woman's Own 117

wording of questions: changes to 10—12; definition of terms 444—5, 499—501; misunderstanding of 143—5, 287—8, 304, 317—18, 338—9, 446; pitfalls in 424; principles of 23—4